THE ELIOT TRACTS

Recent Titles in
Contributions in American History

THE ELIOT TRACTS

With Letters from John Eliot to Thomas Thorowgood and Richard Baxter

Edited with an Introduction by Michael P. Clark

Contributions in American History, Number 199

Westport, Connecticut
London

Library of Congress Cataloging-in-Publication Data

The Eliot Tracts : with letters from John Eliot to Thomas Thorowgood and Richard Baxter
  / edited with an introduction by Michael P. Clark.
     p.   cm. — (Contributions in American history, ISSN 0084-9219 ; no. 199)
    Includes bibliographical references and index.
    ISBN 0-313-30488-2 (alk. paper)
    1. Eliot, John, 1604–1690. 2. Indians of North America—Missions—New
England—History—17th century. 3. Missions—New England—History—17th century. I.
Eliot, John, 1604–1690. II. Thorowgood, Thomas, d. ca. 1669. III. Baxter, Richard,
1615–1691. IV. Clark, Michael, 1950– V. Series.
  E78.N5E45   2003
  266'.0089'97074—dc21   2003042051

British Library Cataloguing in Publication Data is available.

Library of Congress Catalog Card Number: 2003042051
ISBN: 0-313-30488-2
ISSN: 0084-9219

First published in 2003

Praeger Publishers, 88 Post Road West, Westport, CT 06881
An imprint of Greenwood Publishing Group, Inc.
www.praeger.com

Printed in the United States of America

The paper used in this book complies with the
Permanent Paper Standard issued by the National
Information Standards Organization (Z39.48–1984).

10 9 8 7 6 5 4 3 2 1

Copyright Acknowledgments

The editor and publisher gratefully acknowledge permission for use of the following material:

The map of the Praying Towns on p. 6 is from Jean M. O'Brien, *Dispossession by Degrees:
Indian Land and Identity in Natick, Massachusetts, 1650–1790*, Cambridge Studies in North
American Indian History (New York: Cambridge University Press, 1997), 29. It was developed
by Mark Lindberg and Allan Willis of the Cartographic Laboratory at the University of
Minnesota and is reproduced here by permission of the Cartographic Laboratory.

A brief portion of the introduction was originally published in Michael P. Clark, "'Even
without a Metaphor': The Poetics of Apocaplypse in Puritan New England," in *Millennial
Thought in America: Historical and Intellectual Contexts, 1630–1860*, ed. Bernd Engler,
Joerg O. Fichte, and Oliver Scheiding (Trier, Germany: Wissenschaftlicher Verlag, 2002). It
is reprinted here by permision of the publisher.

Contents

Letters

Acknowledgments

I would like to thank the following people for their help at different stages of this project. Peter Goldman sought out and collected copies of the tracts as first published, and Joanna Gislason transcribed them and prepared the initial version of the manuscript. Andrew Newman and Michael Householder helped review and correct the transcript and advised me on other editorial matters from their perspective as doctoral candidates in early American literature at the University of California, Irvine. Their enthusiasm and dedication to our field were invaluable, and in many ways they served as ideal readers for this book. My colleagues Patrick Sinclair and Daniel Schroeter helped clarify passages in Greek, Latin, and Hebrew. My wife, Kate Clark, also contributed editorial advice and formatted the title pages and the body of the text to reproduce the visual organization of the original tracts while increasing their legibility for the contemporary reader. Barbara Caldwell prepared the final version of the manuscript for publication and helped to oversee the last steps of that process. In addition, I am especially indebted to Richard W. Cogley, who reviewed a draft of the introduction and whose comprehensive knowledge of Eliot's work and early American religious thought in general contributed significantly to the accuracy and precision of that essay. Any errors that remain are entirely my own.

Additional material and information about various reprints of the tracts were provided by Marie E. Lamoureux, head of readers' services, American Antiquarian Society, and Romaine Ahlstrom, reference librarian at the Huntington Library. Photographs of the title pages from the original tracts were provided by Sean Daily and John Powell of the Newberry Library. Mark Lindberg, director of the cartography lab at the University of Minnesota, generously permitted the use of a map of the Praying Towns he developed originally for Jean O'Brien's *Dispossession by Degrees: Indian Land and Identity in Natick, Massachusetts, 1650 - 1790* (1997). Approval for the use of the original seal of the Massachusetts Bay Colony was granted by the Public Records Division of the Commonwealth of Massachusetts, Allan Cote, Secretary. Erwin Otto of Wissenschaftlicher Verlag Trier allowed me to use a small portion of my essay that originally appeared in *Millennial Thought in America: Historical and Intellectual Contexts, 1630 - 1860* (2002). I would also like to thank John Dan Eades, former senior editor of the Greenwood Publishing Group, for his encouragement and support at the beginning of this project, and Heather Staines, acquisitions editor at Greenwood, and John Beck, production manager, for seeing it through to the end.

Seal of the Massachusetts Bay Colony. Courtesy of Public Records Division, Office of the Secretary, Commonwealth of Massachusetts

Introduction

This volume collects together for the first time eleven works published in London between 1643 and 1671 and now known collectively as "The Eliot Tracts." This informal title refers to the principal author in most of the tracts, John Eliot. Eliot emigrated to New England in 1631 and was a Puritan teacher and minister at the church in Roxbury in the Massachusetts Bay Colony from 1632 until his death in 1690. He held no other important political or ecclesiastical positions, but he was widely known in England and New England as the "Apostle to the Indians" for his missionary work during the last half of the seventeenth century. Although other authors represented in these tracts include more influential intellectual and political leaders in the colonies—most notably Thomas Shepard and Edward Winslow—it was Eliot who was most closely associated with the missionary project described in these tracts. In addition to personally visiting and preaching to many of the tribes in the colonies of New England, Eliot created and oversaw the relocation of Indian proselytes into fourteen "Praying Towns" that were the most ambitious and controversial aspect of the missionary project. He also translated the entire Bible into a dialect of the Algonquian language, and through his contributions to these tracts and other publications, Eliot provided a theological rationale for the missionaries' work that imbued the enterprise with a doctrinal coherence and millennial urgency.

The Eliot tracts were originally published to help raise funds for missionary work in New England, and to publicize that work as a partial fulfillment of the terms of the original charter for the Massachusetts Bay Colony. In 1629 that charter had granted to the Governor and his deputies the authority to make laws and establish statutes

whereby our said People, Inhabitants there, may be soe religiously, peaceablie, and civilly governed, as their good Life and orderlie Conversacon, maie wynn and incite the Natives of Country, to the Knowledg and Obedience of the onlie true God and Savior of Mankinde, and the Christian Fayth, which in our Royall Intencon, and the Adventurers free Profession, is the principall Ende of this Plantacion.[1]

This objective was reinforced by the seal of the colony, which depicted an Indian standing with open arms and crying, "Come over and help us," an echo of the Macedonian's plea to Paul in Acts (16.9). The British colonists, however, were notoriously lax in their commitment to this "principall Ende" of their plantation in the New World. In 1641, more than twenty years after the colony at Plymouth was founded, seventy-six British ministers supporting a petition to Parliament "for the propagating of the Gospel in America" observed that British colonization had not proceeded "in pitty to mens soules, but in hope to possesse the land of those Infidels, or of gaine by Commerce" (Castell 1641, 6). This conclusion embarrassed the Puritans and encouraged critics such as Robert

Baillie (1645), who claimed that the Massachusetts Bay colonists neglected conversion more than "all that ever crossed the American seas," and that the single exception to that generalization, Roger Williams, began to pay attention to the Indians only after his banishment from Massachusetts. Three years earlier, Thomas Lechford (1642) had made the same charge in a diatribe against the Puritans, *Plain Dealing*, in which he complained that no church in Massachusetts Bay had sent anyone "to learn the Indians' language or to instruct them in the religion."[2] This lack of missionary zeal also contrasted dramatically to the efforts of Catholic priests in the Spanish and French colonies, who had been proselytizing among indigenous peoples for more than 100 years and who had already left a long record of their accomplishments.[3]

England's belated embrace of imperialist expansionism was a source of economic anxiety as well as proto-nationalist embarrassment at being beaten to the New World by most of its European neighbors. Internal disputes among the Spanish about the objectives and tactics of their conquest in New Spain, however, allowed England to take rhetorical advantage of its late start by arguing that they now had a chance to do it right. The Black Legend of horror and atrocities committed against the Indians by the *conquistadores* became an important motif in English writing about the exploration and settlement of British North America (see Maltby 1971). That tradition began in Spain with the publication of Bartolomé de Las Casas's (1552) *Brevíssima relación de la destrucción de las Indias*, and the importance of that work to English propagandists is evident in the translated titles of Las Casas's book, which grew increasingly graphic about Spanish atrocities as the British presence in North American expanded. The first translation of Las Casas appeared in 1583 as *The Spanish Colonie*; another version the same year used the title *Spanish cruelties and tyrannies*; and then, in the midst of Eliot's most concerted missionary efforts, John Phillips (1656) titled his new translation to emphasize the contrast between British and Spanish relations to the natives, "*The Tears of the Indians: being an historical and true Account of the Cruel Massacres and Slaughters of above Twenty Millions of innocent People, Committed by the Spaniards in the Islands of Hispaniola, Cuba, Jamaica, &c. As also, in the Continent of Mexico, Peru, & other Places of the West Indies, To the total destruction of those Countries.* Written in Spanish by Casaus, an Eye-witness of those things; And made English by J.P." The following lines from Phillips's introduction give an idea of the intended response by British readers to Las Casas's account of Spanish conquest: Note well, Phillips says,

the devilish Cruelties of those that called themselves Christians: had you seen the poor creatures [i.e., the Indians] torn from the peace and quiet of their own Habitations, where God had planted them, to labour in a Tormenting Captivity, by many degrees worse than that of Algier, or the Turkish Galleys. The tears of Men can hardly suffice; these are Enormities to make the Angels mourn and bewail the loss of so many departed souls, as might have been converted and redeemed to their eternal Mansions.

We read of old, of the Ten Persecutions wherein the Primitive Christians were destroy'd by the Cruelties of the Heathen Emperours: but we now read of Christians, the Professors of a Religion grounded upon Love and Charity, massacring, where there was no cause of Antipathy, but their own obstinate Barbarism. (b2 recto - b3 verso)

This extraordinary representation of the Indians casts them in the role of the primitive Christians and the Spanish Catholics as heathens, and then claims that it is the Indians who are captives of their foreign tormentors. Both of these images draw upon the growing popularity of the idea that the American Indians were descendants of the Jews, which followed the publication of Thomas Thorowgood's (1650) *Jewes in America*. Equally important to these images was the rabid anti-Catholicism and anti-Spanish sentiment of the English, who were competing with the Spanish in the exploitation of the New World and for the spiritual colonization of the natives' souls. So the authors of the "Epistle Dedicatory" to Eliot's (1663) translation of the Bible into Algonquian observed,

The Southern Colonies of the *Spanish Nation* have sent home from this *American Continent*, much Gold and Silver, as the Fruit and End of their Discoveries and transplantations: that (we confess) is a scarce Commodity in this Colder Climate. But . . . we present this [Bible] and other Concomitant Fruits of our poor Endeavours to Plant and Propagate the Gospel here; which, upon a true account, is as much better then Gold, as the Souls of men are more worth then the whole World. This is a Nobler Fruit (and indeed in the Counsels of All-disposing Providence, was an higher intended End) of *Columbus* his Adventure. (A4 verso)

In this bold claim, the authors not only propose to transmute Spanish gold into Christian souls, but they also appropriate the whole Spanish antecedence in the New World by claiming that the New England missionary effort is what God had in mind all along as the outcome of Columbus's great adventure.

THE ELIOT TRACTS AND ELIOT'S LETTERS TO THOROWGOOD AND BAXTER

Appearing at the height of England's attempt to justify its role in the international imperialism of early modern Europe, the Eliot Tracts thus not only countered accusations about a lack of missionary zeal among the British settlers; they also provided evidence to support the spiritual superiority of England's belated occupation of North America. Together, the tracts constitute the single most sustained and detailed account of British missionary work in the New World in the seventeenth century, and as such they serve as a comparatively modest but important counterpart to the Jesuit *Relations* in New France and to the missionary work described as part of the conquistador narratives of New Spain.[4]

The tracts also contain detailed descriptions of customs, behavior, and beliefs among native peoples in the area of Massachusetts Bay. To be sure, this ethnographic information is filtered through the Eurocentric lens of the British authors, and it is even more obviously subordinated to the religious objectives of the missionaries' work and to the overt and persistent need to justify additional funding to support that work. Any conclusions about native life based on the tracts must therefore be tempered with considerable skepticism about the reliability of these accounts without extensive corroboration by other sources, on the rare occasions when such sources exist.[5] On the other hand, the missionaries' pragmatic accommodations of native culture, including various dialects of the Algonquian language, traditional social practices, native husbandry, and even rhetorical customs, indelibly mark the hybrid nature of the tracts, which are not only a record of the contact but also a product of the most extensive and sophisticated two-way interaction between colonists and native peoples in seventeenth-century British America.[6]

Despite their social and political importance to the role of New England in the transatlantic context of British colonialism, the Eliot Tracts were not treated as a coherent sequence as they appeared, and the quality of the original publications varies from poor to mediocre. The individual tracts were often cobbled together hurriedly by authors and editors struggling to provide support for various measures in Parliament related to the missionary efforts, and their publication over three decades was sporadic, with many years passing between the publication of some tracts. They have received no better treatment by historians since then. The Eliot Tracts have never been printed together, and apart from pieces occasionally incorporated into books and articles, none of the tracts have been reprinted since the nineteenth century, when the Massachusetts Historical Society published the tracts printed from 1647 to 1655 as "Tracts Relating to the Attempts to Convert to Christianity the Indians of New England" (1834), and Joseph Sabin published several tracts in his Sabin's Reprints (1865).[7]

Nor is there agreement on exactly which texts should be included under the general rubric of the Eliot Tracts, or on the criteria for inclusion. In *John Eliot: "Apostle to the Indians,"* Ola Elizabeth Winslow (1966) lists the eleven texts collected in this volume as the Eliot Tracts, even though the first tract, *New England's First Fruits* (London, 1643) was published almost three years before Eliot delivered his first missionary sermon and does not even refer to him. Most contemporary scholars agree with this series of eleven tracts, including Hilary Wyss (2000) and Kristina Bross (1997), who makes a persuasive argument for 1643 as the beginning of concerted missionary efforts in New England.[8] On the other hand, in *John Eliot's Mission to the Indians before King Philip's War*, the most comprehensive and authoritative account to date of British missionary activity in New England, Richard W. Cogley (1999) omits that early tract from his list and begins with the first tract to which Eliot contributed, *The Day-Breaking, If Not the Sun-Rising of the Gospell with the Indians in New England* (London, 1647). The Eliot Tracts are thus reduced to ten, although Eliot is not the principal author of all of those tracts, and Cogley himself describes the earlier *New England's First Fruits* as "by far the richest source for missionary history prior to the start of Eliot's work" (29).

Furthermore, although the five tracts that appeared from 1652 to 1660 were clearly published as a series by the Society for the Propagation of the Gospel in New England (later known as the New England Company), that organization had no clear connection to what is generally considered to be the eleventh of the Eliot tracts, *A Brief Narrative*, written by Eliot and published in 1671. On the other hand, a case could be made for including Experience Mayhew's (1727) *Indian Converts: or, Some Account of the Lives and Dying Speeches of A Considerable Number of the Christianized Indians of Martha's Vineyard, in New England . . .* which Kellaway (1962, 243) calls a "direct descendant" of the Eliot tracts. Although appearing decades after Eliot's death and not directly sponsored by the company, this tract is dedicated to the New England Company as well as to the governor of Massachusetts Bay, and it continues the story of the missionary project that was begun in *The First Fruits*. It also follows the generic forms and discourse of the earlier tracts.

In the absence of consensus on exactly which tracts should be included in the series, the most reasonable principle of inclusion is the significance of the Eliot Tracts as a record of British missionary activity in New England during Eliot's lifetime. That record is best understood when the eleven tracts customarily associated with support for the missionary project are read together as a series, starting with the compilation published by Edward Winslow for that purpose in 1643 and extending through the last tract to which Eliot contributed that was associated with the New England Company in 1671. Consequently, Mayhew's later tract of 1727 has been omitted from this collection, but both *New England's First Fruits* and *A Brief Narrative* have been included.

In addition to the tracts, two important letters by Eliot directly related to his theological defense of the missionary project have been included in this volume: "The Learned Conjectures of Reverend Mr. John Eliot touching the Americans, of new and notable consideration, written to Mr. Thorowgood," which was written in 1652 and published as the preface to the second edition of Thomas Thorowgood's (1660) book, *Jews in America,* and Eliot's letter to Richard Baxter of July 6, 1663, which was published in Richard Baxter's (1696) *Reliquiae Baxterianae.* Thorowgood's argument that the Indians were descendents of the lost tribes of Israel powerfully influenced Eliot's understanding of the significance and future of his missionary project in the 1650s, and these letters expound on the millennialist themes that reinforced and shaped that project at the height of its success.[9] These letters help account for the sudden appearance of millennialist themes in the tracts of that decade, and they also remind readers of Eliot's notoriety as a radical millenarian following the publication of his book *The Christian Commonwealth* in London in 1659. Admired by Fifth Monarchists in England for its projection of a British government inspired by Exodus and scriptural prophecy, after the Restoration the antimonarchical sentiments of this book earned Eliot the enmity of officials in Massachusetts, where it was burned on the Boston Common by the public hangman. Eliot publicly recanted his more extreme political views, but the structure of government proposed for all of England in this book became the model for the first Praying Towns established in Massachusetts Bay. In addition, these letters establish a close connection between Eliot's millennialist speculations and his interest in language, which found its most notable expression in his translation of the Bible into a dialect of Algonquian, but, as these letters show, had its origins in Eliot's understanding of Biblical history and his familiarity with the rudimentary anthropology of early European exploration of the New World.[10]

SCHOLARSHIP ON THE TRACTS

The Eliot Tracts have received relatively little attention from scholars, despite Eliot's long-standing place in the hagiography of British settlement that many textbooks continue to support. The most important exception to this general lack of interest in Eliot's work is Richard W. Cogley's (1999) *John Eliot's Mission to the Indians before King Philip's War*. Drawing extensively on the Eliot Tracts, Cogley traces British missionary efforts among the Indians step by step from the earliest professions of missionary zeal in colonial charters through the failure of Eliot's attempts to use native proselytes to defuse tensions between the Pokanokets and Plymouth Colony on the eve of Metacom's (i.e., King Philip's) War. Cogley contextualizes the missionary project in relation to Eliot's millennialism, and through a precise and detailed analysis of the historical sources he offers a series of important correctives to the generalizations characteristic of earlier histories regarding the motives and consequences of Eliot's missionary efforts.[11] In addition, William Kellaway's (1962) *The New England Company 1649 - 1776* offers a detailed account of the complex transatlantic politics behind the Society for the Propagation of the Gospel in New England, which raised funds to support the missionaries and publish some of the Eliot Tracts, and the Commissioners of the United Colonies, who were responsible for disbursing those funds as well as for overseeing the more general shared concerns of the four colonies of New England. Kellaway's exhaustive history of these organizations explains the strategic role each of the tracts played in the delicate balance among the political, economic, and religious motives that sustained the missionary project in the colonies, and it remains one of the most concrete and precise case studies of the intricate bureaucracy supporting the colonial settlements.[12]

Before the 1960s, few scholars paid much attention to the Eliot Tracts, or to Eliot himself. The earliest overview of missionary work in New England is Daniel Gookin's (1674) *The Historical Collections of the Indians in New England*. Gookin was superintendent of the Indians from 1661 to 1687, and in that role he oversaw affairs of the Praying Towns for the General Court of Massachusetts. Gookin had been involved in the missionary project at an early stage, possibly from the time of Eliot's first sermon to the Indians, and Gookin's dedication to the Indians continued throughout Metacom's War, which earned him the enmity of his British neighbors. Gookin and Eliot were friends; Eliot nominated him for the superintendency, and John Eliot Jr. married Gookin's daughter Elizabeth in 1666. *Historical Collections* reflects Gookin's close personal connection to Eliot and the mission, as does Gookin's (1677) more pessimistic *An Historical Account of the Doings and Sufferings of the Christian Indians in New England*. Neither work pretends to scholarly objectivity, but Gookin's position as superintendent rather than missionary does provide a little distance from the immediate engagement more typical of the letters and reports published in the Eliot Tracts, and Gookin's books constitute the most comprehensive first-hand account of the missionary project.[13]

In 1691, Cotton Mather published a biography of Eliot's life, the tenor of which is evident from the extended title: *The Triumphs of the Reformed Religion in America. The Life of the Renowned John Eliot; a Person justly Famous in the Church of God, Not only as an Eminent Christian, and an Excellent Minister, among the English, But also, As a Memorable Evangelist among the Indians, of New-England; With some Account concerning the late and strange Success of the Gospel, in those parts of the World, which for many Ages have lain Buried in Pagan Ignorance.*[14] Three book-length biographies of Eliot were published in the nineteenth century, and then two more in the 1960s, including Ola Elizabeth Winslow's (1966) nostalgic and oddly anachronistic *John Eliot: "Apostle to the Indians."*[15] All of these biographies are limited by the scant information available about Eliot, whose dedication to his pastoral duties at Roxbury and then to the Indians in the Praying Towns left little trace in the historical record beyond his letters and publications. As a result, like Mather, who always treated lack of information about any biographical subject as a convenient opportunity for erudite flourish and typological elaboration, all of Eliot's biographers have idealized their subject, either by isolating him from the political context of British colonization, or, as in Winslow's case, by casting Eliot's doomed missionary ambitions as the lost idealism of British imperialism in the New World.

Apart from these biographies, the 1960s also saw the first substantial attempts to situate Eliot's missionary work in the broader theological and historical contexts of his time: Sidney H. Rooy's (1965) *The Theology of Missions in the Puritan Tradition; a Study of Representative Puritans: Richard Sibbes, Richard Baxter, John Eliot, Cotton Mather, and Jonathan Edwards*, and Alden T. Vaughan's (1965) influential *New England Frontier: Puritans and Indians, 1620 - 1675*. Rooy's work addresses the doctrinal paradoxes of predestination and conversion in Calvinist evangelism, with some attention to the evolving differences between Puritanism in old and New England. Vaughan's history of colonial New England focuses more on the social and political complexities inherent in early contact between the British and the indigenous peoples of the area. He portrays the motives of the Puritan missionaries as sincere and benign, and the effect of their actions upon the Indians as at least partially beneficial, despite the devastating consequences for the native population. A decade later, Vaughan's thesis was bitterly contested by Francis Jennings (1975) in *The Invasion of America: Indians, Colonialism, and the Cant of Conquest*. Jennings not only emphasizes the terrible consequences of Puritan policies and practices; he links them directly to the motives that led to contact and argues that proclamations of evangelical objectives were never more than a rhetorical disguise for "the missionary racket" of British colonialism (53). Jennings's critique led to a series of revisionist histories that constitute a contemporary Black Legend of the British occupation of New England, including most notably Neal Salisbury's article "Red Puritans" (1974) and book *Manitou and Providence: Indians, Europeans, and the Making of New England, 1500 - 1643* (1982), James Axtell's (1985) *The Invasion Within: The Contest of Cultures in Colonial North America* and George Tinker's (1993) *Missionary Conquest: The Gospel and Native American Cultural Genocide.*

This revisionist condemnation of British imperialism in North America often focused on Puritan New England and at times singled out Eliot himself for his lack of concern with native customs and beliefs, and for his role in the relocation of native peoples into the Praying Towns during the last half of the century. During this same period, however, Greenwood Press published a modern edition of the Eliot's *Indian Dialogues* edited by Henry W. Bowden and James P. Ronda (1980), *John Eliot's Indian Dialogues: A Study in Cultural Interaction.* In the long introduction to this edition, Bowden and Ronda offered a more detailed and nuanced account of Eliot's missionary project, and contextualized it within a brief summary of the social and religious practices of some indigenous cultures in New England. This comparativist presentation of the *Dialogues* helps connect the plausible but manifestly contrived exchanges of Eliot's *Dialogues* to the more complex historical situation behind the contact between missionaries and Indians, turning what might otherwise be dismissed simply as Puritan propaganda into a lens onto the world it aspired to represent. James Holstun's (1983) important essay on Puritan utopianism in *Representations* expanded on Maclear's essay of 1975 and situated Eliot's work squarely within some of the most sophisticated and radical political speculation of the day. Together, this edition and these articles set a new standard for scholarship on Eliot, one that emphasized the intellectual sophistication of his work, its transatlantic context, and the complexity of relations between the Puritan colonists and the native peoples of New England.

The 1990s continued the productive turn of this earlier work. In addition to Cogley's book, there were important essays on Eliot and the Praying Indians by van Lonkhuyzen (1990), Naeher (1989), and Cohen (1993), as well as Timothy J. Sehr's (1984) more general history of the colony. Two other books focused on the peoples of the Algonquian language group and their neighbors in southern New England, Dane Morrison's (1995) *A Praying People: Massachusett Acculturation and the Failure of the Puritan Mission, 1600 - 1690*, and Jean O'Brien's (1997) *Dispossession by Degrees: Indian Land and Identity in Natick, Massachusetts, 1650 - 1790.* Morrison portrays the missionary project from the perspective of the Massachusett Indians. He argues that the Algonquian people, and particularly the Massachusett, participated in that project much more actively than is usually represented. Morrison says that activity was in large part a deliberate attempt by the Massachusett to deal with their devastation by illness in the epidemics that swept through the native populations of New England between 1616 and 1646, and he claims it should be understood as a strategic accommodation of the British presence in the face of that adversity, rather than as assimilation or capitulation to an enemy. Along with George Tinker's chapter on Eliot in *Missionary Conquest,* which reconstructs certain aspects of Massachusett religious beliefs and social mores within the broader historical context of European imperialism in North America,

Morrison's book offers a detailed and concrete account of the role of the indigenous people of southern New England as active participants in, rather than passive victims of, the British missionary project. O'Brien makes a similar argument concerning the people of Natick, the first Praying Town, as they struggled to rebuild their farms and community following the devastating effects of Metacom's War and of the assimilationist ideals that slowly rendered the Indians invisible to most European settlers in New England. The broader historical scope of this work, in conjunction with its focus on a single community, allows O'Brien to trace the concrete persistence of Indian culture in New England in the face of an inexorable evolution from the native "Americans" of the early colonial period to little more than invisible memories for citizens of the Early Republic.[16]

ORIGINS OF THE MISSIONARY PROJECT IN NEW ENGLAND

The first attempts to attain what the Massachusetts Bay charter called the "principall Ende" of the plantation were made on Martha's Vineyard in 1643, when Thomas Mayhew Jr. began preaching to the Wampanoags on the island that his father had colonized only a year earlier (*Light Appearing* 109). That same year, following the efforts of New England agents Thomas Weld and Hugh Peter to raise money in England for charity in the colonies, a pamphlet was published that advertised on its title page an account of "New Englands First Fruits," among which was the "Conversion of some / Conviction of divers, / Preparation of sundry of the Indians.[17] First in the series that would become the Eliot Tracts, *First Fruits* invokes the Black Legend to advocate what Bross (1997) calls the "anti-conquest" theme of the missionary project by emphasizing that, contrary to the Spanish and Catholic precedents, the English had occupied the land without violence and were welcomed by the Indians. The Indians are eager to hear about the Gospel, the authors claim; the only obstacle is the lack of qualified missionaries, which could easily be remedied by contributions from England.

This first pitch for funds was not received enthusiastically; less than £35 was received for the Indians, although it did produce £300 for the new Harvard College (Kellaway 1962, 9 - 10). Nor did the colonists find much evidence in New England of any widespread inclination among the Indians to embrace the New England Way in the first decade of settlement. In 1644, however, five sachems formally submitted themselves and their people to the authority of the General Court. The motives behind this "voluntary" subjugation to British jurisdiction were complex, and they undoubtedly included a hope for sheer survival of groups that were devastated by disease, that had lost most of their land, and that were surrounded by enemies on all sides.[18] Nevertheless, whatever their motives for signing, the terms of the agreements they endorsed included an explicit willingness "to be instructed in the knowledge and worship of God," and the colonists seized upon this opportunity to pass three missionary directives in 1644 - 1645 to begin that instruction (Cogley 1999, 28). The lack of any infrastructure to support that work, coupled with a persistent ambivalence about its theological timeliness, undermined the effort for another two years, but in October 1646 John Eliot was selected to give the first missionary sermon to the Massachusett Indians at Dorchester Mill near the Indian village of Nonantum on the Charles River.

John Eliot was born in 1604 in Widford, England, and attended Jesus College at Cambridge. He received his bachelor's degree in 1622, and in 1629 he served briefly in a school run by Thomas Hooker. In 1631 Eliot emigrated to New England aboard the *Lyon*. He was immediately asked to fill in for pastor John Wilson of the First Church in Boston, which suggests that Eliot had been ordained as a minister before he left England. As soon as a church was gathered at Roxbury, Eliot joined that congregation first as a teacher and then minister, and he remained at Roxbury until his death in 1690. In 1632 he married Hanna Mumford and had six children with her.[19] Eliot also participated in the trial of Anne Hutchinson, supporting the orthodox complaints against her, and he contributed some verses to the *Bay Psalm Book* published in Cambridge in 1640. Little is known about his relations with the Indians before 1646, other than his opposition to Massachusetts Bay's friendship treaty with the Pequots in 1634, and his account of how he learned to speak Algonquian from a Montauk captive by the name of Cockenoe, who had been seized in the Pequot War and was living as a servant in the house of Richard Collicot of Dorchester.[20]

The first sermon at Dorchester Mill, which was delivered with the help of an interpreter, was met with scorn and indifference. Eliot suspected that the sachem Cutshamekin had encouraged his people to resist the missionary's overtures because Cutshamekin feared his authority would be undermined by the English missionary (see *Clear Sun-shine*). Eliot returned to Nonantum in October, accompanied by Thomas Shepard, Daniel Gookin, another Englishman (either John Wilson of Boston or Elder Heath of Roxbury), and Cockenoe. This time Eliot found his audience more receptive; he spoke to the Indians for three hours and then left, distributing gifts of tobacco and apples (Morrison 1995, 43).[21] A week later, the Massachusetts Bay Colony passed measures designed to codify and reinforce this initial receptivity. Those measures included a systematic assignment of responsibility for ministering to the Indians, and the charge to find a place for the converted Indians to live where they could develop a code by which they could live more compatibly among the English. Two other measures explicitly subjected the submitting Indians to the capital law against blasphemy and set fines for idolatry, which was defined as the "outward worship to their false gods and to the devil" (Cogley 1999, 42).[22]

Eliot met with the people of Nonantum three more times before the end of the year, and soon he could point to the conversion of Waban, a minor leader among the Indians, as evidence of the power of the Gospel. In the winter of 1646 the people of Nonantum drew up ten rules that were designed to bring Indian customs into conformity with English mores, and in May 1647 the General Court created a separate judicial order for the converted Indians that established a special status for them under Massachusetts law (see *Day-Breaking*).[23] In 1650, under pressure from the expanding English town of Watertown just across the river, the Nonantum were persuaded to move several miles south along the Charles River, where they were joined by the Neponset, Musketaquid, Pawtuckets, and some Nipmucks to form Natick, the first Praying Town.[24] The missionary project was underway. All it lacked was a reliable source of funds and a means of reporting its successes to supporters in England; both of those needs were met by the Society for the Propagation of the Gospel in New England.

THE SOCIETY FOR THE PROPAGATION OF THE GOSPEL IN NEW ENGLAND

Shortly after the jurisdiction of the General Court was extended to cover the civil affairs of the proselytes, a bill was proposed in Parliament to establish a Society for Propagation of the Gospel in New England.[25] The bill was the product of Edward Winslow's tireless efforts on behalf of the colonies and the missionary project in particular. Winslow had recently been appointed agent for the colonies in England to replace Weld and Peter, the most probable authors of the first Eliot tract, *New England's First Fruits* (1643). Though ostensibly intending to raise funds for the missionary project in New England, Weld's and Peter's dedication to the missionaries was equivocal, to say the least, and *First Fruits* pointedly suggested that that project would also be a likely way to raise funds for Harvard College. Winslow, however, took the promise of Indian conversion made in that earlier tract to be a serious commitment on the part of the colonists to missionary work. On his way over to England, he put together several manuscripts that had been given to him upon his departure and created the second Eliot tract, *The Day-Breaking, if not the Sun-Rising of the Gospell with the Indians in New England* (1647). While in England he received a second manuscript with a long letter from Eliot and a brief epilogue by Thomas Shepard, which Winslow published as *The Clear Sun-shine of the Gospel breaking forth upon the Indians in New-England . . .* By Mr. Thomas Shepard Minister . . . at Cambridge in New-England (1648). The purpose of both tracts was to demonstrate progress toward the conversion of the Indians, and they had the desired effect. In March 1648 the House of Commons finally discussed Winslow's bill shortly after the publication of *The Clear Sun-shine of the Gospel*. Urged on by Winslow, the House referred the bill to the Committee on Foreign Plantations, which prepared it for formal reading in August. The reading was postponed several times, however, and the bill was finally dropped in December 1648.

Winslow persisted in his efforts, and in April 1649 another bill was prepared but, again, its reading was postponed. The next month Winslow published the fourth of the Eliot Tracts, *The Glorious Progress of the Gospel*. In his dedicatory letter, Wilson mentioned the theory that the Indians might be descendents of the ten tribes of Israel, and he reminded Parliament that a new bill was ready. A month later, in June 1649, the bill was read and sent to committee for amendment. After a futile last-minute attempt to attach an amendment that would include a charge to raise funds for Harvard, the bill finally passed. It established a corporation in England consisting of sixteen people, mostly wealthy London merchants, to be called "The President and Society for the Propagation of the Gospel in New-England."[26] The bill further provided for the collection of funds to support the missionary efforts in New England through house-by-house canvassing in England and Wales, and for the disbursement of those funds through the Commissioners of the United Colonies of New England.[27]

The Commissioners of the United Colonies was a group formed in 1643 to oversee the interests of Plymouth, Connecticut, New Haven, and Massachusetts Bay, each of which elected its own representatives to the group. Though they were the only formal intercolonial organization at the time, the Commissioners were never officially recognized by Parliament; nor were they necessarily the most obvious choice for this job, since the group had been formed primarily to protect the colonies against the Indians, as well as against the expansion of Dutch and French interests in the area. As soon as the Commissioners were formally notified of their new responsibility in September 1650, tensions arose between them and the Society. The Commissioners undertook to prescribe how the Society should spend the funds it raised, what kinds of goods it should send the colonists for use or sale, and, in particular, where it should invest in real estate—that is, in New England rather than in England, as the Society planned. In return, the Society told the Commissioners they had to confer with Eliot and Mayhew on the best use of the funds sent to New England, and it required the Commissioners to provide an exact account of all goods bought or sold for the missionaries and Indians. These disputes were partially settled in 1656 when the Society agreed simply to endorse bills of exchange drawn up by the Commissioners for the purchase of goods in the colonies related to the missionary effort, with only an annual limit imposed on their spending. This practical compromise lasted until 1684, when the Commissioners ceased meeting altogether. At that time a new group was formed by the Society—now called the New England Company—with its members appointed directly by the Company rather than elected in the colonies: the Commissioners for Indian Affairs, also known as the Commissioners for Propagation of the Gospel (Kellaway 1962, 199).[28]

The Society was the first Protestant missionary organization in the world, and the first to raise funds by canvassing individuals for small donations. In the first ten years of its existence, it raised almost £16,000, most of which was invested in England to provide a regular income for the mission that averaged £440 per annum from 1662 to 1690.[29] These funds supported Eliot's missionary efforts over these years with salaries and supplies, and they paid for publications associated with Eliot's projects, including, most notably, his Indian Bible and other Algonquian-language works. The Society also funded educational programs for Indian children conducted in both Algonquian and English, and it supported the Indian College at Harvard, where at least four Indians were enrolled in the seventeenth century and one graduated (Cogley 1999, 222). This success was not uncontroversial, however. Critics complained that England should be doing more for the poor at home before it sent its funds abroad, and that the Society's funds did not always wind up being used for the intended purposes. Part of that suspicion was left over from the persistent inability of the first colonial agents, Weld and Peter, to account for monies entrusted to them. Another part was derived from the fact that the Commissioners of the United Colonies clearly had a broader sense of the funding objectives than did most of the Society—including, predictably, persistent attempts by the Commissioners to divert money to Harvard College. Furthermore, Eliot himself continued to agitate for direct funding from several benefactors and to complain publicly about the salary he was paid by the Society (originally set at £20), much to the irritation of both the Society and the Commissioners (Kellaway 1962, 32).

In addition to providing money and supplies for the missionaries, the Society immediately began publishing a series of tracts describing the missionary project in New England, starting with *The Light appearing more and more towards the perfect Day* (1651) and continuing through *A further Account of the progress of the Gospel Amongst the Indians in New England* (1660) and perhaps *A Brief Narrative of the Progress of the Gospel amongst the Indians in New England, in the Year 1670* (1671)—that is, the last six of what are now known as the Eliot Tracts. The Society also wrote and published broadsides and letters of appeal that were sent to ministers along with a copy of the act establishing the Society to encourage the ministers' participation in the project (Kellaway 1962, 25 - 26).[30] Of all the publications supported by the Society, the most unusual were Eliot's translations from the English Bible into the Algonquian language. In *The Light Appearing*, Eliot reports that he has taught an Indian (Job Nesutan) to read and write, and in *Strength Out of Weaknesse* he says many others had acquired at least a rudimentary literacy. Eliot's most immediate goal was to enable the Indians to read religious instruction in preparation for conversion, but his students also assisted Eliot in his ongoing translations of scripture.[31] Eliot first proposed to translate parts of the Bible in a letter to Edward Winslow in 1649, only thirty-eight years after the King James Version of the Bible had been published. That great literary and scholarly enterprise had taken fifty-four men seven years; Eliot completed his translation in fourteen years, working only with some native interpreters who advised him on Algonquian lexicography. In 1653 Eliot's first text in Algonquian, a primer and catechism, was published by the Society and printed by Samuel Green in Cambridge at Harvard College, which had the only operating press in New England.[32] In 1655 the book of Genesis and part of Matthew were printed as an experiment, and in 1659 the Commissioners announced their intention to print 1,000 copies of Eliot's translation of the whole Bible. Eighty pounds of new type were ordered for the press at Cambridge (with extra O's and K's to accommodate Eliot's transcription of Algonquian phonemes), and the next year journeyman printer Marmaduke Johnson was hired in England and shipped to New England to assist Green on the project, along with more than 100 reams of paper (Kellaway 1962, 130).[33] In 1661 the entire New Testament appeared in print in a run of 1,500 copies, and in 1663, complete translations of the Old and New Testaments were printed together in the same 1,180-page volume, along with 500 copies of a psalter in Algonquian, *Mamusse Wunneetupanatamwe Up-Biblum God* (see Eliot's letter to Richard Baxter, July 6, 1663 and Baxter 1696). In April 1664, the new

Governor of what was now the New England Company, Robert Boyle, proudly presented a specially bound presentation copy to King Charles II.[34]

Eliot's literal translations of scripture were serviceable, though neither elegant nor strictly accurate, and in a letter to the Company drafted by Cotton Mather the Commissioners complained, "There are many words of Mr. Elliott's forming which they [the Indians] never understood." The letter goes on to observe that Eliot had "as much difficulty to bring them unto a competent knowledge of the Scriptures, as it would be to get a sensible acquaintance with the English Tongue."[35] Nevertheless, after some debate the Company sponsored another edition of Eliot's Indian Bible in 1685, and the Company continued to publish small quantities of other books in dialects of the Algonquian language after Eliot's death, with translations by Grindal Rawson (who collaborated with Eliot on his last translation, a version of Thomas Shepard's *Sincere Convert*), the minister Samuel Danforth of Taunton, and Experience Mayhew (Kellaway 1962, 147). The main series of Indian books published by the Company ended in 1720 as it had begun over sixty years earlier with the printing of an Indian Primer, this time in both English and Algonquian (Kellaway 1962, 163).[36]

In the first two decades of the eighteenth century there was a brief campaign by some Commissioners to issue another edition of the Indian Bible. At that time, however, the old argument arose about whether it was better to preach to the Indians in Algonquian or to teach the Indians English. Samuel Sewall, by then a Commissioner, argued for reprinting the Bible, largely on practical grounds that the Indians responded better to sermons and texts in their own language. More of the Commissioners opposed the printing, including Cotton Mather. Those opposing the project argued that the money would be better spent Anglicizing the Indians: "It is very sure, the best thing we can do for our Indians is to Anglicize them in all agreeable Instances; and in that of Language, as well as other. They can scarce retain their Language, without a Tincture of other Salvage Inclinations, which do but ill suit, either with the Honor, or with the design of Christianity."[37] By the 1730s the question was settled in favor of English, and the Indian Bible was not reprinted again (Kellaway 1962, 230).

When Charles II gained the throne in 1660 the legal basis for the Society—like all the other ordinances of the Interregnum—was obliterated by the Act of Oblivion and Indemnity, which also undermined the Society's title to the real estate in England that it had acquired as investments. That autumn the Society began working to reestablish its legal foundation, and on February 7, 1662 a new charter was sealed creating the "Company for Propagacion of the Gospell in New England, and the parts adjacent in America," or more simply, "The New England Company" (though New Englanders still commonly referred to it as the "Corporation"). Nine of the original Society's members were appointed to the new Company, along with thirty-six new members and its new Governor Robert Boyle (Kellaway 1962, 46 - 47).[38] Eventually the Company was able to regain ownership to most of the lands it had acquired in the preceding decade; it renewed annuities from several wealthy individuals and resumed its fundraising efforts. Support for the Company diminished somewhat after 1702 when the Anglican Society for the Propagation of the Gospel in Foreign Parts was formed to compete with the Dissenters, who made up the majority of the Company's members.[39] Despite increased competition and continuing criticism from both Anglicans and Catholics, the Company persisted in its dedication to the Indians, and in the first two decades of the eighteenth century it broadened its mission to include a defense of the legal rights of the Indians against the encroachment of English colonists onto lands set aside for the natives of the area (Kellaway 1962, 218).

It was only after the Revolutionary War began that the Company suspended its support for the missionary project in New England, declaring that "this Court do not think themselves warranted by their charter from the Crown in remitting Money to New England so long as that country continues in Arms against his Majesty & their fellow Subjects."[40] After the war was over, the Company still refused to resume support for the missionaries in New England on the grounds that the former colonies were now foreign states and so beyond the bounds of the Company's charter and charge. Despite some debate about the legal merits of that argument, in 1786 the Company finally resolved that its charter no longer extended to New England and decided to transfer its attention entirely to "the King's colony of new Brunswick"—territory covered by the "Parts adjacent to America" phrase in the Company's formal title—thus ending the Company's official involvement with the missionary project in New England (Kellaway 1962, 280).

PRAYING TOWNS

Of all the activities supported by the Company, the most controversial and historically significant was the formation of settlements specifically for native proselytes, which were known as "Praying Towns." Shortly after the Society for the Propagation of the Gospel in New England was established, the first Praying Town was formed at Natick under Eliot's guidance. The site was based on a land grant from the General Court of 2,000 acres along the Charles River near the town of Dedham.[41] Most of the Indians who relocated to Natick came from Nonantum, which was the first Indian town to obtain legal status under colonial law when its inhabitants formally submitted to the jurisdiction of the General Court in 1646, but the civil covenant formed by Praying Indians at Natick in 1650 created the first community of Indian proselytes in New England.

The Praying Towns were organized according to what Morrison (1995) describes as Eliot's three-part strategy of "cohabitation and labor, government and law, and a church covenant" (93). Many of the Indians at Natick continued to live in wigwams, but several English-style structures were built quickly, including a large meetinghouse, several private houses, and a footbridge over eighty feet long spanning the Charles River (Winslow 1966, 126 - 27). Eliot designed a system of government based on Exodus 18: 17 - 26, where Moses's father-in-law Jethro suggests to Moses that he appoint a hierarchical system of leaders for his people based on groups of ten, fifty, one hundred, and so on up to Moses at the top as the general ruler. With fewer than 150 people at first,

Natick offered only a small-scale opportunity to test this theory, but the model was imposed, with the sachem Cutshamekin as the ruler of hundreds, and two rulers of fifties: the aging Totherswamp, and Waban, who also helped adjudicate minor legal matters among the Indians (Cogley 1999, 128; Morrison 1995, 96).[42] A school was soon started with the proselyte Monequassun as schoolmaster, Eliot having already taught him to read and write. In 1660, following several unsuccessful attempts, the first Indian Church was formally gathered at Natick, and by 1675 there were roughly 200 people living there (Mandell 1991; cf. Cogley 1999, 111).[43]

Motives for this relocation were mixed on both sides. Since the European incursion in the early years of the seventeenth century, the Indians of New England, and especially the Massachusett (who were the main focus of Eliot's work in coastal Massachusetts Bay) had been devastated by waves of disease that reduced their numbers, destroyed their kinship groups, undermined the social and political structures of the villages, and in some places literally emptied areas where thousands of people had lived for decades and perhaps centuries. Prior to the great plagues of 1617 - 1619, it is likely there had been up to 90,000 people in the area of southern New England; by 1674 there were fewer than 11,000. Among the Massachusett alone, the population dropped from 4,500 in 1600 to 750 by 1631, and that was reduced even further by the smallpox epidemic of 1633 - 1634 and waves of disease in the early 1640s (see Cook 1976). These changes left the "remnants" vulnerable to pressure from the expanding British population as well as open to attack by their Indian enemies, and at least some of their leaders clearly looked upon cooperation with the English as a realistic accommodation of their diminished situation.[44]

The native people within the culture area of the Northeast Woodlands where the Praying Towns were located lived by a combination of hunting, fishing, and agriculture, with 80 percent of the population engaged in the latter category (Cronon 1983, 42).[45] These Indians were not nomadic hunters, but they were much more mobile than the British population of the area because the Indians tended to plant, move to gather and fish over the summer, and then return to the fields when harvest was ready. Wigwams were the basic housing, and small groups occasionally gathered in more permanent fortified villages, though the population of a village fluctuated greatly over the course of the year. Individual men and women usually formed bonded pairs (and hence produced a family unit recognizable as such by the British), but these pairs also combined to form extended family groups. These groups were further extended by exogamous marriage, and the larger clans were organized into extensive and more formal tribal structures governed by the sachems. Sachems did not usually have the broad political power accorded to them by the English; their authority seldom extended beyond a single village or group of villages in limited proximity. They usually ruled for life, but their authority and influence were based on personal traits rather than governing structures, and their power waxed and waned depending on many factors. This relatively informal foundation for the sachems' power was one reason they occasionally sought out alliances with the English to consolidate their control and protect their villages from incursions by neighboring sachems, the most obvious example being the submission of the sachems to English law in 1644 and the conversion of Cutshamekin in 1647 (Cogley 1999, 54 - 55).

The Algonquians also relied on the power of powwows, or shamans, who were believed to possess the ability to communicate with the spiritual world, cast and cure spells, predict the future, and perform other magical acts common to most shamanistic cultures. Like the sachems, powwows had no permanent structural position in village society, and they could demand no loyalty beyond the persuasive power of their acts. That power was constantly tested against pragmatic outcomes, and powwows were always open to challenge from competitors. As a result, the idea of challenging the local powwow for spiritual eminence was part of the Algonquian culture, as was the custom of shifting allegiance to the more powerful spiritual agent following a successful challenge. The Puritans' rejection of the powwows' authority therefore could be read as continuous with religious and cultural practice among the Indians, and that continuity no doubt contributed to some of the missionaries' success. The most notable example of such an occasion was the widespread conversion of Indians on Martha's Vineyard in 1646, when Indians who had been baptized seemed to escape the effects of a devastating plague sweeping the island (Bowden and Ronda 1980, 33).

The power of the powwows and the more general sacred life of the Algonquian were based on a belief in the spiritual dimension of all lived experience, which included a realm of beings and forces beyond the human individual. That belief led to ritualized contact between individuals and guiding spirits associated with specific places, objects, animals, and especially activities such as hunting and warfare.[46] These contacts were formally associated with ritual practices that prepared the individual (most often a young man) to engage with the world in pursuit of a particular objective, but the presence of spiritual beings called *manitowuk* suffused the visible world of the Algonquians and were thought to influence even the most trivial daily tasks (Bowden and Ronda 1980, 19). This "general religiosity," as Bowden and Ronda call it, made the spiritual thrust of Christianity comprehensible to the Indians quite apart from any real or imagined similarity between the Algonquian Manitou and the Puritan Jehovah that is occasionally mentioned by English missionaries.[47] This shared interest in spiritual experience also resulted in general similarities between Puritan prayer and the personal, ritualized communication with the spiritual world that was part of the Indians' religious practice (Morrison 1995, 31, 57).

More particularly, the crucial role that origin myths played in the culture of the Bay Algonquians predisposed them to curiosity about the story of Genesis, which Eliot at first dismissed as idle curiosity but eventually recognized as genuine philosophical inquiry. The same was true for the connection between Christian notions of sin and punishment and the Indians' haunting sense of guilt and despair at their recent decimation through illness. As Morrison (1995) puts it, the devastating effect of the pestilence and plague years had prepared the Algonquians to be receptive to the idea of a god who punishes his enemies, and to the suggestion of apocalyptical social decay from a previous paradisiacal state: "Eliot's Scriptural exegesis seemed to support their own origin myths, their collective memory of the coming of the epidemics. . . . The understanding of disease as supernaturally inspired and directed, held by both cultures, became the foundation upon which the remnants learned to embrace a common bond with their European neighbors" (31, see also 55). These parallels did not go unnoticed at the time. In *Good Newes from New England,* Edward Winslow (1624) observed that the Indians "by their own traditions [had] some principles of a life after this life, and that good or evill, according to their demeanor in this life" (12). It is unlikely Eliot ever took such beliefs as anything other than ignorant superstition. As he remarked in *Light Appearing*, the Algonquians had "no principles of their own, nor yet wisdome of their own" (131). Nevertheless, as Morrison (1995) puts it, "The standard tools of the Puritan clergy approximated coincidentally, tenuously, yet successfully, the remnant experience" (52), and there are enough reports in the Eliot tracts of syncretic discourse by Indians in religious examinations and responses to sermons to suggest that they found at least some connection between their traditional beliefs and what they heard from the missionaries.

Beyond these general parallels and indirect reports of individuals' speech, it is difficult to measure the extent to which the proselytes found the preaching of the missionaries comprehensible or compatible with their former way of life. To be sure, the pervasive pantheism of Algonquian beliefs, as manifested in their animistic worship of places, objects, and animals, had little in common with the strict monotheism of Puritanism or its iconoclastic distrust of material images, nor was the bibliocentric nature of Calvinist theology compatible with the decidedly more open and flexible oral traditions of the Algonquians. Contrary to Morrison, Bowden and Ronda argue that the Indians must have found the Puritan doctrine of human depravity, hell, and the doctrine of grace versus works utterly incomprehensible given the Indians' more benign view of the visible world and a less-selective vision of the afterlife. Whatever internal adjustments may or may not have been required in the proselytes' beliefs, however, the Indians clearly recognized conversion and relocation into Praying Towns as a major change in their way of life and in themselves, as reflected at the end of Eliot's *Indian Dialogues,* when the "Penitent" native says to John Speen, "I am another man than I was" (Bowden and Ronda 1980, 160). In addition to philosophical differences, there were many social changes that undermined pre-contact customs and the Indians' former everyday life: the shift to permanent residence versus a seminomadic lifestyle, the need for European farming techniques to make the permanently cultivated fields productive, corollary changes in gender roles and generational expectations regarding children and the elderly, and new British names, clothes, and hairstyles, to name only the most obvious examples of how life changed for the Indians who moved into the Praying Towns (Morrison 1995, 84).

Despite these changes, Morrison rejects the stereotype of the converted Indians as new men, and he argues that Indians who switched to English ways did not simply abandon their former way of life. Rather than "assimilation," Morrison describes the Indian's adoption of English ways as an act of "acculturation" (that is, a syncretic integration of traits from two cultures that retains links to both). For example, meetinghouses and clapboard structures existed alongside wigwams, and some of the towns were protected by a palisaded fort, the familiar defensive structure for Algonquian people. There were assemblies of worship, but the people were called by drums rather than expensive English bells (Morrison 1995, 153). As a result, the towns became a contact zone between the two cultures that was inhabited by genuine cultural hybrids, Praying Indians who were also what Neal Salisbury (1982) calls "red Puritans" to emphasize the reciprocal effects of this mimetic exchange of customs, social practices, and cultural identities.[48] Still, the syncretic culture of the Praying Towns undeniably undermined the principal sources of order and cohesion of Indian life. Powwows could not be admitted to the towns unless they submitted to the higher spiritual authority of Puritan missionaries, so their power and social status were immediately diminished.[49] The sachems who moved with their people tended to retain positions of political authority, but their formal submission to British law obviously undermined their autonomy and with it much of their former power. Furthermore, the social cohesion of the exogamous clan seldom survived the move unless an entire village or network of villages moved together, and even then the British emphasis on the pair-bonded family, reinforced by the architecture of single-family houses and enclosed fields that were adopted by many of the Praying Indians, often made the church congregation the only viable source of social cohesion beyond the family. The Algonquian language remained intact among the proselytes and served as an important source of traditional community, but in John Eliot's hands that, too, was to become a tool for British missionary work.

Despite the disruptive effect of the new beliefs and customs and the dislocation of entire clans from their traditional areas, the relative stability and security of the Praying Towns were undoubtedly appealing to a people whose social structures were disintegrating and who were under constant threat from their Indian enemies and hostile colonists. Among the colonists, the spiritual motives for relocating the proselytes were perhaps naïve but undoubtedly sincere, at least for Eliot and the other missionaries and their supporters. Removed from the influence of their heathen neighbors, the proselytes could devote themselves to religious instruction and to adopting the English mores and customs that were so closely associated with spiritual rectitude by the Puritans. The Praying Towns thus pleased the few Puritans who believed that the Indians should be instructed in their own languages and that the Indians' beliefs and rituals should at least be acknowledged while being corrected by Christianity. At the same time, the Praying Towns were viewed as a productive halfway step by others who insisted that complete Anglicization of the Indians was necessary for true civilization and conversion. Less idealistic colonists often supported the relocation of Indians into Praying Towns because in most cases those new towns were farther removed from British settlements, which were constantly expanding and needed more adjacent land. Occasionally, as at Natick and Dedham, the new towns created tensions where none had existed before, but more often they were seen by both sides at least as a short-term solution to mounting tensions over the expansion of the British settlements.

Eliot originally hoped to bring all Praying Indians together at Natick, but shortly after Natick was established, five other Praying Towns were created nearby, partly to accommodate the growing number of proselytes, and partly to respond to the Indians' desires to have towns closer to the traditional homelands of different tribes. The towns were Punkapoag and Wamesit in 1653, and Hassanamesit, Okommakamesit, and Nashobahh in 1654.[50] In 1669 Magunkog was created, completing the group of what Daniel Gookin (1674) called the "old praying towns." Most of these towns were clustered around Natick and populated by Massachusetts and Nipmucks; the only exception was Wamesit, which was located near the juncture of the Concord and Merrimack rivers and mostly inhabited by Pennacook Indians. Following the submission of eight Nipmuck sachems in 1668—motivated by their desire for English protection from their Narragansett enemies—seven new Praying Towns were formed among the Nipmucks along the Quinebaug and Blackstone rivers just south of the original group: Quantisset, Pakachoog, Chabanakongkomun, Wabquisset, Manchage, Maanexit, and Waeuntug. According to Gookin, by the time Metacom's War began in 1675, each of the old towns had about seventy people, and most of the new towns had about ninety inhabitants, for a total of about 1,000 residents of all Praying Towns combined (O'Brien 1997, 81; cf. Bross 2001, 66). According to Eliot, speaking through Piumbukhou in the *Indian Dialogues*, that represented all of the Massachusett Indians and most of the Nipmucks (Bowden and Ronda 1980, 80).

Beyond Massachusetts Bay there were few systematic missionary efforts in the British colonies other than those of the Mayhew family on Martha's Vineyard, where 300 Wampanoags had accepted the mission by 1652. In Connecticut the General Court ordered ministers to begin preaching to the Indians in 1650, but in the absence of anyone with adequate language skills or the evangelical commitment that drove Eliot and Mayhew, these directives produced few results before Metacom's War. The situation in Connecticut was further complicated by the Mohegan sachem Uncas, who resisted the mission, undoubtedly because he feared he would lose power over his people and the tribute that power entailed (Cogley 1999, 205). The Rhode Island Charter of 1663 proclaimed the missionary aims of that colony, but with similarly meager results. There are scattered references in the Eliot Tracts to missionary efforts among the Narragansetts in Rhode Island by Eliot's proselytes in the 1640s and early 1650s, but the Narragansetts were generally resistant to the mission. The efforts were further undermined by hostilities between the two English colonies. In a letter to the Massachusetts General Court in 1654, Roger Williams complained that the Rhode Island Indians had been threatened with death if they refused to accept the mission brought by Eliot's associates. Williams associated this interference from Massachusetts Bay with a more general hostility to the Indians in that colony, which he said was contrary to the objective of conversion—and, not coincidentally, to the continuing independence of Rhode Island from its Puritan neighbor (Cogley 1999, 189).

In Plymouth Colony, missionary efforts were more successful. Eliot first preached to the Nauset Indians in 1647, and by 1675 there were more than 500 Christian Indians in the colony (Cogley 1999, 193). Part of this success was due to the unusual commitment and linguistic abilities of several colonists who oversaw the development of the mission in Plymouth, including Richard Bourne, who founded the praying town of Mashpee in 1660 and served as pastor to the Indian congregation until he died in 1682, and John Cotton Jr., who lived in Plymouth from 1667 to 1697 and advised Eliot on the revision of his Algonquian Bible. These successes have been overshadowed in history, however, by Eliot's failure to convert Metacom and the Pokanokets. In that effort Eliot was assisted by John Sassamon, a Christian Neponset who was living among the Pokanokets in the early 1660s after briefly enrolling at Harvard in 1653, and whom Eliot chose as a teacher for the Pakonokets, ostensibly at Metacom's request. Eliot also sent two Christian Indians, William Ahawton and Anthony, to speak with Metacom, and Eliot later represented that conversation in his *Indian Dialogues* as leading to the imaginary conversion of Metacom. In fact, Metacom's hostility to the mission remained adamant, and, as Cogley points out, the efforts of Eliot's proselytes exacerbated tensions between the Pakonokets and Plymouth Colony that led to war in 1675 (206).[51]

On the eve of Metacom's War there were fourteen Praying Towns and two Indian churches in New England.[52] Life was seldom easy in these towns. Disease remained a problem, and in addition to continuing suspicions and the occasional legal challenge from their English neighbors, the Praying Towns also faced serious threats from the Iroquois in northern New York, especially the Mohawk. Nashobah was hit especially hard, and in *Brief Narrative* Eliot says that he was arming the inhabitants for their own protection against their Indian enemies (6 - 7; see also Morrison 1995, 157 - 158). In 1673 hundreds of Algonquians (including some Praying Indians) were killed in an ambush while returning from an unsuccessful attack on a Mohawk fort, and hostilities continued through the 1680s. Even more significant, by 1675 tensions between Indians and the British had reached a critical stage throughout New England, mostly due to the ever-expanding encroachment of the British settlements on Indian land. The outright seizure of Indian land by the British was quite rare and has been greatly exaggerated by historians, who have conflated the causes with the consequences of colonial expansion. While the effect of that expansion was the undeniable displacement of native peoples along the Eastern seaboard, prior to 1675 most of that expansion had taken place through land purchases from Indians that were entirely legal—under British law, of course, and certainly without a clear sense among the Indians at the beginning of the extent to which the British would permanently occupy the land and close it to use by others.

As the cumulative effect of these sales became more evident to the Indians, resentment grew among some tribes toward the British presence on their former lands. In December 1674 the British at Plymouth were warned about the growing rebellion by Sassamon, who had rejoined the converts at Natick by 1670 after serving as a scribe and translator to Metacom (see Hubbard 1677; also Morrison 1995, 168, and Cogley 1999, 197). In January 1675 Sassamon was found beneath the ice of a pond near his home and quickly buried, but after rumors of foul play the body was exhumed and examined, and no water was found in the lungs. The cause of death was determined to be severe blows to the head. Three Wampanoags were accused of the murder, and in June they were convicted by a jury of twelve Englishmen and six Praying Indians. The three were later executed for that crime despite their protestations of innocence.[53] Two weeks later, on June 24, the town of Swansea was attacked by a band of Wampanoags under the leadership of the sachem Metacom, known to the British as King Philip. Soon some Nipmucks joined the fight on Metacom's side, and even a few Massachusetts living in the Praying Towns briefly fought the British. Metacom and his allies were a formidable force, but in May 1676 Metacom's wife and nine-year-old child were captured by the British and sold into slavery in Bermuda, and the war ended shortly after that when Metacom was killed in August.

Metacom's War was one of the bloodiest wars in the history of North America. Approximately 5,000 Indians were killed, which represented roughly 40 percent of the Indians in southern New England at the time. About half that many colonists were killed, which was roughly 5 to 6 percent of the British population, and nearly half of the British towns and villages in New England were directly affected by the war. The sheer scale of the deaths, coupled with the relatively rare alliance among tribes in the area, terrified the British and reinforced the widespread fear and animosity towards all Indians, even though one-fourth of the Indians in the area remained sympathetic to the British, including most of the Indians in the Praying Towns. Nevertheless, as early as June 1675 all Praying Indians in New England—a group that by this time totaled as many as 4,000 people—were relocated to only five towns.[54] In October the General Court further consolidated these people into two camps: one on Long Island, and another larger camp of about 500 people on Deer Island, where the entire population of Natick and Indians from many other towns remained in great hardship throughout the severe winter of 1675 - 1676. It was only after the English belatedly realized that the Praying Indians might actually aid them in the war against Metacom that a few were released from captivity and used as spies, guides, and warriors by the British. Military leaders praised the skill and bravery of the Indians in their service, and although Gookin (1677) probably exaggerated when he attributed the British victory to the Indian allies, their presence among the British forces undoubtedly contributed significantly to the outcome of the war.

By the end of the war the missionary effort was in shambles. The Praying Towns were in ruins, and almost all of the Algonquian Bibles Eliot had distributed to the Indians had been lost. Perhaps even more devastating was the dramatic reversal of the image of the Praying Indian among the colonists. Before the war the hybrid character of the Praying Indian represented the civilizing effect of colonization, the promise of peaceful coexistence, and, at least for some, New England's role at the forefront of the millennium. It also forced colonists to acknowledge differences among the Indians that reinforced the more practical political and geographical distinctions among tribes and villages familiar to the British settlers. During and after the war the traits of piety and English civilization that had distinguished the Praying Indian from unconverted Indians came to represent the height of hypocrisy and deceit, and some colonists considered the proselytes more of a threat to the English than the overtly hostile Indians. As Nathaniel Saltonstall (1675) put it in *The Present State of New-England, With Respect to the Indian War,* "Care now is taken to satisfie the (reasonable) desires of the Commonalty, concerning Mr. *Eliots Indians.* . . . They that wear the Name of *Praying Indians,* but rather (as Mr. Hezekiah Ushur termed *Preying Indians*) they have made Preys of much English Blood" (19; see also Bross 1997, ch. 6). The former significance of differences between Praying Indians and the unconverted—clothes and hairstyle, the ability to speak English, and even literacy itself—were lost within the binary opposition between Indian and British, and earlier attempts to bridge that difference—conversion among them—were now read as futile, naïve, and even potentially treacherous to the safety of the colonists.[55]

After the war, despite animosity toward all Indians on the part of most colonists and despite continuing suspicions about Praying Indians in particular, Natick and three more of the Praying Towns were rebuilt, and in 1685 a second edition of the Bible was printed.[56] Eliot was seventy-six years old, however, and disabled from the sciatica that had plagued him for much of his life, and he was unable to restore the momentum of missionary work in the preceding three decades. By 1698 there were only 180 inhabitants and 10 church members at Natick, which in many ways had always been the centerpiece of the missionary project. There was also an increasing tendency among the British to relocate both hostile and Christian Indians onto the same reserved land, which encouraged alliances across tribal boundaries and undermined any sense of identification with the English that remained among the Praying Indians. According to Bowden and Ronda (1980, 54), 40 percent of the Massachusett proselytes retained their faith after the war, and Gookin continued to proselytize along with a few other missionaries, but none of these people had the influence or the organizational skills necessary to sustain the mission at its previous level after Eliot died in 1690. The Great Awakening renewed interest in Christianity among some Indians, but the missionary effort in New England was never again able to overcome the lingering hostility and prejudice of the British settlers, nor the resentment of the Indian allies they had abandoned during the war.

Following Eliot's death the Company and Commissioners tried to purchase large pieces of land on Martha's Vineyard and Hogg's Island for the Indians, but resistance by the colonists and continuing legal fights over title to the lands rendered this strategy largely ineffectual. Interest in the Indian languages also waned, but in 1698 two of the few ministers who could speak Algonquian, Grindal Rawson and Samuel Danforth (son of Eliot's famous colleague at Roxbury), were appointed to tour the Indian settlements, preach to them, and report back to the Company on the present state of the missionary effort. They reported that at Natick church membership had dwindled to seven men and three members, with about 170 other men, women, and children in the town (Kellaway 1962, 233 - 236). The Praying Indians on Martha's Vineyard had fared better under the continuous supervision of the Mayhew family, and the history of this success was told by Experience Mayhew (1727) (grandson of Thomas Mayhew Jr.) in *Indian Converts: or some account of the Lives and Dying Speeches of A Considerable Number of the Christianized Indians of Martha's Vineyard, in New England . . . .* Viable populations of 300 to 500 Christian Indians were also reported at Plymouth, Nantucket, Rhode Island, and Cape Cod throughout the first quarter of the 1700s, and in that same period the Commissioners extended their missionary outreach to include the Five Nations in New York, the Pequots and Mohegans in Connecticut, and the Kennebec Indians in Maine (Kellaway 1962, 251).[57] These missions were sustained, albeit somewhat irregularly, until the Revolutionary War, when the disbursement of funds was suspended by the Company prior to the formal withdrawal of support from the former colonies in 1786.

THE THEOLOGY OF CONVERSION: MILLENNIALISM AND THE MISSIONARY PROJECT IN NEW ENGLAND

It is impossible to appreciate the full significance some Puritans ascribed to the missionary project in New England without an understanding of how they understood its place in the widespread millennialist speculation of the period. There was little enthusiasm among Eliot's neighbors for his evangelical ambitions in general. For most of his life Eliot pursued his missionary goals with only a small coterie of associates, and those efforts were funded almost entirely by private money raised in England. Whatever the authors of the Massachusetts Bay charter may have understood as the principal end of the colony, the colonists in New England were faced with a plethora of more immediate practical problems inherent in settling what they considered a foreign and hostile wilderness. While the Indians occasionally may have been helpful to the settlers and might possibly be receptive to the Gospel in time, those traits provided little incentive to support what many colonists thought to be the missionaries' quixotic, if not treasonous, diversion of energy, resources, and land to savages that God himself had marked for extinction on behalf of his chosen people.

In his sermon to the emigrants on the eve of their departure to Massachusetts Bay in 1630, John Cotton explained that God had emptied New England of its former inhabitants to make way for his chosen people, who thus had both spiritual and legal rights to occupy the land.[58] Joined with the Calvinist doctrine of election, which the colonial Puritans extended to encompass not just the individual's salvation but that of the entire nation of saints, this divine mandate for colonization not only encouraged little sympathy for the Indians, but also bore within it justification for the genocidal rage that had erupted in the Pequot War a decade before Eliot began preaching to the Indians.[59] Furthermore, even apart from the mythic demonization of the Indians as Satan's minions, Calvinist doctrine reserved no clear role for the missionary. Predestination and the elevation of free grace over the power of good works seemed to preclude the spiritual efficacy of any missionary effort. Kellaway (1962) even goes so far as to call the New England Way "basically antipathetic to evangelical endeavour," arguing that pastoral obligations to those outside the covenant were "nebulous" at best (5 - 6). Even for those colonists who felt that obligation more than most of their neighbors, there were more specific doctrinal obstacles to overcome. For the Puritans, conversion was based on a profoundly personal, internal experience of grace by the individual, informed by a full knowledge of Christian doctrine that prepared the soul for salvation. That knowledge depended on being able to read the Bible, and to understand the sermons that explicated and applied its words. As illiterate speakers of a language foreign to scripture and to Puritan ministers, the Indians therefore had no way to prepare themselves, and hence were not seen as likely prospects for instruction leading to conversion and confession.

Eliot would attempt to address this obstacle directly in later years by learning Algonquian, teaching the Indians to read, and translating religious works into their language. That solution was always controversial, however, because from the beginning of the missionary project the primary strategy for converting the Indians relied heavily on the notion of *exemplum*, which Cogley (1999, 5) calls the "affective model" of missionary work. Just as Christ served as a model or *exemplum* for Puritan identity and behavior, the colonists in Plymouth and Massachusetts Bay were to serve as *exempla* for the Indians.[60] As John White (1630) put it in *The Planters Plea,* "The greatest advantage must needes come unto the Natives themselves, whom wee shall teach providence and industry, for want whereof they perish oftentimes. . . . Withall, commerce and example of our course of living, cannot but in time breed civility among them, and that by Gods blessing may make way for religion consequently, and for the saving of their soules" (27). This relatively passive approach to conversion provided little impetus for concerted action, even among those colonists dedicated to the missionary objectives. It tended to discourage overt proselytizing and support for translation or any other acknowledgement of Indian discourse, beliefs, or customs, and it was easily reinforced by the more general assimilationist practices that would render the Indians almost invisible to most colonists over the course of the next century.[61]

The most powerful doctrinal support for the missionary project came from the millennialist speculations embraced by many important dissenting theologians on both sides of the Atlantic. From the earliest years of imperial expansion, millenarian nationalists had portrayed the English presence in North America as the latest step in the spiritually inevitable westward expansion of Christianity and British rule.[62] In an English translation of Bartholomew Keckermann's (1621) *Manuductio to Theologie,* readers could find the prediction that "toward the end of the world the true Religion shall be in America" (93 - 95, in Lovejoy 1985, 18). In the 1630s William Twisse wrote to ask Joseph Mede "whether . . . the plantations in the New World might not be the promised New Jerusalem," and by the middle of the seventeenth century speculations about the geographical location of the Fifth Monarchy regularly included New England among other alternatives.[63] According to Geoffrey Nuttall (1957), the church at Arnhem explicitly claimed that the establishment of "Independency" marked the beginning of Christ's reign on earth (148), and no less a light than Thomas Hooker (1648) claimed in the preface to *A survey of the Summe of Church-Discipline* that if the colonists adhered to rigorous requirements for church membership, the Lord would "Lead us all into that truth, *which will lead us into eternall life . . . so our Congregations, may not only be stiled, as* Ezekiels *temple, but be really what was prophesied the Churches should be, in these last daies,* Jehovah Shammah" (C verso; see also Maclear 1975, 229 - 230). Thomas Goodwin, copastor at Arnhem, found in Revelations the prediction that the purification of the church begun by the emigration to New England was the second of "three great transformations prerequisite to the coming of the New Age," and as late as 1662 the New England minister Jonathan Mitchel was still arguing that the millennium would begin in the New World rather than the Old (see Maclear 1975, 230; Tuveson 1968, 97 - 98; Sehr 1984, 197).

As early as 1620, John Cotton was also preaching to the Puritans on the ideas of Thomas Brightman, who was among the first British theologians to argue not only that the millennium would take place on this earth but that it had actually been underway since 1300 (see Bozeman 1988, 198 - 220). (Most British Protestants believed that the millennium would take place in heaven, or that it had already occurred on earth in ancient times before the reign of the Catholic Church.) After emigrating, Cotton (1642 - 1648) further developed his millennialism in two series of lectures delivered in Massachusetts Bay and published as *A Brief Exposition of the whole Book of Canticles*. Cotton argued that two conditions had to be met before the millennium could occur: The Roman Catholic Church would be destroyed at Armageddon, and there would be a general conversion of the Jews. Cotton's argument complicated the rationale for the colonial mission, because according to him the millennium would start in Jerusalem, and only after these two inaugural events would conversion spread to "Gentiles" around the world—including the pagan peoples of the New World. Consequently, although isolated instances of pagan conversions might occur at any time, the success of any more comprehensive missionary efforts would be necessarily limited prior to the millennium. Therefore, the Puritans had little incentive to launch systematic projects to convert the Indians when there was reason to suspect those enterprises would be both premature and futile (cf. Cogley 1999, 12 - 15).

Early in his career Eliot agreed with Cotton that that the Indians were simply more of the Gentiles from whom some "sprinklings and gleaning" might be brought home to Christ.[64] In the late 1640s, however, Edward Winslow informed Eliot about speculation by John Dury, Menasseh Ben Israel, and Thomas Thorowgood that the Indians might be of the Lost Tribes of Israel, and after reading a manuscript of *Jewes in America* that Thorowgood had sent him just before publication in 1650, Eliot was convinced about the Hebraic ancestry of the Indians (Cogley 1986 - 1987, 216 - 217). In two of the early tracts (*The Glorious Progress of the Gospel amongst the Indians in New England* [1649] and *The Light appearing more and more towards the perfect Day* [1651]), Eliot suggests that the descendants of Shem had migrated to North America via an overland route that had since disappeared.[65] The special place of the New World in Eliot's millennialism provided a unique perspective on the missionary project, and it bestowed an immediate spiritual significance on those efforts. Eliot felt compelled to develop an argument that could account for the persistent discrepancy between the recalcitrant reality of the Indians before him and the more cooperative abstractions of millennialist speculation. He found that connection in language, as he explained in a long letter to Thomas Thorowgood that was published as the preface to the second edition of *Jews in America* in 1660. In that letter, Eliot traces the geographical dissemination of the human race around the globe through the fragmentation of the Hebrew language into disparate, mutually incomprehensible languages that reflected the disintegration of the original community into isolated clans. The European discovery of the Indians in the Americas completed the circle of that migration, and Eliot's translation of the Bible into the Algonquin language was therefore a step toward the restoration of linguistic, social, and spiritual unity—a point emphasized three years later in a letter to Richard Baxter, where Eliot proposes to make Hebrew the universal language.

The first edition of Thorowgood's book in 1650 had been met with as much derision as enthusiasm. Parallels between the Indians and the Jews were picked apart by critics, and the very notion that the American savages might be related to the chosen people of the Bible was ridiculed.[66] The skeptical reception of *Jewes in America* began to undermine the influence of millennialist claims about the New World, which had never been widely accepted, and it threatened the missionary efforts that were being partially defended by the speculative genealogies for the North American natives. So, when *Jewes in America* was republished, Eliot's letter to Thorowgood was appended as preface and defense.[67] In the letter, Eliot defends the proposition that the American Indians had Hebraic origins by proposing no less than a sketch of the history of humankind since the flood in twenty pages. His account of the global diaspora begins with an allusion to the "dry bones" of Ezekiel 37—the same passage he used as a text in his first Algonquian sermon—and to the promise in Deuteronomy 28:64 that what has been scattered and forgotten (that is, the Tribes of Israel) will soon be reintegrated and remembered.[68]

Eliot's account of the dispersion of the human race around the globe begins with the flood and traces the migration of Noah's descendants westward into Europe and northern Africa. The exception to this westerly inclination is the descendants of Shem, who found the West too crowded and developed a contrarian taste for migration to the East. Under the leadership of Eber, they settled India, China, and, finally, America, but they remained united as a single people because they all spoke the same language, Hebrew, "which the old world, before the floud did universally speak, being necessary in the paternal government thereof, and the new world also, until the confusion of *Babel*" (Thorowgood 1660, 7 - 8). Unfortunately, time and the huge geographical expanses of this migration inevitably altered the purity of this common language, but Eliot claims to have found vestigial traces of Hebrew in the languages of the American Indians (usually referred to simply as "the

Americans"). These traces prove that the Americans are descendants of Israel, Eliot says, and, even more important, it suggests that their connections to the primitive Church are less mediated by God's wrath than those of "Western" (i.e., European) cultures:

> may it not be worth the searching after, whether all the Easterne world, the posterity of *Eber*, have not more footsteps of the *Hebrew* language, at least in the gramatical frame of the language, than the westerne world hath. It seemeth to me, by that little insight I have, that the gramatical frame of our *Indian* language cometh *neerer to the Hebrew*, than the *Latine*, or *Greek* do: and if so, then may it not be considerable, that the dispersion of the Ten tribes to the utmost ends of the Earth eastward, into the Easterne world . . . hath lesse severity of punishment in it. (19)

According to Eliot, the simultaneous dispersal of the Jews to the West and to the East halted on the Atlantic shores until the sixteenth century, when the expanding European empires completed the circle. As James Holstun (1983) puts it in his brief but trenchant comment on this letter, "The New World is the appointed site for the utopian encounter of clockwise and counterclockwise Israelites: the Indian descendants of Shem and Eber bearing themselves eastward . . . and the Puritan Israelites bearing westward the Hebrew Scriptures with their heretofore undiscovered models for regenerate civility" (133). Eliot's account of the global dispersion of the human race thus achieves a narrative as well as geographical closure with the colonization of New England. There is nowhere left to go. The completion of this worldly circuit clearly represents for Eliot a comprehensive symbolic mapping of material reality that promises to restore the unity lost when language—and the coherent social order it embodied—was fragmented and the pieces scattered in time and space.

In this account Eliot closely identifies the American shore as a point of genealogical, geographical, and linguistic reintegration and closure, and that closure had obvious historical and spiritual implications. He believed it marked the beginning of the end of time, and quite likely could bring about the millennialist transformation of this earth into a form more suitable for the coming reign of Christ. The scriptural form of government he imposed on the Praying Towns was a step toward that transformation, as was the transformation of the Indian souls through conversion. Central to this transformation for Eliot was its symbolic dimension, which created the common ground where what had been scattered in time could find its spiritual reunion. Language was thus of paramount importance to the missionary effort, not only as a practical means of transmitting spiritual knowledge but as a medium for the transformation of minds and souls. Eliot makes this point emphatically in a letter he wrote to Richard Baxter (1696) three years after the appearance of the second edition Thorowgood's book. The letter to Baxter begins with a typical vision of millennial imminence that refers to Eliot's disappointment over the Restoration in England, but he adds, "However black the Cloud is, and big the Storm . . . in these Clouds Christ is coming to set up his Kingdom" (293). Having just finished his Indian Bible, Eliot proposes to translate one of Baxter's books for the Indians and warns Baxter that he is altering a phrase here and there "to speak in their ears, in their own Language" (293). Eliot then mentions that he has heard of a project in England to establish "a universal Character and Language" (294). The practical relevance of this project to Eliot's own efforts as a translator are obvious, but here he is most interested in the project primarily as an aid to missionary work, a "necessary, and a singular Promotion of that great Design of Christ" to spread the rule of the Godly all over the earth. He does, however, modestly offer one suggestion. Rather than trying to devise a new system of symbols to regularize the correspondence between language and the world, Eliot proposes that "the *Hebrew* Language" be embraced as the "most capable to be the instrument of so great a Design" (294). The millennialist, linguistic, and political dimensions of this argument are directly joined to Eliot's missionary preoccupations in a long passage near the end of the letter. Hebrew is ideal for a universal language, Eliot says,

for being the Language which shall be spoken in Heaven, when knowledge will be so enlarged, there will need a spacious Language; and what Language fitter than this of God's own making and composure? And why may we not make ready for Heaven in this Point, by making and fitting that Language, according to the Rules of the divine Artifice of it, to express all imaginable Conceptions and Notions of the Mind of Man, in all Arts and Sciences? Were this done (which is so capable of being done, and it seemeth God hath fitted Instruments to fall to the Work) all Arts and Sciences in the whole Encyclopaedie would soon be translated into it; and all Paganish and prophane Trash would be left out: it would be (as now it is) the purest Language in the World; And it seemeth to me, that *Zeph*.3.9 with other Texts, do prophesie of such a universal and pure Language. Were this done, all Schools would teach this Language, and all the World, especially the Commonwealth of Learning, would be of one, and that a divine and heavenly Lip. . . .
   If unto all this, it may please the Lord to direct his People into a Divine Form of Civil Government . . . this would so much the more advance all Learning, and Religion, and good Government; so that all the World would become a Divine Colledge. And *Lastly,* when Antichrist is overthrown, and a divine Form of Church-Government is put in practice in all Places; then all the World would become Divine. (294 - 295)[69]

Baxter (1696) was unimpressed with the project for a universal language and even more so with Eliot's millennialist revision of it. Noting the general resistance to missionary projects among the English, Baxter speculates that many more might be willing to serve in other lands if they spoke the language of those places. "The Defect of their Languages is their great Discouragement," Baxter says, echoing the common complaint about lack of linguistic training among missionaries to the Indians in New England, but "For the universal Character that you speak of, many have talked of it . . . but no body regards it" (296). After addressing several of Eliot's other questions, Baxter then concludes by gently rebuking what he considers Eliot's millennialist excesses: "As for the divine Government by the Saints which you mention, I dare not expect such great Matters upon Earth, lest I encroach upon the Priviledge of Heaven, and tempt my own Affections downwards, and forget that our Kingdom is not of this World" (297).
   Baxter's remarks express a pessimism that not only rebukes Eliot, but also

contradicts the millennialism characteristic of more conventional Puritanism, though after the Restoration most Puritans had abandoned hope for the reign of Saints on this earth. Eliot himself would retreat from the radical millennialism expressed in the letters and the tracts, and he would later publicly renounce the militant antimonarchical politics of *The Christian Commonwealth.*[70] Nevertheless, at the height of his missionary success in the decades leading up to Metacom's War, Eliot clearly believed that he was engaged in an enterprise that could not only win over the Indians' souls to Christ, but potentially transform New England and the whole world in preparation for Christ's rule on earth. That millennialist ambition united the spiritual, political, and linguistic dimensions of Eliot's missionary work, and in its light the streets of the struggling Praying Towns led directly through the wilderness of New England to a new world at the end of time.

NOTES ON THE TEXTS

This edition of the Eliot Tracts attempts to reproduce key elements in the graphic design of the original publications in a form that is compatible with the constraints and format of contemporary publishing, and is clear and consistent across all of the tracts. The relative size of fonts and the spacing of title pages, section headings, lists, and other significant structural markers in the original tracts have been retained to reflect the visual organization of seventeenth-century printing, but regularized throughout to reduce insignificant variation and to reinforce the coherence of the tracts as a series of related texts. Elaborate lines and borders, ornate initials, and other purely decorative features of the original printings that do not have a clear structural function have not been reproduced; where necessary to clarify divisions in the text, they are represented by single lines and dropped capitals. In cases where the original versions use extensive spacing to divide subsections of the tracts or to separate letters by different authors, a single half-line has been inserted to achieve the same end without extending the length of the volume needlessly.

In addition to reproducing the graphic organization of the original printings, this edition generally retains the spelling and format for citations and references in the original version of the tracts. The most significant exception to that practice is the use of bracketed insertions [. . .] in the text to incorporate material that appears as a marginal notation in the original printings. (The asterisks and occasional superscript letters used in the original to coordinate those marginal notes with the point of reference have been silently deleted.) Inverted, broken, and missing letters have been silently corrected, and the occasional use of "I" for "J" (e.g., "Iob" for "Job") and "V" for "U" is not reproduced. Similarly, the occasional monetary designation "l." has been regularized to "£." Numbering has been regularized, especially in citations, by converting the occasional Roman numeral to Arabic where the latter is clearly the conventional form. The punctuation of Biblical references in the text has been regularized to conform to the predominant practice in the tracts, and the use of quotation marks has been modernized. When the quotation ends in the middle of a line, the closing mark has been inserted in braces: {"}. On the rare occasions when later tracts refer back to pages in earlier tracts, those page references have been retained and the corresponding page in this volume is inserted in braces. The few other editorial interpolations to indicate illegible letters and words, or to clarify otherwise cryptic or misleading abbreviations and references, are enclosed in braces: {. . .}.

THE ELIOT TRACTS

1. Anonymous [Weld, Thomas, Hugh Peter, and Henry Dunster (?)[71]]. *New Englands First Fruits; in respect, First of the Conversion of Some, Conviction of Divers, Preparation of sundry of the Indians* . . . London, 1643. Reprinted by Joseph Sabin, Sabin's Reprints, Quarto Series no. 7. New York, 1865.

Defends New England against charges that it had been remiss in its mission to the Indians and recounts several instances of the Indians' interest in Christianity from the earliest years of contact with the British. Also describes the brutal Pequot War as a foundation for peace necessary to the missionary effort. The second half of the tract describes the beginning of Harvard College.

2. Anonymous [Shepard, Thomas (?)[72]]. *The Day-Breaking, if not the Sun-Rising of the Gospell with the Indians in New England.* London, 1647. Reprinted in the Massachusetts Historical Society *Collections*, Third series, 4 (1834): 1 - 23, but incorrectly attributed to Eliot. Also reprinted by Joseph Sabin, Sabin's Reprints, Quarto Series no. 9. New York, 1865. Sabin attributes the tract to John Wilson.

Describes the missionaries' meetings with the Indians on October 28 and November 11, 1646, including answers to doctrinal questions posed by the Indians following the sermons. Also describes later meetings with the Indians that year, and lists the eight laws drawn up by the Nonantum Indians while the General Court was debating the location of the first Praying Town.

3. Shepard, Thomas. *The Clear Sun-shine of the Gospel breaking forth upon the Indians in New-England.* London, 1648. Reprinted in the Massachusetts Historical Society *Collections*, Third series, 4 (1834): 25 - 67. Also reprinted by Joseph Sabin, Sabin's Reprints, Quarto Series no. 10. New York, 1865.

Claims the original impetus for emigration was to convert the Indians and spread the Gospel, rather than to seek freedom from persecution. This point becomes a persistent motif throughout the tracts. The tract also includes the twenty-seven "Conclusions and Orders" drawn up by the Indians at Concord, and a long letter from Eliot on the progress of the missionary effort. In a brief section on possible millennialist implications of the missionary effort, Shepard claims that the Indians are most likely descendants of the Tartars, and their widescale conversion must therefore await the conversion of the Jews, though individual exceptions to that rule will continue to justify the missionaries' efforts.

4. Winslow, Edward, ed. *The Glorious Progress of the Gospel amongst the Indians of New England.* London, 1649. With an Appendix by J[ames] D[ury]. Reprinted in the Massachusetts Historical Society *Collections*, Third series, 4 (1834): 69 - 98.

Contains letters from Eliot and one from Thomas Mayhew Jr. describing the success of missionary efforts in Massachusetts Bay and on Martha's Vineyard. Stresses the millennialist context of the missionary project much more than Shepard does in *The Clear Sun-shine*, especially in an appendix by John Dury that compares the Indians' speaking in parables to that tendency in the Jews.

5. Whitfield, Henry, ed. *The Light appearing more and more towards the perfect Day, or a farther discovery of the present state of the Indians in New England.* London, 1651. Reprinted in the Massachusetts Historical Society *Collections*, Third series, 4 (1834): 101 - 147. Also reprinted by Joseph Sabin as *A farther discovery of the present state of the Indians in New England, concerning the progress of the gospel among them, manifested by letters from such as preached to them then.* Sabin's Reprints, Quarto Series no. 3. New York, 1865.

First tract published by the Society for the Propagation of the Gospel in New England. Letters by John Eliot (letters 2-6) and Thomas Mayhew (letter 1). In this most radically millennialist of the tracts, Eliot speculates on the Jewish origins of the Indians and describes the scriptural origins of his plan for government at Natick. He also claims that England may have a harder time living up to Christ's rule than do the Indians of New England, because existing structures and attitudes in England will be obstacles to reform.

6. Whitfield, Henry, ed. *Strength out of Weaknesse, Or a Glorious Manifestation of the Further Progresse of the Gospel among the Indians in New England.* London, 1652. Reprinted in the Massachusetts Historical Society *Collections*, Third series, 4 (1834): 149 - 196. Also reprinted by Joseph Sabin, Sabin's Reprints, Quarto Series no. 5, New York, 1865.

Contains letters and reports by Eliot and fourteen other "eminent English Divines," with accounts of a visit to a two-hour worship service at Natick, and of the covenant of rules drawn up at Natick by which the Indians were to form themselves "into the Government of God."

7. Eliot, John, and Thomas Mayhew Jr. *Tears of Repentance: Or, A further Narrative of the Progress of the Gospel amongst the Indians in New-England: Setting forth, not only their present state and condition, but sundry Confessions of sin by diverse of the said Indian.* London, 1653. With a preface by Richard Mather. Reprinted in the Massachusetts Historical Society *Collections*, Third series, 4 (1834): 197 - 260.

Contains two prefaces by Eliot, one to Cromwell and another to the general public; also Thomas Mayhew Jr.'s letter to the New England Company describing his missionary work on Martha's Vineyard. A second letter contains English translations of the some confessions and preliminary conversion narratives and several of the official narratives from the evaluation of the congregation at Natick in 1652. The translations from Algonquian are by Eliot and an Indian interpreter, probably Cockenoe. Richard Mather explains why the narratives were not accepted by the Elders, who denied permission to gather the church at Natick at this time (Mayhew was among the Elders who refused to accept the confessions).[73] *Tears* is also important for Eliot's millennialist claims that the kingdom of Christ is rising up in "these western parts of the world," and that the success of the colonial missionaries indicates the simultaneous conversion of Gentiles and Jews has begun in New England as well as England. This tract also deals directly with some of the devastating effects of the epidemics that continued to sweep through the Indian population.

8. Eliot, John. *A Late and Further Manifestation of the Progress of the Gospel amongst the Indians in New England . . . Being a Narrative of the Examinations of the Indians, about their Knowledge in Religion, by the Elders of the Churches.* London, 1655. Reprinted in the Massachusetts Historical Society *Collections*, Third series, 4 (1834): 261 - 287.

Contains records of the successful examination of the Indian converts in Roxbury in June 1654 that led to the gathering of the church at Natick. Frustrated at the slowness of local Elders to accept the confessions of the Indians at Natick, Eliot here appeals directly to readers in England to recognize the sincerity of the confessions and help persuade the Elders in Massachusetts. In support of his appeal, he recounts further trials of Indian proselytes in 1655.

9. Eliot, John. *A further Accompt of the Progresse of the Gospel amongst the Indians in New England and of the means used effectually to advance the same.* London, 1659. Reprinted by Joseph Sabin, Sabin's Reprints, Quarto Series no. 6. New York, 1865.

Contains several letters on the printing of Eliot's Indian Bible, and accounts of exhortations and sermons by Indians associated with a Fast Day at Natick November 15, 1658.[74] Also includes *Some Helps for the Indians* in English and Algonquian.

10. Eliot, John. *A further Account of the progress of the Gospel Amongst the Indians in New England: being A Relation of the Confessions made by several Indians (in the presence of the Elders and Members of several Churches) in order to their admission into Church-fellowship.* London, 1660.

Describes the process by which a church was gathered at Natick (cf. Morrison 1995, 99 - 119 and O'Brien 1997, 31 - 64). Contains conversion narratives from the eight Indians admitted to Eliot's church at Roxbury before the Natick church was formed. The eight Indians accepted at Roxbury later became the "founding pillars" of the church at Natick.

11. Eliot, John. *A Brief Narrative of the Progress of the Gospel amongst the Indians in New England, in the Year 1670.* London, 1671. Reprinted in *Old South Leaflets* 1:21. Boston: Old South Meeting House, n.d., pp. 1 - 11 (Cogley 1999, 263).

Argues that Praying Indians can be missionaries and diplomats to the unconverted Indians—in this case, the Mohawks threatening the colonies—and so they can serve as a protective hedge between English and hostile Indians. This role for the proselytes is much diminished from the millennialist significance accorded to their conversions in the earlier tracts, but it would become crucially important four years later during Metacom's War.

LETTERS

Eliot, John. "The Learned Conjectures of Reverend Mr. John Eliot touching the Americans, of New and notable consideration, written to Mr. Thorowgood." In Thorowgood 1660, 1 - 28 (pp. 25 - 28 incorrectly paginated).

Defends Thorowgood's contention that the Indians are descendants of the Jews and describes the dispersion of the Jews to the West, through Europe, and to the East, through Asia and across the American continent. The identification of the Indians as Jews establishes the millennialist significance of the missionary project in New England. Cogley (1986 - 1987, 223) proposes the date of composition for this letter as March 1653 - February 1654.

Eliot, John. Letter to Richard Baxter of "this 6th of the 5th" [i.e., July 6] 1663. In Baxter 1696, 293 - 295. Baxter's reply is on pp. 295 - 297.

Asserts faith in the imminence of the millennium despite the discouraging effects of the Restoration in England, and discusses the importance of a universal language to the global spread of Christianity. Eliot proposes Hebrew be used as that language and suggests that it would help establish a "Commonwealth of Learning" compatible with a "Divine Form of Civil Government."

NOTES

1.   See Thorpe (1909, 1857). The Massachusetts Bay Charter from Thorpe is available online through the Avalon Project at Yale Law School; see their website at http://www.yale.edu/lawweb/avalon/states/mass03.htm.

2.   Lechford emigrated to New England but repatriated in 1641 and became an Anglican; Baillie was a Scottish Presbyterian (Cogley 1995, 67). For a discussion of the anti-Puritan critique of missionary inaction in Massachusetts, see Cogley (1999, 67), and Morrison (1995, 38).

In *The Bloody Tenent yet More Bloody*, Roger Williams (1652) complained that "none of the Ministers of New England, nor any person in the whole Countrey, is able to open the *Mysteries of Christ Jesus* in any proprietie of their *speech* or *Language*, without which *Proprietie* it cannot be imagined that *Christ Jesus* sent forth his first *Apostles* or *Messengers*, and without which no people in the World are long wiling to heare of difficult and heavenly matters" (219). Williams's reference to the lack of adequate language skills necessary to provide religious instruction to the Indians is surely a veiled criticism of Eliot's work in Massachusetts Bay, as well as a pitch for the importance of Williams's (1643) own book *A Key into the Language of America*.

The issue of preaching to the Indians in their own language was controversial among the Puritans. It would become the cornerstone of Eliot's early missionary efforts, but John Cotton (1648) argued that Eliot's strategy was at best a stop-gap measure: "Though the *Indians* have been slow to learne our language, especially in matters of Religion (howsoever in Trading they soon understood us:) yet wee have often offered to bring up their *Indian* children in our Schooles, that they might learne to speake to their Countreymen in their own language. But because that might prove long, one of our Elders (Mr. *Eliot*, the Teacher of the Church of Rocksbury) hath (with the consent of the Natives) preached to them first by an Interpreter, but . . . he now preacheth to two Congregations of them in their own language weekly" (77). Responding to Baillie's complaint that the colonists would only instruct Indians who came to them, rather than reaching out to the Indians in their own language, Cotton added, "What if there have not bin any sent forth by an Church to learn the *Indians* language? That will not argue our neglect of minding the work of their conversion. For there be of the *Indians* that live amongst us, and dayly resort to us, and some of them learne our language; and some of us learn theirs" (78 - 79).

Cotton (1648) goes on to dispute Baillie's claim about the success of Roger Williams's missionary efforts once he had been freed from the yoke of Puritan oppression in Massachusetts: "If Mr. *Williams* his speech of the wonderfull great facility hee had of gaining so farre upon the *Indians*, be not too too [sic] prodigally hyperbolicall (as I much fear it is) I thinke his sinne is so much the greater before the Lord. . . . Mr. *Baylie* shall do well to consider, that Mr. *Williams* his speech doth not so much hold forth the facility of the *Indians* to any such conversion, as might fit them for Church-estate, but rather the Hypocrisie and Formalitie of the ordinary Church-Members of Nationall Churches [i.e., the Anglican Church]; which he professeth is so far off from true conversion, 'that it is the subversion of the soules of many Millions in Christendome, from one false worship to another'" (79, 81 - 82).

3.   On a much smaller scale, the Dutch also carried out missionary work in and around the area of New Amsterdam, now New York, and the East Indies. These latter efforts were described by Caspar Sibelius, whose work translated and published in English in 1650 by Henry Jessey as *Of the conversion of Five Thousand and Nine Hundred East-Indians* (Cogley 1999, 207).

Catholic priests among the Spanish and French were often the first to contact native populations and lived among them for extended periods of time, but the British settlement of North America was led by soldiers, explorers, land speculators, and farmers. The few active missionaries among the British tended to follow the lead of their secular predecessors and remained relatively aloof from the people they proselytized (Bowden and Ronda 1980, 26).

Dwight Bozeman's (1988) comprehensive account of professed motives for British emigration to America claims that references to the conversion of the natives were usually overwhelmed by the two most frequently cited motives, the "wish to secure a refuge" from social, political, and economic hardships in England, and a "determination to win 'liberty of the Ordinances'" forbidden to the Puritans in England (97 - 98). Though not necessarily contradictory to the missionary enterprise, these more practical strategic objectives dominated the first two decades of colonization in New England and left little time for the spiritual ambitions described in the literature. Although the conversion of the natives was a common theme in almost all discourse concerning the New World from Columbus on, most historians have concluded that such spiritual claims, though prominent and highly respected in both Catholic and Protestant writings, clearly served more as a conventional rhetorical motif than a primary objective for the imperial enterprises of Spain, France, and England in the sixteenth and seventeenth centuries.

4.   The Jesuits' accounts were originally written in French and usually were in the form of journals or diaries that were published separately. They were collected into

seventy-three volumes and translated into English by R. G. Thwaites as *Jesuit Relations* in 1896 - 1901. Jennings (1975) praises the ethnographic detail of the *Relations* and claims that it is a product of "the Catholic imperative for converting and including the heathen," which "compelled the Catholics to learn something about them in order to do the holy work effectively, while the Protestant principle of elitism worked out in practice to exclusionism and indifference." He goes on to claim that "There is nothing comparable in Protestant literature until we reach the reports of Moravian missionaries in the mid-eighteenth century" (57). The Eliot Tracts stand as a partial refutation of that claim, although there is no question that the Protestant emphasis on "civilizing" the natives as well as converting them resulted in an ethnocentric scorn for most aspects of the indigenous cultures.

5.   The most sustained and detailed attempt to reconstruct pre-contact cultures from the Eliot Tracts is Dane Morrison's (1995) *A Praying People: Massachusett Acculturation and the Failure of the Puritan Mission, 1600 - 1690. See* also O'Brien (1997), Tinker (1993), and Cohen (1993). Bross's (1997) introduction in "Praying Indian" describes many of the problems involved in such reconstructions and the extent to which these scholars can confuse the purely rhetorical conventions of missionary discourse with evidence of "authentic" Indian attitudes and practices.

6.   The extent to which Indians incorporated Christian beliefs into their native traditions—instead of simply abandoning their beliefs for Christian principles, as the missionaries often represented it—has been the object of much study. See Morrison (1995), Naeher (1989), Bowden and Rhonda (1980), Tinker (1993), and O'Brien (1997).

7.   Massachusetts Historical Society (MHS) *Collections*, Third series, 4 (1834): 1 – 287, and Joseph Sabin, Sabin's Reprints, Quarto Series, 1865. See also the reprint of the last tract, *A Brief Narrative*, in the undated *Old South Leaflets* (Boston: Old South Meeting House) 1 - 11, cited in Cogley (1999, 263). More specific bibliographic information about these reprints appears in "Notes on the Texts."

The editors of the MHS volume claim in a prefatory note that they worked from the only extant complete set of the tracts, bound together in a volume at the American Antiquarian Society. That volume is titled on the spine *Indian history tracts*. It includes the tracts reprinted by the MHS plus an English translation of Sibelius's *Of the conversion of Five Thousand and Nine Hundred East-Indians* (1650), W. A. Hubbard's *A narrative of the troubles with the Indians in New-England* (1677), and B. Church's *Entertaining passages relating to Philip's War* (1716). An inscription to the volume reads "Presented to the American Antiquarian Society by William Henry Bass, Boston, July 26th, 1815." (Information provided by a letter from Marie E. Lamoureux, head of readers' services, American Antiquarian Society.)

Images of the individual tracts are now available on microfilm and on the web at Early English Books Online, although one of the tracts in that online series (*Glorious Progress*) is missing a long section of interlinear English Algonquian translation by Thomas Stanton and Abraham Pierson titled "Some Helps for the Indians."

8.   Bross (1997, 1) notes that 1643 also saw the publication of Roger Williams's *Key into the Language of America*, the first recorded fruit of the Mayhew family's proselytizing on Martha's Vineyard, and the probable beginning of Eliot's study of the Algonquian language.

9.   Among other New Englanders, Samuel Sewall was perhaps the most notable proponent of missionary work on millennialist grounds. In the dedicatory letter to *Phaenomena quaedam*, Sewall (1697) claims "The Commendation of *Erasmus*, in his Book entituled *Ecclesiastes*, doth very justly belong to the *English* Nation, upon account of their effectual Desires that the *Americans* might be gospelliz'd. . . . And yet their Praises are to be sung in a higher Note: For I can't but think that either *England*, or *New*

England, or both (Together is best) is the only Bride Maid mentioned by Name in *David's* prophetical *Epithalamium*, to assist at the Great Wedding now shortly to be made." After this diplomatic gesture toward transatlantic unity ("Together is best"), Sewall observes "the *English* Nation, in shewing Kindness to the Aboriginal Natives of *America,* may possibly, shew Kindness to *Israelites* unawares" (A2 recto).

10. Two other works by Eliot also deserve mention in connection with the Eliot Tracts, though neither are ever considered part of the series and have not been included here: Eliot's translation of *The Dying Speeches of Several Indians . . . Dying Speeches and Counsels Of such Indians as dyed in the Lord* (1685), and *Indian Dialogues* (1671), which Eliot published as a guide and catechism for missionaries in the field. Both of these books refer to and elaborate on exchanges between the Indians and missionaries reported in the tracts, but the specific editorial purpose of each book so dominates the account of Indian speech and perspective that they compound, rather than clarify, the already manifestly ethnocentric limits of the tracts themselves. Although the conversions of at least some of the Indians surely were sincere and lasted till their deaths, the contrived doctrinal consistency of deathbed speeches reported in *Dying Speeches* sound more like the overtly fictional conversations in *Indian Dialogues* than the spontaneous exchanges reported in the earlier tracts. What Eliot says in his preface to the *Dialogues* applies to *Dying Speeches* as well: These documents were not intended as historical record but only "to show what might or should have been said" on such occasions. On the importance of *Dying Speeches* see Bross (2001).

11. In addition to Cogley's (1999) book, there were two dissertations completed at the end of the 1990s that focused on Eliot and the missionary project in New England: Bross (1997) and Jalalzai (2000). Bross situates her discussion of the Praying Indians within the transatlantic context represented in earlier work by Holstun (1987) and Bremer (1994). She uses that perspective to articulate what she calls Eliot's "anti-conquest" strategy of peaceful conversion (164), but more important, she reads the accounts of Praying Indians in Puritan texts as a rhetorical strategy designed by the colonists "to construct for themselves a positive identity when all signs seemed to point to Old England's preeminent place in the coming millennium" (3). Bross analyzes the evolution of the image of the Praying Indian as a measure of the colonists' changing view of themselves in relation to England before and after the Restoration, and in so doing restores what has been considered an arcane protoethnology to its proper place within the discourse of transatlantic identity produced by the British occupation of the New World. Jalalzai's thesis is informed by recent postcolonial theory and its contribution to our understanding of colonized subjectivity as applied to the situation of the indigenes of colonial New England. Jalalzai reinforces the ideological critique of British colonialism in the New World characteristic of postcolonial studies and complicates that perspective productively by a more speculative theoretical discourse.

12. See also the more limited account of the Company's earlier years in Winship (1920).

13. Neither book was published during Gookin's lifetime; *Historical Collections* (1792) first appeared in the Massachusetts Historical Society *Collections*, and *An Historical Account* (1836) in the American Antiquarian Society's *Transactions and Collections*. See Cogley (1999, 264, 224 – 230) for a concise biography of Gookin.

14. Years later, in *Magnalia Christi Americana*, Mather (1702) returned to Eliot, but this time gently rebuked what he now saw as Eliot's millennialist excesses: "I confess, that was one, I cannot call it so much *guess* as *wish*, wherein he [Eliot] was willing a little to indulge himself; and that was, *That our* Indians *are the Posterity of the dispersed and rejected Israelites.*" Mather goes on to describe several of what he considers spurious parallels between the Indians and the Jews cited by Eliot as evidence

for his millennialist claims, and then Mather observes that in fact the Indians "have too a great unkindness for our *Swine*; but I suppose that is because our *Hogs* devour the *Clams* which are a Dainty with them" (3.3: 192 - 193; on Mather's rejection of the purportedly Hebraic roots of Algonquian, see Smolinski 1995, 25). The importance of Eliot's millennialist speculations to his missionary project is discussed below.

15. See Moore (1822), Francis (1836), Adams (1847), Caverly (1880), and Harling (1965).

16. O'Brien (1997) argues that after Metacom's War and throughout the eighteenth century, "the English, who as colonists were rootless people by definition, displaced their own dislocation onto Indians. . . . In contrast to the missionary venture, which was premised on fixing Indians in a bounded location, the establishment of a separate social welfare system for Indians entailed a complete discount of the Indians' place. . . . The transformation is quite explicit in the successively worked out (and sometimes overlapping) categories of 'Praying Indian,' 'Friend Indian,' and 'Wandering Indian' which the English deployed to assign Indians to their place in the colonial social order" (209).

This anxiety of dislocation is typical of what postcolonial theorists sometimes call the "settler" mentality of groups that displace indigenous populations to settle in a region but also consider themselves distinct from their metropolitan origins. That attitude is distinguished from that of "colonists," who retain a strong identification with their origins despite their geographical separation from home. See Ashcroft, Griffiths, and Tiffin (1989) and the introduction in Watts (1998). ("Colonist" and "settler" are used interchangeably in this introduction.)

For a more general survey of the way Indians were represented by Europeans in the New World, see Berkhofer (1978). An ethnographic overview of the Indians in New England is available in Bragdon (1996).

17. On Weld's and Peter's work as agents for New England, see Stearns (1934).

18. Cf. Cotton's (1648) account of these laws: "Their *Sachims*, aand *Sagamores* (as they call them to wit, their Governors) have submitted themselves to the government of the *English*, and have willingly subjected themselves to the acceptance of the Ten Commandements, though some of them, doe most stick at the seventh Commandement, as it forbiddeth Polygamy. Neverthelesse otherwise they willingly consent to abandon Adultery and Fornication, and unnaturall lusts" (77).

Most scholars agree that the decimation of the native population of southern New England by disease had left the "remnants" of the epidemic dispirited and defenseless against British expansion, so the Indians had few options beyond capitulation, conversion, and assimilation. Morrison (1995), however, argues that openness to conversion must be understood from the perspective of the Indians as a more active strategy of pragmatic accommodation in the face of a disintegrating social structure, threats from their native enemies to the south and northwest, and the undeniable pressure of British occupation on a land emptied by the recent plagues: The people at Nonantum "now saw themselves as a society of remnants, survivors of a tribe whose existence was contingent upon adopting the beliefs and behaviors of their dominant and thriving puritan neighbors" (3).

19. Hannah Mumford Eliot died in 1687. When Eliot died three years later he was survived only by two of his six children: Joseph, minister at Guilford, Connecticut, and Hannah, his only daughter (Ola Winslow 1966, 184). After relinquishing the pulpit at Roxbury, Eliot spent the last years of his life again as a teacher, this time to African and Indian children near his home. He died on May 20, 1690, at eighty-six.

20. Eliot's opposition to the treaty offended other colonists; see John Winthrop's (1996) *Journal* for November 27, 1634: "It was then informed vs, how mr Eliott the

Teacher of the Churche of Rockesbury had taken occasion in a Sermon to speake of the peace made with the Pekodes, & to laye some blame vpon the magistrates [ministry?] for proceedinge therein without Consent of the people, & for other faylinges (as he conceived) we tooke order that he should be dealt with by mr Cotton mr Hooker & mr weld to be brought to see his error, & to heale it by some public explanation of his meaninge: for the people beganne to take occasion to murmure against vs for it" (136 - 137). See also Tooker (1896), and Ola Winslow (1966, 89). Cf. Jennings' (1975) remark that the captive from whom Eliot learned Algonquian was not a Pequot and therefore probably had not been a combatant in the war against the British. Jennings concludes that the captive had been seized as plunder and made a slave to the colonists (233 - 234). Regardless of his status in the Pequot War, Cockenoe became what Greenblatt (1991) calls a "go-between," figures who emerge in history because of their ability to move between two cultures.

Eliot's ability to preach to the Indians in their language was unusual but not unprecedented. The Mayhews had been preaching to the Indians on Martha's Vineyard ("Nope" in the local dialect) for several years, and Roger Williams was familiar enough with Algonquian to preach to Indians in their local dialects at Plymouth and Providence (Ola Winslow 1966, 85).

21. See also John Cotton's (1648, 77 - 78) account of the first sermon.

22. These latter two measures have received much attention from Jennings (1975) and other historians, who argue that the Puritans' missionary efforts were at best a rationalization and at worse a hypocritical cover for the true aim of subjugating the Indians, stealing their land, and destroying their culture. Cogley (1999, 42) argues that Jennings has little evidence to support his claim about malevolent motives behind the measures, and that the more beneficent explicit claims cannot simply be dismissed. The terrible consequences of these policies cannot be denied, but as they extended the jurisdiction of the Massachusetts General Court to the civil affairs of the Indians, they also gave the missionary effort an authority and direction it had lacked. The legal authority of the colony over the Indians was further codified when, in 1658, at Eliot's suggestion, the Court established an Indian Superintendency devoted exclusively to Indian affairs.

23. Eliot only recorded eight of the ten laws drawn up by the Nonantum and claims the others were lost, which is especially unfortunate since the parallel with the Ten Commandments could hardly have been coincidental among the newly converted Christian Indians. The laws Eliot did record focus on differences between Nonantum and English social practices more than they do on serious crimes or religious belief. Numbers 5 - 8, for example, enforce long hair for women and short hair for men, prohibit women from baring their breasts, and set a five-shilling fine for anyone caught killing lice with his teeth. In *Sun-shine*, however, Eliot says they also made a law enforcing the Sabbath, presumably one of the two that were lost.

At the same time as the Nonantum were forming their laws, a band at Musketaquid, near Concord, drew up a list of twenty-nine "Conclusions and Orders" (*Sun-shine* 39 - 40; see also Morrison 1995, 69). Jennings (1975), Salisbury (1975, 1982), and other historians who focus on the genocidal consequences of the British occupation have argued that the "voluntary" submission of Indians to English law was in fact the product of coercion by the British. Morrison (1995), however, argues that these Indian charters were neither coerced nor evidence of the Indians' capitulation to the English culture that surrounded them. Instead, Morrison says, the charters were developed by the Indians "to provide a sense of structure in functionally fragmented communities" devastated by disease and under pressure from their Indian enemies (69, 70 - 73).

24. The relocation of the Indians into Praying Towns is frequently cited as one of

the most destructive policies of British imperialism in Salisbury (1974) and Jennings (1975), and O'Brien (1997) points out the paradox of dispossessing Indians of their land only to fix the populations in new places more compatible with the British occupation of Indian lands. Morrison (1995) agrees that British expansionism was one motive for moving the Indians from Nonantum, but he also observes that Eliot may have had other reasons for wanting to remove the Indians from the immediate proximity of some English saints who did not provide good role models for the proselytes (76 - 77).

According to Eliot, it was Waban and other Indians at Nonantum who suggested the move; he claims that most of the Nonantum liked the area of Natick and moved there willingly (*Light Appearing*). Eliot also notes that many Algonquians had no desire to live near English settlements (*Glorious Progress*; cf. Morrison 1995, 78). In *Tears of Repentance* Eliot says the Indians first picked the area just south of Nonantum around Cohannet, which had been home to thousands of Algonquians before the epidemics, but the English had already planned to occupy that area. The Indians then selected Natick, eight miles from Dedham, a distance that would quickly be closed by expansion of the English and Indian populations and so became a source of escalating tension between the two groups (*A Late and Further Manifestation*).

25. As early as 1619 the General Assembly at Jamestown had passed laws mandating Indian conversion, and money had been collected for that purpose in 1620, though with little effect (Kellaway 1962, 3). The first English attempt to establish a permanent fund to support missionary work with the Indians in New England came in 1630, when John White proposed in *Planters Plea* setting aside £10,000 from individual donors who, he said, regularly cast away £25 - 50 on "superfluities in apparell, dyet, buildings, &c." (83). In 1641 the petition by William Castell garnered the support of seventy-six ministers in England and Scotland, though it concluded on a pessimistic note, observing that the colonists "are becoming exceeding rude, more likely to turne Heathen, then to turne others to the Christian faith" (10).

26. According to Kellaway (1962), there were only two New Englanders in the original group: Winslow and Herbert Pelham. The first president was William Steele, Recorder of London, who went on to become Lord Chief Justice of Ireland in 1656 (17).

27. See Kellaway (1962, ch. 1). The Society was often known simply as "the Corporation." Historians usually refer to the Society as "the New England Company" or more simply "the Company," but that term was not commonly used at the time until the Society had been dissolved and then reformed after the Restoration in 1662 as the "Company for Propagation of the Gospel in New England and the Parts Adjacent in America."

28. Five of the original Commissioners were reappointed to the new group: Simon Bradstreet, William Stoughton, Joseph Dudley, Peter Bulkeley, Thomas Hinckley (Company Minutes, September 30, 1685, Massachusetts Historical Society ms., in Kellaway 1962, 199). No ministers had been elected Commissioners when the colonies voted on them, but as soon as the Company could appoint people to the post, they began naming prominent colonial ministers including Increase and Cotton Mather (Kellaway 1962, 207 - 208).

29. These figures are based on Cogley (1999, 208 - 209) and Kellaway (1962, 37 - 40). Kellaway reports that by 1653 contributions to the Society totaled £4,500, and by 1658, investments in English real estate had produced an annual income of £600 (39).

30. The work of the Society was reinforced in 1650 by the publication of Thomas Thorowgood's *Jewes in America*, which proposed a millennial context for the missionary effort, and by Casparus Sibelius's (1650) *Of the Conversion of Five Thousand and Nine Hundred East-Indians*, which contains a section on the spread of the Gospel in New

England based on selections taken from the earlier tracts. Letters regarding the missionary work from Eliot and others also appeared in London newspapers and journals.

31. Literacy was a crucial element in the hybrid cultural identity that was emerging among Indian proselytes, and, especially in the earlier years of the missionary project, it was closely associated with conversion and the community of the Praying Towns; see Wyss (2000).

32. On behalf of the Society, the Commissioners ordered a run of 500 to 1,000 copies, but they complained about the poor accuracy of Eliot's translation. They suggested that in the future Eliot be assisted by Thomas Stanton, "Interpreter-General to the United Colonies for the Indian Language" (Kellaway 1962, 126). Eliot refused, accusing Stanton of being insufficiently pious to participate in such a project. The Commissioners continued to express reservations about Eliot's translations until 1660, when the Indian Bible was in press (124). Stanton did finally work on a catechism with Abraham Pierson in the "Narragansett or Pequott" languages, which was published with the Commissioners' support in 1659 at the end of *A further Accompt* and is included in this volume as "Some Helps for the Indians." The title page refers to Stanton and "some others of the most able Interpreters amongst us," but, pointedly, not Eliot.

33. As with many printer's devils, Johnson was a mixed blessing for Green. The Commissioners complained that Johnson was lazy, and, although he had a wife in England, Johnson was soon accused of "obtaining the affections" of Green's daughter through "flattering & allureing expressions." He was convicted and fined £5, but he was allowed to return to work on the Bible. When it was finished he returned to England, but in 1665 he came back to New England, this time with a press of his own, and set up shop near Green in Cambridge (Kellaway 1962, 130 - 132, 136).

34. Charles was apparently not as impressed as the Company might have hoped. Boyle reported to his colleagues that the King "lookd a pretty while upon it, & shewd some things in it to those that had the honour to be about him in his bed-chamber, into which he carryd it, yet the unexpected comming in of an Extraordinary Envoyé from the emperour hindred me from receveing that fuller expression of his grace towards the translators and Dedicators that might otherwise have been expected" (Pilling 1891, 141, in Kellaway 1962, 133).

35. From Samuel Sewall's letter book, in Massachusetts Historical Society *Collections*, sixth series, 1, p. 400 - 403; quoted in Kellaway (1962, 157). For an account of criticisms directed at Eliot's translations, see Kellaway (1962, 124 - 127).

36. The Company had originally planned to have the book translated and printed by John Neesnumun, an Indian preacher at Natick, but he died before the project could be completed. It was finished by Samuel Danforth (Kellaway 1962, 163).

37. Letter from the Commissioners to the Company, drafted by Cotton Mather prior to November 1710 (according to Kellaway), as copied by Samuel Sewall in his book of correspondence, published in Massachusetts Historical Society *Collections* (Kellaway 1962, 156). Cf. Cotton Mather in *India Christiana* (1721), addressing the Commissioners: "A Main Intention which you now have in your view, is, To bring the Rising Generation of the *Indians*, unto a more general Understanding of the *English Language*, and more into the *English Way of Living*" (43, quoted in Kellaway 1962, 228).

38. In addition to his scientific accomplishments, Boyle was committed to spreading the Gospel and helped support the translation of the Bible into Irish and Welsh, languages regarded as almost as "primitive" as Algonquian. He also defended the colonial enterprise in New England and was occasionally asked by the colonists to

represent their interests in London, though in 1681 he wrote a letter to Eliot complaining about religious persecution in Massachusetts Bay (Kellaway 1962, 48).

39. The formation of this new Society was the culmination of over two decades of attacks on the New England Company from Anglicans and Catholics. See, for example, *New England's Faction Discovered* (London, 1690), by "C.D.," who compared the meager results of the Company's efforts unfavorably with the more successful missionary enterprise of the Jesuits (Kellaway 1962, 201). In 1709 additional competition came from the newly chartered Society in Scotland for Propagating Christian Knowledge, though in 1756 those two organizations agreed to cooperate in their fundraising efforts (186).

40. Resolution of the New England Company, May 19, 1779, New England Company Archive, Guildhall Library, London, Ms. 7920/I, pp. 43, 45 - 47, quoted in Kellaway (1962, 277).

41. There was tension between Natick and Dedham from the beginning, and in January 1662 the town of Dedham challenged the Indians' legal right to the land they had been farming for ten years, especially the portion south of the river. Eliot pursued a legal defense of the Indians' right to the land, at one point even claiming that Dedham itself had never obtained formal legal rights to its own land (Morrison 1995, 138, 144). A local jury quickly found in favor of Dedham, but the magistrates refused the verdict and sent the case to the Court of Assistants. The case was settled five months later by the Court of Assistants in favor of the Indians, though a year later the General Court awarded Dedham 8,000 additional acres to expand somewhere other than the area of Natick (see Morrison 1995, ch. 4). For a detailed history of Natick and its importance to the more general role of Indians in colonial society, see O'Brien (1997).

42. This is, of course, the scheme proposed by Eliot (1659) for all of England in *The Christian Commonwealth*. Cogley (1999) argues that Eliot wrote this book around the time he established the town of Natick upon just such a millennial system, though the book was not published until 1659 (76). See O'Brien (1997, ch. 2), for a more extended account of the founding of Natick.

43. See *Tears of Repentance* for Eliot's account of the events leading up to the establishment of an Indian church at Natick. The "gathering" of a church required at least seven people—in this case the Indian proselytes—to present conversion narratives acceptable to Elders from nearby churches. In addition, the applicants had to prove themselves capable of leading and teaching others. These tests were rigorous, and evaluated severely. Morrison (1995) claims that the failure of the Natick proselytes to succeed in their first attempts is an example of the "institutional racism" of Congregationalists in the colonies (119; see 99 - 119 for a detailed account of the efforts to gather a church at Natick). However, even Richard Mather and the people of Dorchester failed in their first attempt to form a church there, so the difficulty was not unique to Indian churches. Interestingly, Mather attended the examination of the Natick Indians and later wrote a preface to Eliot's account of the occasion in which he explains why the confessions were not accepted at that time. The Elders worried that the people of Natick had no one capable of serving as "Pastor and Elder." The Elders also complained that Eliot was the only English translator, invoking the Puritan requirement of two witnesses—and thereby discounting the contributions of Eliot's Indian assistants at the examination. For a more general account of church formation in the colonies, see Hall (1972).

44. Population figures for native populations in the seventeenth century are notoriously vague. These numbers are proposed by Jennings (1975, 29), based on extrapolations from Gookin. Morrison (1995) endorses and updates Jennings's figures based on more recent archeological research, particularly that of Cook (1976) and Snow

(1980). See Jennings (1975, ch. 2) and Morrison (1995, 203 n. 9) for a discussion of the limits and methodologies behind these population figures. Working with somewhat different sources, Russell (1980, 28) arrives at a smaller estimate of 75,000 for the population of New England prior to contact with the British.

45. This brief sketch of Indian customs and beliefs is primarily based on the much more detailed information available in Russell (1980), Cronon (1993), Morrison (1995), and O'Brien (1997).

46. Attempts to reconstruct native beliefs prior to contact with the British can only be speculative and very general because the entry of those beliefs into the historical record was governed almost entirely by English authors through the eighteenth century. The oral transmission of ancestral beliefs to later generations, though culturally important, is not a reliable source for the earlier periods. Morrison (1995) discusses the spiritual life of the Indians throughout *A Praying People*, and Tinker's (1993) account of native beliefs is precise and carefully documented. Bowden and Ronda (1980) offer a brief synopsis in their introduction to the *Indian Dialogues* (28 - 32). Eliot's own record of those beliefs in the tracts (and as represented in the *Dialogues*) has the advantage of immediacy, though like most Puritans he seldom expressed much curiosity about, let alone sympathy for, Indian beliefs and customs in any context.

47. Perhaps the closest analogy between an Indian god and the Jehovah of the Calvinists was the Narragansett supreme spirit Kautantowit. The Massachusett ascribed their fate to Kiehtan and Hobbamock (i.e., Chepian and Abamacho). See Morrison (1995, 11 - 12).

48. Pratt (1992) calls this two-way exchange of cultural practices and icons "transculturation," an adaptation of the ethnographic term that is more commonly applied only to indigenous populations. Pratt also popularized the term "contact zone" to mark those geographical and symbolic spaces where different cultures encounter each other. Bross (1997, 3) notes the relevance of Pratt's work to the Praying Towns, and the postcolonial extension of Pratt's work figures prominently in Jalalzai (2000).

49. Eliot expressed relatively little interest in the powwows. He recognized the efficacy of some native medicine and argued that such cures were not a sin, even though like most Puritans he considered their powwows' claims to spiritual power at best empty and at worst Satanic (see O'Brien 1997, 28). Cogley (1999) argues that Eliot's recognition of the powwows' ability to cure some illnesses allowed them to retain a portion of their power and status among the Indians, and as a result they remained resistant to conversion. On Martha's Vineyard the Mayhews directly contested the power of the powwows from the beginning, and Cogley claims that was one reason why their missionary efforts were more successful than those of Eliot (175 - 176).

50. In addition to Gookin's (1674 - 1677) work, see the general overview of the Praying Towns in the *Historical Collections of the Indians of New England, Massachusetts Historical Society Collections*, first series, 1 (1792): 141 - 226, esp. 180 - 196. Cogley (1999) offers the most detailed contemporary account of the towns, but also see Bross (1997) and Ola Winslow (1966, ch. 13).

51. Jennings (1975, 249 - 252) argues that Eliot's missionary efforts destabilized the colonists' relations with the Indians throughout New England.

52. According to Gookin, in 1674 the areas encompassed by each of the old Indian towns ranged from 2,500 acres (Wamesit) to 8,000 (Hassanamesit and Nashobah). Natick, Punkapog, and Okommakamesit each had 6,000 acres, and Magunkakog 3,000. Populations for all the towns ranged between forty-five people at Chabanakongkomun to well over a hundred at Wabquisset and Natick (see Gookin 1674, 181 - 189; Morrison 1995, 228 - 229, n. 7; and Cogley 1999, Appendix Three).

53. The convicted men were Tobias, his son Wampapaquan, and Mattashunnamo, all *pniese* or wisemen of Metacom's people (Morrison 1995, 169). Wampapaquan was shot, the others hanged. For other accounts of the events surrounding the beginning of Metacom's war, see Leach (1958), Jennings (1975), and Lepore (1998).

54. Natick, Punkapog, Nashobah, Wamesit, and Hassanamesit (see Gookin 1674, 450 - 453; and Morrison 1995, 171 - 172).

55. The idea of a "white" race was only beginning to emerge at this time, ironically through English attempts to distinguish themselves as white in opposition to the Irish (see Allen 1994). The distinction between Indian and British in the literature of the period is therefore not racial in a contemporary sense, though its effect was much the same as that of later racist bigotry. On the importance of such binary categories to the emergence of an "American" identity among the British, see Lepore (1998). On the role of literacy in the evolving sense of identity among Indian proselytes in New England, see Wyss (2000).

56. Soon the General Court further reduced the number of Praying Towns to three: Natick, Punkapog, and Wamesit. Punkapog, and Wamesit were quickly absorbed by their English neighbors (see Gookin 1674; Morrison 1995, 181). Natick's church remained Indian until 1716, when its Indian minister, Daniel Tokkowampait, died. It then became an English church with the Indians as members, following the pattern of other Praying Towns as Indian teachers died and were not replaced (Ola Winslow 1966, 187). By 1763 the Indians at Natick had lost most of their land and political autonomy to English neighbors, and in 1781 Natick finally became an English town (see O'Brien 1997, 209).

57. Joseph Baxter was sent to Maine at this time to compete with the successful Jesuit missionary Sébastien Râle. Baxter contacted Râle, who responded with a 100-page defense of Roman Catholicism, in Latin. Baxter replied in kind, and Râle responded to that with a critique of Baxter's Latin (Kellaway 1962, 259). Competition with the Jesuits drove much of the Company's missionary efforts in the first half of the eighteenth century. Despite the Catholics' considerable head start in New York, for example, the Company reassured the Commissioners that "the Protestants have trugh & the God of truth on their side" (letter, October 31, 1701, New England Company archive ms. 7952, in Kellaway 1962, 266).

58. "Wherein doth this worke of God stand in appointing a place for a people? . . . when he makes roome for a people to dwell there," Cotton (1630) said. It is a "principle in Nature," he adds, "that in a vacant soyle, hee that taketh possession of it, and bestoweth culture and husbandry upon it, his Right it is" (3 - 5). The legal principle of *vacuum domicilium* gave settlers the right to colonize any land that was not occupied and "improved" according to the standards of European agriculture.

59. The most notorious atrocity of that war occurred at Mystic Fort, where 400 to 500 Pequots were killed when a colonial army and its Narragansett allies attacked the Pequot village on the Mystic River, set the village on fire, and then waited outside to slaughter people who tried to escape (Vincent 1637; Underhill 1638). It almost wiped out the entire tribe. Those who were not killed were sold as slaves to other tribes or shipped to the West Indies (see Jennings 1975, 186 - 227, and Vaughan 1979, 144 - 147). In *Of Plymouth Plantation*, William Bradford (1952) celebrates this victory by comparing the burning flesh of the Pequot villagers to a burnt offering to the Lord. Bradford writes, "It was a fearful sight to see them thus frying in the fire and the streams of blood quenching the same, and horrible was the stink and scent thereof; but the victory seemed a sweet sacrifice, and they gave the praise thereof to God, who had wrought so wonderfully for them." Bradford glosses the phrase "sweet sacrifice" as a reference to Leviticus 2:1 - 3, which describes the smell of burning meat offered to the

Lord as a "sweet savour unto the Lord . . . it is a thing most holy of the offerings of the Lord made by fire" (296). For a discussion of the connection between Calvinist doctrine, Puritan rhetoric, and genocidal military policies, see Kibbey (1986).

60. For a discussion of the importance of the *exemplum* in the formation of identity among colonial Puritans, see Bercovitch (1975).

61. On the connection between the missionary project in New England and the more overtly assimilationist policies of the eighteenth century, see O'Brien (1997).

62. The following remarks about Eliot's millennialism are based on Clark (2002, 104-115), portions of which are reprinted here with permission.

63. Twisse, "Fourth Letter" to Mede, March 2, 1634 - 1635, in Mede's 1664, ii, 979, Epistle XLII, quoted in Firth (1979, 223 - 224, n. 67).

64. An excellent summary of the origins and evolution of the ethnographic evidence supporting this speculation may be found in Cogley (1986 - 1987, 212 - 222), who also details the changes in Eliot's attitude toward the Indians as Jews.

65. Eliot's place in the history of millennialism is usually associated with the militant millenarian politics of *The Christian Commonwealth* (1659), where he celebrates the regicide of Charles I as the first step in a spiritual revolution that will transform England into Christ's kingdom: "Christ is the only right Heir of the Crown of England, and of all other Nations; and he has now come to take possession of His Kingdom, making England first in that blessed work of setting up the Kingdom of the Lord Jesus." It was the next part of the sentence that represented colossally bad timing when the book was published on the eve of the Restoration: "in order thereunto, he [God] hath cast down not only the miry Religion, and Government of Antichrist, but also the former form of civil Government, which did stick so fast unto it, until by an unavoidable necessity, it fell with it" (Preface, B2 verso).

What distinguishes this claim from most millennialism, and what at the time associated Eliot's work with the radical millenarianism of the Fifth Monarchists, was the insistence that Christ's kingdom was to be established on the earth as we know it in the present, rather than on some ontological middle ground more hospitable to the spirit, as was argued by others. The latter claim was more characteristic of Protestant millennialism, and much safer, since it did not require the overthrow of existing corporeal social forms. The antimonarchical thrust of *The Christian Commonwealth* scandalized many of Eliot's friends in England and embarrassed his fellow colonists. Eliot later recanted his more radical political arguments, but years after the controversy surrounding *The Christian Commonwealth* Eliot continued to insist on a literal understanding of millennialist promises for Christ's return to earth long after most millennialists had abandoned such claims. See, for example, Eliot's (1665) *Communion of Churches*, where he claims that the New Jerusalem will "the most glorious city that ever shall be on Earth" (see Sehr 1984, 194 - 198).

66. Among the harshest responses to Thorowgood was *Americans No Iewes*. This book was written by Hamon L'Estrange (1652), who describes himself as a knight and explorer, and who claims to have "adventured for the discovery of the North-west passage" (72).

67. Jong (1970), Cogley (1986 - 1987), and Holstun (1983) have commented on this letter and the second edition of Thorowgood's book. Jong proposes a later date of composition, 1655 or 1656. Cogley argues that the letter must have been composed between March 1653 and February 1654 because of what he reads persuasively as a reference to *Tears of Repentance* in 1653 (223, n. 9). Cogley considers the letter in the context of Eliot's attraction to the theory that the Indians were the Lost Tribes of Israel. In the letter to Thorowgood, Eliot argues that the Indians are descendants of Eber, but he

was clearly drawn to the theory of the Lost Tribes and speculated that they had followed the Eberites to America and coexisted with them there. Cogley claims there were two reasons Eliot was attracted to this theory. First, in Deuteronomy 28:64, Moses warns the tribes that "the Lord will scatter you among all peoples, from one end of the earth to the other," which would obviously include Asia and America. Second, while Eliot was composing his letter there was a movement in England to admit the Jews into the country legally for the first time since their banishment by Edward I in 1290. The leading proponents for readmission were John Dury and Menasseh ben Israel, and they argued that if the Jews returned to England, "the universal dimension of Deuteronomy 28.64 would be realized in history" (219).

68. When Eliot had used Ezekiel 37 in his Algonquian sermon of 1646, he interpreted the "dry bones" as a reference to gentiles. To that point Eliot had clearly endorsed the theory that the Indians were descendants of the Tartars, and hence gentiles rather than Jews. Cf. Shepard's similar argument in *Clear Sun-shine*.

69. To this last claim, Eliot adds the following qualification: "or at least, all the World would become Very Divine or very Prophane, *Rev.* 22.11, 15. And so the World should end as it began, *Gen.* 4.26. some calling on the Name of the Lord, and some prophaning it; eminently distinguish'd from each other" (Baxter 1696, 295).

70. On the disappointment of Puritan millennialists following the Restoration, see Toon (1970), Firth (1979), and Capp (1972).

71. Authorship of this tract is unclear, though Cogley (1999) says these men are almost certainly the authors (268, n. 6). Cogley's claim is based on the argument in Stearns (1954, 167).

72. Cogley follows Thomas Werge in attributing this tract to Shepard (Cogley 1999, 278, n. 1).

73. Bross (1997, 130) stresses that Eliot's written presentation of the confessions conflates two very different occasions: the public confessions formally presented in October 1652 and written reports of confessions delivered in private to the Elders well before the public occasion. The Elders judged only the public narratives of conversion, which were delivered orally; they found them insufficient, and expressed reservations about the lack of corroboration for the translations by Eliot and his Indian assistants. Publishing the two sets of confessions together was clearly an attempt by Eliot to convince supporters in England that the church should be approved.

74. Morrison (1995) reads this account as evidence of a syncretic combination of Indian and Christian ritual, since in both cultures fasting was an important aspect of spiritual preparation.

BIBLIOGRAPHY

Adams, Nehemiah. *The Life of John Eliot; With an Account of the Early Missionary Efforts Among the Indians of New England.* Boston: Massachusetts Sabbath School Society, 1847.

Allen, Theodore. *The Invention of the White Race.* Vol. 1. New York: Verso, 1994.

Ashcroft, Bill, Gareth Griffths, and Helen Tiffin. *The Empire Writes Back: Theory and Practice in Postcolonial Literatures.* New York: Routledge, 1989.

Axtell, James. *America Perceived: A View from Abroad in the 17th Century.* West Haven, Conn.: Pendulum Press, 1974.

Axtell, James. *White Indians of Colonial America.* Fairfield, Wash.: Ye Galleon Press, 1979.

Axtell, James. *The Invasion Within: The Contest of Cultures in Colonial North America.*

Oxford: Oxford University Press, 1985.

Axtell, James. *After Columbus: Essays in the Ethnohistory of Colonial North America.* New York: Oxford University Press, 1988.

Axtell, James, ed. *The Indian Peoples of Eastern America: A Documentary History of the Sexes.* New York: Oxford University Press, 1981.

Baillie, Robert. *A Dissuasive from the Errours of the Time.* London, 1645.

Baxter, Richard. *Reliquiae Baxterianae: or, Mr. Richard Baxter's Narrative of the Most Memorable Passages of His Life and Times.* Edited by Matthew Sylvester. London, 1696.

Beaver, R. Pierce. *Church, State, and the American Indian: Two and a Half Centuries of Partnership in Missions between Protestant Churches and Government.* St. Louis, Mo.: Concordia, 1966.

Bercovitch, Sacvan. *The Puritan Origins of the American Self.* New Haven: Yale University Press, 1975.

Berkhofer, Robert F. *The White Man's Indian: Images of the American Indian from Columbus to the Present.* New York: Knopf, 1978.

Bowden, Henry W., and James P. Ronda, eds. *John Eliot's Indian Dialogues: A Study in Cultural Interaction.* Contributions in American History, No. 88. Westport, Conn: Greenwood Press, 1980.

Bozeman, Theodore Dwight. *To Live Ancient Lives: The Primitivist Dimension in Puritanism.* The Institute of Early American History and Culture. Chapel Hill: University of North Carolina Press, 1988.

Bradford, William. *Of Plymouth Plantation, 1620 - 1647.* Edited by Samuel Eliot Morison. New York: Knopf, 1952.

Bragdon, Kathleen J. *Native People of Southern New England, 1500 - 1650.* Norman: University of Oklahoma Press, 1996.

Bremer, Francis J. *Congregational Communion: Clerical Friendships in the Anglo-American Puritan Community, 1610 – 1692.* Boston: Northeastern University Press, 1994.

Bross, Kristina. "'That epithet of praying': The Praying Indian Figure in Early New England Literature." Ph.D. diss., University of Chicago, 1997.

Bross, Kristina. "Dying Saints, Vanishing Savages: 'Dying Indian Speeches' in Colonial New England Literature." *Early American Literature* 36 (2001): 325 - 52.

Broughton, Hugh. *A Require of Agreement to the Groundes of Divinitie Studie.* Middleburg, 1611. Reprinted as *A Require of Consent to Agreement Against Jews, who by us are hardened, and Perish,* in Broughton, Hugh. *The Works of the Great Albionean Divine, Renown'd in Many Nations For rare Skill in Salems and Athnes Tongues, And familiar Acquaintance with all Rabbinical Learning.* London, 1662, 614 - 649.

Capp, B. S., *The Fifth Monarchy Men: A Study in Seventeenth-Century English Millenarianism,* Totowa, N. J.: Rowman and Littlefield, 1972.

Castell, William. *A Petition of W[illiam] C[astell] Exhibited to the High Court of Parliament now assembled, for the propagating of the Gospel in America, and the West Indies: and for the setling of our Plantations there.* London, 1641.

Caverly, Robert Boodey. *Lessons of Law and Life from John Eliot, the Apostle to the Indian Nations of New England.* Boston: Moses H. Sargent and Sons, 1880.

Clark, Michael P. "'Even without a Metaphor': The Poetics of Apocalypse in Puritan New England." In *Millennial Thought in America: Historical and Intellectual Contexts, 1630 - 1860.* Edited by Bernd Engler, Joerg O. Fichte, and Oliver Scheiding. Trier, Germany: Wissenschaftlicher Verlag, 2002.

Cogley, Richard W. "John Eliot and the Origins of the American Indians." *Early*

American Literature 21 (1986 - 1987): 210 - 225.

Cogley, Richard W. *John Eliot's Mission to the Indians before King Philip's War.* Cambridge: Harvard University Press, 1999.

Cohen, Charles. "Conversion among Puritans and Amerindians: A Theological and Cultural Perspective." In *Puritanism: Transatlantic Perspectives on a Seventeenth-Century Anglo-American Faith*, edited by Francis Bremer. Boston: Massachusetts Historical Society, 1993.

Cook, Sherburne F. *The Indian Population of New England in the Seventeenth Century.* Berkeley and Los Angeles: University of California Press, 1976.

Cotton, John. *God's Promise to his Plantation.* London, 1630.

Cotton, John. *A Brief Exposition of the whole Book of Canticles.* London, 1642.

Cotton, John. *The Way of Congregational Churches.* London, 1648.

Cronon, William. *Changes in the Land: Indians, Colonists, and the Ecology of New England.* New York: Hill and Wang, 1983.

D., C. *New England: faction discovered, or, A brief and true account of their persecution of the Church of England. . . .* London, 1690.

Delbanco, Andrew. *The Puritan Ordeal.* Cambridge: Harvard University Press, 1989.

Eliot, John. *The Christian Commonwealth.* London, 1659. Written 1651 - 1652. Facsimile edition, New York: Arno Press, 1972.

Eliot, John. *The Communion of Churches.* Cambridge, 1665.

Eliot, John. *The Holy Bible: containing the Old Testament and the New. Translated into the Indian Language, and Ordered to be printed by the Commissioners of the United Colonies in New England, At the Charge, and with the Consent of the Corporation in England for the Propagation of the Gospel amongst the Indians in New England.* Cambridge, 1663.

Eliot, John. *Indian Dialogues.* Cambridge, 1671.

Eliot, John. *John Eliot and the Indians, 1652 - 1657: Being Letters Address to Rev. Jonathan Hanmer of Barnstaple, England.* Edited by Wilberforce Eames. New York: Adams and Grace Press, 1915.

Eliot, John.tr. *The Dying Speeches of Several Indians . . . Dying Speeches and Counsels of such Indians as dyed in the Lord.* Cambridge, 1685.

Firth, Katharine R. *The Apocalyptic Tradition in Reformation Britain: 1530 - 1645.* New York: Oxford University Press, 1979.

Francis, Convers. *Life of John Eliot, the Apostle to the Indians.* Boston: Hilliard, Gray, 1836.

Freeman, John F. "The Indian Convert: Theme and Variation." *Ethnohistory* 12 (1965): 113 - 128.

Goddard, Ives, and Kathleen J. Bragdon. *Native Writings in Massachusett.* Philadelphia: American Philosophical Society, 1988.

Gookin, Daniel. *An Historical Account of the Doings and Sufferings of the Christian Indians in New England.* 1677. American Antiquarian Society, *Transactions and Collections* 2 (1836): 429 - 525.

Gookin, Daniel. *The Historical Collections of the Indians in New England.* 1674. Massachusetts Historical Society *Collections, first series,* 1 (1792): 141 - 226.

Greenblatt, Stephen. *Marvelous Possessions: The Wonder of the New World.* Chicago: University of Chicago Press, 1991.

Hall, David. *The Faithful Shepherd: A History of the New England Ministry in the Seventeenth Century.* Institute of Early American History and Culture. Chapel Hill: University of North Carolina Press, 1972.

Harling, Frederick Farnham. "A Biography of John Eliot, 1604 - 1690." Ph.D. diss., Boston University, 1965.

Holstun, James. "John Eliot's Empirical Millenarianism." *Representations* 4 (1983): 128 - 153.

Holstun, James. *A Rational Millennium: Puritan Utopias of Seventeenth-Century England and America.* New York: Oxford University Press, 1987.

Hooker, Thomas. *A survey of the Summe of Church-Discipline.* London, 1648.

Hubbard, William. *The Present State of New England, Being a Narrative of the Troubles with the Indians in New-England.* London, 1677.

Jalalzai, Zubeda. "Puritan Imperialisms: The Limits of Identity and the Indian Missions of Massachusetts Bay." Ph.D. diss., State University of New York at Buffalo, 2000.

Jennings, Francis. *The Invasion of America: Indians, Colonialism, and the Cant of Conquest.* Chapel Hill: University of North Carolina Press, 1975.

Jong, James A de. *As the Waters Cover the Seas: Millennial Expectations in the Rise of Anglo-American Missions, 1640 - 1810.* Kampen, Netherlands: Kok, 1970.

Keckermann, Bartholomew. *Manuductio to Theologie.* Translated by T. Vickers. 1621.

Kellaway, William. *The New England Company, 1649 - 1776: Missionary Society to the American Indians.* New York: Barnes and Noble, 1962.

Kibbey, Anne. *The Interpretation of Material Shapes in Puritanism: A Study of Rhetoric, Prejudice, and Violence.* New York: Cambridge University Press, 1986.

Kupperman, Karen Ordahl. *Settling with the Indians: The Meeting of English and Indian Cultures in America, 1580 - 1640.* Totowa, N. J.: Rowman and Littlefield, 1980.

Las Casas, Bartolomé de. *Brevíssima relación de la destrucción de las Indias.* Seville, 1552.

Leach, Douglas Edward. *Flintlock and Tomahawk: New England in King Philip's War.* New York: Norton, 1958.

Lechford, Thomas. *Plaine Dealing.* London, 1642.

Lepore, Jill. *The Name of War: King Philip's War and the Origins of American Identity.* New York: Knopf, 1998.

L'Estrange, Hamon. *Americans No Iewes, or Improbabilities That the Americans Are of That Race.* London, 1652.

Lincoln, Charles H., ed. *Narratives of the Indian Wars, 1675 - 1699.* New York: C. Scribner's Sons, 1913.

Lonkhuyzen, Harold van. "A Reappraisal of the Praying Indians: Acculturation, Conversion, and Identity at Natick, Massachusetts, 1646 - 1720." *New England Quarterly* 63 (1990): 396 - 428.

Lovejoy, David. *Religious Enthusiasm in the New World.* Cambridge: Harvard University Press, 1985.

Maclear, J. F. "New England and the Fifth Monarchy: The Quest for the Millennium." *William and Mary Quarterly,* 3d series. 32 (1975): 223 - 260.

Maltby, William. *The Black Legend in England: The Development of Anti-Spanish Sentiment, 1558 - 1660.* Durham, N.C.: Duke University Press, 1971.

Mandell, Daniel. "'To Live More Like My Christian English Neighbors': Natick Indians in the Eighteenth Century." *William and Mary Quarterly,* 3d series. 48 (1991): 552 - 579.

Mather, Cotton. *The Triumphs of the Reformed Religion in America. The Life of the Renowned John Eliot; a Person justly Famous in the Church of God, Not only as an Eminent Christian, and an Excellent Minister, among the English, But also, As a Memorable Evangelist among the Indians, of New-England; With some Account concerning the late and strange Success of the Gospel, in those parts of the World, which for many Ages have lain Buried in Pagan Ignorance.* Boston, 1691.

Mather, Cotton. *India Christiana.* Boston, 1721.

Mather, Cotton. *Magnalia Christi Americana.* London, 1702. Facsimile edition. New

York: Arno Press, 1972.

Mayhew, Experience. *Indian Converts: or, Some Account of the Lives and Dying Speeches of A Considerable Number of the Christianized Indians of Martha's Vineyard, in New England. . . .* Boston, 1727.

Mede, Joseph. *The Works of Joseph Mede, B. D.*, edited by John Worthington. 2 vols. London, 1664.

Moore, Martin. *Memoirs of the Life and Character of Rev. John Eliot, Apostle of the N.A. Indians.* Boston: T. Bedlington, 1822.

Morrison, Dane. *A Praying People: Massachusett Acculturation and the Failure of the Puritan Mission, 1600 - 1690.* American Indian Studies, vol. 2. New York: Peter Lang, 1995.

Naeher, Robert James. "Dialogue in the Wilderness: John Eliot and the Indian Exploration of Puritanism as a Source of Meaning, Comfort, and Ethnic Survival." *New England Quarterly* 62 (1989): 346 - 368.

New England Company. Resolution of May 19, 1779. New England Company Archive. Guildhall Library, London. Ms. 7920/I.

Nuttall, Geoffrey. *Visible Saints: The Congregational Way, 1640 - 1660*, Oxford: Oxford University Press, 1957.

O'Brien, Jean M. *Dispossession by Degrees: Indian Land and Identity in Natick, Massachusetts, 1650 - 1790.* Cambridge Studies in North American Indian History. New York: Cambridge University Press, 1997.

Phillips, John, trans. *The Tears of the Indians: being an historical and true Account of the Cruel Massacres and Slaughters of above Twenty Millions of innocent People, Committed by the Spaniards in the Islands of Hispaniola, Cuba, Jamaica, &c. As also, in the Continent of Mexico, Peru, & other Places of the West Indies, To the total destruction of those Countries.* Written in Spanish by Casaus, an Eye-witness of those things; And made English by J.P." London, 1656.

Pilling, James Constantine. *Bibliography of the Algonquin Languages.* Washington, D. C.: Government Printing Office, 1891.

Pratt, Mary Louise. *Imperial Eyes: Travel Writing and Transculturation.* New York: Routledge, 1992.

Ronda, James P. "'We Are Well As We Are': An Indian Critique of Seventeenth-Century Christian Missions." *William and Mary Quarterly*, 3d ser., 34 (1977): 66 - 82.

Rooy, Sidney H. *The Theology of Missions in the Puritan Tradition; a Study of Representative Puritans: Richard Sibbes, Richard Baxter, John Eliot, Cotton Mather and Jonathan Edward.* Grand Rapids, Mich.: W. B. Eerdmans, 1965.

Russell, Howard S. *Indian New England before the Mayflower.* Hanover, N.H.: University Press of New England, 1980.

Salisbury, Neal Emerson. *Manitou and Providence: Indians, Europeans, and the Making of New England, 1500 - 1643.* New York: Oxford University Press, 1982.

Salisbury, Neal Emerson. "Prospero in New England: The Puritan Missionary as Colonist." *In Papers of the Sixth Algonquian Conference, 1974.* edited by William Cowan. National Museum of Man, Mercury Series, Canadian Ethnology Service, vol. 23. Ottawa: National Museums of Canada, 1975.

Salisbury, Neal Emerson. "Red Puritans: The 'Praying Indians' of Massachusetts Bay and John Eliot." *William and Mary Quarterly*, 3d. ser., 31 (1974): 27 - 54.

S[altonstall], N[athaniel]. *The Present State of New-England, With Respect to the Indian War.* London, 1675.

Sauer, Carl Ortwin. *Sixteenth Century North America: The Land and the People as Seen by the Europeans.* Berkeley: University of California Press, 1971.

Schwartz, Stuart B., ed. *Implicit Understandings: Observing, Reporting, and Reflecting on the Encounters between Europeans and Other Peoples in the Early Modern Era.* New York: Cambridge University Press, 1994.

Segal, Charles M., and David C. Stineback. *Puritans, Indians, and Manifest Destiny.* New York: G. P. Putnam's Sons, 1977.

Sehr, Timothy J. "John Eliot, Millennialist and Missionary." *The Historian* 46 (1984): 187 - 203.

Sewall, Samuel. *Phaenomena quaedam Apocalyptica ad aspectum Novi Orbis configurata. Or, some few Lines towards a description of the New Heaven as it makes to those who stand upon the New Earth.* Boston, 1697.

Shepard, Thomas. *The Sincere Convert.* London, 1672. Translated into Algonquian by John Eliot and Grindal Rawson. Cambridge, 1689.

Sibelius, Caspar. *Of the conversion of Five Thousand and Nine Hundred East-Indians.* Translated by Henry Jessey. London, 1650.

Smolinski, Reiner. "Israel Redivivus: The Eschatological Limits of Puritan Typology in New England." *New England Quarterly* 63 (1990): 357 - 395.

Smolinski, Reiner, ed. *The Threefold Paradise of Cotton Mather: An Edition of "Triparadisus."* Athens: University of Georgia Press, 1995.

Snow, Dean. *The Archaeology of New England.* New York: Academic Press, 1980.

Stearns, Raymond P. "The Weld - Peter Mission to England." *Publications of the Colonial Society of Massachusetts* 32 (1934), in *Transactions of the Colonial Society of Massachusetts, 1933 - 1937.* Boston: Colonial Society of Massachusetts, 1937: 188 - 246.

Stearns, Raymond P. *The Strenuous Puritan: Hugh Peter, 1598 - 1660.* Urbana: University of Illinois Press, 1954.

Thorowgood, Thomas. *Jewes in America, or Probabilities that the Americans are of that Race,* with an "Epistle" by John Dury. London, 1650. Reprinted as *Jews in America, or, Probabilities, that those Indians are Judaical, made more probable by some additionals to the former conjectures,* with a lengthy preface by John Eliot, "Learned Conjectures." London, 1660.

Thorpe, Francis Newton, ed. *The Federal and State Constitutions Colonial Charters, and Other organic Laws of the States, Territories, and Colonies Now or Heretofore Forming the United States of America.* Vol. 3. Compiled and edited under the act of Congress of June 30, 1906. Washington, D. C.: Government Printing Office, 1909.

Thwaites, Robert Gold, ed. *The Jesuit Relations and Allied Documents, Travels, and Explorations of the Jesuit Missionaries in New France, 1610 - 1791.* 73 vols. Cleveland: Burrows, 1896 - 1901.

Tinker, George. *Missionary Conquest: The Gospel and Native American Cultural Genocide.* Minneapolis: Fortress Press, 1993.

Tooker, William Wallace. *John Eliot's First Indian Teacher and Interpreter, Cockenoe-de-Long Island.* New York, 1896.

Toon, Peter, ed. *Puritans, the Millennium and the Future of Israel: Puritan Eschatology 1600 to 1660.* Cambridge: 1970.

Tuveson, Ernest Lee. *Redeemer Nation: The Idea of America's Millennial Role,* Chicago: University of Chicago Press, 1968.

Underhill, John. *Newes from America or, a New and experimentall discoverie of New England.* London, 1638.

Vaughan, Alden T. *New England Frontier: Puritans and Indians, 1620 - 1675.* New York: Little, Brown, 1965; revised ed. New York: Norton, 1979.

Vincent, Philip. *A True Relation of the Late Battell fought in New England, between the English and the Salvages.* London, 1637.

Watts, Edward. *Writing and Postcolonialism in the Early Republic*. Charlottesville: University Press of Virginia, 1998.

Weis, Frederick L. "The New England Company of 1649 and Its Missionary Enterprises." *Publications of the Colonial Society of Massachusetts* 38 (1948): 134 - 218.

Werge, Thomas. *Thomas Shepard*. Boston: Twayne, 1987.

Williams, Roger. *The Bloody Tenent yet More Bloody*. London, 1652.

Williams, Roger. *A Key into the Language of America*. London, 1643.

White, John. T*he Planters Plea*. London, 1630.

Winship, George Parker. *The New England Company of 1649 and John Eliot*. Publications of the Prince Society, vol. 36. Boston: Prince Society, 1920.

Winslow, Edward. *Good Newes from New England*. London, 1624.

Winslow, Ola Elizabeth. *John Eliot: "Apostle to the Indians."* Boston: Houghton Mifflin, 1966.

Winthrop, John. *The Journal of John Winthrop 1630 - 1649*. Edited by Richard S. Dunn, James Savage, and Laetitia Yeandle. Cambridge: Harvard University Press, 1996.

Wyss, Hilary E. *Writing Indians: Literacy, Christianity, and Native Community in Early America*. Amherst: University of Massachusetts Press, 2000.

Ziff, Larzer, ed. *John Cotton on the Churches of New England*. Cambridge: Harvard University Press, 1968.

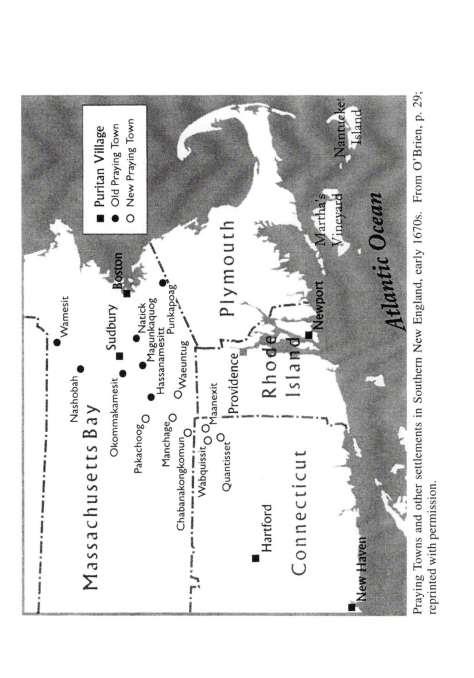

Praying Towns and other settlements in Southern New England, early 1670s. From O'Brien, p. 29; reprinted with permission.

NEVV ENGLANDS FIRST FRUITS;

IN RESPECT,

First of the { Conversion of some, Conviction of divers, Preparation of sundry } of the *Indians*.

2. Of the progresse of *Learning*, in the *Colledge* at CAMBRIDGE in *Massacusets* Bay.

WITH

Divers other speciall Matters concerning that *Countrey*.

Published by the instant request of sundry Friends, who desire to be satisfied in these points by many *New-England* Men who are here present, and were eye or eare-witnesses of the same.

Who hath despised the Day of small things. Zach. 4. 10.

If thou wert pure and upright, surely now he will awake for thee : — And though thy beginnings be small, thy latter end shall greatly encrease. Iob. 8 6,7.

LONDON,

Printed by R.O and G.D. for *Henry Overton*, and are to be sold at his Shop in *Popes-head-Alley.* 1643.

N E W
E N G L A N D S
F I R S T   F R U I T S;

IN RESPECT,

First of the $\left\{\begin{array}{l}\text{Conversion of some,}\\ \text{Conviction of divers,}\\ \text{Preparation of sundry}\end{array}\right\}$ of the *Indians*.

2. Of the progresse of *Learning*, in the *Colledge* at
CAMBRIDGE in *Massacusets* Bay.

WITH
Divers other speciall Matters concerning that *Countrey*.

Published by the instant request of sundry Friends, who desire
to be satisfied in these points by many *New-England* Men
who are here present, and were eye or eare-
witnesses of the same.

Who hath despised the Day of small things. Zach. 4.10.

*If thou were pure and upright, surely now he will awake for thee: – And though
thy beginnings be small, thy latter end shall greatly encrease.* Job 8. 6,7.

LONDON,

Printed by R.O. and G.D. for *Henry Overton*, and are to be
sold at his Shop in *Popes-head-Alley*. 1 6 4 3.

NEW
ENGLANDS
FIRST FRUITS:

1. In respect of the Indians, &c.

He Lord, who useth not to be wanting to the desires of his Servants, as he hath not frustrated the ends of our Transplanting in sundry other respects; so neither in the giving some light to those poore *Indians*, who have ever sate in hellish darknesse, adoring the *Divell* himselfe for their *GOD*: but hath given us some testimony of his gracious acceptance of our poore endeavours towards them, and of our groanes to himselfe for mercy upon those miserable Soules (the very Ruines of Mankind) there amongst us; our very bowels yerning within us to see them goe downe to Hell by swarmes without remedy.

Wherefore we judged it our duty no longer to conceale, but to declare (to the praise of his owe free grace) what *first Fruits* he hath begun to gather in amongst them, as a sure pledge (we are confident) of a greater *Harvest* in his owne time. And wonder not that wee mention no more instances at present: but consider, First, their infinite distance from Christianity, having never been prepared thereunto by any Civility at all. Secondly, the difficulty of their Language to us, and of ours to them; there being no Rules to learne either by. Thirdly, the diversity of their owne Langauge to it selfe; every part of that Countrey having its own Dialect, differing much from the other; all which make their comming into the Gospel the more slow. But what God hath done for some of them, we will declare.

---

1. Many years since at *Plimmouth* Plantation, when the Church did fast and pray for Raine in extreame Drought; it being a very hot and cleare sun-shine day, all the former part thereof; An *Indian* of good quality, being present, and seeing what they were about, fell a wondring at them for praying for raine in a day so unlikely, when all Sunne and no Clouds appeared; and thought that their God was not able to give Raine at such a time as that: but this poore wretch seeing them still to continue in their Prayers, and beholding that at last the

Clouds began to rise, and by that time they had ended their Duty, the Raine fell in a most sweet, constant, soaking showre, fell into wonderment at the power that the English had with their God, and the greatnesse and goodnesse of that God whom they served, and was smitten with terror that he had abused them and their God by his former hard thoughts of them; and resolved from that day not to rest till he did know this great good *God*, and for that end to forsake the *Indians*, and cleave to the English, which he presently did, and laboured by all publique and private meanes to suck in more and more of the knowledge of God, and his wayes. And as he increased in knowledge so in affection, and also in his practice, reforming and conforming himselfe accordingly: and (though he was much tempted by inticements, scoffes and scornes from the *Indians*) yet, could he never be gotten from the *English*, nor from seeking after their God, but died amongst them, leaving some good hopes in their hearts, that his soule went to rest.

2. *Sagamore John*, Prince of *Massaquesets*, was from our very first landing more courteous, ingenious, and to the English more loving then others of them; he desired to learne and speake our Language, and loved to imitate us in our behaviour and apparrell, and began to hearken after our God and his wayes, and would much commend English-men, and their God; saying (*Much good men, much good God*) and being convinced that our condition and wayes were better farre then theirs, did resolve and promise to leave the *Indians*, and come live with us; but yet kept downe by feare of the scoffes of the *Indians*, had not power to make good his purpose; yet went on, not without some trouble of mind, and secret plucks of Conscience, as the sequel declares: for being struck with death, fearfully cryed out of himselfe, that he had not come to live with us, to have knowne our God better: "*But now* (said he) *I must die, the God of the English is much angry with me, and will destroy me; ah,* I *was affraid of the scoffes of these wicked* Indians; *yet my Child shall live with the* English, *and learne to know their God when I am dead; Ile give him to Mr.* Wilson, *he is a much Good man, and much loved me*": so sent for Mr. *Wilson* to come to him, and committed his onely Child to his care, and so died.

3. Divers of the *Indians* Children, Boyes and Girles we have received into our houses, who are long since civilized, and in subjection to us, painfull and handy in their businesse, and can speak our language familiarly; divers of whom can read English, and begin to understand in their measure, the grounds of Christian Religion; some of them are able to give us account of the Sermons they heare, and of the word read and expounded in our Families, and are convinced of their sinfull and miserable Estates, and affected with the sense of Gods displeasure, and the thoughts of Eternity, and will sometimes tremble and melt into teares at our opening and pressing the Word upon their Consciences; and as farre as we can discerne, some of them use to pray in secret and are much in love with us, and cannot indure to returne any more to the *Indians*.

Some of them will not be absent from a Sermon or Family duties if they can help it; and we have knowne some would use to weep and cry when detained by occasion from the Sermon.

Others of them are very inquisitive after God and his wayes; and being themselves industrious in their Calling, will much complaine of other servants idlenesse, and reprove them.

One of them who for some misdemeanour that laid him open to publique punishment, ran away; and being gone, God so followed him, that of his owne accord he returned home, rendred himselfe to Justice, and was willing to submit himselfe, though he might have escaped.

An *Indian* Maid at *Salem*, would often come from the Word, crying out with abundance of teares, concluding that she must burne when she die, and would say, she knew her selfe naught for present, and like to be miserable for ever, unlesse free Grace should prevent it; and after this grew very carefull of her carriage, proved industrious in her place, and so continued.

Another often frequenting the House of one of the Ministers at *Salem*, would tell him the Story of the Bible, even to his admiration, and that he attended upon the Word preached, and loved it; and how he could tell all the Commandements, and in particular each Commandement by itselfe, and how he laboured to keep them all; and yet for all this (said he) [*Me die, and walke in fire,*] that is, when I die, I must to Hell: That Minister asked him why? he answered, because I know not *Jesus Christ*, and pray'd him earnestly to teach him *Jesus Christ*, and after went out amongst the *Indians*, and called upon them to put away all their wives save one, because it was a sinne against English-mans Saviour.

Another *Indian* comming by, and seeing one of the English (who was remote from our jurisdiction, prophaning the Lords day, by felling of a tree, said to him, "*Doe you not know that this is the Lords day*, in *Massaqusetts? much machet man,* that is *very wicked man, what, breake you Gods Day?*

The same man comming into an house in those parts where a man and his wife were chiding, and they bidding him sit downe, he was welcome; he answered, "*He would not stay there, God did not dwell there, Hobamock,* (that is *the Devill) was there,* and so departed.

One of the *Sagamores*, having complaint made to him by some of the English, that his men did use to kill Pigeons upon the Lords day, thereupon forbad them to doe so any more; yet afterwards some of them did attempt it, and climbing the high trees (upon which Pigeons in that Countrey use to make their nests) one of them fell down from off the tree and brake his neck, and another fell down and brake some of his limbs: thereupon the *Sagamore* sent two grave old men to proclaime it amongst his *Indians*, that none of them should kill Pigeons upon the Sabboth day any more.

Another *Indian* hearing of the fame of the *English*, and their God came from a far to see them, and such was this mans love to the *English* and their wayes after he came acquainted with them, that he laboured to transform himselfe into the *English* manners and practises, as if he had been an English man indeed; would be called no more by his *Indian* name, but would be named *William*; he would not goe naked like the *Indians*, but cloathed just as one of our selves; he abhorred to dwell with the *Indians* any longer; but forsaking all his friends and Kindred dwelt wholly with us; when he sate downe to meat with us, if thanks were given before he came in; or if he did eat by himselfe, constantly he would give thanks reverently and gravely, he frequented the word and family duties where he came, and gat a good measure of knowledge beyond ordinary, being a man of singular parts, and would complaine that he knew not Christ, and without him, he said all he did was nothing; hee was so zealous for the Lords day, that (as it was observed) if he saw any profaning it, he would rebuke them, and threaten them to carry them to the Governour.

All which things weighed, we dare not but hope, that many of them, doe belong to the Kingdome of God; and what further time may produce, we leave it to him that is excellent in Counsell, and wonderfull in working.

4. There is also a Blackmore maid, that hath long lived at *Dorchester* in *New England*, unto whom God hath so blessed the publique and private means of Grace that she is not only indued with a competent measure of knowledge in the mysteries of God, and conviction of her miserable estate by sinne; but hath also experience of a saving work of grace in her heart, and a sweet savour of Christ breathing in her; insomuch that her soule hath longed to enjoy Church-fellowship with the Saints there, and having propounded her desire to the Elders of the Church, after some triall of her taken in private, she was called before the whole Church, and there did make confession of her knowledge in the Mysteries of Christ and of the work of Conversion upon her Soule: And after that there was such a testimony given of her blamelesse and godly Conversation, that she was admitted a member by the joynt consent of the Church, with great joy to all their hearts. Since which time, we have heard her much admiring Gods free grace to such a poore wretch as she was; that God leaving all her friends and Kindred still in their sinnes, should cast an eye upon her, to make her a member of Christ, and of the Church also: and hath with teares exhorted some other of the *Indians* that live with us to embrace *Jesus Christ*, declaring how willing he would be to receive them, even as he had received her.

5. The last instance we will give shall be of that famous Indian *Wequash* who was a Captaine, a proper man of person, and of a very grave and sober spirit; the Story of which comming to our hands very lately, was indeed the occasion of writing all the rest: This man, a few years since, feeling and beholding the mighty power of God in our English Forces, how they fell upon the *Pegans*, where divers hundreds of them were slaine in an houre: The Lord, as a God of glory in great terrour did appeare unto the Soule and Conscience of this poore Wretch, that very act; and though before that time he had low apprehensions of our God, having conceived him to be (as he said) but a *Musketto* God, or a God like unto a flye; and as meane thoughts of the English that served this God, that they were silly weake men; yet from that time he was convinced and perswaded that our God was a most dreadfull God; and that one *English* man by the help of his God was able to slay and put to flight an hundred *Indians*.

This conviction did pursue and follow him night and day, so that he could have no rest or quiet because hee was ignorant of the *English mans God*: he went up and down bemoaning his condition; and filling every place where he came with sighes and groanes.

Afterward it pleased the Lord that some *English* (well acquainted with his Language) did meet with him; thereupon as a Hart panting after the water

Brookes, he enquired after God with such incessant diligence that they were constrained constantly for his satisfaction to spend more then halfe the night in conversing with him.

Afterwards he came to dwell amongst the English at *Connecticut*, still travelling with all his might and lamenting after the Lord: his manner was to smite his hand on his breast, and to complaine sadly of his heart, saying it was *much machet*, (that is very evill) and when any spake with him, he would say, *Wequash, no God, Wequash no know Christ*. It pleased the Lord, that in the use of the meanes, he grew greatly in the knowledge of Christ, and in the Principles of Religion, and became thorowly reformed according to his light, hating and loathing himselfe for his dearest sinnes, which were especially these two *Lust* and *Revenge*, this repentance for the former was testified by his temperance and abstinence from all occasions, or matter of provocation thereunto. Secondly, by putting away all his Wives, saving the first, to whom he had most right.

His repentance for the latter was testified by an eminent degree of meeknesse and patience, that now, if any did abuse him, he could lie downe at their feet, and if any did smite him on the one cheeke, he would rather turne the other, than offend them: many trialls hee had from the *Indians* in this case. Thirdly, by going up and downe to those hee had offered violence or wrong unto, confessing it, and making restitution.

Afterwards he went amongst the Indians, like that poore Woman of *Samaria*, proclaiming *Christ*, and telling them what a Treasure he had found, instructing them in the knowledge of the true *God:* and this he did with a grave and serious spirit, warning them with all faithfullnesse to flee from the wrath to come, by breaking off their sinnes and wickednesse.

This course of his did so disturb the Devill, that erelong some of the Indians, whose hearts Satan had filled did secretly give him poyson, which he tooke without suspition: and when he lay upon his death bed, some Indians who were by him, wished him according to the Indian manner, to send for *Powow* (that is to say) a Wizzard; he told them, *If Jesus Christ say that Wequash shall live, then Wequash must live; if Jesus Christ say that Wequash shall dye, then Wequash is willing to dye, and will not lengthen out his life by any such meanes.* Before he dyed, he did bequeath his Child to the godly care of the English for education and instruction and so yielded up his soule into *Christ* his hands.

I cannot omit the testimony of Mr. S[h] a godly Minister in the *Bay*, that wrote to his Friend in *London* concerning this Story, his lines are full plain and pithy his words these,

Wequash the famous Indian at the Rivers mouth is dead, and certainly in heaven; gloriously did the Grace of Christ *shine forth in his conversation, a yeare and a halfe before his death he knew Christ, he loved Christ, he preached Christ up and down, and then suffered Martyrdome for Christ; and when he dyed, he gave his soule to Christ, and his only child to the English, rejoycing in this hope, that the child should know more of Christ then its poore Father ever did.*

Thus we have given you a little tast of the sprincklings of Gods spirit, upon a few Indians, but one may easily imagine, that here are not all that may be produced: for if a very few of us here present, upon very sudden thoughts, have snatcht up only such instances which came at present to hand, you may conceive, that if all in our Plantations (which are farre and wide) should set themselves to bring in the confluence of all their Observations together, much more might be added.

We beleeve one mean amongst others, that hath thus farre wonne these poore wretches to looke after the Gospell, hath been the dealings and carriages, which God hath guided the English in our Patent, to exercise towards them: For,

1. At our entrance upon the Land, it was not with violence and intrusion, but free and faire, with their consents and allowance the chief Sagamores of all that part of the Countrey, entertaining us heartily, and professed we were all much welcome.

2. When any of them had possession of, or right unto any Land we were to plant upon, none were suffered, (to our knowledge) to take one acre from them, but do use to compound with them to content.

3. They have had justice truly exercised towards them in all other particular acts; that as we expect right dealing from them, in case any of them shall trespasse us, we send to their Sagamore, and he presently rights us, or else we summon them to our Court to answer it; so if any of our men offend them, and complaint and proofe be made to any of our Magistrates, or the publique Court (they know) they are sure to be righted to the utmost, by us.

4. The humanity of the English towards them doth much gaine upon them, we being generally wary, and tender in giving them offensive or harsh language, or carriage, but use them fairly and courteously, with loving termes, good looks and kind salutes.

Thus they having first a good esteem of our Persons, (such of them as God intends good unto) are the sooner brought to hearken to our words, and then to serve our God: wheras on the contrary, the wicked, injurious and scandalous carriages of some other Plantations, have bin a mean to harden those poore wofull soules against the English, and all Religion for their sakes; and seale them up under perdition.

Yet (mistake us not) we are wont to keep them at such a distance, (knowing they serve the Devill and are led by him) as not to imbolden them too much, or trust them too farre; though we do them what good we can. And the truth is, God hath so kept them, (excepting that act of the Pequits, long since, to some few of our men) that we never found any hurt from them, nor could ever prove any reall intentions of evill against us: And if there should be such intentions and that they all should combine together against us with all their strength that they can raise, we see no probable ground at all to feare any hurt from them, they being naked men, and the number of them that be amongst us not considerable.

Let us here give a touch also of what God hath done and is further about to doe to divers Plantations of the English, which before that time that God sent light into our coasts, were almost as darke and rude as the Indians themselves.

1. First at Agamenticus (a Plantation out of our jurisdiction) to which one of our Preachers comming and labouring amongst them, was a meanes under

God, not only to sparkle heavenly knowledge, and worke conviction and reformation in divers of them, but conversion also to Christ in some of them, that blesse God to this day, that ever he came thither.

2. Then after that, at Sauco {i.e., Saco} Plantation, which is an hundred miles from us, divers of that place comming often into our coasts and hearing the Word preached, and seeing Gods goings amongst his people there, being much affected went home, and lamented amongst their neighbours their own wofull condition, that lived like heathens without the Gospel, when others injoyed it in great plenty: hereupon with joynt consent two of their chiefe men were sent in all their names, earnestly to intreat us to send a godly Minister to preach the Word unto them: which was doe accordingly, not without good successe to the people there, and divers places about them.

3. After this, towards the end of last Summer, foure more Plantations some of which are divers hundred miles; others of them many hundred leagues from our Plantation) hearing of the goodnesse of God to his people in our parts, and of the light of the Gospel there shining; have done even as *Jacob* did in the Famine time, when he heard there was bread in *Egypt*, he hasted away his Sonnes for Corn, that they might live and not die: in like manner three severall Towns in *Virginia*, as also *Barbados, Christophers* and *Antego,* all of them much about the same time, as if they had known the minds of each other did send Letters and Messengers crying out unto us as the man of *Macedonia* to *Paul, Come and help us* and that with such earnestnesse, as men hunger-starved and ready to die cry for bread; so they cry out unto us in the bowels of compassion for the Lord Jesus sake to send them some helpe. They tell us in some of their Letters that from the one end of the Land to the other, there is none to break the *bread* of *life* unto the *hungry*; and those that should doe it, are so vile, that even drunkards and swearers, cry shame on them.

We had thought (but only for the swelling of our Discourse) to have set down their Letters at large, which they wrote to all our Churches, which spake with such strength of reason and affection, that when they were read in our Congregations, they prevailed with us that for their necessity we spared the bread from our own mouths to save their lives, and sent two of our Ministers for the present to *Virginia*; and when the Ships came away from them they left them in serious consultation, whom to give up to the worke of Christ in the other three places also.

We heare moreover that the Indians themselves in some of the places named did joyne with them in this their suit.

Now from what hath bin said, see the riches of Gods free Grace in Christ, that is willing to impart mercy even to the worst of men, and such as are furthest off cry out with *Paul, Oh the depths, &c.* and let heaven and earth be filled with the glorious praises of God for the same.

And if such as are afarre off, why should not we that are nearer presse in for a share therin, and cry out, as *Esau* did with teares to his Father, when he saw the blessing going away to his younger brother, and himselfe, like to lose it: [*Oh my Father hast thou but one blessing, blesse me also, even me thy first borne, blesse me, oh my Father.*] Else these poore Indians will certainly rise up against us, and with great boldnesse condemn us in the great day of our accompts, when many of us here under great light, shall see men come from the East and from the West, and sit down in the Kingdome of God, and our selves cast out.

2. Let the world know, that God led not so many thousands of his people into the Wildernesse, to see a reed shaken with the wind, but amongst many other speciall ends, this was none of the least, to spread the light of his blessed Gospel, to such as never heard the sound of it. To stop the mouths of the profane that calumniate the work of God in our hands, and to satisfie the hearts of the Saints herin that God had some speciall service for his people there to doe, which in part already we begin to see, and wait upon *Divine Wisdome*, to discover more of his pleasure herin, and upon his Grace to effect, which we beleeve in his time he will so doe, that men shall see and know the wisdome and power of God herin.

3. Shall we touch here upon that apprehension which many godly and wise have conceived, and that from some Scriptures compared, and from other grounds, and passages of Providence collected that (as it's very probable) God meanes to carry his Gospel westward, in these latter times of the world; and have thought, as the Sunne in the afternoon of the day, still declines more and more to the West and then sets: so the Gospel (that great light of the world) though it rose in the East, and in former ages, hath lightened it with his beames; yet in the latter ages of the world will bend Westward, and before its setting, brighten these parts, with his glorious lustre also.

4. See how Gods wisdome produceth glorious effects, from unlikely meanes, and make streight works by crooked instruments: for who would have thought, that the chasing away hence so many godly Ministers, should so farre have promoted the praises of God, and should be a meane to spread the Gospel, when they intended to ruine it: they blew out their lights and they burn clearer: their silencing Ministers have opened their mouths so wide as to sound out his glorious praises, to the uttermost parts of the earth, say with the Psalmist, *This is the Lords doing and it is marvelous in our eyes.*

5. Despise not the day of small things; let none say of us as those scoffers did of their building *Jerusalem, what will these weak jewes do?* but learne to adore God in all his Providence, and wait to see his ends.

6. Lend us, we beseech you (all you that love *Zion*) your prayers and helpe in heaven and earth for the furtherance of this great and glorious worke in our hands; great works need many hands, many prayers, many teares: And desire the Lord to stirre up the bowels of some godly minded, to pitty those poore Heathen that are bleeding to death to eternall death and to reach forth an hand of soule-mercy, to save some of them from the fire of hell by affording some means to maintain some fit instruments on purpose to spend their time, and give themselves wholly to preach to these poore wretches, that as the tender *Samarran* {Samaritan} did to the wounded man, they may pitty them, and get them healed, that even their bowels may blesse them in the day of their visitation, and Christs bowels refreshed by their love, may set it on his own score, and pay them all againe in the day of their accompts.

N E W

E N G L A N D S

F I R S T   F R U I T S:

2. In respect of the Colledge, and the proceedings of *Learning* therein.

1. **A**Fter God had carried us safe to *New England*, and wee had builded our houses, provided necessaries for our liveli-hood, rear'd convenient places for Gods worship, and setled the Civill Government: One of the next things we longed for, and looked after was to advance *Learning* and perpetuate it to Posterity; dreading to leave an illiterate Ministery to the Churches, when our present Ministers shall lie in the Dust. And as wee were thinking and consulting how to effect this great Work; it pleased God to stir up the heart of one Mr. *Harvard* (a godly Gentleman, and a lover of Learning, there living amongst us) to give the one halfe of his Estate (it being in all about {£}1700.) towards the erecting of a Colledge, and all his Library: after him another gave {£}300. Others after them cast in more, and the publique hand of the State added the rest: the Colledge was, by common consent, appointed to be at *Cambridge*, (a place very pleasant and accommodate) and is called (according to the name of the first founder) *Harvard Colledge*.

The Edifice is very faire and comely within and without, having in it a spacious Hall; (where they daily meet at Common Lectures) Exercises, and a large Library with some Bookes to it, the gifts of diverse of our friends; their Chambers and studies also fitted for, and possessed by the Students, and all other roomes of Office necessary and convenient, with all needfull Offices thereto belonging: And by the side of the Colledge a faire *Grammar* Schoole, for the training up of young Schollars, and fitting of them for *Academicall Learning*, that still as they are judged ripe, they may be received into the Colledge of this Schoole: Master *Corlet* is the Mr., who hath very well approved himselfe for his abilities, dexterity and painfulnesse in teaching and education of the youth under him.

Over the Colledge is master *Dunster* placed, as President, a learned conscionable and industrious man, who hath so trained up his Pupills in the tongues and Arts, and so seasoned them with the principles of Divinity and Christianity, that we have to our great comfort, (and in truth) beyond our hopes, beheld their progresse in Learning and godlinesse also; the former of these hath appeared in their publique declamations in *Latine* and *Greeke*, and Disputations Logicall and Philosophicall, which they have beene wonted (besides their ordinary Exercises in the Colledge-Hall) in the audience of the Magistrates, Ministers, and other Schollars, for the probation of their growth in Learning, upon set dayes, constantly once every moneth to make and uphold: The latter hath been manifested in sundry of them, by the savoury breathings of their Spirits in their godly conversation. Insomuch that we are confident, if these early blossomes may be cherished and warmed with the influence of the friends of Learning, and lovers of this pious worke, they will by the help of God, come to happy maturity in a short time.

Over the Colledge are twelve Overseers chosen by the generall Court, six of them are of the Magistrates, the other six of the Ministers, who are to promote the best good of it, and (having a power of influence into all persons in it) are to see that every one be diligent and proficient in his proper place.

2. *Rules, and Precepts that are observd in the Colledge.*

1. When any Schollar is able to understand Tully, or such like classicall Latine Author *ex tempore*, and make and speake true Latine in Verse and Prose, suont aiant Marie; And decline perfectly the Paradigm's of *Nounes* and *Verbes* in the *Greek* tongue: Let him then and not before be capable of admission into the Colledge.

2. Let every Student be plainly instructed, and earnestly pressed to consider well, the maine end of his life and studies is, *to know God and Jesus Christ which is eternall life*, John 17.3. and therefore to lay *Christ* in the bottome, as the only foundation of all sound knowledge and Learning.

And seeing the Lord only giveth wisedome, Let every one seriously set himselfe by prayer in secret to seeke it of him *Prov 2.3.*

3. Every one shall so exercise himselfe in reading the Scriptures twice a day, that he shall be ready to give such an account of his proficiency therein, both in *Theoretticall* observations of the Language, and *Logick*, and in *Practicall* and spirituall truths, as his Tutor shall require, according to his ability, seeing *the entrance of the word giveth light, it giveth understanding to the simple*, Psalm. 119.130.

4. That they eshewing all profanation of Gods Name, Attributes, Word, Ordinances and times of Worship, doe studie with good conscience, carefully to retaine God, and the love of his truth in {t}heir mindes else let them know, that (nothwithstanding their Learning), God may give them up *to strong delusions, and in the end to a reprobate minde.* 2 Thes. 2.11-12. Rom. 1.28.

5. That they studiously redeeme the time; observe the generall houres appointed for all the Students, and the speciall houres for their owne *Classe*: and then diligently attend the Lectures without any disturbance by word or gesture. And if in any thing they doubt, they shall inquire as of their fellowes, so, (in case of *Non satisfaction*) modestly of their Tutors.

6. None shall under any pretence whatsoever, frequent the company and society of such men as lead an unfit, and dissolute life.

Nor shall any without his Tutors leave, or (in his absence) the call of Parents or Guardians, goe abroad to other Townes.

7. Every Schollar shall be present in his Tutors chamber at the 7th. houre in the morning, immediately after the sound of the Bell at his opening the Scripture and prayer, so also at the 5th. houre at night, and then give account of his owne private reading as aforesaid in Particular the third, and constantly attend Lectures in the Hall at the houres appointed? But if any (without necessary impediment) shall absent himself from prayer or Lectures, he shall be lyable to Admonition, if he offend above once a weeke.

8. If any Schollar shall be found to transgresse any of the Lawes of God, or the Schoole, after twice Admonition, he shall bee lyable if not *adultus*, to correction, if *adultus*, his name shall be given up to, the Overseers of the Colledge, that he may bee admonished at the publick monethly Act.

3. ***The times and order of their Studies, unlesse experience shall shew cause to alter.***

T He second and third day of the weeke, read Lectures, as followeth.
To the first yeare at 8th. of the clock in the morning *Logick*, the first three quarters, *Physicks* the last quarter.

To the second yeare, at the 9th. houre, *Ethicks* and *Politicks*, at convenient distances of time.

To the third yeare at the 10th. *Arithmetick* and *Geometry*, the three first quarters, *Astronomy* the last.

Afternoone,

The first yeare disputes at the second houre.

The 2d. yeare at the 3d. houre.

The 3d. yeare at the 4th. every one in his Art.

The 4th. day reads Greeke.

To the first yeare the *Etymologie* and *Syntax* at the eigth houre.

To the 2d. at the 9th. houre, *Prosodia* and *Dialects*.

Afternoone.

The first yeare at 2d. houre practice the precepts of *Grammar* in such Authors as have variety of words.

The 2d. yeare at 3d. houre practice in *Poêsy, Nonnus, Duport*, or the like.

The 3d. yeare perfect their *Theory* before noone, and exercise *Style, Composition, Imitation, Epitome*, both in Prose and Verse, afternoone.

The fift day reads Hebrew, and the Easterne Tongues.

Grammar to the first yeare houre the 8th.

To the 2d. *Chaldee* at the 9th. houre.

To the 3d. *Syriack* at the 10th. houre.

Afternoone.

The first yeare practice in the Bible at the 2d. houre.

The 2d. in *Ezra* and *Danel* at the 3d. houre.

The 3d. at the 4th. houre in *Trostins* New Testament.

The 6th. day reads Rhetorick to all at the 8th. houre.

Declamations at the 9th. So ordered that every Scholler may declaime once a moneth. The rest of the day *vacat Rhetoricis Studiis.*

The 7th. day reads Divinity Catecheticast at the 8th. houre, Common places at the 9th. houre.

Afternoone.

The first houre reads history in the Winter,

The nature of plants in the Summer

The summe of every Lecture shall be examined, before the new Lecture be read.

Every Schollar, that on proofe is found able to read the Originalls of the *Old* and *New Testament* in to the Latine tongue, and to resolve them *Logically*; withall being of godly life and conversation; And at any publick Act hath the Approbation of the Overseers and Master of the Colledge, is fit to be dignified with his first Degree.

Every Schollar that giveth up in writing a *System*, or *Synopsis*, or summe of *Logick*, Naturall and Morall *Phylosophy*, *Arithmetick*, *Geometry*, and *Astronomy*: and is ready to defend his *Theses* or positions: withall skilled in the Originalls as abovesaid: and of godly life & conversation: and so approved by the Overseers and Master of the Colledge, at any publique *Act*, is fit to be dignified with his 2d. Degree.

---

4. *The manner of the late Commencement, expressed in a Letter sent over from the Governour, and diverse of the Ministers, their own words these.*

THe Students of the first Classes that have beene these foure yeeres trained up in University Learning (for their ripening in the knowledge of the Tongues, and Arts) and are apprved for their manners as they have kept their publick Acts in former yeares, our selves being present, at them; so have they lately kept two solemne Acts for their Commencement, when the Governour, Magistrates, and the Ministers from all parts, with allsorts of Schollars, and others in great numbers were present, and did heare their Exercises; which were Latine and Greeke Orations, and Declamations, and Hebrew Analasis, Grammaticall, Logicall & Rhetoricall of the Psalms: And their Answers and Disputations in Logicall, Ethicall, Physicall, and Mettaphysicall Questions; and so were found worthy of the first degree, (commonly called Batchelour) pro more Academiarum in Anglia: Being first presented by the President to the Magistrates and Ministers, and by him, upon their Approbation, solemnly admitted unto the same degree, and a Booke of Arts delivered into each of their hands, and power given him to read Lectures in the Hall upon any of the Arts, when they shall be thereunto called, and a liberty of studying in the Library.

All things in the Colledge are at present, like to proceed even as wee can wish, may it but please the Lord to goe on with his blessing in Christ, and stir up the hearts of his faithfull, and able Servants, in our owne Native Country, and here, (as he hath graciously begun) to advance this Honourable and most *hopefull worke. The beginnings whereof and progresse hitherto (generally) doe fill our hearts with comfort, and raise them up to much more expectation, of the Lords goodnesse for hereafter, for the good of posterity, and the Churches of Christ Jesus.*

BOSTON in New-England,

September the 26.

1642.   Your very loving
                                                          friends, &c.

A Copie of the Questions given and maintained by the *Commencers* in their publick Acts, printed in *Cambridge* in *New-England*, and reprinted here *verbatim*, as followeth.

Spectatissimis Pietate, et Illustrissimis Eximia

Virtute Viris, D. *Johanni Winthropo*, inclytæ Massachu-
Setti Coloniae Gubernatori, D. Johanni Endicotto Vice-
Guvernatori D. *Thom. Dudleo*, D. *Rich. Bellinghamo*,
D. *Joan. Humphrydo*, D. *Israel. Stoughtone*.

Nec non Reverendis pientissimisque viris *Joanpi Cottono, Joan, Wilsono,
Joan. Davenport, Tho. Weldo. Hugoni Peiro, Tho. Shepardo*, Collegij
Harvardensis nov. *Cantabr.* inspectoribus fidelissimis, cæterisq;
Magistratibus, & Ecclesiarum quidem Coloniæ Pres-
byteris vigilantissimis,

Has Theses Philologicas, & Philosophicas, quas Deo duce, Præside
Henrico Dunstero palam pro virili propugnare conabuntur,
(honoris & observantiae gratia) dicant consecranique in artibus
liberalibus initiati Adolescentes.

Benjamin Woodbrigius.	*Henricus Saltonstall.*	*Nathaniel Brusterus.*
Georgius Downingus.	*Johannes Bulklesus.*	*Samuel Belinghamus.*
Gulielmus Hubbardus.	*Johannes Wilsonus.*	*Tobias Bernardus.*

Theses Philologicas.

GRAMMATICAS.

L Inguarum Scientia est utilissima.
  Literæ non exprimunt quantum vocis Organa efferunt.
3. Hæbræa est Linguarum Mater.
4. Consonantes & vocales Hæbreorum sunt coætaneæ.
5. Punctationes chatepha æ syllabam proprie non efficiunt.
6. Linguarum Græca est copiosissima
7. Lingua Græca est ad accentus pronuntianda.
8. Lingua Latina est eloquentissima.

RHETORICAS.

R Hetorica specie differt a Logica.
  In Elocutione perspicuitati cedit ornatus, ornatui copia.
3. Actio primas tenet in pronuntiotione.
4. Oratoris est celare Artem.

LOGICAS.

U Niversalia non sunt extra intellectum.
Omnia Argumenta sunt relata.
3. Causa *sine qua non* non est peculiaris causa a quatuor reliquis   generalibus,
4. Causa & Effectus sunt simul tempore.
5. Dissentanea sunt æque nota.
6. Contrarietas est tantum inter duo,
7. Sublato relato tollitur correlatum.
8. Genus perfectum æqualiter communicatur speciebus.
9. Testimonium valet quantum testis.
10. Elenchorum doctrina in Logica non est necessaria.
11. Axioma contingens est, quod ita verum est, ut aliquando falsum esse possit.
12. Præcepta Artium debent esse κατὰ πάντος, καθ' αυτὸ, καθ' ολον ωγωτον .

Theses Philosophicas.

ETHICAS.

P Hilosophia practica est eruditions meta.
Actio virtutis habitum antecellit.
3. Voluntas est virtutis moralis subjectum.
4. Voluntas est formaliter libera.
5. Prudentia virtutum difficillima.
6. Prudentia est virus intellectualis & moralis.
7. Justitia mater omnium virtutum.
8. Mors potius subcunda quam aliquid culpæ perpetrandum.
9. Non injuste agit nisi qui libens agit.
10. Mentiri potest qui verum dicit.
11. Juveni modestia summum Oranmentum.

PHYSICAS.

C Orpus naturale mobile est sujbectum Phisicae
Materia secunda non potest existere sine forma.
3. Forma est accidens.
4. Unius rei non est nisi unica forma constitutiva.
5. Forma est principium individuationis.
6. Privatio non est principium internum.
7. Ex meris accidentibus non fit substantia.

8. Quicquid movetur ab alio movecur.
9. In omni motu movens simul est cum mobili.
10. Cœlum non movetur ab intelligentiis.
11. Non dantur orbes in cœlo.
12. Quodlibe. Flementum habet unam ex primis qualitatibus sibi maxime propriam.
13. Putredo in humido fit a calore externo.
14. Anima non fit ex traduce.
15. Vehemens sensibile destruit sensum.

METAPHISICAS.

O Mne ens est bonum.
  Omne creatum est concretum.
3. Quicquid æternum idem & immensum.
4. Bonum Metaphysicum non suscipit gradus.

Thus farre hath the good hand of God favoured our beginnings: see whether he hath not engaged us to wait still upon his goodnesse for the future, by such further remarkable passages of his providence to our Plantation in such things as these:

1. In sweeping away great multitudes of the Natives by the small Pox a little before we went thither, that he might make room for us there.

2. In giving such marveilous safe Passage from first to last, to so many thousands that went thither, the like hath hardly been ever observed in any Sea-voyages.

3. In blessing us generally with health and strength, as much as ever (we might truly say) more than ever in our Native Land; many that were tender and sickly here, are stronger and heartier there. That wheras diverse other Plantations have been the graves of their Inhabitants and their numbers much decreased: God hath so prospered the climate to us, that our bodies are hailer, and Children there born stronger, wherby our number is exceedingly increased.

4. In giving us such peace and freedome from enemies, when almost all the world is on a fire that (excepting that short trouble with the Pequits) we never heard of any sound of Warres to this day. And in that Warre which we made against them Gods hand from heaven was so manifested, that a very few of our men, in a short time pursued through the Wildernesse, slew and took prisoners about 1400 of them, even all they could find, to the great terrour and amazement of all the Indians to this day: so that the name of the Pequits (as of *Amaleck.*) is blotted out from under heaven there being not one that is, or, (at least) dare call himselfe a Pequit.

5. In subduing those erronious opinions carryed over from hence by some of the Passengers, which for a time infested our Churches peace but (through the goodnesse of God) by conference preaching, a generall assembly of learned men, Magistrates timely care, and lastly, by Gods own hand from heaven, in

most remarkable stroaks upon some of the chief fomenters of them; the matter came to such an happie conclusion, that most of the seduced came humbly and confessed their Errours in our publique Assemblies and abide to this day constant in the Truth; the rest (that remained obstinate) finding no fit market there to vent their wares, departed from us to an Iland farre off; some of whom also since that time, have repented and returned to us, and are received againe into our bosomes. And from that time not any unsound, unsavourie and giddie fancie have dared to lift up his head, or abide the light amongst us.

6. In settling and bringing civil matters to such a maturity in a short time amongst us having planted 50. Townes and Villages, built 30. or 40. Churches, and more Ministers houses; a Castle, a Colledge, Prisons, Forts, Cartwaies, Causies many, and all these upon our owne charges, no publique hand reaching out any helpe: having comfortable Houses, Gardens, Orchards, Grounds fenced, Corne fields &c. and such a forme and face of a Common wealth appearing in all the Plantation, that Strangers from other parts, seeing how much is done in so few yeares, have wondred at Gods blessing on our indeavours.

7. In giving such plenty of all manner of Food in a Wildernesse insomuch, that all kinds of Flesh amongst the rest, store of Venison in its season. Fish both from Sea and Fresh water. Fowle of all kinds, wild & tame; store of Whit-Meale, together with all sorts of English Graine, aswell as Indian, are plentifull amongst us; as also Rootes, Herbs and Fruit, which being better digested by the Sun, are farre more faire pleasant and wholsome then here.

8. In prospering Hempe and Flaxe so well, that its frequently sowen, spun, and woven into linnen Cloath: (and in a short time may serve for Cordage) and so with Cotton-wooll, (which we may have at very reasonable rates from the Ilands) and our linnen Yarne, we can make Dimittees and Fustions for our Summer cloathing. And having a matter of a 1000. Sheep, which prosper well, to begin withall, in a competent time we hope to have wollen Cloath there made. And great and small Cattel, being now very frequently killd for food; their skins will afford us Leather for Boots and Shoes, and other uses: so that God is leading us by the hand into a way of cloathing.

9. In affording us many materialls, (which in part already are, and will in time further be improved) for Staple commodities, to supply all other defects: As

1. Furres, Bever, Otter, &c.

2. Clapboord, Hoops, Pipestaves, Masts.

3. English Wheat and other graine for *Spaine* and West Indies; and all other provisions for Victualling of Shippes

4. Fish as Cod, Haddock, Herrings, Mackerill, Basse, Sturgeon, Seales, Whales, Sea-horse.

5. Oyle of sundry sorts, of Whale, Sea-horse, &c.

6. Pitch and Tarre, Rosen and Turpentine, having Pines, Spruce, and Pitch-trees in our Countrey to make these on.

7. Hempe and Flaxe.

8. Mineralls discovered and proved, as of Iron in sundry places, Black-lead (many other in hopes) for the improving of which, we are now about to carry over Sevants and instruments with us,

9. (Besides many Boates, Shallops, Hows, Lighters, Pinnaces) we are in a way of building Shippes, of an 100, 200, 300, 400. tunne, five of them are already at Sea; many more in hand at this present, we being much incouraged herein by reason of plenty and excellencie of our Timber for that purpose, and seeing all the materialls will be had there in short time.

10. In giving of such Magistrates, as are all of them godly men, and members of our Churches, who countenance those that be good, and punish evill doers, that a vile person dares not lift up his head; nor need a godly man to hang it down, that (to Gods praise be it spoken) one may live there from yeare to yeare, and not see a drunkard, heare an oath, or meet a begger. Now where sinne is punished, and judgement executed, God is wont to blesse that place, and protect it, *Psal.* 106.30, *Jer.* 5.1, *Jos.* 7.25 with 8.1.*e. contra Esa.{Isaiah}* 20.21.

11. In storing that place with very many of his own people, and diverse of them eminent for godlinesse. Now where his people are, there is his presence, and Promise *to be in the middest of them, a mighty God to save, and to joy over them with singing,* Zeph.3.17.

12. Above all our other blessings, in planting *his own Name,* and *precious Ordinances* among us; (we speak it humbly, and in his feare) our indeavour is to have all his own Institutions, and no more then his own and all those in their native simplicity, without any humane dressings; having a liberty to injoy all that God Commands, and yet urged to nothing more then he Commands. Now *Where soever he records his Name, thither he will come and blesse,* Ex. 20.24.

Which promise he eath already performed to very many soules in their effectuall conversion to Christ, and the edification of others in their holy Faith, who daily blesse God that ever he carried them into those parts.

All which blessings names we looke upon as an earnest-penny of more to come. If we seeke his face, and serve his Providence, wee have no cause to doubt, that he for his part will faile to make seasonable supplies unto us.

1. By some meanes to carry on to their perfection our staple trades begun.

2. By Additions of Ammunition and Powder.

3. By maintenance of Schooles of Learning especially the Colledge, as also additions of building to it, and furnishing the Library.

4. By stirring up some well-minded to cloath and transport over poore children Boyes and Girles, which may be a great mercy to their bodies and soules and a help to us, they being super abundant here, and we wanting hands to carry on our trades, manufacture and husbandry there.

5. By stirring up some to shew mercy to the *Indians,* in affording maintenance to some of our godly active young Schollars, there to make it their worke to studie their Language converse with them and carry light amongst them, that so the Gospell might be spread into those darke parts of the world.

Ob. But all your own cost and ours also will be lost, because there can be no subsistence there for any long time. For,

1. Your ground is barren,

Answ. 1. If you should see our goodly Corne-fields, neere harvest you would answer this your selfe. Secondly, how could it be thin, that we should have *English* Wheat at 4. S *per* bushell, and *Indian* at 2.8. and this not only for ready-money, but in way of exchange. Thirdly, that in a wildernesse in so few yeares, we should have corne enough for our selves and our friends that come over, and much to spare.

2. *Obj.* Your ground will not continue above 3 or 4 yeares to beare corne.

Answ. Our ground hath been sowne and planted with corne these 7.10.12. yeares already by our selves, and (which is more than can be said here of *English* Land) never yet summer tild: but have borne corne, every yeare since we first went, and the same ground planted as long by the *Indians* before, and yet have good crops upon it still, and is like to continue as ever: But this is, (as many other slanders against that good Land{)} against all sense, reason and experience.

3. *Obj.* But you have no money there.

Answ. It's true we have not much though some there is, but wee have those staple commodities named, they will (still as they are improved) fetch money from other parts. Ships, Fish, Iron, Pipestaves, Corn, Bever, Oyle, &c will help us with money and other things also.

2. Littl money is raised in coyne in *England*, how then comes it to abound, but by this meane?

3. We can trade amongst our selves by way of exchange, one commodity for another, and so doe usually.

4. *Obj.* You are like to want clothes hereafter.

Answ. I. Linnen Fustians Dimettees we are making already. Secondly, Sheepe are comming on for woollen cloath. Thirdly, in meane time we may be supplied by way of trade to other parts. 4th. Cor{illeg.}ant, Deere, Seale; and Moose Skins (which are beasts as big Oxen, and their skins are buffe) are there to be had plentifully, {w}hich will help this way, especially for servants cloathing.

5. *Obj.* Your Winters are cold.

Answ. True, at sometimes when the wind blowes strong at *Nor-West*: but it holds not long together, and then it useth to be very moderate for a good space. First the coldnesse being not naturall (that place being 42. degrees) but accidentall. Secondly, The cold there is no impediment to health, but very wholsome for our bodies, insomuch that all sorts generally, weake and strong had scarce ever such measure of health in all their lives as there. Thirdly, Its not a moist and foggie cold, as in *Holland*, and some parts of *England*, but bright, cleare, and faire wether, that men are seldome troubled in Winter with coughes and Rheumes. Fourthly, it hinders not our imployment, for people are able to worke or travell usually all the Winter long, so there is no losse of time, simply in respect of the cold. Fiftly good fires (wood being so plentifull) will make amends.

6. *Ob.* Many are growne weaker in their estates since they went over.

Answ. Are not diverse in *London* broken in their Estates? and many in *England* are growne poore, and thousands goe a begging (yet wee never saw a beggar there) and will any taxe the City or Kingdome, and say they are unsubsistable places?

Secondly their Estates now lie in houses, Lands, Horses, Cattel, Corne &c.

though they have not so much money as they had here, and so cannot make appearance of their wealth to those in *England*, yet they have it still, so that their Estates are not lost but changed.

3. Some mens Estates may be weaker through great and vast common charges, which the first planters especially have bin at in making the place subsistable and comfortable, which now others reape the fruit of, unknowne summes lye buried underground in such a worke as that is.

4. Some may be poore (so we are sure) many are rich, that carried nothing at all that now have House Land, Corne, Cattel, &c and such as carry something are much encreased.

7. *Ob.* Many speake evill of the place.

Answ. Did not some doe so of the Land of *Canaan* it selfe yet *Canaan* was never the worse and themselves smarted for so doing. Secondly some have been punished there for their Delinquencies, or restrained from their exorbitances; or discountenanced for their ill opinions and not sufferd to vent their stuffe: and hence being displeased take revenge by slanderous report. Thirdly, Let such if any such there be as have ought to alleadge, deale fairely and above board, and come and justifie any thing against the Country to our faces while we are here to answer, but such never yet appeared in any of our presence to avouch any thing in this kinde, nor (we beleive) dare do it without blushing.

8. *Ob.* Why doe many come away from thence?

Answ. Doe not many remove from one Country to another, and yet nonelikes the Country the lesse because some depart from it? Secondly, few that we know of intend to abide here, but doe come on some speciall busines and purpose to returne. Thirdly of them that are come hither to stay, (on our knowledge) some of the wisest repent them already, and wish themselves there againe. Fourthly as some went thither upon sudden undigested grounds, and saw not God leading them in their way, but were carryed by an unstayed spirit so have they returned upon as sleight headlesse, unworthy reasons as they went. Fiftly others must have elbow-roome, and cannot abide to be so pinioned with the strict Government in the *Common-wealth*, or Discipline in the Church, now why should such live there; as *Ireland* will not brooke venemous beasts, so will not that Land vile persons, and loose livers. Sixtly, though some few have removed from them, yet (we may truly say) thousands as wise as themselves would not change their place for any other in the World.

FINIS.

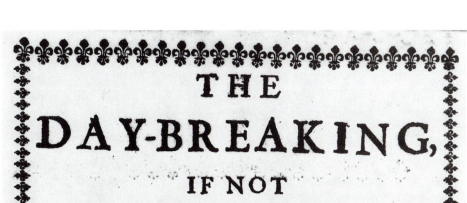

THE
DAY-BREAKING,
IF NOT
The Sun-Rising
OF THE
GOSPELL

With the
INDIANS in New-England.

Zach. 4. 10.
Who hath despised the day of small things?
Matth. 13. 13.
The Kingdome of heaven is like to a graine of mustard seed.
Ibid. Verse 33.
The Kingdome of heaven is like unto Leven.

LONDON,
Printed by *Rich. Cotes,* for *Fulk Clifton,* and are to bee
sold at his shop under Saint *Margarets* Church on
New-fish-street Hill, 1647.

THE

DAY-BREAKING,

IF NOT

The Sun-Rising

OF THE

GOSPELL

With the

INDIANS in New-England.

Zach. 4. 10.
Who hath despised the day of small things?
Matth. 13. 13.
The Kingdome of heaven is like to a graine of mustard seed.
Ibid. Verse 33.
The Kingdome of heaven is like unto Leven.

LONDON,
Printed by *Rich. Cotes,* for *Fulk Clifton*, and are to bee
sold at his shop under Saint *Margarets* Church on
New-fish-street Hill, 1647.

To the Reader

Ee that pen'd these following Relations, is a Minister of Christ in New England, so eminently godly and faithfull, that what he here reports, as an eye or an eare witnesse, is not to be questioned; Were he willing his name should bee mentioned, it would bee an abundant, if not a redundant, Testimoniall to all that know him.

Nathan. Warde.

A

TRUE RELATION

OF

Our beginnings with the *INDIANS*.

Pon *October* 28, *1646*. four of us (having sought God) went unto the *Indians* inhabiting within our bounds, with desire to make known the things of their peace to them, A little before we came to their *Wigwams*, [Indian houses or tents made of barks or matts.] five or six of the chief of them met us with English salutations, bidding us much welcome; who leading us into the principall *Wigwam* of *Waaubon*, [The name of an Indian] we found many more *Indians*, men, women, children, gathered together from all quarters round about, according to appointment, to meet with us, and learne of us. *Waaubon* the chief minister of Justice among them exhorting and inviting them before thereunto, being one who gives more grounded hopes of serious respect to the things of God, then any that as yet I have knowne of that forlorne generation; and therefore since wee first began to deale seriously with him, hath voluntarily offered his eldest son to be educated and trained up in the knowledge of God, hoping as hee told us, that he might come to know him, although hee despaired much concerning himself; and accordingly his son was accepted, and is now at school in *Dedham*, whom we found at this time standing by his father among the rest of his *Indian* brethren in English clothes.

They being all there assembled, we began with prayer, which now was in English, being not so farre acquainted with the *Indian* language as to expresse our hearts herein before God or them, but wee hope it will bee done ere long, the *Indians* desiring it that they also might know how to pray; but thus wee began in an unknowne tongue to them, partly to let them know that this dutie in hand was serious and sacred, (for so much some of them understand by what is undertaken at prayer) partly also in regard of our selves, that wee might agree together in the same request and heart sorrowes for them even in that place where God was never wont to be called upon.

When prayer was ended it was a glorious affecting spectacle to see a company of perishing, forlorne outcasts, diligently attending to the blessed word of salvation then delivered; professing they understood all that which was then taught them in their owne tongue; it much affected us that they should smell some things of the Alablaster box broken up in that darke and gloomy habitation of filthinesse and uncleane spirits. For about an houre and a quarter the Sermon continued, wherein one of our company ran thorough all the principall matter of religion, beginning first with a repetition of the ten Commandements, and a briefe explication of them, then shewing the curse and dreadfull wrath of God against all those who brake them, or any one of them, or the least title of them, and so applyed it unto the condition of the *Indians* present, with much sweet affection; and then preached Jesus Christ to them the onely meanes of recovery from sinne and wrath and eternall death, and what Christ was, and whither he was now gone, and how hee will one day come againe to judge the world in flaming fire; and of the blessed estate of all those that by faith beleeve in Christ, and know him feelingly: he spake to them also (observing his owne method as he saw most fit to edifie them) about the creation and fall of man, about the greatnesse and infinite being of God, the maker of all things, about the joyes of heaven, and the terrours and horrours of wicked men in hell, perswading them to repentance for severall sins which they live in, and many things of the like nature; not medling with any matters more difficult, and which to such weake ones might at first seeme ridiculous, untill they had tasted and beleeved more plaine and familiar truths.

Having thus in a set speech familiarly opened the principal matters of salvation to them, the next thing wee intended was discourse with them by propounding certaine questions to see what they would say to them, that so wee might skrue by variety of meanes something or other of God into them; but before wee did this we asked them if they understood all that which was already spoken, and whether all of them in the *Wigwam* did understand or onely some few? and they answered to this question with multitude of voyces, that they all of them did understand all that which was then spoken to them. We then desired to know of them, if they would propound any question to us for more cleare understanding of what was delivered; whereupon severall of them propounded presently severall questions, (far different from what some other *Indians* under *Kitshomakin* [The name of one of the chiefe Indians about us {i.e., Cutshamekin}] in the like meeting about six weekes before had done, *viz* 1. What was the cause of Thunder. 2. Of the Ebbing and Flowing of the Sea. 3. Of the wind) but the questions (which wee thinke some speciall wisedom of God directed these unto) (which these propounded) were in number six.

[1. *Quest.*] How may wee come to know Jesus Christ?

[*Answ.*] [1]. Our first answer was, That if they were able to read our Bible, the book of God, therein they should see most cleerely what Jesus Christ was: but because they could not do that; therefore,

[2.] Secondly, we wisht them to thinke, and meditate of so much as had been taught them; and which they now heard out of Gods booke, and to thinke much and often upon it, both when they did lie downe on their Mats in their *Wigwams*, and when they rose up, and to goe alone in the fields and woods, and muse on it, and so God would teach them; especially if they used a third helpe, which was,

[3.] Prayer to God to teach them and reveale Jesus Christ unto them, and wee told them; that although they could not make any long prayer as the English could, yet if they did but sigh and groane, and say thus; Lord make mee know Jesus Christ, for I know him not, and if they did say so againe and againe with their hearts that God would teach them Jesus Christ, because hee is such a God as will bee found of them that seeke him with all their hearts, and hee is a God hearing the prayers of all men both *Indians* as well as *English*, and that *English* men by this meanes have come to the knowledge of Jesus Christ.

[4.] The last helpe wee gave them was repentance, they must confesse their sinnes and ignorance unto God, and mourne for it, and acknowledge how just it is, for God to deny them the knowledge of Jesus Christ or anything else because of their sinnes.

These things were spoken by him who had preached to them in their owne language, borrowing now and then some small helpe from the Interpreter whom wee brought with us, and who could oftentimes expresse our minds more distinctly then any of us could; but this wee perceived, that a few words from the Preacher were more regarded then many from the *Indian* Interpreter.

[2 *Quest.*] One of them after this answer, replyed to us, that hee was a little while since praying in his *Wigwam*, unto God and Jesus Christ, that God would give him a good heart, and that while hee was praying, one of his fellow *Indians* interrupted him, and told him, that hee prayed in vaine, because Jesus Christ understood not what *Indians* speake in prayer, he had bin used to heare *English* man pray and so could well enough understand them, but *Indian* language in prayer hee thought hee was not acquainted with it, but was a stranger to it, and therefore could not understand them. His question therefore was, whether Jesus Christ did understand, or God did understand *Indian* prayers.

[*Answ.*] This question sounding just like themselves, wee studied to give as familiar an answer as wee could, and therefore in this as in all other our answers, we endeavoured to speake nothing without clearing of it up by some familiar similitude; our answer summarily was therefore this, that Jesus Christ and God by him made all things, and makes all men, not onely *English* but *Indian* men, and if hee made them both (which wee know the light of nature would readily teach as they had been also instructed by us) then hee knew all that was within man and came from man, all his desires, and all his thoughts, and all his speeches, and so all his prayers, and if hee made *Indian* men, then hee knowes all *Indian* prayers also: and therefore wee bid them looke upon that *Indian* Basket that was before them, there was black and white strawes, and many other things they made it of, now though others did not know what those things were who made not the Basket, yet hee that made it must needs tell all the things in it, for (wee said) it was here.

[3 *Q*] Another propounded this question after this answer, Whether English men were ever at any time so ignorant of God and Jesus Christ as themselves?

[*Ans{w}.*] When wee perceived the root and reach of this question, wee gave them this answer, that there are two sorts of English men, some are bad and naught, and live wickedly and loosely, (describing them) and these kind of English men wee told them were in a manner as ignorant of Jesus Christ as the *Indians* now are; but there are a second sort of English men, who though for a time they lived wickedly also like other prophane and ignorant English, yet repenting of their sinnes, and seeking after God and Jesus Christ, they are good men now, and now know Christ, and love Christ, and pray to Christ, and are thankfull for all they have to Christ, and shall at last when they dye, goe up to heaven to Christ, and we told them all these also were once as ignorant of God and Jesus Christ as the *Indians* are, but by seeking to know him by reading his booke, and hearing his word, and praying to him, &c. they now know Jesus Christ, and just so shall the *Indians* know him if they so seeke him also, although at the present they bee extremely ignorant of him.

[4 *Q*] How can there be an Image of God, because it's forbidden in the second Commandement?

[*Answ.*] Wee told them that Image was all one Picture, as the Picture of an *Indian*, Bow and Arrowes on a tree, with such little eyes and such faire hands, is not an *Indian* but the Picture or Image of an *Indian*, and that Picture man makes, and it can doe no hurt nor good. So the Image or Picture of God is not God, but wicked men make it, and this Image can doe no good nor hurt to any man as God can.

[5 *Q*] Whether, if the father bee naught, and the child good, will God bee offended with that child, because in the second Commandement it's said, that hee visits the sinnes of fathers upon the children?

[*Answ.*] Wee told them the plainest answer we could thinke of *viz.* that if the child bee good, and the father bad, God will not bee offended with the child, if hee repents of his owne and his fathers sinnes, and followes not the steps of his wicked father; but if the child bee also bad, then God will visit the sins of fathers upon them, and therefore wisht them to consider of the other part of the promise made to thousands of them that love God and the *Evangenesh Jehovah, i.e.* the Commandments of Jehovah.

[6 *Quest.*] How all the world is become so full of people, if they were all once drowned in the Flood?

[*Answ.*] Wee told them the story and causes of *Noahs* preservation in the Arke at large, and so their questioning ended; and therefore wee then saw our time of propounding some few questions to them, and so take occasion thereby to open matters of God more fully.

[*Quest.* 1.] Our first question was, Whether they did not desire to see God, and were not tempted to thinke that there was no God, because they cannot see him?

[*Answ.*] Some of them replyed thus; that indeed they did desire to see him if it could bee, but they had heard from us that hee could not be seene, and they did beleive that though their eies could not see him, yet that hee was to bee seene with their soule within: Hereupon we sought to confirme them the more, and asked them if they saw a great *Wigwam*, or a great house, would they thinke that *Racoones* [A beast somewhat like a Fox.] or Foxes built it that had no wisedome? or would they thinke that it made it selfe? or that no wise workman made it, because they could not see him that made it? No but they would beleeve some wise workman made it though they did not see him; so should they beleeve concerning God, when they looked up to heaven, Sunne, Moone, and Stars, and saw this great house he hath made, though they do not see him with their eyes, yet they have good cause to beleeve with their soules that a wise God, a great God made it.

[*Quest.* 2.] We knowing that a great block in their way to beleiving is that there should bee but one God, (by the profession of the English) and yet this God in many places; therefore we asked them whether it did not seeme strange that there should bee but one God, and yet this God in *Massachusets*, at *Conectacut*, at *Quimipeiock*, [Three Indian names of places where the English sit downe.] in old England, in this *Wigwam*, in the next every where.

Their answer was by one most sober among them, that indeed it was strange, as everything else they heard presented was strange also, and they were wonderfull things which they never heard of before; but yet they thought it might bee true, and that God was so big every where [That Hee was present every where.]: whereupon we further illustrated what wee said, by wishing them to consider of the light of the Sun, which though it be but a creature made by God, yet the same light which is in this *Wigwam* was in the next also, and the same light which was here at *Massachusets* was at *Quinipeiock* also and in old England also, and every where at one and the same time the same, much more was it so concerning God.

[3 *Quest.*] Whether they did not finde somewhat troubling them within after the commission of sin, as murther, adultery, theft, lying, &c. and what they thinke would comfort them against that trouble when they die and appeare before God, (for some knowledge of the immortality of the soule almost all of them have.)

[*Answ.*] They told us they were troubled, but they could not tell what to say to it, what should comfort them; hee therefore who spake to them at first concluded with a dolefull description (so farre as his ability to speake in that tongue would carry him) of the trembling and mourning condition of every soul that dies in sinne, and that shall be cast out of favour with God.

Thus after three houres time thus spent with them, wee asked them if they were not weary, and they answered, No. But wee resolved to leave them with an appetite; the chiefe of them seeing us conclude with prayer, desired to know when wee would come againe, so wee appointed the time, and having given the children some apples, and the men some tobacco and what else we then had at hand, they desired some more ground to build a Town together, which wee did much like of, promising to speake for them to the generall Court, that they might possesse all the compasse of that hill, upon which their Wigwams then stood, and so wee departed with many welcomes from them.

A true relation of our coming to the Indians the second time.

UPon November 11. 1646. we came the second time unto the same Wigwam of *Waawbon*, where we found many more Indians met together then the first time wee came to them: and having seates provided for us by themselves, and being sate downe a while, wee began againe with prayer in the English tongue; our beginning this time was with the younger sort of Indian children in Catechizing of them, which being the first time of instructing them, we thought meet to aske them but only three questions in their own language, that we might not clog their mindes or memories with too much at first, the questions (asked and answered in the Indian tongue) were these three, 1. *Qu* Who made you and all the world? *Answ.* God. 2. *Qu.* Who doe you looke should save you and redeeme you from sinne and hell? *Answ.* Jesus Christ. 3. *Qu.* How many commandements hath God given you to keepe? *Answ.* Ten. These questions being propounded to the Children severally, and one by one, and the answers being short and easie, hence it came to passe that before wee went thorow all, those who were last catechized had more readily learned to answer to them, by hearing the same question so oft propounded and answered before by their fellowes; and the other Indians who were growne up to more yeares had perfectly learned them, whom wee therefore desired to teach their children againe when wee were absent, that so when wee came againe wee might see their profiting, the better to encourage them hereunto, wee therefore gave something to every childe.

This Catechisme being soone ended, hee that preached to them, began thus (speaking to them in their owne language) *viz, Wee are come to bring you good newes from the great God Almighty maker of Heaven and Earth, and to tell you how evill and wicked men may come to bee good, so as while they live they may bee happy, and when they die they may goe to God and live in Heaven.* Having made this preface, hee began first to set forth God unto them by familiar descriptions, in his glorious power, goodnesse, and greatnesse, and then set forth before them what his will was, and what hee required of all men even of the Indians themselves, in the ten commandements, and then told them the dreadfull torment and punishment of all such as breake any one of those holy commandements, and how angry God was for any sinne and transgression, yet notwithstanding hee had sent Jesus Christ to die for their sinnes and to pacifie God by his sufferings in their stead and roome, if they did repent and beleeve the Gospell, and that hee would love the poore miserable Indians if now they sought God and beleeved in Jesus Christ: threatning the sore wrath of God upon all such as stood out and neglected such great salvation which now God offered unto them, by those who sought nothing more then their salvation: thus continuing to preach the space of an houre, we desired them to propound some questions; which were these following. Before I name them it may not be amisse to take notice of the mighty power of the word which visibly appeared especially in one of them, who in hearing these things about sinne and hell, and Jesus Christ, powred out many teares and shewed much affliction without affectation of being seene, desiring rather to conceale his griefe which (as was gathered from his carriage) the Lord forced from him.

[1.*Quest.*] The first Question was suddenly propounded by an old man then present, who hearing faith and repentance preacht upon them to finde salvation by Jesus Christ, hee asked whether it was not too late for such an old man as hee, who was neare death to repent or seeke after God.

[*Answ.*] This Question affected us not a little with compassion, and we held forth to him the Bible, and told him what God said in it concerning such as are hired at the eleventh houre of the day: wee told him also that if a father had a sonne that had beene disobedient many yeares, yet if at last that sonne fall downe upon his knees and weepe and desire his father to love him, his father is so mercifull that hee will readily forgive him and love him; so wee said it was much more with God who is a more mercifull father to those whom hee hath made, then any father can bee to his rebellious childe whom he hath begot, if they fall downe and weepe, and pray, repent, and desire forgivenesse for Jesus Christ's sake; and wee farther added that looke as if a father did call after his childe to returne and repent promising him favour, the childe might then bee sure that his father would forgive him; so wee told them that now was the day of God risen upon them, and that now the Lord was calling of them to repentance, and that he had sent us for that end to preach repentance for the remission of sins, and that therefore they might bee sure to finde favour though they had lived many yeares in sinne, and that therefore if now they did repent it was not too late as the old man feared, but if they did not come when they were thus called, God would bee greatly angry with them, especially considering that now they must sinne against knowledge, whereas before we came to them they knew not any thing of God at all.

[2 *Quest.*] Having spent much time in clearing up the first question, the next they propounded (upon our answer) was this, *viz.* How come the English to differ so much from the Indians in the knowledge of God and Jesus Christ, seeing they had all at first but one father?

[*Answ.*] Wee confessed that it was true that at first wee had all but one father, but after that our first father fell, hee had divers children some were bad and some good, those that were bad would not take his counsell but departed from him and from God, and those God left alone in sinne and ignorance, but others did regard him and the counsell of God by him, and those knew God, and so the difference arose at first, that some together with their posterity knew God, and others did not; and so wee told them it was at this day, for like as if an old man an aged father amongst them have many children, if some of them bee rebellious against the counsell of the father, he shuts them out of doores, and lets them goe, and regards them not, unlesse they returne and repent, but others that will bee ruled by him, they learne by him and come to know his minde; so wee said English men seek God, dwell in his house, heare his word, pray to God, instruct their children out of Gods booke, hence they come to know God; but Indians forefathers were a stubborne and rebellious children, and would not heare the word, did not care to pray nor to teach their children, and hence Indians that now are, do not know God at all: and so must continue unlesse they repent, and returne to God and pray, and teach their children what they now may learne: but withall wee told them that many English men did not know God but were like to *Kitchamakins* drunken Indians; Nor were wee willing to tell them the story of the scattering of *Noahs* children since the flood; and thereby to shew them how the Indians come to bee so ignorant, because it was too difficult, and the history of the Bible is reserved for them (if God will) to be opened at a more convenient season in their owne tongue.

[3. *Quest.*] Their third Question was, How may wee come to serve God?

[*Answ.*] Wee asked him that did propound it whether he did desire indeed to serve him? and hee said, yes. Hereupon wee said, first, they must lament their blindnesse and sinfulnesse that they cannot serve him; and their ignorance of Gods booke (which wee pointed to) which directs how to serve him. Secondly, that they could not serve God but by seeking forgivenesse of their sinnes and power against their sinnes in the bloud of Jesus Christ who was preached to them. Thirdly, that looke as an Indian childe, if he would serve his father, hee must first know his fathers will and love his father too, or else he can never serve him, but if hee did know his fathers will and love him, then he would serve him, and then if hee should not doe some things as his father commands him, and yet afterwards grieve for it upon his knees before his father, his father would pity and accept him: so wee told them it was with God, they must labour to know his will and love God, and then they will bee willing to serve him, and if they should then sin, yet grieving for it before God he would pity and accept of them.

[4. *Quest.*] Their fourth Question was, How it comes to passe that the Sea water was salt, and the Land water fresh.

[*Answ.*] 'Tis so from the wonderfull worke of God, as why are Strawberries sweet and Cranberries [A Berry which is ripe in winter and very sowre, they are called here Bea Berries.] sowre, there is no reason but the wonderfull worke of God that made them so: our study was chiefly to make them acknowledge God in his workes, yet wee gave them also the reason of it from naturall causes which they lesse understood, yet did understand somewhat appearing by their usuall signes of approving what they understand.

[5 *Quest.*] Their fifth Question was, that if the water was higher then the earth, how comes it to passe that it doth not overflow all the earth?

[*Answ.*] Wee still held God before them, and shewed that this must needes bee the wonderfull worke of God, and we tooke an apple and thereby shewed them how the earth and water made one round globe like that apple; and how the Sun moved about it; and then shewed them how God made a great hole or ditch, into which hee put the waters of the Sea, so that though it was upon the earth and therefore above the earth, yet wee told them that by making so deepe a hole the waters were kept within compasse that they could not overflow, just as if Indians making a hole to put in much water, the water cannot overflow nor runne abroad, which they would if they had no such hole; so it was with God, it was his mighty power that digged a hole for all Sea-waters, as a deepe ditch, and there by God kept them in from overflowing the whole earth, which otherwise would quickly drowne all.

[6 *Quest.*] They having spent much conference amongst themselves about these Questions and the night hastening, we desired them to propound some other Questions, or if not, we would aske them some, hereupon one of them asked us; If a man hath committed adultery or stolen any goods, and the Sachim doth not punish him, nor by any law is hee punished, if also he restore the goods he hath stolen, what then? whether is not all well now? meaning that if Gods Law was broken and no man punished him for it, that then no punishment should come from God for it, and as if by restoring againe an amends was made to God.

[*Answ.*] Although man be not offended for such sinnes yet God is angry, and his anger burnes like fire aginst all sinners: and here wee set out the holinesse and terrour of God in respect of the least sinne; yet if such a sinner with whom God is angry fly to Jesus Christ, and repent and seeke for mercy and pardon for Christ's sake, that then God will forgive and pity. Upon the hearing of which answer hee that propounded the question drew somewhat backe and hung downe his head as a man smitten to the very heart, with his eyes ready to drop, and within a little while after brake out into a complaint, Mee little know Jesus Christ, otherwise he thought he should seeke him better: we therefore told him, that looke as it was in the morning at first there is but a little light, then there is more light, then there is day, then the Sun is up, then the Sun warmes and heates, &c. so it was true they knew but little of Jesus Christ now, but wee had more to tell them concerning him hereafter, and after that more and after that more, untill at last they may come to know Christ as the English doe; and wee taught them but a little at a time, because they could understand but little, and if they prayed to God to teach them, he would send his Spirit and teach them more, they and their fathers had lived in ignorance untill now, it hath beene a long night wherein they have slept and have not regarded God, but now the day-light began to stirre upon them, they might hope therefore for more ere long, to bee made knowne to them.

Thus having spent some houres with them, wee propounded two Questions.

[1 *Quest.*] What do you remember of what was taught you since the last time wee were here?

[*Answ.*] After they had spoken one to another for some time, one of them returned this answer, that they did much thanke God for our comming, and for what they heard, they were wonderfull things unto them.

[2 *Quest.*] Doe you beleeve the things that are told you, *viz*, that God is *musquantum, i.e.* very angry for the least sinne in your thoughts, or words, or workes?

[*Answ.*] They said yes, and hereupon wee set forth the terrour of God against sinners, and mercy of God to the penitent, and to such as sought to know Jesus Christ, and that as sinners should bee after death, *Chechainuppan, i.e.* tormented alive, (for wee know no other word in the tongue to expresse extreame torture by) so beleevers should after death *Wowein wicke Jehovah, i.e.* live in all blisse with *Jehovah* the blessed God: and so we concluded conference.

Having thus spent the whole afternoone, and night being almost come upon us; considering that the Indians formerly desired to know how to pray, and did thinke that Jesus Christ did not understand Indian language, one of us therefore prepared to pray in their owne language, and did so for above a quarter of an houre together, wherein divers of them held up eies and hands to heaven; all of them (as wee understood afterwards) understanding the same; but one of them I cast my eye upon, was hanging downe his head with his rag before his eyes weeping; at first I feared it was some sorenesse of his eyes, but lifting up his head againe, having wiped his eyes (as not desirous to be seene) I easily perceived his eyes were not sore, yet somewhat red with crying; and so held up his head for a while, yet such was the presence and mighty power of the Lord Jesus on his heart that hee hung downe his head againe, and covered his eyes againe and so fell wiping and wiping of them weeping aboundantly, continuing thus till prayer was ended, after which hee presently turnes from us, and turnes his face to a side and corner of the Wigwam, and there fals a weeping more abundantly by himselfe, which one of us perceiving, went to him, and spake to him encouraging words; at the hearing of which hee fell a weeping more and more; so leaving of him, he who spake to him came unto mee (being newly gone out of the Wigwam) and told mee of his teares, so we resolved to goe againe both of us to him, and speake to him againe, and wee met him comming out of the Wigwam, and there wee spake againe to him, and he there fell into a more aboundant renewed weeping, like one deeply and inwardly affected indeed, which forced us also to such bowels of compassion that wee could not forbeare weeping over him also: and so wee parted greatly rejoycing for such sorrowing.

Thus I have as faithfully as I could remember given you a true account of our beginnings with the Indians within our owne bounds; which cannot but bee matter of more serious thoughts what further to doe with these poore Natives the dregs of mankinde and the saddest spectacles of misery of meere men upon earth: wee did thinke to forbeare going to them this winter, but this last dayes worke wherein God set his seale from heaven of acceptance of our little, makes those of us who are able, to resolve to adventure thorow frost and snow, lest the fire goe out of their hearts for want of a little more fewell: to which wee are the more incouraged, in that the next day after our being with them, one of the Indians came to his house who preacht to them to speake with him, who in private conference wept exceedingly, and said that all that night the Indians could not sleepe, partly with trouble of minde, and partly with wondring at the things they heard preacht amongst them; another Indian comming also to him the next day after, told him how many of the wicked sort of Indians began to oppose these beginnings.

Whence these Indians came here to inhabit is not certaine, his reasons are most probable who thinke they are Tartars passing out of *Asia* into *America* by the straits of *Anian*, who being spilt by some revenging hand of God upon this continent like water upon the ground are spread as farre as these *Atlanticke* shores, there being but few of them in these parts in comparison of those which are more contiguous to the *Anian* straits, [Straits of Anian: Fabled straits otherwise known as the Northwest Passage.] if wee may credit some Historians herein: what ever these conjectures and uncertainties bee, certaine it is that they are inheritors of a grievous and fearefull curse living so long without Ephod or Teraphim, and in nearest alliance to the wilde beasts that perish; and as God delights to convey blessings of mercy to the posterity of some, in respect of his promise to their fathers, so are curses entailed and come by naturall descent unto others, for some great sinnes of their Ancestors, as no doubt it is in respect of these. Yet notwithstanding the deepest degeneracies are no stop to the overflowing grace and bloud of Christ, when the time of love shall come, no not to these poore outcasts, the utmost ends of the earth being appointed to bee in time, the Sonne of Gods possession.

Wee are oft upbraided by some of our Countrymen that so little good is done by our professing planters upon the hearts of Natives; such men have surely more spleene then judgement, and know not the vast distance of Natives from common civility, almost humanity it selfe, and 'tis as if they should reproach us for not making the windes to blow when wee lift ourselves, it must certainly be a spirit of life from God (not in mans power) which must put flesh and sinewes unto these dry bones; if wee would force them to baptisme (as the Spaniards do about *Cusco, Peru,* and *Mexico,* having learnt them a short answer or two to some Popish questions) or if wee would hire them to it by giving them coates and shirts, to allure them to it (as some others have done{)}, wee could have gathered many hundreds, yea thousands it may bee by this time, into the name of Churches; but wee have not learnt as yet that art of coyning Christians, or putting Christs name and Image upon copper mettle. Although I thinke we have much cause to bee humbled that wee have not endeavoured more then wee have done their conversion and peace with God, who enjoy the mercy and peace of God in their land. Three things have made us thinke (as they once did of building the Temple) it is not yet time for God to worke, 1. Because till the Jewes come in, there is a seale set upon the hearts of those people, as they thinke from some Apocalypticall places. 2. That as in nature there is no progresses *ab extremo ad extremum,* so in religion such as are so extreamly degenerate, must bee brought to some civility before religion can prosper, or the word take place. 3. Because wee want miraculous and extraordinary gifts without which no conversion can bee expected amongst these; But me thinkes now that it is with the Indians as it was with our New English ground when we first came over, there was scarce any man that could beleeve that English graine would grow, or that the Plow could doe any good in this woody and rocky soile. And thus they continued in this supine unbeliefe for some yeares, till experience taught them otherwise, and now all see it to bee scarce inferiour to Old English tillage, but beares very good burdens; so wee have thought of our Indian people, and therefore have beene discouraged to put plow to such dry and rocky ground, but God having begun thus with some few it may bee they are better soile for the Gospel then wee can thinke: I confesse I think no great good will bee done till they bee more civilized, but why may not God begin with some few, to awaken others by degrees? nor doe I expect any great good will bee wrought by the English (leaving secrets to God) (although the English shall surely begin and lay the first stones of Christs Kingdome and Temple amongst them) Because God is wont ordinarily to convert Nations and peoples by some of their owne country men who are nearest to them, and can best speake, and most of all pity their brethren and countrimen, but yet if the least beginnings be made by the conversion of two or three, its worth all our time and travailes, and cause of much thankfulnesse for such seedes, although no great harvests should immediately appeare; surely this is evident, first that they never heard heart-breaking prayer and preaching before now in their owne tongue, that we know of, secondly, that there were never such hopes of a dawning of mercy toward them as now, certainely those aboundant teares which wee saw shed from their eies, argue a mighty and blessed presence of the spirit of Heaven in their hearts, which when once it comes into such kinde of spirits will not easily out againe.

The chiefe use that I can make of these hopefull beginnings, besides rejoycing for such fainings, is from *Esay.* {Isaiah} 2.5. *Oh house of Israel, let us walke in the light of the Lord;* Considering that these blinde Natives beginne to looke towards Gods mountaine now.

The observations I have gathered by conversing with them are such as these.

1. That none of them slept Sermon or derided Gods messenger: Woe unto those English that are growne bold to doe that, which Indians will not, Heathens dare not.

2. That there is need of learning in Ministers who preach to Indians, much more to English men and gracious Christians, for these had sundry philosophicall questions, which some knowledge of the arts must helpe to give answer to; and without which these would not have been satisfied: worse then Indian ignorance hath blinded their eies that renounce learning as an enemy to Gospell Ministeries.

3. That there is no necessity of extraordinary gifts nor miraculous signes alway to convert Heathens, who being manifest and professed unbeleevers may expect them as soone as any; (signes being given for them that beleeve not I *Cor.* 14.22.) much lesse is there any need of such gifts for gathering Churches amongst professing Christians, (signes not being given for them which beleeve,) for wee see the Spirit of God working mightily upon the hearts of these Natives in an ordinary way, and I hope will, they being but a remnant, the Lord using to shew mercy to the remnant; for there be but few that are left alive from the Plague and Pox, which God sent into those parts, and if one or two can understand they usually talke of it as wee doe of newes, it flies suddainely farre and neare, and truth scattered will rise in time, for ought we know.

4. If English men begin to despise the preaching of faith and repentance, and humiliation for sinne, yet the poore Heathens will bee glad of it, and it shall doe good to them; for so they are, and so it begins to doe; the Lord grant that the foundation of our English woe, be not laid in the ruine and contempt of those fundamentall doctrines of faith, repentance, humiliation for sin, &c. but rather relishing the novelties and dreames of such men as are surfeited with the ordinary food of the Gospell of Christ. Indians shall weepe to heare faith and repentance preached, when English men shall mourne, too late, that are weary of such truths.

5. That the deepest estrangements of man from God is no hinderance to his grace nor to the Spirit of grace for what Nation or people ever so deeply degenerated since *Adams* fall as these Indians; and yet the Spirit of God is working upon them?

6. That it is very likely if ever the Lord convert any of these Natives, that they will mourne for sin exceedingly, and consequently love Christ dearely, for if by a little measure of light such heart-breakings have appeared, what may wee

thinke will bee, when more is let in they are some of them very wicked, some very ingenious, these latter are very apt and quick of understanding and naturally sad and melancholly (a good servant to repentance,) and therefore there is the greater hope of great heart-breakings, if ever God brings them effectually home, for which we should affectionately pray.

A third meeting with the Indians.

N *Ovember 26.* I could not goe my selfe, but heard from those who went of a third meeting; the Indians having built more Wigwams in the wonted place of meeting to attend upon the Word the more readily. The preacher understanding how many of the Indians discouraged their fellowes in this worke, and threatning death to some if they heard any more, spake therefore unto them, about temptations of the Devill, how hee tempted to all manner of sinne, and how the evill heart closed with them, and how a good heart abhorred them; the Indians were this day more serious then ever before, and propounded divers questions againe; as 1. Because some Indians say that we must pray to the Devill for all good, and some to God; they would know whether they might pray to the Devill or no. 2. They said they heard the word humiliation oft used in our Churches, and they would know what that meant? 3. Why the English call them Indians, because before they came they had another name? 4. What a Spirit is? 5. Whether they should beleeve Dreames? 6. How the English come to know God so much and they so little? To all which they had fit answers; but being not present I shall not set them downe: onely their great desire this time was to have a place for a Towne and to learne to spinne.

Sir, I did thinke I should have writ no more to you concerning the Indians; but the Ship lingers in the Harbour, and the Lord Jesus will have you see more of his conquests and triumphes among these forlorne and degenerate people; surely hee heares the prayers of the destitute and that have long lien downe in the dust before God for these poore prisoners of the pit: surely some of these American tongues and knees must confesse him, and bow downe before him: for the Saturday night after this third meeting (as I am informed from that man of God who then preached to them) there came to his house one *Wampas* [The name {of} an Indian] a wise and sage Indian, as a messenger sent to him from the rest of the company, to offer unto him his owne sonne and three more Indian children to bee trained up among the English, one of the children was nine yeares old, another eight, another five, another foure: and being demanded why they would have them brought up among the English, his answer was, because they would grow rude and wicked at home, and would never come to know God, which they hoped they should doe if they were constantly among the English.

This *Wampas* came also accompanied with two more Indians, young lusty men, who offered themselves voluntarily to the service of the English that by dwelling in some of their families, they might come to know Jesus Christ; these are two of those three men whom wee saw weeping, and whose hearts were smitten at our second meeting above mentioned, and continue still much affected, and give great hopes; these two are accepted of and received into two of the Elders houses, but the children are not yet placed out because it is most meet to doe nothing that way too suddainly, but they have a promise of acceptance and education of them either in learning or in some other trade of life in time convenient, to which *Wampas* replyed that the Indians desired nothing more.

These two young men who are thus disposed of, being at an Elders house upon the Sabbath day night, upon some conference with them, one of them began to confesse how wickedly he had lived, and with how many *Indian* women hee had committed filthinesse, and therefore professed that hee thought God would never looke upon him in love. To which hee had this answer, that indeed that sinne of whoredome was exceeding great, yet if hee sought God for Christs sake to pardon him, and confesse his sinne and repented of it indeed, that the Lord would shew him mercy; and hereupon acquainted him with the story of Christs conference with the Samaritan woman, *John* 4. and how Jesus Christ forgave her although shee lived in that sinne of filthinesse, even when Christ began to speake to her: whereupon he fell a weeping and lamenting bitterly, and the other young man being present and confessing the like guiltinesse with his fellow, hee burst out also into a great mourning, wherein both continued for above halfe an houre together at that time also.

It is wonderfull to see what a little leven and that small mustardseed of the Gospell will doe, and how truth will worke when the spirit of Christ hath the setting of it on, even upon hearts and spirits most uncapable; for the last night after they had heard the word this third time, there was an English youth of good capacitie who lodged in *Waaubon's Wigwam* that night upon speciall occasion, and hee assured us that the same night *Waaubon* instructed all his company out of the things which they had heard that day from the Preacher, and prayed among them, and awaking often that night continually fell to praying and speaking to some or other of the things hee had heard, so that this man (being a man of gravitie and chiefe prudence and counsell among them, although no *Sachem*) [That is King] is like to bee a meanes of great good to the rest of his company unlesse cowardice or witchery put an end (as usually they have done) to such hopefull beginnings.

The old man who askt the first question the second time of our meeting (*viz.* whether there was any hope for such old men or no) hath six sonnes, one of his sonnes was a *Pawwaw*, [That is Sorcerers and Witches] and his wife a great *Pawwaw*, and both these God hath convinced of their wickednesse, and they resolve to heare the word and seeke to the devill no more. This, the two *Indians* who are come to us acquaint us with, and that they now say, that *Chepian, i.e.* the devill is naught, and that God is the author onely of all good as they have been taught. Hee therefore who preacheth to the *Indians* desired them to tell him who were *Pawwaws* when hee went againe to preach amongst them; and upon speciall occasion this *Decemb.* 4. being called of God to another place where the *Indians* use to meet, and having preacht among them, after the Sermon, hee that was the *Pawwaw* of that company was discovered to him, to whom hee addressed himselfe and propounded these questions, *viz.* 1. Whether doe you thinke that God or *Chepian* is the author of all good? he answered, God. 2. If God bee the author of all good, why doe you pray to *Chepian* the devill? The *Pawwaw* perceiving him to propound the last question with a sterne countenance and unaccustomed terrour, hee gave him no answer, but spake to other *Indians* that hee did never hurt any body by his *Pawwawing*, and could not bee got by all the meanes and turnings of questions that might bee, to give the least word of answer againe; but a little after the conference was ended, hee met with this *Pawwaw* alone and spake more lovingly and curteously to him, and askt him why hee would not answer, he then told him that his last question struck a terrour into him and made him afraid, and promised that at the next meeting hee would propound some question to him as others did.

And here it may not bee amisse to take notice of what these two *Indians* have discovered to us concerning these *Pawwaws*: for they were askt how they came to bee made *Pawwaws*, and they answered thus, that if any of the *Indians* fall into any strange dreame wherein *Chepian* appeares unto them as a serpent, then the next day they tell the other *Indians* of it, and for two dayes after the rest of the *Indians* dance and rejoyce for what they tell them about this Serpent, and so they become their *Pawwaws*: Being further askt what doe these *Pawwaws*, and what use are they of; and they said the principall imployment is to cure the sick by certaine odde gestures and beatings of themselves, and then they pull out the sicknesse by applying their hands to the sick person and so blow it away: so that their *Pawwaws* are great witches having fellowship with the old Serpent, to whom they pray, and by whose meanes they heale sicke persons, and (as they said also) will slew {?} many strange juglings to the wonderment of the *Indians*. They affirmed also that if they did not cure the sick party (as very often they did not) that then they were reviled, and sometime killed by some of the dead mans friends, especially if they could not get their mony againe out of their hands, which they receive aforehand for their cure.

Wee have cause to be very thankfull to God who hath moved the hearts of the generall court to purchase so much land for them to make their towne in which the *Indians* are much taken with, [*This town the Indians did desire to know what name it should have, and it was told them it should bee called* Noonatomen, *which signifies in English rejoycing, because they hearing the word, and seeking to know God, the English did rejoyce at it; and God did rejoyce at it, which pleased them much; & therefore that is to be the name of their towne.*] and it is somewhat observable that while the Court were considering where to lay out their towne, the *Indians* (not knowing of any thing) were about that time consulting about Lawes for themselves, and their company who sit downe with *Waaubon*; there were ten of them, two of them are forgotten.

Their Lawes were these.

1. That if any man be idle a weeke, at most a fortnight, hee shall pay five shillings.

2. If any unmarried man shall lie with a young woman unmarried, hee shall pay twenty shillings.

3. If any man shall beat his wife, his hands shall bee tied behind him and

carried to the place of justice to bee severely punished.

4. Every young man if not anothers servant, and if unmarried, hee shall be compelled to set up a *Wigwam* and plant for himselfe, and not live shifting up and downe to other *Wigwams*.

5. If any woman shall not have her haire tied up but hang loose or be cut as mens haire, she shall pay five shillings.

6. If any woman shall goe with naked breasts they shall pay two shillings six pence.

7. All those men that weare long locks shall pay five shillings.

8. If any shall kill their lice betweene their teeth, they shall pay five shillings. This Law though ridiculous to English eares yet tends to preserve cleanlinesse among *Indians*.

'Tis wonderfull in our eyes to understand by these two *Indians*, what Prayers *Waaubon* and the rest of them use to make, for hee that preacheth to them professeth hee never yet used any of their words in his prayers, from whom otherwise it might bee thought that they had learne them by rote, one is this.

> *Amanaomen   Jehovah   tehassen metagh.*
> Take away   Lord   my stony heart.
>
> Another.
>
> *Cheehesom   Jehovah   kekowhogkow,*
> Wash   Lord   my soule.
>
> Another.

Lord lead mee when I die to heaven.

These are but a taste, they have many more, and these more enlarged then thus expressed, yet what are these but the sprinklings of the spirit and blood of Christ Jesus in their hearts? and 'tis no small matter that such dry barren and long-accursed ground should yeeld such kind of increase in so small a time. I would not readily commend a faire day before night, nor promise much of such kind of beginnings, in all persons, nor yet in all of these, for wee know the profession of very many is but a meere paint, and their best graces nothing but meere flashes and pangs, which are suddenly kindled and as soone go out and are extinct againe, yet God doth not usually send his Plough & Seedman to a place but there is at least some little peece of good ground, although three to one bee naught: and mee thinkes the Lord Jesus would never have made so fit a key for their locks, unlesse hee had intended to open some of their doores, and so to make way for his comming in. Hee that God hath raised up and enabled to preach unto them, is a man (you know) of a most sweet, humble, loving, gratious and enlarged spirit, whom God hath blest, and surely will still delight in, & do good by. I did think never to have opened my mouth to any, to desire those in England to further any good worke here, but now I see so many things inviting to speak in this businesse, that it were well if you did lay before those that are prudent and able these considerations.

1. That it is prettie heavy and chargeable to educate and traine up those children which are already offered us, in schooling, cloathing, diet and attendance, which they must have.

2. That in all probabilitie many *Indians* in other places, especially under our jurisdiction, will bee provoked by this example in these, both to desire preaching, and also to send their children to us, when they see that some of their fellowes fare so well among the English, and the civill authoritie here so much favouring and countenancing of these, and if many more come in, it will be more heavy to such as onely are fit to keepe them, and yet have their hands and knees infeebled so many wayes besides.

3. That if any shall doe any thing to incourage this worke, that it may bee given to the Colledge for such an end and use, that so from the Colledge may arise the yeerly revenue for their yeerly maintenance. I would not have it placed in any particular mans hand for feare of cousenage or misplacing or carelesse keeping and improving; but at the Colledge it's under many hands and eyes chief and best of the country who have been & will be exactly carefull of the right and comely disposing of such things; and therefore, if any thing bee given, let it bee put in such hands as may immediatly direct it to the President of the Colledge, who you know will soone acquaint the rest with it; and for this end if any in England have thus given any thing for this end, I would have them speake to those who have received it to send it this way, which if it bee withheld I thinke 'tis no lesse then sacriledge: but if God moves no hearts to such a work, I doubt not then but that more weake meanes shall have the honour of it in the day of Christ.

A fourth meeting with the Indians.

THis day being *Decemb. 9.* the children being catechised, and that place of *Ezekiel* touching the dry bones being opened, and applyed to their condition; the *Indians* offered all their children to us to bee educated amongst us, and instructed by us, complaining to us that they were not able to give any thing to the English for their education: for this reason there are therefore preparations made towards the schooling of them, and setting up a Schoole among them or very neare unto them. Sundry questions also were propounded by them to us, and of us to them; one of them being askt what is sinne? hee answered a naughty heart. Another old man complained to us of his feares, *viz.* that hee was fully purposed to keepe the Sabbath, but still hee was in feare whether he should goe to hell or heaven; and thereupon the justification of a sinner by faith in Christ was opened unto him as the remedy against all feares of hell. Another complayned of other *Indians* that did revile them, and call them Rogues and such like speeches for cutting off their Locks, and for cutting their Haire in a modest manner as the New-English generally doe; for since the word hath begun to worke upon their hearts, they have discerned the vanitie and pride which they placed in their haire, and have therefore of their owne accord (none speaking to them that we know of) cut it modestly; they were therefore encouraged by some there present of chiefe place and account with us, not to feare the reproaches of wicked *Indians*, nor their witch-craft and *Pawwaws* and poysonings, but let them know that if they did not dissemble but would seeke God unfaignedly, that they would stand by them, and that God also would be with them. They told us also of divers *Indians* who would come and stay with them three or foure dayes, and one Sabbath, and then they would goe from them, but as for themselves, they told us they were fully purposed to keepe the Sabbath, to which wee incouraged them, and night drawing on were forced to leave them, for this time.

F I N I S.

THE
Clear Sun-shine of the Gospel
BREAKING FORTH
UPON THE
INDIANS
IN
NEVV-ENGLAND.
OR,
An Historicall Narration of Gods
Wonderfull Workings upon sundry of the
INDIANS, both chief Governors and Common-people,
in bringing them to a willing and desired submission to
the Ordinances of the Gospel; and framing their
hearts to an earnest inquirie after the knowledge
of God the Father, and of Jesus Christ
the Saviour of the World.

By Mr. THOMAS SHEPARD Minister of the Gospel of
Jesus Christ at *Cambidge* in *New-England*.

Isaiah 2. 2, 3. *And it shall come to passe in the last dayes, that the mountain of the
Lords ouse shall bee established in the top of the mountains, and shall bee exalted
above the hills; and all Nations shall flow unto it.
And many people shal go and say, Come ye and let us go up to the mountain of the Lord,
to the house of the God of Jacob, and he will teach us of his wayes, and we will walk
in his paths: for out f Zion shall go forth the Law, and the word of the Lord from
Jerusalem.*

London. Printed by R. *Cotes* for *John Bellamy* at the three golden
Lions in *Cornhill* near the Royal Exchange, 1648.

THE
Clear Sun-shine of the Gospel
BREAKING FORTH
UPON THE
INDIANS
IN
NEW-ENGLAND
OR,
An Historicall Narration of Gods
Wonderfull Workings upon sundry of the
INDIANS, both chief Governors and Common-people,
in bringing them to a willing and desired submission to
the Ordinances of the Gospel; and framing their
hearts to an earnest inquirie after the knowledge
of God the Father, and of Jesus Christ
the Saviour of the World

By Mr. THOMAS SHEPARD Minister of the Gospel of
Jesus Christ at *Cambridge* in *New-England.*

Isaiah 2.2,3. *And it shall come to passe in the last dayes, that the mountain of*
the Lords house shall bee established in the top of the mountains, and
shall bee exalted above the hills; and all Nations shall flow unto it.
And many people shal go and say, Come ye and let us go up to the mountain of
the Lord, to the house of the God of Jacob, and he will teach us of his
wayes, and we will walk in his paths for out of Zion shall go forth the
Law, and the word of the Lord from Jerusalem.

London, Printed by *R. Cotes* for *John Bellamy* at the three golden
Lions in *Cornhill* near the Royall Exchange, 1648.

RIGHT HONOURABLE

THE

LORDS & COMMONS

Assembled

In High Court of Parliament.

Right Honorable,

T Hese *few* sheets *present* unto your view a *short* but welcome *discourse* of the visitations of the *most High* upon the *saddest* spectacles of degeneracy upon earth, The *poore Indian People*: the *distance* of place, (if our *spirits* be right) will be no *lessening* of the mercy, nor of our *thankefulnesse*, That *Christ* is glorified, that the *Gospel* doth any where find *footing*; and successe is a *mercy* as well worthy the *praise* of the *Saints* on Earth, as the *joy* of the *Angels* in heaven. The *report* of this mercy is *first* made to you, who are the *Representative* of this Nation, That in you *England* might bee stirred up, to be Rejoycers in, and Advancers of these promising beginnings. And because to you an *account* is *first* due of the *successe* of the Gospel in those *darke* corners of the World, which have been so much *inlightned* by Your favour, *enlivened* by Your resolutions, *encouraged* by Your fore-past indeavours for God, & hope stil being parts of Your selves, to be *further* strengthned by Your benigne aspects and bountifull influences on them.

The present *troubles* have not so far *obliterated* and worn out the sad *impressions* which *former* times have made upon our spirits, but we can *sadly* remember those *destructive* designes which were on foot, and carried on for the *Introduction* of so great *evils* both into *Church* and *State*; In order to which it was the *endeavour* of the *Contrivers* and *Promoters* of those designes, *to wast* the number of the godly, as those who would never be brought to *comply* in such destructive enterprises; which was attempted by *banishing* and *forcing* some abroad, by *burthening* and *afflicting* all at home. Among those who *tasted* of the *first*, I say not the *worst* sort of their cruelty, were these our *Brethen*, who to enjoy the *liberties* of the Gospel, were *content* to sit downe, and pitch their *tents* in the *utmost* parts of the Earth, hoping that there they might be out of the *reach* of their malice, as they were assured they were beyond the *bounds* of their love. God who doth often make mans *evill* of sin, serviceable to the *advancement* of the *riches* of his owne Grace; The most *horrid* act that ever was done by the *sonnes* of men, the *murther* of Christ, God made *serviceable* to the highest *purposes* of Grace and mercy that ever *came* upon his breast; That God doth shew that hee had *mercifull* ends, in this their *malicious* purpose: as hee suffer'd *Paul* to be cast into prison, to *convert* the Jaylor, to be shipwrackt at *Melita*, to *preach* to the *barbarous*, [Acts 6.30, 33, 34. Acts 28.1-11] so he *suffer'd* their way to be *stopped* up here, and their persons to be *banished* hence, that hee might *open* a passage for them in the Wildernesse, and make them instruments to draw soules to him, who had been so long *estranged* from him.

It was the end of the *adversary* to suppresse, but Gods to *propagate* the Gospel; theirs to *smother* and put out the light, Gods to *communicate* and disperse it to the *utmost* corners of the Earth; that as one saith of *Paul, his blindnesse gave light to the whole World,* [Cæcitas *Pauli* totius orbis illuminatio. Act 9.9.] so we hope God will make their distance and *estrangednesse* from us, a meanes of *bringing* many near and in to acquaintance with him.

Indeed *a long time* it was before God let them see any *farther* end of their comming over, then to *preserve* their consciences, *cherish* their Graces, *provide* for their sustenance: But when *Providences* invited their return, he let them *know* it was for some farther Arrand that hee *brought* them thither, giving them some *Bunches* of Grapes, some *Clusters* of Figs in *earnest* of the prosperous *successe* of their endeavours upon those *poor outcasts*: The *utmost* ends of the earth are *designed* and promised to be *in time* the possessions of Christ, And *hee sends his Ministers into every place where he himself intends to come*, and take possession. Where the *Ministery* is the *Harbinger* and goes before, Christ and *Grace* will *certainly* follow after. [Psal. 2.8 Isa. 58.10-12. Isa. 41.9-10 Luke 10.1.]

This little we see is *something* in hand, to earnest to us those things which are in hope; something in *possession*, to assure us of the *rest* in promise, when the *ends* of the earth shall see his glory, and *the Kingdmes of the world shall become the Kingdomes of the Lord and his Christ, when hee shall have Dominion from Sea to Sea, and they that dwell in the wilderness shall bow before him.* [Psal 22.27 Rev. 11.15 Psal. 72.8-11] And if the *dawn* of the *morning* be so delightfull, what will the *clear* day be? If the *first fruits* be so precious, what wil the *whole harvest* be? if some *beginnings* be so ful of joy, what will it be when God shall *perform* his *whole* work, when *the whole earth shall be full of the knowledge of the Lord, as the waters cover the Sea,* [Isa. 11.9-10] and East and West shal sing together the song of the Lamb?

In *order* to this what doth God *require* of us, but that we should *strengthen* the hands, *incourage* the hearts of those who are at *work* for him, *conflicting* with difficulties, *wrestling* with discouragements, to *spread* the Gospel, & in that, the *fame* and honor of this Nation, to the *utmost* ends of the earth? It was the *design* of your *enemies* to make them *little*, let it be your *endevor* to *make* them *great*, their *greatnesse* is your strength. Their enemies threatned *their* hands should *reach* them for evil, God *disappointed* them; And let your *hands* reach them now for good; there is enough in them to speak then fit *objects* of your incouragement, they are men of *choice* spirits, not *frighted* with dangers, *softned* with allurements, nor *discouraged* with difficulties, *preparing* the way of the Lord in those *unpassable* places of the earth, dealing with such *whom* they are to *make* men, before they can *make* them Christians. They are such who are *impressed* for your service in the *service* of Christ, can *stand* alone, but desire to have *dependence* on you, they feare not the *malice* of their enemies, but *desire* the countenance and incouragement of their friends; And shal your *Honors* in *consideration* of their *former* sufferings, their *present* service, and *reall* deservings, *help the day of small things among them*; shal you interest them in your assistances, as you are interested in their affections, you wil thereby not only *further* these *beginnings* of God by *incouraging* their hearts, and *strengthning* their hands to *work* for him, but also (as we humbly conceive) much add to the *comfort* of your owne *accounts* in the day of the Lord, and lay greater obligations on them *yet more* to *pray* for you, to *promote* your counsels, and together with us your *unworthy servants* to *write down* themselves,

Yours humbly devoted in the service of the Gospel.

Stephen Marshall	*John Downam*	*Tho. Goodwin*
Jeremy Whitaker	*Philip Nye*	*Tho. Case*
Edm. Calamy	*Syd. Symptson*	*Simeon Ashe*
William Greenhill	*William Carter*	*Samuel Bolton.*

TO THE

Godly and well affected of

this Kingdome of *E N G L A N D* ;

who pray for, and rejoyce in, the

thrivings of the Gospel of our

L O R D   J E S U S.

Christian Reader,

*I*F ever thou hadst experience of this day of power, these visitations of Christ *upon thine own spirit; I suppose thee to be one who hast* embarqu'd *many prayers for the* successe *of the Gospel in these* darke corners *of the earth; to* strenghten *thy faith,* inlarge *thy heart, and assure thy soul that God is a* God hearing prayers: *An* account *is here given to thee of the* conquests *of the Lord Jesus upon these poor out-casts, who have thus long been estranged from him, spilt like* water *upon the ground and none to gather them. Formerly thou had,* The Day-break, *some* dawnings *of light, after a long and black night of darkeness, here thou seest* the sun is up, *which wee hope* will rejoice like the strong man to run its race, *scattering those thick clouds of darknesse, and* shining *brighter and brighter* till it come to a perfect day. *These few sheets give thee* footing *for such thoughts, and some further* incouragements *to wait & pray for the* accomplishment *of such things. Here thou mayst see, the* Ministry *is precious,* the feet of them who bring glad tidings beautifull, Ordinances *desired, the* Word *frequented and attended, the* Spirit *also going forth in* power *and efficacy with it, in* awakening *and* humbling *of them, drawing forth those* affections *of sorrow, and expressions of* tears *in abundance, which no tortures or* extremities *were ever observed to* force *from them, with* lamenting: *we read here, their leaving of sinne, they* forsake *their* former *evill wayes, and set up* fences *never to returne, by making* laws *for the* punishment *of those sins wherein they have lived, and to which they have been so much addicted. They set up* prayers *in their families* morning *and* evening, *and are in* earnest *in them; And with more* affection *they* crave *Gods blessing upon a little parched corn, &* Indian *stalks, then many of us do upon our greatest plenty and abundance. They rest on the Lords day, and make laws for the* observation *of it, wherein they* meet *together to pray & instruct one another in the things of God, which have* *been* communicated *to them. They renounce their* diabolicall *Charmes and Charmers, and many of those who were* practitioners *in these sinfull and soulundoing Arts, being made naked,* convinced *and ashamed of their evill,* forsake their way, and betake themselves to prayer, preferring the Christian Charm, *before their* diabolical Spells [Isa{iah}. 26.16. לחש Incantatio, mussitatio. Jer. 8.17. Eccles. 10.11.]: *herein God making good that promise Zeph.* 2.11. I will famish al the Gods of the earth, (*which he doth by withdrawing the worshippers, and throwing contempt upon the worship*) And men shal worship me alone every one from his place, even all the Isles of the Heathens.

All these are hopefull presages *that God is* going *out in his* power *and grace to* conquer *a people to himself; That he begins to cast an* owning *look on them, whom he hath so long* neglected & despised [Act. 14.16 Acts 17.30. υπεριδων *And indeed God may wel seek out for other* ground *to sow the seed of his* Ordinances *upon, seeing the* ground *where it hath been* sown *hath brought forth no* better *fruit to him; he may well* bespeak *another people to himself, seeing he* finds *no better* entertainment *among the people he hath* espoused *to him, and that by so many* mercies, priviledges, indeerments, ingagements. *We have as many* sad symptoms *of a* declining, *as these poor outcasts have* glad presages *of a* Rising Sun among them. *The* Ordinances *are as much* contemned *here, as* frequented *there; the* Ministery *as much* discouraged *here, as* embraced *there;* Religion *as much* derided, *the* ways *of godliness as much* scorned *here, as they can be* wished *and desired there; generally wee are* sick *of plenty, wee surfet of our abundance, the worst of surfets, and with our* loathed Manna *and* disdained *food, God* preparing *them a* Table *in the wilderness; where our* satieties, *wil be their* sufficiencies; *our* complaints, *their* contents; *our* burthens, *their* comforts; *if he cannot have an* England *here, he can have an* England *there; &* baptize & adopt them into those *priviledges, which wee have* looked *upon as our burthens. We have* sad decayes *upon us, we are a* revolting *Nation, a people* guilty *of great* defection *from God. Some fall from the* worship *of God to their old* superstitions, *and corrupt worship, saying with those in Jeremy,* It was better with us then now. *Some fall from the* doctrin *of grace to errors, some to* damnable, *others to* defiling, *some to* destructive, *others to* corruptive *opinions. Some fal from* professed *seeming holynes, to sin & profanenes; who like* blazing *comets did shine* bright *for a time, but after have* set *in a* night *of darknes. We have many* sad symptoms *on us, we* decay *under all the* means *of nourishment, are* barren *under all Gods* sowings, dry *under al the* dews, *droppings showres of heaven, like that* Country *whereof* Historians *speak, where drought causeth dirt, and showres causeth dust. [Siccitas dat lutum, imbres pulverem.] And what doth God* threaten *herein, but to* remove *the* Candlesticks, *to take away the Gospel, that* pretious *Gospel, the* streams *whereof have brought so many* ships *laden with blessings to our shoar, that Gospel under the* shadow *whereof we have* sate down and been *refreshed these many years? where the* power *is lost, God will* not long *continue the* form, *where the* heat *is gone, he wil not long* continue the light. *The* temple *did not* preserve *the Jews when their* hearts *were the* Synagogues *of Satan, nor shall* any outward *priviledge* hold us up, when the inward power *is down in our spirits. God hath* forsaken *other* Churches *as eminent as ever* England *was: where are the* churches *of* Asia, *once* famous *for the gospel, for general* Councels, *now places for* Zim *and* Ochim, *their* habitation *desolate? where are those* ancient *people of the Jews who were (segulla micol hagnâmim)* his peculiar and chosen people of al nations? *they are* scattered *abroad as a curse, and their* place *knows them no more. And shall I tel you? God hath no* need *of us, he can cal them* Gnammi, *his people, who were* Lo gnammi, *not his people, and them* beloved, *who were not* beloved. *Indeed he hath* held *up us, as if he had not* known *where to have* another *people, if he should* forsake *us; we have been a* Goshen, *when others have been an* Egypt, *a* Canaan, *when others an* Akeldama, *the* garden *of God, when others have been a wildernesse, our* fleece *hath been* wet, *when others have been* dry: *But* know, *God hath no need of us, he can* want *no people if he* please *to call; If he speake,* all the ends of the world shall remember and turn unto the Lord, and all the kindreds of the Nations shall worship before him [Psal. 22.27-28. & Esa. {Isaiah} {11}.9-10]. *If he set up his* standard, to him shal the Gentiles flock, *and* the earth shall be full of the knowledge of the Lord, as the waters cover the sea. *It is not for* need *but for* love *that God abides with* England, *and there is nothing out of himselfe the* incentive *of this love* [Amat deus, non aliunde hoc habet, sed ipse est unde amat. Aug.]: *there can be no* reason *given why God should* fence *us, and* suffer *other places to lye* wast, *that we should bee his* Garden, *and other places a* Wildernes, *that he should* feed *us with the* bread *of Heaven, and* suffer *others to* starve, *men of the same mould, his* offspring *as well as we, and such (did he* conquer *to himselfe) were likely to doe him* more *service, bring him* more *glory then we have done. Wee see something here done in order to such a work, our* Harvest *is much over, we see little incomes, there we see the* fields are ripe for harvest; *here the* ministry *is contemned,* there *the* feet of them that brings glad tydings are beautifull; *we have* outlived *the power and efficacy of Ordinances, there God goes forth with* life *and power; we can* outfit *the most speaking and* winning discoveries *of Christ, there every* notion, *breeds* motion *in them; the* glory *of the Lord is* much departed *from us, there his* rising *is conspicuous and glorious. The* blind *man found it* good to *be in the* way *where Christ came: And who would be in* Ægypt *when there is* light *in* Goshen? *Oh that* England *would be* quickned by *their risings, and* weep *over her own declinings! What a* wonder *is it that they should doe so* much, *and we* so little, *that they should be* men *in their infancy, and we such* children *in our* manhood, *that they so* active, *we so* dead? *That which was* Hieroms *complaint may be ours,* O that Infidelity should do that which those who professe thenmselvs beleevers cannot do! *We have the* light *of former times, but* want *the* heat, *knowledge* abounds *as the* waters cover *the sea, but we* want *the salt; we have a* form *of Godlinesse, but want the* power: *And it wil be* smal *comfort should God* continue *to us the form, and* cary *to others the* power, *to suffer us to* wast *our selvs with* unnecessary *brangles (which are the* sweat *of the times) and in the mean to* cary *the life and* power *of* Religion *unto others.* [Hea! Quod præstat infidelitas, quod non præstitit fides. Ignis qui in parentibus fuit Calidus, in nobis

Lucidus.]

Let these poor Indians *stand up* incentives *to us, as the Apostle set up the* Gentiles *a* provocation *to the Jews* [Rom 11.14]*: who knows but God gave life to* New England, *to* quicken Old, *and hath* warmed *them, that they might* heat *us,* raised *them from the dead, that they might* recover *us from that consumption, and those sad* decayes *which are come upon us?*

This smal Treatise *is an* Essay *to that end, an* Indian Sermon, *though you will not* hear *us, possibly when some* rise *from the* dead *you will* hear *them. The main* Doctrin *it preacheth unto all, is to* value *the Gospel,* prize *the Ministry,* loath *not your Manna, surfet not of your plenty, be* thankfull *for mercies,* fruitfull *under means:* Awake *from your slumber,* repair *your decayes,* redeem *your time,* improve *the seasons of your peace;* answer *to cals, open* to knocks, attend *to whispers,* obey *commands; you have a* name *you live, take heed you bee not* dead, *you are* Christians *in shew, be so* indeed: *least as you have* lost *the power, God take away from you the form also.*

And you that are Ministers *learn by this not to* despond *though you see not* present *fruit of your labors,* though you fish all night and catch nothing. *God hath a* fulnesse *of time to* perform *all his purposes. And the* deepest *degeneracies, &* widest *estrangements from God, shall be no* bar *or obstacle to the* power *and freenesse of his owne grace when that* time *is come.*

And you that are Merchants, *take* incouragement *from hence to* scatter *the beames of light, to* spread *and propagate the* Gospel *into those dark* corners *of the earth; whither you* traffick *you take much from them, if you can* carry *this to them, you wil make them an* abundant *recompence. And you that are* Christians *indeed, rejoice to see the* Curtaines *of the Tabernacle inlarged, the* bounds *of the Sanctuary extended,* Christ *advanced, the* Gospel *propagated, and* souls *saved. And if ever the love of God did* center *in your hearts, if ever the* sense *of his goodness hath* begot *bowels of compassion in you, draw them forth* towards *them whom God hath* singled *out to be the* objects *of his grace and mercy; lay out your prayers, lend your assistance to carry on this* day of the Lord *begun among them. They are not able (as* Moses *said) to* bear the burthen of that people alone, *to make* provision *for the* children *whom God hath given them; & therefore it is requisite the* spiritual community *should help to bear part with them. Many of the* young ones *are given and taken in, to be* educated *& brought up in* Schooles, *they are* naked *and must be* clad, *they* want *al things, and must be* supplied. *The Parents also, and many others being convinced of the evill of an* idle life, *desire to be* employed *in honest labor, but they want* instruments and tooles *to set them on work, and* cast-garments *to throw upon those bodies,* that their loins may blesse you, *whose* souls *Christ hath* cloathed. *Some* worthy persons *have given much; and if God shall* move *the heart of others to* offer willingly *towards the buildings of Christ a* Spirituall temple, *it will certainly* remain *upon their account, when the* smallest rewards *from God, shall be better then the greatest layings out for God. But we are making a relation, not a collection; we leave the whole to your Christian consideration, not doubting but they who have tasted of mercy from God, will be ready to exercise compassion to others, & commend you unto him* who gave himself for us, that hee might redeem us from all iniquity, and purifie *as well as purchase* unto himself a peculiar people, zealous of good works. [Tit.9.14 {i.e., Titus 2.14}].

Stephen Marshall	*John Downam*	*Tho. Goodwin*
Jer.Whitaker	*Philip Nye*	*Tho. Case*
Edmund. Calamy	*Sy. Sympson*	*Simeon Ashe*
William Greenhill	*William Carter*	*Samuel Bolton*

THE
C L E A R E S U N S H I N E

OF THE

G O S P E L L,

Breaking forth upon the **INDIANS**

in *New-England.*

Much Honored and deare Sir,

T Hat glorious and sudden rising of Christ Jesus upon our poore *Indians* which began a little before you set saile from these shores, hath not beene altogether clouded since, but rather broken out further into more light and life, wherewith the most High hath visited them; and because some may call in question the truth of the first relation, either because they may thinke it too good newes to be true, or because some persons maligning the good of the Countrey, are apt, as to aggravate to the utmost any evill thing against it, so to vilifie and extenuate any good thing in it: and because your selfe desired to heare how farre since God hath carried on that worke, which your owne eyes saw here begun; I shall therefore as faithfully and as briefly as I can, give you a true relation of the progresse of it, which I hope may be a sufficient confirmation of what hath been published to the world before, having this as the chiefe end in my owne eye, that the precious Saints and people of God in *England,* beleeving what hath been and may bee reported to them, of these things, may help forward this work together with us by their prayers and prayses, as we desire to doe the like for the worke of Christ begun among them there. I dare not speake too much, nor what I thinke about their conversion, I have seen so much falsenesse in that point among many English, that I am slow to beleeve herein too hastily concerning these poore naked men; only this is evident to all honest hearts that dwell neer them, and have observed them, that the work of the Lord upon them (what ever it bee) is both unexpected and wonderfull in so short a time; I shall set downe things as they are, and then your selfe and others to whom these may come, may judge as you please of them.

Soon after your departure hence, the awakening of these *Indians* in our Towne raised a great noyse among all the rest round about us, especially about

Concord side where the *Sachim* [An inferiour Prince.] (as I remember) and one
or two more of his men, hearing of these things and of the preaching of the
Word, and how it wrought among them here, came therefore hither to
Noonanetum [An Indian town so called.] to the *Indian* Lecture, and what the
Lord spake to his heart wee know not, only it seems hee was so farre affected, as
that he desired to become more like to the English, and to cast off those *Indian*
wild and sinfull courses they formerly lived in; but when divers of his men
perceived their *Sachims* mind, they secretly opposed him herein; which
opposition being known, he therefore called together his chiefe men about him,
& made a speech to this effect unto them, *viz.* "That they had no reason at all to
oppose those courses the English were now taking for their good, for (saith hee)
all the time you have lived after the *Indian* fashion under the power and
protection of higher *Indian Sachems*, what did they care for you? they onely
fought their owne ends out of you, and therefore would exact upon you, and
take away your skins and your *Kettles* & your *Wampam* from you at their own
pleasure, & this was al that they regarded: but you may evidently see that the
English mind no such things, care for none of your goods, but onely seeke your
good and welfare, and in stead of taking away, are ready to give to you;" with
many other things I now forget, which were related by an eminent man of that
town to me. What the effect of this speech was, we can tell no otherwise then as
the effects shewed it; the first thing was, the making of certain Lawes for their
more religious and civill government and behaviour, to the making of which,
they craved the assistance of one of the chiefe *Indians* in *Noonanetum*, a very
active *Indian* to bring in others to the knowledge of God; desiring withall an
able faithful man in *Concord* to record and keep in writing what they had
generally agreed upon. Another effect was, their desire of Mr. *Eliot* [Teacher of
the Church of *Roxbury*, that preacheth to the *Indians* in their own Language.]
coming up to them, to preach, as he could find time among them; and the last
effect was, their desire of having a Towne given them within the bounds of
Concord neare unto the English. This latter when it was propounded by the
Sachim of the place, he was demanded why hee desired a towne so neare, when
as there was more roome for them up in the Country. To which the *Sachim*
replyed, that he therefore desired it because he knew that if the *Indians* dwelt far
from the English, that they would not so much care to pray, nor would they be
so ready to heare the Word of God, but they would be all one *Indians* still; but
dwelling neare the English he hoped it might bee otherwise with them then. The
Town therefore was granted them; but it seemes that the opposition made by
some of themselves more malignantly set against these courses, hath kept them
from any present setling downe; and surely this opposition is a speciall finger of
Satan resisting these budding beginnings; for what more hopefull way of doing
them good then by cohabitation in such Townes, neare unto good examples, and
such as may be continually whetting upon them, and dropping into them of the
things of God? what greater meanes at least to civilize them? as is evident in the
Cusco and *Mexico Indians*, more civill then any else in this vast Continent that
wee know of, who were reduced by the politick principles of the two great
conquering Princes of those Countries after their long and tedious wars from

these wild and wandering course of life, unto a setling into particular Townes and Cities: but I forbear, only to confirme the truth of these things, I have sent you the orders agreed on at *Concord* by the *Indians*, under the hand of two faithfull witnesses, who could testifie more; if need were, of these matters: I have sent you their owne Copy and their own hands to it, which I have here inserted.

Conclusions and Orders made and agreed upon by *divers Sachims and other principall men amongst the Indians at* Concord, *in the end of the eleventh moneth, Au. 1646.*

1. THat every one that shall abuse themselves with wine or strong liquors, shall pay for every time so abusing themselves, 20 *s.*
2. That there shall be no more *Pawwowing* amongst the *Indians.* And if any shall hereafter *Pawwow* [Pawwows are Witches or Sorcerers that cure by help of the devill.], both he that shall *Powwow*, & he that shall procure him to *Powwow*, shall pay 20 *s.* apeece.
3. They doe desire that they may be stirred up to seek after God.
4. They desire they may understand the wiles of Satan, and grow out of love with his suggestions, and temptations.
5. That they may fall upon some better course to improve their time, then formerly.
6. That they may be brought to the sight of the sinne of lying, and whosever shall be found faulty herein shall pay for the first offence 5 *s.* the second 10 *s.* the third 20 *s.*
7. Whosoever shall steale any thing from another, shall restore fourfold.
8. They desire that no *Indian* hereafter shall have any more but one wife.
9. They desire to prevent falling out of *Indians* one with another, and that they may live quietly one by another.
10. That they may labour after humility, and not be proud.
11. That when *Indians* doe wrong one to another, they may be lyable to censure by *fine* or the like, as the *English* are.
12. That they pay their debts to the *English.*
13. That they doe observe the Lords-Day, and whosoever shall prophane it shall pay 20 *s.*
14. That they shall not be allowance to *pick Lice,* as formerly, and eate them, and whosoever shall offend in this case shall pay for every louse a penny.
15. They will weare their *haire* comely, as the English do, and whosoever shall offend herein shall pay 5 *s.*
16. They intend to reforme themselves, in their former greasing themselves, under the Penalty of 5 *s* for every default.

17. They doe all resolve to set up prayer in their *wigwams,* [A Wigwam is such a dwelling house as they live in.] and to seek to God both before and after meate.

18. If any commit the sinne of fornication, being single persons, the man shall pay 20 *s.* and the woman 10 *s.*

19. If any man lie with a beast he shall die.

20. Whosoever shall play at their former games shall pay 10 *s.*

21. Whosoever shall commit adultery shall be put to death.

22. Wilfull Murder shall be punished with death.

23. They shall not disguise themselves in their mournings, as formerly, nor shall they keep a great noyse by howling.

24. The old Ceremony of the Maide walking alone and living apart so many dayes 20 *s.*

25. No *Indian* shall take an English mans *Canooe* [A Canooe is a small Boate.] without leave under the penaltie of 5*s.*

26. No *Indian* shall come into any *English* mans house except he first knock: and this they expect from the *English.*

27. Whosoever beats his wife shall pay 20 *s.*

28. If any *Indian* shall fall out with, and beate another *Indian*, he shall pay 20 *s.*

29. They desire they may bee a towne, and either to dwell on this side the *Beare Swamp*, or at the East side of Mr. *Flints Pond.*

Immediatly after these things were agreed upon, most of the *Indians* of these parts, set up Prayer morning and evening in their families, and before and after meat. They also generally cut their haire, and were more civill in their carriage to the *English* then formerly. And they doe manifest a great willingnesse to conform themselves to the civill fashions of the *English.* The Lords day they keepe a day of rest, and minister what edification they can to one another. These former orders were put into this forme by Captaine *Simond Willard* of *Concord,* whom the *Indians* with unanimous consent intreated to bee their Recorder, being very solicitous that what they did agree upon might be faithfully preserved without alteration.

Thomas Flint.   *Simon Willard.*

These things thus wrought in a short time about *Concord* side, I looke upon as fruits of the ministery of the Word; for although their high esteem bred lately in them, especially the chief and best of the *English*, together with that mean esteem many of them have of themselves, and therefore will call themselves sometimes *poore Creatures*, when they see and heare of their great distance from others of the English; I say, although these things may be some causes of making these orders and walking in these courses, yet the chiefe cause seemes to bee the power of the Word, which hath been the chiefe cause of these Orders, and therefore it is that untill now of late they never so much as thought of any of these things.

I am not able to acquaint you very much from my owne eye and eare witnesse of things, for you know the neare relation between me and the fire side usually all winter time, onely I shall impart two or three things more of what I have heard and seen, and the rest I shall relate to you as I have received from faithfull witnesses, who testifie nothing to me by their writings, but what is seene in the open Sun, and done in the view of all the world, and generally known to be true of people abiding in these parts wee live in.

As soone as ever the fiercenesse of the winter was past, March.3.1647. I went out to *Noonanetum* to the *Indian* Lecture, where Mr. *Wilson*, Mr. *Allen*, of *Dedham*, Mr. *Dunster*, beside many other Christians were present; on which day perceiving divers of the *Indian* women well affected, and considering that their soules might stand in need of answer to their scruples as well as the mens; & yet because we knew how unfit it was for women so much as to aske questions publiquely immediatly by themselves; wee did therefore desire them to propound any questions they would bee resolved about by first acquainting either their Husbands, or the Interpreter privately therewith: whereupon we heard two questions thus orderly propounded; which because they are the first that ever were propounded by *Indian* women in such an ordinance that ever wee heard of, and because they may bee otherwise usefull, I shall therefore set them downe.

The first question was propounded by the wife of one *Wampooas* a well affected *Indian, viz.* "Whether (said she) do I pray when my husband prayes if I speak nothing as he doth, yet if I like what he saith, and my heart goes with it?{"} (for the *Indians* will many times pray with their wives, and with their children also sometime in the fields) shee therefore fearing lest prayer should onely be an externall action of the lips, enquired if it might not be also an inward action of the heart, if she liked of what he said.

The second question was propunded by the Wife of one *Totherswampe*, her meaning in her question (as wee all perceived) was this, *viz.* "Whether a husband should do well to pray with his wife, and yet continue in his passions, & be angry with his wife?{"} But the modesty and wisdome of the woman directed her to doe three things in one, for thus shee spake to us, *viz.* "Before my husband did pray hee was much angry and froward, but since hee hath begun to pray hee was not angry so much, but little angry{"}: wherein first shee gave an honorable testimony of her husband and commended him for the abatement of his passion; secondly, shee gave implicitly a secret reproofe for what was past, and for somewhat at present that was amisse; and thirdly, it was intended by her as a question whether her husband should pray to God, and yet continue in some unruly passions; but she wisely avoyded that, lest it might reflect too much upon him, although wee desired her to expresse it that was not her meaning.

At this time (beside these questions) there were sundry others propounded of very good use, in all which we saw the Lord Jesus leading them to make narrow inquiries into the things of God, that so they might see the reality of them. I have heard few Christians when they begin to looke toward God, make more searching questions that they might see things really, and not onely have a notion of them: I forbeare to mention any of them, because I forget the chiefe of them; onely this wee tooke notice of at this dayes meeting, that there was an aged *Indian* who proposed his complaint in propounding his question concerning an unruly disobedient son, and "what one should do with him in case of obstinacy and disobedience, and that will not heare Gods Word, though his Father command him, nor will not forsake his drunkennesse, though his father forbid him?{"} Unto which there were many answers to set forth the sinne of disobedience to parents; which were the more quickned and sharpned because wee knew that this rebellious sonne whom the old man meant, was by Gods providence present at this Lecture: Mr. *Wilson* was much inlarged, and spake so terribly, yet so graciously as might have affected a heart not quite shut up, which this young *desperado* hearing (who well understood the *English* tongue) instead of humbling himself before the Lords Word, which touched his conscience and condition so neare, hee was filled with a spirit of Satan, and as soone as ever Mr. *Wilsons* speech was ended hee brake out into a loud contemptuous expression; *So*, saith he: which we passed by without speaking againe, leaving the Word with him, which we knew would one day take its effect one way or other upon him.

The latter end of this yeare Mr. *Wilson*, Mr. *Eliot*, and my selfe were sent for by those in *Yarmouth* to meet with some other Elders of *Plimouth patent*, to heare and heale (if it were the will of Christ) the difference and sad breaches which have been too long a time among them, wherein the Lord was very mercifull to us and them in binding them up beyond our thoughts in a very short time, in giving not only that bruised Church but the whole Towne also a hopefull beginning of setled peace and future quietnesse; but Mr. *Eliot* as hee takes all other advantages of time, so hee tooke this, of speaking with, and preaching to the poore *Indians* in these remote places about *Cape Cod*: in which journey I shall acquaint you with what all of us observed.

Wee first found these *Indians* (not very farre from ours) to understand (but with much difficulty) the usuall language of those in our parts, partly in regard of the different dialect which generally varies in 40. or 60. miles, and partly and especially in regard of their not being accustomed unto sacred language about the holy things of God, wherein Mr. *Eliot* excells any other of the *English*, that in the *Indian* language about common matters excell him: I say therefore although they did with much difficulty understand him, yet they did understand him, although by many circumlocutions and variations of speech and the helpe of one or two Interpreters which were then present.

Secondly, wee observed much opposition against him, and hearing of him at the day appointed, especially by one of the chiefest *Sachims* in those parts, a man of a fierce, strong and furious spirit whom the *English* therefore call by the name *John:* who although before the day appointed for preaching, promised very faire that he would come and bring his men with him; yet that very morning when they were to bee present, he sends out almost all his men to Sea, pretending fishing, and therefore although at last he came late himselfe to the Sermon, yet his men were absent, and when he came himself, would not seem to understand anything, although hee did understand as some of the *Indians* themselves then told us, when Mr. *Eliot* by himself and by them inquired of him if he understood what was spoken: yet he continued hearing what was said with a dogged looke and a discontented countenance.

Thirdly, notwithstanding this opposition wee found another *Sachim* then present willing to learne, and divers of his men attentive and knowing what was said: and in the time which is usually set apart for propounding questions, an aged *Indian* told us openly, "That these very things which Mr. *Eliot* had taught them as the Commandements of God, and concerning God, and the making of the world by one God, that they had heard some old men who were now dead, to say the same things, since whose death there hath been no remembrance or knowledge of them among the *Indians* untill now they heare of them againe.{"} Which when I heard solemnly spoken, I could not tell how those old *Indians* should attaine to such knowledge, unlesse perhaps by means of the *French* Preacher cast upon those coasts many yeers since, by whose ministry they might possibly reape and retaine some knowledge of those things; this also I hear by a godly and able Christian who hath much converse with them; that many of them have this apprehension now stirring among them, *viz,* "That their forefathers did know God, but that after this, they fell into a great sleep, and when they did awaken they quite forgot him,{"} (for under such metaphoricall language they usually expresse what eminent things they meane:) so that it may seeme to be the day of the Lords gracious visitation of these poore Natives, which is just as it is with all other people, when they are most low, the wheele then turnes, and the Lord remembers to have mercy.

Fourthly, a fourth and last observation wee tooke, was the story of an *Indian* in those parts, telling us of his dreame many yeers since, which he told us of openly before many witnesses when we sate at meat: the dreame is this, hee said "That about two yeers before the *English* came over into those parts there was a great mortality among the *Indians*, and one night he could not sleep above half the night, after which hee fell into a dream, in which he did think he saw a great many men come to those parts in cloths, just as the *English* now are apparelled, and among them there arose up a man all in black, with a thing in his hand which hee now sees was all one *English* mans book; this black man he said stood upon a higher place then all the rest, and on the one side of him were the *English*, on the other a great number of *Indians*: this man told all the *Indians* that God was *moosquantum* or angry with them, and that he would kill them for their sinnes, whereupon he said himself stood up, and desired to know of the black man what God would do with him and his *Squaw* and *Pappooses* but the black man would not answer him a first time, nor yet a second time, untill he desired the third time, and then he smil'd upon him, and told him that he and his *Papooses* should be safe, and that God would give unto them *Mitchen, (i.e.)* victualls and other good things, and so hee awakened.{"} What similtude this dream hath with the truth accomplished, you may easily see. I attribute little to dreams, yet God may speak to such by them rather then to those who have a more sure Word to direct and warn them, yet this dream made us think surely this *Indian* will regard the black man now come along them rather then any others of them: but whether Satan, or fear, and guilt, or world prevailed, we cannot say, but this is certaine, that he withdrew from the sermon, and although hee came at the latter end of it, as hoping it had been done, yet we could not perswade him then to stay and hear, but away he flung, and we saw him no more till next day.

From this third of *March* untill the latter end of this Summer I could not be present at the *Indian* Lectures, but when I came this last time, I marvailed to see so many *Indian* men, women and children in *English* apparell, they being at *Noonanetum* generally clad; especially upon Lecture dayes, which they have got partly by gift from the *English*, and partly by their own labours, by which some of them have very handsomely apparelled themselves, & you would scarce know them from *English* people. There is one thing more which I would acquaint you with, which happened this Summer, *viz. June 9.* the first day of the Synods meeting at *Cambridge*, where the forenoon was spent in hearing a Sermon preached by one of the *Elders* as a preparative to the worke of the Synod, the afternoon was spent in hearing an *Indian* Lecture where there was a great confluence of *Indians* all parts to heare Mr. *Eliot*, which we conceived not unseasonable at such a time, partly that the reports of Gods worke begun among them, might be seen and beleeved of the chief who were then sent and met from all the Churches of Christ in the Countrey, who could hardly beleeve the reports they had received concerning these new stirs among the *Indians*, and partly hereby to raise up a greater spirit of prayer for the carrying on of the work begun upon the *Indians*, among all the Churches and servants of the Lord Jesus: The Sermon was spent in shewing them their miserable conditions without Christ, out of *Ephes.*2.1. that they were dead in trespasses and sinnes, and in pointing unto them the Lord Jesus, who onely could quicken them.

When the Sermon was done, there was a convenient space of time spent in hearing those questions which the *Indians* publikely propounded, and in giving answers to them; one question was, *What Countrey man Christ was, and where he was borne?*

Another was, *How farre off that place was from us here?*

Another was, *Where Christ now was?*

And another, *How they might lay hold on him, and where, being now absent from them?* with some other to this purpose; which received full answers from severall hands. But that which I note is this, that their gracious attention to the Word, the affections and mournings of some of them under it, their sober propounding of divers spirituall questions, their aptnesse to understand and beleeve what was replyed to them, the readinesse of divers poore naked children to answer openly the chief questions in Catechism which were formerly taught them, and such like appearances of a great change upon them, did marvellously affect all the wise and godly Ministers, Magistrates, & people, and did raise their hearts up to great thankfulnesse to God; very many deeply and abundantly mourning for joy to see such a blessed day, and the Lord Jesus so much known and spoken of among such as never heard of him before: So that if any in *England* doubt of the truth of what was formerly writ, or if any malignant eye shall question and vilifie this work, they will now speak too late, for what was here done at *Cambridge* was not set under a Bushell, but in the open Sunne, that what *Thomas* would not beleeve by the reports of others, he might be forced to beleeve, by seeing with his own eyes and feeling Christ Jesus thus risen among them with his own hands.

I have done with what I have observed my self; I shall therefore proceed to give you a true relation of what I have heard from others, and many faithfull witnesses have seene: and first I shall speake a little more of the old man who is mentioned in the story now in print; this old man hath much affection stirred up by the Word, and comming to Mr. *Eliots* house (for of him I had this story) Mr. *Eliot* told him that because he brought his wife & all his children constantly to the Lecture, that he would therefore bestow some Cloths upon him, (it being now winter & the old man naked:) which promise he not certainly understanding the meaning of, asked therefore of another *Indian* (who is Mr. *Eliots* servant and very hopefull) what it was that Mr. *Eliot* promised him? he told him that hee said hee would give him some Cloths; which when hee understood, hee affectionately brake out into these expressions, *God I see is mercifull*: a blessed, because a plain hearted affectionate speech, and worthy *English* mens thoughts when they put on their Cloths; to thinke that a poor blind *Indian* that scarce ever heard of God before, that he should see not only God in his Cloths, but mercy also in a promise of a cast off worne sute of Cloths, which were then given him, and which now he daily weares. But to proceed;

This same old man (as I think a little before hee had these Cloths) after an *Indian* Lecture, when they usually come to propound questions; instead of asking a question, began to speak to the rest of the *Indians*, and brake out into many expressions of wondring at Gods goodnesse unto them, that the Lord should at last look upon them and send his Word as a light unto them that had been in darknesse and such grosse ignorance so long; me wonder (saith he) at God that he should thus deale with us. This speech expressed in many words in the *Indian* Language, and with strong actings of his eyes and hands, being interpreted afterward to the *English*, did much also affect all of them that were present this Lecture also.

There were this winter many other questions propounded, which were writ down by Mr. *Edward Jackson* one of our Town, constantly present at these Lectures, to take notes both of the questions made by the *Indians* and returned by Mr. *Eliot* to them; this man having sent me in his notes, I shall send you a tast of some of them.

1. *Why some men were so bad, that they hate those men that would teach them good things?*

2. *Whether the devill or man were made first?*

3. *Whether if a father prayes to God to teach his sons to know him, and he doth teach them himself and they will not learn to know God, what should such fathers doe?* (this was propounded by an old man that had rude children.)

4. A *Squaw* [Indian woman.] propounded this question, *Whether she might not go & pray in some private place in the woods, when her husband was not at home, because she was ashamed to pray in the Wigwam before company?*

5. *How may one know wicked men, who are good and who are bad?*

6. *To what Nation Jesus Christ came first unto, and when?*

7. *If a man should be inclosed in Iron a foot thick and thrown into the fire,*

what would become of his soule, whether could the soule come forth thence or not?

8.   *Why did not God give all men good hearts that they might bee good?*

9.   *If one should be taken among strange Indians that know not God, and they would make him to fight against some that he should not, and he refuse, and for his refusall they kill him, what would become of his soule in such a case?* This was propounded by a stout [They hold that all their stout and valiant men have a reward after death.] fellow who was affected.

10.   *How long it is before men beleeve that have the Word of God made known to them?*

11.   *How they should know when their faith is good, and their prayers good prayers?*

12.   *Why did not God kill the Devil that made all men so bad, God having all power?*

13.   *If we be made weak by sinne in our hearts, how can we come before God to sanctifie a Sabbath?*

There were many more questions of this kind, as also many Philosophical, about the Sunne, Moon, Stars, Earth and Seas, Thunder, Lightning, Earthquakes, &c. which I forbear to make mention of, lest I should clog your time with reading, together with the various answers to them: by these you may perceive in what streame their minds are carried, and that the Lord Jesus hath at last an enquiring people among these poor naked men, that formerly never so much as thought of him; which questionings and enquiries are accounted of by some as part of the whitenings of the harvest toward, wherever they are found among any people, the good and benefit that comes to them hereby is and will be exceeding great.

We had this year a malignant drunken *Indian*, that (to cast some reproach, as wee feared, upon this way) boldly propounded this question, Mr. *Eliot* (said he) *Who made Sack? who made Sack?* but he was soon snib'd by the other *Indians*, calling it a *Papoose* question [That is a childish question.], and seriously and gravely answered (not so much to his question, as to his spirit) by Mr. *Eliot*, which hath cooled his boldnesse ever since, while others have gone on comfortably in this profitable and pleasant way.

The man who sent me these and the like questions with their severall answers in writing, concluded his letter with this story, which I shall here insert, that you may see the more of God among these poore people: "Upon the 25. of *Aprill* last (saith he) I had some occasion to go to speak with *Wabun* [An Indian Sachim.] about Sunrising in the morning, and staying some half an hours time, as I came back by one of the *Wigwams*, the man of that *Wigwam* was at prayer; at which I was so much affected, that I could not but stand under a Tree within hearing, though I could not understand but little of his words, and consider that God was fulfilling his Word, *viz. The ends of the earth shall remember themselves and turne unto him;* and that Scripture, *Thou art the God that hearest prayer, unto thee shall all flesh come.*

Also this present *September* I have observed one of them to call his children to him from their gathering of Corne in the field, and to crave a blessing, with much affection, having but a homely dinner to eate.{"}

These things me thinks should move bowels, and awaken *English* hearts to be thankfull, it is no small part of Religion to awaken with God in family prayer, (as it seemes these doe it early) and to crave a blessing with affectionate hearts upon a homely dinner, perhaps parcht Corne or *Indian* stalks: I wish the like hearts and wayes were seen in many *English* who professe themselves Christians, and that herein and many the like excellencies they were become *Indians*, excepting that name, as he did in another case, except his bonds: and that you may see not only how farre Religion, but civility hath taken place among them, you may be pleased therefore to peruse this Court Order, which is here inserted.

The Order made last Generall Court at Boston *the 26. of* May, 1647. *concerning the* Indians, &c.

U Pon information that the *Indians* dwelling among us, and submitted to our government, being by the Ministry of the Word brought to some civility, are desirous to have a course of ordinary Judicature set up among them: It is therefore ordered by authority of this Court, that some one or more of the Magistrates, as they shall agree amongst themselves, shall once every quarter keep a Court at such place, where the *Indians* ordinarily assemble to hear the Word of God, and may then hear and determine all causes both civill and criminall, not being capitall, concerning the *Indians* only, and that the *Indian Sachims* shall have libertie to take order in the nature of Summons or Attachments, to bring any of their own people to the said Courts, and to keep a Court of themselves, every moneth if they see occasion, to determine small causes of a civill nature, and such smaller criminall causes, as the said Magistrates shall referre to them; and the said *Sachims* shall appoint Officers to serve Warrants, and to execute the Orders and Judgements of either of the said Courts, which Officers shall from time to time bee allowed by the said Magistrates in the quarter Courts or by the Governour: And that all fines to bee imposed upon any *Indian* in any of the said Courts, shall goe and bee bestowed towards the building of some meeting houses, for education of their poorer children in learning, or other publick use, by the advice of the said Magistrates and of Master *Eliot*, or of such other Elder, as shall ordinarily instruct them in the true Religion. And it is the desire of this Court, that these Magistrates and Mr. *Eliot* or such other Elders as shall attend the keeping of the said Courts will carefully indeavour to make the Indians understand our most usefull Lawes, and the principles of reason, justice and equity whereupon they are grounded, & it is desired that some care may be taken of the *Indians* on the Lords dayes.

Thus having had a desire to acquaint you with these proceedings among the *Indians*, and being desirous that you might more fully understand, especially from him who is best able to judge, I did therefore intreat my brother *Eliot* after some conference about these things, to set down under his own hand what he hath observed lately among them: which I do therefore herein send unto you in his owne hand writing as he sent it unto mee, which I think is worthy all Christian thankfull eares to heare, and wherein they may see a little of the Spirit of this man of God, whom in other respects, but especially for his unweariednesse in this work of God, going up and down among them and doing them good, I think we can never love nor honour enough.

The Letter of Mr. Eliot *to* T.S. *concerning the late work of God among the* Indians.

Deare Brother,

A T your desire I have wrote a few things touching the *Indians* which at present came to my mind, as being some of those passages which took principall impression in my heart, wherein I thought I saw the Lord, and said the finger of God is here.

That which I first aymed at was to declare & deliver unto them the Law of God, to civilize them, wch course the Lord took by *Moses*, to give the Law to that rude company because of transgression, *Gal.* 3.19. to convince, bridle, restrain, and civilize them, and also to humble them. But when I first attempted it, they gave no heed unto it, but were weary, and rather despised what I said. A while after God stirred up in some of them a desire to come into the *English* fashions, and live after their manner, but knew not how to attain unto it, yea despaired that ever it should come to passe in their dayes, but thought that in 40. yeers more, some *Indians* would be all one *English*, and in an hundred yeers, all *Indians* here about, would so bee: which when I heard, (for some of them told me they thought so, and that some wise *Indians* said so) my heart moved within mee, abhorring that wee should sit still and let that work alone, and hoping that this motion in them was of the Lord, and that this mind in them was a preparative to imbrace the Law and Word of God; and therefore I told them that they and wee were already all one save in two things, which make the only difference betwixt them and us: First, we know, serve, and pray unto God, and they doe not: Secondly, we labour and work in building, planting, clothing our selves, &c. and they doe not: and would they but doe as wee doe in these things, they would be all one with *English* men: they said they did not know God, and therefore could not tell how to pray to him, nor serve him. I told them if they would learn to know God, I would teach them: unto which they being very willing, I then taught them (as I sundry times had indeavored afore) but never found them so forward, attentive and desirous to learn till this time, and then I told them I would come to their *Wigwams*, and teach them, their wives and children, which they seemed very glad of; and from that day forward I have not failed to doe that poore little which you know I doe.

I first began with the *Indians* of *Noonanetum*, as you know; those of *Dorchester mill* not regarding any such thing: but the better sort of them perceiving how acceptable this was to the *English,* both to Magistrates, and all the good people, it pleased God to step in and bow their hearts to desire to be taught to know God, and pray unto him likewise, and had not I gone unto them also, and taught them when I did, they had prevented me, and desired me so to do, as I afterward heard.

The effect of the Word which appears among them, and the change that is among them is this: First, they have utterly forsaken all their *Powwaws*, and given over that diabolicall exercise, being convinced that it is quite contrary to praying unto God; yea sundry of their *Powwaws* have renounced their wicked imployment, have condemned it as evill, and resolved never to use it any more; others of them, seeing their imployment and gaines were utterly gone here, have fled to other places, where they are still entertained, and have raised lies, slanders, and an evill report upon those that heare the Word, and pray unto God, and also upon the English that indeavour to reclaime them and instruct them, that so they might discourage others from praying unto God, for that they account as a principall signe of a good man, and call all religion by that name, praying to God; and beside they mock and scoffe at those Indians which pray, and blaspheme God when they pray; as this is one instance. A sober *Indian* going up into the countrey with two of his sons, did pray (as his manner was at home) and talked to them of God and Jesus Christ: but they mocked, & called one of his sons *Jehovah,* and the other *Jesus Christ*: so that they are not without opposition raised by the *Powwaws*, and other wicked Indians.

Againe as they have forsaken their former Religion, and manner of worship, so they doe pray unto God constantly in their families, morning and evening, and that with great affection, as hath been seen and heard by sundry that have gone to their *Wigwams* at such times; as also when they goe to meat they solemnly pray and give thanks to God, as they see the English to doe: so that that curse which God threatens to poure out upon the families that call not on his name, is through his grace, and tender mercy stayed from breaking forth against them, and when they come to English houses, they desire to be taught; and if meat bee given them, they pray and give thanks to God: and usually expresse their great joy, that they are taught to know God, and their great affection to them that teach them.

Furthermore they are carefull to instruct their children, that so when I come they might be ready to answer their Catechize, which by the often repeating of it to the children, the men and women can readily answer to.

Likewise they are carefull to sanctifie the Sabbath, but at first they could not tell how to doe it, and they asked of mee how they should doe it, propounding it as a question whether they should come to the English meetings or meet among themselves; they said, if they come to the English meetings they understand nothing, or to no purpose, and if they met together among themselves, they had none that could teach them. I told them that it was not pleasing to God, nor profitable to themselves, to hear and understand nothing, nor having any that could interpret to them. Therefore I counselled them to meet together, and desire those that were the wisest and best men to pray, and then to teach the rest such things as I had taught them from Gods Word, as well as they could; and when one hath done, then let another do the like, and then a third, and when that was done aske questions, and if they could not answer them, then remember to aske me, &c. and to pray unto God to help them therein: and this is the manner how they spend their Sabbaths.

They are also strict against any prophanation of the Sabbath, by working, fishing, hunting, &c. and have a Law to punish such as are delinquents therein by a fine of 10 s. and sundry cases they have had, wherein they have very strictly prosecuted such as have any way prophaned the Sabbath. As for example, upon a Sabbath morning *Cutchamaquin* the *Sachim* his wife going to fetch water met with other women, and she began to talk of worldly matters, and so held on their discourse a while, which evill came to *Nabantons* eare, who was to teach that day (this *Nabanton* is a sober good man, and a true friend to the English ever since our comming) so he bent his discourse to shew the sanctification of the Sabbath, & reproved such evils as did violate the same; & among other things worldly talk, and thereupon reproved that which he heard of that morning. After hee had done, they fell to discourse about it, and spent much time therein, hee standing to prove that it was a sinne, and she doubting of it, seeing it was early in the morning, and in private; and alledging that he was more to blame than she, because he had occasioned so much discourse in the publick meeting: but in conclusion they determined to refer the case to me, and accordingly they did come to my house on the second day morning and opened all the matter, and I gave them such direction as the Lord directed me unto, according to his holy Word.

Another case was this, upon a Lords day towards night two strangers came to *Wabans Wigwam* (it being usual with them to travaile on that day, as on any other; (and when they came in, they told him that at a place about a mile off they had chased a *Rackoone*, and he betook himself into an hollow tree, and if they would goe with them, they might fell the tree and take him: at which tidings, *Waban* being willing to be so well provided to entertain those strangers (a common practice among them, freely to entertain travailers and strangers) he sent his two servants with them, who felled the tree, and took the beast. But this act of his was an offence to the rest, who judged it a violation of the Sabbath, and moved agitation among them: but the conclusion was, it was to bee moved as a question upon the next Lecture day; which was accordingly done, and received such answer as the Lord guided unto by his Word.

Another case was this, upon a Lords day their publick meeting holding long, and somewhat late, when they came at home, in one *Wigwam* the fire was almost out, and therefore the man of the house, as he sate by the fire side took his Hatchet and split a little dry peece of wood, which they reserve on purpose for such use, and so kindled his fire, which being taken notice of, it was thought to bee such a worke as might not lawfully be done upon the Sabbath day, and therefore the case was propounded the Lecture following for their better information.

These instances may serve to shew their care of the externall observation of the Sabbath day.

In my exercise among them (as you know) wee attend foure things, besides prayer unto God, for his presence and blessing upon all we doe.

First, I catechize the children and youth; wherein some are very ready & expert, they can readily say all the Commandements, so far as I have communicated them, and all other principles about the creation, the fall, the redemption by Christ, &c. wherein also the aged people are pretty expert, by the frequent repetition thereof to the children, and are able to teach it to their children at home, and do so.

Secondly, I Preach unto them out of some texts of Scripture, wherein I study all plainnesse, and brevity, unto which many are very attentive.

Thirdly, if there be any occasion, we in the next place go to admonition and censure; unto which they submit themselves reverently, and obediently, and some of them penitently confessing their sins with much plainnesse, and without shiftings, and excuses: I will instance in two or three particulars; this was one cafe, a man named *Wampoowas*, being in a passion upon some light occasion did beat his wife, which was a very great offence among them now (though in former times it was very usuall) and they had made a Law against it, and set a fine upon it; whereupon he was publikly brought forth before the Assembly, which was great that day, for our Governor and many other English were then present: the man wholly condemned himself without any excuse: and when he was asked what provocation his wife gave him? he did not in the least measure blame her but himself, and when the quality of the sinne was opened, that it was cruelty to his own body, and against Gods Commandement, and that passion was a sinne, and much aggravated by such effects, yet God was ready to pardon it in Christ, &c. he turned his face to the wall and wept, though with modest indeavor to hide it; and such was the modest, penitent, and melting behavior of the man, that it much affected all to see it in a Barbarian, and all did forgive him, onely this remained, that they executed their Law notwithstanding his repentance, and required his fine, to which he willingly submitted, and paid it.

Another case of admonition was this, *Cutshamaquin* the *Sachim* having a son of about 14. or 15. yeers old, he had bin drunk, & had behaved himself disobediently, and rebelliously against his father and mother, for which sinne they did blame him, but he despised their admonition. And before I knew of it, I did observe when I catechized him, when he should say the fift Commandement, he did not freely say, *Honor thy father*, but wholly left out *mother*, and so he did the Lecture day before, but when this sinne of his was produced, he was called forth before the Assembly and hee confessed that what was said against him was true, but hee fell to accuse his father of sundry evils, as that hee would have killed him in his anger, and that he forced him to drink Sack, and I know not what else: which behavior wee greatly disliked, shewed him the evill of it, and Mr. *Wilson* being present laboured much with him, for hee understood the English, but all in vaine, his heart was hard and hopelesse for that time, therefore using due loving perswasions, wee did sharply admonish him of his sinne, and required him to answer further the next Lecture day, and so left him; and so stout he was, that when his father offered to pay his fine of 10 s. for his drunkennesse according to their Law, he would not except it at his hand. When the next day was come, and other exercises finished, I called him forth, and he willingly came, but still in the same mind as before. Then wee turned to his father, and exhorted him to remove that stumbling block out of his sonnes way, by confessing his own sinnes whereby hee had given occasion of hardnesse of heart to his sonne; which thing was not suddain to him, for I had formerly in private prepared him thereunto, and hee was very willing to hearken to that counsell, because his conscience told him he was blameworthy; and accordingly he did, he confessed his maine and principall evils of his own accord: and upon this advantage I took occasion to put him upon confession of sundry other vices which I knew hee had in former times been guilty of, and all the Indians knew it likewise; and put it after this manner, Are you now sorry for your drunkennesse, filthines, false dealing, lying, &c. which sinnes you committed before you knew God? unto all which cases, he expressed himself sorrowfull, and condemned himself for them: which example of the *Sachim* was profitable for all the Indians. And when he had thus confessed his sinnes, we turned againe to his sonne and laboured with him, requiring him to confesse his sinne, and intreat God to forgive him for Christ his sake, and to confesse his offence against his father and mother, and intreat them to forgive him, but he still refused; and now the other Indians spake unto him soberly, and affectionatly, to put him on, and divers spake one after another, and some severall times. Mr. *Wilson* againe did much labour with him, and at last he did humble himself, confessed all, and intreated his father to forgive him, and took him by the hand, at which his father burst forth into great weeping: hee did the same also to his mother, who wept also, and so did divers others; and many English being present, they fell a weeping, so that the house was filled with weeping on every side; and then we went to prayer, in all which time *Cutshamaquin* wept, in so much that when wee had done the board he stood upon was all dropped with his teares.

Another case of admonition was this, a hopefull young man who is my servant, being upon a journey, and drinking Sack at their setting forth, he drank too much, and was disguised; which when I heard I reproved him, and he humbled himself, with confession of his sinne, and teares. And the next Lecture day I called him forth before the Assembly, where he did confesse his sinne with many teares.

Before I leave this point of admonition, if I thought it would not bee two tedious to you, I would mention one particular more, where we saw the power of God awing a wicked wretch by this ordinance of admonition. It was *George* that wicked *Indian*, who as you know, at our first beginnings fought to cast aspersions upon Religion, by laying slanderous accusations against godly men, and who asked that captious question, *who made Sack?* and this fellow having kild a young Cow at your Towne, and sold it at the Colledge instead of *Moose*, covered it with many lies, insomuch as Mr. *Dunster* was loath he should be directly charged with it when we called him forth, but that wee should rather inquire. But when he was called before the Assembly, and charged with it, he had not power to deny it, but presently confessed, onely hee added one thing which wee think was an excuse; thus God hath honored this ordinance among them.

Fourthly, the last exercise, you know, we have among them, is their asking us questions, and very many they have asked, which I have forgotten, but some few that come to my present remembrance I will briefly touch.

One was *Wabbakowets* question, who is reputed an old *Powwaw*, it was to this purpose, seeing the English had been 27. yeers (some of them) in this land, why did wee never teach them to know God till now? had you done it sooner, said hee, wee might have known much of God by this time, and much sin might have been prevented, but now some of us are grown old in sin, &c. To whom we answered, that we doe repent that wee did not long agoe, as now we doe, yet withall wee told them, that they were never willing to hear till now, and that seeing God hath bowed their hearts to be willing to hear, we are desirous to take all the paines we can now to teach them.

Another question was, that of *Cutshamaquin*, to this purpose, Before I knew God, said he, I thought I was well, but since I have known God and sin, I find my heart full of sin, and more sinfull then ever it was before, and this hath been a great trouble to mee; and at this day my heart is but very little better then it was, and I am afraid it will be as bad againe as it was before, and therefore I sometime wish I might die before I be so bad again as I have been. Now my question is, whether is this a sin or not? This question could not be learned from the English, nor did it seem a coyned feigned thing, but a reall matter gathered from the experience of his own heart, and from an inward observation of himself.

Another question was about their children, Whither their little children goe when they dye, seeing they have not sinned?

Which question gave occasion more fully to teach them originall sin, and the damned state of all men: And also, and especially it gave occasion to teach them the Covenant of God, which he hath made with all his people, and with their children, so that when God chooses a man or a woman to be his servant, he chooses all their children to be so also: which doctrin was exceeding gratefull unto them.

Another great question was this, when I preached out of *I Cor.* 6.9,10,11. old Mr. *Brown*, being present, observed them to be much affected, and one especially did weep very much, though covered it what hee could; and after that there was a generall question, which they sent unto mee about, by my man, as the question of them all, *Whether any of them should goe to Heaven, seeing they found their hearts full of sinne, and especially full of the sinne of lust,* which they call *nanwunwudsquas,* that is, mad after women; and the next meeting, being at *Dorchester mill,* Mr. *Mather* and Mr. *Wareham,* with divers others being present, they did there propound it, expressing their feares, *that none of them should bee saved;* which question did draw forth my heart to preach and presse the promise of pardon to all that were weary and sick of sinne, if they did beleeve in Christ who had died for us, and satisfied the justice of God for all our sinnes, and through whom God is well pleased with all such repenting sinners that come to Christ, and beleeve in him; and the next day I took that Text, *Matth.* 11.28,29. and this doctrin some of them in a speciall manner did receive in a very reverent manner.

There is another great question that hath been severall times propounded, and much sticks with such as begin to pray, namely, *If they leave off* Powwawing, *and pray to God, what shall they do when they are sick?* for they have no skill in physick, though some of them understand the vertues of sundry things, yet the state of mans body, and skill to apply them they have not: but all the refuge they have and relie upon in time of sicknesse is their *Powwaws*, who by antick, foolish and irrationall conceits delude the poore people; so that it is a very needfull thing to informe them in the use of Physick, and a most effectuall meanes to take them off from their *Powwawing*. Some of the wiser sort I have stirred up to get this skill; I have shewed them the anatomy of mans body, and some generall principles of Physick, which is very acceptable to them, but they are so extreamely ignorant, that these things must rather be taught by sight, sense, and experience then by precepts, and rules of art; and therefore I have had many thoughts in my heart, that it were a singular good work, if the Lord would stirre up the hearts of some or other of his people in England to give some maintenance toward some Schoole or Collegiate exercise this way, wherein there should be Anatomies and other instructions that way, and where there might be some recompence given to any that should bring in any vegetable or other thing that is vertuous in the way of Physick; by this means we should soon have all these things which they know, and others of our Countreymen that are skilfull that way, and now their skill lies buried for want of incouragement, would be a searching and trying to find out the vertues of things in this countrey, which doubtlesse are many, and would not a little conduce to the benefit of the people of this Countrey, and it may bee of our native Countrey also; by this meanes wee should traine up these poore *Indians* in that skill which would confound and root out their *Powwaws*, and then would they be farre more easily inclined to leave those wayes, and pray unto God, whose gift Physick is, and whose blessing must make it effectuall.

There is also another reason which moves my thought and desires this way, namely that our young Students in Physick may be trained up better then yet they bee, who have onely theoreticall knowledge, and are forced to fall to practise before ever they saw an Anatomy made, or duely trained up in making experiments, for we never had but one Anatomy in the Countrey, which Mr. *Giles Firman* (now in England) did make and read upon very well, but no more of that now.

This very day that I wrote these things unto you, I have been with the *Indians* to teach them, as I was wont to doe, and one of their questions among many other was to know what to say to such *Indians* as oppose their praying to God, and beleeving in Jesus Christ, and for their own information also, What get you, say they, by praying to God, and beleeving in Jesus Christ? you goe naked still, and you are as poore as wee, and our Corne is as good as yours, and wee take more pleasure then you; did we see that you got any thing by it, wee would pray to God and beleeve in Jesus Christ also as you doe? Unto which question I then answered them. First, God giveth unto us two sorts of good things, one sort are little ones, which I shewed by my little finger; the other sort are great ones, which I shewed by my thumbe, (for you know they use and delight in demonstrations:) the little mercies are riches, as cloths, food, sack, houses, cattle, and pleasures, these are little things which serve but for our bodies a little while in this life; the great mercies are wisdome, the knowledge of God, Christ, eternall life, repentance, faith, these are mercies for the soule, and for eternall life: now though God do not yet give you the little mercies, he giveth you that which is a great deale better, which the wicked *Indians* cannot see. And this I proved to them by this example; when *Foxun* the *Mohegan* Counseller, who is counted the wisest *Indian* in the Country, was in the *Bay*, I did on purpose bring him unto you; and when he was here, you saw he was a foole in comparison of you, for you could speak of God and Christ, and heaven and repentance and faith, but he sate and had not one word to say, unlesse you talked of such poor things as hunting, wars, &c. Secondly, you have some more cloths then they, and the reason why you have no more is because you have but a little wisdome, if you were more wise to know God, and obey his Commands, you would work more then you do, for so God commandeth, *Six dayes thou shall work, &c.* and thus the English do: and if you would bee so wise as to worke as they do, you should have cloths, houses, cattle, riches as they have, God would give you them.

This day they told me this news, that some of them having been abroad in the Country at *Titacut*, divers of those *Indians* would be glad to know God, and to pray unto God, and would be glad if I would come and teach them, but some of them opposed and would not. They askt me this day, why God made the Rainbow. These things are now fresh in my mind, that makes me so large in them, but I'le forbeare any more of their questions of this nature.

There do sundry times fall out differences among them, and they usually bring their cases to me, and sometimes such, as it's needfull for me to decline; where I may, I advise them to some issue. One great case that hath come severall times to mee, is about such debts as they owe by gaming, for they have been great gamesters, but have moved questions about it, and are informed of the unlawfulnesse of it, and have thereupon wholly given over gaming for any wagers, and all games wherein is a lot, onely use lawfull recreations, and have a Law against unlawfull gaming; but other *Indians* that are of another mind, come and challenge their old debts, and now they refuse to pay, because it was a sinne so to game, and they now pray to God, and therefore must not pay such sinfull debts. Now the case being serious, and such as I saw a snare underneath, the first counsaile they had was, who ever would challenge such a debt should come to our Governor, and he would take order to rectifie the matter. But the Creditors liked not that way, and therefore soon after there came another case of the same kinde, and an issue was very necessary, therefore I first dealt with the creditor, and shewed him the sinfulnesse of such games, and how angry God was at them; and therefore perswaded him to be content to take half his debt, unto which he very willingly condescended; then I dealt with the debtor, and askt him if he did not promise to pay him all that debt? and he answered yea, he did so; then I shewed him that God commands us to performe our promises, and though he sinned in gaming, he must repent of that, but seeing he hath promised payment, he should sin to break his promise: at which he was utterly silenced; but then I asked him, if hee would willingly pay half, if I should perswade the other to accept it; yea said hee very willingly, and so the matter ended: and in this way they usually end such cases since that time. Their young men, who of all the rest, live most idlely and dissolutely, now begin to goe to service, some to *Indians*, some to *English*; and some of them growing weary, broak out of their services, and they had no help among them for it; so that some propounded what they should doe to remedy that evill; they were answered, that the English bring such servants to the Court, and our Magistrates rectifie those evills; then they desired that they might have a Court among them for government, at which motion wee rejoyced, seeing it came from themselves, and tended so much to civilize them, since which time I moved the Generall Court in it, and they have pleased to order a way for exercising government among them: the good Lord prosper and blesse it.

They moved also as you know for a School, and through Gods mercy a course is now taken that there be Schooles at both places where their children are taught.

You know likewise that wee exhorted them to fence their ground with ditches, stone walls, upon the banks, and promised to helpe them with Shovels, Spades, Mattocks, Crows of Iron; and they are very desirous to follow that counsell, and call upon me to help them with tooles faster then I can get them, though I have now bought pretty store, and they (I hope) are at work. The women are desirous to learn to spin, and I have procured Wheels for sundry of them, and they can spin pretty well. They begin to grow industrious, and find something to sell at Market all the yeer long: all winter they sell Brooms, Staves, Elepots, Baskets, Turkies. In the Spring, Craneberies, Fish, Stawberies; in the Summer Hurtleberries, Grapes, Fish; in the Autumn they sell Craneberries, Fish, Venison, &c. and they find a good benefit by the Market, and grow more and more to make use thereof; besides sundry of them work with the English in Hay time, and Harvest, but yet it's not comparable to what they might do, if they were industrious, and old boughs must be bent a little at once; if we can set the young twiggs in a better bent, it will bee Gods mercy. Deare brother I can go no further, a weary body, and sleepy eyes command me to conclude, if I have not satisfied your desire in this little I have wrote, let me understand it from you, and I shall be willing to do my indeavour: and thus with my deare love remembred to your self and your beloved yoakfellow, and desiring your prayers for Gods grace and blessing upon my spirit and poor indeavours, I take leave at this time and rest

Roxbury this 24. of   *Your loving brother in*

   Septemb.   *our Saviour Christ,*

   1647.   J O H N   E L I O T.

Let me adde this Postscript, that there be two reasons that make me beleeve the Lords time is come to make a preparative at least for the comming of his grace, and kingdome among them. First, that he hath bowed their hearts, who were as averse, and as farre off from God, as any heathen in the world; and their hearts begin to bow more and more. Secondly, because the Lord hath raised a mighty spirit of prayer in this behalfe in all the Churches.

This Relation of Mr. *Eliots* I know many things therein to be true, & all the rest I have heard confirmed by credible persons, eye & eare witnesses of these things, and they are familiarly known in these parts. I know also that Mr. *Eliot* writes (as his spirit is) modestly and sparingly, and speaks the least in sundry particulars; for in his story of the repentance and publike admonition of his own man, page 23 {128}. hee saith he manifested many teares in publike, but I heard it from many then present that there were so many, as that the dry place of the *Wigwam* where hee stood was bedirtied with them, powring them out so abundantly. *Indians* are well known not to bee much subject to teares, no not when they come to feele the sorest torture, or are solemnly brought forth to die; and if the Word workes these teares, surely there is some conquering power of Christ Jesus stirring among them, which what it will end in at last, the Lord best knows. If Mr. *Brightmans* interpretation of *Daniels* prophesie be true, that *Anno* 1650. Europe will hear some of the best tidings that ever came into the world, *viz.* rumors from the Easterne Jews, which shall trouble the Turkish tyrant and shake his Pillars when they are comming to repossesse their own land, for which they will be wrastling (if my memory failes not, according to his notion) about 40. yeers; I shall hope then that these Westerne *Indians* will soon come in, and that these beginnings are but preparatives for a brighter day then we yet see among them, wherein East & West shall sing the song of the Lambe: but I have no skill in prophesies, nor do I beleeve every mans interpretation of such Scripture; but this is certain, God is at work among these; and it is not usual for the Sun to set as soon as it begins to rise, nor for the Lord to Jesus to lose an inch of ground in the recovering times of his Churches peace and his own eclipsed and forgotten glory, (if these bee such times) untill hee hath won the whole field, and driven the Prince of darknesse out of it, who is but a bold usurper of the Lord Jesus inheritance, to whom are given the utmost ends of the earth. When *Charles* the Great had broken the chief power of the barbarous and fierce *Saxons* in *Germany*, he made this the onely article of peace, that they should entertain such a Gospel as good then as the degenerate Christian world could affoord, and for that end admit of a Monastery among them of such men as might instruct them, and this course prevailed, if wee may beleeve *Crantzius* the Historian of those times [Crantzius lib.1.ch,1,2.]; and shall wee think that when the Lord Jesus hath set up not a Monastery of workes but Churches of Saints in these coasts to encourage the ministry and this work of Christ, that his blessed Gospel cannot or shall not in these dayes take some effect since it hath broke so far? I dare conclude nothing, onely it will be our comfort in the day of our accounts, that wee have endeavored something this way; and it may be this very indeavour shall be our peace. *Gildas* our British Historian observing that one cause why God let loose the *Saxons* to scourge and root out the *Britaines*, was their deep carelesnesse of communicating unto them the Christian Religion, when they had their spirits at fit advantage: but I dare not discourse of these matters.

One thing more I remember concerning Mr. *Eliots* conference with a *Narraganset Sachim* a sober man this yeer; after that he had taught this *Sachim* the Law of God, and had shewen him the means of salvation by Christ; he then asked him if he did know and understand those things? and he said, yes. He then asked him if he did beleeve them? but hee could not get any answer from him that way, but did seeme to take them into more serious thoughts. He then asked him, why they did not learn of Mr. *Williams* who hath lived among them divers yeers? and he soberly answered that they did not care to learn of him, because hee is no good man but goes out and workes upon the Sabbath day; I name it not to shew what glimmerings nature may have concerning the observation of the Sabbath, but to shew what the ill example of English may doe, and to see what a stumbling block to all Religion the loose observation of the Sabbath is, however mans shifting wits may find out evasions, to get loose from out of that net.

But this may serve to satisfie your own or others desires concerning the progresse of the Gospel among the *Indians*: the Lord Jesus seemes at this day to bee turning upside down the whole frame of things in the world, Kings, Parliaments, Armies, Kingdomes, Authorities, Churches, Ministers, and if out of his free grace hee looks not upon these hopefull beginnings, these will be so turned also; for opposition there is from men and devils against it, and I have feared in my own heart that within these few moneths there hath been some coolings among the best of these *Indians*; but wee find it so also among many people that are *English* in their first work, but the Lord Jesus revives again; and therefore Mr. *Eliot* of late having told them that hee was afraid that they began to bee weary, they took it to heart, and propounded in my hearing at a late *Indian* Lecture at *Noonanetum* many profitable questions, viz. *When they prayed and heard the Word aright? and how they might know when they were weary of them? And what time it might bee before the Lord might come and make them know him? And what the first sinne of the Devils was?* (Hee discoursing to them about the danger of Apostasie.) At this time they are (as you may perceive by Mr. *Eliots* writings) about fencing in their ground and Town given them some hundreds of Acres, with a stone fence, for which end Mr. *Eliot* provides them Mattocks, Shovels and Crowes of Iron, &c. and to encourage their slothfulnesse, promised to give a groat or six pence a rod, if they would thus farre attend their own good, and work for themselves: all the poor *Indians* at *Noonanetum* are generally clad with such cloths as wee can get them, and the *Wigwams* of the meanest of them equallize any *Sachims* in other places, being built not with mats but barks of Trees in good Bignesse, the rather that they may have their partitions in them for husbands and wives togeather, and their children and servants in their places also, who formerly were never private in what nature is ashamed of, either for the sun or any man to see. It's some refreshing to thinke that there is (if there was no more but) the name of Christ sounding in those darke and despicable *Tartarian* Tents; the Lord can build them houses in time to pray in, when hee hath given unto them better hearts, and when perhaps hee hath cursed and consumed theirs who have disdained to give that worship and homage to Christ in their seiled houses, which poor *Indians* rejoyce to give to him in their poor Tents and *Wigwams*: I desire you to gather what stock of prayers you can for them. I had almost forgot to tell you of Mr. *Eliots* going up the Country lately with Mr. *Flint*, Captain *Willard* of *Concord*, and sundry others, towards *Merrimath* River unto that *Indian Sachim Passaconnaway*, that old Witch and *Powwaw*, who together with both his sons, fled the presence of the light, and durst not stand their ground, nor be at home when he came, pretending feare of being killed by a man forsooth that came only with a book in his hand, and with a few others without any weapons only to bear him company and direct his way in those deserts; but in it you may see the guilt of the man, & that *Satan* is but a coward in his Lyons skin even upon his own dunghill, as also the hatred and enmity against the Word which is in some, which argues that the attention which others give to it, is a power of God, and not meerly to flatter and get favour with the English: but the rest of *Passaconnawaies* men attended to the things which were spoken and asked divers questions, the *Indians* in our parts accompanying Mr. *Eliot* and giving blessed examples to the others herein, as also in saying Grace before and after meat, praying in their *Wigwams* with them, and some of them singing of Psalmes, which they have learnt among the English: discoursing also with them about the things of God. It is somewhat observable (though the observation bee more cheerfull then deep) that the first Text out of which Mr. *Eliot* preached to the *Indians* was about the dry bones, *Ezek*. 37. where it's said, *Vers*. 9,10. *that by prophesying to the wind, the wind came and the dry bones lived;* now the Indian word for Wind is *Waubon*, and the most active *Indian* for stirring up other *Indians* to seek after the knowledg of God in these parts, his name is *Waubon*, which signifies Wind, (the *Indians* giving names to their children usually according to appearances of providences) although they never dreamt of this, that this their *Waubon* should breathe such a spirit of life and incouragement into the rest of the *Indians*, as hee hath indeavored in all parts of the Countrey, both at *Concord, Merrimeck* and elsewhere; but some of the *Indians* themselves that were stir'd up by him took notice of this his name and that Scripture together, and the English also have much observed him herein, who still continues the same man, although we thinke there be now many others whom he first breathed encouragement into that do farre exceed him in the light and life of the things of God: Mr. *Eliot* also professing that he chose that Text without the least thought of any such application in respect of *Waubon*.

There have been many difficult questions propounded by them, which we have been unwilling to engage our selves in any answer unto, untill wee have the concurrence of others with us.

First, suppose a man before hee knew God, hath had two wives, the first barren and childlesse, the second fruitfull and bearing him many sweet children, the question now propounded was, *Which of these two wives he is to put away?* if hee puts away the first who hath no children, then hee puts away her whom God and Religion undoubtedly binds him unto, there being no other defect but want of children: if hee puts away the other, then he must cast off all his children with her also as illegitimate, whom hee so exceedingly loves. This is a case now among them, and they are very fearefull to do any thing crosse to

Gods will and mind herein.

Secondly, suppose a man marry a *Sqaw*, and shee deserts and flies from her husband, and commits adultery with other remote *Indians*, but afterward it come to passe that shee hearing the Word, and sorry for what shee hath done, she desires to come to her husband againe, who remaines still unmarried; *Whether should this husband upon her repentance receive her againe? and whether is he not bound thereunto so to doe?*

At the last Lecture at *Noonanetum* this *September*, there were divers questions asked: one was propounded by an old *Sqaw*, a Widow: viz. *If when men know God, God loves them, why then is it that any one are afflicted after that they know him?* I shall mention no more, but conclude with the solemn speech of a sober and hopefull *Indian* at this Lecture, whose name is *Wampooas*, who in stead of propounding a question fell into these expressions, viz. "That because wee pray to God, other *Indians* abroad in the countrey hate us and oppose us, the English on the other side suspect us, and feare us to be still such as doe not pray at all; but (saith he) God who knowes all things, he knowes that wee do pray to him.{"} To which speech Mr. *Eliot* replyed, that it was true indeed, that some of the English did so far suspect them for sundry reasons; but I doe not so, and others of us, who know you and speake with you, we do not so think of you; and then gave them gracious and serious incouragements to goe forward and make more progresse in the things of God. This their own testimony of themselves being propounded with much sweetnesse and seriousnesse of affection, may be the last, although it be the least confirmation of some inward worke among them; which I looked upon as a speciall providence that such a speech should be spoken and come to my eare just at such a time as this, wherein I was finishing the story, to confirme in some measure what hath been written; the Lord himself I beleeve and no man living, putting these words into their own hearts, to give this modest testimony concerning themselves. The beginning of this enlargement of Christs Kingdome should inlarge our hearts with great joy. If I should gather and summe up together the severall gracious impressions of God upon them from what hath been scattered here and there in the story, I thinke it might make many Christians ashamed, who may easily see how farre they are exceeded by these naked men in so short a time thus wrought upon by such small and despicable means. My brother *Eliot* who is Preacher to them, professing he can as yet but stammer out some peeces of the Word of God unto them in their own tongue; but God is with him, and God is wont to be *maximus in minimis*, and is most seene in doing great things by small meanes. The Sword of Gods Word shall and will pierce deep, even when it is half broken, when the hand of a mighty Redeemer hath the laying of it on: and the Scripture herein is, and must be fulfilled, that as soon as the heathen heare Christ they shall submit, *Psal.* 18.43,44. and such nations whom Christ knew not shall run unto him, *Isaiah.* 55.5. The fall of the unbeleving Jewes was the rising of the Gentiles; my prayer to God therefore for *Europe* is, that the fall of the Churches, (little bettered by the devouring Sword which is still thirsty) may not bee the rising of these *American* Gentiles, never pitied till now. I wish that *Alstedius* [Alsted in Apoc.]

prophesie herein may never prove true; but rather that the rising of these may be a provoking and raising up of them, especially of the English, to lament after that God whom they have forsaken; and to lament after him, together with us, for these poor *Indians* who never yet knew him.

Sir, I had ended these relations once or twice, but the stay of the Vessell increaseth new matter; which because 'tis new and fresh, you shall have it as I heard of it from a faithfull hand: There were sundry questions propounded at the *Indian* Lecture at *Noonanetum* this *Octob*.13. by the *Indians*: the first was propounded to Mr. *Eliot* himself upon occasion of his Sermon out of *Ephes.* 5.11. *Have no fellowship with unfruitfull workers of darknes*, viz. *What English men did thinke of* Mr. Eliot *because he came among wicked Indians to teach them?*

Secondly, *Suppose two men sinne, the one knowes he sinneth, and the other doth not know sinne, will God punish both alike?*

Thirdly, *Suppose there should be one wise Indian that teacheth good things to other Indians, whether should not he be as a father or brother unto such Indians he so teacheth in the wayes of God?* This last question seemes to argue some motions stirring in some of their hearts to pity and teach their poor Countreymen; and surely then will bee the most hopefull time of doing good among them, when the Lord shall raise up some or other like themselves to go among them and preach the Word of life unto them with fatherly or brotherly bowels; and yet I limit not the most High, who can make use of what Instruments hee pleaseth for this work. I shall conclude therefore with a story I had both by writing and word of mouth, from a faithfull man [Mr. Edward Jackson.] which hee saw with his own eyes this *Octob*.7. There was one of the *Indians* at *Noonanetum*, hath had a child sick of a Consumption many a day, and at that time died of it; when it was dead, some of the *Indians* came to an honest man to enquire how they should bury their dead; the man told them how and what the English did when they buried theirs; hereupon rejecting all their old superstitious observances at such sad times (which are not a few) they presently procured a few boards, and buy a few nayles of the *English*, and so make a pretty handsome Coffin, (for they are very dextrous at any thing they see once done) and put the child into it, and so accompanied it to the grave very solemnly, about 40. *Indians* of them: when the earth was cast upon it and the grave made up, they withdrew a little from that place, and went all together and assembled under a Tree in the Woods; and there they desired one *Tutaswampe* a very hopefull *Indian* to pray with them; now although the *English* do not usually meet in companies to pray together after such sad occasions, yet it seemes God stird up their hearts thus to doe; what the substance of their prayer was I cannot certainly learn, although I have heard some things that way, which I therefore name not, onely I have and shall indeavour to get it, if it bee possible for the poor *Indian* to expresse the substance of it, and so shall send it if the ship stayes long, onely this is certaine by him who was occasionally an eye and eare witnesse of these things, that they continued instant with God in prayer for almost half an houre together, and this godly mans words to mee (who understands a little of their language) are these; that this *Tutaswampe* did expresse such zeale in prayer with such variety of gracious expressions, and abundance of teares, both of himself and most of the company, that the woods rang againe with their sighes and prayers; and (saith he) I was much ashamed of my self and some others, that have had so great light, and yet want such affections as they have, who have as yet so little knowledge. All this he saw standing at some good distance alone from them under a Tree.

Thus you see (Sir) that these old obdurate sinners are not altogether senselesse of Gods afflicting hand and humbling providences; and though naturall affection may be much stirring in such times, yet you see how God begins to sanctifie such affections among them: and I wish that many English were not outstript herein by these poor *Indians*, who have got the start I feare of many *English*, that can passe by such sad providences without laying them in this manner to heart. I confesse these and many such things which wee see in divers of them, do make some to thinke that there is more of God and his Spirit in some of their hearts then we yet can discover, and which they hope will break out in time.

Thus you have a true, but somewhat rent and ragged relation of these things; it may be most sutable to the story of naked and ragged men: my desire is that no mans Spectacles may deceive him, so as to look upon these things either as bigger or lesser, better or worser then they are; which all men generally are apt to doe at things at so great distance, but that they may judge of them as indeed they are, by what truth they see here exprest in the things themselves. I know that some thinke that all this worke among them is done and acted thus by the *Indians* to please the *English*, and for applause from them; and it is not unlikely but so 'tis in many, who doe but blaze for a time; but certainly 'tis not so in all, but that the power of the Word hath taken place in some, and that inwardly and effectually, but how far savingly time will declare, and the reader may judge of, by the story it self of these things. Some say that if it be so, yet they are but a few that are thus wrought upon; Be it so, yet so it hath ever been, *many called, few chosen:* and yet withall I beleeve the calling in of a few *Indians* to Christ is the gathering home of many hundreds in one, considering what a vast distance there hath been between God and them so long, even dayes without number; considering also how precious the first fruits of America will be to Jesus Christ, and what seeds they may be of great harvests in after times; and yet if there was no great matter seen in these of grown yeers, their children notwithstanding are of great hopes both from *English* and *Indians* themselves, who are therefore trained up to Schoole, where many are very apt to learne, and who are also able readily to answer to the questions propounded, containing the principles and grounds of all Christian Religion in their own tongue. I confesse it passeth my skill to tell how the Gospel should be generally received by these *American* Natives, considering the variety of Languages in small distances of places; onely hee that made their eares and tongues can raise up some or other to teach them how to heare, and what to spake; and if the Gospel must ride circuit, Christ can and will conquer by weake and despicable meanes, though the conquest perhaps may be somewhat long. The beginnings and foundations of the *Spaniard* in the Southerne parts of this vast continent, being laid in the blood of nineteene

Millions of poor innocent Natives (as *Acosta* the Jesuite a bird of their own nest relates the story) shall certainly therefore bee utterly rooted up by some revenging hand; and when he is once dispossest of his Golden Mansions and Silver Mines, it may be then the oppressed remnant in those coasts also may come in. In the meane while if it bee the good pleasure of Christ to look upon any of the worst and meanest of these outcasts in these Coasts of *New-England*, let us not despise this day of small things, but as the Jews did of old, so let us now cry mightily to God and say, and sing, *Let the people praise thee O God, yea let all the people praise thee, then shall the earth bring forth her increase, and God even our God will blesse us.*

I have sent you two witnesses beside my own of the truth
of the Indian story printed, you may publish them if
you please as they have writ, and subscrib'd with their
own hands.

THOMAS SHEPHARD.

FINIS.

THE
Glorious Progress
OF THE
GOSPEL,
AMONGST THE
Indians in New England.

MANIFESTED

By three Letters, under the Hand of that famous Instrument of the Lord Mr. JOHN ELIOT, And another from Mr. *Thomas Mayhew* jun: both Preachers of the Word, as well to the *English* as *Indians* in *New England*.

WHEREIN

The riches of Gods Grace in the effectuall calling of many of them is cleared up: As also a manifestation of the hungring desires of many People in sundry parts of that Country, after the more full Revelation of the Gospel of *Jesus Christ*, to the exceeding Consolation of every Christian Reader.

TOGETHER,

With an Appendix to the foregoing Letters, holding forth Conjectures, Observations, and Applications. By *I. D.* Minister of the Gospell.

Published by EDWARD WINSLOW

Mal. 1.11. *From the rising of the Sun, even unto the going down of the same, my Name shall be great among the Gentiles, and in every place incence shall be offered unto my Name, and a pure Offering; for my Name shall be great among the Heathen, saith the Lord of Hosts.*

LONDON, Printed for *Hannah Allen* in *Popes-head-Alley.* 1649.

Photo courtesy of the Newberry Library, Chicago.

THE
Glorious Progress
OF THE
G O S P E L,
AMONGST THE
Indians in New England.
MANIFESTED

By three Letters, under the Hand of that famous Instrument of the Lord Mr. JOHN ELIOT,
And another from Mr. *Thomas Mayhew* jun: both Preachers of
the Word, as well to the *English* as *Indians* in *New England*.

W H E R E I N

The riches of Gods Grace in the effectuall calling of
many of them is cleared up: As also a manifestation of the hungring
desires of many People in sundry parts of that Country, after the
more full Revelation of the Gospel of *Jesus Christ*, to the
exceeding Consolation of every Christian Reader.

TOGETHER,

With an Appendix to the foregoing Letters, holding forth Conjectures, Observations, and Applications.
By I {J}. D. Minister of the Gospell.

Published by EDWARD WINSLOW

Mal. 1.11. *From the rising of the Sun, even unto the going down of the
same, my Name shall be great among the Gentiles, and in every place incence shall be offered unto my Name, and a pure Offering; for my Name
shall be great among the Heathen, saith the Lord of Hosts.*

LONDON, Printed for *Hannah Allen* in *Popes-head-Alley*. 1649.

TO THE

RIGHT HONOURABLE

THE

Parliament of England

AND THE COUNCELL

OF STATE.

Right Honourable,

That former Narative called, *The clear Sunshine of the Gospel, breaking forth upon the Indians in New England;* dedicated to your Honours by divers Reverend and eminent Ministers of the Gospell in and about the City of London, found such acceptance in your House, as it begat a debate amongst your selves, how the Parliament of England might be serviceable to the Lord Jesus, to help forward such a work begun; which conduced so abundantly to the glory of God, and good of men in the salvation of their soules. And in order thereunto your Honours were pleased to refer it to the Committee of forraign plantations, to prepare and bring in an Ordinance *for the encouragement and advancement of Learning and Piety in New England,* as appeareth by your Order March 17, 1647. This Honourable Committee with great readiness and chearfulness took it into their serious consideration, and presented the result of their mature debates to this honourable House: But so many and weighty have been the occasions and businesses of the House, that however the nature of the work and my duty (being appointed Agent though unworthy) on the behalf of New-England to this Parliament: yet durst not presse too hard to interrupt the great affaires your Honours have been in hand withall. Nevertheles, I do now crave leave, humbly to acquaint you, that what was then judged deficient in the power granted to the Feoffees in that Ordinance, is since corrected and amended, and attendeth your Honours leisure for compleating and finishing the same.

Undoubtedly the common enemy of mans salvation hath rejoyced that this work so happily begun, hath not as yet received that countenance and encouragement from hence, which your Honours intended and resolved many months since. Nevertheles, I trust the most wise God hath turned this appearing losse into gaine, by affording your Honours and the Nation a more clear account of the reall and glorious Progres of the Gospel among those poor Indians in

AMERICA, by such Intelligence I very lately received from thence, under the hands of those Reverend & learned Ministers, which are principally employed in preaching the Gospel to them in their own Language. And as I am daily and earnestly called upon to publish the same, that the whole Nation may be acquanted therewith: So I took it to be my duty to present it in the first place to this honourable HOUSE, and the Councel of State; that your HONOURS might perceive how these poor Creatures cry out for help; Oh come unto us, teach us the knowledge of God, tarry longer with us, come and dwell amongst us, at least depart not so soon from us. And others of them whose dwellings are near the Habitations of the English, (whose hearts God hath touched) calling for and demanding a free and full participation of all the Ordinances of Jesus Christ. All which, and much more is evidently held forth in the following Narrative, which I have with all faithfulnes collected and transcribed, according as I received the same from persons that were Actors therein, and are of known Integrity.

There are two great questions Right Honourable, which have much troubled ancient and modern writers, and men of greatest depth and ability to resolve: the first, what became of the ten Tribes of Israel, that were carried into Captivity by the King of Siria, when their own Countrey and Cities were planted and filled with strangers? The second is, what Family, Tribe, Kindred, or people it was that first planted, and afterwards filled that vast and long unknown Countrey of America? Now however I confesse questions are sooner asked then resolved; yet let me acquaint your Honors, that a godly Minister of this City writing to Rabbi-ben-Israel, a great Dr. of the Jewes, now living at Amsterdam, to know whether after all their labor, travells, and most diligent enquiry, they did yet know what was become of the ten Tribes of Israel? His answer was to this effect, if not in these words, That they were certainly transported into America, and that they had infallible tokens of their being there. Unto which if I may take the boldnesse to adde what my self, with many others in New England have observed in the practice of the Indians there, in relation to some things enjoyned in the ceremonial Law of Moses, about the purification of weomen, which no men at this day do observe, nor beside the Jewes were ever known in that strictness to observe, as these Indians there daily do: As also is the principles of the most grave and sober amongst them, not only in reference to a Deity, the soule of man, the immortality of the soule, and an eternity after death in happines or misery; but also their manifold daily expressions, bewailing the losse of that knowledge their Ancestors had about God, and the way of his Worship; the general deluge, and of one man only that ever saw God, which they hold forth to be a long time since, (even with the greatest expression of length of time that may be) which certainly I believe to be *Moses*. As also if many other Circumstances well known to many, (but not fit to be at large expressed in any Epistle) be duly considered, It is not lesse probable that these Indians should come from the Stock of *Abraham*, then any other Nation this day known in the world: *E*specially considering the juncture of time wherein God hath opened their hearts to entertain the Gospel, being so nigh the very years, in which many eminent and learned Divines, have from Scripture grounds, according to their apprehensions foretold the conversion of the *Jewes*. However Right Honourable, the work of communicating and encreasing the light of the Gospel is glorious in reference to *Jewes & Gentiles*. And as God hath set a signall marke of his presence upon your Assembly, in strengthning your hands to redeem and preserve the civill Rights of the Common-weale: so doubtlesse may it be a comfortable support to your Honours in any future difficulties, to contemplate, that as the Lord offered you (in this designe) an happy opportunity to enlarge and advance the Territories of his Sonnes Kingdom: So he hath not denyed you (as I am confident he will not) an heart to improve the same; and in as much as lies in you to make all the Nations of the Earth, the Kingdoms of the Lord, and of his Christ; that so your Honours may still preserve your interest in his favour, which is and shall be the prayers of

Your Honours most humble Servant,

EDWARD WINSLOW.

THE

GLORIOUS PROGRESSE

of the Gospel amongst the *Indians*

in *New-England.*

I N the year of our Lord, 1646. it seemed good to the most high God, to stirre up some reverend Ministers of the Gospel in *New-England,* to consider how they might be serviceable to the Lord Jesus, as well towards the Natives of that Countrey, (as to their owne Congregations and Churches, over which the Lord had set them) in bringing them to a right understanding of God and hemselves; and so by degrees to hold forth unto them that Salvation by Jesus Christ to all that should beleeve and obey his Commands; perswading themselves, that God might have a select people amongst these Heathens, and that for that end amongst many others he had planted so many Christian Congregations so neer them. And however the English were not wholly negligent this way, but had in sundry parts of the Countrey long before brought divers to a pretty competency of right understanding in the mystery of salvation, who lived orderly, and dyed hopefully; yet till such time as they were more generally acquainted with our conversation amongst our selves, and with our demeanor towards them, as well in peace, as in such warres they had unavoidably drawn upon themselves; whereby they had such experience of the justice, prudence, valour, temperance, and righteousnesse of the *English*, as did not onely remove their former jealousies and feares concerning us, and convict them of their owne uneven walking; but begat a good opinion of our persons, and caused them to affect our Laws and Government.

Till now (together with the want of language) we had but some few that were wrought upon; But in this acceptable year of the Lord, (being it seems the appointed season for their visitation) God having stirred up these Ministers to seek a Blessing upon their endeavours, and direct them in a right way; they found the answer of their prayers by the good acceptation they had amongst the poore *Indians* where they first went, &c. who soon became in love also with our Religion, and mightily hungred and thirsted after the Knowledge of God in

Christ, as was published and made apparant to this Nation by a short Treatise, called, *The day-breaking, if not the Sun-rising of the Gospel with the Indians in New-England.*

In the year 1647. being here upon some speciall service for the Countrey, Letters came to my hands with some Papers from Mr. *Tho. Shepard*, Pastor of the Church at *Cambridge* there, which held forth a greater warmth of heavenly heat upon their (former frozen) spirits; which I communicated to some eminent Ministers of and neere the City of *London; viz.* Mr. *Marshall*, Mr. *Downham*, Mr. *Thomas Goodwin*, Mr. *Whitaker*, Mr. *Nye*, Mr. *Case*, Mr. *Calamy*, Mr. *Sydrack Simpson*, Mr. *Ash*, Mr. *Greenhill*, Mr. *Carter*; and Mr. *Bolton*: And such was the esteem these reverend men had of it, as by two severall Epistles under their hands they recommended it to the Parliament of *England*, as a thing worthy their notice, care, and furtherance: And secondly, to the godly and well-affected of this Nation, who pray for, and rejoyce in the thrivings of the Gospel of our Lord Jesus. This Narrative was also published, and called, *The clear Sun-Shine of the Gospel breaking forth upon the Indians in New-England.*

In the year 1648. our Letters miscarried many of them, in that the Ship that brought them was taken by the Prince of *Wales*, to the Countries great prejudice, as well as many other Vessels and their lading formerly; by which miscarriage I was wholly hindred from giving any further account till this instant, 1649.

And now having received some Letters, and others brought to me by divers of quality here residing at present, that appertaine to *New-England;* and being exceedingly pressed to publish them by many godly and well-affected of the City and parts adjacent, I shall by Gods help publish them all, or so many of them as concernes the *Indian* work; and if any doubt my faithfulnesse herein, (as I hope none will that know me) I shall most willingly shew them the Originalls themselves. And before I come to this years Letters, I received from Mr. *Eliot,* shall begin with one came to my hands, (dated *Nov.* 1647.) after the last Treatise was put out. And I the rather take this course; lest the young man should be discouraged in his labours so hopefully begun; his name is Mr. *Mayhew*, who teacheth the Word both to *English* and *Indians* upon an Island called formerly *Capawack*, by us *Morthas Vineyard*, by which you may see 'tis not one Minister alone that laboureth in this great work: His Letter followeth:

S I R,   [Mr. Mayhews Letter from Capawack. Novemb. 18, 1647.]

THe encouragements I met withall touching the *Indians* conversion, next unto Gods glory, and his gracious promises was, the notable reason, judgement, and capacitie that God hath given unto many of them; as also their zealous enquiring after true hapinesse, together with the knowledge I had of their tongue, besides severall providences which hath advantaged my progresse therein; as for instance:

1. There was one *Ieogiscat* about 60. years of age, who was sick of a consuming disease, insomuch as the *Indian Pawwawwes* gave him over for a dead man: Upon which resolution of all the *Pawwawes* [Such as cure by

devillish sorcery, and to whom the devil appeares sometimes.] in the Island, the sick distressed Heathen upon a Lords day came unto mee (the rest of the *English* being then present) to desire me to pray unto God for him: And so when I had by reasoning with him convinced him of the weaknesse and wickednesse of the *Pawwaws* power; and that if health were to be found, it must be had from him that gave life, and breath, and all things; I commended this case unto the Lord, whereof he rejoyced, gave me thanks, and he speedily recovered unto his former strength.

2. In this present year 1647. the eldest sonne of one *Vakapenessue*, a great Sagamore of the Island, being very sick, took occasion to send for me to come unto him; and when I came unto him, I found him not more weak in body, then strong in earnest desires, that I should pray unto God for him; so I instructed him, and prayed for him: And when I had ended, of his own accord he spake these words, *Taubot mannit nuh quam Cowin. viz.* I thank thee God, I am heavy to sleep; and so I left him holding forth good affections: But shortly after he was changed altogether, and contrary to the perswasion of other *Indians* of severall Townes, sought againe unto Witches. The Heathen seeing this, they forsook the *Wigwam* [The Indians so call their houses.], saying, We leave the house for the Devill and them that would tarry. This newes being brought me, I much mervailed thereat, yet sent him this message, *viz.* Tell *Saul;* (for the sick man was by the *English* so called) that when I was with him, I thought as then I told him, that he would live; because he sought for life unto the living God, where if anywhere it was to be found: But tell him now, that I think he will dye. I also added the example of *Ahaziah*, who because he had the knowledge of the great God, and sought unto an inferiour God; God was angry with him, and killed him: And so for that this *Saul* was informed of the true God, and is fallen from him to the earthen gods here below; that God will kill him also; and so it shortly came to passe.

3. Not long after a *Sagamore* [A Prince or Ruler amongst them.], called, *Towanquattick* had his eldest sonne, whose name is *Sachachanimo*, very sick of a Feaver; this young man sent for me to come unto him; and when I came, his father and himself desired me to pray for him, the which I did in their owne language, and promised to come againe unto him very shortly, if he mended not, and use some other meanes also for his recovery: When I came againe unto him, I found him very ill, asked him (together with his friends) whether they were willing I should let him blood? acquainting them that we used so to do in such cases. After some consideration, they consented thereunto, notwithstanding the *Pawwaws* had told them before, that he should dye, because he sought not unto them: so I bound his arme, and with my Pen-knife let him blood; he bled freely, but was exceeding faint, which made the Heathen very sad; but in a short time, he begun to be very cheerfull, whereat they much rejoyced, &c. So I left them, and it pleased the Lord the man was in a short time after very well.

In these providences the Lord hath manifested both mercy and judgement, and it is, that he may raise up the Tabernacle of *David* that is fallen, and close up the breaches thereof, and raise up its ruines, and build it as in the dayes of old, that they may possesse the Covenant of *Edom*, and of all the Heathen which are called by my Name, saith the Lord that doth this.

But I pray you take notice of a speech of *Towanquattick* (being the Father of the young man recovered) who lamenting the losse of their knowledge said unto me, *That a long time agon, they had wise men, which in a grave manner taught the people knowlege, but they are dead, and their wisedome is buried with them: and now men live a giddy life in ignorance till they are white headed, and though ripe in yeares, yet then they go without Wisedom unto their graves.* [An indian speech worthy our consideration.] He also told me; that *he wondred the English should be almost thirty yeers in the Country, and the Indians fools still; but he hoped that the time of knowledge was now come;* wherefore himself with others desired me to give them an Indian meeting, to make known the word of God unto them in their own tongue. And when he came to me to accomplish his desire thereabout, he told me, that *I should be to them, as one that stands by a running River, filling many vessels: Even so should I fill them with everlasting knowledge.* [The better sort of them are full of such like expressions, affecting to speak in Parables.] So I undertook to give them a meeting once a moneth; but as soon as the first exercise was ended, they desired it oftner then I could well attend: but once a Fortnight is our setled course. This I present to your consideration; entreating you to present us unto the Lord for wisedome, to preach unto the Heathen the unsearchable riches of Christ, that so the root of *Jesse* standing for an Ensigne of the people, the Gentiles may seek unto it, and his rest shall be glorious, *Amen.*

Great Harbour in the Vineyard   Yours in the best Bonds

18. *of the* 9. 1647.   *Tho. Mahew, junior.*

In the next place, I shall present you with some Letters of that painfull yet unwearied Minister of the Gospel, Mr. John Eliot, *who notwithstanding his faithfull labours in teaching that Church or Congregation of the English, over which the Lord hath set him at* Roxbury *in the Government of the* Massachusets, *yet taketh all occasions, (neglecting no opportunity, whether more remote, or neere at hand) to advance the glory of God, in calling those poor heathen to the saving knowledge of Jesus Christ, and satisfying those hungry soules by administring the bread of life unto them. And however I cannot give you his first large Letter (as he tearmes it) being sent by Way of* Spaine, *and by that meanes not yet come to my hands, yet take his second in his own words, which will minister abundance of sweet consolation to every Christian Reader, that God should in these latter times so magnifie his glorious grace in extending his everlasting mercies to those poor naked Indians. His Letter followeth.*

Worthy Sir, [Mr. Eliots 2. Letter in 48. concerning the progresse of the Gospel among the Indians.]

Y Our cordiall and faithfull endeavours, &c. I am bold now by the way of *Virginia*, to trouble you with a few lines, to expresse the thankfulnesse of my heart unto you for that one part of your care, love, and labour in furthering this work of preaching Christ to these poor *Indians*, and declaring to them the way of eternall life and salvation; which work I blesse the Lord goeth on not without successe, beyond the ability of the Instruments: It is the Lord, the Lord only who doth speak to the hearts of men, and he can speak to theirs, and doth, (blessed be his name) so effectually, that one of them I beleeve verily is gone to the Lord: a woman [A precious testimony of an indian woman conceived to dye a Christian.], who though she was not the first that came into the knowledge of Christ and the Gospel, yet she was the first of ripe yeares that hath dyed since I taught them the way of salvation by Jesus Christ, and the onely one. And though of the living I will not say much, yet of the dead I may freely speak; After I began to preach unto them, her husband and she did quickly come in; and after she came, she was a diligent hearer; and out of desire to live where the word of God was taught, they fetched all the corne they spent, sixteen miles upon their backs from the place of their planting: She was industrious, and did not goe about to *English* houses a begging, as sundry doe, (though it is well reformed now with many of them) but kept home, kept her children to labour, making baskets to sell, &c. She quickly learned to spin well (for I got some wheels, but want meanes to supply them and order them.) Her life was blamelesse after she submitted to the Gospel, and was exemplary: She was the first woman that asked a question (by another man propounded for her) which was this: *When my Husband prayeth in his house, my heart thinketh what he prayeth; whether is this praying to God aright or no?* I thought it a fit question for a woman. She dyed of a sicknesse she took in childbed: I severall times visited her, prayed with her, asked her about her spirituall estate? *She told me: she still loved God, though he made her sick, and was resolved to pray unto him so long as she lived, and to refuse powwawing.* She said also, *that she beleeved God would pardon all her sins, because she beleeved that Jesus Christ dyed for her; and that God was well pleased in him, and that she was willing to dye, and beleeved to goe to Heaven, and live happy with God and Christ there.*

It may be you may mervell at, and scarce credit such expressions: but they are the points of Catechisme which I constantly teach the Children; and the Children can very readily answer me in them; and they be truths now familiarly known by the attentive hearers, whereof she was one. And moreover of her own accord, she called her children to her, especially two up-grown daughters, which she had before she married this man, and said to them, *I shall now dye, and when I am dead, your Grand-Father and Grand-mother, and Unckles, &c. will send for you to come live amongst them, and promise you great matters, and tell you what pleasant living it is among them; But doe not beleeve them, and I charge you never hearken unto them, nor live amongst them; for they pray not to God, keep not the Sabbath, commit all manner of sinnes and are not punished for it: but I charge you live here, for here they pray unto God, the Word of God is taught, sins are supressed, and punished by Lawes; And therefore I charge you live here all your dayes.* [A precious dying speech of an indian woman to her children.] And soon after this she dyed, and it fell out indeed as she had said, for there was earnest sending and soliciting for the maids to live with them: so that the case was propounded to me on a Lecture day; and their Father in law opposed it, not only as adjudging it evill, but because of their mothers charge; and by this meanes I came to know the Story. And though they doe, as you know, abhor the remembrance of their dead friends; yet when I take occasion to speak of her, and my reasons of hope that she is gone to heaven, they entertian it with joy, and sometimes with teares: I have been too tedious in this Story, yet I doubt not but it will be acceptable unto you.

For the further progresse of the work amongst them, I doe perceive a great impediment [Note what hinders the progresse of the Gospel amongst them.]; Sundry in the Country in divers places would gladly be taught the knowledge of God and Jesus Christ, and would pray unto God, if I could goe unto them, and teach them where they dwell: but to come to live here among or neer to the *English*, they are not willing, because they have neither tooles, nor skill, nor heart to fence their grounds; and if it be not well fenced, their Corne is so spoyled by the *English* Cattell, and the English so loath to restore when they want fence, that its a very great discouragement to them and me; so that few come to dwell at the neer places where I ordinarily teach, onely some strangers do come to hear, and away again: So that I plainly see, the way to do them good must be this. A place must be found (both for this and sundry other reasons I can give) some what remote from the English, where they must have the word constantly taught, and government constantly exercised, meanes of good subsistance provided, incouragements for the industrious, meanes of instructing them in Letters, Trades, and Labours, as building, fishing, Flax and Hemp dressing, planting Orchards, &c. Such a project in a fit place, would draw many that are well minded together: but I feare it will be too chargeable, though I see that God delighteth in small beginnings, that his great name may be magnified.

Few of our Southern Indians incline this way, onely some of *Tihtacutt*. Young *Ousamequin* is an enemy to praying to God, and the old man too wise to look after it. Our *Cutshamoquin* hath some subjects in *Marthas* Vineyard, and they hearing of his praying to God, some of them doe the like there, with some other ingenious Indians, and I have intreated Mr. *Mahew* (the young Schooler, son to old Mr. *Mayhew*) who preacheth to the English, to teach them; and he doth take pains in their Language, and teacheth them not without successe, blessed be the Lord. And truly I think all the Ministers that live neer them should do well to do the like. I have earnestly solicited many so to do, and I hope God will in his time bow their hearts thereunto. But I perceive our Western Indians up into the Inland do more earnestly embrace the Gospel. *Shawanon* the great *Sachym* of *Nashawog* doth embrace the Gospel, and pray unto God. I have been foure times there this Summer, and there be more people by far, then be amongst us; and sundry of them do gladly hear the word of God, but it is neer 40. miles off, and I can seldom goe to them; whereat they are troubled, and desire I should come oftner, and stay longer when I come.

There is a great fishing place upon one of the Falls of *Merimack* River called *Pautucket*, where is a great confluence of Indians every Spring, and thither I have gone these two yeares in that season, and intend so to doe the next Spring (if God will.) Such confluences are like Faires in *England*, and a fit season it is to come then unto them, to teach them to know God, and Jesus Christ, and call upon his name. For whereas there did use to be gaming and much evill at those great meetings, now there is praying to God, and good conference, and observation of the Sabbath, by such as are well minded; and no open prophanesse suffered as I heare of, and my coming amongst them is very acceptable in outward appearance. This last Spring I did there meet old *Papassaconnaway*, who is a great *Sogamore*, and hath been a great Witch in all mens esteem (as I suppose your self have often heard) and a very politick wise man. The last yeare he and all his sonnes fled when I came, pretending feare that we would kill him: But this yeare it pleased God to bow his heart to heare the word; I preached out of Malachi 1.11. which I thus render to them; *From the rising of the Sun, to the going down of the same, thy name shall be great among the Indians, and in every place prayers shall be made to thy name, pure prayers, for thy name shall be great among the Indians.* Whence I shewed them, what mercy God had promised to them; and that the time was now come wherein the Lord did begin to call them to repentance, and to beleeve in Christ for the remission of their sins, and to give them an heart to call upon his name, forsaking their former wayes of *pawwawing*, and praying to the Devill, &c. And when I had done preaching, they began to propound questions, and one of them propounded this; If it be thus as you teach, then all the world of Indians are gone to hell to be tormented for ever, untill now a few may goe to Heaven and be saved; Is it so? These principles of a twofold estate after this life, for good and bad people, Heaven and Hell, I put amongst the first questions that I instruct them in, and catechise the children in; and they doe readily embrace it for a truth, themselves by their own traditions having some principles of a life after this life, and that good or evill, according to their demeanour in this life. After a good space, this old *Papassaconnoway* speak to this purpose, that indeed he had never prayed unto God as yet, for he had never heard of God before, as now he doth. And he said further, that he did beleeve what I taught them to be true. And for his owne part, he was purposed in his heart from thenceforth to pray unto God, and that hee would perswade all his sonnes to doe the same, pointing at two of them who were there present, and naming such as were absent. His sonnes present, especially his eldest sonne (who is a Sachim [The same signification with Sagamore viz one bearing rule among them.] at *Wadchuset*) gave his willing consent to what his father had promised, and so did the other who was but a youth. And this act of his was not onely a present motion that soon vanished, but a good while after he spake to Capt. *Willard*, who tradeth with them in those parts for *Bever* and *Otter Skins,* &c. that he would be glad if I would come and live in some place thereabouts to teach them, and that Capt. *Willard* would live there also: And that if any good ground or place that hee had would be acceptable to me, he would willingly let me have it. I doe endeavour to engage the *Sachims* of greatest note to accept the Gospel, because that doth greatly animate and encourage such as are well-affected, and is a damping to those that are scoffers and opposers; for many such there be, though they dare not appeare so before me.

Thus you see by this short intimation, that the sound of the Word is spread a great way; yea, farther then I will speake of; and it appeareth to me, that the Fields begin to look white unto the Harvest. Oh that the Lord would be pleased to raise up many labourers into this Harvest! But it is difficult, not only in respect of the language, but also in respect of their barbarous course of life and poverty; there is not so much as meat, drink, or lodging for them that go unto them to preach among them, but we must carry all things with us, and somewhat to give unto them: So that the coming of Jesus Christ into these parts of the world, is not as he formerly came amongst the Gentiles, a poore underling, and his servants poore, living upon the Gospel where it was accepted among the rich Gentiles: But Christ will come unto these, rich, potent, above them in learning, riches, and power; and they shall flock unto the Gospel, thereby to receive externall benificence and advancement, as well as spirituall grace and blessings. And thus I bend my selfe to doe to my poor ability: I never go unto them empty, but carry somewhat to distribute among them; and so likewise when they come unto my house, I am not willing they should go away without some refreshing, neither do I take any gratuity from them unrewarded; and indeed they doe account, that they have nothing worth the giving unto me; onely once when I was up in the Countrey, a poore creature came to me as I was about to take Horse, shaking me by the hand, and with his other hand thrust something into my hand, I looked what it was, and it was a penny-worth of *Wampom* [A beade they make, and is highly esteemed among the Indians, equal to money with us.], upon a strawes end; I seeing so much hearty affection in so small a thing, I kindly accepted, onely inviting him to my house, that I might there shew my love to him.

There is another great fishing place about threescore miles from us, whether I intend (God willing) to go next Spring, which belongeth to the forenamed *Papassaconnaway*; which journey, though it be like to be both difficult and chargeable for horse and men, in fitting provisions, yet I have sundry reasons which bow and draw my heart thereunto. I desire your prayers to the Lord for me and for them, that the Lord would open my mouth to speak in his Name to their understandings, that with their hearts they may embrace that message which from the Lord I shall bring unto them.

They have no meanes of Physick at all, onely make use of *Pawwawes* when they be sick, which makes them loath to give it over: But I finde, by Gods blessing, in some meanes used in Physick and Chyrurgery, they are already convinced of the folly of *Pawwawing*, and easily perswaded to give it over utterly as a sinfull and diabolicall practice: but I much want some wholsome cordialls, and such other medicines as I have here mentioned in the inclosed.

The *Indians* about us which I constantly teach, do still diligently and desirously attend, and in a good measure practice (for the outward part of Religion, both in their families and Sabbaths) according to their knowledge; and by degrees come on to labour. I should be over-tedious and troublesome to you to runne into particulars, onely let me give you a taste of their knowledge by their Questions, a few whereof I did sometimes set downe, though I have slipped many, and very materiall ones; these questions being asked at sundry times, and at sundry meetings of the *Indians*.

Quest. *How many good people were in* Sodome *when it was burnt?*

I know not how to pray to Christ and the Spirit, I know a little how to pray to God?

Doth the Devill dwell in us as we dwell in an house?

When God saith, Honour thy Father, doth he mean three Fathers? Our Father, and our Sachim, and God.

When the Soule goes to heaven, what doth it say when it comes there? And what doth a wicked Soule say when it commeth into Hell?

If one sleep on the Sabbath at meeting, and another awaketh him, and he be angry at it, and say, its because he is angry with him that he so doth, Is not this a sinne?

If any talk of another mans faults, and tell others of it when hee is present to answer, is not that a sinne?

Why did Christ dyo in our stead?

Seeing Eve *was first in sinne, whether did she dye first?*

Why must we love our enemies, and how shall we doe it?

How doth Christ redeem and deliver us from sinne?

When every day my heart thinks I must dye, and goe to hell for my sins, what shall I doe in this case?

May a good man sin sometimes? Or may he be a good man, and yet sin sometimes?

If a man think a prayer, doth God know it, and will he blesse him?

Who killed Christ?

If a man be almost a good man, and dyeth; whither goeth his soule?

How long was Adam good before he sinned?

Seeing we see not God with our eyes, if a man dream that he seeth God, doth his soule then see him?

Did Adam see God before he sinned?

Shall we see God in Heaven?

If a wicked man pray, whether doth he make a good prayer? or when doth a wicked man pray a good prayer?

If a man repent, doth God take away his sinnes, and forgive him?

Whether did God make hell before Adam sinned?

If two families dwell in one house, and one prayeth, and the other not, what shall they that pray do to them that do not?

Did Abimeleck *know* Sarah *was Abrahams wife?*

Did not Abraham *sin in saying she is my sister?*

Seeing God promised Abraham *so many children, like the starres for multitude, why did he give him so few? and was it true?*

If God made hell in one of the six dayes, why did God make Hell before Adam *had sinned?*

Now the Indians desire to goe to Heaven, what shall we do that we may go thither when we dye?

How shall I bring mine heart to love Prayer?

If one man repent, and pray once in a day, and another man often in a day; whether doth one of them go to Heaven, the other not? or what difference is there?

I finde I want wisdome, what shall I do to be wise?

Why did Abraham *buy a place to bury in?*

Why doth God make good men sick?

How shall the Resurrection be, and when?

Doe not Englishmen spoile their soules, to say a thing cost them more then it did? and is it not all one as to steale?

You say our body is made of clay, what is the Sunne or Moone made of?

If one be loved of all Indians good and bad, another is hated of all saving a few that be good, doth God love both these?

I see why I must feare Hell, and do so every day. But why must I feare God?

How is the tongue like fire, and like poyson?

What if false Witnesses accuse me of murther or some foul sin?
What punishment is due to lyars?

If I reprove a man for sinne, and he answer, why doe you speak thus angerly to me: Mr. Eliot *teacheth us to love one another, is this well?*

Why is God so angry with murtherers?

If a wife put away her husband because he will pray to God, and she will not, what must be done in this case?

If there be young women pray to God, may such as pray to God marry one that will not pray to God? Or what is to bee done in this case?

Whether doth God make bad men dream good Dreames?

What is Salvation?

What is the Kingdome of Heaven?

If my wife doe some work in the house on the night before the Sabbath, and some work on the Sabbath night, whether is this a sin?

If I doe that which is a sinne, and do not know it is a sin, what will God say to that?

Whether is faith set in my heart, or in my minde?

Why did Christ dye for us, and who did kill him?

By these questions you may see they somewhat savour the things of God and Christ, and that their soules be in a searching condition after the great points of Religion and Salvation. And I will say this solemnly, not suddenly, nor lightly, but before the Lord, as I apprehend in my conscience, were they but in a setled way of Civility and Government cohabiting together, and I called (according to God) to live among them, I durst freely joyne into Church-fellowship amongst them, and could finde out at least twenty men and women in some measure fitted of the Lord for it, and soone would be capable thereof: And we doe admit in charity some into our Churches, of our owne, of whose spirituall estate I have more cause of feare, then of some of them: But that day of Grace is not yet come unto them. When Gods time is come, he will make way for it, & enable us to accomplish it. In the meane time, I desire to wait, pray, and beleeve. But I will proceed no further at this time to trouble you with these things, though I doubt not but they will be acceptable tidings to your heart, and will be an occasion of quickning your prayers for them, and for me also, that utterance may be given mee, and further knowledge of their language, wherein for want of converse, I can make but slow progresse. Thus commending you to the Grace, guidance and protection of God in Christ, I rest,

Yours to be commanded in Jesus Christ,

Roxbury this 12.
Of Nov. 1648.

J O. E L I O T.

In the next place I shall offer a second Letter of his, written to a Gentleman of New-England, *here residing at present, upon his urgent occasions; wherein the Reader may have further light concerning this great work now begun.* Take his Letter as it followeth.

Sir,

Y Our faithfull and true love to Jesus Christ is expressed evidently to my heart, among other waies very much in your solicitous thoughts and care about the good of these poor Indians, and the furtherance of their conversion. God guided your discretion very seasonably in the Letters and Tokens you were pleased to send to those leading men, which reallity of love was very thankfully accepted by them, and they desire thanks to be returned for it, &c.

Your project for their Apparell which you first mention, is very fitting, but all the difficulty will be to get so much cloath as you speak of: Yet this they doe; some old things I have gotten and given them, and some they buy; and they carefully keep them till meeting times, and many of them at such times are pretty handsome, both men, women, and children also: And whereas some good people may think fitting to send some gifts that way for them, you shall find directions here inclosed, what will best sute with their condition.

Your next project for imployment of them in planting Orchards and Gardens, it suiteth very well with my apprehensions, and I have encouraged them that way, and have promised them many hundred trees, which I reserve in nurseries for them, & hope they shall set them out, or some of them the next Spring. The onely remora the fensing in of an Orchard, we yet being upon the fencing in of a great Corne field, where they have made (I think) 200. rod of ditching already, setting two rayles in the top, and are to stone up the banks as they raise stones in planting: And when the field is fenced, then they shall fence Orchards, but they are hindred for want of Tooles, and by bad Tooles discouraged; their skill also being weak though the tooles were good, but of 30. or 40. I have scarce any left. But we must endeavour to get a Magazine for them of all manner of Tooles, &c. They had Sawyers at work last winter, and will have more this winter (I hope) for they saw very good board and planke, and could I be amongst them oftner, they would both attend it better, and doe things more orderly.

They are willing to follow my advice in any reasonable thing: onely I am confident of what you write, they must not be bent too hard at first, and I find not many that do so duly consider that point as your self; but because they be not in all points of labour as the *English* be, think all is too little or no purpose. Its hard to look upon the day of small things with patience enough. I finde it absolutely necessary to carry on civility with Religion: and that maketh me have many thoughts that the way to doe it to the purpose, is to live among them in a place distant from the *English*, for many reasons; and bring them to co-habitation, Government, Arts, and trades: but this is yet too costly an enterprize for *New-England*, that hath expended it self so far in laying the foundation of a Common-weale in this wildernesse.

For their Schooling, a Gentleman in *London* (whose name I could never learn) did give ten pounds towards it the last yeare, which I thus disposed of; five pounds I gave to a grave woman in *Cambridge*, who taught the Indian children last yeare; And God so blessed her labours, that they came on very prettily. The other five pounds I gave to the School-master of *Dorcester*, and thither the Children of those Indians that lived thereabout went, with a like good successe, if not better, because the children were bigger and more capable. This {£}10. bill Captain *Harding* paid here, and was to take it at *London*: but I heare nothing from him, no do I know whether the Gentleman will continue his gift: I feare for want of meanes both these Schooles will fall; and the Children like to lose all that they have gotten the first yeare, which is a work had need be closely followed: because they are to learn our language as well as to read; onely I take my constant course of catechising them every Lecture day, and I thank the Lord, they are (many of them) very ready in their answers in the principles of Religion. And in that exercise I endeavour also to use them to good manners.

Some of *Sudbury* Indians, some of *Concord* Indians, some of *Mestick* Indians, and some of *Dedham* Indians are ingenious, and pray unto God, and sometimes come to the place where I teach to heare the word. *Linn* Indians are all naught save one, who sometimes commeth to heare the word, and telleth me that hee prayeth to God: and the reason why they are bad is, partly and principally because their *Sachim* is naught, and careth not to pray unto God [Bad Governours have an evill inflence upon the people.]: But I am over-wearisome unto you, and therefore will go no further at this time; onely this one thing more, where as it hath pleased you to allow 40.s. to the payment of a man who should direct the Indians about their labour, and in planting of Orchards; I shall be so bold as to appoint such as have deserved it to call for it, and it shall be employed God willing to their best furtherance as neer as I can.   And thus desiring God, &c. I remaine.

Roxbury this 13. Of   *Yours to be commanded any thing in*
the 9. 1649.   *Christ Jesus*   John Eliot.

Another Letter Courteous Reader dated in February *last, I received also from this our Indian Evangelist (if I may so terme him) and because it is replenished with many pithy questions of the Indians, which imply a further progresse in knowledge; and sundry other considerable passages worthy observation, and very delightfull to a Christian spirit, I thought it my duty to publish it to the world, that so it might be a meanes to stir up all that are faithfull in Christ Jesus by prayer and otherwise to help forward this precious work begun, so much conducing to the glory of God, and the good of men.* His Letter followeth.

Much respected and longed for in the Lord,

WEre you not about the Lords businesse, and Instrument in his hand to manage some special affaires wherein his glory is much concerned, your long absence could not but be imbittered with manifold troubles to your own spirit, as it is like to be with losses and inconveniencies to your outward estate; but I trust the Lord will have a speciall regard to all, &c. I perceive others to be silent in giving you information about the progresse of the Lords work amongst the poor Indians, and therefore I thought it necessary to do it, knowing it will add to your comfort to heare that the Lord is still at worke, but I have done it more largely already in Letters by Mr. *Usher*, by way of *Maligo* [These Letters and Passengers are not yet come into England.], as also by Mr. *Bracket* of *Braintree*, by the way of *Virginia*, in Letters both to your self, and also to Mr. *Pelham*, &c. I only write now by this Ship, lest it coming in before the other Ships, you should receive some discouragement concerning the work, as if it were sunk in the beginning; but blessed be the Lord it is not so, although the progresse is yet small: It is a day of small things, an Embrio which the Lord expecteth should be furthered by the prayers of the Saints and Churches: And therefore I earnestly begg your prayers, that the Lord would thrust forth more Labourers into this Harvest; and because the meanes is exceeding small and inconsiderable for so vast an enterprize as this is: there is the more eminent need of Faith and Prayer, that the Lord himself, by his speciall grace, favour, and providence, would appear in this matter: for the Lord must raigne in these latter dayes, and more eminently & observably, overtop all Instruments and meanes: And I trust he will mightily appear in this businesse, as in other parts of the world.

I have intimated in my other Letters, what good hopes I have of sundry of them, and that they begin to *enquire after baptisme and Church Ordinances, and the way of worshipping God as the Churches here do* [They shall ask the way to Syon. Jer.50.5.]; but I shewing them how uncapable they be to be trusted therewith, whilst they live so unfixed, confused, and ungoverned a life, uncivilized and unsubdued to labor and order; they begin now to enquire after such things. And to that end, I have propounded to them that a fit place be found out for Cohabitation, wherewith they may subsist by labor, and settle themselves in such a way: And then they may have a Church, and all the Ordinances of Christ amongst them. These and other things tending that way, I have propounded to them, and they seeme to me to accept them gladly, and the longer they consider, and the more they confer together of them, the more acceptable they are unto them: And I wayting to see how the Lord would carry on this work by the wise and gracious eye & hands of his providence, I took this to be one *speciall and eminent smile of God*, upon the work that he had stirred up, the *Parliament of England* to take it into consideration, and to order the Committee of Lords and Commons for forraigne Plantations to think of some meet way how they might best advance it: And indeed the way you mention in your Letter which they have taken, *(which I trust is perfected long before this time,)* I conceive to be a way of God, and not only very acceptable to me, but honourable to themselves, and the Nation, to be engaged in so pious and charitable a work, if meanes may hereby be procured to a thorow carrying on the same.

I have also intimated in my other Letters, and sent word again in this, what manner of provisions [It would be neither pleasing nor profitable to mention them, and therefore are left out.] of all sorts wil be necessary to be sent over, and that special care be had that the tooles for labour of all sorts may be of a good temper and well made; otherwise they will be discouraged; &c. the particulars as well for Phisick and Surgery, as for Cloathing and Instruments for labour of all sorts is inclosed therein: But I will trouble you no further at this time with what I have written in my other Letters, hoping the Lord will bring them to your hands: onely I shall intimate such things as have occurred since the writing of my former Letters.

There is an *Indian* living with Mr. *Richard Calicott* of *Dorchester*, who was taken in the *Pequott* Warres, though belonging to *Long* Island; this Indian is ingenious, can read; and I taught him to write, which he quickly learnt, though I know not what use he now maketh of it: He was the first that I made use of to teach me words, and to be my Interpreter. Now of late, the Lord hath stirred up his heart to joyn unto the Church at *Dorchester*, and this day I am going to the Elders, meeting, to the examination and Tryall of this young man, in preparation for his admission into the Church.

Likewise since I purposed to write to you of these matters, I have taken care to note such Questions as they propound, and I shall here set down such as have been propounded by them since my last Letters: For by them you may guesse at the progresse they make in knowledge.

Questions.

Hy have not beasts a soul as man hath, seeing they have love, anger, &c. as man hath?

How is the spirit of God in us? And where is it principally present? [The indwelling of the spirit in us is mysterious.]

Why doth God punish in hell for ever? Man doth not so, but after a time lets them out of prison again. And if they repent in hell, why will not God let them out again?

What is Faith?

Whether do you think I have Faith?

How shall I know when God accepts my prayers? [A choice spirit looks after his prayers.]

How doth Christ make peace betwixt God and man? And what is the meaning of that point?

Why did the *Jewes* give the Watchmen money to tell a lye?

If I heare Gods Word when I am young, and do not believe, but when I am old I believe: what will God say?

In wicked dreames doth the soule sin? [See Eccles. 5.7.]

Doth the soule in Heaven know things done here on earth?

Doth the soule in *Heaven* remember what it did here on earth before he dyed?

Who first gave Lawes to men?

What is Law?

If my heart be full of evil thoughts, [A soft and serious spirited Christian eyes his thoughts.] and I repent and pray, and a few houres after it is full again, and I repent and pray again; and if after this it be full of evill thoughts again, what will God say?

Why did the earth shake at Christs Resurrection?

What meaneth this, That God will not hold him guiltlesse that taketh his name in vaine?

What force of wicked men is lawfull, and what is not?

What if a Minister weare long hayre, as some other men do, what will God say?

If a man will make his Daughter marry a man whom she doth not love, what will God say? [Forced marriages scrupled by Indians.]

Why doth Christ compare the Kingdom of heaven to a net?

Why doth God so hate them that teach others to commit sin?

SIR,

I Am now streightned in time, and must hasten away my Letters: I can proceed no further at present, and therefore with earnest desires of your Prayers, I commit you to the gracious protection of the Lord, who hath hitherto helped, and will never faile those that trust in him.

Roxbury this   Yours in any service
2. of the 12.   I can in Jesus
   1648.   Christ

John Elliot

AN

APPENDIX TO THE

foregoing Letters, holding forth

Conjectures, Observations, and Apply-

cations of them.

He works of the Lord are great, sought out of all them that love them, saith the Psalmist, Psal. 111.3 {i.e., Psalms 111.2}. The word which we render, *sought out*, hath a mighty *Emphasis* in it. Tis a word used sometimes to *Denote* the *Elaborate care* of digging and *searching into mines.* And sometimes its made use of to express the *accurate labors of those who comment upon writings.* Indeed there is a *golden mine* in every work of God; and the *foregoing* Letters to a gracious eye, are as a discovery of a far more precious *mine* in *America,* then those *Gold* and *Silver* ones of *India:* For they bring tidings of the *unsearchable riches of Christ* revealed unto poor soules in those parts.

Or if thou wilt (Reader) thou mayest eye *this work of God* as a full *text:* affording matter, both for *Theoretick,* and *practick* conclusions.

I must professe for my self, I could not passe over so rich a mine without diging nor let passe so full a *text* (as this work of God in *America*) without some short comment: which the request of the worthy Publisher of these precious papers, hath prevailed with me to affix, and publish as an Appendix.

The palpable and present acts of providence, doe more then hint the approach of Jesus Christ: And the Generall consent of many judicious, and godly Divines, doth induce *considering minds* to beleeve, that the conversion of the Jewes is at hand. Its the expectation of some of the wisest Jewes now living, that about the year 1650. *Either we Christians shall be Mosaick, or else that themselves Jewes shall be Christians.* The serious consideration of the preceding Letters, induceth me to think, that there may be at least a remnant of the *Generation of Jacob in America,* (peradventure some of the 10. Tribes dispersions.) And that those sometimes poor, now precious *Indians* (mentioned in those Letters) may be as the *first fruits* of the glorious harvest, of *Israels redemption.* The observation is not to be sleighted (though the observer [Mr. *Shepherd in the clear Sunshine, & pag.* 33 {135}.] modestly said it was *more cheerfull then deep*) that the first Text out of which Mr. *Eliot* preached, was about the dry bones, Ezek. 37.9.10. *That by prophesying to the wind, the wind came and the dry bones lived:* It may be there is not much weight in the observation, that the word which the Indians use for wind, is *Waubon:* and that an *Indian* of that name is, and hath been very sedulous for their conversion: Yet to me there is ground for a very weighty thought; that, that portion of Scripture should be first of all openned to them, which clearly foretold the conversion of *Israel, i.e.* The 10. Tribes universally understood, and peculiarly meant by the name or notion of *Israel,* when distinct from *Judah,* as in that prophesy it is) Why may we not at least *conjecture,* that God by a special finger pointed out that text to be first openned, which immediately concerned the persons to whom it was preached: Especially, if (as some credibly affirme) that the *Jewes of the Netherlands* (being intreated thereunto) *informe that after much inquiry they found some of the ten Tribes to be in America.* When our Lord came to *Nazaret,* and standing up to read: Its said there was delivered unto him the book of *Isaias,* and he openned the book, and found it written, *The spirit of the Lord is upon me, &c.* The bringing of that Scripture to our Lords hands so providentially, was a hint (at least) that the present hearers were in an eminent manner concerned in that prophesie. What ever maybe in this observation (which I humbly offer to the *searching thoughts of judicious persons*) I am much inclined to conjecture, that there is a sprinkling at least of *Abrahams seed* in these parts, The reasons of my inclination hereunto are these,

1. *They have (at least) a traditionall knowledge of God, as the maker of heaven and earth.* Its true, they talk of other Gods; but yet they hold that the chief God is he, *who made all things.* Which agnition of God, was peculiar to the *Jewes,* in opposition to the *Gentiles:* Hence it was, that when they were Captives in *Babylon:* this was that *Character,* by which they were taught to distinguish the true God (which the *Gentiles* knew not) that he was the *Maker of all things.* Jer. 10.16.

2. *What ever they attribute unto others, this they peculiarly attribute unto this God,* viz. *that all things both good and evill, are managed by his Providence,* and if they doe but hurt themselves, they say 'tis a note of Gods displeasure: Hence

3. Before ever any of them received any instruction from our *English,* by tradition they were taught, and did *upon observation of a bad year, or other ill successe, meet and weep as unto God; acknowledging it to be his hand of displeasure upon them: And on the other side, upon a good year, or good successe in any businesse, as of War, &c. they used to meet and make a kind of acknowledgement of thanks to God* for it.

4. It is very observable; that they are *carefull to preserve the memory of their Families, mentioning Unckles, Grand-Fathers, and Grand-mothers, &c.* and much studying the advancing of their houses and kindred. A thing which hath a great tang of, and affinitie to the *Jewes* care of preserving the memoriall of their *Tribes.*

5. Those of them who have been wrought upon, tell of *some face of Religion, Wisedom, and manners which long agoe* their Ancestors had, but that it was lost.

6. (To omit other grounds of this conjecture) The *better and more sober sort of them, delight much to expresse themselves in parables.* [See pag. 5.{150}] A thing peculiar to the Jewes, as those who read their writings, or consider Christs manner of expressing himself, will easily see.

These and the like considerations prevaile with me to entertain (at least) a *Conjecture,* that these *Indians in America,* may be *Jewes* (especially of the ten Tribes.) And therefore to hope that the work of Christ among them, may be as a preparatory to his own appearing.

If these reasons prevaile not with thee (Reader) to give quarter to my conjecture, yet I cannot but perswade my self, that the former Letters soberly & duly weighed, will cause thee to subscribe with me to this conclusion, that, *the work of God among the Indians in America, is glorious, and to be admired by all those, who look after and rejoyce in the appearance of our Lord Jesus,* Surely the *Sun of Righteousnesse* is risen, *with healing vertue under his wings,* upon those poor hearts, who sate *in darknesse, and the shadow of death.* And these godly persons who fled into *America* for shelter from *Prelaticall persecution,* doe now appeare to be carried there by a sacred and sweet providence of Christ, to make known his name to those poor soules, who have been *Captives to Satan* these many Ages. The Christians when scattered abroad, went to and fro preaching the word. And I wish from my soul, that all these *Ministers of the Dispertion* (as I may call them) in *New-England;* would stirre up themselves to this work of the Lord, which (now it seems) he intended in his carrying of them thither. Surely these tydings as they are *grounds of rejoycing* to others a far off; so they should be much more *incouragements of putting to the hand* of such as are there unto this harvest of the Lord. And so much the rather, because the Gospel in its advancement amongst these *Western Indians,* appeares to be *not in word only* (as it was by the *Spaniards* among their Indians) *but also in power, and in the Holy Ghost, and in much assurance:* Doe not these true reports shew *what manner of entrance the Gospel hath among them: and how they turn unto God from Idols* (from their *pawwawes*) to serve the *living and true God,* and to *look for his sonne* from Heaven, &c. [1Thes.1. See the Womans speech pag. 7 {151 - 152}. Observation.]

(*Reader*) I intreat thee to beare with me, if in *Commenting upon this work of* God, I offer a few notes to declare that in truth this work of God is not only in the *Letter,* but in the *Spirit* and power of the *Gospel.* These things I note (and pray doe thou) to this purpose.

1. The questions which are moved by the Indians comming and come in, are such as are of great and weighty concernment; And such as indeed evince a more then common working of the spirit by the word on them. Such are those that concerne *spirituall joyning in prayer,* and a *knowledge of Gods acceptation thereof.* Those questions also that relate to the *marrying of the godly with the wicked:* (much like that of the *Corinthians* to *Paul.* 1 *Cor.*7. and 2 *Cor.*8.) and those that concern *the evill of thoughts and dreames, &c.* See and consider the

Questions.

2. The full casting off their *Pawwaws*; and not seeking to them: Although they much idolized them, and albeit they know not as yet, any meanes of help when sick, but them.

3. Their sweet and affectionate melting under the word of grace: and their exceeding hungring and thirsting after the enjoyment thereof. Together with enquiry after *Syon*, and their great joy they declare in their hopes thereof. [Vide pag. 27 {159}.]

4. Lastly, and especially the real, and undenyable evidences of the work of grace in power upon some particular persons mentioned: and particular that of the *woman* in whom I cannot but note these things

1. Her desire to live by the ordinance of the word, although with great trouble. [pag. 6,7 {151 - 152}.]

2. Her Exemplarines of life, after the Lord did work upon her.

3. Her resolutions to love God, though he made her sick. Oh! could she love God, except *he loved her first?*

4. Her belief that God was well pleased with her in Christ, and hereupon her willingnesse to dye, in assurance of going to Heaven.

5. Her care of her Children upon her first knowing of God: and her charging them not to live with their kindred, pressing it chiefly with this, that *they prayed not,* and that they *committed sin, and were not punished*: Oh holy and high attainment! To see an *evill in sinning and not being punished.* This was the great evill threatned. *Hosea 9.14.*

[Application.] What doe all these things declare? but this: That Christ hath made the *day of his power* to arise upon those poor soules: In making them *a willing people*: And what improvement should we make of this comment upon the work of the Lord, if not this or the like;

First, To study and search into the works of the Lord, to see how he counterplots the enemy in his designes: In making the late Bishops persecuting of the Godly tend to the promoting of the Gospel.

Secondly, To take heed of dispising the *day of small things*. It being Gods way to lay most glorious workes upon little and despicable foundations: And to advance the Treasury of the Gospel in earthen vessels, even to the ends of the Earth,

Thirdly, To be ashamed of, and bewaile our want of affection to, and estimation of that glorious Gospel, and those great things of Christ: which these poor Heathens upon the little Glymmerings and tasts so exceedingly value and improve.

Fourthly: Doth not the observation of the preceeding reports, clearly confirme the *Doctrine of the Sabboth*, and the *practise of prayer*: Oh tremble ye *Sabboth slighters,* and *duty-dispisers*, Christ hath witnesses against you in *America!* Be ashamed ye pretended – *Men* and *fathers* in Christ for comming short of *Babes and Children!* In truth the very light of Nature will condemne you. Prayer in all ages (and that not mentall, but verball, and expresse) hath been that by which the Deity hath been *agnized* and worshipped. The *converted Heathens* in *New-England,* goe beyond you, O ye, *Apostate Christians* in

England!

Lastly, be incouraged to put to your helping hand unto the work of the Lord. And to that end,

1. *Arise ye heads of our Tribe in Old England*, and extend your help to further Christs labourers in *N.-England*. Rather steal from your sleep an houre, then suffer that good Ordinance to lye asleep so long; which if drawn into an Act, will exceedingly further this blessed work. Surely if you were petitioned to in the name of Christ, and his Gospel, to give money out of your own purse to exalt him in furthering it. Durst you deny it? How much lesse can you deny the passing of an Act to enable some to receive and dispose what others would gladly give. The work is so clear, that you need not many houres to debate it: And I hope you are so willing that I shall not need more words to presse it, only let me add this that as Ministers, so Statists do finde personall examples, the most powerfull motives to practick doctrines.

2. *Rouze up your selves my Brethren; ye Preachers of the Gospel*, this work concernes you. Contrive and plot, preach for, and presse the advancement hereof. Its cleare you may do much: Let not this be your condemnation, that you did nothing.

3. *Come forth ye Masters of money*, part with your Gold to promote the Gospel; Let the gift of God in temporal things make way, for the Indians receipt of spiritualls. If you give any thing *yearly*, remember Christ will be your Pensioner. If you give any thing into *banke,* Christ will keep *account* thereof, and reward it. You hear of what things are necessary in order to the advancement of that one *thing necessary*. Rest assured of this, what ever you give will be well and wisely improved. And as far as the Gospel is mediately advanced by your money, be sure you will be remembered.

But to winde up all, *Fall down O all ye who love the Lord Jesus: & bow your knees to his father & yours in his name, to prosper the progresse made of the Gospel among the Indians in N-England.* Pray that an effectuall door may be openned there. Remember Mr. *Eliot.* Forget not Mr. *Mayhew*, and all other that labour in the work. Pray for them that Christs work may prosper in their hands. Christ calls upon you by these Letters, and saith. *The harvest is great, but the Labourers are few, pray ye therefore the Lord of the harvest to send forth Labourers into his vineyard.* If you thus heare Christ, and obey his voice, you shall accomplish the end of this Appendix, and exceedingly rejoyce the heart of the Author thereof, who is

> *An unworthy Labourer in Christs work here,*
> *And an ardent desirer of further progresse*
> *thereof in* New-England.

J.   D.

FINIS.

The Light appearing more and more towards the perfect Day.

OR,

A farther Discovery of the present state of the *INDIANS*

IN

New-England,

Concerning the Progresse of the *Gospel* amongst them.

Manifested by Letters from such as preacht to them there.

Published by *Henry Whitfeld*, late Pastor to the Chuch of Christ at *Gilford* in *New-England*, who came late thence.

Zeph. 2. 11. *The Lord will famish all the gods of the earth, and men shall worship him, every one from his place, even all the Iles of the Heathen.*

London, Printed by *T. R.* & *E. M.* for *John Bartlet*, and are to be sold at the Gilt Cup, neer St. *Austins* gate in *Pauls* Church-yard. 1651.

The Light appearing more and more towards the perfect Day.

O R,

A farther Discovery of the present state of the *I N D I A N S*

I N

New -England,

Concerning the Progresse of the *Gospel* amongst them.

Manifested by Letters from such as preacht to them there.

Published by *Henry Whitfeld*, late Pastor to the Church of Christ at *Gilford* in *New-England*, who came late thence.

Zeph. 2.11. *The Lord will famish all the gods of the earth, and men shall worship him, every one from his place, even all the Iles of the Heathen.*

London, Printed by *T. R. & E. M.* for *John Bartlet,* and are to be sold at the Gilt Cup, neer St. *Austins* gate in *Pauls* Church-yard. 1 6 5 1.

The Lord, *who is wonderful in Councel, and excellent in working*, hath so wrought, that the scorching of some of *his people* with the *Sun of persecution,* hath been the enlightning of those who were *not his people*, with the *Sun of righteousnesse.* This present Narrative gives testimony, That our dear Brethren whowith-draw from the heat of trouble in *Old England*, have been used as Instruments in the Lords hand to draw som (I might say many) of the poor Heathens to behold and rejoyce in the light of the everlasting Gospel in *New-England.* Surely 'tis cause of greater glorying that any of those Heathens have found the way of life and salvation among our brethren, then that our brethren have found place and safety (yea, then though they should finde the richest merchandize of gold and silver) among those Heathens. And how much doth it become Christians to let Heathens see that they seek *them* more then *theirs*; That the gaining of them to Christ is more in their eye, then any worldly gaine.

Joseph Caryl.

THE

PARLIAMENT

OF

England

And the

COUNCEL of STATE.

Right Honorable,

Ow abundantly the Lord hath enlarged the hearts, and raised the resolutions of this present Parliament to serve him, the many good things, and great things done by you, sufficiently witnesse, and will be acknowledged, at least in another generation. It is not the smallest in the eyes of those that look up to God for you, both in Old England and New, that you have so readily contributed your power, upon the first notice of the manifestation of Gods gracious work upon the Indians, by an Act published by you, for promoving the same.

In order whereunto I crave leave in all humility to represent (having lived some yeers in the Countrey, and lately came thence) how happily the Lord carrieth on his work there, which I have done in this small Treatise following.

And for your more full satisfaction, give leave to remove such false surmises and aspersions, suggested on purpose to retard the work. Some are heard to question the affections of New-England towards the Parliament, and present state; To which I must answer; that the Magistrates, Ministers, and generally the people of New-England, so farre as I know or have observed, or can learn, have been faithful and cordial to the Parliament from the first, and do own this present Government, and Common-wealth, giving in this as a reall argument, in being your Honours Remembrancers at the throne of grace, both praying to God for you in your straits, and praising God for the enlargment of his good hand upon you. Others endeavour more directly to prejudice the work, by suggesting that the charity of the wel-affected hath been abused, in that there is no such work, or that there is a greater noise made of it in the world then there is cause; To this I can safely answer, that there hath been, I beleeve in no mans observation, greater faithfulnesse found in any businesse, both for truth of relation in what hath passed, or disposing what hath been contributed; the *persons that are concerned in it, whether they be the Corporation established by you, or that have the managing of it in* New-England, *being persons of known integrity, and much honoured of all that know them, in this very respect; Most of these accounts I have seen, both what monies have been received and disbursed, both what, how, and to whom. These also are ready to give your Honours satisfaction about this, if need require, and it will be an ease, and an honour to them to be called to such an account.*

And now the way being thus cleared, I proceed to make it my humble request to your Honours, that you would be pleased to accept of this my humble acknowledgment, and thankful remembrance of what you have already done; and that it would not be troublesome to you to be intreated, and stirred up by my meannesse, to proceed in the continuance of your favour, as to the whole Country, so especially towards this work, that your hands may be still held up to the farther advance, and perfecting these happy beginnings. And as you have given it feet, so you would give it wings, that it may get above al difficulties, which may be cast in the way. Truly the work is honorable, and worthy your care, and inmost affections, and to be laid in your bosomes, that it may feel the warmth and influence of your favour, and best respects, it tending so much to the good of the souls of these poor wild creatures, multitudes of them being under the power of Satan, and going up and downe with the chains of darknesse ratling at their heels. This I may also say for your Honours encouragement, there is farre greater cause of promoting this work then formerly, there being more persons, and places which have received the Gospel amongst them. Our Lord Christ and his truth gets ground, and the Devil loseth, they daily break from him, and renounce him, and all his cursed works of darknesse, as you will find in this following Narrative. *And lastly, let me adde but this, The Lord hath given the uttermost ends of the earth to Jesus Christ for his inheritance, let therefore your hands go on (Noble Worthies) to help him in taking the possession of his own, who hath kept you in* yours *with an out-stretched arme. But I shall be no farther troublesome to your Honours; The most wise and strong God, for Christs sake, strengthen your hearts and hands, sit amongst you in your daily assemblings, and help you to guide the Ship of this Common-wealth, under your care, in these tossing and troublesome times, that there may be peace and safety found for such as are quiet in the Land; and let me have the favour to be looked upon by you, as*

Your Honours to serve you
in the things of Jesus Christ,

Henry Whitfeld.

Christian Reader.

I Have adventured to put this smal Treatise *in thy hand, and to give some account of the publishing of it, conceiving it a means to advance that common comfort, which all good Christians do share in with the Angels of heaven, about the conversion of sinners to God. This will appear by shewing there is a doore of hope opened for the poore Indians, of whom it may be thou hast not yet heard; I thought also by relating the truth of things, as they stand at present, concerning the* Indians *you have heard of, and Gods dealing with them, I might undeceive such as are either apt, or do beleeve, that things reported of them are but a fable, and a device or engine used by some to cheat good people of their money, and so discourage them from yeelding any help towards this great work. The Lord forgive them this great sinne, that have raised these evill reports.*

Understand therefore (good Reader) that my selfe intending (by Gods help) my returne into my native Countrey; It pleased the Lord by his providence, before we could come to the place where we were to take ship for England, *that, by reason of contrary winds, we were faine to put in at an Iland called* Martins Vineyard [Some call it Marthaes Vineyard.], *which is the most Southerly Iland that lies in that tract of Land called* New England, *where there is a small Plantation, and a Church gathered, where we stayed about ten dayes, in which time I had the more leasure and opportunity to informe my selfe of the state of the Indians there; having heard formerly that divers of them began to taste the knowledge of Christ: For this end I had recourse to Mr.* Mahu, *who is the Pastor of the Church, and having attained a good understanding in the Indian tongue, and can speak it well, hath laid the first foundation of the knowledge of Christ amongst the Indians there by preaching unto them; who gave me full information of what I desired. I had also speech with some of the Indians (Mr.* Mahu *being my Interpreter.) Above the rest my desire was to speak with the Indian who now preacheth unto them every Lords day twice, whose name is* Hiacoomes, *who seemed to me to be a man of a prompt understanding, of a sober and moderate spirit, and a man well reported of for his conversation both by the English and Indians. I thought him to be about 30 yeers of age; with this man I had often speech, and I asked him divers questions about Christian Religion, and about his own estate before God. I remember once I asked him these questions.* 1. Whether he had found sorrow for sin, as sin. 2. Whether he had sorrowed for his sins as they had pierced Christ. 3. Whether he had found the Spirit of God as an inward comforter to him; *Unto all which he gave me a very good satisfactory and Christian answer. After this I had the opportunity to go to a private meeting of the Indians (of which you shall understand more in the Letter following) with Mr.* Mahu, *where having spent three or foure houres in Questions and Answers, which passed too and fro between the Indians and my self; at our parting I desired that one of them would desire a blessing upon what they had heard for their edification, which was accordingly done; for they chose out a young man who prayed a quarter of an houre, and somewhat more, with great reverence and affection, as farre as I could judge by his voyce and outward deportment: Master* Mahu *also told me that he had many pertinent and significant expressions in his prayer; so that God hath poured on some of them the gift, and I hope the spirit of prayer.*

The next day we rode to the Indians Lecture, where Mr. Mahu *preached and catechised their children, who answered readily and modestly in the Principles of Religion; some of them answered in the English, some in the Indian tongue. Thus having seen a short model of his way, and of the paines he took, I made some enquiry about Mr.* Mahu *himself, and about his subsistance, because I saw but small and slender appearance of outward conveniences of life, in any comfortable way; the man himself was modest, and I could get but little from him; but after, I understood from others how short things went with him, and how he was many times forced to labour with his own hands, having a wife and three small children which depended upon him, to provide necessaries for them; having not halfe so much yeerly coming in, in a setled way, as an ordinary labourer gets there amongst them. Yet he is chearfull amidst these straits, and none hear him to complain. The truth is, he will not leave the work, in which his heart is engaged; for upon my knowledge, if he would have left the work, and imployed himself otherwhere, he might have had a more competent and comfortable maintenance. I mention this the rather, because I have some hope, that some pious minde, that reads this, might be inwardly moved to consider his condition, and come to his succor for his encouragement in this great work.*

At my parting from this Iland I desired Mr. Mahu *that he would take the pains to write me the Story of Gods dealing with the Indians, from the first time of their coming thither, to this present time; which he accordingly did, and I received before my going out of the Countrey; which Letter of his to me, finding many remarkable passages in it, I thought fit to publish it, that the Lord might have the glory of his free grace, in regard of these poor Heathens who seeme to be the dregs and refuse of* Adams *lost posterity; and to put an edge upon the prayers and prayses of Gods people, the fruit of which will returne into their owne bosomes. And if there be a right set of spirit in you, you will blesse God for such as present such kinde of matter to you, and do put an opportunity into your hands, whereby you may any way be instrumental to promote the Kingdome of our Lord Christ.*

The Letter written with his own hand followeth.

S I R,

YOu being by especial providence of God, brought amongst us, and while you were here looking into the present mercy of God that these Indians were blessed with, you found an occasion farther to enquire what the former dispensations of God have beene to bring them hitherto. Now assuring my self that it is from your desire that the Lord may be glorified in the salvation of these poor Indian souls, I shall, by the assistance of God, declare the truth, and that which shall, by his grace, administer also a ground of prayer to be put unto the God of all blessings in Jesus Christ for us; and I hope, unto any, whom the Lord shall call to the like service, a blessed experience of the Lords workings, turning all things, yea seeming hinderances, to the furtherance of the work of grace amongst them.

Now for your satisfaction, you may please to know that this work amongst the Indians had its first rise and beginning in the yeere 1643. When the Lord stirred up the heart of an Indian, who then lived neer to the English Plantation, whose name is *Hiacoomes*, a man of a sad & a sober spirit, unto whose *Wigwam* or house some of the English repairing, & speaking to him about the way of the English, he came to visit our habitations and publike meetings, thinking that there might be better wayes and means amongst the English, for the attaining of the blessings of health and life, then could be found amongst themselvs: Yet not without some thoughts and hopes of a higher good he might possibly gain thereby, at which time I took notice of him, and had oft discourse with him, inviting him to my house every Lords day at night. About this time it so fell out, that this Indian went with some English men to a little Iland, where meeting a surly *Sagamore* [By this name they call their kings and Governors] whose name was *Pake Ponesso*, who reproached him for his fellowship with the English, both in their civil and religious wayes, railing at him for his being obedient to them: *Hiacoomes* replyed that he was gladly obedient to the English, neither was it for the Indians hurt he did so; Upon which the Sagamore gave him a great blow on the face with his hand; but there being some English men present, they would not suffer the Sagamore to strike him again. The poor Indian thus wronged, made this use of it, and said, *I had one hand for injures, and the other for God, while I did receive wrong with the one, the other laid the greater hold on God.*

There was a very strange disease this yeare amongst the Indians, they did run up and down till they could run no longer, they made their faces as black as a coale, snatched up any weapon, spake great words, but did no hurt; I have seen many of them in this case. The Indians having many calamities fallen upon them, they laid the cause of all their wants, sicknesses, and death, upon their departing from their old heathenish ways, only this man held out, and continued his care about the things of God: and being desirous to read, the English gave him a Primer, which he stil carries about with him.

[1644] Now whilst *Hiacoomes* was feeling after God, he met with another tryall; for going into an Indian house where there were many Indians, they scoffed at him with great laughter, saying, *Here comes the English man,* who by their noyse awaked his old enemy *Pakeponesso,* who was asleep, who joyning with the other Indians, told him, *I wonder* (said he) *that you that are a young man, having a wife and two children, should love the English and their wayes, and forsake the Pawwawes; what would you do if any of you should be sick? Whither would you go for help? I say, if I were in your case there should nothing draw me from our gods and Pawwawes.* At this time he replyed nothing, but told a friend of his that he then thought in his heart that the God in heaven did know and heare all the evill words that *Pakeponesso* spake. Thus the changing of his way caused much hatred to him, neither was there so much as the least appearance of any outward argument amongst us, that might weigh against it.

After this there fell a great judgment of God on this Sagamore; for in the night when he and his company were in the Wigwam, [An Indian house or Wigwam is made with smal poles like an arbour covered with mats, and the fire is in the midst, over which they leave a place for the smoak to go out at.] it beginning to raine, he and a young man stood up upon the floor of planks which lay about two foot from the ground, to put a Matt over the Chimnie, there came a great flash of lightning, and after it thunder not very loud, yet full of the vengeance of God, which killed the young man out-right, and strook *Pakeponesso* down dead for a long time, and he fell off from the floore of planks along upon the ground with one legge in the fire, and being much burned, it was took out by some that lay in the other side of the Indian house. Now *Hiacoomes* (as himself saith) did remember his former thoughts of God, and then thought God did answer him, and that he was brought more to rejoyce in God, and rest more upon him.

[1645] Now in these times, as I did endeavour the good of these Heathens by discourse with diverse of them, so in particular with *Hiacoomes*, who did communicate that knowledge he had amongst those he could; for some of them could not endure the light he brought; some were more attentive to hear, and more ready to follow the truth, yet they did not well behold the Majesty of the Lord by these personal particular works; at last the Lord sent an universal sicknes, and it was observed by the Indians, that they that did but give the hearing of good counsel, did not taste so deeply of it, but *Hiacoomes* and his family in a manner not at all. [1645] This put the Indians who dwell about six miles from us, upon serious consideration of the thing, being much affected, that he which had exposed himself to such reproaches and troubles, should receive more blessings then themselves; hereupon they sent a messenger to *Hiacoomes*, who was with him about the break of day, and delivering his message, told him that he was come to pray him to go presently to *Myoxeo* the chief man of that place, and he should have a reward for his labour; for the Indians were very desirous to know from him all things that he knew, and did, in the wayes of God; so he being glad of the opportunity, went with the messenger, and when he came, there were many Indians gathered together, amongst which was *Towanquatick* the Sagamore; then after many requests (the general whereof was this, that he would shew his heart unto them, how it stood towards God, and what they must do) he shewed unto them all things he knew concerning God the Father, Sonne and Holy Ghost; *Myoxeo* asking him how many Gods the English did worship, he answered one God, whereupon *Myoxeo* reckoned up about 37. principal gods he had, and shall I (said he) throw away these 37. gods for one? *Hiacoomes* replyed, what do you think of your self? I have throwne away all these, and a great many more some yeers ago, yet am preserved as you see this day; you speak true said *Myoxeo*; therefore I will throw away all my gods too, and serve that one God with you. *Hiacoomes* told them all, he did fear this great

God only, and also in a speciall manner that the Son of God did suffer death to satisfie the wrath of God his Father, for all those that did trust in him, and forsake their sinnes, and that the spirit of God did work these things in the hearts of men, and that himself did feare this great God only, was sorry for his sinnes, desiring to be redeemed by Jesus Christ, and to walk in Gods commandments; this, with many truths more he shewed unto them, As *Adams* transgression, and the misery of the world by it, and did conclude, that if they had such hearts as he, they should have the same mercies. He reckoned up to them many of their sins, as having many gods, going to Pawwawes; and *Hiacoomes* told me himself, that this was the first time that ever he saw the Indians sensible of their sins; formerly they did but hear it as a new thing, but not so nearly concerning them, for they were exceeding thankful, saying, also *now we have seen our sins.* Thus it pleased the Lord to give both light and courage to this poore Indian; for although formerly he had been a harmlesse man amongst them, yet, as themselves say, not at all accounted of, and therefore they often wondered that he which had nothing to say in all their meetings formerly, is now become the Teacher of them all; I must needs give him this testimony, after some yeers experience of him, that he is a man of a sober spirit, and good conversation, and as he hath, as I hope, received the Lord Jesus Christ in truth, so also I look upon him to be faithful, diligent, and constant in the work of the Lord, for the good of his own soul and his neighbours with him.

Now, after these things it pleased God to move the heart of *Towanquatick*, encouraged by some others amongst them, to desire me to preach unto them. [*Though I have written this passage to Mr.* Winslow *in my Letter to him, which is printed, yet it is not so full a story {as} here, and therefore I have added it.*] At my coming, this man spake thus unto me; *That a long time agon they had wise men, which in a grave manner taught the people knowledge; but they are dead, and their wisdome is buried with them, and now men live a giddy life, in ignorance, till they are white headed, and though ripe in yeeres, yet then they go without wisdome to their graves.* He told me that he wondered the English should be almost thirty yeers in the Country and the Indians fools still; but he hoped the time of knowledge was now come; wherefore himself with others desired me to give them an Indian meeting, to make known the word of God to them in their own tongue; and when he came to me to accomplish his desire thereabout, he told me *That I should be to them as one that stands by a running river filling many vessels,* even so should I fill them with everlasting knowledge; So I undertook to give them a meeting once a moneth; but as soone as the first Exercise was ended, they desired it oftner then I could well attend it, but once in a fortnight in our setled course. He hath also since told me the reason why he desired me to preach to them, as that he was greatly desirous to have the Indians grow more in goodnesse, to have their posterity inherit blessings when he was dead; and himself was desirous to put the Word of God to his heart, to repent, and throw away his sins, and to be better, and after he was dead, to inherit a life in heaven.

Now there be three things in this beginning that were greatly inquired into. 1. Earthly riches, what they should get. 2. What approbation they should get from other Sagamores and Governors. 3. How they should come off from the Pawwawes; but in neither of these could they finde that which might give motion to a carnal minde; for the first kept off many, I have had much discourse with several of them about it, wherein they have strongly stood for their own meetings, wayes and customes, being in their account more profitable then ours, wherein they meet with nothing but talking and praying. The second also remaines an obstacle, the Sagamores generally are against the way. The third is the strongest cord that binds them to their own way, for the Pawwawes by their witchcraft keep them in feare, many of the Indians got over the two first difficulties, and in some measure the third; now there were about twelve which came to the meeting as it were halting between two opinions, others came to hear and see what was done, for although they had heard and seen something of the one God of heaven, yet such was their unspeakable darknesse, their captivity in sin, and bondage to the Pawwawes, that they hardly durst for feare take the best way, for though a few of them were better enlightned, yet the Heathen round about stuck fast in their old brutishnesse.

[1647] We had not long continued the meeting, but the Sagamore *Towanquatick* met with a sad tryal, for he being at a Weare where some Indians were a fishing, where also was an English man, as he lay along upon a matt on the ground asleep, by a little light fire, the night being very dark, an Indian came down, as being ready fitted for the purpose, and being about six or eight paces from him, let flie a broad headed arrow, purposing by all probability to drench the deadly arrow in his heart blood, but the Lord prevented it; for notwithstanding all the advantages he had, instead of the heart he hit the eye-brow, which like a brow of steele turned the point of the arrow, which, glancing away, slit the top of his nose to the bottome. [This man when I was in the Iland I often saw and spake with, seeing also the skar upon the eye-brow and nose.] A great stirre there was presently, the Sagamore sate up, and bled much, but was not much hurt through the mercy of God; the darknesse of the night hid the murtherer, and he is not discovered to this day. The next morning I went to see the Sagamore, and I found him praising God for his great deliverance, both himself and all the Indians, wondering that he was yet alive. The cause of his being shot, as the Indians said, was for his walking with the English; and it is also conceived, both by them and us, that his forwardnesse for the meeting was one thing, which (with the experience I have had of him since) gives me matter of strong perswasion that he beares in his brow the markes of the Lord Jesus.

After this, through the mercy of God, we proceeded on with the meeting, to the rejoycing of some Indians, and the envie of the rest, who derided and scoffed at those that did follow the Lecture, and in their way of wickednesse blaspheming the Name of God, which damped the spirits of some of them for a time in the wayes of God, and hindering others from looking thitherward, but the Lord gave courage and constancy to some of them, especially to *Hiacoomes* and *Towanquatick* who was hurt with the arrow, who were not ashamed of the way of God.

[1648] And hereupon they made farther progresse in the way of God, for without any knowledge thereof, they appointed a meeting, [Although I was present at this meeting from the beginning to the end it was done without my privity or putting them on upon it, but it came meerly from themselvs.] and there came some younger men, and brought with them the ancient men of their kindred and acquaintance to speak for them, whereof the very old man that your self saw and heard at the meeting, was one, who began the meeting with a relation of the old customes of the ancient Heathen, preferring them before those wayes of their own they were now in, yet acknowledging they were farre inferior to those wayes of God they had now begun: Then twelve of the young men went and took *Sacochanimo* [This was Towanqueticks eldest sonne.] by the hand one by one and told him that they did love him, and would go with him in Gods way, and some of them made a long speech to him to this purpose; and the old men encouraged them in their way, & desired them never to forget those promises they had now made; then one of the young men told me the ground of their meeting, *viz.* They were sorry to see that the meeting did go on no more strongly, and that there were no more at it, and that they were desirous to strengthen themselves in the way of God, to have good hearts, and one heart, and to walk together in love in the wayes of God. So after they had eaten together the victuals of their own providing, and we had sung part of a *Psalme* in their own language, and I had prayed with them, they returned with the manifestation of much joy and thankfulnesse; and this I can say, they are generally constant in the way of God, and I have great hopes of some of them, blessed be his name.

[1649] After this it pleased the Lord to stirre up the hearts of the Indians to appoint another meeting, and many Indians being met, they fell to a great discourse about the Pawwawes power to kill men, and there were many stories told of the great hurt they had done by their witchcraft many wayes (here you must know, that though the Indians many of them were brought by the knowledge they had of God, to renounce the Pawwawes help in time of sicknesse or otherwise, yet they found it hard to get from under the yoake of cruelty that they and their forefathers had so long groaned under; for I know some, that then groaned under it, acknowleged that they did see that in God which would free them from it, if they had but confidence to trust in him. Then the question was asked, Who is there that doth not fear the Pawwawes? answer was made by some who favoured them, there is not any man which is not afraid of the Pawwawes; then looking upon *Hiacoomes*, who was one that protested most against them, told him that the Pawwawes could kill him; he answered they could not; they asked him againe, why? he told them, because he did beleeve in God and trust in him, and that therfore all the Pawwaws could not do him any hurt; Then they all wondered exceedingly when he spake thus so openly. Then divers of them said one by one, though before I was afraid of the Pawwawes, yet now, because I hear *Hiacoomes* his words, I do not fear them, but beleeve in God too. Then the meeting at this time was carried on, and *Hiacoomes* is desired by the Indians to reckon up their sins unto them; he presently found 45. or 50. and as many good duties; his work was very well liked, and in the conclusion twenty two Indians were found to resolve against those evils, and to walk with God, and attend the word of God. [1650] But I may not here forget an Indian called *Hummanequem*, who exceeded all the rest, to the wonderment of the Indians; he with much sorrow, hatred, and courage, related about twenty of his own sins, and professed to follow the one God against all opposition; He told them he was brought into this condition by *Hiacoomes* his counsel from the Word of God, which at first he said he liked not, afterwayes laid it by him as a thing to be considered, not knowing well what to do; at last, looking over things again, he came to this resolution which you have now heard; I confesse this action makes me think he spake more then from a natural principle, considering that the man hath been since an earnest seeker of more light both publike and private; as also for refusing the help of a Pawwaw which lives within a bow shoot of his doore, when his wife was three dayes in travel, and waited patiently upon God, till they obtained a merciful deliverance by prayer.

And whilst we were making progresse in the work of the Lord on a Lecture day, an Indian stood up, and said he had been a sinner, and committed many evill things, but now was sorry for them, and did repent, desired to forsake his sins, and to walk in Gods way. Then he went to the Sagamore *Towanquetick*, and took him by the hand, saying, *I do love you, and do greatly desire to go along with you for Gods sake*; the like also he said to some others, and then came to me in like manner, saying, *I pray love me, and I do love you, and am desirous to go with you for Gods sake*; so he was received with many thanks, and since I know him to be diligent and laborious. I confesse I marvelled to see them act with such a spirit, but I considered, it was sutable to their own meeting in 48.

Now the Indian accompanied his friend that suddenly lost his two sons; he I say remaining still in his obstinacy, is also found out, and feeles the wrath of God, being stricken with a dead Palsie, all one side of him, but his eye and eare; The dead Palsie is a strange and unwonted disease among the Indians; I have beene sometimes with him; when I spake to him, he fetched many sighs; he is at this day a living and a dead monument of the Lords displeasure, having hurt himself most, and done them most good he hated.

Another thing is a remarkable combate between two Indians and a Pawwaw, who, on the Lords day after meeting, came in very angry, saying, I know the meeting Indians are lyars; you say you care not for the Pawwawes; then calling two or three of them by name, and railing at them, told them that they were deceived, for the Pawwawes could kill all the meeting Indians if they did set about it; with that one of the young men replyed with much courage, saying, it is true, I do not fear the Pawwawes, neither do I desire any favour at their hands, pray kill me if you can. And *Hiacoomes* told him also that he would be in the midst of all the Pawwawes of the Iland that they could procure, and they should do their utmost they could against him, and when they did their worst by their witchcrafts to kill him, he would without feare set himself against them, by remembering *Jehovah*; he told him also that he did put all the Pawwawes under his heel, pointing unto it; which answers did presently silence the Pawwawes devillish spirit, and had he nothing to say, but that none but *Hiacoomes* was able so to do.

I have observed the wise disposing hand of God in another Providence of his; there have not as I know, any man, woman or child died of the meeting Indians since the meeting began, untill now of late the Lord took away *Hiacoomes* his child which was about five dayes old; he was best able to make a good use of it, and to carry himself well in it, and so was his wife also; and truly they gave an excellent example in this also, as they have in other things; here were no black faces for it as the manner of the Indians is, nor goods buried with it, nor hellish howlings over the dead, but a patient resigning of it to him that gave it; There were some English at the burial, and many Indians to whom I spake something of the Resurrection, and as we were going away, one of the Indians told me he was much refreshed in being freed from their old customes, as also to hear of the Resurrection of good men and their children to be with God.

There are now by the grace of God thirty nine Indian men of this meeting, besides women that are looking this way, which we suppose to exceed the number of the men, though not known by open entrance into Covenant as the men, but are now near it. These in general have the knowledge of the fundamental points of Religion; your self when you were with us, had some tryal of it; it was a great while my maine work to administer light in general to them; and there now, through mercy, appears some life, hoping that some of them have received this great mercy of God in Christ. This is a great incouragement to me, as also that their hearts are engaged in the way of the Lord for the salvation of their own souls upon Gods ends. One of these meeting Indians said (and I hope feelingly) that if all the world, the riches, plenty, and pleasures of it were presented without God, or God without all these, I would take God. And another said, that if the greatest Sagamore in the Land should take him in his armes, and proffer him his love, and riches and gifts to turn from his way, he would not go with him from this way of God. I heard one of them of his own accord (and to the same purpose) in complaining against head knowledge and lip prayers, without heart holinesse, loathing the condition of such a man, saying, I desire my heart may taste the word of God, repent of my sinnes, and leane upon the Redemption of the Lord Jesus Christ. Some of them having a discourse with *Vzzamequin* {Wossamegon} a great Sachem or Governour on the maine Land (coming amongst them) about the wayes of God, he enquired what earthly good things came along with them, and demanding of them what they had gotten by all they had done this way? one of them replyed, we serve not God for cloathing, nor for any outward thing. I have observed many such like passages; but my occasions at present will not permit me to set them down, I only bring you those things which are most ready in my minde.

The last thing that I took special notice of, is, the receiving of the five men when your self was present, into the meeting Indian number, one of them (the young man you saw) was sent at first about two or three months before by one of the greatest Pawwawes upon the Iland to learn and spy what was done at the meeting, and carry him word, but at the last he learned so much as he then openly profest to hate the Pawwawes and their witchcrafts, and that he did repent of his sinnes, and desired to go with the meeting Indians in Gods ways;

another said he desired to joyn with the meeting Indians that he might have a renewed good heart, the other were much like affected, only one of them reckoned up the commandments, and as he proceeded he protested against the sins forbidden, and professed obedience to the duties commanded; the last answered the question put to him by your self, *viz.* by what power they did think to do this? who answered, First, by his good desire; and secondly, by the help and blessing of Jesus Christ.

Just now whilst I am a writing, there comes an Indian unto me and tels me his minde in these words, I shall long for your returne back again out of the Bay, that we may hear the good word of God; the former sins of my heart in the time of my youth I now remember; when I hear the word of God, and when I walk in the woods alone, I have much talk with God, and great repentance for my sins, and now I throw behind me all my strange gods, and my heart goes right to God in prayer.

The way that I am now in (through the grace of God) for the carrying on of this great work, is by a Lecture every fortnight, whereunto both men women and children do come; and first I pray with them, teach them, chatechise their children, sing a Psalm, and all in their own language. I conferre every last day of the week with *Hiacoomes* about his subject matter of preaching to the Indians the next day, where I furnish him with what spiritual food the Lord is pleased to afford me for them, wherein God hath much assisted him for his own and their spiritual good and advantage, who is diligent and conscionable to hold forth the grace of Christ to the Indians. For this purpose your fervent and frequent prayers together with all those who rejoyce in advancing the Scepter of Christ, are by me earnestly desired, and for me that I may preach him amongst the Heathen, to the praise of the excellency of his own power, and not mine; and that the Indians in this small beginning, being Gods husbandry, and Gods building, may be a fruitful glorious spreading Vine, and builded together for an habitation of God through the Spirit, unto whom I commend you in Jesus, and in him rest.

From Great Harbor   *Yours in the Lord to*
in Martins *Vineyard*
Sept. 7. 1 6 5 0   *be commanded,*

THOMAS MAYHOW.

N*Ow to speak somewhat farther of the proceeding of the things of Christ amongst the Indians of* Mattacusets *and thereabouts since the last book came forth; Somewhat I saw and understood concerning those Indians which are under the care of Mr.* Eliot, *unto whom I repaired at my coming from* Martins Vineyard, *who acquainted me with the state of things amongst the Indians as they were at present; at which time I rode with him to the* Water-town *Indians, and heard him preach to them, and catechize their children in the*

Indian tongue; who wrote also by me to Mr. Winslow, *the Agent of the Countrey; which Letter together with some other sent since the last publication by the Presse, the Corporation of* New England *desired me that they might be joyned and printed with this written by Master* Mahu*; which letters here follow.*

Much honoured Sir,

Y Our very loving aceptance of my Letters doth engage me very much unto you, but especially your cordial rejoycing in the progresse of this work of the Lord among these poor Indians. Sir, I shall first answer some material things in your Letter. First, for that opinion of *Rabbi-ben-Israel* which you mention, I would intreat you to request the same godly Minister (nay I hope he hath already done it) to send to him to know his grounds, and how he came to that Intelligence, when was it done, which way were they transported into *America*, by whom, and what occasion, how many, and to what Parts first, or what steps of intimation of such a thing may there be. I had some thoughts in my heart to search the Original of this People, that I might finde under what Covenant and Promise their fore-fathers have been, for the help of my faith; for *Jehovah* remembers and giveth being to ancient Promises. What had become of us sonnes of *Japhet,* if the Lord had not remembred that (and such like ancient Promises). *God shall perswade* Japhet *to dwell in the Tents of* Shem. If these people be under a Covenant and Promise as ancient as *Shem* and *Eber*, it is a ground of faith to expect mercy for them.

Now this I have thought, that it seemeth to me as clear in the Scripture, that these are the children of *Shem* as we of *Japhet,* [*Gen.* 10.] and *Shem* was a great man in the Church, and to whom *Abraham* paid *Tythes*; for I beleeve he was *Melchisedceck*; yea it seemeth to me probable that these people are Hebrews, of *Eber*, whose sonnes the Scripture sends farthest East (as it seemeth to me) and learned *Broughton* put some of them over into *America*, and certainly this Country was peopled Eastward from the place of the *Arks* resting, seeing the finding of them by the West is but of yesterday: Now *Eber* was also a great man in the Church; *Abraham* the Hebrew, saith the text; and how often in the Scriptures doth the Lord use that blessed word of *Grace* and *Covenant, I am the God of the Hebrewes?* besides there be sundry Prophesies in Scripture, *unto the goings down of the Sunne*; and let it be considered whether *America* be not to be accounted among the places that are the goings down of the Sunne unto those places where those Promises were promulgated; And when the Lord inlarged the Promise to *Jacob* (as the light and extent of grace hath ever been encreasing and enlarging) he promised to make him a Nation and a multitude of Nations, which so farre as we regard a litteral accomplishment, is in part accomplisht in the Nation of the Jewes, and the other part remaineth (as it may seem) to be accomplisht in the lost Israelites scattered in the world, principally, if not wholly, amongst the sons of *Japhet* and *Shem*; and our God who can and will gather the scattered and lost dust of our bodies at the Resurrection, can and will finde out these lost and scattered Israelites, and in finding up them, bring in with them the Nations among whom they were scattered, and so shall *Jacobs* Promise extend to a multitude of Nations indeed; and this is a great ground of faith for the conversion of the Easterne Nations, and may be of help to our faith for these Indians; especially if *Rabbi Ben-Israel* can make it appeare that some of the Israelites were brought into *America*, and scattered here, or if the Lord shall by any meanes give us to understand the same.

These meditations upon Scripture grounds do minister comfort & encouragement to my heart with others also, as, *That all Languages shall see his Glory, and that all Nations and Kingdoms shall become the Kingdoms of the Lord Jesus;* and this I desire to do, to look unto Scripture grounds only; *Oh this precious this perfect Word of God!* You intimate also how zealously worthy Mr. *Owen* did prosecute this work; the Lord reward him, and the Lord accept him in all his holy labours. Likewise you intimate how acceptable this work is to the Parliament, that blessed Assembly, whom the Lord Christ hath delighted to make instrumental to begin to set up the longed for, prayed for, and desired Kingdome of the Lord Jesus; for we may see in some measure the accomplishment of that Prophesie of Christ, *Luke* 21.25. The peaceable summer beginning to arise out of these distressed times of perplexity, all those signes preceding the glorious coming of Christ are accomplishing, and a thick black cloud is gathered, a cloud of blood, confusion, Heresies and Errors, and the thickest and most portentous black part of that cloud is the Toleration of the most grosse and convicted impieties under the pretence of conscience, which misapplication of the Sword of Authority (if it should awhile prevaile) cannot be innocent, and will undoubtedly prolong the storme and delay of the reigne of Christ; But notwithstanding all this black cloud, who seeth not the glorious coming of the Lord Jesus breaking through this cloud, and coming with power and great glory? He is King of Kings and reigneth over Kings; for where Justice reignes, Christ doth reigne; and that Antichristian principle for man to be above God, whether the Pope in the Church, or Monarches in the Common-wealth, is thrown to the ground. He that is above the Law, is above the Word; and he that is above the Word, is above Christ; Christ reigneth not over such as be above his Law: But behold, now Christ reigneth, and gloriously breaks forth in the brightnesse of his coming, and will in his time scatter all this thick black cloud, yea the thickest of it. Now this glorious work of bringing in and setting up the glorious kingdome of Christ, hath the Lord of his free grace and mercy put into the hands of this renowned Parliament and Army; Lord put it into all their hearts to make this designe of Christ their main first and chiefest endeavour, according to the Word, *Seek first the Kingdom of heaven and the righteousnesse thereof, and all other things shall be added.* And when the Lord Jesus is about to set up his blessed Kingdome among these poore Indians also, how well doth it become the spirit of such instruments in the hand of Christ to promote that work also, being the same businesse in some respect which themselves are about by the good hand of the Lord.

Surely Sir, your chief work of this nature now is to follow this Indian work which sticks in the birth for want of means. You would marvel if I should tell you how they long to come into a way of civility by co-habitation, and by forming government among themselves, that so they being in such order might have a Church and the Ordinances of Christ among them; but want of a Magazine of all sorts of tools and materials for such a work, is the present impediment.

The Lord is wiser then man, and his time is best; I will not say any thing now for farther direction about what is requisite for the work which the Lord is preparing their hearts unto; my former Letters have said enough that way, partly to you, and partly to Mr. *Pelham*, whose Letters I hope you have seen as containing sundry things necessary for your view; and I doubt not but your wisdome will readily adde what is lacking in what I have projected; only let me say this, that I dayly still see more evidence that that is the very way which the Lord would have us take at present.

Let me, I beseech you, trouble you a little farther with some considerations about this great Indian work which lyeth upon me, as my continual care, prayer, desire and endeavour to carry on, namely for their schooling and education of youth in learning, which is a principal means for promoting of it for future times; If the Lord bring us to live in a Towne and Society, we must have speiial care to have Schools for the instruction of the youth in reading, that they may be able to read the Scriptures at least. And therefore there must be some Annual revenew for the maintaining of such Schoolmasters and Dames; Besides, I do very much desire to translate some parts of the Scriptures into their language, and to print some Primer in their language wherein to initiate and teach them to read, which some of the men do much also desire, and printing such a thing will be troublesome and chargable, and I having yet but little skill in their language (having little leasure to attend it by reason of my continual attendance on my Ministry in our own Church) I must have some Indians, and it may be other help continually about me to try and examine Translations, which I look at as a sacred and holy work, and to be regarded with much fear, care, and reverence; and all this is chargable; therefore I look at that as a special matter on which cost is to be bestowed, if the Lord provide means, for I have not means of my own for it. I have a family of many children to educate,and therefore I cannot give over my Ministry in our Church whereby my family is sustained to attend the Indians to whom I give, and of whom I receive nothing, nor have they any thing to give: so that want of money is the only thing in view that doth retard a more full prosecution of this work unto which the Lord doth ripen them apace.

Moreover, there be sundry prompt, pregnant witted youths, not vitiously inclined, but well disposed, which I desire may be wholly sequestred to learning, and put to Schoole for that purpose, had we means; and I suppose ten pounds *per Annum* to be paid in *England*, will maintaine one Indian youth at Schoole, and halfe ascore such Gifts or Annuities would by the blessing of God greatly further this work so farre as concerns that particular.

I had thought to have set down some of their Questions, wherby you might perceive how these dry bones begin to gather flesh and sinnews; but partly I have them not ready, for I have not leasure to set them down at present, and they soone slip my memory, and I did it in all my last Letters, and may do it again, if the Lord will, hereafter. And therefore thus much at present, being cald off to hasten to seale up my Letters, the Lord Jesus blesse you, sanctifie and keep you in all your labours and travels, and accept you, and all your works, and return you again unto us in due season here to see Gods blessing with your eyes upon those poore souls, for whose sakes you have laboured, and the Lord supply your absence to all yours; and so commending you to the Lord and to the word of his grace which is able to sanctifie and save you, I rest

Roxbury, this 8.   *Your Brother and fellow*
of the 5. 49.   *labourer for the good*
                                                  of the poor Indians.
                                                  JOHN ELIOT.

Worthy and much esteemed in the Lord.

I T is no small encouragement unto my spirit, not only to go on unweariably in this enterprize which the Lord hath set my heart upon, but also to expect a great blessing therein; only I must intimate two *Redundances*, one is *page* 8 {152}. where there is a great (I) redundant which maketh the sence untrue; but if left out, the sence is both good and true; for (I) was not the Nominative case or efficient of that Verb, or Act of intreating Mr. *Mahu* to teach them, but it was the Indians Act, and so I said, and so is the sence if that (great I) be left out. A second *Redundancie* is *page* 17 {159}. (though misfigured and no matter) where you put the title of *Evangelist* upon me, which all men take, and you seeme so to put it for that extraordinary office mentioned in the *New Testament*; I do beseech you to suppresse all such things, if ever you should have occasion of doing the like; let us speak and do, and carry all things with all humility; it is the Lord who hath done what is done, and it is most becoming the spirit of Jesus Christ to lift up Christ, and our selves lie low; I wish that that word could be obliterated if any of the books remain.

Now seeing it is so great a comfort to you to hear how the Lord is pleased to carry on this work, I shall relate unto you some passages, whereby you may see in what frame they be; I had, and still have, a great desire to go to a great fishing place, *Namaske* upon *Merimak*; and because the Indians way lyeth beyond the great River which we cannot passe with our horses, nor can we well go to it on this side the river, unlesse we go by *Nashaway*, which is about, and bad way, unbeaten, the Indians not using that way; I therefore hired a hardy man of *Nashaway* to beat out a way and to mark trees, so that he may Pilot me thither in the spring, and he hired Indians with him and did it; and in the way passed through a great people called *Sowahagen Indians*, some of which had heard me at *Pautuket* and at *Nashaway*, and had carried home such tydings, that they were generally stirred with a desire that I would come and teach them; and when they saw a man come to cut out a way for me that way, they were very glad; and when he told them I intended to come that way the next spring, they seemed to him full of joy, and made him very welcome. But in the Spring, when I should have gone, I was not well, it being a very sickly time, so that I saw the Lord prevented me of that journey; yet when I went to *Pautuket* another fiishing place, where from all parts about they met together, thither came divers of these *Sowahegen* Indians, and heard me teach, and I had conference with them; and among other things, I asked whether *Sowahegen* Indians were desirous to pray to God; they answered; yea, I asked how many desired it; they answered *wamu*, that is, *All,* and with such affection as did much affect those Christian men that I had with me in company.

The chief *Sachim* of this place *Pautuket,* and of all *Mermak* in *Papassaconnoway,* whom I mentioned unto you the last yeere, who gave up himself and his sonnes to pray unto God, this man did this yeer shew very great affection to me, and to the Word of God; he did exceeding earnestly, importunately invite me to come and live there and teach them; he used many arguments, many whereof I have forgotten: but this was one, *that my coming thither but once in a yeere, did them but little good, because they soone had forgotten what I taught, it being so seldome, and so long betwixt the times;* further he said, *That he had many men, and of them many nought, and would not beleeve him that praying to God was so good, but if I would come and teach them, he hoped they would beleeve me;* He farther added, that I did, *as if one should come and throw a fine thing among them, and they earnestly catch at it, and like it well, because it looks finely, but they cannot look into it to see what is within it, and what it is within, they cannot tell whether something or nothing, it may be a stock or a stone is within it, or it may be a precious thing; but if it be opened, and they see what is within it, and see it precious, then they should beleeve it* (so said he) *you tell us of praying to God,* (for so they call all Religion) *and we like it well at the first sight, and we know not what it is within, it may be excellent, or it may be nothing, we cannot tell, but if you would come unto us, and open it unto us, and shew us what it is within, then we should beleeve that it is so excellent as you say, when we see it opened;* Such elegant arguments as these did he use, with much gravity, wisdome and affection; and truly my heart much yearneth towards them, and I have a great desire to make our Indian Towne that way; yet the Lord by the Eye of Providence seemeth not to look thither, partly because there is not a competent place of due encouragement for subsistence; which would spoyle the work; and partly because our Indians which are our first and chief materials in present view, are loth to go Northward, though they say they will go with me any whether; but it concerneth me much not to lead them into temptation of scarity, cold and want, which may damp the progresse of the Gospel; but I rather think where ever I begin the first Towne, (if I live) I must begin more townes then one, or oh that the Lord would raise up more and more fit labourers into this harvest.

Another Indian, who lived remote another way, asked me if I had any children? I answered yea; he asked how many? I said sixe; he asked how many of them were sonnes? I told him five; then he asked whether my sonnes should teach the Indians to know God as I do? at which question I was much moved in my heart, for I have often in my prayers dedicated all my sonnes unto the Lord to serve him in this service, if he will please to accept them therein; and my purpose is to do my uttermost to traine them up in learning, whereby they may be fitted in the best manner I can to serve the Lord herein, and better preferment

I desire not for them then to serve the Lord in this travel; and to that purpose I answered him, and my answer seemed to be well pleasing to them, which seemed to minister to my heart some encouragement, that the Lords meaning was to improve them that way, and he would prepare their hearts to accept the same.

There is another aged *Sachem* at *Quabagud* threescore miles Westward, and he doth greatly desire that I would come thither and teach them, and live there; and I made a journey thither this summer, and I went by *Nashaway*; but it so fell out that there were some stirres betwixt the *Nazagenset* and *Monahegen* Indians, some murder committed, &c. which made our Church doubtful at first of my going, which when the *Nashaway Sachem* heard, he commanded twenty armed men (after their manner) to be ready, and himself with these twenty men; besides sendry of our neer Indians went along with me to guard me, but I took some English along with me also, so that hereby their good affection is manifested to me, and to the work I have in hand; here also I found sundry hungry after instruction, but it pleased God to exercise us with such tedious raine, and bad weather, that we were extreme wet, insomuch that I was not dry night nor day from the third day of the week unto the sixth, but so travelled, and at night pull off my boots, wring my stockins, and on with them again, and so continued; the rivers also were raised, so as that we were wet in riding through; but that which added to my affliction was, my horse tyred, so that I was forced to let my horse go empty, and ride on one of the mens horses which I took along with me, yet God stept in and helped; I considered that word of God, *2 Tim* 2,3. *Endure hardship as a good Souldier of Christ*; with many other such like meditations, which I think not meet to mention now. And I thank the Lord, neither I nor my company took any hurt; but the Lord brought us in safety and health home again.

Because, both Mr. *Pelham* and your self do so heartily, and with such good affection send commendations and greetings unto our Indians which pray unto God, I will tell you what a good occasion was ministred unto me, through the goodnesse of God, by a question which one of them propounded the next meeting as I remember) after I had received my Letters, and I must first tell you the occasion of the question.

There had been at that time some strange Indians among them which came to see them who prayed to God, as one from *Martins Vineyard,* who is helpful to Mr. *Mahu* to tell him words, &c. and I think some others, *when those strangers came,* and they perceived them to *affect Religion,* and had mutual conference about the same, there was very great *gladnesse of heart* among them, and they made these strangers exceeding welcome; Hereupon did the Question arise, namely what is the reason, that when a strange Indian comes among us whom we never saw before, *yet if he pray unto God, we do exceedingly love him: But if my own Brother, dwelling a great way off, come unto us, he not praying to God, though we love him, yet nothing so as we love that other stranger who doth pray unto God.*

This question did so clearly demonstrate that which the Scripture calleth *love of the Brethren,* that I thought it was useful; first to try others of them, whether they found the same in their hearts; I therefore asked them, how they found it in theis hearts? And they answered, that they all found it so in their hearts, and that it had been a matter of discourse among themselves, *wondring at it, what the reason of it should be*, which was no small comfort and encouragement unto my spirit; Then in my answer I asked them what should be the reason that the godly people in *England,* 3000. miles off, who never saw them, yet hearing that they pray to God, do exceedingly rejoyce at it, and love them, and send them tokens of their love, and then I reckoned up what had been sent them, and mentioned some names to them, and farther told them that their love was so great unto them, that they would send them over a great deale more; and in special, I hoped they would send us such materials as be requisite to make a Towne, and mentioned some such things as I have named in the Catalogue I sent to you, and asked them if they could tell the reason of it; they answered no; this being the same with their question; and then I shewed the unity of spirit, &c. And thus you see the occasion and way of communicating the good will and love of the Saints in *England,* unto them, so as that they might taste a spiritual blessing, and finde some edification of their souls by those outward blessings which they received. And whereas some, (as I am informed) who came from us to *England,* are no better friends to this work then they should, and may speak slightly of it: I do intreat that such may be asked but this question; Did they so much regard to look after it here, as to go three or four miles to some of our meetings, and to observe what was said and done there? if not, how can they tell how things be? if they say they were, I desire to know what they except against? If they say the Indians be all nought because such as come loytering and filtching about in our Townes are so; Wish them to consider how unequal that judgment is, if all the English should be judged by the worst of them; and any should say they be all such, this were to condemne the righteous with the wicked. Had I leasure, I would insert a few more of their questions, that you might perceive how flesh and sinewes begin to gather upon these dry bones; but I cannot at this time attend it; the present work of God among them is to gather them together to bring them to Political life, both in Ecclesiastical society and in Civil, for which they earnestly long and enquire, and some aged ones say, *Oh that God would let me live to see that day*; I allude to that in *Ezekiel,* not because I have any light to perswade me these are that people there mentioned, only they be dry and scattered bones, if any be in the world; and the work of God upon all such dry bones I beleeve will be in many things *Symmetricall*; But the work of the day is to civilize them, and it will be very chargeable, and because in your Letters to Mr. *Cotton,* you desired that he and I should speak with the Commissioners what was fitting to send over for this work, we could not speak with the Commissioners of other Colonies, nor write to have any seasonable return, nor could we communicate the state of the businesse unto them, but what was feasible we have done.

Now dear Sir, it may be you will desire to know what kinde of Civil Government they shall be instructed in; I acknowledge it to be a very weighty consideration; and I have advised with Mr. *Cotton* and others about it, and this I propound as my general rule through the help of the Lord; they shall be wholly governed by the Scriptures in all things both in Church and State; they shall have no other Law-giver; the Lord shall be their Law-giver, the Lord shall be their Judge, the Lord shall be their King, and he will save them; and when it is so the Lord reigneth, and unto that frame the Lord will bring all the world ere he hath done, but it will be more difficult in other Nations who have been adulterate with their *Antichristian* or humane wisdome; they will be loth to lay downe their imperfect own Star-light of excellent Lawes, in their conceits, for the perfect Sun-light of the Scripture, which through blindnesse they cannot see.

England long since had happy experience of it, and it is often in my heart to desire they would pitch there in this present great change they are about; this is certaine, that all formes and Lawes of mans invention will shake, be unsetled; and many will doubt of subjecting to any way man can devise; and they will never rest till they come up to the Scriptures, and when they produce Scripture grounds for all they do, it will answer and satisfie all godly consciences, and awe the rest, and stop their mouths unlesse they will cavill against divine wisdome. It is the very reason why the Lord in this houre of temptation will bring Nations into distresse and perplexity, that so they may be forced to the Scriptures; the light whereof hath sole authority to extricate them out of their deep perplexities; and therefore all Governments are and will be shaken, that men may be forced to pitch upon the firme and unshaken foundation, *the Word of God*, this is doubtlesse the great designe of Christ in these later dayes; Oh that mens eyes were open to see it, and when the world is brought into this frame, then Christ reigneth; and when this is, Government shall be in the hands of the Saints of the most high.

But I forget my self; this is not my present work, it is my desire and prayer; my work is to endeavour the setting up Christ Kingdome among the Indians.

Sir, you tell me of one that will publish reasons to prove (at least) some of the ten Tribes are in *America*, it would be glad tydings to my heart; and when Mr. *Dudley* heard of it, he said that Captaine *Cromwell*, who lately dyed at *Boston,* told him that he saw many Indians to the Southward Circumcised, and that he was oft conversant among them, and saw it with his eyes, and that he was undoubtedly certaine of it; this is Captaine *Cromwels* testimony, and it seemeth to be one of the most probable arguments that ever I yet heard of; unlesse the Lord shall please to clear it up that they are some of those dry bones which *Ezekiel* speaketh of.

Mr. *Mahew*, who putteth his hand unto this Plough at *Martins Vineyard*, being young, and a beginner here, hath extreme want of books; he needeth *Commentaries* and *Common Places* for the body of Divinity, that so he might be well grounded and principled; if therefore the Lord bring any meanes into your hand, I desire you would (by the help of some godly Divine) send him over such books as may be necessary for a young Scholer; I will name no books, he needs all; I beseech you put some weight upon it, for I desire he might be furnished in that kinde, and other supplies will be needful for him.

And for my self I have this request (who also am short enough in books) that I might be helped to purchase my brother *Weld* his books, the summe of the purchase is ({£}34.) I am loth they should come back to *England* when we have so much need of them here, and without ready money there I cannot have them; if therefore so much money might be disbursed for me, it would be a blessing to me, but it is on condition that all his books here be comprehended, else I will not give so much for them.

One thing more I shall mention, *viz.* if the work go on, and you send us means, then this may be considerable, which some have advised me, whether it might not be good to send me over a Carpenter or two young men-servants; but if you should approve it, I desire they may be godly, and well conditioned, of a good spirit, for they must be imployed among the Indians, and if they should be naught, and of an ill disposition they might do a great deal of hurt, but if they be honest & meek and well spirited, it may be a great furtherance of the work, I wholly leave it to your wisdom.

Having some leasure by the Ships delay I will insert a few questions which they have propounded. *viz.*

If a man know Gods Word, but beleeve it not; and he teach others, is that good teaching? and if others beleeve that which he teacheth, is that good beleeving, or faith? upon this question I asked them, how they could tell when a man knoweth Gods Word that he doth not beleeve it? They answered me, *When he doth not do in his practice answerable to that which he knoweth.*

If I teach on the Sabbath that which you have taught us, and forget some, Is that a sin? and some I mistake and teach wrong, Is that a sin?

Do all evill thoughts come from the Devill, and all good ones from God?

What is watchfulnesse?

How shall I finde happinesse?

What should I pray for at night, and what at morning, and what on the Sabbath day?

What is true Repentance, or how shall I know when this is true?

How must I wait on God?

Shall we see Christ at the day of Judgment?

Can we see God?

When I pray for a soft heart, why is it still hard?

Can one be saved by reading the book of the creature? This question was made when I taught them, That God gave us two books, and that in the book of the creature, every creature was a word or sentence, &c.

You said God promised Moses *to go with him, how doth he go with us?*

When such die as never heard of Christ, whether do they go?

When the wicked die, do they first go to heaven to the judgment seate of Christ to be judged, and then go away to hell?

What is the meaning of the word Hebrews?

Why doth God say, I am the God of the Hebrews?

When Christ arose, whence came his soul? When I answered from heaven; It was replyed, *How then was Christ punished in our stead? Or when did he suffer in our stead, afore death, or after?*

When I pray every day, why is my heart so hard still, even as a stone?

How doth God arise, and we worship at his feet, what meaneth it? This was when I preached out of *Psal.132.*

Why did they eate the Passeover, with loynes girt, and shooes on their feet?

What meaneth, arise O Lord into thy resting place?

What meaneth, hunger and thirst after righteousnesse, and they blessed?

What meaneth, thou shalt not coven any thing that is thy neighbours?

If one purposeth to pray, and yet dieth before that time, whether goeth his soul?

If I teach on the Sabbath something that some other Englishman taught me, the Indians do not like it, if it be not that which you have taught, is this well?

Why must we be like Salt?

If I do not love wicked men, nor good men, am I good?

What meaneth that, love enemies and wicked men?

Doth God know who shall repent, and beleeve, and who not? When I answered in the affirmative, then it was replyed, *Why then did God use so much meanes with* Pharoah?

What meaneth that his wife shall be like a Vine, and his children like young plants?

What meaneth, that blessed are they that mourn?

When I see a good example, and know that it is right, why do I not do the same?

What meaneth lifting up hands to God?

Whot anger is good, and what is bad?

Do they dwell in severall houses in heaven, or altogether, and what do they?

How do you know what is done in heaven?

If a child die before he sinne, whether goeth his soul? By this question, it did please the Lord, clearly to convince them of original sin, blessed be his name.

If one that prayes to God, sins like him that prayes not, is not he worse? And while they discoursed of this point, and about hating of wicked persons, one of them shut it up with this, *They must love the man and do him good, but hate his sin.*

Why do Englishmen so eagerly kill all snakes?

May a man have good words and deeds and a bad heart, and another have bad words and deeds, and yet a good heart?

What is it to eate Christ his flesh and drink his blood, what meaneth it?

What meaneth a new heaven and a new earth?

Much honoured and respected in the Lord Jesus.

Y Our faithful and unwearied paines about the Lords work for the good of his dear children here, and for the furtherance of the Kingdome of Christ among these poor Indians, shall doubtlesse be had in remembrance before the Lord, not through merit, but mercie.

By former Letters sent by Mr. *Saltonstall*; I informed you of the present state of the Indian work, and though I might adde farther matters, yet I shal forbear, only this, still they continue constant, and earnestly desire to set upon the way of cohabitation & prepare for their enjoyment of that great blessing to gather a Church of Christ among them; and since the writing of my last a *Nipnet Sachem* hath submitted himself to pray unto the Lord, and much desireth one of our chief ones to live with him and teach him and those that are with him.

You wrote (I thank you) much encouraging to lose no time, and follow the work, though I borrow materials, but I durst not do so, the work is great, as I informed you in my former Letters; and I fear, lest it should discourage you, nor would I be too hasty to run before the Lord do clearly (by Scripture rules) say go; nor on the other side would I hold them too long in suspence, there may be weaknesse that way to their discouragement, but it is the Lords work, and he is infinite in wisdome, and he will suit the work in such a time and place as shall best attain his appointed ends and his great glory.

Touching the way of their Government, I also intimated the purpose of my heart, that I intend to direct them according as the Lord shall please to help and assist to set up the Kingdome of Jesus Christ fully, so that Christ shall reigne both in Church and Common-wealth, both in Civil and Spiritual matters; we will (through his grace) fly to the Scriptures, for every Law, Rule, Direction, Form, or what ever we do. And when everything both Civil & Spiritual are done by the direction of the word of Christ, then doth Christ reigne, and the great Kingdome of Jesus Christ which we weight for, is even this that I do now mention; and by this means all Kingdomes and Nations shall become the Kingdomes of Christ, because he shall rule them in all things by his holy word; humane wisdome in learned Nations will be loth to yeeld to Christ so farre, much lesse will Princes and Monarches readily yeeld so farre to stoop to Christ, and therefore the Lord will shake all Nations, and put them into distresse and perplexity, and in the conclusion they will be glad to stoop to Christ. But as for these poore Indians they have no principles of their own, nor yet wisdome of their own (I mean as other Nations have) wherein to stick; and therefore they do most readily yeeld to any direction from the Lord, so that there will be no such opposition against the rising Kingdome of Jesus Christ among them; yet I foresee a cloud of difficulties in the work, and much obscurity and trouble in some such respects, as I think not meet to mention, only by faith I do see through this cloud: I beleeve the faithful promises of Christ shall be accomplisht among them, and the Lord Jesus shall reigne over them gloriously, *Oh my heart yearneth over distressed perplexed England*, and my continual prayer unto the Lord for them is, that he would be pleased to open their hearts and eyes, and let them see their opportunity to let in Christ, and to advance his Kingdome over them; yea, my hope is, that he will not leave tampering with them untill he hath brought it to passe; Oh the blessed day in *England* when the Word of God shall be their *Magna Charta* and chief Law Book; and when all Lawyers must be Divines to study the Scriptures; and should the Gentile Nations take up *Moses* policie so farre as it is morall and conscionable, make the Scriptures the foundation of all their Lawes, who knoweth what a door would be opened to the

Jewes to come in to Christ; I wrote likewise by my last to intreat for some encouragement to Master *Mahu* who preacheth to the Indians, and that some monies may be laid out in books for him; for young Sholars in *New-England* are very poor in books, as he is in extreme want.

Dear Sir,

Be helpful in prayer to our work, and above all gatherings, gather prayers; I mean, put the Saints in minde that they pray much about it, as they do both there and here.

Truly Sir,

The spirit of prayer that is daily going about this matter, is a very great encouragement for all our meetings, through mercie, ring of it; I would intimate some more questions which they have propounded since my last, for they are fruitful that way, but partly I fear I shall want time, yet my heart saies, it may comfort you, and therefore I will set down a few, so many as I have noted down since my last.

If but one parent beleeve, what state are our children in?

How doth much sinne make grace abound? I having made use of that Text.

If so old a man as I repent, may I be saved? The wisdome of God drew forth this question next to interpret the former.

When we come to beleeve, how many of our children doth God take with us, whether all only young ones, or at what age?

What meaneth that, Let the trees of the Wood rejoyce?

What meaneth that, That the Master doth not thank his servant for waiting on him?

What meaneth that, We cannot serve two masters?

Can they in Heaven see us here on Earth?

Do they see and know each other? Shall I know you in heaven?

Do they know each other in Hell?

When English-men choose Magistrates and Ministers, how do they know who be good men, that they dare trust?

Seeing the boody sinneth, why should the soule be punished, and what punishment shall the body have?

If all the world be burnt up, where shall hell be?

What is it to beleeve in Christ?

What meaneth, that Christ meriteth eternal life for us?

What meaneth that, Covet not they neighbours house, &c?

What meaneth that, The woman brought to Christ a box of Oyle, and washt his feet with tears. &c?

What meaneth that of the two debtors, one oweth much, another but little?

If a wicked man prayeth, and teacheth, doth God accept, or what saies God?

At what age may maids marry?

If a man be wise, and his Sachem *weak must he yet obey him?*

We are commanded to honour the Sachem, *but is the* Sachem *commanded to lovve us?*

When all the world shall be burnt up, what shall be in the roome of it; an old womans question yester day?

What meaneth God, when he saeys, yee shall be my Jewels? This was asked from my text last time, *Exod.* 19.5. for so I rendred the word peculiar treasure.

You may perceive many of the questions arise out of such texts as I handle, and I do endeavour to communicate as much Scripture as I can; *The word of the Lord converteth, sanctifieth and maketh wise the simple*; sometimes they aske weaker questions then these, which I mention not, you have the best; and when I am about writing, I am more careful in keeping a remembrance of them; it may be the same question may be again and again asked at several places, and by several persons; The Lord teach them to know Christ, *whom to know is eternal life*; I shall intreat your supplications at the throne of grace, under the tender wing whereof I leave you, being forced by the time, and rest

Roxbury this 29. *of*
   the 10*th* 49.

              Your respectful and loving
              brother and fellow-labourer
              in the Indian work.

JOHN ELIOT.

Much honoured and beloved in Christ, &c.

I Heard of the health and welfare of your family not long since, though the sharpnesse and depth of snowes this later part of winter did more shut up and hinder intercourse then ever I knew in *New-England*.

I shall principally attend to give you intelligence about the Indians, touching whom, I know not that you are like to have intelligence by others; The Lord hath shewed them a very great testimony of his mercy this winter, in that when formerly the English had the Pox much, they also had the same; but now though it was scattered in all or most of the Townes about them, yet the Lord hath preserved them from it; And that which maketh this favour of God the more evident and conspicuous, is this; That there is a company of profane Indians that lately are come to a place near *Wamouth*, not farre from our Indians, who do not onely refuse to pray unto God, but oppose and apprehend that they were sent thither, if not by the policie of some *Pawwaws*, yet by the instigation of Sathan, on purpose to seduce the younger sort from their profession, and discourage others; and indeed they being so neer, had that effect evidently in some of the younger sort. Now it pleased God that this company of wicked Indians, were smitten with the Pox, and sundry cut off, and those which were cut off, were of the worst and mischievous of them all; which Providences, all the good Indians do take a great notice of, and doth say that the Lord hath wrought a wonder for them; and it seemeth to me that the Lord hath blest this good Providence of his to be a strong ingagement of their hearts to the Lord.

The work of the Lord through his grace doth still go on as formerly, and they are still full of questions, and mostly they now be, to know the meaning of such Scriptures as I have translated and read, and in a poor measure expounded to them, they long for to proceed in that work which I have in former Letters mentioned; namely to cohabit in a Towne, to be under the government of the Lord, and to have a Church and the Ordinances of Christ among them; this Spring the Lord seemed to put some of them upon such streights, about a convenient place of planting, as if his Providence had meant to call us to a present setting upon the work, but partly by reason of the undetermination about the place where, but principally for want of means, wherewith it is yet deferred, though I see a necessity to speed it forward, for they have been now long in the expectation, and if I should still fail them, it would both discourage them, and embolden their adversaries to despise the work (for all the Country of Indians are in an expectation of it) yea by this delay that hath been, Sathan hath taken this advantage to my great grief;   That whereas at my first preaching at *Nashawog* sundry did imbrace the word, and called upon God, and *Pau wauing* was wholly silenced among them all; yet now, partly being forty miles of; and principally by the slow progresse of this work, Sathan hath so embolned the Pawwawes, that this winter, (as I hear to my grief) there hath been Paw-wauing again with some of them.

The reason why there is still a delay of laying the foundation of the work is this, because we must see first whether any supply is like to be had from *England* (for our sins and bad times may disappoint our greatest hopes) and if any, what measure, that we may by that be guided what foundation and beginning to make; their condition and the necessary frame of this work requireth a liberall stock to begin withall, and liberall supply to carry it on; And therefore to begin the work before the Lord hath discovered his providing providence this way, by the rule of prudence may not be; nor can I manifest unto the Church that God doth call me to that work, untill I may lay before them, (at least some) present means to begin the work, and some probable hopes of supply; and untill that be done, the Church hath no rule to give me up to that work; nor I a rule to require it; only I do (through the Lords help) continually go on to teach them, as for these three yeers and a half I have done, instructing them, and preparing them as well as I can against such time as the Lord, who hath promised to guide us by his eye and voyce, shall manifestly call us to go forward with that work which we wait to see accomplished.

I forbear to mention any thing about the materials requisite, and manner of proceedings, having done that in my former Letters, by the first ship especially, and also by the second; both which Vessels I trust the Lord hath brought in safe to you long ere this time. I was in great hopes to have heard some encouragement by fishing ships, but not one being this yeere come, nor tydings any other way, we are put to sad thoughts how it may fare with *England*, but we cease not to pray continually in that behalf, and this expectation of mine is one ingagement of my heart to be the more earnest both for *England* and for your self also.

Roxbury this 18. *of*   *Your loving friend and brother*
    the 2^d   1650.   *in our Lord Jesus*

JOHN ELIOT.

Much respected and beloved in our Lord Jesus.

GOd is greatly to be adored in all his Providences, and hath evermore wise and holy ends to accomplish that which we are not aware of; and therefore although he may seem to crosse our ends with disappointments after all our pains and expectations, yet he hath farther and better thoughts then we can reach unto, which will cause us to admire his love and wisdome, when we see them accomplished; and yet he is gracious to accept of our sincere labours for his name, though he disappoint them in our way, and frustrate our expectations in our time; yea, he will fulfill our expectations in his way, and in his time, which shall finally appeare to the eye of faith, a better way then ours, and a fitter time then ours; his wisdome is infinite.

For the work of the Lord among the Indians, I thank his Majesty he still smileth on it, he favoureth and blesseth it; through his help that strengthneth me, I cease not in my poor measure to instruct them; and I do see that they profit and grow in knowledge of the truth, and some of them in the love of it, which appeareth by a ready obedience to it; and to testifie their growth in knowledge, I will not (though I could do it if need were) trouble you with their questions; but I will only relate one story which fell out about the fifth month of this yeere; Two of my hearers travelled to *Providence* and *Warwick* where *Gorton* liveth, and there they spent a Sabbath, and heard them in some exercises, and had much conference with them; for it seemeth they perceiving that they had some knowledge in Religion, and were of my hearers; they endeavour to possesse their minds with their opinions. When they came home, the next Lecture day, before I began the exercise, the company being not fully come together, one of them asked me this question; *What is the reason, that seeing those English people, where he had been, had the same Bible that we have, yet do not speake the same things?* I asked the reason of his question; he said, *because his brother and he had been at* Providence *and at* Warwick, *and he perceived by speech with them, that they differ from us; he said they heard their publike exercise, but did not understand what they meant,* (though the man understandeth the English Language pretty well) But afterwards said he, *we had much speech*; I asked him in what points; and so much as his brother and he could call to minde, he related as followeth.

First, said he, *they said thus, they teach you that there is a Heaven and a Hell; but there is no such matter;* I asked him what reason they gave; *he answered, that he said there is no other Heaven, then what is in the hearts of good men; nor no other Hell, then what is in the hearts of bad men;* Then I asked, and what said you to that; saith he, *I told them, I did not beleeve them, because Heaven is a place whether good men go after this life is ended; and Hell is a place whether bad men go when they die, and cannot be in the hearts of men;* I approved of this answer. I asked what else they spake? he answered, *they spake of Baptism,* and said, *that they teach you that Infants must be baptized, but that is a very foolish thing;* I asked him what reason they gave? He said, *because Infants neither know God nor Baptisme, nor what they do, and therefore it is a foolish thing to do it;* I asked him what he said to that? He said, *he could not say much, but he thought it was better to baptize them while they be young, and then they are bound and engaged; but if you let them alone till they be grown up, it may be they will flie off, and neither care for God nor for Baptisme;* I approved of this answer also, and asked what else they spake of? He said farther, *they spake of Ministers,* and said, *they teach you that you must have Ministers, but that is a needlesse thing.* I asked what reason they gave? He said, *they gave these reasons,* First, *Ministers know nothing but what they learn out of Gods book, and we have Gods book as well as they and can tell what God saith.* Again, *Ministers cannot change mens hearts, God must do that, and therefore there is no need of Ministers.* I asked him what he said to that? He said, *that he told them, that we must do as God commands us, and if he commands to have Ministers, we must have them. And farther I told them, I thought it was true, that Ministers cannot change mens hearts; but when we do as God bids us, and hear Ministers preach, then God will change our hearts.* I approved this answer also. I asked what else they spake of? He said, *They teach you that you must have Magistrates, but that is needlesse, nor ought to be.* I asked what reason they gave? He said, *That they gave this reason, because Magistrates cannot give life, therefore they may not take away life; besides, when a man sinneth, he doth not sinne against Magistrates, and therefore why should they punish them? but they sinne against God, and therefore we must leave them to God to punish them.* I asked him what he said to that, he answered, *I said to that as to the former, we must do as God commands us; If God command us to have Magistrates, and commands them to punish sinners, them we must obey.* I approved this also.

I asked farther what they said; then both of them considered a while, and said, *they could remember no more,* only they said somewhat of the Parliament of *England,* which they did not understand. And by such time as we had done this conference, the company was gathered together, and we went to Prayer, and I did solemnly blesse God who had given them so much understanding in his truth, and some ability to discerne between Truth and Error, and an heart to stand for the Truth, and against Error; and I cannot but take it as a Divine Testimony of Gods blessing upon my poor labours; I afterwards gave him an answer to his first question, *viz. Why they having the same Bible with us, yet spake not the same things?* And I answered him by that Text, 2 *Thes.* 2.10,11.

Because they received not the love of the truth that they might be saved, for this cause God shall send them strong delusions that they should beleeve a lye. This text I opened unto them; I will adde no more at present to manifest their proficiency in knowledge.

The present work of the Lord that is to be done among them, is to gather them together from their scattered kinde of life; First, unto Civil Society, then to Ecclesiastical, and both by the Divine direction of the Word of the Lord; they are still earnestly desirous of it; and this Spring that is past, they were very importunately desirous to have been upon that work, and to have planted corne in the place intended; but I did disswade, and was forced to use this reason of delay, because I hoped for tools, and meanes from *England,* whereby to prosecute the work this Summer. But when ships came, and no supply, you may easily think what a damping it was; and truly my heart smote me, that I had looked too much at man and meanes, in stoping their earnest affections with that barre which proved a Blank. I began without any such respect, and I thought that the Lord would have me so to go on, and only look to him for help, whose work it is; and when I had thus looked up to the Lord, I advised with our Elders and some other of our Church, whose hearts consented with me; then I advised with divers of the Elders at *Boston* Lecture, and Mr. *Cottons* answer was, *my heart sayeth, go on, and look to the Lord onely for help*, the rest also concuring; So I commended it to our Church, and we sought God in a day of fasting and prayer about it, (together with other causes) and have been ever since a doing, according to our abilities; and this I account a favour of God, that that very night, before we came from our place of meeting, we had notice of a Ship from *England* whereby I received Letters, and some encouragement in the work from private friends; a mercy which God had in store, but unknown to some, and so contrived by the Lord, that I should receive it as a fruit of prayer.

The place also is of Gods providing, as a fruit of prayer; for when I, with some that went with me, had rode to a place of some hopefull expectation, when we came to it, it was in no wise sutable; I went behind a Rock, and looked to the Lord, and committed the matter to him; and while I was travelling in Woods, Christian friends were in prayer at home; and so it was, that though one of our company fell sick in the Woods, so that we were forced home with speed; yet in the way home, the Indians in our company, upon enquiry describing a place to me, and guiding us over some part of it, the Lord did both by his providence then, and by after more diligent search of the place, discover that there it was his pleasure we should begin this work. When grasse was fit to cut, I sent some Indians to mow, and others to make some hay at the place, because we must oft ride thither in the Autumn when grasse is withered and dead, and especially in the Spring before any grasse is come, and there is provision for our horses; this work was performd well, as I found when I went up to them with my man to order it. We must also of necessity have an house to lodge in, meet in, and lay up our provisions and clothes, which cannot be in *Wigwams.* I set them therefore to fell and square timber for an house, and when it was ready, I went, and many of them with me, and on their shoulders carried all the timber together, &c. These things they chearfully do; but this also I do, I pay them wages carefully for all such works I set them about, which is good encouragement to labour. I purpose, God willing, to call them together this Autumne to break and prepare their own ground against the Spring, and for other necessary works, which are not afew, in such an enterprize. There is a great river which divideth between their planting grounds and dwelling place, through which, though they easily wade in Summer, yet in the Spring its deep, and unfit for daily passing over, especially of women and children; therefore I thought it necessary, that this Autumne we should make a foot Bridge over, against such time in the Spring as they shall have daily use of it; I told them my purpose and reason of it, wished them to go with me to do that work, which they chearfully did, and with their own hands did build a Bridge eighty foot long, and nine foot high in the midst, that it might stand above the floods; when we had done, I cald them together, prayed, and gave thanks to God, and taught them out of a portion of Scripture, and at parting I told them, I was glad of their readinesse to labour, when I advised them thereunto; and in as much as it hath been hard and tedious labour in the water, if any of them desired wages for their work, I would give it them; yet being it is for their owne use, if they should do all this labour in love, I should take it well, and as I may have occasion, remember it; they answered me, they were farre from desiring any wages when they do their own work; but on the other side they were thankful to me that I had called them, and counselled them in a work so needful for them, whereto I replyed, I was very glad to see them so ingenuous.

This businesse of praying to God (for that is their general name of Religion) hath hitherto found opposition only from the *Pawwawes* and profane spirits; but now the Lord hath exercised us with another and a greater opposition; for the *Sachems* of the Country are generally set against us, and counter-work the Lord by keeping off their men from praying to God as much as they can; And the reason of it is this, They plainly see that Religion will make a great change among them, and cut them off from their former tyranny; for they used to hold their people in an absolute servitude, insomuch as what ever they had, and themselves too were at his command; his language was, as one said (*amne meum*) now they see that Religion teaches otherwise, and puts a bridle upon such usurpations; Besides their former manner was, that if they wanted money, or if they desired any thing from a man, they would take occasion to rage and be in a great anger; which when they did perceive, they would give him all they had to pacifie him; for else their way was to suborne some villain (of which they have no lack) to finde some opportunity to kill him: *This keeps them in great awe of their Sachems*, and is one reason why none of them desire any wealth, only from hand to mouth, because they are but servants, and they get it not for themselves; But now if their *Sachem* so rage, and give sharp and cruell language, instead of seeking his favour with gifts (as formerly) they will admonish him of his sinne; tell him that is not the right way to get money; but he must labour, and then he may have money, that is Gods command, &c. And as for Tribute, some they are willing to pay, but not as formerly. Now these are great temptations to the *Sachems*, and they had need of a good measure both of wisdome and grace to swallow this Pill, and it hath set them quite off; And I suppose that hence it is, that (I having requested the Court of Commissioners for a general way to be thought of to instruct all the Indians in all parts, and I told the Indians that I did so, which they would soon spread; and still in my prayers, I pray for the *Monohegens, Narragansets, &c.*) the *Monohegen* Indians were much troubled lest the Court of Commissioners should take some course to teach them to pray to God; and *Unkus* their *Sachem* went to *Hartford* this Court (for there they sate) and expressed to Elder *Goodwin* his feare of such a thing, and manifested a great unwillingnesse thereunto; this one of our Commissioners told me at his coming home.

This temptation hath much troubled *Cutshamoquin* our *Sachem*, and he was raised in his spirit to such an height, that at a meeting after Lecture, he openly contested with me against our proceeding to make a Town; and plainly told me that all the *Sachems* in the Countrey were against it, &c. When he did so carry himself, all the Indians were filled with fear, their countenances grew pale, and most of them slunk away, a few stayed, and I was alone, not any English man with me; But it pleased God (for it was his guidance of me, and assistance) to raise up my spirit, not to passion, but to a bold resolution, telling him it was Gods work I was about, and he was with me, and I feared not him, nor all the *Sachems* in the Country, and I was resolved to go on do what they can, and they nor he should hinder that which I had begun, &c. And it pleased God that his spirit shrunk and fell before me, which when those Indians that tarried saw, they smiled as they durst, out of his sight, and have been much strengthned ever since; and since I understand that in such conflicts their manner is, that they account him that shrinks to be conquered, and the other to conquer; which alas I knew not, nor did I aime at such a matter, but the Lord carried me beyond my thoughts and wont; after this brunt was over, I took my leave to go home, and *Cutshamoquin* went a little way with me, and told me that the reason of this trouble was, because the Indians that pray to God, since they have so done, do not pay him tribute as formerly they have done; I answered him that once before when I heard of his complaint that way, I preached on that text, *Give unto Cæsar what is Cæsars, and unto God what is Gods*; and also on *Rom.* 13. naming him the matter of the texts (not the places of which he is ignorant). But he said its true, I taught them well, but they would not in that point do as I taught them; And further he said, this thing are all the *Sachems* sensible of, and therefore set themselves against praying to God; and then I was troubled, lest (if they should be sinfully unjust) they should both hinder and blemish the Gospel and Religion; I did therefore consult with the Magistrates and Mr. *Cotton* and other Elders; Mr. *Cottons* text by Gods providence, the next Lecture gave him occasion to speak to it, which I fore knowing advised some that understood English best, to be there; and partly by what they heard, and by what I had preached to the like purpose, and told them what Mr. *Cotton* said, &c. they were troubled, and fell to reckon up what they had done in two yeers past, a few of them that lived at one of the places I preached unto; I took down the particulars in writing, as followeth. At one time they gave him twenty bushels of corne, at another time more then six bushels; two hunting dayes they killed him fifteen Deeres; they brake up for him two Acres of Land, they made for him a great house or Wigwam, they made twenty rod of fence for him, with a Ditch and two Railes about it, they paid a debt for him of 3.li.10.s. only some others were contributors in this money; one of them gave him a skin of Beaver of two pound, at his returne from building, besides many dayes works in planting corne altogther, and some severally; yea they said they would willingly do more if they would govern well by justice, and as the word of God taught them; when I heard all this, I wondred, for this cometh to neere 30.li. and was done by a few, and they thought it not much if he had carried matters better; and yet his complaint was, they do nothing; But the bottome of it lieth here, he formerly had all or what he would; now he hath but what they will; and admonitions also to rule better, and he is provoked by other *Sachems*, and ill counsel, not to suffer this, and yet doth not know how to help it; hence arise his tentations, in which I do very much pity him. Having all this information what they had done, and how causelesse his complaint and discontent was, I thought it a difficult thing to ease his spirit, and yet clear and justifie the people, which I was to endeavour the next day of our meeting after the former contestations, therefore I was willing to get some body with me; And by Gods providence, Elder *Heath* went with me, and when we came there, we found him very full of discontent, sighing, sower looks, &c. but we took no notice of it.

I preached that day out of the fourth of *Matthew*, the temptations of Christ; and when I came at that temptation, of the Devils showing Christ the kingdomes and glories of the world, thereby to tempt him from the service of God, to the service of the Devill; I did apply it wholly to his case, shewing him the Devill was now tempting him, as he tempted Christ; and Sathan sheweth him all the delights and dignities, and gifts and greatnesse that he was wont to have in their sinfull way; Satan also tels him he shall lose them all if he pray to God, but if he will give over praying to God he shall have them all again; then I shewed him how Christ rejected that temptation, and exhorted him to reject it also, for either he must reject the temptation, else he will reject praying to God; if he should reject praying to God, God would reject him.

After our exercise was ended, we had conference of the matter, and we gave him the best counsel we could (as the Lord was pleased to assist) and when we had done, Elder *Heath* his observation of him was, that there was a great change in him, his spirit was very much lightned, and it much appeared both in his countenance and carriage, and he hath carried all things fairly ever since.

But the temptation still doth work strongly, in the Countrey the *Sachems* opposing any that desire to submit themselves to the service of the Lord, as appeareth sundry wayes; some that began to listen, are gone quite back; I meane *Sachems* and some people that have a mind to it, are kept back; this last Lecture day one came in and submitted himself to call on God, and said he had been kept back this half yeer by opposition, but now at last the Lord hath helped and emboldned him to break through all opposition.

Thus Sathan seeketh to beat off these poore creatures from seeking after the Lord by opposing the highest powers they have against the Lord and this work of his, knowing that the light of the Gospel and kingdome of Jesus Christ (if it once get footing) will scatter and dissipate that darknesse whereby his kingdome is maintained; But I beleeve verily that the Lord will bring great good out of all these oppositions, nay I see it already, (though I see not all, I beleeve more then I can see; you who can know the thoughts of Gods love to his people, it is yet a secret) but this I see, that by this opposition the wicked are kept off from us, and from thrusting themselves into our society, at least sundry are, who else might croud in among us and trouble us; besides it is become some tryall now, to come into our company and call upon God; for besides the forsaking of their *Pauwaus*, (which was the first triall) and their old barbarous fashions and liberty to all sinne, and some of their friends and kindred, &c. Now this is added, they incurre the displeasure of their *Sachems*, all which put together, it cannot but appear there is some work of God upon their hearts, which doth carry them through all these snares, and adde to this, that if upon some competent time of experience, we shall finde them to grow in knowledge of the principles of Religion, and to love the wayes of the Lord the better, according as they come to understand them, and to yeeld obedience to them, and submit to this great change, to bridle lust by lawes of chastity, and to mortifie idlenese by labour, and desire to traine up their children accordingly; I say if we shall see these things in some measure in them, what should hinder charity from hoping that there is grace in their hearts, a spark kindled by the Word and Spirit of God that shall never be quenched; and were these in a fixed cohabitation, who could gain-say their gathering together into a holy Church-Covenant and election of Officers? and who can forbid that they should be baptized? And I am perswaded that there be sundry such among them, whom the Lord will vouchsafe so far to favour and shine upon, that they shall become a Church, and a Spouse of Jesus Christ, and among whom the pure and holy Kingdome of Christ shall arise, and over whom Christ shall reigne, ruling them in all things by his holy word.

But though this trouble and oppsition is turned (and shall be more) unto a spiritual gaine, yet it behoveth us not to be secure, and regardlesse of our safety; for if the Adversary should discerne us naked and weak, and see an opportunity, who knoweth what their rage and Sathans malice may stirre them up unto to work us a mischief? Nay, it is our duty to be vigilant, and fortifie our selves the best we can, thereby to put the enemy out of hope to hurt us, and to prevent them from attempting any evill against us, if it be the will of God; and to that end we purpose (if the Lord will) to make a strong Palizado (wanting means of doing better) and if we cannot get any Guns, Powder, Shot, Swords, &c. we will make us Slings, Bowes, and other Engines, the best the Lord will please to direct us for our safety; and when we have used the best meanes we can, I hope the Lord will help us to trust in his great name, to make that our strong Tower to flie unto.

I see the Lord delighteth to appear himself in the work, and will have us content our selves with little, low, poor things, that all the power and praise may be given to his great name; Our work in civilizing them will go on the more slowly for want of tools; for though I have bought a few for them, we can do but little, for alas afew will set but afew on work, and they be very dear too; had I store of hoses this Autumne either to lend them or sell them at moderate prizes, we should prepare (by Gods blessing) good store of ground for corne against next yeere; and had I wherewith to buy corne to carry up to the place, and have it in a readinesse to supply them, that so they might tarry at their work, and not be shut off through necessity to go get food, that also would be a great furtherance; and had we but means to maintaine a discreet diligent man to work with them, and guide them in work, that also would much further the work; and many such things I could propound as very requisite unto the work, but I lay my hand upon my mouth, I will say no more, I have left it with the Lord, who hath hitherto appeared, and he will appear for his own eternal praise in shining upon the day of our smal things in his due season.

The blessing of God upon this work doth comfortably, hopefuly, & successefuly, appear in the labours of my brother *Mahu* at *Martins Vineyard,* insomuch that I hope they also will be after awhile ripe for this work of Civility and Cohabitation, if once they see a successeful pattern of it, and I doubt not but they will (as these do) ere long, desire Church-fellowship, and the Ordinances of Gods worship; the cloud increaseth, and the Lord seemeth to be coming in among them, they are very desirous to have their children taught, which is one argument that they truly love the knowledge of God; as on the contrary, it is a great ground of doubt of the truth of grace in that mans heart, when he hath not an heart to take care to traine up his children in the truth and in the practise of all godlinesse, but this care is in them, and it is pity it should not be furthered by all meanes; I have intreated a woman living neer where they dwell, to do that office for their children, and I pay her for it; but when they go to their plantation, we shall be in a streight for help that way; the Indians so well like the parties who performeth that service, that they intreat them to go with them, which I look at as a finger of God; they are I hope a godly couple, and might be a blessing to them, had we meanes to encourage them unto so difficult an enterprize, for it is a great matter to go and live among such a people; but in that case also, I look up to the Lord, and leave it with his holy care and wisdome; and if the Lord move any hearts to help in this work, I desire that the care of their schooling may be among the chiefest cares.

If the Lord please to prosper our poor beginnings, my purpose is, (so for as the Lord shal enable me to give attendance unto the work) to have schoole exercises for all the men by daily instructing of them to read and write, &c. Yea if the Lord affords us fit instruments, my desire is, that all the women may be taught to read; I know the matter will be difficult every way, for English people can only teach them to read English; and for their own Language we have no book; my desire therefore is to teach them all to write, and read written hand, and thereby with pains taking, they may have some of the Scriptures in their own Language; I have one already who can write, so that I can read his writing well, and he (with some paines and teaching) can read mine; I hope the Lord will both inlarge his understanding, and others also to do as he doth; and if once I had some of themselves able to spell aright, write and read, it might further the work exceedingly, and will be the speediest way.

Sir, When I had gone thus farre in my Letters, by a Ship that came in, you wrote unto our Governour touching the two Libraries, my brother *Welds* and

Mr. *Jenners*, and of the willingnesse of the Corporation to discharge for them, for which cause I do humbly thank the Worshipful Corporation, all the Christian and much respected Gentlemen my loving friends. And Sir, I thank you for all your faithful pains in this work, and the more I am obliged thereunto, because herein I am like to partake of the fruit of your labours, the Lord Jesus give you a full reward.

Whereas you require the Catalogue of both Libraries, it shall be done (if God will) but I am to go into the Countrey to the Indians now, and have much businesse, therefore know not whether I can do it by this Ship, if I can I will.

This last Court of Commissioners sate at *Hartford Conecticot*, so that I could not speak with them, but this course I took by our Governours advice; our General Court gave him, with some other, power to give instructions to our Commisioners; therefore all my requests I did write unto him, and he gave them in his Instructions to our Commissioners, so they went strong.

 Sir,

I have done at present, Mr. *Whitfeld* will informe you farther in any particulars if need be: The Lord of heaven blesse and assist you in all your wayes, and I beg your prayers for me still, and so rest

Roxbury this 21   *Yours in our Lord Jesus.*
 of the 8th. {16}50

                JOHN ELIOT.

The Conclusion.

A*Nd now (loving Reader) having brought thee along through these Divine dispensations of Gods merciful dealing with the Indians, I shall briefly acquaint thee with the workings of my own thoughts under the apprehension of these things.[Ainsw]*

First, I see plainly the fulfilling of that Divine truth and promise spoken of by David, *Psal.* 138.2. *Thou hast magnified thy Word above all thy Name, i.e. The Word in the Gospel brought and preached to men. The Lord hath made this Word the only outward instrumental means to bring home these wandring sinners; to this Word they have attended from the first; from this they have received their light; unto this they have given up themselves; without this they will not stirre; from this they will not depart; from hence they have their peace, and have seen good dayes under the Kingdome of our Lord Christ.*

Secondly, the Lord hath now declared one great end he had of sending many of his people to those ends of the earth; for besides that the Lord hath made that Land a place of rest, and a little sanctuary to them in these troublesome times, and hath made it a place where many, very many have been brought home to Christ, even amongst themselves [Ezek. 11.1]; *so now apparently in the conversion of many of the Heathens, who sing and rejoyce in the wayes of the Lord.*

Thirdly, when *I looked on my dear native Country (in the bulke and masse of them) there is one above doth know, that my heart melteth towards it, desiring the Lord to give me grace to sorrow in secret for millions of them, who were never yet acquainted with what many of these poore Indians have felt and found of the things of Christ, and that multitudes of such who hold forth a profession of Christian Religion, yet fall short of them, in regard of their belief and practise. Here I helped my self by comparing the one with the other, and that in divers particulars.*

1. *These Indians are found (to speak of such whose hearts the Lord hath opened by his Word and Spirit) to prize Ordinances, and such as bring the Light to them, even that poor Indian, whose best clothing is a simple skin about him, of whom you read in the first Letter, yet they honour him for his works sake, and for those gifts, piety, and modesty they see in him; Here Ministers of Christ are despised, though many of them are eminent for parts, wisdome, and known integrity.*

2. *These Indians are plain-hearted seek for Christ to enjoy him for himself; they receive the Truth in the love of it, and obey it without shifting or gain-saying; Here men have their own ends to tend to in matter of Religion, take up the forme, and let the power lie, as not serving their turn, have evasions to get from under the authority of the truth, and the Majesty of the Rules of Christ; here is rending and tearing of wits, whilst we wrangle one another out of the truth, till love and peace be lost.*

3. *These Indians are industrious and pursue the things of their salvation, rest they cannot, have it they must, what ever it cost them, bearing up strongly against all opposition: We have weak and bed-rid dispositions, sunk down into a sottish and sensuall way; in many the kingdome of Hell suffers violence, and none can withstand them, but thither they will.*

4. *These mourn and weep bitterly, and are pained under the sight and sense of their sins, when convinced of them; that some of them have been known to have wet with their teares the places weere they have stood. We here for the most part, the Lord knowes, live with dry eyes, and hard hearts, and sleight spirits.*

5. *They are careful and constant in duties of worship, both in private and family prayer, hearing the Word, observation of the Sabbath, meet often together, and will pray together as occasion serves, converse lovingly together, are teachable, patient, and contented. O that there were such hearts in us! O that their example did not shame multitudes of us who are fearfully guilty of omitting what the very light of Nature cals for from us! For this my heart is sad, fearing that if the Lord do not mightily step in, the next generation will be betrayed to Ignorance of the* Truth *as it is in* Jesus, *to Delusions and Profanenesse, and be rendred odious to all our neighbour Nations; and that these Indians will rise up in judgment against us and our children at the last day. Brethren, the Lord hath no need of us, but if it please him, can carry his Gospel to the other side of the world, and make it there to shine forth in its glory, brightnesse, power and purity, and leave us in Indian darknesse.*

And concerning these Indians, who have tasted how gracious the Lord is, though it cannot be expected but that the Devil should be like himself, by the counter-working of this blessed work, both by himself and his instruments, so as to cause many of them to totter, back slide, and fall away from what they have professed; yet I have ground to conceive and hope, that there is such a candle lighted amongst the Indians in those parts which shall not be put out till Christ comes to judgment, for the accomplishment of which he shall not cease to pray, who is

Your loving friend in
all Christian duties.

HENRY WHITFELD.

FINIS.

STRENGTH
OUT OF
WEAKNESSE;
Or a Glorious
MANIFESTATION
Of the further Progresse of
the Gospel among the *Indians*
in NEVV-ENGLAND.

Held forth in Sundry Letters
from divers Ministers and others to the
Corporation established by Parliament for
promoting the Gospel among the Heathen in *New-England*; and to particular
Members thereof since the last Treatise to that effect, Published by
Mr *Henry Whitfield* late Pastor
of *Gilford* in *New-England*.

CANT. 8. 8.

*Wee have a little Sister, and she hath no breasts : what
shall we doe for our Sister, in the day that she shall be
spoken for?*

LONDON;
Printed by *M. Simmons* for *John Blague* and
Samuel Howes, and are to be sold at their
Shop in *Popes-Head-Alley.* 1 6 5 2.

STRENGTH

OUT OF

WEAKNESSE;

Or a Glorious

MANIFESTATION

Of the further Progresse of
the Gospel among the *Indians*
in NEW - ENGLAND.

Held forth in Sundry Letters

from divers Ministers and others to the
Corporation established by Parliament for
promoting the Gospel among the Heathen in *New-England*; and to particular
Members thereof since the last Treatise to that effect, Published by
Mr. *Henry Whitfield* late Pastor
of *Gilford* in *New-England.*

C A N T. 8. 8.

*Wee have a little Sister, and she hath no breasts : what
shall we doe for our Sister, in the day that she shall be
spoken for?*

LONDON;

Printed by *M. Simmons* for *John Blague* and
Samuel Howes, and are to be sold at their
Shop in *Popes-Head-Alley.* 1 6 5 2.

TO THE

SUPREAME AUTHORITIE

OF THIS NATION,

The Parliament of the Common-

Wealth of E N G L A N D.

That the Fathers joy at the returning of a Spend-thrift Sonne, ought to have an influence upon the whole Family of Heaven and Earth, that is called after his name, to worke their suitable affections, and conformity to him selfe, cannot be questioned by any true childe thereof. Behold then, Right Honourable, a call thereunto, Poore Prodigalls, who have not only with our selves lost that rich Treasure of grace and holinesse, wherewith in our Common roote and Fountaine we were entrusted, but also in a course of Rebellion for many Generations wasted the remainder of Natures Riches to the utmost degeneracy that an Immortall rationall being is obnoxious unto, not returning a farre off, but rejoycing in the imbraces of their Father, and enterteined with his flesh and bloud, who was slaine and sacrificed for them.

The ayme of our walking with God here is to come up to some conformitie to them, who behold his face and doe his Will in Heaven: amongst them there is joy at the Repentance of one Sinner, and shall not wee finde sweetnesse in the first fruits of a barren Wildernesse in the shining of a beame of light into the darknesse of another World, giving hope of a plentifull harvest, and a glorious day to ensue. Let men take heed, lest by despising the day, and opposing the Worke of the Lord towards those poore Sonnes of *Adam*, notwithstanding all their zealous profession, they proclaime themselves to pursue a Carnall Interest; by which they declare the enlargement of the Dominion of Jesus Christ is of no Concernment unto them.

Wee are by many Pledges assured better things of you Right Honourable, and such as accompany zeale for the House of our God, and therefore the ensuing Testimonialls of the progresse of the Worke of the Gospel being sent unto us, wee make bold humbly to present them to you; partly that we may invite you as the friends of Jesus Christ, to rejoyce with him that some sheepe of his, who were lost, are found; and partly to lay before you, as matter of your rejoycing, some such fruits of the putting forth of your Authoritie, and investing us therewith for the carrying on this most glorious undertaking, as may encourage your selves and all others that love the Lord Jesus, to goe on through him who doth enable you unto future reall expressions of love and zeale thereunto. Wee shall not need to draw forth any particulars from the ensuing Narrative, to give you a taste of that Spirit whereinto these poore Creatures are sweetly baptized; Wee hope your delight in the Worke of God will inforce a leasure, to view the whole, this in Generall wee may say, that in the Wildernesse are waters broken out, and streames in the Desert, the parched ground is become a Poole, and the thirsty Land-springs of water: in the Habitation of Dragons where each lay, there is grasse with Reeds and Rushes, the Lord hath powred water upon him that is thirstie, and flouds upon the dry ground; He hath powred his Spirit on the seeds of the Heathen, & his blessing on their Off-spring, they spring up as among the grasse, as willowes by the water-courses: One sayes I am the Lords, and another calls himselfe by the name of *Jacob*, and another subscribes with his hand unto the Lord, and sirnames himselfe by the name of *Israel*. The Lord hath done a new thing, and wee know it, he hath made a way in the Wildernesse, and Rivers in the Desert, the beast of the feild doth honour him, the Dragons, and the Owles because he gives waters in the Wildernes, and Rivers in the Desert, to give drinke to his People his chosen. So that upon the Report heere read unto us, wee cannot but glorifie God with those Primitive beleevers, and say, then hath God also to the poore naked Indians granted Repentance unto life. Their outward wants and streights have often been presented unto you; wee shall not need to repeate them, blessed be the Lord, and blessed be you of the Lord that your hearts have been stirred up to give encouragement unto this Worke, and to open a Doore for the reliefe of those Eminent Instruments in the hand of the Lord who there carry it on, who though they communicate to them Spiritualls yet are so farre from receiving of their Temporalls, that they impart unto them a Portion of their own dayly bread, and provision necessary from their owne subsistence.

The good Lord lay the weight and concernment of this Worke upon your spirits, and wee no way doubt that you will in any way be wanting to the Publique improvement of this blessed opportunitie, for the enlargement of the Kingdome of him whom our Soules doe love: There is a vexation of spirit, which through their formalitie and unbeliefe, hath encompassed many Professors, that whereas they have with much seeming earnestnes cryed out for mercies; when they have been bestowed, they have thought scorne of them: so did the Jewes in the busines of their Messias, and many at this day amongst our selves in the great works of the Providences of God: It is so with some to this breaking forth of light amongst the Indians, desiring it before it began, despising it in its very beginnings, the Lord lay it not unto their charge, and keep all our spirits in an holy admiration and reverence of the powerfull efficacy of his eternall and unchangeable purposes, which through so many sinfull Generations (falling in their Rebellion) hath preserved a seed to himselfe, whereof he will take care that one graine fall not to the Ground.

Your Honors to serve you in promoting the Gospel of Christ.

Signed in the name and by appointment of the Corporation.

William Steele, President.

To the R E A D E R.

Christian Reader;

Hese ensuing Letters doe represent unto thee, and to the
Churches, the outgoings of Christ, as a *Light to the Gentiles*, that
the grace which *brings Salvation* hath appeared unto them also in
the furthest parts of the Earth, for the accomplishment of that
ancient and glorious Promise; I will give thee for a Light to the
Gentiles, that thou may'st be my Salvation to the Ends of the
Earth, (*Isa.* 49.6.) The People of God have been greatly affected with the
appearances of Christ, when he hath rode forth upon a *red Horse* to the
destruction of his Enemies; for he is *glorious in his Apparell*, even when his
garments are dipt in bloud, but much more when he rides forth upon a *white
Horse*, for the Conversion of Soules, and goes on *Conquering and to Conquer.*

Wee have therefore thought fit to commend this great worke of Christ unto
the view of all the Saints, under these following Considerations.

First, *Hereby the Kingdome of Christ is enlarged*, and the promise made
unto him in the Covenant between him and his Father accomplished, his
Dominion shall be from Sea to Sea, and from the floud unto the Worlds end,
[*Arma diaboli Gentes erant; fide autem Gentium vulneratus, caput quod
habebat, amisit.* Amb. In Psal. 118.] therefore his designe is upon all the
Kingdomes of the Earth, that he may take possession of them for himselfe, they
shall all *become the Kingdomes of the Lord and of his Christ*, Revel. 11.15.
And the *Kingdome and Dominion under the whole Heaven*, being so possessed
by Christ, *shall be given to the Saints of the most High*, Dan. 7.18. Our prayer
is, *Thy Kingdome come*, to see the promise made unto Christ fullfilled, and the
Prayers of the Saints answered, should be matter of great rejoycing unto us, and
of high Praises unto God.

Secondly, *The glorious Gospel of Christ is hereby Propagated*, which is the
Scepter of his Kingdome, the *Rod of his Power*, which wee pray may *run and be
glorified.* And when we consider, by how many (even amongst us) the Gospel
is rejected, for men reject the *Councell of God* against themselves: by how
many it is resisted, for there are *many adversaries*, and by how many the Gospel

is perverted, being made *another Gospel*, by strange Interpretations; one of the great acts of *sacriledge* of our times, stealing the sence of the Scripture from the words of the Scripture. Now to see the Gospel lifted up *as an Ensigne to the Nations*, and they to *flow unto it*, should be matter of great rejoycing to the soules of those who love the Gospel in sinceritie. [ἀντικείμενοι I Cor. 16.9 ἀντιδιατιθέμενοι 2 *Tim.* 2.25 ιερόσυλοι, τὸν νοῦν τῶν γραμμένων κλίπτοντες, Nazian.]

Thirdly, *Hereby the soules of men are rescued out of the snare of the Devill*, in which they were before held captive at his will; The Lord hath manifested that there is a *seed according to the Election of grace*, even amongst these also as well as other Gentiles, that the Lord hath visited them to take out of them *a people for his Name*, yea that even they who in a more immediate manner among them worshipped the Devill, their Witches call'd in their language *Pawwawes*, that even these should be deliver'd, *Satan falling from Heaven like lightning before the Gospel*, should greatly exalt free grace in our hearts; the great Love of God, is Love to Soules, and our tenderest compassion should be manifested in pittying of Soules, neither know wee any other ordinary way that the Lord has appointed but the preaching of the Gospel for the winning of Soules to himselfe: *That being the Power of God to Salvation.*

Fourthly, *Hereby the fullnes of the Gentiles draws neere to be accomplished*, that the calling of the *Jewes* may be hastned: the Scripture speaks of a *double conversion* of the *Gentiles*, the first before the conversion of the *Jewes*, they being *Branches wilde by nature* grafted into the *True Olive Tree* in stead of the *naturall Branches* which are broken off. This fullnesse of the *Gentiles* shall come in before the conversion of the *Jewes*, and till then *blindnesse hath hapned unto Israel*, Rom.11.25. [*Brightman in Cant.8.8. Mede in Apoc. Cap.7.p.56.*] The Second, after the conversion of the Jewes, as appeares Acts 15.16,17. *After this I will returne and will build againe the Tabernacle of David which is fallen downe, and I will build again the ruines thereof, and I will set it up; that the residue of men might seek after the Lord, and all the Gentiles upon whom my Name is called sayth the Lord.* Hence it appeares that there are some *Gentiles*, upon whom the Lords Name is called that are a people to him, even whilst the *Tabernacle of David* lyes in its ruines; and when he hath built againe this *Tabernacle of David*, that there are a residue of men, the remainder of the *Gentiles* that shall enquire after the Lord, and worship him, together with those *Gentiles* that were formerly converted, and upon whom his Name was called. The first conversion of the *Gentiles* in *its fullnesse* makes way for the coming in of the *Jewes*, the *King of the East*, therefore to see this worke goe on, should cause the people of God to lift up their heads, and expect that the Time of the fullfilling that Promise is neere.

Fifthly, *That the Lord hath blessed the labours of our Brethren*, who were driven out from among us: A gracious heart as he prayes for, so he cannot but rejoyce in the successe of other mens labours as well as his owne, so the worke which is Gods may prosper, who ever be the Instrument; 'tis enough to him. When *Peter* gave an account to the Apostles and Brethren of the Conversion of *Cornelius* and his family, who were, as it were the *first fruits of the Gentiles*, they all glorified God, saying; *Then hath God also to the Gentiles granted Repentance unto life,* Act. 11.18. And if they could rejoyce in the Conversion of the *Gentiles* which they knew would be with the rejection of the *Jewes,* how much more should wee rejoyce in this great worke, who may grow together upon the same good Olive Tree! That when other Nations who have planted in those furthest parts of the Earth, have onely sought their owne advantage to possesse their Land, Transport their gold, and that with so much covetousnesse and cruelty, that they have made the name of Christianitie and of Christ an abomination, that the Lord should be pleased to make use of our Brethren that went forth from us to make manifest *the savour of Christ* among the people, and to winne their soules to him; How should wee rejoyce that the Lord hath so farre prosper'd such an undertaking. It was a holy ambition in *Paul* to *preach the Gospel where Christ was not named,* that he might not glory in another mans line: It is certainly a great honour to be Instrumentall to bring soules to Christ, who before never heard of his Name.

Sixthly, *This wee hope may be but the first fruits of those great Nations unto Christ,* the Lord doth not usually *cause to bring forth and then shut the wombe,* Isa. 66.9. Let no man despise the day of *small things,* the Lord hath opened *a great doore,* which we hope Satan shall never be able any more to shut.

Such Considerations as these, have filled and affected our hearts, in the reading and meditation of this great worke of the Lord, and wee hope being communicated, may be a good means to awaken the godly and faithfull of this Nation, to observe the Presence and appearances of God amongst his people there, that wee also may say; *What shall we doe for our Sister in the day that shee shall be spoken for?* Shall we not be abundant in Prayer, that the Lord would yet further blesse their holy endevours? Shall wee not labour to strengthen their hands by ministering to them of our aboundance? that they may not be discouraged in so eminent a service, one of the greatest workes that hath been upon the wheele in this latter age, for to contribute to the offering up of Soules to Christ, must needs be a Sacrifice of a very sweet smelling savour unto God. This wee humbly offer unto all those that love the Lord Jesus in sinceritie, and remaine

Thine in the furtherance of the Gospel,

W. Gouge	*Phillip Nye.*
Edm: Calamy.	*William Bridge.*
Simon Ashe.	*Henry Whitfeld.*
Wil: Spurstowe.	*Sidrach Simpson.*
Jer: Whitaker.	*William Strong.*
Lazarus Seaman.	*Joseph Caryl.*
George Griffith.	*Ralph Venning.*

STRENGTH
OUT OF
WEAKNESSE;
Or a Glorious
MANIFESTATION
Of the further Progresse of
the Gospel among the *Indians*
in NEW–ENGLAND.

AS every worke of God tending to the rescuing of deluded Soules out of the snares of the Devill, so even this Glorious worke of Gods grace hath met with many discouragements by various kinds of objections cast abroad by divers sorts of people, and even by some that came from New-England it selfe, who having lived remote from the worke done, and either not affecting the instruments therein imployed, or not going to the places of their Exercise, that they might see and heare the gracious operations of the Spirit of God amongst them, may easily misreport the proceedings of Gods goodnesse therein. Yet neverthelesse God having called us to be exercised in a worke of this Nature, wherein his Glory and the Salvation of so many of the lost sonnes of Adam are concerned; wee have taken up a Resolution by his gracious Assistance to improve the power and trust by Authoritie of Parliament committed to us to the utmost, least it be laid to our Account amongst others the obstructors of it in the great day of the Lord.

But as wee meete with discouragements, so, through mercy, wee are not without incouragements of many sorts. Viz.

1. This worke of Gods grace growes in New-England, not onely in the places where the Gospel was formerly preached to the Indians; But God hath stirred up two Eminent Ministers in two other parts of the Countrey, to labour in the worke, not without successe answerable; as Mr William Leveridge neere Sandwich in the Government of New Plymouth, sixtie miles from the place where Mr Eliot teacheth, and Mr Richard Blindman at Pecoat, a place formerly subdued by the English, and is a place about the same distance from Sandwich another way, an account whereof you will have in the following Treatise.

2. Where the Act of Parliament for the Collection meets with Gospel-spirited Ministers and people, there wee finde a good account of it comparatively; God

having stirr'd up the hearts of some Eminent Christians to contribute in a considerable manner; some by charging their Lands with a yearely Revenue to the Corporation for that end for ever: and others by sending in good summes of money, subscribing to pay yearely so much whilst they live. And one Gentleman (leaving two sonnes of tender age)having appointed by his Will, in case they dye without issue, that an estate of two hundred pound per annum, *should be setled upon the Corporation for ever, and the rest of his estate for the like uses in the foure Northerne Counties of* England.

3. That God hath wrought a resolution in us of the Corporation (wherein wee trust hee will inable us to persist (viz.) *to contribute our labour and paines freely to this worke, without the least diminution of the Stocke. And if any desire to be satisfied what our receipts, disbursements, or manner of proceedings are, our Bookes are open at* Coopers Hall, London, *betweene the houres of Tenne and Twelve every* Saturday, *where they may without offence see what is given, and by whom, when brought in, and how imployed or improved.*

'Tis very strange to see what a multitude of objections are darted against this pure piece of Christianitie, yea by some, whom otherwise wee have charitable thoughts of, and how exceedingly the worke is impeded thereby, and however through mercy wee are able to answer every one of them sufficiently, yet wee forbeare to particularize them, least wee should reflect too much on some, our Consciences telling us, that as the worke is of God, and really such as is held forth, so he onely can satisfie the Spirits of Men, and will doe it in due season, and in the meane time blesse his owne worke being able to carry it on, who delighteth oft times in small meanes, that his gracious operations may the more be seene.

This is the fifth Treatise hath been published to the world in this kinde (but the first by the Corporation) every one of them exceeding each other, wherein a most apparant growth and progresse doth appeare amongst the poore Natives.

That wee have now to offer to the publique view is a farther account of that living, growing, spreading power of Godlinesse amongst them. And first wee shall begin with some remarkeable passages of divine providence in a Letter received from Mr John Eliot *(who was the first Minister the Lord stirred up to promote this worke) bearing date the* 28th *of* April 1651. *to one of our selves.*

Much Honored and

Beloved in C H R I S T.

THe Providence of G O D giving this unexpected opportunitie of sending, I thought it my duty not to omit it, that so the Saints and people of God with you, especially your selfe, with the rest of the Worshipfull Corporation, might understand the progresse and present state of this worke of the Lord among the *Indians*, for wee meete with changes of providence and tryalls in this our day of small things. It hath [By this name they call their kings and Governors]pleased the Lord to try them, so soone as they have but tasted of his holy wayes. For our natures cannot live without Physicke, nor grace without affliction, more or lesse, sooner or later. The winter before this last past it pleased God to worke wonderfully for the *Indians*, who call upon God in preserving them from the small Pox, when their prophane Neighbours were cut off by it. This winter it hath pleased God to make lesse difference, for some of ours were also visited with that disease, yet this the Lord hath done for them, that fewer of them have dyed thereof, then of others who call not upon the Lord. Onely three dyed of it, (but five more young and old) of other diseases: Now (through the Lords mercy) they are well, though not without ordinary infirmities, which befall Mankinde. In matters of Religion they goe on, nor onely in attendance on such meanes as they have, not onely in knowledge, which beginneth to have some clearenesse in the Fundamentall poynts of Salvation; but also in the practice and power of Grace, both in constant care in attendance on the worship of God on Sabbath dayes and Lecture-dayes, especially proftting in the gift of prayer, and also in the exercise of love to such as be in affliction, either by sicknesse or povertie. I have seene lively Actings of Charitie out of Reverence to the Command of the Lord, when such as had not that principle were farre from such workes of mercy, it pleased God to try them in the time of the Pox, for some of them did hazard their owne lives (for to them it is very mortall) in obedience to the Command of the Lord, to shew mercy to them that were sicke, and some were infected thereby, and fell sicke and lay with much chearefullnesse and patience under Gods hand, and through the Lords mercy are well againe; others who did shew mercy in that case escaped the sicknesse to the praise of God. Likewise God is pleased to try their Charitie by an old Paraliticke or Palsie sick-man, whose owne Children being prophane and tyred with the burthen of him (his retentive power of houlding excrements being loosened) and having a loosenesse, sometimes he is very noysome and burthensome) they forsooke him, and he had perished, but that the Lord stirred up (by the word of his grace) their hearts to shew mercy to him, for he was while he was sicke at six shilling a weeke charge, for wee offered twelve-pence a night to any to tend him, and for meere hyre none would abide it, but out of mercy and Charitie some of the Families did take care of him, and gave freely some weeks, and others were payd out of their publique money, namely, such as hath been taken off, such as have been Transgressors by Fine or Mulct: and still he is at foure shillings a weeke charge being better in health, in so much that all their publique money is spent, and much more, and wee have Collections among them for the same use. The old man who hath been and still is wise, doth wisely testifie that their love is sincere, and that they truely pray to God, and I hope so doth he, and shall be saved. I could with a word speaking in our Churches have this poore man relieved, but I doe not, because I thinke the Lord hath done it, for the tryall of their grace, and exercise of their love, and to traine them up in works of Charitie, and in the way of Christ to make Collections for the poore. I see how the Lord provideth to further the progresse of the Gospel, by these tryalls and afflictions, yea there be more passages of this winters worke, wherein the Lord hath taught us by the Crosse. For one of our first and principall men is dead, which though it be a great blow and damping to our worke in some Respects, yet the Lord hath not left the rest to discouragement thereby, nay the worke is greatly furthered, for hee made so gracious an end of his life, and imbraced death with such holy submission to the Lord, and was so little terrified at it, as that it hath greatly strengthened the Faith of the living to be constant, and not to feare death, greatly commending of the death of *Wamporas*, for that was his name, I thinke he did more good by his death, then he could have done by his life: one of his sayings was, That God giveth us three mercies in this world; the first is health and strength; the second is food and cloaths; the third is sicknesse and death; and when wee have had our share in the two first, why should wee not be willing to take our part in the third? for his part he was: I heard him speake thus, and at other times also, and at his last he so spake, and it so tooke with them, that I observe it in their prayers, that they so reckon up Gods dispensations to them, his last words which he spake in this world were these; *Jehova Aninnumah Jesus Christ*, (that is) Oh, Lord, give mee Jesus Christ; and when hee could speake no more, he continued to lift up his hands to Heaven, according as his strength lasted, unto his last breath; so that they say of him he dyed praying; when I visited him the last time that I saw him in this world (not doubting but I shall see him againe with Christ in Glory) one of his sayings was this: Foure yeares and a Quarter since, I came to your house, and brought some of our Children to dwell with the *English*, now

I dye, I strongly intreate you (for that is their phrase) that you would strongly intreate Elder *Heath* (with whom his Sonne liveth) and the rest, which have our Children, that they may be taught to know God, so as that they may teach their Countrymen, because such an example would doe great good among them, his heart was much upon our intended worke, to gather a Church among them, I told him I greatly desired that he might live (if it were Gods will) to be one in that worke, but if he should now dye he should goe to a better Church, where *Abraham*, and *Isaac*, and *Jacob*, and *Moses*, and all the dead Saints were with Jesus Christ in the presence of God in all happinesse and Glory; he said he feared not death, he was willing to dye, and turning to the Company which were present, hee spake unto them thus; *I now shall dye, but Jesus Christ calleth you that live to goe to* Naticke, *that there the Lord might rule over you, that you might make a Church, and have the Ordinance of God among you, believe in his Word, and doe as hee commandeth you:* With many such words exhorting them, which they could not heare without weeping. A little before his death hee spake many gracious words unto them, wherein one passage was this; *Some delight to heare and speake idle and foolish words, but I desire to heare and speake onely the words of God, exhorting them so to doe likewise*: his gracious words were acceptable and affecting, that whereas they used to flie and avoyde with terrour such as lye dying, now on the contrary they flocked together to heare his dying words, whose death and buriall they beheld with many teares; nor am I able to write his Storie without weeping.

Another affliction and damping to our worke was this, that it hath pleased God to take away that *Indian* who was most active in Carpentrey, and who had framed me an house with a little direction of some *English*, whom I sometime procured to goe with mee to guide him, and to set out his worke: hee dyed of the Pox this winter, so that our house lyeth, not yet raised, which maketh my aboade amongst them more difficult, and my tarriance shorter then else I would, but the Lord helpeth me to remember that he hath said, *Endure thou hardnesse as a good Souldier of Jesus Christ*. These are some of the gracious tryalls and Corrections the Lord hath exercised us withall, yet he hath mingled them with much love and favour in other respects; for it hath pleased God this winter much to inlarge the abilitie of him whose helpe I use in translating the Scriptures, which I account a great furtherance of that which I most desire, namely, to communicate unto them as much of the Scriptures in their owne language as I am able. Besides, it hath pleased God to stirre up the hearts of many of them this winter to learne to reade and write, wherein they doe very much profit with a very little helpe, especially some of them, for they are very ingenuous. And whereas I had thoughts that wee must have an *Englishman* to be their Schoole-Master, I now hope that the Lord will raise up some of themselves, and enable them unto that worke, with my care to teach them well in the reason of the sounds of Letters and spelling, I trust in the Lord that wee shall have sundry of them able to reade and write, who shall write every man for himselfe so much of the Bible as the Lord shall please to enable me to translate. Besides those workes which concerne Religion and Learning, wee are also a doing (according to the measure of our day of small things) in the civill part of this worke wee have set out some part of the Towne in severall Streets, measuring out and dividing of Lots, which I set them to doe and teach them how to doe it: many have planted Apple-Trees, and they have begun diverse Orchards, its now planting-time, and they be full of businesse, yet wee are doing some publicke workes; the last weeke I appointed our Lecture to be at a Water which is a common passage, and where the Fish wee call *Alewives* come, there wee built a bridge, and made a wyre to catch Fish, and being many of them, some wee appointed to one worke, and some to another, through the blessing of God wee brought both these workes to perfection: we also have begun a Pallizadoe Fort, in the midst whereof wee intend a meeting-house and Schoole-house, but wee are in great want of Tooles, and many necessaries, and when wee cannot goe wee must be content to creepe; this present weeke I am going to Pawtucket, the great Fishing place upon Merimek where I heare sundry doe expect my coming, with a purpose to submit themselves unto the Lords hand. Sir, I doe earnestly beg your prayers both for mee and for this worke of the Lord which he hath set mee about,

Roxbury the 28th*: of*   *John Eliott.*
the 2[d]*:* 1 6 5 1.

The former Letter of Mr Elliots *came to hand about six Moneths before the latter, and thats the reason you have another of his followeth next after his former, whereby the Reader may see and observe the constant goodnes of God in carrying on his owne worke, notwithstanding all the opposition of Men. Every day bringing forth as it were additionall improvements, to the praise of God, who delighteth so much in this his day of small things.*

Worshipfull and much honoured in the L O R D.

I T is through the grace of Christ, who hath called you into the fellowship of his Kingdome, that you are willing to take such care and paines for the advancement and furtherance of his Kingdome, and the Lord fill your hearts with the Consolations of his holy Spirit, whose spirit hee hath set to seeke his glory in promoting the Gospel of Jesus Christ, and because the fruite of our Labours coming in with a blessing, is a great meanes to quicken the heart to be constant in that worke which the Lord delighteth to prosper and blesse. It is my duty to let you understand how it pleaseth the Lord to prosper and proceed in this worke of his among the *Indians*; for the promoting whereof you travaile with care and paines, that so you may goe on with the more Comfort, and the better know how to direct your prayers unto the Lord in that behalfe. I will not trouble you with rehearsall of such things as I have already this yeare written about unto our honoured Friend Mr *Winslowe*, so farre as I can call to minde what I wrote, hoping in the Lord that the Ships are safely arrived, and my Letters come unto his hands. I know not whether I have yet mentioned our Schoole, which through the Lords mercy wee have begun, though wee cannot yet be constant in it, wee have two men in some measure able to teach the youth with my guidance, and inspection. And thus wee order the Schoole: The Master daily prayeth among his Schollers, and instructeth them in Catechisme for which purpose I have compiled a short Catechisme, and wrote it in the Masters booke, which he can reade, and teach them; and also all the Copies he setteth his Schollers when he teacheth them to write, are the Questions and Answers of the Catechisme, that so the Children may be the more prompt and ready therein: wee aspire to no higher learning yet, but to spell, reade, and write, that so they may be able to write for themselves such Scriptures as I have already, or hereafter may (by the blessing of God) translate for them; for I have no hope to see the Bible translated, much lesse printed in my dayes. Therefore my chiefe care is to Communicate as much of the Scriptures as I can by writing: and further, my scope so to traine up both men and youths, that when they be in some measure instructed themselves, they may be sent forth to other parts of the Countrey, to traine up and instruct others, even as they themselves have been trained up and instructed. This consideration doth make mee very carefull to put on the Schoole, and attend it with what diligence I can, although I cannot as yet doe in it, what I desire. There be severall providences of God appearing to worke, which make mee thinke that the most effectuall and generall way of spreading the Gospel will be by themselves, when so instructed as I have above mentioned; as for my preaching, though such whole hearts God hath bowed to attend, can picke up some knowledge by my broken expressions, yet I see that it is not so taking, and effectuall to strangers, as their owne expressions be, who naturally speake unto them in their owne tongue. To the end therefore that they may be the better able to teach others, I doe traine them up, and exercise them therein: when I am among them on the Lords dayes, appointing two, each Sabboth to exercise, and when they have done, then I proceed, and assuredly I finde a good measure of abilitie in them, not onely in prayer (wherein they exceed my expectation) but in memory to rehearse such Scriptures as I have read unto them and expounded; to expound them also as they have heard mee doe, and apply them. And now also the Schoole-Master taking the care of catechizing the Children, I leaving that to him doe catechize the men, examining and trying their knowledge, which yet I am wary in doing, least I should dampe and discourage the weake. These things I attend with the more intention, because it seemeth to mee God will imploy these first instructed to instruct others, of which I have sundry experiences, some I shall instance; it pleased Mr *Winthrop* (son unto our late Honoured Governour now at rest) to advise mee to send two discreete men to the greatest and most potent *Sachem* among the *Naragansets*, to answer such Questions as they might propound, and to stirre them up to call on God. I did accordingly, and sent him a Present by them; but the proud *Sachem* did little lesse then despise the offer, though hee tooke the Present; So they thought they should have returned without successe; but when they came among the people, especially such as were a little more remote from the great and proud ones, they received them with great gladnesse; one Company taking one of ours among them, others taking the other of our men amongst them; they asked them many Questions, expressed their readinesse to call upon God, if they had any to teach them: expressing likewise that they did not expect their *Sachems* would pray to God, because they were so proud: by which I doe perceive that the Lord is preparing a plentifull harvest, and not onely by this, but by many other Evidences. There is a great Countrey lying betweene *Conectacott* and the *Massachusets,* called *Nipnet*, where there be many *Indians* dispersed, many of which have sent to our *Indians*, desiring that some may be sent unto them to teach them to pray unto God. And sometimes some of our best men doe goe to severall places for a little while, and returne againe, and not without successe. These things being so, the worke which wee now have in hand will be as a patterne and Copie before them, to imitate in all the Countrey, both in civilizing them in their order, government, Law, and in their Church proceedings and administrations; and hence great care lyeth upon mee to set them right at first, to lay a sure foundation for such a building, as I foresee will be built upon it, and in this matter I greatly need pray: The order of proceeding with them, is first to gather them together from their scattered course of life, to cohabitation and civill order and Government, and then to forme them (the Lord having fitted them) into visible Church-state, for the guidance whereof, I have instructed them, that they should looke onely into the Scriptures, and out of the word of God fetch all their Wisedome, Lawes, and Government, and so shall they be the Lords people, and the Lord above shall Reigne over them, and governe them in all things by the word of his mouth. Sundry of these which pray unto God have formerly subjected themselves unto the *English*; So that in this Government among themselves they doe reserve themselves in that poynt to owne them as their superiours, to make appeales unto them as neede may require, and experience for these many yeares shew, that though they have so subjected themselves, yet the onely benefit they have is protection: as for hearing and determining their causes, the difference of language, and paucitie of Interpreters prohibits, and if their causes come, they be so longsome, and yet of small importance, that it is of necessitie, that either they must have no government, as hitherto it hath been, or else they must have it among themselves. Besides, all or many of their differences and causes they usually brought to mee, which was not convenient, and I was willing to avoyde: themselves also found great need that some should be over them, to judge their causes, and end differences, and much desired it. Therefore upon the sixt day of the sixt Moneth of this present yeare (their Pallizadoe Fort being finished) they had a great meeting, and many came together from diverse parts, though sundry were hindred and came not at that time, where, with prayer to God I read and expounded to them the 18th of *Exodus*, (which I had done severall times before) and finally they did solemnly choose two Rulers among themselves, they first chose a Ruler of an Hundred, then they chose two Rulers of Fifties, then they chose Ten or Tithing Men (so I call them in *English*) for so they were called (as is reported) in *England*, when *England* did flourish happily under that kinde of Government. And lastly, for that dayes worke every man chose who should be his Ruler of ten, the Rulers standing in order, and every man going to the man he chose, and it seemed unto mee as if I had seene scattered bones goe, bone unto his bone, and so lived a civill politicall life, and the Lord was pleased to minister no small comfort unto my spirit, when I saw it. After this worke was ended, they did enter into Covenant with God, and each other, to be the Lords people, and to be governed by the word of the Lord in all things. The words of which Covenant are these in *English*. *Wee doe give our selves and our Children unto God to be his people, Hee shall rule us in all our affaires, not onely in our Religion, and affaires of the Church (these wee desire as soone as wee can, if God will) but also in all our workes and affaires in this world, God shall rule over us. Isa. 33.22. The Lord is our Judge, the Lord is our Law-giver, the Lord is our King, Hee will save us; the Wisedome which God hath taught us in his Booke, that shall guide us and direct us in the way. Oh Jehovah, teach us wisedome to finde out thy wisedome in thy Scriptures, let the grace of Christ helpe us, because Christ is the wisedome of God, send thy Spirit into our hearts, and let it teach us, Lord take us to be thy people, and let us take thee to be our God.*

This Act of forming themselves into the Government of God, and entring into this Government is the first publique Record among the *Indians*, and for ought I know the first that ever was among them: and now our next worke is to prepare them for Church-estate, to which end I doe instruct them, that the Visible Church of Christ is builded upon a lively confession of Christ, and Covenanting to walke in all the Administrations of the publique worship of God, under the Government and Discipline of Jesus Christ. I doe therefore exhort them to try their hearts by the word of God to finde out what change the Lord hath wrought in their hearts, and this is the present worke wee have in hand.

Give mee leave (much honoured Friends) to goe a little backe in my relation, that I might be more particular, because these Letters I prepared in the sixt Moneth after they had chosen their Officers, as I was propounding and teaching them the above-written Covenant, for that I did often before wee did solemnely accomplish it, that so they might doe it as an Act of knowledge and faith. Now let mee relate the order of our proceeding: Having againe and againe read this Covenant to them, and instructed them in the meaning of it, it pleased God to wrack Mr *Webbers* Ship at *Conahasset*, though the Lord dealt favourably; most goods were saved, though much spoyled: this was on the first day of the 7th Moneth, wherefore at a Lecture at *Natik* on the 10th of the same Moneth, I informed them of the plentifull supply which the Lord had made your selves his instruments to send unto them for the furtherance of this our worke, and also how the Lord had frowned upon it, and undoubtedly it was a fruit of sinne, and therefore the Lord called them to repentance, and make peace with God: besides wee were beginning a great worke of civill Cohabitation and Government, and they wanted wisdome to carry on such a worke, and the Lord had promised, *if any want wisdome aske it of God, who gives liberally,* citing that of *James* which I had formerly preached on. Moreover, wee were in preparation for a Church-state, and that was a great matter to seeke the Lord in; and lastly, they having chosen Rulers, and intending to enter into a Covenant, to promise unto

God to be his people, and to be ruled in all things by his Word. Gods appointment is that such a Covenant should be entred into, in a solemne day of fasting and prayer, and all these causes concurred, to put us on unto that worke. Now though wee never yet had kept such a day unto the Lord, yet I had instructed them therein, for in the Spring wee had a generall day of humiliation in all the Churches; and thereupon they moved this question; *Why the English often fasted and prayed, and I never yet taught them so to doe*: to which I did answer, by that of Christ unto the Disciples, but told them, that when wee set upon the great workes of God to be his people, governed by his Word, and to gather a Church, then they should be called of God unto it, &c. and now it came to passe, my motion they deliberated on with some conference (as their manner is) and finally did consent unto it, then I told them, it was needfull they should pray and teach that day; sundry of them and wee agreed, that all such as were called to be Rulers should exercise that day, or so many as wee had time for their exercise. Before that day came, even then when it was appointed *Cutshamoquin*, the chiefe *Sachem*, and therefore chosen the chiefe (for hee is constant in his profession, though doubtfull in respect of the throughnesse of his heart) was in the Countrey neere *Narraganset*, about appeasing some strife among some *Sachems*. In which Journey some of those bad *Indians* and *Cutshamoquin* with them did buy much strong Water at *Gortons* Plantation, and had a great drinking, from which the wiser sort did withdraw themselves, but *Cutshamoquin* was in it, though not unto drunkennesse, yet his Act was scandalous. Before wee solemnly appeared before God, and made the above-written-Covenant, I advised with Mr *Cotton* about it, and his Counsaile was to add these words in the beginning: *Wee are the sonnes of Adam, wee and our forefathers have a long time been lost in our sinnes, but now the mercy of the Lord beginneth to finde us out againe; therefore the grace of Christ helping us, wee doe give our selves and our Children, &c.*

When the day came, this Act of *Cutshamoquin* being broken out, wee suffered not him to teach; onely he began the day with confession of his sinne, and made a short prayer, wherein he confessed, Satan acted in his heart, begged pardon, and that the Spirit of God might dwell in him, and act in him for time to come, and so ended.

Then another of them began with prayer, and for his Text tooke that in the 7th of *Luke 36.* to the end, (though they doe not know the Booke, Chapter, or Verse, but distinguish my Lectures by the first materiall word in it) *Christ being invited by Symon the Pharisee, the Woman washt his feete with her teares, &c.* At which *Symon* stumbling, Christ spake the parable of the two Debtors, both freely forgiven, with the application, all which he repeated pretty well, and after his teaching he prayed againe and ended. The second tooke for his Text the *Lords Prayer*, because it is, said he, a day of prayer. The third tooke for his Text the 7th of *Matthew 19.* to the end, *Every tree that bringeth not forth good fruit is cut downe, &c.* And upon that parable of the two Builders, on the rocke the first, the other on the sand, &c. By this time the day was well up, then I taught out of the 9th of *Ezra 3.& 9.* where I described a day of fasting, and the right carriage of it; yet by the parable of a Nut, I shewed that outward acts are as the shell, which is necessary, but a broken and believing heart is the kernell, and so ended the forepart of the day. After a little respite (in which time a Question came to mee, if it were lawfull to take a pipe of Tobacco) we met againe, the first took his Text, *Job*.3.16.22. and his Preface was, *I reade or rehearse this, and let every one reade it in his owne heart.* The second took his Text, *Matth.* 13.24. to 31. from the parable of him that *sowed good seed, and the enemie came and while they slept sowed tares, &c.* The third took his Text, *Luke* 3ᵈ.4,5,6. ver. *Prepare yee the way of the Lord, make his paths straight, &c.* By this time night drew on, then I took for my Text, *Deut.* 29. and the 1.to16. where *Israel* entred into Covenant with the Lord: and finally our Covenant in the forerecited words I expressed, and they joyntly consented unto; first the Rulers, then all the people, then was the Collections for the poore, and by dark night wee finished our worke. Thus have I briefly described that blessed day wherein these poore soules solemnely became the people of the Lord: this was on the 24ᵗʰ day of the 7ᵗʰ Moneth, 1651.

Upon the 8ᵗʰ of the *Oct.* Moneth, which was our next Lecture (for it is in that place but once in a fortnight, I houlding a Lecture each other weeke still at any other place) it pleased our Governour with many others attending him, to visit our poore workes and day of small things, where they viewed our house, our Fort, our Bridge, advised about a place for a Mill, &c.) At the season they came unto our Lecture, and observed the carriage and behaviour of things and men: among other things one of our *Indians* did (as we are wont) exercise, which they tooke so much notice of, and were so farre affected with, as that it pleased the Governour to advice me to write the substance of that which he spake, which is as followeth; his Text was *Matth.*13.44,45,46. *Againe, the Kingdome of heaven is like unto treasure hid in a feild, the which when a man hath found, he hideth and for joy thereof goeth and selleth all that he hath, and buyeth the feild: 45. Againe, the Kingdome of heaven is like unto a Marchant man seeking goodly pearles: 46. Who when he had found one pearle of great price, he went and sould all that he had and bought it.* The substance of these words he did twice rehearese, then for instruction he first propounded what is this treasure which is hid in a feild? he answered it is Repentance for sinne, faith in Christ, and pardon of sinne and all grace, as also praying to God, the worship of God, and his appointments, which are the meanes of Grace, on which he dilated, shewing what excellent pearles these are, exhorting all to account so of them, and on this point he did much insist: secondly, he asked what is the Feild where these pearles are to be found? he answered the Church of Christ, which they did desire to constitute in this place, and to that end come thither to dwell: Thirdly, he asked what is it to sell all that a man hath to buy this Feild? He answered, to part with all their sinnes, and to part with all their old Customes, and to part with their friends and lands, or any thing which hindereth them from coming to that place, where they may gather a Church, and enjoy all these pearles; and here he insisted much to stirre them up, that nothing should hinder them from Gathering together into this place where they might enjoy such a mercy.

Then he proceeded to the second parable, and his first Question was, Who is the Marchant man, that seeketh goodly pearles? he answered, it is all you *Indians* which pray to God, and repent of sinne, and come to heare the word of God, you come to seeke for excellent pearles; and here also he insisted: his second Question was, What is this pearle of great price? now in answer to this Question he did not pitch it on Christ alone, and shew the worth and price of Christ: but he did pitch it on faith in Jesus Christ, and repentance for sinne, and stood upon the excellency and necessitie thereof. And this was the greatest defect I observed in his Exercise, which seeing I undertake to relate that which none but my selfe understood, I dare not but truely relate, because the Lord heard all, and I must give an account of this relation before him: His next question was, What is meant by all the Riches he had? he answered, his sinnes, his evill Customes, his evill manners, in which he formerly tooke much pleasure; And here he dilated also: Lastly he asked how did he sell them all, and buy the pearle? he answered, by casting away & forsaking all his sinnes, mourning and repenting of them, praying to God, and believing in Jesus Christ. And here he fervently dilated, and so ended; and this according to the best of my memory and observation, is the substance of what he delivered. Whereby you may observe the manner of my teaching them, for they imitate mee, as for our method of preaching to the *English* by way of Doctrine, reason, and use, neither have I liberty of speech, for that way of teaching being very unskilfull in their Language, nor have they sufficient abilitie of understanding to profit by it, so well as by this way, whereof you have herein a little Taste.

Jo: Eliot

The next Letter good Reader (for we place them according to their severall dates) is one that came from Mr John Wilson *that reverend holy man, who is Pastor of the Church of Christ at* Boston *in* New England, *who accompanying the Governour, together with Mr* Eliot *and sundry others to their new Towne built by the Converted* Indians, *where they purpose by Gods permission to cohabite together, that so they may enjoy all those Ordinances the Lord Jesus hath left unto his Church. Now what Mr* Wilson *there saw, heard, and observed, that he hath written over to us, and we have published for thy information and consolation.*

Honoured and ever deare Sir.

Ouching the worke of God among the *Indians,* for ought I heare or see from them that are most conversant therein, as Mr *Eliot,* Mr *Mahew,* and Mr *Leverich,* with whom I have made diligent enquiry; It doth prosperously succeed to their great encouragement, and ours in the Lord. There was here some few weekes since, the prime *Indian* at *Martins Vineyard* with Mr *Mahewe (Humanequinn)* a grave and solemne Man, with whom I had serious discourse, Mr *Mahewe* being present as Interpreter between us, who is a great proficient both in knowledge and utterance, and love, and practice of the things of Christ, and of Religion, much honoured and reverenced, and attended by the rest of the *Indians* there, who are solemnely Covenanted together, I know not how many, but between thirtie or fortie at the least, and receive none into their Fraternitie, or Combination, but those which give good proofe of their upright desires, to their Conscience, in their professions and Conversations, who when Mr *Mahewe* cannot be with them (as at many set times he is) doth in the weeke time instruct himselfe from Mr *Mahews* mouth, and prepare for their instruction on the Lords day, which they conscionably observe, and have their constant solemne meetings together: This man where he was, had communion on the Lords day with Mr *Eliots Indians* neere *Dorchester* Mill, unto whom he preached or declared, what he had learned himselfe from the Scripture, some two houres together, with solemne prayer before and after, and then ended with a *Psalme,* such as at home is wont to be sung among his usuall hearers. The Lords day after he was in our Assembly, the Boate then being ready to carry him home by the next opportunitie, and truely my reverence to him was such, as there being no roome I prayed our brethren to receive that good *Indian* into one of their pewes, which they did forenoone and afternoone, and at meale, I perceived by him that he had understanding of what he heard. Mr *Leverich* being lately here and at my house, (who also preached at our new Church) I conferred with him about the beginnings and progresse of the Lords worke, among his neighbouring *Indians* at *Sandwich*, and did heare from him, what did my heart good. And therefore when he tooke his leave of me I requested him that he would doe me the favour at his returne home, to send me a briefe story of that good hand of God which was there upon them, *ab origine*, which I thanke him he did soone after, and I thought not amisse to inclose it, as it came to me, being written with his owne hand, not doubting but it would adde unto your rejoycing in the Lord. About a fortnight since, there was a Lecture to be of Mr *Eliot*, at *Naticke*, the new *Indian* Towne, where he useth frequently to preach to them, besides what he doth neere home (on either side) and many times doth keepe the Lords day with them, whereof having some notice, and that the Governour Mr *Endicot* intended then to be there, my Cosin *Nawson* and I with some other, did prepare to ride thither, the Governour and his Sergeants lying at *Dedham*, which is within seaven or eight miles of the Towne, and we at Mr *Jacksons* neere *Watertowne* Mill) in like distance in the next morning after we had been some houres there where we found Mr *Eliot*, and by that time we had viewed all things, the Governour came with about twentie horsemen from *Dedham*, and made a like view, after which the Lecture or Sermon began in the Fort, which the *Indians* have made of whole trees very hansome and firme, which is neere a faire house which the *Indians* have built after the *English* manner high and large (no *English*-mans hand in it, save that one day or two they had an *English*-Carpenter with them to direct about the time of rearing, with chimneys in it: In which Mr *Eliot* & those which accompany him use to lye, and the Schoole-Master (*Indian* was there teaching the Children) who doth reade and spell very well himselfe, and teacheth them to doe the like (besides writing) and as there is a large Roome below, so there is a like chamber above, in a Corner whereof Mr *Eliot* hath a little Roome inclosed, and a bed & bed-sted therein, and in the same Chamber the *Indians* doe as in a Wardrope hang up their skinnes, and things of price, as counting them there to be very safe, as well when the dores be open, as when they be locked; they have laid out three long faire streets there, two on this side the River, and one on that, and have severall house-lots apportioned severally to every one, which doe or be to inhabite there, and in many of them there are fruit-trees already planted, and they are building *English* houses for themselves, meane while living in *Wigmoones*, whereof there is good store neere the hill side, at present there being a goodly plaine from the plaine towards *Dedham*) over the River (that is, *Charles* River) they have made a firme high foote-bridge archwise to walke to and fro, having heaped on the bottome tymbers huge stones, the more to fortifie it, and it was a great encouragement to them, that the last yeare, (when a like bridge made by the *English* in the new *Dedham* Village called *Medefield*, some foure or five miles from them) was throwne downe by the force of the flouds or Ice, yet theirs did stand firme and upright. But to returne to the Fort, and to the busines of the day, that is Round and Capacious, and they have prepared there a large Canopie of Matts upon poles for Mr *Eliot* and the chiefe of his Company to sit under, and other sorts for themselves and other hearers. The *Saneps* or men by themselves and the *Squaes* or women by themselves, besides the *English* then present, (which were about thirtie) there were I thinke not fewer then a hundred men women and young ones; among the *Indians* there be some greater proficients in knowledge, and of better utterance by farre then their fellowes, Grave and serious men, whom Mr *Eliot* hath trained up (or the Lord rather by his instructions and directions) to instruct and exhort the rest of the *Indians* in their Lords day and other meetings, when he cannot come to them himselfe. There be some five of these, one of them was prepared before we came, and appointed to begin this Exercise: the further relation of the manner of this *Indians* behaviour in preaching, together with the substance of that Sermon being before set downe by Mr *Eliot* may be never omitted: other particulars in order to the exact description of the *Indian* Fort and buildings in Mr *Eliots* Letter is defective are here supplyed. This man being of middle age, and clad all in *English* apparell (as most if not all others of them are) sitting in the midst, on a stoole, under the shelter, did begin with prayer very solemnely, standing up for some halfe quarter of an houre, then sitting downe spake unto them of the two Parables, concerning the Feild wherein the treasure hid, and the wise Marchant selling all for the pearle; wee understood him not (save Mr *Eliot*) excepting now and then a word or two, he discoursed to them some three quarters of an houre at the least, with great devotion, gravitie, decency, readines and affection, and gestures very becomming, and sundry mentions he made of Jesus Christ, specially in the beginning, and towards the ending, as if he were the scope of all, and the rest of the *Indians*; diverse old men and women, and the younger did joyne and attend with much Reverence, as if much affected therewith; then he ended with prayer as he beganne. Then Mr *Eliot* prayed and preached in the *Indian* Language for some houre more, about coming to Christ, and bearing his yoake. This Text was translated by him from the Scripture into *English*, speaking with much authoritie, and after his latter prayer the *Indian* Schoole-Master read out of his Booke one of the *Psalmes* in meeter, line by line, translated by Mr *Eliot* into *Indian*, all the men and women, &c. singing the same together in one of our ordinary *English* tunes melodiously. I should have said that after Mr *Eliots* Sermon there were two or three grave *Indians* that propounded to Mr *Eliot*, each of them a Question, very pertinent to the matter he handled about the yoake of Christ, and coming to Christ, which he answered, interpreting unto us both their Questions, and the summe of his owne Answers. After this the Lord did stirre up my heart to make an Exhortation to the *Indians*, which Mr *Eliot* expounded to them, and also the Governours Speech, which God did stirre him up too unto the same purpose, declaring our joy to see such beginnings, and warning them of the great danger if they should decline from what they had already come unto, either in their knowledge, affection, or Christian practice, incouraging them against what might dampe or deterre.

Then all of us taking us to our horses left Mr *Eliot* and them together, the Governour and his Company to lye at *Dedham*, and the rest of us when wee had rid two or three miles with them did returne into our owne way towards our former lodging, having been every one of us much refreshed in our spirits in what we saw, & were informed of, *viz.* of God amongst them. Not long before this, travelling with Mr *Eliots* brother I conferred in the way seriously with him about these *Indians*, for he useth to accompany his brother, and is a right godly and diligent man, desiring to know what solidity he found by experience in them. Who did acquaint mee that there was difference between them as between the *English*, some being lesse serious then others, and lesse spirituall; but that there was a considerable Company of solide ones that were constant and forward in good duties, as well on the weeke dayes as on the Lords. And that he had purposely sometimes in the darke walked the Round, as it were alone, and found them in their severall Families as devout in prayer, &c. as if there had been any present to observe: and that carried it very modestly, utterly refusing to receive any reliefe from Mr *Eliots* Table, choosing rather to live on the provisions at home, which came in by their owne labour; and when once Mr *Eliots* owne provisions failed (hee being detained among them sundry dayes beyond his intent) they soone tooke notice, and of their owne accord did bring unto him varietie of the best which they had themselves, and he professed unto mee that upon all his best observation, there was a very hopefull beginning amongst them of the Grace & Kingdome of our Lord Jesus. The Lord vouche-safe to be the *Omega* among them as well as the *Alpha* of this blessed change.

Your most loving Friend,

Boston: 27: 8ber
{16}51.   *and Brother in Christ,*

John Wilson.

As Mr Wilson *was stirred up in himselfe to send us the Relation of his owne observations upon his journey with Mr* Eliot, *so he having received some precious lines from an able Minister of the Gospel, viz. Mr* Leverich *of* Sandwich *in the Government of* New Plymouth, *whom the Lord had stirred up to labour also in the conversion of the* Indians*: the eares seeming as it were white unto harvest, and the labourers but very few, he adventures to put in his sickle, not without hopefull successe, as will appeare in his following lines. And for the discouragements mentioned in his Letter, know that divers of his people having cast off all the Ordinances of God in his Church, at last came to be seduced by every idle spirit that came amongst them, to be led into such fancies as we are ashamed to mention. And so this good man upon this occasion turned to the* Indians, *where he meets with an abundant blessing upon his endeavours.*

Reverend Sir.

I Salute you in the Lord, I shall trouble you onely with two things, first, the mooving causes inducing mee to set upon this worke: Secondly, with what successe I have hitherto been entertained, by the blessing of God upon my weake endeavours. For the first of these, I suppose its not unknowne to your selfe, amongst many others, what singular exercise I have had in these parts, and what singular Conflicts I have met withall in my travails amongst our owne Countreymen, divers of them transported with their (though not singular) Fancies, to the rejecting of all Churches and Ordinances by a new cunning, and I perswade my selfe one of the last but most pernicious plot of the Devill to undermine all Religion, and introduce all Atheisme and profanenesse, if it were possible, together with which, I have observed a spirit of Pharisaisme and formalitie too, too evidently creeping upon and strongly possessing others generally, besides other discouragements I shall forbeare to mention, which considered divers of our brethren, together with my selfe, upon consultation had together, were resolved to moove together else whether, where wee might hope for more and better encouragement, as touching our Communion, if God so pleased: but were disswaded by divers our honoured Friends, both by their Letters and more private Councells, unto whom we gave way, at least for the present: not long after having an hopefull *Indian* in my house, he propounds to mee a motion of teaching the *Indians* neere us. And sometime after Mr *Eliot* invites mee to the same worke by his Letters: then I thought with my selfe I must stay, and began to tast the motion with more affection, resolving, that if God would please to sit up roomes of others with the accesse of such forlorne Creatures, and bring in such as wandred in the highwayes, lanes, and hedges; and Call in the lame, and halt, and blind, in stead of those Contemners, it would be a mercy; and by no other respects in this world was my breast inclined unto this worke, and to attend God in it. As touching the second, for matter of successe and incouragement, I cannot but reckon this one, and that not the least, that though the *Indian* tongue be very difficult, irregular, and anomalous, and wherein I cannot meete with a Verbe Substantive as yet, nor any such Particles, as Conjunctions, &c. which are essentiall to the severall sorts of axioms, and consequently to all rationall and perfect discourses, and that though their words are generally very long, even *sesquipedalia verba*, yet I finde God helping, not onely my selfe to learne and attaine more of it in à short time, then I thinke I could or did of Latine, Greeke, or Hebrew, in the like space of time, when my memory was stronger, & when all known rules of Art are helpfull to fasten such notions in the minde of the learner; but also the *Indians* to understand mee fully (as they acknowledge) so farre as I have gone. I am constrained by many ambages and circumlocutions to supply the former defect, to expresse my selfe to them as I may. The next encouragement I may not without ground omit to mention is this, that it pleaseth God to helpe some of these poore Creatures to looke over and beyond the Examples of some of our looser sort of *English*: which I looke upon as a great stumbling blocke to many. It's to be lamented that the name of God so generally professed by those looser sort of *English*, should be so generally polluted by them, and blasphemed by Heathens, through the occasion of their loosenes and deniall of the power of godlinesse, yet God gives some of theirs a spirit of discerning between precious and vile, and a spirit of Conviction, to acknowledge (oh that ours would lay it to heart) there is no difference between the worst *Indians*, and such *English*, saying, *they are all one Indians*, yea and further, to put a like difference between such *Indians* amongst themselves here and elsewhere, as appeare to be more serious in their Inquiries after God, and conscientious according to their light, and such others that are more slight, and meere pretenders to Religions. Thirdly, for more particular observations. 1. God hath brought some of them to a sence of their sinnes, and a feare of his justice. Here I shall insert an example or two, one of them being to repeate such Principles I had begun to traine them in, in a Catechisticall way (for my penury confines mee to this method at present, and I hope it may be never the worse for them) was a good while before he could speake, having his countenance sad before (and as I have understood since a weeke together after our former exercise) and in speaking the teares all the while trickling downe his Cheekes: After being demanded by mee what was the matter of his sadnesse, he answers mee, he did now understand that God was a just God, and for himselfe he had been very wicked, even from a childe. And another, whom I used as my Interpreter now and then in teaching them, falls suddenly and publiquely into a bitter passion, crying out, and wringing his hands, out of the like apprehension of his Condition, as he told mee afterwards, and I finde no one of them (daring men) to speake of their good hearts, but some more some lesse sensible of the Contrary. Secondly, God hath brought some of them to some Evangelicall Conviction, one acknowledging that though he and others leave their former evills, and should keepe Gods Commandements, yet without Christ they must goe to hell. Thirdly, Two or three of them have complained of the hardnesse of their hearts, and are questioning of Remedies. Fourthly, Speaking to them of the mercy of God in Christ, one of them tells publiquely it did him more good to heare of Christ, then to heare of all earthly good things, I would faine hope for seeds of Faith in such. Fifthly, Two of them I deale withall, particularly for personall evills, by name for the sinne of Fornication, which they were carried away into, which my *Indian* acquainting my selfe with after our exercise I spake unto, shewing them the evills of this sinne, and aggravating of it by the knowledge they now had of God, &c. and exhorting them to Repentance, and to seeke mercy in Christ; whereupon one of them fell into bitter weeping, presently the other though his heart was shut up at present, yet not long after, and with longer continuance sayd, I have observed in others a sence of temptations, spirituall bondage, which they expressed naturally thus; one saith that he and the Devill were all one Souldiers, and this in sadnesse of spirit and speech: another laying his hands upon his knees and hammes, complaines he was as a man tyed in Cords, and prayes to God to be unloosed, and in generall they are observed divers of them to pray with much affection, mourning; in so much that they are in this respect a wonderment to their Companions, who enquired what is the matter, why they doe so, &c.

A fourth encouragement to mee is this, I finde the Devill bestirring himselfe, and betaking of himselfe to his wonted practice of stirring up oppositions against this worke by his Instruments, as fearing the ruine of his Kingdome, their Countrymen manifesting their hatred, threatning they shall not plant, hunt, &c. as before; yea the Controversie or enmitie rather arises between Parents and Children, &c. Lastly, and not long before I was last with you in the Bay upon a second day in the morning before they went away, there came to me to the number of twentie of them, voluntarily professing one by one their desire to feare God, promising that they would leave their sins (some intermixing acknowledgements of their sins and ignorance: and one that *English* and *Indians* knew shee had been very wicked) hereunto calling *Jehovah* to witnes; and this to doe all their dayes, as long as they live: some bringing their Children, and causing them to make the like profession; whereupon I was the more stirred towards them in my spirit (though I acknowledge I was loath to make an absolute engagement) to promise them I would endevour to be as helpfull to them as I could in teaching them: which when I had done, they gave mee thankes publiquely; and since this, they living some seaven miles from us, have built a *Wigwam* of purpose neere our Towne to receive them when they come on the Lords dayes; and truely Sir, they are so attentive in hearing, that it grieves me I cannot speake to them as I desire, they seeming to be hungry, and I wanting bread for them. And thus Sir, you have a naked Narration of our proceedings, with the events fallen out by Gods providence within not many moneths. It is I believe a day of small things, and so lookt at by our *English* many of them, who surely would have perished in their darknesse, if all others should have contemned them as they these, I pray God they perish not in the light, however I am resolved to bable to them as I may, considering that out of the mouthes of babes God ordaines praise, and found strength to still the enemie, &c. the beginnings of Gods great works are often in great obscuritie, where he appoints the end to be glorious. Also I remember one sowes and another reaps, which where ever they be, such as are faithfull shall rejoyce together. I doubt not Sir, of your fervent prayers (which I doe further beg of you and others that know how to pitty lost ones) for my selfe and poore *Indians*; that the Lord will prosper our endeavours this way, and water them with his abundant blessings in Jesus Christ, that the day-spring from on high may visit such poore soules as are in darknesse, and the shadow of death, and bring them to life in Jesus Christ.

Sandwich this 22th *of*
   the 7th. 1 6 5 1.   *William Leverich.*

The next Letter is a testimoniall from a private hand of what Mr Leverich *mentions in his to Mr.* Wilson, *where we may see some fruits of his labours testified by a neighbour of his at* Sandwich, *which is fiftie miles from that place, where Mr* Eliot *hath taught other* Indians *for divers years: but we doe not a little rejoyce to heare that Mr* Leverich *is engaged in this worke, because he is a grave learned knowing and a prudent Christian; one indeed from whom by Gods blessing we may expect much good.*

Oncerning the *Indians* I have seene and heard more this Sommer then ever I did before, I have seene some *Indians* crave a blessing before meate, and returne thankes after meate, pray morning and evening, some of them doe frequent our meetings, they come constantly eight or tenne miles every Saturday, and the Monday they returne home againe, while our Exercise doth last, they doe attend diligently, but understand but little, but when that is done Mr *Leverich* and they doe put questions one to another, and Mr *Leverich* hath an *Indian,* that speakes good *English*, and he is Interpreter. There is a man that lives neere us, that comes from an Island that is called *Martins Vineyard*, where is a Minister that speakes good *Indian*, he doth preach to them every weeke, he hath told me that that Minister told him, that there are some of them *Indians*, that are able to give a better reason of their Faith, then some of the Members of their Church; some of them will preach, and they have private meetings, and keepe very good orders.

Sandwich 22th *Sep-*
   tember. 1 6 5 1.   *Anthoney Bessey.*

The next Letter we present thee withall good Reader, is one from Mr Mayhew, *whom God hath honoured with abundant successe in making his labours the instrumentall meanes to turne many of the Heathens from their evill wayes to the Lord our God. This he not onely wrote to Mr* John Whitfield, *who is a Minister in* Winchester, *but also to a Member of our Corporation, being the same Narrative word for word for ought we discerne, wherein appeareth a mighty progresse in godlines since our last Treatise published by Mr* Henry Whitfield *upon his comming hither from* New England. *God not onely daily adding to their number such as in Charity we conceive appertain to his Election: but stirred them up (being neere two hundred persons) to enter into a more close way of the Gospel, declaring themselves to be the worshippers of the everliving God. With many other things ministring much consolation to every Christian heart, to see these very* Powwawes *fall off from the worship of Devills, and embrace the glad tydings of Salvation.*

Reverend and dearly beloved in Christ Jesus.

S I R,

Hat you have done in the *Indian* busines, and concerning my selfe in particular, doe give good testimony of your holy desires to further the worke of the Lord amongst them. The good providence of God in bringing you unto us, and the free engaging of your selfe in this worke of the Lord, and that upon the best ground, did fully perswade my heart of your faithfullnesse therein, and of an inward blessing from God upon us thereby; although I should never have seene a returne in outward supplies, as now through mercy I have, as an acceptable and very helpfull fruit of Christian goodnes and bounty, received from your selfe and Christian Friends, that the Lord hath stirred up both to pray earnestly, and contribute freely for the promoting of the worke of the Lord in my hand amongst the poore *Indians*. Sir, assure your selfe, and let all our beloved Friends know, that what is done by you together in this behalfe, doth not onely strengthen my hands, and give me advantage to be more helpful to the *Indians*, but also is a further encouragement unto my heart from the Lord to doe to the utmost of my power in this service he hath called me unto, and wherein he hath afforded me his gracious presence unto this day; and not onely in supporting me therein, but also in some remarkeable passages of his power and mercy amongst the Indians, those miserable Captives, something whereof your selfe have been an eye witnes unto; and have already heard, yet now being further advantaged through the grace of God appearing with us, and knowing it will be acceptable to your selfe, and our dearely beloved Christian Friends, that long for and rejoyce in the gracious appearance of Jesus Christ in his Kingly Soveraigntie and power, where he hath not formerly been knowne, I shall by the helpe of God certifie you how the Lord hath carried on his own worke with us since your departure from us.

It pleased the Lord who had drawne the *Indians* from the *Pawwaws* to worship himselfe, whereat the *Pawwaws* were much discontented, yet now to perswade two of themselves to run after those that followed hard after God, desiring that they might goe with them in the wayes of that God whose name is *Jehovah*; and they came much convinced of their sinnes that they had lived in, and especially of their *Pawwawing*, saying, I throw it from mee with hatred of it, being sorry that ever I medled with it. And now I have heard of *Jehovah*, by his helpe I put it under my feete, and hope to trample it downe in the dust with the Devill and *Pawwawnomas* (or imps) I throw it into the fire, and burne it. Thus they fully made knowne unto all both by word and gesture, and by more such like expressions they then used, not onely their indignation against it, but that they would never make use of it more. One of them did then discover the bottome of his witchcraft, confessing that at first he came to be a *Pawwaw* by Diabolicall Dreames, wherein he saw the Devill in the likenesse of foure living Creatures; one was like a man which he saw in the Ayre, and this told him that he did know all things upon the Island, and what was to be done; and this he said had its residence over his whole body. Another was like a Crow, and did looke out sharply to discover mischiefes coming towards him, and had its residence in his head. The third was like to a Pidgeon, and had its place in his breast, and was very cunning about any businesse. The fourth was like a Serpent, very subtile to doe mischiefe, and also to doe great cures, and these he said were meere Devills, and such as he had trusted to for safetie, and did labour to raise up for the accomplishment of any thing in his diabolicall craft but now he saith, that he did desire that the Lord would free him from them, and that he did repent in his heart, because of his sinne.

The other said his Conscience was much troubled for his sinne, and they both desired the Lord would teach them his wayes, have mercy upon them, and pardon their sinnes, for Jesus Christ his sake: and truely it did give to us who were present a great occasion of praising the Lord, to see those poore naked sonnes of *Adam*, and slaves to the Devill from their birth to come toward the Lord as they did, with their joynts shaking, and their bowells trembling, their spirits troubled, and their voyces with much fervency, uttering words of sore displeasure against sin and Satan, which they had imbraced from their Childhood with so much delight, accounting it also now their sinne, that they had not the knowledge of God.

Secondly, that they had served the Devill, the Enemy both of God and Man.

Thirdly, that they were so hurtfull in their lives, and were also thankfull that now through the blessing of God they had an opportunitie to be delivered out of that dangerous Condition. The *Indians* did all much rejoyce to see the *Pawwaws* turne from their wicked wayes to serve the Lord. Not long after the *Pawwaws* had forsaken their old way, on a Lecture day after Exercise diverse *Indians* desired to become the servants of the Lord, amongst whom was a *Pawwaw*, called *Tequanonim*, who was of great esteeme and very notorious; for he as they said, and in their ignorance conceived, never did hurt to any, but alwayes good, endeavouring the good and preservation of the *Indians*; whereunto also he was accompted by them to be strongly provided. And as himselfe said he had been possessed from the Crowne of the head to the soal of the foote with *Pawwawnomas*, not onely in the shape of living Creatures, as Fowles, Fishes, and creeping things, but Brasse, Iron, and Stone. It was therefore the more to be acknowledged the worke of God, that he should forsake this way, his friends, his gaine, to follow the Lord, whose wayes are so despisable in the eyes of devillish minded men. This *Pawwaw* declaring by what meanes the Lord tooke him off this devillish Trade, said that he had heard some things from my Father, who tooke occasion to discourse with him about the way of true happinesse, that he should never forget, blessed be God, his Counsell had so good an effect, as I hope it hath on many others. It pleased the Lord who will have all the gods of the earth to be terrible unto him; For he meeting *Mumanequem* in the wood by accident, told him that he was glad he had an opportunitie to speake his minde unto him, for he had many searchings of heart about his *Pawwawing*, and did thinke it was not a good way, and that God was angry with him for it; for said he my wife hath been a long time sicke, and the more I *Pawwaw* for her, the sicker she is; And this doth agree with an observation of the *Indians* of this Island, *viz.* that since the Word of God hath been taught unto them in this place, the *Pawwaws* have been much foyled in their devillish taskes, and that instead of curing have rather killed many; but in a word the fruit of this and all other meanes was a publique manifestation of hatred to his former wayes, wondering he was yet alive who was so sinfull, and that he desired to be better, and to believe in Christ, for whose sake onely, he did believe his sinnes could be pardoned, and that he did desire to heare the word of God. This man hereby hath made those of his own house to be his Enemies; his wife, his children, and most of his friends and kindred, who remaine obstinate still, whereby he meets with many troubles & temptations: one of his brethren being very sicke did earnestly desire that he would *Pawwaw* for him, which he refused, his brother told him that he might keep it private, but he still refused, telling him that notwithstanding that, if he should answer his desire, he should breake his Covenant, and sinne against God; and therefore would not.

There came pressing in at the same time about fiftie *Indians*, desiring to joyne with the worshippers of God in his service. It would be too long for mee to set downe what every one said before they entred into Covenant, onely this I may not omit, that all of them came confessing their sinnes, some in speciall the naughtinesse of their hearts, others in particular, actuall sinnes they had lived in: and also they all desired to be made better, and to attend unto the Word of God, to that end looking onely to Christ Jesus for salvation. I observed also that they generally came in by Families, bringing also their Children with them, saying, I have brought my Children too, I would have my Children serve God with us, I desire that this son and this daughter may worship *Jehovah*, and if they could but speake, their parents would have them say something, to shew their willingnesse to serve God: And when the Commandements were repeated, they all acknowledged them to be good, and made choice of *Jehovah* to be their God, promising by his helpe to walke according to his Counsells: And when they were received by them that were before in this generall Covenant, it was by lowde voyces giving thanks to God that they were met together in the wayes of *Jehovah*: this is all before the end of the yeare 1 6 5 0.

And now through the mercy of God there are an hundred ninetie-nine men, women, and children, that have professed themselves to be worshippers of the great and everliving God. There are now two meetings kept every Lords day, the one three miles, the other about Eight miles off my house: *Hiacomes* teacheth twice a day at the nearest, and *Mumanequem* accordingly at the farthest, the last day of the weeke they come unto me to be informed touching the subject they are to handle: And the Lord doth much assist them, blessed be the name of the Lord. I have also undertaken to keepe by the helpe of God two Lectures amongst them, which will be at each once a fortnight: And I hope it will be by the blessing of God very profitable unto them. This winter I intend, if the Lord will, to set up a Schoole to teach the *Indians* to reade, *viz.* the Children, and also any young men that are willing to learne, whereof they are very glad. I am also endeavouring their Cohabitations with all convenient speed, that so they may be more helpfull one to another; and also the better advantaged to carry on that worke they have set upon to Gods glorie, and their owne comfort. And what I have written concerning the *Pawwawes*, and the fiftie *Indians*, that were admitted to those that worshipped God in one day: There were diverse *English* both eye and eare witnesses thereof, as well as my selfe, and wee could not but acknowledge much of the Lords power and goodnesse to be visible amongst them, who without being driven by power, or allured by gifts, were so strongly carried against those wayes they so much loved, to love the way that nature hates. Let us therefore magnifie the Lord, who alone doth this, and seeke unto him to doe more and more still, that so one generation may praise his works to another, and that so both wee and them may abundantly utter the memory of his great goodnesse and power, In that new song, *Revelations* 5.9. untill that wee all meete together in Heaven, and *sing glorious praises unto him that sitteth upon the Throne, and unto the Lambe for ever and ever.* In whom I heartily recommend you unto God, desiring to be recommended by you, and in him to rest.

From the Vineyard this

16th of October. 1651.　　　　　　　　　　*Yours to be commended in*

and for the Lord Jesus.

Thomas Mayhew.

The next Letter you meete withall came from the present Governour of the Massachusets, *directed to the President of our Corporation; and another of the Members thereof, which we thought good to publish, that every Christian Reader may partake in the same consolation, wherewith he and we are comforted; and joyne with us in prayer to the Lord of the Harvest, that he would provide more labourers to enter upon this soule-saving worke, and enlarge the hearts of all his people in this Nation towards the same.*

Much Honoured and beloved in the Lord Jesus.

I Esteeme it not the least of Gods mercies that hath stirred up the hearts of any of the people of God to be instrumentall in the inlarging of the kingdome of his deare Sonne here amongst the Heathen *Indians*, which was one end of our comming hither, and it is not frustrated. It was prophesied of old, and now begins to be accomplished, *Psal.* 2.8. Neither can I but acknowledge the unspeakeable goodnesse of God that gives us favour in the fight of our Countrymen to helpe on with so large a hand of bountie, so glorious a worke, provoked thereunto by your worthy selves, the chiefe Actors of so good a designe, let mee (with leave) say confidently, you will never have cause to repent it; For the worke is Gods, and he doth own it, the labour there hath been yours, and your Master will reward it. I thinke Religion and Conscience binde mee to seeke unto God for you, and to praise him with you, for what is alreadie begun. The Foundation is layd, and such a one that I verily believe the gates of Hell shall never prevaile against. I doubt not but the building will goe on apace, which I hope will make glad the hearts of Thousands. Truely Gentlemen, had you been eare and eye-witnesses of what I heard and saw on a Lecture-day amongst them about three weekes since, you could not but be affected therewith as I was. To speake truely I could hardly refraine teares for very joy to see their diligent attention to the word first taught by one of the *Indians*, who before his Exercise prayed for the manner devoutly and reverently (the matter I did not so well understand) but it was with such reverence, zeale, good affection, and distinct utterance, that I could not but admire it; his prayer was about a quarter of an houre or more, as wee judged it; then he tooke his Text, and Mr *Eliot* their Teacher tould us that were *English* the place, (there were some Ministers and diverse other godly men there that attended mee thither) his Text was in *Matthew* 13.44,45,46. He continued in his Exercise full halfe an houre or more as I judged it, his gravitie and utterance was indeed very commendable, which being done Mr *Eliot* taught in the *Indian* tongue about three quarters of an houre as neere as I could guesse; the *Indians*, which were in number men & women neere about one hundred, seemed the most of them so to attend him (the men especially) as if they would loose nothing of what was taught them, which reflected much upon some of our *English* hearers. After all there was a *Psalme* sung in the *Indian* tongue, and *Indian* meeter, but to an *English* tune, read by one of themselves, that the rest might follow, and he read it very distinctly without missing a word as we could judge, and the rest sang chearefully, and prettie tuneablie. I rid on purpose thither being distant from my dwelling about thirty-eight or fortie miles, and truely I account it one of the best Journeys I made these many yeares. Some few dayes after I desired Mr *Eliot* briefely to write mee the substance of the *Indians* Exercise, which when he went thither againe, namely, to *Naticke*, where the *Indians* dwell, and where the *Indian* taught, he read what he remembred of it first to their Schoole-Master, who is an *Indian* and teacheth them and their Children to write, and I saw him write also in *English*, who doth it true and very legible, and asked him if it were right, and he said yea, also he read it unto others, and to the man himselfe, who also owned it. To tell you of their industry and ingenuitie in building of an house after the *English* manner, the hewing and squaring of their tymber, the sawing of the boards themselves, and making of a Chimney in it, making of their groundsells and wall-plates, and mortising, and letting in the studds into them artificially, there being but one *English*-man a Carpenter to shew them, being but two dayes with them, is remarkeable. They have also built a Fort there with halfe trees cleft about eight or ten Inches over, about ten or twelve foote high, besides what is intrenched in the ground, which is above a quarter of an acre of ground, as I judge. They have also built a foote bridge over *Charles* River, with Groundsells and Spurres to uphold it against the strength of the Flood and Ice in the Winter; it stood firme last Winter, and I thinke it will stand many Winters. They have made Drummes of their owne with heads and brases very neatly and artificially, all which shewes they are industrious and ingenuous. And they intend to build a Water-Mill the next Sommer, as I was tould when I was with them. Some of them have learnt to mow Grasse very well. I shall no further trouble you with any more relation at this time concerning them. But a word or two further with your patience concerning other *Indians*. The worke of God amongst the *Indians* at *Martins Vineyard*, is very hopefull and prosperous also. I mist of Mr *Mayhew* their Teacher, who was lately at *Boston*, and therefore cannot give you a particular account thereof at this present time; yet I cannot but acquaint you what other motions there are touching other *Indians*. There came to us upon the 20th of this instant Moneth, at the generall Court one *Pummakummin* Sachem of *Qunnubbágge*, dwelling amongst or neere to the *Narragansets*, who offered himselfe and his Men to worship God, and desired that some *English* may be sent from the *Massachusets* Government to plant his River, that thereby he may be partaker of Government, and may be instructed by the *English* to know God. Wee shall I hope take some care and course about it, and I hope wee shall have more helpe to carry on that worke also; For there are some Schollers amongst us who addict themselves to the study of the *Indian* Tongue. The Lord in mercy recompence it into your Bosomes, all that labour of love vouchsafed to the poore *Indians*, which are the hearty prayers and earnest desire of; much honoured.

Boston the 27th *of*

the Eight. 1651.

*Your loving Friend in all
service of Christ,*

John Endecott.

The next thing we present the reader withall is a private passage from one in New England *to his godly Friend here, who was so much affected therewith, as he found out our Treasurer of the Corporation, by name Mr* Richard Floyd *at the* Meremaide *in* Cheapside, *and desired it might be published to the world amongst other things, when we should publish and print what we received of like nature. And how ever it is but briefe in it selfe, yet full of sweetnesse and plainnes of spirit which we offer to thy view.*

THe best News I can write you from *New England* is, the Lord is indeed converting the *Indians*, and for the refreshing of your heart, and the hearts of all the Godly with you. I have sent you the Relation of one *Indian* of two yeares profession, that I tooke from his owne mouth, by an Interpreter, because he cannot speake or understand one word of *English*.

The first Question was;

Q. How did you come first to any sight of sinne?

A. His answer was, before the Lord did ever bring any English *to us, my conscience was exceedingly troubled for sinne, but after Mr* Mahew *came to preach, and had been here some time, one chiefe* Sagamore *did imbrace the Gospel, and I hearing of him, I went to him, and prayed him to speake something to mee concerning God, and the more I did see of God, the more I did see my sinne, and I went away rejoycing, that I knew any thing of God, and also that I saw my sinne.*

Q. I pray what hurt doe you see in sinne?

A. Sinne, sayth he, is a continuall sicknesse in my heart.

Q. What further evill doe you see in sinne?

A. I see it to be a breach of all Gods Commandements.

Q. Doe you see any punishment due to man for sinne?

A. Yea, sayth he, I see a righteous punishment from God due to man for sinne, which shall be by the Devills in a place like unto fire not that I speake of materiall fire, (sayth he) where man shall be for ever dying and never dye.

Q. Have you any hope to escape this punishment?

A. While I went on in the way of Indianisme I had no hope, but did verily believe I should goe to that place, but now I have a little hope, and hope I shall have more.

Q. By what meanes doe you look for any hope?

A. Sayth he, by the satisfaction of Christ.

I prayed the Interpreter, to tell him from mee that I would have him thinke much of the satisfaction of Christ, (and so he told him) I prayed him to returne mee his Answer.

A. I thanke him kindly for his good Counsell, it doth my heart good, sayd he, to heare any man speak of Christ.

Q. What would you think if the Lord should save you from misery?

A. If the Lord, said he, would save me from all the sinne that is in my heart, and from that misery, I should exceedingly love God, and sayth he, I should love a man that should doe mee any good, much more the Lord, if he should doe this for mee.

Q. Doe you thinke that God will doe you any good for any good that is in you?

A. Though I beleeve that God loves man that leaves his sinne, yet I beleeve it is for Christs sake.

Q. Doe you see that at any time God doth answer your prayers?

A. Yea, sayth he, I take every thing as an Answer of prayer.

Q. But what speciall answer, have you taken notice of?

A. Once my wife being three dayes and three nights in labour, I was resolved never to leave praying, till she had deliverance, and at last God did it, and gave her a sonne, and I called his name Returning, *because all the while I went on in Indianisme I was going from God, but now the Lord hath brought mee to him backe againe.*

By this time Captaine *Gooking* came to us, and he asked him this Question:

Q. What he would thinke if he should finde more affliction and trouble in Gods wayes, then he did in the way of Indianisme.

A. His answer was, when the Lord did first turne mee to himselfe and his wayes, he stripped mee as bare as my skinne, and if the Lord should strip mee as bare as my skinne againe, and so big Saggamore *should come to mee, and say, I will give you so big* Wampom, *so big* Beaver, *and leave this way, and turne to us againe: I would say, take your riches to your selfe, I would never forsake God and his wayes againe.*

This is a Relation taken by my selfe, *William French.*

The last Letter we offer to the Readers view, is a Letter directed to one of our selves from Mr Thomas Allen, *who came lately from* New England, *and is now setled in the Ministery at* Norwitch *in* Norfolke, *wherein he beareth witnes to the reallitie and truth of this worke of the Lord in* New England *begun upon the* Indians, *against all such that raise up false reports against the same, or such as labour to weaken the same, by lessening the number of such as are wrought upon by the power of the Gospel preached to them.*

Honored Sir;

IT seemes that some of late have been so impudently bold (which I cannot sufficiently wonder at) as to report and publiquely affirme, that there was no such thing as the preaching and dispersing of the Gospel amongst the Natives in *New England*: verily Sir, I doe beleeve that the Devill himselfe (who is the Father of Lyes) would not, yea durst not have uttered such a notorious untruth as that was. Now although I confesse I have not been present at the places where the *Indians* are wont to meete, to heare such as doe preach unto them, by reason of my bodily weaknes, and indisposition to travell so farre into the Wildernesse, yet thus much I can testifie (if my Testimony may be of any use) being lately come over from *New-England*; that there are divers persons in severall places, who doe take paines, and labour in that Worke there, *viz.* not onely Mr *Eliot* of *Roxbury*, who hath preached among them for many yeares up & downe in the Jurisdiction of the *Massachusets*; and Mr *Mahew*, who for a good while hath taken paines amongst the *Indians* at an Island called *Martins Vineyard;* but of late also Mr *Leveridge* in the Jurisdiction of *Plymouth*, and Mr *Blynman*, who lives now in a new Plantation in the *Pequotts* Countrey. As for the successe of the preaching of the Gospel unto the Natives, I have heard Mr *Eliot* affirme, that he is so well perswaded of the Worke of grace in some of them, as that he could comfortably joyne in Church-fellowship with them: Mr *Mahew* also (who came to see mee a little before my coming from thence) told me that after Mr *Whitfeilds* coming thence (for he had been upon that Island, as he came to the Bay, and was present also with Mr *Mahew* amongst the *Indians*) there were neer upon one hundred (I think he said Ninety and odd) persons of them more who came in to heare him preach unto them, and some *Pawaws* also, and one of some Eminency amongst them, who did acknowledge his Evill in such doings, and made a Declaration of the manner how he came at the first to be a *Pawaw*, the which also Mr *Mahew* did relate unto mee. Sir, that there is such a work in hand in *New-England* as the preaching of the Gospel unto the Natives there, all the Magistrates and Ministers and people in that place (who know any thing) will be readie to attest, and therefore such as dare affirme the contrary, may as well say, that the Sunne doth not shine at Noone day, when the skie is cleere, and doe indeed deserve a Publique Witnesse to be borne against them, for such a Publique, and so notorious an untruth; The good Lord humble them deeply for it, if it be his good will, and pardon it to them through his grace in Christ.

Thus Sir, not having further at this present to be troublesome unto you, desiring an Interest in your earnest prayers for mee, beseeching the Lord to let his presence and blessing be with you, and upon your great and weighty businesses, I take leave, resting.

Norwich 8^d. 11th
1 6 5 1.

Your humble Servant in the Lord,
Thomas Allen.

The Corporation to the Reader.

T **T** *Hus having presented thee* Christian Reader *with a view of those things that God hath brought to our hands, which we of the Corporation conceive our selves bound in duty to publish to the world, looking upon it as one meanes to advance the work in the hearts of Gods people, and to stirre them up thereby to contribute more freely towards the carrying on the same: The reason wherefore* *we have published so many testimonialls, and shall insert more, is because too many that come from thence labour to blast the worke, by reporting here that there is no such worke afoote in the Countrey: or if it be it is but for the loaves, & if any be truely converted, 'tis not above five or seaven at most? These things as they are very grievous to us to heare, so we take God to witnes, that as we are in sincerity exercised in a great deale of care and travell to carry on the worke: so we publish to the world no more then what we have received, and beleeve to be really true. And if these testimonies related in the foregoing discourse, be not sufficient to satisfie any still doubting spirit, there are some eminent Gentlemen come from thence, who are ready to resolve them in the truth hereof, as Mr* Edward Hopkins, *late Governour of* Conectacutt, *Mr* Francis Willowby, *(and others) a late Magistrate of the* Massachusets. *Besides if any shall repaire to* Coopers Hall, *we shall be willing to shew them the originall Copies we have received, which we have transcribed for the Presse: the time for any to repaire thither is Saturday every weeke between the houres of ten and twelve in the Morning, where our Corporation sit, and where we shall gladly take paines to satisfie the doubts of any: and thinke nothing too much wherein we may be serviceable to the Lord Jesus in a worke having so much tendency to his glory in the propagation of his Kingdome.*

Signed in the name and by the appointment of the said Corporation by *William Steele* Esquire, President.

F I N I S.

Tears of Repentance:

Or, A further
Narrative of the Progreſs of the *Goſpel*
Amongſt the

INDIANS
IN
NEW-ENGLAND:

Setting forth, not only their preſent ſtate
and condition, but ſundry Confeſſions of ſin
by diverſe of the ſaid *Indians*, wrought upon
by the ſaving Power of the Goſpel; Together
with the manifeſtation of their *Faith* and *Hope*
in *Jeſus Chriſt*, and the Work of Grace upon
their Hearts.

Related by Mr. *Eliot* and Mr. *Mayhew*, two Faithful Laborers
in that Work of the Lord.

Publiſhed by the Corporation for propagating the Goſpel there, for the
Satisfaction and Comfort of ſuch as wiſh well thereunto.

Iſay, 42. 3. *A bruiſed Reed ſhall he not break, and the ſmoaking*
Flax, ſhall be not quench.

London: Printed by *Peter Cole* in *Leaden-Hall*, and are to Sold at
his Shop, at the Sign of the Printing-Preſs in Cornhil,
near the Royal Exchange. 1653.

Tears of Repentance:

Or, A further

Narrative of the Progress of the *Gospel*

Amongst the

I N D I A N S
I N
N E W - E N G L A N D :

Setting forth, not only their present state and condition, but sundry Confessions of sin by diverse of the said *Indians*, wrought upon by the saving Power of the Gospel; Together with the manifestation of their *Faith* and *Hope* in *Jesus Christ*, and the Work of Grace upon their Hearts.

Related by Mr. *Eliot* and Mr. *Mayhew*, two Faithful Laborers in that Work of the Lord.

Published by the Corporation for propagating the Gospel there, for the Satisfaction and Comfort of such as wish well thereunto.

Isay, 42.3.   A bruised Reed shall he not break, and the smoking Flax, shall he not quench.

London: Printed by *Peter Cole* in *Leaden-Hall*, and are to Sold at his Shop, at the Sign of the Printing-Press in Cornhil, near the Royal Exchange.   1653.

TO
HIS EXCELLENCY
The Lord General
CROMWEL.

WHat *the Jews once said of their Centurion,* He loved our Nation, and built us a Synagogue, *the same may we affirm upon a more Noble Accompt of Your Lordship, and of those faithful Centurions and Soldiers under Your Conduct; by how much the Adventure of your Lives in the Cause of God, for the Good of your Country, is a more infallible Demonstration of your Love to it: for as much as the King of Saints, is also King of Nations, and when he shall be the desire of all Nations, will prove their safest Interest.*

Upon consideration whereof, it was but equal that Mr. Eliot *a faithful Laborer of Christ in spreading the* Everlasting Gospel *to the Poor* Indians, *should prefix Your Lordships Name to his Relation of the Progress of Divine Grace amongst them: And with his Judgment, We of the Corporation, who are subordinately intrusted, do so far concur, especially moved there unto by that liberal and Exemplary Contribution to this Glorious Work lately promoted by Your Lordship, and Your Officers with the Army, that we thought not fit either to sever that Narrative, and this of Mr.* Mayhew's, *or to send them abroad under any other Name to the Publick View.*

Coopers-Hall, *London,*
   March, 26. 1653.

Signed in the Name, and by
   the Appointment of the
   said Corporation, by

William Steel, President.

To the much Honored Corporation in London, Chosen to Place of Publick Trust for the promoting of the Work of the Lord among the Indians *in* N E W - E N G L A N D.

Worthy Sirs,

IT hath not been from any disrespect to your selves, that I have not formerly directed to your Presence, and presented into your Hand, what have already been let go, which made Relation of the Work of God among the *Indians* in this Island (commonly called *Martins Vineyard*) This year there was an opportunity not to be refused, of certifying the Right Worshipful *John Endicot* Esquire, Governor of the *Massachussets* in *New-England* of what I had to communicate concerning the *Indians*, from whose hand also you will receive it; but yet I may not for several causes, neglect the writing to your selves the same things, with more particulars since adjoyned, in the conclusion to accompany the former unto your Pious and Prudent consideration, to which they are committed to be (as I have received them from God) the tokens of more Grace in store to be bestowed on Indian Souls.

Highly esteemed in the Lord Jesus,

WHen the Lord first brought me to these poor Indians on the *Vinyard*, they were mighty zealous and earnest in the Worship of False gods, and Devils; their False gods were many, both of things in Heaven, Earth, and Sea: And there they had their Men-gods, Women-gods, and Children-gods, their Companies, and Fellowships of gods, or Divine Powers, guiding things amongst men, besides innumerable more feigned gods belonging to many Creatures, to their Corn, and every Colour of it: The Devil also with his Angels had his Kingdom among them, in them; account him they did, the terror of the Living, the god of the Dead, under whose cruel power and into whose deformed likeness they conceived themselves to be translated when they died; for the same word they have for *Devil,* they use also for a *Dead Man,* in their Language: by him they were often hurt in their Bodies, distracted in their Minds, wherefore they had many meetings with their *Pawwaws* (who usually had a hand in their hurt) to pacifie the Devil by their Sacrifice, and get deliverance from their evil; I have sometimes marvelled to see the vehemency of their Spirits, which they acted with no less bodily violence therein. The *Pawwaws* counted their Imps their Preservers, had them treasured up in their bodies, which they brought forth to hurt their enemies, and heal their friends; who when they had done some notable Cure, would shew the Imp in the palm of his Hand to the Indians; who with much amazement looking on it, Deified them, then at all times seeking to them for cure in all sicknesses, and counsel in all cases: This Diabolical way they were in, giving heed to a multitude of Heathen Traditions of their gods, and many other things, under the observation whereof, they with much slavery were held, and abounding with sins, having only an obscure Notion of a god greater than all, which they call *Mannit*, but they knew not what he was, and therefore had no way to worship him.

What an entrance I had at first amongst these miserable Heathen, how called thereunto, and what success God blessed us with, hath been in some measure already published, which will I hope through the dew of Gods blessing from Heaven, have such a gracious increase, that the blossoming and budding time shal at least be acknowledged, and by many more God blessed for it, in the growth of the fruit to more maturity; Since it hath pleased God to send his Word to these poor captivated men (bondslaves to sin and Satan) he hath through mercy brought two hundred eighty three Indians (not counting yong children in the number) to renounce their false gods, Devils, and Pawwaws, and publickly in set meetings, before many witnesses, have they disclaimed the Divinity of their formerly adored multitude, defied their tyrannical Destroyer the Devil, and utterly refused the help of the Pawwaws in any case; neither have they at any time, either by threatnings or flatteries been drawn thereto, although their lives have been in hazard; yea, eight of their Pawwaws have forsaken their Devillish craft, and profitable trade as they accounted it, for to embrace the Word and Way of God. The Indians which do pray to God, were not compelled thereto by power, neither also could they be allured by gifts, who received nothing for about seven years time, much less that which counterpoyse their troubles, and exceed to the drawing of them from the beloved waies of their own Worships: Surely it were great uncharitableness, and derogatory from the glory of God, to think that none of these are truly changed, and that God himself by his Word and Spirit, hath not in mercy prevailed in their hearts against these evils; nay, may we not hope and be perswaded by this, and some other appearances of God amongst them, that some of them are truly turned to God from Idols, to serve the Living and true God? Serve him, through mercy they do in some hopeful Reformations, walking inoffensively and diligently in their way, which I hope will more plainly appear when they are in a way more hopeful (by the blessing of God to their further well-being) which I hope will be in the best time.

I cannot but take notice of this good providence of God by the way, That he hath mercifully preserved all the Indians which call upon his Name (from the beginning of the Work unto this day) from all extraordinary evil, whereby the Devil and Witches use to torment the Bodies and Minds of Men, not one of them or their children (as I know) or have heard have been touched by them in this kind (only a Pawwaw or two, have not been delivered from his Imps presently after his renouncing of them, but for some time have had the sence of them in his Body with much pain:) The mischief that the Pawwaws and Devils usually do to the common Indian this way, is both by outward and bodily hurt, or inward pain, torture, and distraction of mind, both which I have seen my self: To accomplish the first, the Devil doth abuse the real body of a Serpent, which comes directly towards the man in the house or in the field, looming or having a shadow about him like a man, and do shoot a bone (as they say) into the Indians Body, which sometimes killeth him. An instance whereof I can give, whereby it may the more plainly appear, that it is a great mercy to be delivered therefrom; and it is of a youth, who living with his Parents upon a neck of Land, they did not pray unto *Jehovah*, yet their Neighbors who lived there with them, did; This Youth was hurt after the same manner, and then presently his Parents pulled down the house they lived in, and fled to an Island near by, where I saw the Indian thus hurt in his Thigh, he was grievously tormented, and his Kindred about him mourning, not knowing where to find any comfort; or help, for cure could not be had from their gods or Pawwaws: I then took the opportunity to reason with them about their way, with the best wisdom God gave me, but all in vain, for they would not hear to seek the true God, notwithstanding he had shewn his displeasure so apparantly against them for their former refusing of Him, but they still followed on their wonted Serpentine Machinations: The Pawwaws, and their devillish train, with their horrible outcries, hollow bleatings, painful wrestlings, and smiting their own bodies, sought deliverance, but all in vain, for he died miserably. Hereby, and by several other things, I perceive that they are not (in a manner) indifferent, whether they serve their own gods or not, or change them (as some think) for they are naturally like the Heathens of *Chittim* and *Kedar*, which would not change their gods, which yet are no gods; when God blames his people for changing their glory for that which doth not profit; I hope therefore that it is something of Grace, that many chuse to worship the true God. But touching the former vexing mischiefs, a *Sachem*, and no good friend to the work, could not but acknowledg the blessing of God among the Praying Indians; When I came over (said he) at the further end of the Island, there was a storm (mentioning the aforesaid evils, with some more) but when I came to this end I found a calm, the Praying Indians were all well, they arose in the morning, Prayed to God, and went about their business, and they are not hurt nor troubled like the other Indians: And the Pawwaws themselves, some of them do say, That they cannot make their Power seize on any of them: Questionless they have tried their Skill, and Satan hath not been wanting to assist them, who is so unwilling to fall down from his Rule, and to be driven from his old Possessions. A Pawwaw told me, who was of no small note among the Heathen formerly, and also with the best, now he hath forsaken his Pawwawing, That after he had been brought by the Word of God to hate the Devil, and to renounce his Imps (which he did publickly) that yet his Imps remained still in him for some months tormenting of his flesh, and troubling of his mind, that he could never be at rest, either sleeping or waking: At length one time when I went down to keep the farthest Lecture about seven miles off, he asked me some Questions, whereof this was one, *viz.* That if a Pawwaw had his Imps gone from him, what he should have instead of them to preserve him? Whereunto it was Answered, That if he did beleeve in Christ Jesus, he should have the Spirit of Christ dwelling in him, which is a good and a strong Spirit, and will keep him so safe, that all the Devils in Hell, and Pawwaws on Earth, should not be able to do him any hurt; and that if he did set himself against his Imps, by the strength of God they should all flee away like Muskeetoes: He told me, That he did much desire the Lord, it might be so with him. He further said, That ever since that very time God hath in mercy delivered him from them, he is not troubled with any pain (as formerly) in his Bed, nor dreadful visions of the night, but through the blessing of God, he doth lie down in ease, sleeps quietly, wakes in Peace, and walks in safety, for which he is very glad, and praises God.

This last spring, the Indians of their own accord made a motion to me they might have some way ordered amongst them, as a means whereby they might Walk in good Subjection to the Law of God, whereunto they desired to enter into Covenant; they told me that they were very desirous to have their sins suppressed which God did forbid, and the duties performed, which he hath Commanded in his Word; and thereunto they desired me to inform them, what punishment the Lord did appoint to be inflicted on those which did break any part of His Law, for they were very willing to submit themselves to what the will of the Lord is in this kind. I was not willing on the sudden to draw forth in writing an Answer to their desire, but rather chose to take a longer time of Consideration in a Work of so great Concernment, and refer them to the Word of God, shewing them many places for their information, most whereof they had heard of formerly: They also further desired, That they might have some men Chosen amongst them with my father and my self, to see that the Indians did walk orderly, and that such might be incouraged, but that those which did not, might be dealt with acording to the word of the Lord; I could not but approve and incourage the motion, seeing they spake not as those in *Psal.* 2.3. *Let us break their bands asunder and cast away their cords from us*, but sought totall subjection and strict obedience to God: yet I told them that it was a matter of great weight, shewing them many things which I thought necessary for them to know, but needless now to relate. A day of fasting and prayer to repent of our sins, and seek the gracious help of our God for Christ Jesus sake, we appointed; and another shortly after to finish the work in: Some of the Indians spake something for their benefit; and about ten, or twelve of them prayed, not with any set Form like Children, but like Men indued with a good measure of the knowledg of God, their own wants, and the wants of others, with much affection, and many Spiritual Petitions, favoring of a Heavenly mind; and so are they streitned in respect of help from man, that it appears the more plainly to be the Dictates of Gods Spirit. A Platform of the Covenant in Answer to their desires, I drew forth the same morning in the Indian Language, which I have here sent in English.

Wee the distressed Indians *of the* Vineyard (*or* Nope, the Indian name of the Island) *That beyond all memory have been without the True God, without a Teacher, and without a Law, the very Servants of Sin and Satan, and without Peace, for God did justly vex us for our sins; having lately through his mercy heard of the Name of the True God, the Name of his Son Christ Jesus, with the holy Ghost, the Comforter, three Persons, but one most Glorious God, whose Name is* **J E H O V A H:** *We do praise His Glorious Greatness, and in the sorrow of our hearts, and shame of our faces, we do acknowledg and renounce our great and many sins, that we and our Fathers have lived in, do run unto him for mercy, and pardon for Christ Jesus sake; and we do this day through the* *blessing of God upon us, and trusting to his gracious help, give up our selves in this Covenant, Wee, our Wives, and Children, to serve* **J E H O V A H:** *And we do this day chuse* **J E H O V A H** *to be our God in Christ Jesus, our Teacher, our Law-giver in his Word, our King, our Judg, our Ruler by his Magistrates and Ministers; to fear God Himself, and to trust in Him alone for Salvation, both of Soul and Body, in this present Life, and the Everlasting Life to come, through his mercy in Christ Jesus our Savior, and Redeemer, and by the might of his Holy Spirit; to whom with the Father and Son, be all Glory everlasting.* Amen.

After I had often read this Covenant and expounded it unto them, they all with free Consent willingly and thankfully joyned therein, and desired *Jehovah* his blessing for Jesus Christ his sake, the Lord be gracious to our beginnings.

Within two or three weeks there came an Indian to me in business, and by the way he told me, that some Indians had lately kept a day of Repentance to humble themselves before God in prayer, and that the word of God which one of them spake unto, for their Instruction, was *Psal.* 66.7. *He ruleth by his Power for ever, his eyes behold the nations, let not the rebellious exalt themselves.* I asked him what their end was in keeping such a day? He told me those six things: First, they desired, That God would slay the rebellion of their hearts. Secondly, That they might love God, and one another. Thirdly, That they might withstand the evil words and temptations of wicked men, and not to be drawn back from God. Fourthly, That they might be obedient to the good Words and Commands of their Rulers. Fiftly, That they might have their sins done away by the Redemption of Jesus Christ. And Lastly, That they might walk in Christs way.

Now for the state of things with us, we are by the help of God about to begin a Town that they may Cohabit and carry on things in a Civil and Religious way the better; The praying Indians are constant attenders to the word of the Lord, and some of them (I hope) conscionable seekers after the knowledg of God, and themselves, and not without obtaining (by the grace of God) some saving benefit to their own Souls, which will by his own blessing, in the best time, more plainly appear. About 30. Indian Children are now at School, which began the Eleventh day of the Eleventh month. 1651. They are apt to learn, and more and more are now sending in unto them. The Barbarous Indians, both men and women, do often come on the Lecture dayes, and complaining of their ignorance, disliking their sinful liberty, and refusing the helps, and hopes of their own power, seek Subjection to *Jehovah*, to be taught, governed, and saved by him, for Jesus Christs sake. The Name of the Lord alone be praised for what is begun; What is further needfull, I earnestly desire may be fervently prayed for, and expected by faith, to be effected, and finished by the gracious hand of God, who have laid the foundation, and will not leave his own works unperfect, which is the comfort of an unworthy Laborer in the Lords Vinyard, and an earnest desirer to be remembred at the Throne of Grace.

Having a little more liberty, I shall certifie you of something more, which I have taken notice of amongst the poor Indians.

I observed that the Indians when they chose their Rulers, made choyce of such as were best approved for their godliness, and most likely to suppress sin, and encourage holiness, and since they have been forward upon all occasions, to shew their earnest desire thereof. There was Indian that was well approved for his Reformation, that was suspected to have told a plain Lye for his Gain; the business was brought to the publick Meeting, and there it was notably sifted with zeal and good affection; but at length the Indian defending himself with great disdain, and hatred for such an evil, proved himself clear, and praised God for it. The same Indian was a little before, very sick, and he told me that when he thought he should die, he did so love God, that he was not unwilling to die, and leave his wife, and children, or any thing else, but that he was only desirous to live for this cause, That he might be more taught by the Word of God, and be helpful to teach the Indians the Way of God.

I have also observed how God is pleased to uphold some of these poor Indians against opposition. I was once down towards the further end of the Island, and lodged at an Indians house, who was accounted a great man among the Islanders, being the friend of a great *Sachem* on the *Mayn;* this *Sachem* is a great Enemy to our Reformation on the Island: At this mans house when I had sate a while, his son being about thirty years old, earnestly desired me in his Language, to relate unto him some of the ancient Stories of God; I then spent a great part of the night (in such discourse as I thought fittest for them) as I usually do when I lodg in their houses, what he then heard (as expressed) did much affect him: And shortly after he came and desired to joyn with the praying Indians to serve *Jehovah*, but it was to the great discontentment of the *Sachems* on the *Mayn*, and those Indians about him: News was often brought to him that his life was laid in wait for, by those that would surely take it from him, they desired him therfore with speed to turn back again; The man came to me once or twice, and I perceived that he was troubled, he asked my counsel about removing his Habitation, yet told me, That if they should stand with a sharp weapon against his breast, and tell him that they would kill him presently, if he did not turn to them, but if he would, they would love him, yet he had rather lose his life than keep it on such terms; for (said he) when I look back on my life as it was before I did pray to God, I see it to be wholly naught, and do wholly dislike it, and hate those naughty waies; but when I look on that way which God doth teach me in his Word, I see it to be wholly good; and do wholly love it. Blessed be God that he is not overcome by these temptations.

The next thing I judg also worthy to be observed, My Father and I were lately talking with an Indian who had not long before almost lost his life by a wound his Enemies gave him in a secret hidden way, the mark whereof, he had upon him, and will carry it to his grave: This man understanding of a secret Plot that was to take away his Enemies life, told my Father and I, That he did freely forgive him for the sake of God, and did tell this Plot to us that the mans life might be preserved: This is a singular thing, and who among the Heathen will do so?

I observe also that the Indians themselves do indeavor to propagate the knowledg of God, to the glory of God and the good of others: I heard an Indian (after I had some discourse with the Indians in the night) ask the *Sachem*, and many others together, how they did like that counsel they heard from the word of God: They answered, very wel; then said he, why do you not take it? Why do you not do according to it? He further added, I can tell you why it is, Because you do not see your sins, and because you do love your sins; for as long as it was so with me, I did not care for the Way of God; but when God did shew me my sins, and made me hate them, then I was glad to take Gods Counsel: this I remember he spake, with some other things, with such Gravity and truth, that the *Sachem* and all the company was not able to gain-say.

Myoxeo also lately met with an Indian, which came from the *Mayn* who was of some note among them; I heard that he told them of the great things of God, and of Christ Jesus, the sinfulness and folly of the Indians, the Pardon of sin by Christ, and of a good life; and so were they both affected, that they continued this discourse two half nights, and a day, until their strength was spent: He told them in particular, how a Beleever did live above the world, that he did keep worldly things alwaies at his feet (as he shewed him by a sign) That when they were deminished, or increased, it was neither the cause of his Sorrow, or joy, that he should stoop to regard them, but he stood upright with his heart Heavenward, and his whol desire was after God, and his joy in him. Now Much honored in the Lord, and all that love Christ Jesus in truth, let me prevail with you that we may be presented by you at the Throne of Grace in his worthiness to obtain those blessings, that concerns his Kingdom and Glory; our comfort and Salvation: And you are, and shall also be, ever humbly so prayed for, by him, who is

From the Vinyard the
    22. of October, 1652.

          Yours obliged, and ever
          to be commanded in the
          Work of the Lord Jesus

          Thomas Mayhew.

To His Excellency, the Lord General *Cromwel*; Grace, Mercy, and Peace be Multiplied.

Right Honorable,

ENvy it self cannot deny that the Lord hath raised and improved You in an Eminent manner to overthrow Antichrist, and to accomplish, in part, the Prophesies and Promises of the Churches Deliverance from that Bondage: In all which Service, the Lord hath not only kept Your Honor unsteined, but also caused the Lustre of those precious Graces of Humility, Faith, Love of Truth, and Love to the Saints, &c.

with which, through His Free Grace, He hath enriched You, to shine forth abundantly beyond all exception of any that are, or have been Adversaries to Your Proceedings. Now as the design of Christ in these daies is double, namely, First, To overthrow Antichrist by the Wars of the Lamb; and Secondly, To raise up His own Kingdom in the room of all Earthly Powers which He doth cast down, and to bring all the World subject to be ruled in all things by the Word of His mouth. And as the Lord hath raised and improved You, to accomplish (so far as the Work hath proceeded) the first part of His Design, so I trust that the Lord will yet further improve You, to set upon the accomplishment of the second part of the design of Christ; not only by indeavoring to put Government into the hands of Saints, which the Lord hath made You eminently careful to do, but also by promoting Scripture Government and Laws, that so the Word of Christ might rule all. In which great Services unto the Name of Christ, I doubt not, but it will be some Comfort to Your heart to see the Kingdom of Christ rising up in these Western Parts of the World; and some confirmation it will be, that the Lords time is come to advance and spread His Blessed Kingdom, which shall (in his season) fill all the Earth: and some incouragement to your heart, to prosecute that part of the Design of Christ, namely, That Christ might Reign. Such Considerations, together with the Favorable Respect You have alwaies shewed to poor New-England, *hath imboldned me to present unto Your Hand, these first Confessions of that Grace which the Lord hath bestowed upon these poor Natives, and to publish them under the protection of Your Name, begging earnestly the continuance of Your Prayers for the further proceeding of this gracious Work: And so committing Your Honor to the Lord, and to the Word of His Grace, and all Your weighty Affairs to His Heavenly Direction, I rest*

Your Honors to serve You,
in the Service of Christ

JOHN ELIOT.

To the READER.

Christian Reader,

I *Know thy Soul longeth to hear Tydings of Gods grace powred out upon these goings down of the Sun, because the Spirit of God by the Word of Prophesie, useth to raise up and draw forth such actings of Faith, as accord with the accomplishment of those Prophesies, when the time of their accomplishment is come. When* Israel *was to return from* Babylon, *the Spirit by the word of Prophesie, raised up such actings of*

Faith, as were put forth in the exercise of all gifts necessary for the accomplishment thereof. Daniel *prayeth.* Zerubbabel *hath a Spirit of Ruling, the peoples affections are loose from their dwellings, and have a Spirit of Traveling.* Ezra, Nehemiah, *and all the rest of the Worthies of the Lord, are raised at that time to accomplish what is Prophesied. In these times the Prophesies of* Antichrist *his down fall are accomplishing. And do we not see that the Spirit of the Lord, by the word of Prophesie, hath raised up men, instruments in the Lords hand, to accomplish what is written herein. And the Spirit of Prayer, and expectation of Faith is raised generally in all Saints, by the same word of Prophesie. In like manner the Lord having said* That the Gospel shall spread over all the Earth, even to all the ends of the Earth; and from the riseing to the setting Sun; all Nations shal become the Nations, and Kingdoms of the Lord and of his Christ. *Such words of Prophesie hath the Spirit used to stir up the servants of the Lord to make out after the accomplishment thereof: and hath stirred up a mighty Spirit of Prayer, and expectation of Faith for the Conversion both of the* Jewes, *(yea all* Israel*) and of the* Gentiles *also, over all the world. For this Cause I know every beleeving heart, awakened by such Scriptures, longeth to hear of the Conversion of our poor* Indians, *whereby such Prophesies are in part begun to be accomplished. Yea, the Design of Christ being to erect his own Kingdom, in the room of all those Dominions, which he doth, and is about to overturn: You shall see a Spirit by such words of Prophesie powred forth upon the Saints (into whose hands Christ will commit the manageing of his Kingdom on Earth) that shall carry them forth to advance Christ to rule over men in all affairs, by the word of his mouth, and make him their only Law-giver, and supream Judge, and King.*

It is a day of small things with us: and that is Gods season to make the single beauty of his humbling Grace, to shine in them, that are the veriest ruines of mankind that are known on earth; as Mr. Hooker *was wont to describe the forlorn condition of these poor* Indians. *I see evident demonstrations that Gods Spirit by his word hath taught them, because their expressions, both in Prayer, and in the Confessions which I have now published, are far more, and more full, and spiritual, and various, then ever I was able to express unto them; in that poor broken manner of Teaching which I have used among them. Their turning Doctrins into their own experience, which you may observe in their Confessions, doth also demonstrate the Teachings of Gods Spirit, whose first special work is Application. Their different Gifts likewise, is a thing observable in their Confessions, wherein it is not to be expected that they should be all Eminent, it is not so in any Society of men; but in that there be some among them that are more eminent, it is a sign of Gods favor, who is raising up among themselves, such as shall be his instruments to conveigh a blessing unto the rest. Their frequent phrase of Praying to God, is not to be understood of that Ordinance and Duty of Prayer only, but of all Religion, and comprehendeth the same meaning, with them, as the word [Religion] doth with us: And it is observable, because it seemeth to me, That the Lord will make them a Praying people: and indeed, there is a great Spirit of Prayer powred out upon them, to my wonderment; and you may easily apprehend, That they who are assisted to express such Confessions before men, are not without a good measure of inlargement of Spirit before the Lord.*

The points of Doctrine that are here and there dropped in their Confessions, may suffice at present for a little taste to the Godly discerning Saints, That they are in some measure instructed in the chief points of Salvation, though there be no Doctrinal Confession on purpose set down to declare what they have learned, and do beleeve.

If any should conceive that that word which they so often use [I thought, or I think] should need explication, as a godly Brother did intimate to me on the Fast day, let this suffice, That it is to be Construed by the present Matter: For sometimes it is a thought of Faith; sometime of Fear; sometime of Unbelief; sometime of Carnal Reason; and sometime of Ignorance.

Lastly, It is plainly to be observed, That one end of Gods sending so many Saints to NEW-ENGLAND, *was the Conversion of these* Indians. *For the Godly Counsels, and Examples they have had in all our Christian Families, have been of great use, both to prepare them for the Gospel, and also to further the Lords work in them, as you may evidently discern in most of their Confessions.*

Beloved Reader, I have no more to say as necessary to Prepare for the following Matter, only to beg, yea earnestly to beg the continuance of all your Prayers; by the power whereof (through the Grace and Intercession of Christ) I beleeve this wheele of Conversion of these Indians, *is turned: and my Heart hath been always thereby encouraged, to follow on to do that poor little I can, to help forward this blessed Work of Spreading and Exalting the Kingdom of our dear Savior Jesus Christ, under the direction and protection of whose Word and Grace, by Faith committing you; I rest,*

Your unworthy Brother,

in our dear Savior,

JOHN ELIOT.

To the Christian Reader.

THE Amplitude, and large Extent of the Kingdom of Jesus Christ upon Earth, when *the Heathen shall be his Inheritance, and the uttermost parts of the Earth his Possession; and when all Kings shall fall down unto him, and all Nations do him service, all contrary Kingdoms and Powers being broken in pieces and destroyed,* is a thing plainly and plentifully foretold and promised in the Holy Scriptures; *Psal.* 2.8. and 22.27. and 72.11. and 86.9. *Dan.* 2.35. 44,45. and 7.26,27. *Zech.* 14.9. And although as yet our Eyes have never seen it so, nor our Fathers afore us, many Nations and People having hitherto been overspread, and overwhelmed in Pagan Blindness and Ignorance, having scarce ever heard of Christ, or of His Name; and many others that in some sort have heard of Him, having no more Grace but to make and maintain Opposition against Him, and against His Kingdom, some more professedly, and others more covertly and under fairer pretence, as in the great Dominions of the *Turk*, and of the *Pope*, is apparent; yet *the time is coming when things shall not thus continue, but be greatly changed and altered, because the Lord hath spoken this Word, and it cannot be that his Word should not take effect:* And if the Lord have spoken it, his People have good ground and reason to beleeve it, and to say as the holy Apostle in another case, *I beleeve God that it shall be even as it was told me, Act.* 27.25. Yea, to beleeve it and wait for it, as for that which in Gods appointed and due time shall surely come to pass, and not fail, as *Hab.* 2.3. And not only so, but heartily to desire it, and fervently to pray for it, as a thing wherein the Glory of God, and of Jesus Christ is not a little concerned and interessed; for if the multitude of People be the Kings Honor, *Prov.* 14.28. it must needs be the Honor of Christ Jesus the King of *Sion,* when multitudes of People do submit unto Him as to their King; and therfore it should be earnestly craved of God by all his Saints in their Prayers, that so it may be, according as the Sanctifying of Gods Name, and the coming of his Kingdom are the two first Petitions in that Rule and Pattern of Prayer commanded, and taught by our Savior to His Disciples, *Matth.* 6.9,10. And no man needs to doubt but that those things which are matter for Faith and Prayer to be exercised about their accomplishment, are matters of Thanksgiving when once they come to pass.

Which being so, the godly Christian, who shall read or hear this ensuing Relation concerning the workings of Gods Grace towards these Indians in *New-England*, and the Confessions of sundry amongst them, will, I doubt not, see abundant cause of thanksgiving to the Lord therein. For hereby it will appear, That the Kingdom of the Lord Jesus which every faithful soul, doth so much desire to see enlarged, is now beginning to be set up where it never was before, even amongst a poor people, forlorn kind of Creatures in times past, who have been without Christ, and without God in the world, they and their Fathers, for I know not how many Generations; yea, so far from knowing and acknowledging God in Christ, that they have been little better than the Beasts that perish. But now they that were far off, the Lord is at work to make them neer unto himself by the Blood of Jesus, as *Eph.* 2.13. that they which in time past were not a People, might ere long become the People of God; and they be called Beloved, which were not Beloved; and in the place where it was said unto them, *Ye are not my People,* that there ere long, they might be called, *The Children of the Living God,* as I *Pet.* 2.10. *Rom.* 9.25,26. which is the Lords doing, and it ought to be marvelous in our eyes. And the truth is, there are many marvels in it; marvelous free-grace, and riches thereof, to look upon a People so wretched and unworthy; yea, it were marvelous Grace so much as once to offer the Salvation of God in Christ to any such as they are, being not only the poor and maimed, halt and blind, but also, as it is in *Luk,* 14.21. ranging and roving in the High-waies, and Hedges; and yet behold, even these are not only invited, but their hearts inclined to come in. Mavelous Wisdom and Power is in it also, that of matter so rugged, and unlikely the Lord should ever frame and fashion any gracious and holy building to Himself, which I hope He is now a doing. And to say no more, His mervelous Soveraignty and Liberty is therein to be observed also, who till now of late hath seen meet never to look after this People, but hath suffered them all this while to walk in their own waies, waies of Sin, and waies of Death: yea, and though there hath been Plantations of the English in the Country now 20. years and more, yea, some a matter of 30. years, or thereabout, yet of all this time (except some little workings in a few) no considerable work of Grace hath appeared amongst the Indians till now of late; so true is that saying, *The times and seasons, the Father hath put them in his own Power, Act.* 1.7.

If any shall say, Oh but, we are doubtful whether any sound and saving work be yet wrought in them or no: Such an one I would wish seriously to weigh and consider the ensuing Confessions, and then perhaps he will be better satisfied touching this Point; for there he shall find many expressions favoring of their clear sight and sence of sin, and that not only of gross and external sins, but also of such as are more inward in the Heart and Soul: Also he shall find expressions tending to shew their expecting all righteousness and salvation by Christ alone. Now considering how the Work of the Spirit of God is said by Christ Himself to consist in great part in convincing of sin, and of righteousness; of sin in mens selves, and of righteousness in Christ, *Joh.* 16.9. And considering also, how the least beginnings of Grace are accepted of him that would not break the bruised Reed, nor quench the smoaking Flax, *Matth.* 12.20. And lastly, considering how it were not reasonable to expect such ripeness in these people, as might be expected and found in others, who have had more time and means, and better help and breeding than these have had: If these things I say be considered, it may be an Inducement to hope the best in charity concerning the Work of Grace in their Souls, as Charity hopeth all things, beleeveth all things, *1 Cor.* 13. But thus much at the least I conceive is cleer, and cannot be denied that since the Word of God hath been taught and preached among them, the Spirit of the Lord hath been working thereby in the hearts of many of them such Illumination, such Conviction, &c. as may justly be looked at (if not as a full and through Conversion, yet) as an hopeful beginning and preparation thereto, if the Lord be pleased to go on with what he hath begun, as I hope he will. And if there were no more but only an hopeful beginning, and preparative to Conversion, yet even this were matter of much comfort to the Saints, and of thanksgiving to the Lord; as it was in *Israel* at the building of the Temple, when no more was yet done, but only the foundation laid, *Ezr.* 3.10,11. yet even then they sung for joy, giving praise and thanksgiving to the Lord: How much more should it be so, if the Work of Regeneration be already truly wrought in any of them, as I hope it is in sundry; In such case, how ever it be with men on Earth, sure there is joy in Heaven amongst the Angels of God, when there is so much as one sinner that is truly brought home to God by Repentance, *Luke* 15.7,10.

But how shall we know that the Confessions here related, being spoken in their Tongue, were indeed uttered by them in such words, as have the same signification and meaning with these that are here expressed, for we have only the testimony of one man to assure us of it? It is true, we have only the testimony of one man for it; but yet it is such an one, as is unwillingly alone in this matter, having seriously endeavored to have had divers other Interpreters present at *Natick* that day, but could not obtain what he did desire and endeavor herein; a man whose pious and painful labors amongst this People, have rendred him approved and highly honored in the eyes of his Brethren about him, for indefatigable diligence, and earnest love to the Lord Jesus, and their poor souls; a man whose integrity and faithfulness is so well known in these Parts, as giveth sufficient satisfaction to beleev that he would not wittingly utter a falshood in any matter whatever, and much less so many falshoods, & that in such a publick manner, in the view of God & the World, as he must needs have done if he have coyned these Confessions of his own head, and have not to his best understanding truly related them in our Tongue, according as they were uttered by them in theirs.

If any shall then ask, If there be such a Work of God amongst them, Why were they not combined and united into Church-Estate, when there was that great Assembly at *Natick,* on the thirteenth of *Octob.* last? Such an one many do well to consider, that the material Temple was many yeers in building, even in the daies of *Solomon,* who wanted no helps and futherances thereunto, but was abundantly furnished therewith, and longer in Re-edifying after the Captivity; and therefore no marvel if the building of a Spiritual Temple, an holy Church to Christ, and a Church out of such rubbish as amongst Indians, be not begun and ended on a sudden; It is rather to be wondered at, that in so short a time, the thing is in so much forwardness as it is. Besides, It is a greater matter to have Indians accepted and owned as a Church amongst themselves, and so to be invested with all Church-power as a Church, when yet they are not furnished with any to be an able Pastor and Elder over them, by whom they might be directed and guided in all the Affairs of the Church, and Administrations of the House of God: this I conceive is a far greater matter than the admitting of them as Members into any Church or Churches of the English already so furnished; which latter (for ought I know) might speedily be done, and with much satisfaction, if it were suitable in regard of their different Language, and the remoteness of their Habitations, whereas to the former there seems to be a great necessity, or expediency at the least, that they should first be provided of some to be afterward set over them in the Lord. Even amongst the English, when any company amongst us have united themselves into Church-Estate, it hath been usual that they have had one or other amongst them upon whom their eyes have been set, as intending them to be Pastors or Teachers to them; afterward, when once they should be combined as a Church, and where it hath so been, they have found the comfort and benefit of it; whereas those few that have proceeded otherwise, have found trouble and inconveniency therein. And if it be so amongst the English, who usually have better abilities, how much more amongst the Indians, whose knowledg and parts must needs be far less? Not to insist upon the Rehearsal of those two Reasons mentioned by the Reverend Author of this Relation, *viz.* The shortness of the time to furnish the Work that day, and the want of Interpreters, of whom there was not any present but himself.

Concerning which Reasons, I can freely ad my testimony, that those two were the principal, if not the only Reasons which that day were insisted on, and publickly rendred for deferring the Inchurching of them to another time.

It may be some have thought, and I hear some have spoken little less, That this whol business of the Indians, of which there have been so many speeches in Old *England* and New, is but a devise and design to get money, and that there is indeed no such matter as any Work of Gods grace amongst that People. But if there were any truth in this saying or Surmise, I marvel why the Magistrates and Elders then present at *Natick*, did upon the reasons rendred, advise the deferring of the inchurching of the Indians that day, and why they did not rather hasten forward the Work without any more ado, or longer delay. For the report of a Church of Indians would in all likelihood have more prevailed for the end alledged, than all that hath been reported hitherto But our attending in this business to the Honor of Jesus Christ, and the good of this poor peoples souls, and so to that which Rule and right Reason required, rather than to what might seem conducible for wordly advantage, may be a sufficient witness of our sincerity, contrary to the conceit and surmise afore mentioned, and a sufficient confutation of it. And yet though they be not combined into Church-Estate, there is so much of Gods Work amongst them, as that I cannot but count it a great evil, yea, a great injury to God and his goodness for any to make light or nothing of it. To see and to hear Indians opening their mouths, and lifting up their hands and their eyes in solemn Prayer to the Living God, calling on him by his Name **J E H O V A H**, in the Mediation of Jesus Christ, and this for a good while together; to see and hear them exhorting one another from the Word of God; to see them and hear them confessing the Name of Christ Jesus, and their own sinfulness, sure this is more than usual. And though they spake in a language of which many of us understood but little, yet we that were present that day, we saw them, and we heard them perform the duties mentioned, with such grave and sober countenances, with such comely reverence in gesture, and their whol carriage, and with such plenty of tears trickling down the cheeks of some of them, as did argue to us that they spake with much good affection, and holy fear of God, and it much affected our hearts. Nor is it credible to me, nor for ought I know to any that was present that day, that in these things they were acted and led by that Spirit which is wont to breath amongst Indians, the Spirit of Satan, or of corrupt Nature, but that herein they had with them another Spirit.

But if there be any work of Grace amongst them, it would surely bring forth, and be accompanied with the Reformation of their disordered lives, as in other things, so in their neglect of Labor, and their living in idleness and pleasure. I confess the Allegation is weighty, and I deny not but some sober and godly persons, who do heartily wish well to this work, have been as much troubled in their minds touching this particular as any that I know of. But yet somthing may be said in answer therto, & chiefly this, That since the Word of God came amongst them, and that they have attended thereto, they have more applied themselves unto Labor than formerly: For evidence whereof, appeal my be made to what was seen at *Natick* that day, and is still to be seen in that place, I mean the Grounds that they have fenced in, and clawed and broken up, and especially their capacious Meeting-house, the Dimensions whereof are expressed in the Relation: little did I think when I saw that Fabrick, but that some English Carpenter or other had had the chief hand in the framing and erecting of it; and that more hands than Indians, yea, and more English than one had been employed about it. But now understanding that the Indians alone were the Builders of it, it is a good testimony to me both of their industry, and likewise of their Skill; for where these are utterly wanting, yea, where there is not some good measure of them, such a Building I conceive could never be raised. It is true, that considering the manner of their bringing up, being little accustomed to labor, but the contrary, it is not much to be marveled if they be not comparable therein to some English, who from their Child-hood have been trained up thereto; yet we see they are coming to it, and I hope will fall to it more and more; let all that love their souls, pray for them that they may, yea, let all that love the Lord Jesus Christ pray for them, that the Work of God may still prosper amongst them, that many more of them may be turned from darkness to light, and from the power of Satan unto God; and that being converted they may be preserved in Christ, and be built up in him to further growth and perfection, from day to day. And let unfeigned thanksgiving be rendred to the Lord by his Saints for all that is already wrought amongst them: And Oh, let the English take heed, both in our dear Native Country, and here, lest for our unthankfulness, and many other sins, the Lord should take the Gospel from us, and bestow our mercy therein upon them, as upon a Nation that would yeeld the fruits thereof in better sort than many of us have done. The sins of the Jewish Nation to whom the Gospel was first preached, provoked God to take his Kingdom from them, and to call in the Gentiles: yet it appeareth by *Rom.* 11.11-14,31. that this mercy vouchsafed to the Gentiles, shall in time provoke the Jews to an holy Jealousie, and Emulation, to look after that mercy again that once they refused, that so through the mercy bestowed on the Gentiles, they (I mean the Jews) might at last again obtain mercy. Happy were the English if we could yeeld the fruits of Gods Gospel, that it might not be taken from us; and happy also if the mercy coming to these Indians (though not yet taken from us) might provoke us so to do, that so the Kingdom of God, the Gospel of Salvation, being not taken from us, and given to them, but though given to them, yet might still continue with us, and with our Posterity from Generation to Generation.

Dorchester in New-England
  this 13th *of* 10ber 1652.

RICH. MATHER.

A brief Relation *of the Proceedings of the Lords Work among the* INDIANS, *in reference unto their Church-Estate; The Reasons of the not accomplishing thereof at present: With some of their* Confessions; *whereby it may be discerned in*

some measure, how far the Lord hath prepared among them
fit Matter for a C H U R C H.

THese *Indians* (the better and wiser sort of them) have for some
years inquired after Church-Estate, Baptism, and the rest of
the Ordinances of God, in the observation whereof they see
the Godly English to walk. I have from time to time, delayed
them upon this point, That until they were come up unto Civil
Cohabitation, Government, and Labor, which a fixed
condition of life will put them upon, they were not so capable
to be betrusted with that Treasure of Christ, lest they should scandalize the
same, and make it of none effect, because if any should through temptation fall
under Censure, he could easily run away (as some have done) and would be
tempted so to do, unless he were fixed in an Habitation, and had some means of
livelihood to lose, and leave behind him: such Reasons have satisfied them
hitherunto. But now being come under Civil Order, and fixing themselves in
Habitations, and bending themselves to labor, as doth appear by their works of
Fencings, Buildings &c. and especially in building, without any English
Workmans help, or direction, a very sufficient Meeting-House, of fifty foot
long, twenty five foot broad, neer twelve foot high betwixt the joynts, wel
sawen, and framed (which is a specimen, not only of their singular ingenuity,
and dexterity, but also of some industry) I say this being so, now my argument
of delaying them from entering into Church-Estate, was taken away. Therefore
in way of preparation of them thereunto, I did this Summer call forth sundry of
them in the dayes of our publick Assemblies in Gods Worship; sometimes on
the Sabbath when I could be with them, and somtimes on Lecture daies, to make
confession before the Lord of their former sins, and of their present knowledg of
Christ, and experience of his Grace; which they solemnly doing, I wrote down
their Confessions: which having done, and being in my own heart hopeful that
there was among them fit matter for a Church, I did request all the Elders about
us to hear them reade, that so they might give me advice what to do in this great,
and solemn business; which being done on a day appointed for the purpose, it
pleased God to give their Confessions such acceptance in their hearts, as that
they saw nothing to hinder their proceeding to try how the Lord would appear
therein. Whereupon, after a day of Fasting and Prayer among our selves, to seek
the Lord in that behalf, there was another day of Fasting and Prayer appointed,
and publick notice thereof, and of the names of Indians were to confess, and
enter into Covenant that day, was given to all the Churches about us, to seek the
Lord yet further herein, and to make solemn Confessions of Christ his Truth and
Grace, and further to try whether the Lord would vouchsafe such grace unto
them, as to give them acceptance among the Saints, into the fellowship of
Church-Estate, and enjoyment of those Ordinances which the Lord hath
betrusted his Churches withal. That day was the thirteenth of the eighth month.

When the Assembly was met, the first part of the day was spent in Prayer
unto God, and exercise in the Word of God; in which my self first; and after
that, two of the Indians did Exercise; and so the time was spent till after ten, or

near eleven of the clock. Then addressing our selves unto the further work of the day, I first requested the reverend Elders (many being present) that they would ask them Questions touching the fundamental Points of Religion, that thereby they might have some tryal of their knowledg, and better that way, than if themselves should of themselves declare what they beleeve, or than if I should ask them Questions in these matters: After a little conference hereabout, it was concluded, That they should first make confession of their experience in the Lords Work upon their hearts, because in so doing, it is like something will be discerned of their knowledg in the Doctrines of Religion: and if after those Confessions there should yet be cause to inquire further touching any Point of Religion it might be fitly done at last. Whereupon we so proceeded, and called them forth in order to make confession. It was moved in the Assembly by Reverend Mr. *Wilson*, that their former Confessions also, as well as these which they made at present might be read unto the Assembly, because it was evident that they were daunted much to speak before so great and grave an Assembly as that was, but time did not permit it so to be then: yet now in my writing of their Confessions I will take that course, that so it may appear what encouragement there was to proceed so far as we did; and that such as may reade these their Confessions, may the better discern of the reality of the Grace of Christ in them.

The first which was called forth is named Totherswamp, *whose former Confession read before the Elders, was as followeth:*

BEfore I prayed unto God, the English, when I came unto their houses, often said unto me, Pray to God; but I having many friends who loved me, and I loved them, and they cared not for praying to God, and therefore I did not: But I thought in my heart, that if my friends should die, and I live, I then would pray to God; soon after, God so wrought, that they did almost all die, few of them left; and then my heart feared, and I thought, that now I will pray unto God, and yet I was ashamed to pray; and if I eat and did not pray, I was ashamed of that also; so that I had a double shame upon me: Then you came unto us, and taught us, and said unto us, *Pray unto God*; and after that, my heart grew strong, and I was no more ahsamed to pray, but I did take up praying to God; yet at first I did not think of God, and eternal Life, but only that the English should love me, and I loved them: But after I came to learn what sin was, by the Commandements of God, and then I saw all my sins, lust, gaming, &c. (he named more.) You taught, That Christ knoweth all our hearts, and seeth what is in them, if humility, or anger, or evil thoughts, Christ seeth all that is in the heart; then my heart feared greatly, because God was angry for all my sins; yea, now my heart is full of evil thoughts, and my heart runs away from God, therefore my heart feareth and mourneth. Every day I see sin in my heart; one man brought sin into the World, and I am full of that sin, and I break Gods Word every day. I see I deserve not pardon, for the first mans sinning; I can do no good, for I am like the Devil, nothing but evil thoughts, and words, and works. I have lost all likeness to God, and goodness, and therefore every day I sin against God, and I deserve death and damnation: The first man brought sin first, and I do every day ad to that sin, more sins; but Christ hath done for us all righteousness, and died for us because of our sins, and Christ teacheth us, That if we cast away our sins, and trust in Christ, then God will pardon all our sins; this I beleeve Christ hath done, I can do no righteousness, but Christ hath done it for me; this I beleeve, and therefore I do hope for pardon. When I first heard the Commandements, I then took up praying to God, and cast off sin. Again, When I heard, and understood Redemption by Christ, then I beleeved Jesus Christ to take away my sins: every Commandement taught me sin, and my duty to God. When you ask me, Why do I love God? I answer, Because he giveth me all outward blessings, as food, clothing, children, all gifts of strength, speech, hearing; especially that he giveth us a Minister to teach us, and giveth us Government; and my heart feareth lest Government should reprove me: but the greatest mercy of all is Christ, to give us pardon and life.

Totherswamp
The Confession which he made on the Fast day before the great Assembly, was as followeth:

I Confess in the presence of the Lord, before I prayed, many were my sins, not one good word did I speak, not one good thought did I think, not one good action did I doe: I did act all sins, and full was my heart of evil thoughts: when the English did tell me of God, I cared not for it, I thought it enough if they loved me: I had many friends that loved me, and I thought if they died, I would pray to God: and afterward it so came to pass; then was my heart ashamed, to pray I was ashamed, & if I prayed not, I was ashamed; a double shame was upon me: when God by you taught us, very much ashamed was my heart; then you taught us that Christ knoweth all our harts: therefore truly he saw my thoughts, and I had thought, if my kindred should die I would pray to God; therfore they dying, I must now pray to God: and therefore my heart feared, for I thought Christ knew my thoughts: then I heard you teach, *The first man God made was named* Adam, *& God made a Covenant with him, Do and live, thou and thy Children; if thou do not thou must die, thou and thy Children:* And we are Children of *Adam* poor sinners, therefore we all have sinned, for we have broke Gods Covenant, therefore evil is my heart therefore God is very angry with me, we sin against him every day; but this great mercy God hath given us, he hath given us his only Son, and promiseth, That whosoever beleeveth in Christ shall be saved: for Christ hath dyed for us in our stead, for our sins, and he hath done for us all the words of God, for I can do no good act, only Christ can, and only Christ hath done all for us; Christ have deserved Pardon for us, and risen again, he hath ascended to God, and doth ever pray for us; therefore all Beleevers Souls shall goe to Heaven to Christ. But when I heard that word of Christ, Christ said *Repent and Beleeve*, and Christ seeth *who Repenteth*, then I said, dark and weak is my Soul, and I am one in darkness, I am a very sinful man, and now I pray to Christ for life. Hearing you teach that Word that the Scribes and Pharisees said *Why do thy Disciples break the Tradition of the Fathers?* Christ answered, *Why do ye make void the Commandements of God?* Then my heart feared that I do so, when I teach the Indians, because I cannot teach them right, and thereby make the word of God vain. Again, Christ said *If the blind lead the blind they will both fall into the ditch;* Therfore I feared that I am one blind, and when I teach other Indians I shal caus them to fall into the ditch. This is the love of God to me, that he giveth me all mercy in this world, and for them al I am thankfull; but I confess I deserve Hell; I cannot deliver my self, but I give my Soul and my Flesh to Christ and I trust my soul with him for he is my Redeemer, and I desire to call upon him while I live.

This was his Confession which ended, Mr. *Allin* further demanded of him this Question, How he found his heart, now in the matter of Repentance

His answer was; I am ashamed of all my sins, my heart is broken for them and melteth in me, I am angry with my self for my sins, and I pray to Christ to take away my sins, and I desire that they may be pardoned.

But it was desired that further Question might be forborn, lest time would be wanting to here them all speak.

Then Waban *was called forth, whose Confession was as followeth; no former confession of his being read unto the Elders.*

B Efore I heard of God, and before the English came into this Country, many evil things my heart did work, many thoughts I had in my heart; I wished for riches, I wished to be a witch, I wished to be a Sachem; and many such other evils were in my heart: Then when the English came, still my heart did the same things; when the English taught me of God (I coming to their Houses) I would go out of their doors, and many years I knew nothing; when the English taught me I was angry with them: But a little while agoe after the great sikness, I considered what the English do, and I had some desire to do as they do; and after that I began to work as they work; and then I wondered how the English come to be so strong to labor; then I thought I shall quickly die, and I feared lest I should die before I prayed to God; then I thought, if I prayed to God in our Language, whether could God understand my prayers in our Language; therefore I did ask Mr. *Jackson,* and Mr. *Mahu,* If God understood prayers in our Language? They answered me, God doth understand all Languages in the World. But I do not know how to confess, and little do I know of Christ; I fear I shall not beleeve a great while, and very slowly; I do not know what grace is in my heart, there is but little good in me; but this I know, That Christ hath kept all Gods Commandements for us, and that Christ doth know all our hearts; and now I desire to repent of all my sins: I neither have done, nor can do the Commandements of the Lord, but I am ashamed of all I do, and I do repent of

all my sins, even of all that I do know of: I desire that I may be converted from
all my sins, and that I might beleeve in Christ, and I desire him; I dislike my
sins, yet I do not truly pray to God in my heart: no matter for good words, all is
the true heart; and this day I do not so much desire good words, as throughly to
open my heart: I confess I can do nothing, but deserve damnation; only Christ
can help me and do for me. But I have nothing to say for my self that is good; I
judg that I am a sinner, and cannot repent, but Christ hath deserved pardon for
us.

> This Confession being not so satisfactory as was desired, Mr. *Wilson* testified,
> that he spake these latter expressions with tears, which I observed not,
> because I attended to writing; but I gave this testimony of him, That his
> conversation was without offence to the English, so far as I knew, and
> among the Indians, it was exemplar: His gift is not so much in expressing
> himself this way, but in other respects useful and eminent; it being
> demanded in what respect, I answered to this purpose, That his gift lay in
> Ruling, Judging of Cases, wherein he is patient, constant, and prudent,
> insomuch that he is much respected among them, for they have chosen him
> a Ruler of Fifty, and he Ruleth well according to his measure. It was
> further said, they thought he had been a great drawer on to Religion; I
> replyed, so he was in his way, and did prevail with many; and so it rested.

The next that was called, was William *of* Sudbury, *his Indian
Name is* Nataôus; *his former Confession read before the
Elders, was as followeth:*

I Confess that before I prayed, I committed all manner of sins, and served
many gods: when the English came first, I going to their Houses, they spake
to me of your God, but when I heard of God, my heart hated it; but when they
said the Devil was my god, I was angry, because I was proud: when I came to
their houses I hated to hear of God, I loved lust in my own house and not God, I
loved to pray to many gods. Five years ago, I going to English houses, and they
speaking of God, I did a little like of it, yet when I went again to my own house,
I did all manner of sins, and in my heart I did act all sins, though I would not be
seen by man. Then going to your house, I more desired to hear of God; and my
heart said, I will pray to God so long as I live: then I went to the Minister Mr.
Browns house, and told him I would pray as long as I lived; but he said I did not
say it from my heart, and I beleeve it. When *Waban* spake to me that I should
pray to God, I did so. But I had greatly sinned against God, and had not
beleeved the Word, but was proud: but then I was angry with my self, and
loathed my self, and thought God will not forgive me my sins. For when I had
been abroad in the woods I would be very angry, and would lye unto men, and I
could not find the way how to be a good man: then I beleeved your teaching,
That when good men die, the Angels carry their souls to God; but evil men

dying, they go to Hell, and perish for ever, I thought this a true saying, and I promised to God, to pray to God as long as I live. I had a little grief in my heart five years ago for my sins: but many were my prides; somtime I was angry with my self, and pityed my self; but I thought God would not pardon such a proud heart as mine is: I beleeve that Christ would have me to forsake my anger; I beleeve that Christ hath redeemed us, and I am glad to hear those words of God; and I desire that I might do al the good waies of God, and that I might truly pray unto God: I do now want Graces, and these Christ only teacheth us, and only Christ hath wrought our redemption, and he procureth our pardon for all our sins; and I beleeve that when beleevers dy, Gods Angels carry them to Heaven: but I want faith to beleeve the Word of God, and to open my Eyes, and to help me to cast away all sins; and Christ hath deserved for me eternall life: I have deserved nothing my self; Christ hath deserved all, and giveth me faith to beleeve it.

William of Sudbury:
His Indian Name is
N A T A Ô U S.

The Confession which he made on the fast day before the great Assembly was as followeth.

BEfore I prayed to God, I commited all sins; and serving many gods. I much despised praying unto God, for I beleeved the Devil, and he did dayly teach me to sin, and I did them: somtimes hearing of God my heart did hate it, and went to my own house, because I did love to commit all sin there. About Six years ago, a little I liked to hear of God, and yet I hated that which was good: hearing that *Cutshamoquin* prayed, then I thought I will pray also: a year after, I heard of praying to God, and I went to Mr. *Browns* house and told him I will pray to God as long as live; he said, I doubt of it, and bid me cut off my hair and I did so presently; and then I desired to be like God, and Jesus Christ, and to call on him, but I found it very hard to beleeve; yet I thought, I wil pray as long as I live. Hearing that Word, That Christ dyed for us, was buried & rose again, and hearing of that Word also, Seek peace & imbrace the Word: then I began to beleeve that Christ died for us, for sin; and I saw my heart very full of sin. And hearing that word, That Christ went to the Mount *Olivet*, and ascended, I beleeved and thought, Oh that God would pardon me; but I fear he will not, because I have been so long time a sinner. Somtime I am angry with my self, for my many Evil thoughts in my heart; and to this day I want grace, and cannot confess, because I have been so great a sinner: and this day I confess, a little I pray, and that I can pray but a little and weakly. When I heard that word of God, That all from the rising to the setting Sun shall pray I first under stood it not, and wondered how it should be: after I saw that when they beleeve and obey God, then he will teach them to do right things, and God will teach us to do al things for God, sleeping and waking to be with God. But still do foolishly, and not according to my prayer: I cannot get pardon of my sins, for my sins are great in thought, word, and deed: and no man can cast off his own sins, but that is the work of Christ only to work it in us; a man cannot make a right prayer but when Christ assisteth him; then we shall do all things well. I beleeve that Christ is God, and the Son of God because when he dyed, he rose again, and he dyed for our sins; and I beleeve he is in Heaven and ever prayeth for us, and sendeth his gospel unto us: and I am angry with my self, because I do not beleeve the word of God, and gospel of Jesus Christ.

The next which was called forth was Monequassun, *who is our School-master; whose former Confession, read before the Elders, was as followeth.*

I Confess my sorrow for all my sins against God, and before men: When I first heard instruction, I beleeved not, but laughed at it, and scorned praying to God; afterward, when we were taught *Cohannet* (that is the place where he lived) I still hated praying, and I did think of running away, because I cared not for praying to God; but afterwards, because I loved to dwell at that place, I would not leave the place, and therefore I thought I will pray to God, because I would still stay at that place, therefore I prayed not for the love of God, but for love of the place I lived in; after that I desired a little to learn the Catechisme on the Lecture daies, and I did learn the ten Commandements, and after that, all the points in the Catechisme; yet afterwards I cast them all away again, then was my heart filled with folly, and my sins great sins; afterwards by hearing, I began to fear, because of my many sins, lest the wise men should come to know them, and punish me for them; and then again I thought of running away because of my many sins: But after that I thought I would pray rightly to God, and cast away my sins; then I saw my hypocricy, because I did ask some questions, but did not do that which I knew: afterward I considered of my question, and thought I would pray to God, and would consider of some other Question, and I asked this, Question, *How should I get Wisdom?* and the Answer to it did a little turn my heart from sin, to seek after God; and I then considered that the Word of God was good; then I prayed to God because of the Word of God. The next Lecture day you taught that word of God, *If any man lack Wisdom, let him ask it of God, who giveth freely to them that ask him, and upbraideth no man, James, 1.5.* Then again a little my heart was turned after God, the Word also said, *Repent, mourn, and beleeve in Jesus Christ:* this also helped me on. Then you taught, *That he that beleeveth not Christ, and repenteth not of sin, they are foolish and wicked; and because they beleeve not, they shall perish:* then I thought my self a fool, because I beleeved not Christ, but sinned every day, and after I heard the Word, I greatly broke the Word. But afterward I heard this promise of God, *Who ever repenteth and beleeveth in Christ, God will forgive him all his sins, he shall not perish;* then I thought, that as yet, I do not repent, and beleeve in Christ: then I prayed to God, because of this his Promise; and then I prayed to God, for God and for Christ his sake: after that again I did a little break the Word of Christ. And then I heard some other words of God, which shewed me my sins, and my breakings of Gods word; and sometimes I thought God and Christ would forgive me, because of the promise to them that beleeve in Christ, and repent of sin, I thought I did that which God spake in the Promise. Then being called to confess, to prepare to make a Church at *Natick*, I loved *Cohannet;* but after hearing this instruction, *That we should not only be Hearers, but Doers of the Word,* then my heart did fear. And afterward hearing that in *Matthew*, Christ saw two brethren mending their Nets, he said, *Follow me and I will make you Fishers of men,* presently they followed Christ; and when I heard this, I feared, because I was not willing to follow Christ to *Natick*; they followed Christ at his Word, but I did not, for now Christ saith to us, *follow Me:* then I was much troubled, and considered of this Word of God. Afterward I heard another word, the blind men cryed after Christ and said, *Have mercy on us thou Son of David,* but after they came to Christ, he called them, and asked them, *What shall I do for you?* they said, *Lord open our eyes*; then Christ had pity on them, and opened their eyes, and they followed Christ; when I heard this, my heart was troubled, then I prayed to God and Christ to open mine eyes, and if Christ open my eyes, then I shall rejoyce to follow Christ: then I considered of both these Scriptures, and I a little saw that I must follow Christ. And now my heart desireth to make confession of what I know of God, and of my self, and of Christ: I beleeve that there is only one God, and that he made and ruleth all the World, and that he the Lord, giveth us al good things: I know that God giveth every day all good mercies, life, and health, and all; I have not one good thing, but God it is that giveth it me, I beleeve that God at first made man like God, holy, wise, righteous; but the first man sinned, for God promised him, *If thou do my Commandements, thou shalt live, and thy children; but if thou sin, thou shalt die, thou and thy children;* this Covenant God made with the first man. But the first man did not do the Commandements of God, he did break Gods Word, he beleeved Satan; and now I am full of sin, because the first man brought sin; dayly I am full of sin in my heart: I do not dayly rejoyce in Repentance, because Satan worketh dayly in my heart, and opposeth Repentance, and all good Works; day and night my heart is full of sin. I beleeve that Jesus Christ was born of the *Virgin Mary*; God promised her she should bear a Son, and his Name should be J E S U S, because he shall deliver his people from their sins: And when Christ came to preach, he said, *Repent, because the Kingdom of Heaven is at hand;* again Christ taught, *Except ye repent, and become as a little child, ye shall not enter into the Kingdom of Heaven;* therefore humble your selves like one of these little children, and great shall be your Kingdom in Heaven. Again Christ said, *Come unto me all ye that are weary and heavy laden with sin, and I will give you rest: take up my Cross, and Yoak, learn of me, for I am meek, and ye shall find rest to your souls, for my yoak is easie, and burden light:* these are the Words of Christ, and I know Christ he is good, but my works are evil: Christ his words are good, but I am not humble; but if we be humble and beleeving in Christ, he pardons all our sins. I now desire to beleeve in Jesus Christ, because of the word of Christ, that I may be converted and become as a little Child. I confess my sins before God, and before Jesus Christ this day; now I desire all my sins may be pardoned; I now desire repentance in my heart, and ever to beleeve in Christ; now I lift up my heart to Christ, and trust him with it, because I beleeve Christ died for us, for all our sins, and deserved for us eternal life in Heaven, and deserved pardon for all our sins. And now I give my soul to Christ because he hath redeemed: I do greatly love, and like repentance in my heart, and I love to beleeve in Jesus Christ, and my heart is broken by repentance: al these things I do like wel of, that they may be in my heart, but because Christ hath all these to give, I ask them of him that he may give me repentance, and faith in Christ, and therefore I pray and beseech Christ dayly for repentance and faith; and other good waies I beg of Christ dayly to give me: and I pray to Christ for al these gifts and graces to put them in my heart: and now I greatly thank Christ for all these good gifts which he hath given me. I know not any thing, nor can do any thing that is a good work: even my heart is dark dayly in what I should do, and my soul dyeth because of my sins, and therefore I give my soul to Christ, because I know my soul is dead in sin, and dayly doth commit sin; in my heart I sin, and all the members of my body are sinful. I beleeve Jesus Christ is ascended to Heaven through the clouds, and he will come again from Heaven. Many saw Christ go up to Heaven, and the Angels said, even so he will come again to judg all the world; and therefore I beleeve Gods promise, That all men shall rise again when Christ cometh again, then all shall rise, and all their souls comes again because Christ is trusted with them, and keeps their souls, therefore I desire my sins may be pardoned; and I beleeve in Christ; and ever so long as I live, I will pray to God, and do all the good waies he commandeth.

Monequassun,

The Confession which he made on the Fast day before the great Assembly was as followeth

I Confess my sins before the Lord, and before men this day: a little while since I did commit many sins, both in my hands and heart; lusts, thefts, and many other sins, and that every day: and after I heard of praying to God, and that others prayed to God, my heart did not like it, but hated it, yea and mocked at it; and after they prayed at *Cohannet* I stil hated it, and when I heard the Word I did not like of it, but thought of running away, because I loved sin: but I loved the place of my dwelling, and therfore I thought I wil rather pray to God, and began to do it; a little I desired to learn the ten Commandements of God, and other points of Catechisme; and then a little I repented, but I was quickly weary of repentance, and fell again to sin, and full of evil thoughts was my heart: and then I played the Hypocrite, and my heart was full of sin: I learned some things, but did not do what God commanded, but I sinned and playd the Hypocrite; somethings I did before man, but not before God. But afterward I feared because of my sins, and feared punishment for my sins, therefore I thought again I would run away; yet again I loving the place, would not run away, but would pray to God: and I asked a Question at the Lecture. which was this, *How I should get wisdom?* the Answer made me a little to understand: but afterward I heard the word *If any man lack wisdom, let him ask it of God, who giveth liberally to all that ask, and upbraideth none.* But then I did fear Gods anger, because of all my sins, because they were great. Afterward hearing that Word, That Christ is named *Jesus,* because he redeemeth us from all our sins: I thought Christ would not save me; because I repent not, for he saveth only penitent Beleevers; but I am not such an one, but still a dayly sinner. Afterward hearing that Word, *Blessed are they that hunger and thirst after righteousness, for they shall be filled:* then I thought I am a poor sinner, and poor is my heart: then I prayed to God to teach me to do that which he requireth, and to pray aright. Afterward hearing that word, *Who ever looks upon a Woman to lust after her, hath already committed Adultry with her in his heart;* then I thought I had done all manner of sins in the sight of God, because he seeth lust in the heart, and knoweth all the evil thoughts of my heart; and then I did pray unto God, *Oh! give me Repentance and Pardon.* Afterwards when I did teach among the Indians, I was much humbled because I could not reade right, and that I sinned in it; for I saw that when I thought to do a good work, I sinned in doing it, for I knew not what was right, nor how to do it. In the night I was considering of my sins, and could not find what to do: three nights I considered what to do, and at last God shewed me mercy, and shewed me what I should do. And then I desired to learn to read Gods Word, and hearing that if we ask wisdom of God, he will give it, then I did much pray to God, that he would teach me to reade. After a years time, I thought I did not rightly seek, and I thought I sinned, because I did not rightly desire to read Gods Word, and I thought my praying was sinful, and I feared, how should I, my wife, and child be cloathed, if I spend my time in learning to reade; but then God was merciful to me, and shewed me that Word, *Say not, what shall I eat, or drink, or wherewith shall I be cloathed, wicked men seek after these; but first seek the Kingdom of Heaven, and these things shall be added to you;* then I prayed God to teach me this word, and that I might do it: and then I desired to read Gods word, what ever I wanted. Afterward hearing that we must make a Town, and gather a Church at *Natick,* my heart disliked that place; but hearing that word, *That Christ met two Fishers, and said, follow me, and I will make you fishers of men, and they presently left all and followed him;* hearing this, I was much troubled, because I had not beleeved Christ, for I would not follow him to make a Church, nor had I done what he commanded me, and then I was troubled for all my sins. Again hearing that word, *That the blind man called after Christ, saying, thou Son of* David *have mercy on me; Christ asked him what he would have him do, he said, Lord open my eyes;* and presently Christ gave him sight, and he followed Christ: then again my heart was troubled, for I thought I still beleeve not, because I do not follow Christ, nor hath he yet opened mine eyes: then I prayed to Christ to open mine eyes, that I might see what to do, because I am blind and cannot see how to follow Christ, and do what he commandeth, and I prayed to Christ, Teach me Lord what to do, and to do what thou sayest; and I prayed that I might follow Christ: and then I thought I will follow Christ to make a Church. All this trouble I had to be brought to be willing to make a Church: and quickly after, God laid upon me more trouble, by sickness and death; and then I much prayed to God for life, for we were all sick, and then God would not hear me, to give us life; but first one of my Children died, and after that my Wife; then I was in great sorrow, because I thought God would not hear me, and I thought it was because I would not follow him, therefore he hears not me: then I found this sin in my heart, That I was angry at the punishment of God: but afterward I considered, I was a poor sinner, I have nothing, nor Child, nor Wife, I deserve that God should take away all mercies from me; and then I repented of my sins, and did much pray, and I remembred the promise to follow Christ, and my heart said, I had in this sinned, that followed not Christ, and therefore I cryed for pardon of this sin: and then hearing of this Word, *Who ever beleeveth in Christ, his sins are pardoned, he beleeving that Christ died for us;* and I beleeved. Again hearing that Word, *If ye be not converted, and become as a little Child, you cannot go to Heaven;* then my heart thought, I do not this, but I deserve Hell fire for ever; and then I prayed Christ, Oh! turn me from my sin, and teach me to hear thy Word; and I prayed to my Father in Heaven: and after this, I beleeved in Christ for pardon. Afterward I heard that Word, That it is a shame for a man to wear long hair, and that there was no such custom in the Churches: at first I thought I loved not long hair, but I did, and found it very hard to cut it off; and then I prayed God to pardon that sin also: Afterward I thought my heart cared not for the Word of God: but then I thought I would give my self up unto the Lord, to do all his Word. Afterward I heard that word, *If thy right foot offend thee, cut it off, or thy right hand, or thy right eye; its better to go to Heaven with one foot, or hand, or eye, than having both to go to Hell;* then I thought my hair had been a stumbling to me, therefore I cut it off, and grieved for this sin, and prayed for pardon. After hearing that word, *Come unto me all ye that are weary and heavie laden with your sins, and I will give rest to your souls;* then my heart thought that I do dayly hate my sins, Oh! that I could go to Christ! and Christ looketh I should come unto him, therfore I will go unto him, and therfore then I prayed, Oh! Christ help me to come unto thee: and I prayed because of all my sins that they may be pardoned. For the first man was made like God in holiness, and righteousness, and God gave him his Covenant; but *Adam* sinned, beleeving the Devil, therefore God was angry, and therefore all we Children of *Adam* are like the Devil, and dayly sin, and break every Law of God, full of evil thoughts, words, and works, and only Christ can deliver us from our sins, and he that beleeveth in Christ is pardoned; but my heart of my self cannot beleeve: Satan hath power in me, but I cry to God, Oh! give me faith, and pardon my sin, because Christ alone can deliver me from Hell; therefore I pray, Oh! Jesus Christ deliver me. Christ hath provided the new Covenant to save Beleevers in Christ, therefore I desire to give my soul to Christ, for pardon of all my sins: the first Covenant is broke by sin, and we deserve Hell; but Christ keepeth for us the new Covenant, and therfore I betrust my soul with Christ. Again, I desire to beleeve in Christ, because Christ will come to judgment, and all shall rise again, and all Beleevers in this life shall then be saved; therefore I desire to beleeve Christ, and mortifie sin as long as I live; and I pray Christ to help me to beleeve: and I thank God for all his mercies every day: and now I confess before God that I loath my self for my sins and beg pardon.

Thus far he went in his Confession; but they being slow of speech, time was far spent and a great assembly of English understanding nothing he said, only waiting for my interpretation, many of them went forth, others whispered, and a great confusion was in the House and abroad: and I perceived that the graver sort thought the time long, therfore knowing he had spoken enough unto satisfaction (at least as I judged) I here took him off. Then one of the Elders asked, if I took him off, or whether had he finished? I answered, That I took him off. So after my reading what he had said, we called another.

The next who was called forth was Ponampam, *who had formerly twice made confession, and both read before the Elders. His first Confession was as followeth.*

W Hen God first had mercy on us, when they first prayed at *Noonanetam*, I heard of it, and the first word that I heard was, *That all from the rising of the sun to the going down thereof, shall pray unto God;* and I thought, Oh! let it be so. After I considered what the word may be, and understood by it, That God was mercyfull; afterwards when you alwayes came to us, I only heard the word, I did not understand it, nor meditate on it, yet I found that all my doings were sins against God; then I prayed unto God. Afterwards I heard, That God would pardon all that beleeve in Christ! and quickly after I saw my sins to be very many; I saw that in every thing I did, I sinned: & when I saw these my sins against God, I was weary of my self, & angry with my self in my heart; but the free mercy of God, caused me to hear his word, and then I feared because every day sin was in my heart, and I thought in vain I looked to Christ: Then hearing this word of Christ, that Christ taught through every town, and village, *Repent and beleeve.* If any one repent, and mourn, and beleeve, I will pardon him; then my heart thought I will pray to God as long as I live: but somtimes my heart was ashamed, and somtimes my heart was strong, and God seeth my heart: I now desire to repent, and beleeve in Christ, and that Christ will pardon me, and shew mercy to us all.

Ponampam,
His Second Confession was as followeth:

WHen I prayed not unto God I ever sinned every day: but when *Noonanetam Indians* first prayed, I heard of it, and three nights I considered whether I should pray or no, but I found not how to pray unto God, but how not to pray: but then I heard Gods free mercy in his word, call all to pray, *from the rising of the Sun to the going down thereof;* yet presently I lost that word, and sinned again, and committed many sins. Then Gods free mercy shewed me in the Catechism, *That God made all the World,* yet my heart did not beleeve, because I knew I sprung from my Father and Mother: I did alwaies act many sins, because I was born in sin, and in vain I heard Gods word. Then I heard Gods Word, That Christ was made man, yet I did but hear it, though I thought it might be true: I thought I would cast off all sin, but then I found that I loved them very much. I heard Gods promise to *Abraham, To increase his Children as the Stars for number,* but I beleeved not, because he had but one Son: and thus I cast off the word, and committed sins. I heard also from the word, That all men are not alike to God, some are first to God, [or preferred before other;] but I did not beleeve it because all men die alike; therefore they are not the Sons of God, and God is not their Father: So still I beleeved not the Word, but broke Gods Word dayly, and in vain I heard Gods Word. Afterward I heard that Word of God to *Moses, I'le be with thy mouth, for who maketh the seeing Eye, or hearing Ear, is it not I?* saith the Lord: then I understood a little of God, and of his Word; but still I acted much sin. Afterward I heard that Word of Free-Grace, *Repent, and beleeve the Gospel, and who ever beleeve shall be saved;* then my heart beleeved, then I saw I had prayed but afore man, & so was my hearing or any other duty: and I saw other of my sins against God; and then I saw that my heart did not beleev as it should, & I desired to be open in my doings; I saw I brake every command of God: yet presently I lost this, and the Word of Christ was of little worth unto me; and I saw I loved sin very much. Then again I heard that word, That all shall pray from the rising to the sitting Sun; then I thought I will pray to God, and yet only my tongue prayed. Then again I heard the Catechism, That God made *Adam* and *Eve,* and al the world, and a little I beleeved that word. Afterward I heard another word, *That they are Bastards, not Sons, whom God afflicts not:* I did a little think this to be a truth, and then I prayed more unto God, and yet I saw I feared man more than God: but notwithstanding, I have prayed unto God from that day unto this day; yet I see *I* sin every day. When I heard that Word that God spake to *Moses* in the Mount by a Trumpet, and said, *Thou shalt not have any other God, thou shalt not lust, nor lye, nor kill, &c.* I saw all these I had broken; I heard the Word, but sinned in what I heard: I heard that my heart must break and melt for sin, and beleeve in Christ, and that we should try our hearts if it be so; yet I could try but little, nor find but little, but still I sinned much. I heard that Word, That they which cast off God, God will cast off them; and I feared lest God should cast me away, because of my sins: I was ashamed of my sins, and my heart melted, and I thought I wil give my self to God and to Christ, and do what he will for ever;

and because of this promise of pardon to al that repent and beleeve, my heart desireth to pray to God as long as I live.

Ponampam;

The Confession he made on the Fast day, before the great Assembly was as followeth:

B Efore I prayed unto God, I committed all manner of sins; and when I heard the Catechism, *That God made me,* I did not beleeve it, because I knew I sprang from my Father and Mother, and therefore I despised the Word, and therefore again I did act all sins, and I did love them. Then God was merciful to me, to let me hear that Word, That al shal pray from the rising to the sitting Sun; and then I considered whether I should pray, but I found not in my heart that all should pray: but then I considered of praying, and what would become of me if I did not pray, and what would become of me, if I did pray; but I thought if I did pray, the *Sachems* would be angry, because They did not say, pray to God, and therefore I did not yet pray; but considering of that word, that all shall pray, I was troubled, and I found in my heart that I would pray unto God; and yet I feared that others would laugh at me, and therefore I did not yet pray. Afterward God was yet merciful to me, and I heard that God made the World, and the first man, and I thought it was true, and therefore I would pray to God, because he hath made all; and yet when I did pray, I thought I prayed not aright, because I prayed for the sake of man, and I thought this to be a great sin. But then I wondered at Gods free mercy to me, for I saw God made me, and giveth me all mercies: and then was I troubled, and saw that many were my sins, and that I do not yet beleeve; then I prayed, yet my heart sinned, for I prayed only with my mouth: and then I repented of my sins, and then a little I considered and remembred Gods love unto us: but I was a sinner, and many were my sins, and a little I repented of them; and yet again I sinned, and quickly was my heart full of sin: then again was my heart angry with my self, and often I lost all this again, and fell into sin. Then I heard that word, *That God sent* Moses *to* Egypt, *and promised I will be with thee;* that promise I considered, but I thought that in vain I did seek, and I was ashamed that I did so: and I prayed, Oh God teach me truly to pray, not only before man, but before God, and pardon al these my sins. Again I heard that word, that Christ taught through every Town and Village, *Repent and beleeve, and be saved,* and a little I beleeved this word, and I loved it, and then I saw all my sins, and prayed for pardon. Again I heard that word, He that casteth off God, him will God cast off; and I found in my heart, that I had done this, and I feared because of this my sin, lest God should cast me off, and that I should for ever perish in Hell, because God hath cast me off, I having cast of God: then I was troubled about Hell, and what shall I do if I be damned! Then I heard that word, If ye repent and beleeve, God pardons all sins; then I thought, Oh that I had this, I desired to repent and beleeve, and I begged of God, Oh give me Repentance and Faith, freely do it for me; and I saw God was merciful to do it, but I did not attend the Lord, only sometimes; and I now confess I am ashamed of my sins, my heart is broken, and melteth in me; I am angry at my self; I desire pardon in Christ; I betrust my soul with Christ, that he may do it for me.

By such time as this man had finished, the time was far spent, and he was the fift in number, their speeches being slow, and they were the more slow at my request, that I might write what they said; & oft I was forced to inquire of my interpreter (who sat by me) because I did not perfectly understand some sentences, especially of some of them: these things did make the work long-som, considering the inlargement of spirit God gave some of them; and should we have proceeded further, it would have been sun-set before the Confessions in likelyhood would have been finished, besides all the rest of the work that was to be done to finish so solemn a work; and the place being remote in the woods, the nights long and cold and people not fitted to lie abroad, and no competant lodgings in the place for such persons, and the work of such moment as would not admit an hudling up in hast. And besides all this, though I had fully used all fit means, to have all the Interpreters present that I could, that so the interpretation might not depend upon my single testemony, yet so it was that they all failed, and I was alone (as I have been wont to be in this work) which providence of God was not to be neglected in so solemn a business. Wherfore the Magistrates, Elders, and Grave Men present, advised together what to do, and the Conclusion was, Not to proceed any further at present, yet so to carry the matter, as that the Indians might in no wise be discouraged, but encouraged; to which end, one of the Elders was requested to speak unto the English, the two above said Reasons, *viz.* The want of Interpreters, And want of Time, to finish at this time so solemn a Work; but to refer it to a more fitting time. And I was desired to declare it to the Indians, which I did to this purpose, That the Magistrates, Elders, and other Christian People present, did much rejoyce to hear their Confessions, and advised them to go on in that good way; but as for the gathering a Church among them this day, it could not be; partly, Because neither Mr. *Mayhew,* nor Mr. *Leveridg,* nor any Interpreter was here (for whom they knew I had sent, some of themselves being the Messengers to carry Letters time enough) and it was Gods Ordinance, That when any were to judg a Case, though they could beleeve one Witness, yet they could not judg under two or three. Also I told them, That themselves might easily see there was not time enough to finish so solemn a work this day; therefore they advised, and God called to refer it to a fitter season; in which advice they rested: And so was the Work of that day, with prayers unto God, finished; the accomplishment being referred to a fitter season.

As for my self, the Lord put it into the hearts of the Elders, to speak unto me words of Comfort, and acceptance of my poor Labor, expressing their loving fear, lest I should be discouraged by this disappointment: I shall therefore nakedly declare, and open my very heart in this Matter. The Lord he knoweth, that with much fear, and care I went about this work, even unto the sensible wasting, and weakning of my natural strength, knowing that the investing these young Babes in Christ, with the highest, and all the external priviledges of the Church, the Spouse of Jesus Christ on Earth, would have drawn upon me much more labor and care, lest they should in any wise scandalize the same; unto which I have now more time assigned me by the Lord to prepare them, yea, and a greater advantage than I had before, because this dispensation of the Lord, doth give me occasion to instruct them of their need to be filled with deeper apprehensions of the weight and solemnity of that great Work, though it is most true, that they also came on unto it with many fears, and questions, what they should do when they should be a Church: When therefore I saw the Lord by the Counsel of his Servants (which is an holy reverend Ordinance of Christ) and by his Providence denying me the help of all Interpreters, having many witnesses how much care and pains I took every way I knew, to be supplied therein; and that the work it self was extended by the Lords gracious inlarging them in their Confessions, so that the day was not sufficient to accomplish it; I say, when I saw the Lord speaking that delatory word, I cannot express what a load it took off my heart, and I did gladly follow the Lord therein, yea, and I bless the Lord for that day, that it was carried so far as it was, for the cause of Christ hath many waies gained by it, many hundreds of the precious Saints, being much comforted and comfirmed in their hopes of this work of Christ among them, and their faith and prayers much quickned by what they heard and saw. And because all witnesses failed me, let me say but this, I began, and have followed this work for the Lord according to the poor measure of grace received, & not for base ends. I have been true & faithful unto their souls, and in writing and reading their Confessions, I have not knowingly, or willingly made them better, than the Lord helped themselves to make them, but am verily perswaded on good grounds, that I have rather rendered them weaker (for the most part) than they delivered them; partly by missing some words of weight in some Sentences, partly by my short and curt touches of what they more fully spake, and partly by reason of the different Idioms of their Language and ours.

Now follow those Preparitory Confessions, which were read before the Elders, most of them.

The first that made a publick Confession, and was took in Writing, was Peter, *a Ruler of Ten among them, a Godly man, who quickly after he had made this Confession, fell sick, and died, and now injoyeth the fruit of his Faith, the end of his Hope, the salvaion of his Soul, among the Blessed; where I am perswaded he shall be found in the great day. His Confession was as followeth.*

WHen I first prayed to God, I did not fear God, but I feared perdition, because the English had told me, that all should be damned, that call not upon God. But now I konw that God made all the world, and I fear him; now I beleeve that which you teach is true; Now I beleeve that God calleth us to *Natik*, that here we may be ruled by God, and gather a Church; now I beleeve that it is Gods Command, that we should labor Six dayes, and keep the Sabbath on the Seventh day: now my heart is greatly abased for all my sins; for we see though we pray to God we are ready to offend each other, and be angry with each other, and that we love not each other as we should do; and for this I grieve & my heart crieth: now I remember that God saith thou shalt not lust, but before I prayed to God I was full of lusts. God saith, We must have but one Wife, and at first did make but one man and one woman; but I followed many women. God saith, Remember to keep the Sabbath day holy; but I did hunt, or shoot, or any thing on the Sabbath day: many other sins I committed; but now I see them, and wil cast them away because they are vile, and God forbiddeth them: when I prayed first my sins were not pardoned, for my praying is worth nothing: now I am humbled, and mourn for my sins and yet cannot deliver my self nor get pardon, therfore I trust Christ with my soul.

The next Confession was made by John Speene, *as followeth. His first confession was this,*

WHen I first prayed to God, I did not pray for my soul but only I did as my friends did, because I loved them; and though I prayed to God, yet I did not fear sin, nor was I troubled at it. I heard that when good men die, their souls go to God, and are there happy, but I cannot say that I beleeved it. Afterward my heart run away into the country, after our old wayes, and I did almost cast off praying to God. A little while after that, I saw that I had greatly sinned, and then I saw all my sins, afore I prayed to God, and since I prayed to God, and I saw that God was greatly angry for them, and that I cannot get pardon for them; but yet my heart saith I will pray to God as long as I live: I thought God would not pardon me, and yet I would cast away my sins. I did greatly love hunting, and hated labor: but now I beleeve that word of God, which saith, Six dayes thou shalt labor. and God doth make my body strong to labor.

John Speene,
This Confession being short in some main points, he afterward made Confession as followeth.

WHen I first prayed I prayed not for my soul, but for the sake of men, I loved men, and for their sakes I prayed to God. Before I prayed many were my sins, and my heart was heaped full, and ran over in all manner of lusts and sins. After I heard of praying to *God,* I let it fall and regarded it not; after I came to hear the word, I sometimes feared, but soon lost it again. Then my heart ran away after our former courses, and then what ever I heard I lost, because my heart was run away; and many were my sins, and therfore I could not get pardon, because my heart run away, and many were my sins, and I did indeed go into the Country. But afterwards, I hearing the Catechism, I desired to learn it, and then I beleeved that when Beleevers die, their souls go to God, and are ever happy; when Sinners die, their souls go to Hel, and are ever tormented; and that when Christ judges the world, our bodies rise again, and then we shall receive the judgment of Christ; the good shal stand at his right hand, the bad at his left: this I beleeved was true, and then I saw all my great follies and evils: and now my heart desired to lay by hunting, and to work every day; and this is Gods Command, and therfore a good way; God said, Thou shalt work six daies, and if thou work, thou shalt eat; therfore I beleeve it, and my heart promiseth that I will this do as long as I live. Now I see I did great folly, for now I hear that God saith *Work*; and now I fear because God hath afflicted me, in taking away my brother a Ruler: now I am troubled, I fear I sinned in not beleeving our Ruler, because now God hath taken him away; he taught me good words, but I beleeved them not, and now I repent because Christ calleth me to it: great is the punishment of God in taking away our Ruler; and now I pray, and say to Christ, Oh Jesus Christ I have sinned: I beleeve that if I repent and be humbled, and pray not only outwardly but inwardly, and beleeve in Christ, then God will pardon all my sin; but I cannot get pardon of sin, I cannot deserve pardon, but only Christ hath merited pardon for us: I cannot deliver my self from all my sins, but Christ redeemeth, and delivereth from all sin: I deserve not one mercy of God, but Christ hath merited all mercies for us.

The next are the Confessions of Robin Speene, *who three several times came forth, and confessed as followeth. His first Confession:*

I Was ashamed because you taught to pray to God, and I did not take it up; I see God is angry with me for all my sins, and he hath afflicted me by the death of three of my children, and I fear God is still angry, because great are my sins, and I fear lest my children be not gone to Heaven, because I am a great sinner, yet one of my children prayed to God before it died, and therefore my heart rejoyceth in that. I remember my Panwaning [for he was a *Panwan*] my lust, my gaming, and all my sins; I know them by the Commandements of God, and God heareth and seeth them all; I cannot deliver my self from sin, therefore I do need Christ, because of all my sins, I desire pardon, and I beleeve that God calls all to come to Christ, and that he delivereth us from sin.

Robin Speen,
His Second Confession.

I Have found out one word more: great are my sins, and I do not know how to repent, nor do I know the evil of my sins; only this one word, now I confess I want Christ, this day I want him; I do not truly beleeve nor repent: I see my sin, and I need Christ, but I desire now to be redeemed: and I now ask you this Question, *What is Redemption?* "I answered him, by shewing him our estate by Nature, and desert, the price which Christ paid for us, and how it is to be applied to every particular person; which done, he proceeded in his Confession thus: I yet cannot tell whether God hath pardoned my sins, I forget the Word of God; but this I desire, that my sins may be pardoned, but my heart is foolish, and a great part of the Word stayeth not in my heart strongly. I desire to cast all my sins out of my heart: but I remember my sins, that I may get them pardoned, I think God doth not yet hear my prayers in this, because I cannot keep the Word of God, only I desire to hear the Word, and that God would hear me.

Robin Speen,
His Third Confession.

O Ne word more I cal to mind, Great is my sin! this saith my heart; I have found this sin, when I first heard you teach, that all the world from the rising to the sitting Sun should pray to God, I then wondered at it, and thought, I being a great sinner, how shal I pray to God; and when I saw many come to the Meeting, I wondred at it: But now I do not wonder at that work of God, and therefore I think that I do now greatly sin: and now I desire again to wonder at Gods Works, and I desire to rejoyce in Gods good waies. Now I am much ashamed, and fear because I have deserved eternal wrath by my sins: my heart is evil, my heart doth contrary to God, and this I desire, that I may be redeemed, for I cannot help my self, but only Jesus Christ hath done al this for me, and I deserve no good, but I beleeve Christ hath deserved all for us; and I give my self unto Christ, that he may save me, because he knoweth eternal life, and can give it; I cannot give it to my self, therefore I need Jesus Christ, my heart is full of evil thoughts; and Christ only can keep my soul from them, because he hath paid for my deliverance from them.

The next are the Confessions of Nishohkou; *who twice made preparitory Confessions; the first of which only, was read before the Elders.*

G OD in Heaven is merciful, and I am sinful: when I first heard the Word of God, I neither saw nor understood; but after, when you taught these words,

Be wise, Oh all ye people, and beleeve in Jesus Christ, then I prayed unto God; yet afterwards I sinned, and almost forsook praying to God. Afterward I understood, That God who made all the World was merciful to sinners: and truly I saw my heart very sinful, because I promised God to pray as long as I live, but my heart hath not so done. Again I promised God I will follow Christ in al things, and now I find my heart backward, and not so forward to make a Church. God promiseth, If foolish ones pray to God for Wisdom he will give it: this Promise I beleeve, but I find my heart full of temptations; but now I promise God, as in the *Psalm,* [Psalm: 101.2.] All my works shal be done in wisdom, for I confess al my works and words, have been foolish. God is wise and good, but I am foolish. God who hath made the World, sent his own Son Jesus: and Jesus Christ hath died for us, and deserved for us, pardon and life, this is true; and he hath done for me all Gods Commandements, for I can do nothing, because I am very sinful. God in Heaven is very merciful, and therfore hath called me to pray unto God. *G*od hath promised to pardon al their sins, who pray unto God, and beleeve in the Promise of Christ, and Christ can give me to beleeve in him.

When he had made this Confession, he was much abashed, for he is a bashful man; many things he spoke that I missed, for want of through understanding some words and sentences: therfore before the Fast day he made another Confession, which was not read before the Elders; which was as followeth.

Nishohkou

I Am dead in sin, Oh! that my sins might die, for they cannot give life, because they be dead: before I prayed to God, I did commit all filthynesse, I prayed to many gods, I was proud, full of lusts, adulteries, and all other sins, and therefore this is my first Confession, that God is mercifull, and I am a sinner, for God have given unto me instruction and causeth me to pray unto God, but I only pray words; when I prayed, I sometimes wondered, and thought true it is that God made the world, and me: and then I thought I knew God, because I saw these his works, and then I was glad somtimes, and gave thanks; yet presently again I did not rejoyce in it. Again somtimes I thought, now I do wel because I pray and work not on the Sabbath daies, but come to the Meetings, and hear the Word of God: But afterward again, I thought I do not wel, because true it is, That yet I do not truly pray; for now I see I sin when I pray, because there is nothing but sin in my mouth, or hand, or heart, and all sins are there, for of these my sins my heart is full, because my heart doth sometimes lust, and steal, and the like. Again, I was not only proud before I prayed, but now I am proud. Again, sometimes my heart is humbled, and then I pray, Oh God have mercy on me, and pardon these my sins; yet sometimes I know not whether God did either hear my prayer, or pardon my sins. Again, afterwards I thought I had greatly sinned, because I heard of the good way of praying unto God, but I do wickedly because I pray not truly, yea, sometimes I have much ado to pray with my mouth, and therfore I sin. I heard of that good way, to keep the Sabbath, and not to work on that day, and I did so: but yet again I sinned in it, because I did not reverence the Word of God; yea, and sometimes I thought that working on the Sabbath was no great matter. Again, I heard it was a good way to come to the Meetings, and hear the word of God, and I desired to do it; but in this also I sinned, because I did not truly hear: yea, sometimes I thought it no great matter if I heard not, and cared not to come to hear, and still I so sinned. Then I thought God was angry, because I have greatly sinned; desiring to do well, and yet again to sin. When I desired to do well, then I sinned, and in all things I sinned. But afterward I was angry with my self, and thought I will not sin again; and what God saith, is good, but I am sinful because I have done all these evils. Again, sometimes my heart is humbled, and then I repent, and say, Oh God and Jesus Christ, have mercy on me, and pardon my sins. Now I desire truly to pray; now I desire to reverence the Word every Sabbath day: now I desire to hear the Word of God truly; now I desire to bend my heart to pray, and it may be God will hear me: but quickly after a temptation cometh to my heart, and I did not desire it. Again, sometimes I did think, true it is I can do nothing of my self, but Jesus Christ must have mercy on me, because Christ hath done for me all Gods Commandements and good Works, therfore my heart saith, Oh Jesus give me desires after thee: sometimes I think it is true, I have greatly sinned against God, but great are his mercies: sometimes I hear the Word on the Sabbath day, and he giveth it me, [that is, maketh it my own] sometimes I say the great and mighty God is in Heaven, but these are but words, because I do not fear this great and mighty God; and I sometimes regard not Gods Word, and make it of none effect, because I do not that which is good, but commit sin: sometimes I say I know Christ, because I know he died for us, and hath redeemed us, and procured pardon for us: yet again I say I sin, because I beleeve not Christ, for that only is right to beleeve in Christ, and do what he saith; but I think I do this in vain, because I yet do not truly beleeve in Jesus Christ, nor do what he commandeth, and therefore my heart plays the hypocrite; and now I know what is hypocrisie, namely, when I know what I should do, and yet do it not. Sometimes I think I am like unto Satan, because I do al these sins, and sin in all things I do; if I pray I sin, if I keep Sabbath I sin, if I hear Gods Word I sin, therefore I am like the Devil. Now I know I deserve to go to Hell, because all these sins I have committed: then my heart is troubled, and I say, Oh God and Christ pardon all my sin, for I cannot pardon my sins my self; for the first man brought sin into the world, and therfore I am sinful, therfore I pray thee O Lord pardon all the sins which I have done. Again, sometimes my heart is humbled, and I desire to fear God, because he is a great God, and I desire to do what he saith, and now I desire to do the right way, and now I desire to beleeve Jesus Christ; and sometimes I think it may be God will hear me, it may be he will pardon me, yet again I think I cannot be ashamed of sin; but now I am ashamed of all my sins, and my heart is broken, and all these my sins I cast off, and take heed of: yet then again I sometimes say to God, I cannot my self be humbled, or break my heart, or cast off sin, but I pray thee O Jesus help me to do it.

Again, sometimes I confess this is true, I cannot redeem my self, nor deliver my self, because of all these my many sins; truly, full is my heart of sin in every thing, all my thoughts, my words, my looks, my works are full of sin; true this is, therefore I cannot deliver my self from sin; Oh redeem thou my soul from Hel and torment, for I like not to do it with my own hand, therfore I desire Jesus Christ, that I may delight in him; take thou me and my soul, because thou hast done Gods word, and all good works for me, and hast procured pardon for all my sins, and hast prepared pardon in Heaven, therfore I desire, Oh I desire pardon: but I somtimes think Christ doth not delight in me because I do much play the hypocrite, but if I truly beleeve then he will pardon, but true faith I cannot work; Oh Jesus Christ help me, and give it me.

Another who made Confession, is named *Magus; which is as followeth:*

H Eretofore I beleeved not, that God made the world, but I thought the world was of it self, and all people grew up in the world of themselves. When any bid me pray to God, I said I cannot, and none of our Rulers beleeve or pray to God; yet I went about to seek how to pray to God, I told the wise men, I seek how to pray to God, and all of them could not find how to pray to God. Afterward I had a desire to pray God, lest I should lose my soul, but my heart run away, and I could not find how to pray to God, and therefore I thought of going away; yet I also thought if I do go away, I shall lose my ground. But after this I heard of Gods anger against me, and I beleeved it; for God made the first man good, and told him if he did well he should live, and this day I beleeve all men should do so: and then I thought I will pray as long as I live, and I will labor, because Gods promise is, If we labor we shall eat; and I see that that is a true word; for they that do labor do eat [that is, have wherewith to be fed] I see that sin alwaies hath continued, from the beginning of the world. I beleeve that word which God told *Eve,* That in sorrow she should bring forth Children, and I see it dayly to be true. I beleeve that word of God, that sin brings misery, and all shall die, because by sin, we break all the Commands of God: I have been full of lusts, and thefts, &c. all my life, and all the time I have lived. I have done contrary to the Command of *God.* And I am now grieved, now I hear of all my sins: I beleeve Christ doth convert me to *God,* and he calleth Children, and old men, and all men to turn unto *God,* and from their sins; he calleth to sorrow and repentance, and ever to beleeve in Christ; and who ever doth this, shall be ever blessed in Heaven; but if he do it not, he perisheth: if he trun not from sin, dying, he shall go to Hell for ever. I think also, that so long as I live, God doth give me life. I beleeve that we ought to gather into a Church, to serve God as long as we live. But I do not know whether yet God hath pardoned my sins, or not; but I know Christ, and I know he hath already dyed for me, because I cannot redeem my self.

Another who made Confession, was named Poquanum; *which was as followeth. His first Confession.*

A Great while ago the English would tell me of God but I hated it, and would go out of doors, when they so spake unto me, and I murmured at it. When the Indians first prayed to God, I did not think there was a God, or that the Bible was Gods Book, but that wise men made it: When some prayed to God, I went with them, but I did not know God. Afterward my mind was changed thus far, That I desired to be wise, as others were, but yet I knew nothing of God; yea, after I prayed to God, I still did think there was no God. Afterward I found this in my heart, That we pray to God for our souls; then I thought all my praying was nothing, because I was so foolish that I never thought of dying: but after, I learned, That all must die, and good mens souls go to Heaven; and then I thought of dying, and of my soul: but then I thought we prayed for nothing but that our souls might go to Heaven; I knew nothing of Christ. But after, when the Children were Catechised, and taught the ten Commandements, I hearkned, and by them I came to know that there was a God, and that there was sin against God; and hereby God made me to see all my sins, both before I prayed to God, and since; and I saw Gods anger against me for my sins, before, and since I prayed, because sometimes I came not to the Meeting; brake my word, regarded not my children, and I see sin in me, and therfore I do greatly fear Gods anger.

Poquanum;
His Second Confession was as followeth:

B Efore I prayed unto God, I greatly sinned, I prayed to many gods, and used Panwaning, Adultery, Lust, Lying, and al other sins, and many were my sins, evil thoughts, evil words, and nothing else but evil, hatred, and pride, and all sins against God, coveting other mens goods; when I stole, I added lying to it when I had done; I was very proud, I much hated many men, and loved them not because I was angry with them; and thus I did every day: I would slander my neighbors, great was my pride, I was dayly angry with my neighbors, my heart was alwaies full of such waies. When the English said, Pray to God, I cared not for God, because I loved sin, nor did I desire that God should forgive my sin. Afterward I heard the word, That if we truly pray, mourn for sin, cast off sin, desire to hear the word, and beleeve in Christ, God will then pardon, and when he dieth Christ will lead him to Heaven: I much rejoyced to hear of this pardon, but I must truly beleeve in Christ, else I shal not have pardon; and first I thought God will not pardon me, because I still sinned. But afterward I heard, That though we should pray as long as we live, and never sin more, yet that was of no value; but we must beleeve in Christ, else there is no pardon; and this I rejoyced at.

Another who made Confession, is named Nookau, *which is as followeth. His first Confession.*

F Ive years ago, before I prayed I was sick, I thought I should die; at which I was much troubled, and knew not what to do; then I thought, if there be a God above, and he give life again, then I shall beleeve there is a God above, and God did give me life: and after that I took up praying to God. Now I beleeve God, one God that made all the World, and governeth it, yet this I only said with my mouth, I did not truly beleeve it in my heart. Then I understood, That God made the first man good, and like God, but he sinned, and we have lost Gods Image, and are like the Devil, and deserve Hell and Damnation: this I now know, and see that I am foolish, and sometime think not of God in an whol day, sometime I do think of God every day; sometime my heart greatly sinneth, then sometime I presently fear, but again sometimes I am slow to fear; I am very foolish because I do not understand the Word, but break the Word of God. I beleeve the Catechism we learn to be according to the Word of God; but the writings of the Bible are the very Words of God, and the Spirit of God is the Word, and that God giveth all things that are good: I now see my sins before I prayed unto God, and since, and I beleeve that God seeth them all: and my heart feareth, because I do not yet forsake my sins, and I think God will not forgive me, because my heart is wicked; I know not when Christ forgiveth my sins, others may know, but I desire that my sins may be pardoned for Christ his sake.

Nookau,
His Second Confession.

B Efore I prayed to God, I greatly sinned every day, I was proud, and lived in adultery, lying, &c. and my heart alwaies full of evil thoughts, and when the English would instruct me, I then thought my waies evil, but the business of praying to God, good; then I did think, if I could first understand, then I would pray to God, and I was glad to hear of any that did pray to God. When I heard that word at *Gohannet, Who ever lacketh wisdom, let him ask it of God;* let fools pray to God, and he will give them wisdom: I thought I was a fool, and I beleeved that Word of God. I heard that word of the dry bones, God bid them hear, and promised to put flesh, and sinews, and skin upon them, and make them live; therefore I desired to hear, because I beleeved the dry bones, and that I was one that did not know God: afterward I was glad of praying to God. Sometimes I beleeved not God, and God will not look on such, alwaies I thought God will not forgive me. I wondred at all that prayed to God, because I thought God had given them wisdom: then I thought I am glad I pray to God. Sometime my heart is broken because I shall lose all in this world, and lose my soul also, because I beleeve not, for all the Words of God are true which he hath taught me. Now this day I think I will confess the truth; Because I have sinned, I want Jesus Christ: and I will truly confess God, because of that word of Christ, *He that confesseth me before men, him will I confess before my Father:* I wonder at this Instruction, I desire to confess my heart.

Another who made his Confession is named Antony, *upon whom the Lord was pleased the last Winter to lay an heavy stroke; for he and another Indian being at work sawing of Board, and finishing the Peece, they laid it so short, and the Rowl not so stedfast, insomuch that this man being in the Pit directing to lay the Piece, and the other above ordering thereof, it slipped down into the Pit upon this mans head, brake his neather Chap in two, and cracked his Skull, insomuch that he was taken up half dead, and almost strangled with blood; and being the last day of the week at night I had no word until the Sabbath day, then I presently sent a Chyrurgion, who took a discreet order with him; and God so blessed his indeavors, as that he is now well again, blessed be the Lord: and whereas I did fear that such a blow in their Labor might discourage them from Labor, I have found it by Gods blessing otherwise; yea, this man hath performed a great part of the sawing of our Meeting-House, and is now sawing upon the School-house, and his recovery is an establishment of them to go on; yea, and God blessed this blow, to help on the Work of Grace in his soul; as you shall see in his Confession, which followeth.*

BEfore I prayed to God I alwaies committed sin, but I do not know all my sins, I know but a little of the sins I have committed, therefore I thought I could not pray to God, because I knew not al my sins before I prayed to God, and since I heard of praying to God: formerly when the English did bid me pray unto God, I hated it, and would go out of their houses, when they spake of such things to me. I had no delight to hear any thing of Gods Word, but in every thing I sinned; in my speeches I sinned, and every day I broke the Commands of God. After I heard of praying to God, that *Waban* and my two brothers prayed to God, yet then I desired it not, but did think of running away; yet I feared, if I did run away some wicked men would kill me, but I did not fear God. After when you said unto me, pray, my heart thought, I will pray; yet again I thought, I cannot pray with my heart, and no matter for praying with words only: but when I did pray, I saw more of my sins; yet I did but only see them, I could not be aware of them, but still I did commit them: and after I prayed to God, I was still full of lust, and then a little I feared. Sometimes I was sick, and then I thought God was angry, and then I saw that I did commit all sins: then one of my brothers died, and then my heart was broken, and after him another friend, and again my heart was broken: and yet after all this I broke my praying to God, and put away God, and then I thought I shall never pray to God: but after this I was afraid of the Lord, because I alwaies broke my praying to God, and then my heart said, God doth not hear my prayer. When I was sick, and recovered again,

I thought then that God was merciful unto me. Hearing that word of God, *If you hear the Word of God, and be forgetful hearers, you sin against God;* then I thought God will not pardon such a sinner as I, who dayly did so, and broke my praying to God. When I heard the Commandements, I desired to learn them, and other points of Catechism, but my desires were but small, and I soon lost it, because I did not desire to beleeve: then sometimes I feared Gods anger because of al my sins; I heard the Word and understood only this word, *All you that hear this day, it may be you shall quickly die,* and then I quickly saw that God was very angry with me. Then God brake my head, and by that I saw Gods anger; and then I thought that the true God in Heaven is angry with me for my sin, even for al my sins, which every day I live, I do. When I was almost dead, some body bid me now beleeve, because it may be I shal quickly die, and I thought I did beleeve, but I did not know right beleeving in Christ: then I prayed unto God to restore my health. Then I beleeved that word, *That we must shortly appear before Jesus Christ;* then I did greatly fear lest if I beleeved not, I should perish for ever. When I was neer death, I prayed unto God, *Oh Lord give me life, and I will pray to God so long as I live,* and I said, *I will give my self, soul, and body to Christ:* after this, God gave me health, and then I thought, truly, God in Heaven is merciful; then I much grieved, that I knew so little of Gods Word. And now sometimes I am angry, and then I fear because I know God seeth it; and I fear, because I promised God when I was almost dead, that if he giveth me life, I will pray so long as I live; I fear lest I should break this promise to God. Now I desire the pardon of all my sins, and I beg faith in Christ, and I desire to live unto God, so long as I live; I cannot my self get pardon, but I dayly commit sin, and break Gods Word, but I look to Christ for pardon.

Another who made His Confession is named Owussumag; *which is as followeth:*

W Hen I first heard that *Waban* prayed to God, and after that many more prayed. I first feared praying to God, and instruction, and I hated instruction by the Word of God, and alwaies I laughed at them who prayed to God; and I alwaies thought I will yet more commit sin: and I went into the Country, and there I acted much lust, adultry, and the like, and all my Neighbors, we did together seek after wickedness, and every day I was proud, and of high or open eyes. When some of my neighbors began to pray, I went away into the Country, but I could find no place where I was beloved. Then I heard, That when beleevers die, they go to Heaven, when sinners die they go to Hel; and my heart considered, What good will it be if my soul go to Heaven? But two years ago, I began to think, I had sinned against God; and then somtimes I feared, yet again sinned; but my fear was of man, not of God: Then ever my heart said I should be better, if I would pray to God, and somtimes I beleeved that which I was taught, yet again, last year, I sought to go away afar off, but I could think of no place, but I should be in danger to be killed. Then again I much rembred my sins: and again I thought, What will become of me, if I die in my sins? and then I thought it was good for me to pray unto God so long as I live; and then my heart turned to praying unto God, and I did pray, and my heart feared when I heard the word read and taught, and I was glad to hear the Word of God; and then I purposed to pray as long as I live. Sometime I did dayly see my sins and fear, for I cannot get pardon, only in Jesus Christ. Then I heard that word, *I thank thee oh Heavenly father, that thou hast revealed these things to babes;* and that word, *that we must forgive each other:* then I saw that I beleeved not one word from Christ, not any word of God; and dayly my heart wept, that Christ might pardon all my sins against God and Christ: and now unto this day my heart saith I desire the good waies of praying to God, but I cannot know them of my self, but Jesus Christ must teach me them. When I heard, That only Christ must pardon our sins, and that for Christ God will pardon our sins, this day I rejoyce to hear that word of God, and all that Christ hath taught me: and now I purpose, That while I live, I will pray unto God, and Jesus Christ only: and this day I see I cannot know how to find good thoughts; but this day I desire pardon for all my sins, and to cast them away.

Another who made Confession, is named Ephraim, *his Indian Name I have forgotten. It is as followeth:*

ALL the daies I have lived, I have been in a poor foolish condition, I cannot tell all my sins, all my great sins, I do not see them. When I first heard of praying to God, I could not sleep quietly, I was so troubled, ever I thought I would forsake the place because of praying to God, my life hath been like as if I had been a mad man. Last yeer I thought I would leave all my sins, yet I see I do not leave off sinning to this day; I now think I shall never be able to forsake my sins. I think sometimes the Word of God is false, yet I see there is no giving over that I might follow sin, I must pray to God; I do not truly in my heart repent, and I think that God wil not forgive me my sins; every day my heart sinneth, and how will Christ forgive such an one? I pray but outwardly with my mouth, not with my heart; I cannot of my self obtain pardon of my sins: I cannot tell all the sins that I have done if I should tell you an whol day together: I do every morning desire that my sins may be pardoned by Jesus Christ; this my heart saith, but yet I fear I cannot forsake my sins, because I cannot see all my sins: I hear, That if we repent and beleeve in Christ, all our sins shall be pardoned, therefore I desire to leave off my sins.

This poor Publican was the last which made his Confession before I read them
    unto the Elders, and the last of them I shall now publish. I will shut up
    these Confessions with the Confession (if I may so call it) or rather with
    the Expression, and manifestation of faith, by two little Infants, of two
    yeers old, and upward, under three yeers of age when they died and
    departed out of this world.
                        The Story is this,

THis Spring, in the beginning of the yeer, 1652. the Lord was pleased to afflict sundry of our praying Indians with that grievous disease of the Bloody-Flux, whereof some with great torments in their bowels died; among which were two little Children of the age above-said, and at that time both in one house, being together taken with that disease. The first of these Children in the extremities of its torments, lay crying to God in these words, *God and Jesus Christ, God and Jesus Christ help me;* and when they gave it any thing to eat, it would greedily take it (as is usual at the approach of death) but first it would cry to God, *Oh God and Jesus Christ, bless it,* and then it would take it: and in this manner it lay calling upon God and Jesus Christ untill it died: The mother of this Child also died of that disease, at that time. The Father of the Child told me this story, with great wonderment at the grace of God, in teaching his Child so to call upon God. The name of the Father is *Nishohkou,* whose Confession you have before.

Three or four daies after, another Child in the same house, sick of the same disease, was (by a divine hand doubtless) sensible of the approach of death, (an unusual thing at that age) and called to its Father, and said, *Father, I am going to God,* several times repeating it, *I am going to God.* The mother (as other mothers use to do) had made for the Child a little Basket, a little Spoon, and a little Tray: these things the child was wont to be greatly delighted withal (as all children will) therefore in the extremity of the torments, they set those things before it, a little to divert the mind, and cheer the spirit: but now, the child takes the Basket, and puts it away, and said, *I will leave my Basket behind me, for I am going to God, I will leave my Spoon and Tray behind me* (putting them away) *for I am going to God:* and with these kind of expressions, the same night, finished its course, and died.

The Father of this child is named *Robin Speen,* whose Confessions you have before, and in one of them he maketh mention of this child that died in faith. When he related this story to me, he said, He could not tell whether the sorrow for the death of his child, or the joy for its faith were greater, when it died.

These Examples are testimony, That they teach their children the knowledg and fear of God, whom they now call upon; and also that the Spirit of God co-worketh with their instructions, who teacheth by man, more than man is able to do.

I have now finished all that I purpose to publish at this time; the Lord give them Acceptance in the hearts of his Saints, to engage them the more to pray for them; and Oh! that their judgings of themselves, and breathings after Christ, might move others (that have more means than they have, but as yet regard it not) to do the like, and much more abundantly.

F I N I S.

A Late and Further

MANIFESTATION

OF THE

Progreſs of the GOSPEL

AMONGST THE

INDIANS

IN

Nevv-England.

Declaring their conſtant Love and Zeal to
the Truth: With a readineſſe to give
Accompt of their Faith and Hope; as of
their deſires in Church Communion to be Partakers of
the Ordinances of
CHRIST.

Being a Narrative of the Examinations of the Indians, *about
their Knowledge in Religion, by the Elders of the Churches.*
Related by Mr JOHN ELIOT.

Publiſhed by the CORPORATION, eſtabliſhed by
Act of Parliament, for Propagating the Goſpel there.

Acts 13. 47. *I have ſet thee to be a light to the Gentiles, that
thou ſhouldeſt be for Salvation unto the Ends of the Earth.*

LONDON: Printed by *M.S.* 1 6 5 5.

Photo courtesy of the Newberry Library, Chicago.

A Late and Further

MANIFESTATION

OF THE

Progress of the GOSPEL

AMONGST THE

INDIANS

IN

New-England.

Declaring their constant Love and Zeal to
the Truth: With a readinesse to give
Accompt of their Faith and Hope; as of
their desires in Church Commu-
nion to be Partakers of
the Ordinances of
CHRIST.
Being a Narrative of the Examinations of the Indians, *about their
Knowledge in Religion, by the Elders of the Churches.*
Related by Mr JOHN ELIOT.

Published by the CORPORATION, established
by *Act of Parliament,* for Propagating the Gospel there.

Acts 13.47. *I have set thee to be a light to the Gentiles, that
thou shouldest be for Salvation unto the Ends of the Earth.*

LONDON: Printed by *M. S.* 1 6 5 5.

WEE *having perused the ensuing* Narration, *written by Master* Eliot, *doe conceive it fit to be Printed, That thereby the Servants of God in* England *may be further enlarged in their Praises to God for his free Grace wonderfully manifested in beginning and so succesfully carrying on the hoped for Conversion of the* Indians. *And also that they may be much encouraged to continue their Prayers, and liberall Contributions for the finishing and perfecting of this blessed and glorious undertaking, so much conducing to the Glory of God, the Salvation of soules, and the Inlargement of the Kingdome of Christ upon Earth.*

May 13. 1655.

H: Whitfeild. Edm: Calamy.
Simeon Ashe. John Arthur.

To all that pray and wait for the

Prosperity of *S I O N*, and the increase
of the Kingdome of our Lord Jesus
Christ to the ends of the Earth.

Grace and Peace be multiplied.

Beloved Brethren.

AS, The *One thing* which ye have desired of the Lord, and which yee have sought after, is, that your selves might dwell in the house of the Lord all the dayes of your lives, to behold the beauty of the Lord, and to enquire in his Temple: So, I am much assured that the next thing which yee have desired of the Lord, and which ye have earnestly sought after, is, that they who have hitherto been strangers to, might dwell also in the house of the Lord all the dayes of their lives, to behold the beauty of the Lord, and to enquire in his Temple; yea, that they might be a house and a Temple of the Lord. This being the gratious designe of your holy breathings unto God, and of your liberall contributings unto men, ye cannot but rejoyce to hear of any thing which looketh like, much more which really is a fruit and return of such breathings and contributings. Holy prayers and zealous endeavours are very sweet in their acts, but they are much more sweet in their effects and is issues. It should mightily encourage the seed of *Jacob* to pray, because God hath said, that he hath not said to the seed of *Jacob, seeke yee me in vaine.* But how should it provoke the seed of *Jacob* to give thanks, when they find that they have not sought the Lord in vaine? and that their labours have not been in vaine in the Lord?

Beloved Brethren, yee may now see and tast the fruit of those Prophecies, which ye have been helping to the birth. *The Wildernesse and solitary places are glad, the desert rejoyceth and blossemeth, as the Rose it blossometh abundantly, and rejoyceth even with joy and singing. The glory of Lebanon is given to it, the excellency of Carmell and Sharon, these see the glory of the Lord, and the excellency of our God.*

This little Book of Observations and Experiences gives you a brief and faithfull Narrative of the increasing glory of Christ by the Progresse of the

Gospel in *New-England:* It tells you how Christ hath there led captivity captive, and given gifts for men, yea, for the rebellious, that the Lord God might dwell among them. Where the strong man Armed kept the house (for many Ages and Generations, and all was in peace:) there now (Christ) *A stronger then he,* hath come upon him, and hath (in many examples) overcome him and taken from him all his Armour wherein he trusted, and divided his spoyles: Now Christ keeps the house, which Satan formerly kept; yea, they who were kept by Satan as his house, are now ready and earnestly desire to be built up as a house for Christ. The poor, naked, ignorant *Indians,* who lately knew no civill Order, now beg to be brought into Church Order, to live under the Government, and enjoy the holy Ordinances of our Lord Jesus Christ, in the purest way of Gospel-worship.

May we not now (*Beloved*) make mention of *Rahab* and *Babylon* to them that know Christ? *Behold Philistia, and Tyre, with Ethiopia, this man was borne there; and of Sion* (in *New-England*) *it may be said, this and that man* (of the wild, rude, and barbarous *Indians*) *was borne there.* Read this short discourse, and it will tell you that the Lord hath blessed the labours of the Messengers of *Sion* in *New-England,* with the Conversion of some (I may say, of a considerable number) of the *Indians,* to be a kind of first fruits of his (new) Creatures there. O let old *England* rejoyce in this, that our brethren who with extream difficulties and expences have Planted themselves in the *Indian Wildernesses,* have also laboured night and day with prayers and tears and Exhortations to Plant the *Indians as a Spirituall Garden,* into which Christ might come and eat his pleasant fruits. Let the gaining of any of their souls to Christ, and their turning to God from Idols to serve the living and true God, be more pretious in our eyes then the greatest gaine or return of Gold and Silver. This gaine of soules is a *Merchandize* worth the glorying in upon all the *Exchanges,* or rather in all the *Churches* throughout the world. *This Merchandize is Holinesse to the Lord:* And of this the ensuing Discourse presents you with a Bill of many particulars, from your spirituall *Factory in New-England,* as the improvement of your former adventures thether, for the promoting of that heavenly Trade; as also for an encouragement not only to all those who have freely done it already, to adventure yet more, but also for the quickning of those who hitherto have not done it, now to underwrite themselves Adventurers for the advancement of so holy and hopefull a designe. I shall adde only this one word, That, *Whosoever shall thus Adventer for Christ, shall have Christ for his Insurer.* To his Grace and Blessing I recommend both you and this Blessed Work, who am

Dearly Beloved,

A hearty well-wisher to the Propagation of the Gospel; and your Servant for Christs sake

JOSEPH CARYL.

A BRIEF
NARRATION
OF THE
INDIANS
PROCEEDINGS

In respect of

Church - Estate,
AND
How the Case standeth at the present
with us.

FTER I had spent my poor labours among the *Indians* for the space of neer four years, it pleased God to stir up in them a great desire of partaking in the Ordinance of Baptism, and other Ecclesiasticall Ordinances in way of Church Communion. But I declared unto them how necessary it was, that they should first be Civilized, by being brought from their scattered and wild course of life, unto civill Co-habitation and Government, before they could, according to the will of God revealed in the Scriptures, be fit to be betrusted with the sacred Ordinances of Jesus Christ, in Church-Communion. And therefore I propounded unto them, that they should look out some fit place to begin a Towne, unto which they might resort, and there dwell together, enjoy Government, and be made ready and prepared to be a People among whom the Lord might delight to dwell and Rule.

When they understood the mind of God in this matter, they were desirous to set upon the work: The reallity of which desires, the living have actually expressed, by their performance thereof (in some poor measure) and some of them dying, left their earnest affections and desires with the rest, to set upon that work; especially *Wampooas,* a godly man, of whose death and exhortations that way, I have made some mention in some former Letters.

We accordingly attended thereunto, to search for a fit place, and finally, after sundry journeyes and travells to severall places, the Lord did by his speciall providence, and answer of prayers, pitch us upon the place where we are at *Natick.* Unto which place my purpose at first was to have brought all the Praying *Indians* to Co-habit together: But it so fell out (by the guidance of God, as it now appeareth) that because the *Cohannet Indians* desired a place which they had reserved for themselves, and I finding that I could not at that time pitch there without opposition from some *English,* I refused that place, and pitched at *Natick,* where I found no opposition at present. This choyce of mine did move in the *Cohannet Indians* a jealousie that I had more affection unto those other *Indians,* then unto them. By which occasion (together with some other Providences of God, as the death of *Cutshamoquin,* and the coming of *Josias,* to succeed in the Sachemship in that place) their minds were quite alienated from the place of *Natick,* though not from the work, for they desire to make a Towne in that fore-mentioned place of their owne, named *Ponkipog,* and are now upon the work. And indeed, it now appeareth to be of the Lord, because we cannot have competent accommodations at *Natick,* for those that be there, which are about fifty Lots, more or lesse. And furthermore, by the blessing of God upon the work, there are People, partly prepared, and partly preparing for three Townes more. Insomuch, as that it is most evident, that had I proceeded according to my first intentions, to have called them all unto that one place, we must have been forced very quickly to have scattered againe, for want of accommodations for so great a company of Inhabitants, and so have discouraged them at our first onset of drawing them from their scattered way of living, unto Co-habitation: seeing it would have brought them unto such wants and streights as they could not have grapled withall, but rather would have been occasioned to think there were insuperable difficulties in this enterprise: Whereas in lesser companies they may find a more plentifull and better course of life then they found in that former way out of which they are called; as through Gods mercy, and the bounty of good people in *England,* whose love layeth the foundation-stone of the work, they doe already feele and find at *Natick,* and begin to find at *Ponkipog.*

In prosecution of this work in the year 1650 we began by the Lords assistance our first Towne at *Natick,* where we built a Fort, and one dwelling-house. In the year 51 after Fasting and Prayer about that matter, they gave up themselves and their Children to be governed by the Lord, according to his word, in all wayes of civility, and chose among themselves Rulers of ten, fifty, and an hundred, according to the holy Patterne, so far as they could: In which way of Government the Lord hath not a little owned them, and blessed them.

In the year 52 I perceiving the grace of God in sundry of them, and some poor measure of fitnesse (as I was perswaded) for the enjoyment of Church-fellowship, and Ordinances of Jesus Christ, I moved in that matter, according as I have in the Narration thereof, briefly declared. In the year 53 I moved not that way, for these Reasons.

I having sent their Confessions to be published in *England,* I did much desire to hear what acceptance the Lord gave unto them, in the hearts of his people there, who daily labour at the Throne of grace, and by other expressions of their loves, for an holy birth of this work of the Lord, to the praise of Christ, and the inlargement of his Kingdome. As also my desire was, that by such Books as might be sent hither, the knowledge of their Confessions might be spread here, unto the better and fuller satisfaction of many, then the transacting thereof in the presence of some could doe. These Books came by the latter Ships (as I remember) that were bound for *New-England,* and were but newly out when they set saile, and therefore I had not that answer that year, which my soule desired, though something I had which gave encouragement, and was a tast of what I have more fully heard from severall this year, praised be the Lord.

Besides, there fell a great damping and discouragement upon us, by a jealousie too deeply apprehended, though utterly groundlesse, *viz.* That even these praying *Indians* were in a conspiracy with others, and with the *Dutch,* to doe mischief to the *English.* In which matter, though the ruling part of the People looked otherwise upon them, yet it was no season for me to stir or move in this matter, when the waters were so troubled. This businesse needeth a calmer season, and I shall account it a favour of God when ever he shall please to cause his face to shine upon us in it. Yet this I did the last year, after the Books had been come a season, there being a great meeting at *Boston,* from other Colonies as well as our owne, and the Commissioners being there, I thought it necessary to take that opportunity to prepare and open the way in a readinesse against this present year, by making this Proposition unto them; namely, *That they having now seen their confessions, if upon further triall of them in point of knowledge, they be found to have a competent measure of understanding in the fundamentall points of Religion; and also, if there be due testimony of their conversation, that they walke in a Christian manner according to their light, so that Religion is to be seen in their lives; whether then it be according to God, and acceptable to his people, that they be called up unto Church-estate?* Unto which I had I blesse the Lord, a generall approbation.

Accordingly this year 54 I moved the Elders, that they would give me advice and assistance in this great businesse, & that they would at a fit season examine the *Indians* in point of their knowledge, because we found by the former triall, that a day will be too little (if the Lord please to call them on to Church-fellowship) to examine them in points of Knowledge, and hear their Confessions, and guide them into the holy Covenant of the Lord. Seeing all these things are to be transacted in a strange language, and by Interpreters, and with such a people as they be in these their first beginnings. But if they would spend a day on purpose to examine them in their knowledge, there would be so much the more liberty to doe it fully and throughly (as such a work ought to be) as also when they may be called to gather into Church-Communion, it may suffice that some one of them should make a Doctrinall Confession before the Lord and his people, as the rule of faith which they build upon, the rest attesting their consent unto the same: And themselves (the Elders I mean, if the Lord so far assist the *Indians,* as to give them satisfaction) might testifie that upon Examination they have found a competency of knowledge in them to inable them unto such a work and state. And thus the work might be much shortned, and more comfortably expedited in one day. I found no unreadinesse in the Elders to further this work.

Some dispute there was about Officers in the Church, if they should be found fit matter to proceed, of which I shall anon speak God-willing.

They concluded to attend the work, and for severall Reasons advised that the place should be at *Roxbury,* and not at *Natick,* and that the *Indians* should be called thither, the time they left to me to appoint, in such a season as wherein the

Elders may be at best liberty from other publick occasions. The time appointed was the 13 of the 4 moneth; mean while I dispatched Letters unto such as had knowledge in the Tongue, requesting that they would come and help in Interpretation, or attest unto the truth of my Interpretations. I sent also for my Brother *Mayhu*, who accordingly came, and brought an Interpreter with him. Others whom I had desired, came not. I informed the *Indians* of this appointment, and of the end it was appointed for, which they therefore called, and still doe, when they have occasion to speak of it, *Natootomuhteáe kesuk, A day of asking* Q.*uestions*, or, *A day of Examination*. I advised them to prepare for it, and to pray earnestly about it, that they might be accepted among Gods people, if it were the will of God.

It pleased God so to guide, that there was a publick Fast of all the Churches, betwixt this our appointment, and the accomplishment thereof: which day they kept, as the Churches did, and this businesse of theirs was a Principall matter in their Prayers.

It hath pleased God to lay his hand in sicknesse upon *MoneQ.uassun* our *Natick* Schoolmaster, so that we greatly wanted his help and concurrence in this businesse. Yea, and such is his disease (*viz.* an *Ulcer* in his Lungs) that I fear the Lord will take him away from us, to the great hinderance of our work, in respect of humane means: *Lord increase our faith!*

There fell out a very great discouragement a little before the time, which might have been a scandall unto them, and I doubt not but Satan intended it so; but the Lord improved it to stir up faith and Prayer, and so turned it another way: Thus it was. Three of the unsound sort of such as are among them that pray unto God, who are hemmed in by Relations, and other means, to doe that which their hearts love not; and whose Vices Satan improveth to scandalize and reproach the better sort withall; while many, and some good People are too ready to say they are all alike. I say three of them had gotten severall quarts of Strong-water, (which sundry out of a greedy desire of a little gaine, are too ready to sell unto them, to the offence and grief of the better sort of *Indians,* and of the godly *English* too) and with these liquors, did not onely make themselves drunk, but got a Child of eleven years of age, the Son of *Toteswamp,* whom his Father had sent for a little Corne and Fish to that place near *Watertowne,* where they were. Unto this Child they first gave too spoonfulls of Strong-water, which was more then his head could bear; and another of them put a Bottle, or such like Vessell to his mouth, and caused him to drink till he was very drunk; and then one of them domineered, and said, *Now we will see whether your father will punish us for Drunkennesse* (for he is a Ruler among them) *seeing you are drunk with us for company;* and in this case lay the Child abroad all night. They also fought, and had been severall times Punished formerly for Drunkennesse.

When *Toteswamp* heard of this, it was a great shame and breaking of heart unto him, and he knew not what to doe. The rest of the Rulers with him considered of the matter, they found a complication of many sins together.

1. The sin of Drunkennesse, and that after many former Punishments for the same.

2. A willfull making of the Child drunk, and exposing him to danger also.

3. A degree of reproaching the Rulers.

4. Fighting.

Word was brought to me of it, a little before I took Horse to goe to *Natick* to keep the Sabbath with them, being about ten dayes before the appointed Meeting. The Tidings sunk my spirit extreamly, I did judge it to be the greatest frowne of God that ever I met withall in the work, I could read nothing in it but displeasure, I began to doubt about our intended work: I knew not what to doe, the blacknesse of the sins and the Persons reflected on, made my very heart faile me: For one of the offendors (though least in the offence) was he that hath been my Interpreter, whom I have used in Translating a good part of the Holy Scriptures; and in that respect I saw much of Satans venome, and in God I saw displeasure. For this and some other acts of Apostacy at this time, I had thoughts of casting him off from that work, yet now the Lord hath found a way to humble him. But his Apostacy at this time was a great Tryall, and I did lay him by for that day of our Examination, I used another in his room. Thus Satan aimed at me in this their miscarrying; and *Toteswamp* is a Principall man in the work, as you shall have occasion to see anon God-willing.

By some occasion our Ruling Elder and I being together, I opened the case unto him, and the Lord guided him to speak some gracious words of encouragement unto me, by which the Lord did relieve my spirit; and so I committed the matter and issue unto the Lord, to doe what pleased him, and in so doing my soul was quiet in the Lord. I went on my journey, being the 6 day of the week; when I came at *Natick*, the Rulers had then a Court about it. Soon after I came there, the Rulers came to me with a Question about this matter, they related the whole businesse unto me, with much trouble and grief.

Then *Toteswamp* spake to this purpose, *I am greatly grieved about these things, and now God tryeth me whether I love Christ or my Child best. They say, They will try me; but I say, God will try me. Christ saith, He that loveth father, or mother, or wife, or Child, better then me, is not worthy of me. Christ saith, I must correct my Child, if I should refuse to doe that, I should not love Christ. God bid Abraham kill his Son, Abraham loved God, and therefore he would have done it, had not God with-held him. God saith to me, onely punish your Child, and how can I love God, if I should refuse to doe that?* These things he spake in more words, and much affection, and not with dry eyes: Nor could I refraine from teares to hear him. When it was said, The Child was not so guilty of the sin, as those that made him drunk; he said, *That he was guilty of sin, in that he feared not sin, and in that he did not believe his counsells that he had often given him, to take heed of evill company; but he had believed Satan and sinners more then him, therefore he needed to be punished.* After other such like discourse, the Rulers left me, and went unto their businesse, which they were about before I came, which they did bring unto this conclusion, and judgement, They judged the three men to sit in the stocks a good space of time, and thence to be brought to the whipping-Post, & have each of them twenty lashes. The boy to be put in the stocks a little while, and the next day his father was to whip him in the School, before the Children there; all which Judgement was executed. When they came to be whipt, the Constable fetcht them one after another to the

Tree (which they make use of instead of a Post) where they all received their Punishments: which done, the Rulers spake thus, one of them said, *The Punishments for sin are the Commandements of God, and the worke of God, and his end was, to doe them good, and bring them to repentance.* And upon that ground he did in more words exhort them to repentance, and amendment of life. When he had done, another spake unto them to this purpose, *You are taught in Catechisme, that the wages of sin are all miseries and calamities in this life, and also death, and eternall damnation in hell. Now you feele some smart as the fruit of your sin, and this is to bring you to repentance, that so you may escape the rest.* And in more words he exhorted them to repentance. When he had done, another spake to this purpose, *Heare all yee people* (turning himselfe to the People who stood round about, I think not lesse then two hundred, small and great) *this is the Commandement of the Lord, that thus it should be done unto sinners; and therefore let all take warning by this, that you commit not such sins, least you incur these Punishments.* And with more words he exhorted the People. Others of the Rulers spake also, but some things spoken I understood not, and some things slipt from me: But these which I have related remained with me.

When I returned to *Roxbury,* I related these things to our Elder, to whom I had before related the sin, and my grief: who was much affected to hear it, and magnified God. He said also, That their sin was but a Transient act, which had no Rule, and would vanish: But these Judgements were an Ordinance of God, and would remaine, and doe more good every way, then their sin could doe hurt, telling me what cause I had to be thankfull for such an issue: Which I therefore relate, because the Lord did speak to my heart, in this exigent, by his words.

When the Assembly was met for Examination of the *Indians,* and ordered, I declared the end and Reason of this Meeting, and therefore declared, That any one, in due order, might have liberty to propound any Questions for their satisfaction. Likewise, I requested the Assembly, That if any one doubted of the Interpretations that should be given of their Answers, that they would Propound their doubt, and they should have the words scanned and tryed by the Interpreters, that so all things may be done most clearly. For my desire was to be true to Christ, to their soules, and to the Churches: And the trying out of any of their Answers by the Interpreters, would tend to the satisfaction of such as doubt, as it fell out in one Answer which they gave; the Question was, *How they knew the Scriptures to be the word of God?* The finall Answer was, Because they did find that it did change their hearts, and wrought in them wisedome and humility. This Answer being Interpreted to the Assembly, my Brother *Mahu* doubted, especially of the word *[Hohpoóonk]* signifying *Humility,* it was scanned by the Interpreters, and proved to be right, and he rested satisfied therein. I was purposed my selfe to have written the Elders Questions, and the *Indians* Answers, but I was so imployed in propounding to the *Indians* the Elders Questions, and in returning the *Indians* Answers, as that it was not possible for me to write, unless I had caused the Assembly to stay upon it, which had not been fitting; therefore seeing Mr. *Walton* writing, I did request him to write the Questions and Answers, and help me with a Copy of them, which I thank him, he did, a Copy whereof I herewith send to be inserted in this place, on which, this only I will animadvert, That the Elders in wisdome thought it not fit to ask them in Catechisticall method strictly, in which way Children might Answer: But that they might try whether they understood what they said, they traversed up and downe in Questions of Religion, as here you see.

Postscript.

L ET the Reader take notice, That these Questions were not propounded all to one man, but to sundry, which is the reason that sometime the same Q.uestions are propounded againe and againe. Also the number Examined were about eight, namely. so many as might be first called forth to enter into Church-Covenant, if the Lord give opportunity.

THE
EXAMINATION
OF THE
I N D I A N S
AT
Roxbury,

The 13th Day of the 4th Month, 1 6 5 4.

Hat is God?

Answ: An Ever-living Spirit.

Q. *What are the Atributes of God?*

A. God is Eternall, Infinite, Wise, Holy, Just.

Q. *In which of these are we like unto God?*

A. In Wisedome, Holinesse, and Righteousnesse: But in Infinitenesse and Eternity, God is onely like himselfe.

Q. *How many Gods are there?*

A. There is one onely God.

Q. *Have not some Indians many Gods?*

A. They have many Gods.

Q. *How doe you know these Gods are no Gods?*

A. Before the English came we knew not but that they were Gods, but since they came we know they are no Gods.

Q. *What doe you find in the true God, that you find not in false Gods?*

A. I see in the English many things, that God is the true God.

Q. *What good things see you in the English?*

A. I see true love, that our great *Sachems* have not, and that maketh me think that God is the true God.

Q. *Doe you love God?*

A. A little I love God, my heart wanteth wisedome, but I doe desire to love him.

Q. *Why doe you love God?*

A. Because we are taught this, that when we dye, we must goe to God, and live ever with him.

Q. *Who among the Indians shall goe to God, and what are the signes that they shall goe to God?*

A. Every man that truly believeth in Jesus Christ shall goe to heaven.

Q. *Whether have you not many jealousies and feares that you love not God in truth?*

A. I hope I have some love to God, but I know that I have but little knowledge of him, I hope I love him.

Q. *How doe you understand that God ruleth in your heart?*

A. Before I prayed to God, I knew nothing of God, but since I have been taught, I desire to believe.

Q. *What is faith in Jesus Christ?*

A. I confesse I deserve to be damned for ever, and I am not able to deliver my selfe, but I betrust my soule with Jesus Christ.

Q. *Whether doth not your soule groane within you, under the sense of unbelief, and other sins?*

A. Since I have been taught, I find my selfe very weak, there is a little in me, sometimes my heart mournes, sometimes I desire more.

Q. *How doe you know the word of God is Gods word?*

A. I believe the word that you teach us, was spoken of God.

Q. *Why doe you believe it?*

A. Therefore I believe it to be the word of God, because when we learn it, it teacheth our hearts to be wise and humble.

Q. *Whether are you not your sins, and the temptations of* Hobbomak *more strong since, then before you prayed to God?*

A. Before I preyed to God, I knew not what Satans temptations were.

Q. *Doe you know now?*

A. Now I have heard what Satans temptations are.

Q. *What is a temptation of the Devill in your heart, doe you understand what it is?*

A. Within my heart there are Hypocrisies, which doe not appear without.

Q. *Whether doe not you find this a principall temptation from the wickednesse of your heart, to drive you away from Christ, and not to believe the gracious Promises in Jesus Christ? Or whether when you find wickednesse in your heart, you are not tempted, that you cannot believe?*

A. My heart doth strongly desire to goe on in sin, but this is a strong temptation, but Faith is the work of Jesus Christ.

Q. *Why doe some believe in Christ, and not others, what maketh the difference?*

A. Because Satan speaks to some, and bids them not believe, and they hearken to him, and God speaks to others, and they believe God.

Q. *Why doe they believe God?*

A. It is the work of the Spirit of God, teaching them to believe in Jesus Christ.

> Another Indian being asked what he could say further to it, he Answered, *Jesus Christ sendeth his Spirit into their hearts, and teacheth them.*

Q. *What moveth Jesus Christ to send his Spirit, whether any thing in your selfe?*

A. I believe, the Promise of God.

Q. Whether doe you indeed believe there is a God, Christ, Heaven, Hell, whether have you any doubts concerning these things, or no?

A. I doe but a little know my owne thoughts, but God throughly knoweth my heart, I desire to believe these things, I desire not to be an Hypocrite.

> *It being put to another Indian for further answer, he answered,* My heart desires truly to pray unto God, and I more and more desire to believe these things. When I am taught by the word Preached, I desire to believe in particular, I desire to believe as long as I live.

Q. What is the Word of God?

A. That wherein God hath written his Will, and therein taught the way to Heaven.

Q. What is sin?

A. There is the root sin, an evill heart; and there is actuall sin, sin is a breaking of the Law of God.

Q. Wherein doe you breake the Law of God?

A. Every day in my heart, words, and works.

Q. Why are you troubled for sin, that none ever knew but your selfe?

A. I fear God, and Jesus Christ.

Q. What doe you believe about the immortality of the soule, and resurrection of the body? doth the soule dye when the body dyeth?

A. I believe, when the body of a good man dyeth, the Angels carry his soule to heaven, when a wicked man dyeth, the Devills carry his soule to hell.

Q. How long shall they be in that state?

A. Untill Christ cometh to Judgement.

Q. When Christ cometh to judge the world, what then shall become of them?

A. The dead bodies of all men shall rise againe,

Q. Whether shall they ever dye any more?

A. Good men shall never dye any more.

Q. Whether doe you believe that these very bodies of ours shall rise againe?

A. This body which rots in the earth, this very body, God maketh it new.

Q. Who is Jesus Christ?

A. Jesus Christ is the Son of God, yet borne man, and so both God and man.

Q. Why was Christ Jesus a man?

A. That he might dye for us.

Q. Why is Christ Jesus God?

A. That his death might be of great value.

Q. Why doe you say, Christ Jesus was a man that he might dye, doe onely men dye?

A. He dyed for our sins.

Q. What reason or justice is there, that Christ should dye for our sins?

A. God made all the world, and man sinned, therefore it was necessary Christ should dye to carry men up to Heaven. God hath given unto us his Son Jesus Christ, because of our sins.

The Question being put to another for further Answer, his
Answer was, *That God so loved the word, that he gave
his onely begotten Son, that whosoever believeth in him
should not perish, but have everlasting life.*

Q. *What is God?*

A. An Ever-living Spirit.

Q. *What are the Attributes of God?*

A. As before.

Q. *In these Attributes wherein are we like God?*

A. As before.

Q. *How many Gods are there?*

A. One onely God, but he is three, the Father, the Son, and the Holy Ghost?

Q. *What is Eternall?*

A. Man is not like God in Eternall being.

Q. *What is infinite?*

A. All the World hath an end, but God hath no end.

Q. *Had God any beginning?*

A. No, but he is ever.

Q. *Was there alwayes an Heaven and Earth, how came they to be?*

A. *Jehovah* made them, and Governeth them all.

Q. *Were they ever?*

A. No.

Q. *How did God make the world?*

A. Onely the Will of God.

Q. *Out of what matter did God make the world?*

A. Not of any thing at all.

Q. *How long was God making the world?*

A. Six dayes.

Q. *How cometh it to passe that the Sun riseth and setteth, that there is
winter and Summer, day and night?*

A. All are the work of God.

Q. *Now the world is made, can it keepe it selfe? By whose strength is it kept
together?*

A. God preserveth it, he made it, and keeps it all.

Q. *In what condition was man made?*

A. Very good, like unto God.

Q. *What is the Image of God in man?*

A. Holinesse, Wisedome, and Righteousnesse.

Q. *Was there then any sin in the soule of man?*

A. No.

Q. *What Covenant did God make with Adam?*

A. A Covenant of Works, *Doe this and live,* thou and thy Children, *Sin, and
dye,* thou and thy Children.

Q. *How many Commandements are there?*

A. Ten.

Q. *What is the first Commandement?*

A. God spake these words, and said, *Thou shalt have no other God but me.*

Q. What was the sin of Adam?

A. He believed the Devil, and eat of the Tree in the midst of the Garden, of which God commanded him not to eat.

Q. When Adam *sinned, what befell him?*

A. He lost the Image of God.

Q. What is the Image of God, which he lost?

A. Wisedome, Holinesse, and Righteousnesse.

Q. To whom is man now like?

A. He is like unto Satan.

Q. What is the likenesse to Satan?

A. He is Unholy, Foolish, and Unrighteous.

Q. How many kinds of sin are there?

A. An evill heart, and evill works

Q. What doe you call it?

A. We daily break Gods Commandements, and there is the root sin.

Q. What is the wages of sin?

A. All miseries in this life, and death, and damnation.

Q. Whose wages is death?

A. All unbelievers.

Q. Seeing but one man Adam *sinned, how come all to dye?*

A. Adam deserved for us all, that we should dye.

> *The Question being put to another for further answer, he answered,* Adam *was the first man, and father of all men, and in him we sinned.*

Q. Who is Jesus Christ?

   A. Christ is God, born like man, God and man in one person.

Q. Why was Christ man?

A. That he might dye.

Q. Why was Christ God?

A. That his death might be of great value.

Q. How many are the Offices of Christ?

A. Three. A Priest, a Prophet, a King.

Q. What Sacrifice did Christ offer?

A. His owne body.

Q. What hath Christ done for us?

A. He hath dyed for us.

Q. What death dyed Christ for us? Who put him to death?

A. Wicked men.

Q. What else hath Christ done for us?

A. He hath kept all the Commandements of God for us, and also dyed for us.

Q. What hath Christ deserved, or merited for us?

A. Pardon of sin, and eternall life.

Q. The same question was asked another, *What hath Christ merited?*

A. Pardon of all our sins, because he paid a ransome, the favour of God, and Eternall life.

Q. *What else hath Christ done for us?*

A. He rose again, and ascended into Heaven.

Q. *What doth Christ in heaven for us?*

A. He appeareth for us before God, he prayeth for us, and giveth us the New Covenant.

Q. *What is the New Covenant?*

A. The Covenant of Grace, Repent and believe in Christ, and be saved.

Q. *Shall all men be saved by Jesus Christ?*

A. All that believe in Christ shall goe to heaven, and be saved.

Q. *Why doth they heart desire Jesus Christ more then sin, and thy former Idolls?*

A. Before we prayed to God, I did not desire Jesus Christ, I did desire my sins, but now I see my need of Jesus Christ.

Q. *Why doe you need Christ?*

A. When I dye, Christ carrieth my soule to heaven.

> *The same put to another for further answer, he answered,* We need Jesus Christ, because we are full of sinne.

Q. *How doth Christ work Grace in our hearts?*

A. I beleive Christ hath sent his Spirit into my heart by his word.

Q. *What is repentance for sinne?*

A. I am ashamed of my selfe, and broken is my heart, I hate, and am aware of all sin.

Q. *What most of all breaks your heart, why is your heart broken?*

A. Because I have sinned against God.

Q. *What see you in sin that breaks your heart?*

A. It is not my owne work, but Christ sends his Spirit, and breaks my heart.

Q. *What doth he put into your heart, that causeth your heart to break?*

A. The Spirit.

Q. *What wounds your heart most, because you sin, or because you must goe to hell?*

A. Because we must goe to hell.

Q. *When you heare that* Adam *by his sin deserved eternall death, and when you hear of the grace of God sending Jesus to save you, which of these break your heart most?*

A. Pardon of sin goeth deepest.

Q. *What worke of the Spirit finde you in your heart?*

A. The Spirit of God breaketh my heart to repent of all my sin, and turneth me from sin to believe in Jesus Christ.

Q. *Whether have you found at any time any such worke in your selfe?*

A. I am ashamed of my selfe, I doe not throughly find it in my heart to be so.

Q. *When God sendeth his Spirit, what doth it worke in us?*

A. A change of the heart.

Q. *What change hath God wrought in you of late, which was not in you in former times?*

A. The Spirit turneth us from our sins, to believe in Jesus Christ.

Q. Doe you finde this in your heart, that your heart is turned from your sins?

A. I find my heart turned, I leave my stealing, lying, lust, and now my heart believeth in Jesus Christ.

Q. Doe you believe in Jesus Christ?

A. I doe believe in Jesus Christ.

Q. What is it to believe in Jesus Christ?

A. I confesse I deserve to be damned, and am not able to deliver my selfe, and therefore I doe give up my selfe unto Jesus Christ, and trust in him, casting away my sins.

Q. Why doe you cast away your sins?

A. They make me that I cannot love Jesus Christ.

Q. Is there any Promise set home on your heart that comforteth you, what Promise doe you remember?

A. I believe the Promise of God, that he will pardon believers in Jesus Christ.

So far they proceeded in Questions and Answers.

Some or other of the Elders did severall times publickly call upon the Interpreters, to be attentive to all things that passed, because they must relye upon their testimony, or to that purpose, praying them to speak if they doubted of any thing.

In the conclusion, the Elders saw good to call upon the Interpreters to give a publick testimony to the truth of Mr. *Eliots* Interpretations of the *Indians* Answers, which Mr. *Mahu,* and the two Interpreters by him, did, all speaking one after another, to this purpose, *That the Interpretations which Mr.* Eliot *gave of their Answers, was for the substance the same which the Indians answered, many times the very words which they spake, and alwayes the sense.*

WILLIAM WALTON.

WHen the day was well spent, in this above-written manner, some that were aged desired that an end might be put unto this work for this time, because by this tast which they had, they saw that which gave them comfortable satisfaction. Then I desired that (if it might be without prejudice to any) they might be further tryed with Questions about Christ, and grace wrought in us by the Spirit; and about the Ordinances of Christ (concerning which, no Questions had been yet propounded) and also about the estate of man after death, of the resurrection of the dead, and of the last Judgement, wherein they were, through the grace of Christ, in some measure instructed. But it was said, that they did perceive that they were instructed in points of Catechisme, by what they had heard from them. When they came to a conclusion, one of the Elders (*viz.* Mr. *Ezek: Rogers*) having first privately conferred with such of the Elders as sate near him, spake words of acceptance and encouragement both to me, and to the *Indians*, in the name of the rest. But Mr. *Walton* did not write them, and therefore I omit the rehearsing of them.

This great and solemne work of calling up these poor *Indians* unto that Gospel light and beauty of visible Church-estate, having now passed through a second Tryall: In former whereof, they expressed what experience they had found of Gods grace in their hearts, turning them from dead works, to seek after the living God, and salvation in our Saviour Jesus Christ. In this second they have in some measure declared how far the Lord hath let in the light of the good knowledge of God into their soules, and what tast they have of the Principles of Religion, and doctrine of salvation. Now the Question remaineth, *What shall we further doe? And when shall they enjoy the Ordinances of Jesus Christ in Church-estate?*

The work is very solemne, and the Question needeth a solemn Answer. It is a great matter to betrust those with the holy priviledges of Gods house, upon which the name of Christ is so much called, who have so little knowledge and experience in the wayes of Christ, so newly come out of that great depth of darknesse, and wild course of life; in such danger of polluting and defiling the name of Christ among their barbarous friends and Countrey-men; and under so many doubts and jealousies of many people; and having not yet stood in the wayes of Christ so long, as to give sufficient proof and experience of their stedfastnesse in their new begun profession. Being also the first Church gathering among them, it is like to be a pattern and president of after proceedings, even unto following Generations. Hence it is very needfull that this proceeding of ours at first, be with all care and warinesse guided, for the most effectuall advancement of the holinesse and honour of Jesus Christ among them.

Upon such like grounds as these, though I and some others know more of the sincerity of some of them, then others doe, and are better satisfied with them: Yet because I may be in a temptation on that hand, I am well content to make slow hast in this matter, remembring that word of God, *Lay hands suddenly upon no man* Gods works among men, doe usually goe on slowly, and he that goeth slowly, doth usually goe most surely, especially when he goeth by counsell. *Sat cito si sat bene*, the greater proof we have of them, the better approbation they may obtain at last. Besides, we having had one publick meeting about them already this summer, it will be difficult to compasse another, for we have many other great occasions, which may hinder the same, and it is an hard matter to get Interpreters together to attend such a work, they living so remote. The dayes also will soon grow short, and the nights cold, which will be an hindrance in the attendance unto the accomplishment of that work, which will most fitly be done at *Natick*.

But above all other Reasons this is greatest, that they living in sundry Towns and places remote from each other, and labourers few to take care of them, it is necessary that some of themselves should be trained up, and peculiarly instructed, unto whom the care of ruling and ordering of them in the affaires of Gods house may be committed, in the absence of such as look after their instruction. So that this is now the thing we desire to attend, for the comfort of our little *Sister that hath no breasts*, that such may be trained up, and prepared, unto whom the charge of the rest may be committed in the Lord. And upon this ground we make the slower hast to accomplish this work among them. Mean while I hope the Commissioners will afford some encouragement for the furtherance of the instruction of some of the most godly and able among them, who may be in a speciall manner helpfull unto the rest, in due order and season.

And thus have I briefly set down our present state in respect of our Ecclesiasticall proceedings. I beg the prayers of the good people of the Lord, to be particularly present at the Throne of Grace, in these matters, according as you have hereby a particular Information how our condition is. And for me also, who am the most unfit in humane reason for such a work as this, but my soule desireth to depend and live upon the Lord Jesus, and fetch all help, grace, mercy, assistance, and supply from him. And herein I doe improve his faithfull Covenant and Promises, and in perticular, the Lord doth cause my soule to live upon that word of his, *Psal.* 3 7.3,4,5,6,7. wherein I have food, rayment, and all necessaries for my selfe and Children (whom I have dedicated unto the Lord, to serve him in this work of his, if he will please to accept of them) and this supply I live upon in these rich words of gracious Promise, *vers.* 3. *Trust in the Lord, and doe good, dwell in the Land, and verily thou shalt be fed.*

Herein also I find supply of grace to believe the conversion of these poor *Indians, &* that not only in this present season, in what I doe already see, but in the future also, further then by mine eye or reason I can see. Which supply of grace, I live upon in those words of his gracious Promise, which I apply and improve in this particular respect, *vers.* 4. *Delight thy selfe also in the Lord, and he shall give thee the desires of thy heart.*

Herein also I find supply of grace to believe, that they shall be in Gods season, which is the fittest, brought into Church-Estate; faith fetching this particular blessing out of the rich Fountaine of those gracious words of Promise, *Commit thy way unto the Lord, trust also in him, and he shall bring it to passe.*

Herein also my soule is strengthned and quieted, to stay upon the Lord and to be supported against all suspitious jealousies, hard speeches, and unkindnesses of men touching the sincerity and reallity of this work, and about my carriage of matters, and supply herein. Which grace my soule receiveth by a particular improvement of that rich treasury of the Promise in these words, *vers.* 6. *And he shall bring forth thy righteousnesse as the light, and thy judgement as the noon day.* And herein likewise I find supply of grace, to wait patiently for the Lords time, when year after year, and time after time, I meet with disappointments. Which grace I receive from the commanding force of that gracious Promise, *vers.* 7. *Rest in the Lord, and wait patiently for him, fret not thy selfe,* either for one cause, or for another. Thus I live, and thus I labour, here I have supply, and here is my hope, I beg the help of prayers, that I may still so live and labour in the Lords work, and that I may so live and dye.

T*He Corporation (appointed by Act of Parliament) for Propagation of the Gospel amongst the Heathen Natives in*

New-England, *desire all men to take notice, That such as desire to be satisfied how the moneys Collected, are disposed of, may (if they please) repaire to* Coopers Hall, London, *any* Saturday, *between the houres of Nine and Twelve in the forenoone, where the said Corporation meet.*

FINIS.

A further Accompt

of the Progresse of the

GOSPEL

amongst the *INDIANS*

IN

NEW-ENGLAND,

AND

Of the means used effectually to advance the same.

SET FORTH

In certaine Letters sent from thence declaring a purpose of Printing the Scriptures in the *Indian* Tongue into which they are already Translated.

With which Letters are likewise sent an Epitome of some Exhortations delivered by the *Indians* at a fast, as Testimonies of their obedience to the Gospell.

As also some helps directing the *Indians* how to improve naturall reason unto the knowledge of the true God.

LONDON, Printed by *M. Simmons* for the Corporation of *New-England*, 1659.

A further Accompt

of the Progresse of the

G O S P E L

amongst the *I N D I A N S*

I N

NEW-ENGLAND,

AND

Of the means used effectually to advance the same.

S E T   F O R T H

In certaine Letters sent from thence declaring a
purpose of Printing the Scriptures in the
Indian Tongue into which they are already
Translated.

With which Letters are likewise sent an Epitome of some Exhortations delivered by the *Indians* at a fast, as Testimonies of their obedience to the Gospell.
As also some helps directing the *Indians* how to
improve naturall reason unto the knowledge
of the true God.

LONDON, Printed by *M. Simmons* for the Corporation of New-England, 1659.

TO THE
CRISTIAN READER.

Beloved Brethren,

A S it is the Ardent prayer of all that love the Lord Jesus in sincerity, that his Kingdome may be enlarged, and the glorious light of the Gospell may shine forth into all Nations, that all the ends of the world may see the salvation of our God, that the Stone cut out without hands may become so great a mountaine as to fill the Earth, that the Idols may be utterly abolished, and the Gods of the Earth famished, and that all the Isles of the Heathen may worship the only true God [Psal. 67.3-5. Psal. 22.27, 98.3. Dan. 2.25. Isa. 2.18. Zeph 2.11.]: so the strange & scarcely to be paraleld concussions which have been in the world of late yeares, and so still continue, may seeme to be no improbable harbingers of the more glorious manifestations of Christ thereunto, in answer to those desires of his servants. For the Shaking of all Nations maketh way for the coming of him, who is the desire of all Nations. The wind, and the earthquake, and the fire did usher in the still voyce which spoke unto Eliah [Hag. 2.7. 1 King. 19.11,12,13.]. When the Spirit came down upon the Apostles, there was a sound as of a rushing mighty wind, and the house was shaken, when the people therein were to be filled with the holy Ghost [Act. 2.2.].

How much those winds and shakings which carried many good men out of Old into New England have made way to the publishing of the name of Christ in those barbarous places. How the day of small things hath not been altogether despicable there, How the leaven of the Gospell doth still continue to season more of the lump, as it hath by many former published specimina been demonstrated, so these papers now printed by the care of the Corporation for New-England do give us further evidence & assurance thereof. And truly it cannot but be matter both of abundant thanksgivings to God, to find poor Americans speking the languag of Canaan [Isa. 19.18.], subscribing with their hand unto the Lord, and sirnaming themselves by the name of Israel [Isa. 44.5.] & also of great comfort and encouragement unto all those whose hearts the

Lord hath stirred up, either here in a way of liberall contribution, to honour him with their substance, and to bring their Silver and Gold unto the name of the Lord, that their merchandize may be Holinesse unto him [Prov. 3.9. Numb 15.19. Isa 60.9. Isa. 23.18.]: *or there, in a way of labour and service, setting their heart and hand to snatch poor souls as* brands out of the fire, *to see such a signall blessing upon their paines and prayers, and such seeds of the* Everlasting Gospel *come up in so barren and desolate a soile, making way unto a plentifull harvest for those who shall after enter upon their labours. No monies, no studies will make a more ample returne then those which are up in heaven, which are laid laid out upon building the house of God* [1 Tim. 6.17,18,19.]. *If* David *and his princes did praise the Lord, for that they were able* to offer so willingly *towards the Erecting of a* materiall Temple, *for which was gathered one of the greatest summs, as some learned judge, that we read of in any history, how much reason have we to blesse God when he giveth us hearts to offer willingly towards the building of* living and spirituall Temples, *and when he letteth us see so glorious a returne to our prayers, contributions, and labours in the conversion of many souls unto God.* [1Chron. 29.14. Nehem. 4.6. Exod. 35.5. Brierwood de rummis Indæorum, *cap*.6].

To the end that God may be glorified, good men, who have already furthered this excellent work, may be comforted, and others excited and provoked to put to their hand unto the advancement thereof, are these papers published, being testimonies of the great zeale and care of our Brethren there to promote the Gospell, and of the blessing of God on their labours, in the professed subjection *of many poor soules thereunto.*

Two great works we find here further undertaken in order to that service.

The one some helps and directions to the *Indians* how to improve their naturall reason unto the knowledg of the true God. *The reason why there is so short and imperfect a* specimen *given of it is, because the ships came away from* New-England, *before any more of the Copy was wrought off from the presse. It is a work likely to be by the blessing of God of singular use to the natives there, and a very proper and necessary course for those to take who would convert and perswade* Pagans *to beleeve the Truth.*

The Lord was pleased at the first preaching of the Gospel *to confirme it with* signs and wonders following *for the more speedy planting of it by only twelve, and those possibly aged men, in so many places of the world* [Mark 16.20. Act. 14.3. Heb. 2.4.]. *And how farre he may still bear witnesse thereunto, not only by the holy lives of Christians, but by eminent and remarkable providences, which may tantamount to miracles, I shall not here inquire. But certainly here may be much use made of* naturall reason, *to demonstrate unto* Pagans *the falsenesse of the way they are in, and so to prepare a way for entertainment of the Truth. Though the Doctrine of the* Gospel *be* supernaturall, *and not investigable by humane disquisition, be{i}ng made known to men and Angells onely by the* Revelation *of the Holy Spirit* [I Cor. 2.9,10 Gal.1.12. Matth.16.17.]: *yet when it is revealed, the awakening of* Legall impressions *in the* naturall conscience, *will provoke men to attend, & prepare them to entertain it, when it shall be preached unto them.*

1. *All men have in them a desire of* Happinesse, *and an aversation from misery* [Aristot. Ethic {illeg.}].

2. *All men more or lesse have some indeleble impressions of a* Godhead, *which cannot be utterly worne out, heathen Philosophers have acknowledged that no nation in the world is so barbarous where the confession and adoration of a Deity is not to be found.* [Nulla gens est neq; tam immansueta, neq; tam sera, quæ non, etiamsi ignoret qualem habe re deum deceat, tamen habendum sciat. Cicero de legibus, lib. I. Deum agnoscis ex operibus ejus Tuscul. qu. Q I. Nulla gens tam sera, nemo omnium tam immanis, cujus mentem non imbuerit dei opinio.]

3. *There are innate præsensions of the* Immortality *of the soul within it selfe, for Heathen Philosophers have by the light of nature discover'd and acknowledg'd it* [*Pluto* in Phædro, et apud *Plutarch* consolat ad *Appollon. Cicero* de senectute. Senec. Epst. 118. consolat ad *Polyb c.* 28. Ibid. Senec Ep. 118.]

4. *There is a natural* σωλήρησις *or habit of* morall *and practicall principles, and consequently there are naturall impressions of guilt and fear upon the conscience, and tacit evidences of judgment due unto the workers of iniquity,* An heathen Poet [Juvenal. Tertul{ian}. lib. de Testimonio aminæ.] *could say,* Frigida mens est Criminibus, tacitâ sudant præcordia culpâ.

5. *There being in all men a naturall desire of* Good, *and a naturall Testimony of Conscience that* God *is the giver of it, so that when evills are upon them which they cannot remove themselves, they naturally call out for a divine helpe above them to give them deliverance; from hence it cometh to passe, that there are innate apprehensions of some* Religion *necessary, in order to the knowledge and service of a* God, *as a requisite* means *to the obtaining of so desireable an end as* Happinesse *is.*

6. *Since it is exactly consonant to right reason, that he to whom service is due, should direct and prescribe the way whereby he will be served (for to serve another is to do that which he willeth to be done:) It is therefore necessary that the way of service and* Religion *be revealed unto us from God.*

7. *Because these premises are indelebly written in the minds of men by nature, Therefore* Satan *not being able, as* Prince of this world [Joh. 12.31. 16.11] *alone, to carry men on in a quiet way of wickednesse, without some face of* Religion *and worship amongst them, hath invaded the name of a* God, *and made himselfe* God of this world [2 Corr. 4.4], *and as a* God, *hath set up various wayes of* wicked worship *consistent with his other principles and laws of* wicked lusts, *thereby to bind men the faster unto himselfe,* ut fiant miseris delicta religiosa, *as* Cyprian *speaks, that men might be tied by their Religion unto wickednesse.*

Now the work of Christ *in the* Gospel *is.* 1. *As he is* Prince of righteousnesse *to destroy the* lusts *and works of the Devill.* 2. *As he is* God blessed for ever, *to abolish the* Idols, *to famish the Gods, and to turne men from vanities unto the living God which made heaven and earth.* [Heb. 7.2. I Joh 3.8. Rom. 9.5 Act. 14.15.].

This to doe, we may in this manner proceed with an heathen who knows not God. We may convince him by his own naturall and implanted light.

1. *That there is a* God *who is righteous and holy, who cannot be deceived, will not be mocked.*

2. *That this God hath implanted in all men a light and* law of nature *by which they are to walk* [Rom. 2.14,15].

3. *That he, with whose soul we deale, hath violated that light and law of nature, and is thereby become a* sinner [Rom. 1.29,30. 3.9.].

4. *That sinne is attended with* guilt *and punishment, & bindeth the sinner over unto* death *and judgment* [Rom. 1.32].

5. *That there is in him a naturall desire to be delivered from* death *and to be happy.*

6. *That he is not able by any strength or power of his own to free himselfe from death, or to make himselfe happy.*

7. *That that way of worship and service which he trusteth in for this deliverance, will never be able to effect it for him. For the vanity of* Idolatrous *and* Satanicall *worship may by evidence of Reason, and by the inherent characters of impurity and absurdity within it selfe, be demonstrated. By that way the Lord in Scripture usually doth disprove it.* Deut. 4.28. Psal. 115.4,8. Isa. 41.24,28. Isa. 44.9,20. Isa. 46.1.9. Jer. 10.3,11. Habak. 2.18,20. Act. 14.15,17. Act 17.23,31. Rom. 1.23,25.

8. *Being thus brought into straits and extremities, and reduced* ad impossibile *very self-love, awakened by the spirit of bondage, will dictate unto a man, when he is convinced of being utterly out of the way, to inquire* what he shall do to be saved, *and to listen unto that, which is by credible persons reported to be the right way* [Acts 16.30.].

9. *Being thus perswaded to look into the* Gospel, *which is represented unto him as the alone way unto salvation. He findeth inherent characters of* purity, Sanctity, *and spiritual* beauty *in it. He considereth the* miracles *and* Martyrdomes *whereby it hath been confirmed (which he hath no more reason to distrust then the truth of any other history) He considereth the* prevalency *of it in the world by the ministry of twelve poor men, notwithstanding all the persecutions which have been from time to time raised against it. He considereth the holy lives of the Professors of it, whereby the wicked lusts which his impure religion alloweth, are shamed and rebuked. He considereth the* nature of it *wholly contrary to carnall and secular interests, no way complying with, or giving the least countenance unto any sinfull delights: so that it is evident that it was not contrived or obtruded upon men by humane wisdome, or to gratifie any carnall designe upon these and the like considerations being set on by the finger of the holy Spirit, he is perswaded to beleeve the Gospel, and by beleeving comes to reape those Joyes and comforts as make him know whom he hath beleeved* [Pet. 1.8. *Rom.* 15.13.2 *Tim.* 1.12].

The other work which is set about in order to the premoting of the Gospel *amongst the poor Indians is the* translating of the Scripture *into their tongue, and Printing it for their use, which as it is a necessary and an excellent worke, and a work of great labour (in consideration whereof the Reverend Translator deserveth great thanks and encouragement) so will it be a worke of cost and charges to provide paper, workmen, and letters for so large a work. And therefore, as men, when the foundation of a goodly building is going about, will lay a stone with their own hands, to shew some bounty and encouragement to the workmen who are to carry it on; so the laying of this* foundation stone *seemeth to call unto all those whose hearts the Lord hath made willing, to give in their helping hand and chearfull assistance, unto a work tending so immediately to the Salvation of souls and glory of that God, who hath promised, That* they who sow bountifully shall reape bountifully, *who will* multiply their seed sown, and increase the fruit of their righteousnesse. *Certainly if Christ look on the supplies which are given to his poor brethren for their* bodily *reliefe, as given to* himselfe; *much more will he accept and reward the endeavours of those, who lay out their* bounty, *as he did his* blood, *for the good of mens souls, and for the advancement of his kingdome. To his blessing I commend you, and this excellent service*

1 Aprill 1659.

> Yours, and the Churches
> Servant in our Com-
> mon Lord.

Ed: Reynolds.

This following Letter is sent from the Commisioners for the united Colonies of *New-England* in *New-England*, and directed as followeth.

For the much honoured Corporation for the propagation of the Gospel amongst the Indians *in* New-England, *these present.*

Honoured and worthy Gentlemen.

BY our last of 16th instant, we certified you of our purpose to send Mr *Peirsons* Chatichisme by the first opportunity to be Printed in *England*; Since which time; it is come unto our hands but upon further consideration in regard of the hazard of sending, and difficulty of true Printing it; without a fit overseer of the presse by one skilled in the language; we have chosen rather to have it printed here; and accordingly have taken order for the same; and hope it will be finished within three months, we have sent you herewith the accounts of this years disbursements in reference to the *Indian* work, & shall be ready to attend your advice in any particular therein mentioned. Many charges will be dayly growing, but we hope there will be sufficient in Mr *Ushers* hands to discharge the same till the Spring: and for after supply to carry on the work be pleased to take notice that we have drawn upon you three Bills of Exchange of one tenure and date for five hundred pounds to be payd to Mr *John Harwood* for the use of Mr *Hezekiah Usher*, and have taken his Bill to satisfie so much here, according to his former agreement with us, we pray you to take care it be duely paid at the day, without which the worke cannot be comfortably carryed on, it is our joynt and unfeigned desires with you; that those gifts and contributions may be improved according to the pious minds of the Donors; for the promoting the knowledge of God in Jesus Christ amongst these poore Natives; and we hope and beleeve there is a reall good effect in severall places, which that it may dayly increase to the bringing of many poor souls to heaven, is the earnest prayer of

Boston 22. *Sept.*
1658.

GENTLEMEN,
Your very loving friends and Servants,
The Commissioners of the
united Colonies.

John Endicott President	*John Winthorpe*
Simon Bradstreete	*John Talcot*
Thomas Prence	*Francis Newman*
Josiah Winslow	*William Leete*

A Letter from Mr *John Eliot* directed unto Mr *Richard Floyd* Treasurer of the corporation for *New England*.

To his much respected and Christian friend Mr Floyd *Treasurer of the Corporation for promoting Religion among the* Indians *in New-England.   these present.* {sic}

Christian Friend and Beloved in the Lord.

Fter Salutations in the Lord Jesus. I shall not trouble you with any thing at present save this one businesse of moment, touching the Printing of the Bible in the *Indian* Language, touching which businesse sundry of the Elders did petition unto the Commissioners, moving them to further it, as a principall means of promoting Religion among them. And God so guided (without mans contrivance) that I was there when it came in. They moved this doubt whether the Translation I had made was generally understood? to which I answered, that upon my knowledge it was understood as farre as *Conecticot* [*Conecticot* is about 100 miles up in the Country.]: for there I did read some part of my Translation before many hundred English Witnesses, and the *Indians* manifested that they did understand what I read, perfectly, in respect of the language, they further questioned whether I had expressed the Translation in true language? I answered that I feared after times will find many infirmities in it, all humane works are subject to infirmity, yet those pieces that were printed, *viz. Genesis* and *Matthew,* I had sent to such as I thought had best skill in the language, and intreated their animadversions, but I heard not of any faults they found. When the Commissioners ended their meeting, they did commit the further consideration of this matter to our Commissioners, as I understand, of whom our Governour is president. Therefore at the coming away of this Ship, I repaired to the Governour about it. I proposed this expedient, for the more easie prosecution of this work, *viz.* that your selves might be moved to hire some honest young man, who hath skill to compose (and the more skill in other parts of the work, the better) send him over as your servant, pay him there to his content, or ingage payment, let him serve you here in *New-England* at the presse in *Harvard* Colledge, and work under the Colledg Printer, in impressing the Bible in the *Indian* language, and with him send a convenient stock of Paper to begin withall. The Governour was pleased to send for Mr *Norton* to advise in it, who came and did heartily further it, whereupon the Governour promised to write unto your selves, and propose the matter, which also I doe, and doe earnestly intreat your assistance herein. And I beseech the Lord to bow your hearts, and incourage you in promoting so good a work, so profitable for the furtherance of Religion, which to further in the best manner, I know is already the bent of your hearts, and your constant prayer and indeavour, and thus committing you, and all your weighty affaires unto the Lord, I rest

Roxbury this 28 of   *Yours to serve you in the*
  the 10th 1 6 5 8.   *Service of Christ.*

John Elliot.

A Letter from *John Endicott* Esq; President of the Commissioners for the united Colonies in *New-England* to the Corporation here in *ENGLAND*.

For Mr Richard Floyd *Treasurer and the rest of the Gentlemen of the Corporation for the affaires of* New-England.   *these.*

Honourable Gentlemen.

I Have been moved by divers able and godly men here with us to propound unto your pious consideration, whether it be not needful for the better instruction of the *Indians* amongst us in the true knowledge of God, to get the whole Bible of the old and new Testament, which is already Translated into the *Indian* tongue, to be printed; Many here with us Divines and others judge it a thing that will be acceptable to God, and very profitable for the poor Heathens. If your selves doe so esteeme of it too, it will be necessary to provide paper and letters and such things as may further the work, as also a Journey man Printer to be helpefull under Mr *Greene* our Printer to expedite the work. This is only propounded to your serious consideration, which if God please to put into your hearts to further, being so good a work; It will rejoyce the hearts of many godly ones here, and I doubt not of many there also. The rest of the Commissioners being gone home to their own dwellings, and none left here at Boston of the Commissioners but my selfe: and the Ship being ready to set sayle I have made bold to write these few lines unto you, and leave the issue of all to God, and your godly wisdomes: Mr *Eliot* will be ready at all times to correct the sheets as fast as they are Printed, and desireth nothing for his paines. I shall not trouble you further at this time, but shall desire the Lord so to guide you in all your affaires; as God may have the glory of all, and your selves comfort and peace. So prayeth

Boston the 28 of   *Your Unworthy*
Decem. 1658.   *Servant.*

John Endicott.

Here followes another Letter from Mr *John Eliot* of *New England,* directed to the Corporation, *viz.*

To the Honourable Corporation for spreading the Gospell among the Poor *Indians* in New England.
these present.

Christian Gentlemen, and much honoured in the Lord.

Y Our constant prayers and paines for the promoting of the Kingdome of Christ Jesus in these ends of the earth, among these our poor Indians, is a work of sweet favour unto the Lord: and your labour of love bestowed therein; shall be assuredly rewarded, when the Lord shall say unto you (out of the riches of his free Grace) Come ye blessed of my Father, &c. and, what you did unto them, you did it unto me, and in that day, Blessed is the man who hath his hands full of such free will offerings. The Lord hath give us the amazing blow to take away my brother Mayhew [Mr Mayhew was cast away coming over from New-England, with an Indian who was a Preacher amongst the Indians]. His aged Father doth his endeavour to uphold the worke among the poor Indians, whom by letters I have incouraged what I can, and moved in his behalfe, our Commissioners, and they have given him some incouragement, so that the work in that place is not fallen to the ground, I blesse the Lord for it. As for the work among us, I shall for the present be silent, for severall Reasons, only let the work it selfe speake. I am bold to present you here inclosed, with a few notes which my Sonne and I gathered up, which were delivered by the persons here named, in a day of fasting and prayer; out of which short notes you may see what life is in the work. The very reason of my gathering up these notes; was because my Sonne (who had not been at a fast among us before) was very much affected with what they delivered, so far as he understood them, and when I had communicated these notes to some, they were very well relished, & thereby I was imboldened to present them to your selves, not knowing, but (if the Lord please) thereby you may have more reall information of their state and progresse, then by any thing which were meet for me to say. For my selfe I feele my strength to decay, and I am not able to doe and bear what I have done, and although temptation may sometime breed waverings, yet my soul doth desire & beleeve, that I shall live and dye in the work. And as I have dedicated my sons to serve the Lord in this work (if he please to accept them) so I doe it as they come up; and this yeare my second son having taken his first degree in the Colledge, I presented him also unto our Commissioners, and he is accepted unto the work: which mercy my soul doth greatly rejoyce in, and I humbly beg your prayers for them, that the Lord would bow their green spirits unto the worke, and inable them to overlooke the difficultyes and discouragements which lye in the way, and thus committing you unto the Lord, and to the guidance of his holy Word, I rest

Roxbury this 10th of   *Yours to serve you*
   the 10th, 1658.   *in the Service of*
                                                   our dear Savior.

                                          John Eliot.

Here followeth a Briefe Epitomy of such Exhortations as
these Indians hereafter named, did deliver upon a late
day of fasting and prayer at *Natick*, much more
largely, 15th of the 9th month, 1658.

The causes of this fast were partly in preparation for gathering a Church, and because of much rain, and sicknesse and other tryalls.

An Exhortation from Waban, *an* Indian,

The Text of Scripture he spake of was,

Matth. 9. 12,13.

12. *But when Jesus heard that, he said unto them, they that be whole need not a Physitian, but they that are sick.*

13. *But goe ye and learne what that meaneth; I will have mercy and not sacrifice; for I came not to call the righteous, but sinners to Repentance.*

I am a poor weak man, and know but little, and therefore I shall say but little.

These words are a similitude, that as some be sick, and some well; and we see in experience that when we be sick, we need a Phisitian & goe to him, and make use of his Phisick; but they that be well doe not so, they need it not and care not for it: So it is with soul-sicknesse; and we are all sick of that sicknesse in our souls, but we know it not: we have many at this time sick in body, for which cause we do fast and pray this day, and cry to God; but more are sick in their souls: we have a great many diseases and sicknesses in our souls [he instanced, as Idlenesse, neglect of the Sabboth, Passion, *&c.*] Therefore what should we doe this day? goe to Christ the Phisitian; for Christ is a Physitian of souls; he healed mens bodies, but he can heale souls also: he is a great Physitian, therefore let all sinners goe to him. Therefore this day know what need we have of Christ, and let us goe to Christ to heale us of our sins, and he can heale us both soul and body. Again, what is that lesson, which Christ would have us learne, that *he came not to call the righteous, but sinners to repentance.* What! Doth not God love them that be righteous? Doth he not call them to him? Doth not God love righteousnesse? Is not God righteous? *Answ.* The righteous here are not meant those that are truly righteous, but those that are Hypocrites; that seem righteous, and are not; that think themselves righteous, but are not so indeed; such God calleth not, neither doth he care for them: but such as see their sins, and are sick of sin, them Christ calleth to repentance, and to believe in Christ, therefore let us see our need of Christ, to heale all our diseases of soul and body.

Delivered at the same time by Nishokhou, *another* Indian.

The Text he spake of was,
Gen. 8.20,21.

20. *And* Noah *built an Altar unto Jehovah, and took of every clean Beast, and of every clean fowle, and offered burnt offerings on the Altar.*
21. *And the Lord smelled a sweet Savour; and the Lord said in his heart, I will not againe curse the ground any more for mans sake; for the imaginations of mans heart is evill from his youth, neither will I again smite any more every thing living as I have done.*

A little I shall say, according to that little I know.

IN that *Noah* sacrificed to God he shewed himself thankfull; in that he worshiped God, he shewed himselfe godly; in that he sacrificed clean beasts, he shewed that God is an holy God, pure and clean, and all that come to God, and worship him, must be pure and clean: and know that we must by repentance purge our selves, and cleanse our hearts from all sin; which is a work we are to doe this day.   In that he sacrificed, it was the manner of worshiping God in old times: but what sacrifices must we offer now? *Answ.* By that *Psal.* 4.5. *Offer to God the sacrifices of righteousnesse, and trust in the Lord.* These are true and spirituall sacrifices which God requireth at our hands. Sacrifices of Righteousnesse, that is, we must look to our hearts, and Conversation, that they be righteous, and then we shall be acceptable to God, when we worship him. but if we be unrighteous and unholy, and wicked, we shall not be accepted, our sacrifices are nought. Againe, *we must trust in the Lord*: for who else should we trust in, we must believe in the word of God; for if we doubt of God, and doubt of his word, then our sacrifices are little worth; but if we trust stedfastly in the Lord then our sacrifices are good. Again, what kind of sacrifices must we offer? *Answ.* We must offer such as *Abraham* offered; and what sacrifice did he offer. *Answ.* see *Gen.* 22. 12. *Now I know that thou fearest me, seeing thou hast not withheld thy son, thy only son from me*; he had but one dearly beloved son, and he offered him to God; & then God saith, *I know thou fearest me, because thou hast not withheld thy son*: This was to sacrifice indeed and in truth; so we must sacrifice indeed, and in truth, but God doth not require us to sacrifice our sons, but our beloved sins, our dearest sins: God calleth us this day to part with all our sins, though never so beloved, and we must not withhold any of them from him: if we will not part with all, it is not a right sacrifice: we must part with those sins we love best, and then we offer a good sacrifice. Again, God smelt a sweet savour in *Noahs* sacrifice, & so when we offer such worship to God as is cleane, and pure and sacrifice as *Abraham* did, then God accepts our sacrifice. Again, God manifested his acceptance of *Noahs* sacrifice, by promising to drown the world no more, but gave him fruitfull times and seasons. God hath chastized us of late with such raines, as if he would drown us, and he hath drowned and spoiled a great deale of hay, and threatens to kill our Cattel, and for this we fast and pray this day; now if we offer a spirituall sacrifice, clean and pure as Noah did, then God will smell a savour of rest in us, as he did in *Noah*, and then he will withhold the Rain, and give us fruitfull seasons.

These two before mentioned did exercise the fore part of the day (besides what we did) the four next exercised in the afternoon. The first of which was

Antony.

The Scripture which he grounded his exercise upon was
Matth. 6.16,17,18.

16. *Moreover, when ye fast, be not as the Hypocrites, of a sad countenance, for they disfigure their face, that they may appeare unto man to fast: Verily, I say unto you, they have their reward.*
17. *But thou when thou fastest, anoint thine head, and wash thy face.*
18. *That thou appear not unto men to fast but unto thy father that is in secret, and thy Father that seeth in secret, shall reward thee openly.*

A little I'le speak, according to that poor little I know

THe Doctrine that Christ teacheth us in these words, is the Doctrine of fasting and prayer; and the duty we doe this day, is to practice this Doctrine, for God calleth us this day to fasting and prayer. There be many causes of prayer to God this day; as to prepare our hearts for Church-covenant, and Ordinances, and to pray for the taking away our sicknesse, and these great rains [here he did enumerate sundry causes of seeking God] But why must we fast? *Answ.* That we might the more effectually mourn for sin. If any of you bury a child or a friend, then you will mourn, and fast too, for if we offer you meat, you will refuse it, yea you cannot eat, because your heart is so full of sorrow: no matter for meat then, your tears, and sighs, and sorrows fill you so, that you cannot eat; so that fasting is an help to mourning. Now this day is a day of mourning, and what doe we mourn for? not for a child or a friend, but a greater matter; we must mourn for our sins, and we should be so filled, and possessed with mourning for our sins, that we should forget hunger, ye so afflicted in our hearts, that we cannot eat though it should be offered to us: our hearts should be so full of sorrow, that we cannot be an hungry nor eat. Againe we fast that we might repent of our sins, and amend our lives, according to that *Matt.* 3.8. *bring forth therefore fruits meet for Repentance.* This is a day of Repentance, we must therefore fast this day, so as becometh Repentance, therefore we must confesse our sins, and we must morn for our sins, and we must forsake our sins, for these are works meet for Repentance. Again, *we must not be like hypocrites in our fasting, for they disfigure their faces*, and seem to men as if they mourned and fasted, and repented, but in their hearts they doe not so, and therefore God who knoweth what is in the heart, and seeth in secret, he doth know their hypocrisie, and so he knoweth our hypocrisie, if we come here, and appear to man as if we fasted, and yet in our hearts we fast not, if we do not mourn and repent for sin, we do not fast, God doth not account that to be a fast. Again, such as fast an hypocritical fast, they shall be sure to be rewarded, and what reward will God give to such as fast like hypocrites? I answer, that you may see what the wages of hypocrites is, *Mat.* 25.51. *shall cut him asunder, & appoynt him his portion with the hypocrites, there shall be weeping and gnashing of teeth*, and this is evill wages: and therefore let us be moved, to keep a right fast this day, by repenting of our sins, and amending of our lives, and then the Lord will reward us openly, if he see that our hearts are right before him.

The next that followed was *John Speene.*

The Scripture he spake of was,
Matth. 9.14,15.

14. *Then came to him the disciples of* John, *saying, why doe we and the Pharisees fast oft, but thy Disciples fast not.*
15. *And Jesus said unto them, can the children of the Bridechamber mourn, as long as the Bridegroom is with them, but the dayes will come, when the Bridegroom shall be taken from them, and then they shall fast.*

A little I will say, for I can say but little, for I am weak and know but little.

His is a Parable, as when young people are at a wedding, there is feasting, and joy, and mirth, but no sorrow, nor mourning, nor weeping: So when Christ is with his people, he brings joy and comfort with him, and fills their hearts with comfort: but if he be angry, and depart from his people, and leave them to afflictions, then there is sorrow, and mourning, and weeping, and fasting, as it is this day with us; for we are called to fasting this day, because of the great raine, and great floods, and unseasonable weather, whereby the Lord spoileth our labours: our corne is much spoiled with the wet: so that the Lord doth threaten us with want of food; also our hay is much spoiled, so that God threatneth to starve and kill our Cattel: also we have great sicknesse among us; so that many are dead: the burying place of this Town hath many graves, and so it is in all our Towns among the praying *Indians*. Also in our houses are many sick, and a great many are crazy, and weak, and not well; God threatneth to kill us, and therefore surely he is angry, and what maketh him angry? we may be sure it is our sins, for we are great sinners. This day is therefore a day of Repentance, of fasting, and of mourning. And what are we to doe in this day of fasting? *Answ.* We must search out all our sins, and with hearty Repentance forsake them. And when we goe about to search out our sins, we must remember that there be three places where we must search for sin: First, in our hearts; Secondly, in our words; 3ly, in our works and doings, and in all these places we find too many, but especially in our hearts; for there be evill thoughts, and the root sin [that is to say Originall sin: for so we call it in their language] and therefore it is a great work to search our hearts, & find out the roots of sin: and if any doe say it is an hard work, and I know not how to doe it: I answer, it is true, it is hard work, but therefore we must take so much the more paines, and care to doe it, as we doe about hard work If any say I cannot tell how to find out my sins: I answer, we must this day pray unto the Lord to help us to find them out, and to forsake them, for he knoweth them all.

Againe, another cause of our fasting this day, is to prepare us to make a church of Christ among us: and if you say what must we doe to prepare for Church-estate. I answer we must repent of our sin, and make our selves clean, we must get cleannesse of heart, when we come neer unto God, according to that *Mat. 3. 2. Repent for the Kingdome of heaven is at hand.*

Againe, to prepare us for church estate, we must pray unto God, to send his Spirit into our hearts, because the Spirit of God will convert us, and purge our hearts, and sanctifie us, and teach us to pray, and comfort us, and will never leave us, till he have brought us to the Kingdome of heaven (as you know we are taught in our catechisme) And it is the gift of God to send his Spirit into our hearts, and Christ hath promised to doe it for us, as the word of God speaketh, *Mat. 3. 11. I indeed baptize you with water unto repentance, but he that cometh after me is mightier then I, whose shooes I am not worthy to bear: he shall baptize you with the holy ghost, and with fire.* Where we see that *John* did baptize them with water, but Christ doth baptize them with the holy ghost & fire; we desire to be baptized by man, and man baptizeth with water, and that is a sign of Repentance; but we must look for the baptisme of Christ, & he giveth us his Spirit, that is his baptizing. And when Christ baptizeth with his Spirit that doth more then water can doe, for the Spirit doth purge our soules, and maketh our hearts pure and clean.

Again, he baptizeth with fire, what is that? I *Ans.* not outward fire, but spirituall, and it is a similitude, thus: what will fire doe? I answer, you all know what fire will do; for when your Tobacco-pipes are filthy, foule, stinking, unfit for your use, you cast them into the fire, and that doth not burn them up, but burneth up all their filth, and maketh them clean and sweet, & fit for your use. So our hearts are filthy, and unfit for Gods use, but cast our hearts into the word, for there the Spirit is, and then the Spirit of God will burn out all our filth and sin, and make us sweet, and fit for the Lords use.

Another that preacht, *Piumbubbon.*

The Scripture which he did insist upon was,
Matth. 5.1. ad 10.

1. *And seeing the multitude, he went up into a Mountain and when he was set his 'Disciples came unto him, and, he opened his mouth, and taught them saying,*
2. *Blessed are the poore in Spirit,* &c.

I will speak but a little, because I am a poor creature.

Ere we see that when Christ saw the Multitude come together, he taught them; in like manner you all being come together, this day Christ teacheth you, for it is Christ, that teacheth us all by his word, and these are Christ his words, which I speak unto you, and therefore heare ye Christ this day, for all these words of blessing Christ doth speak this day unto this multitude.

1. For poverty of spirit, we are the most poor, feeble, despicable people in the world, but let us look in what case our spirits be, for if our hearts be answerably poor, and low, as our outward condition is, then we are in the way to be made truly rich, for the Kingdome of heaven is promised to such as are poor in spirit.

2. For mourning this is a day of mourning, and not so much for afflictions, as for our sins, now if we doe truly and heartily mourn for our sins, then the blessing is promised to us and God will find a time and way to comfort us.

3. Again, They that be meek and patient are blessed, therefore those that be froward and passionate and make strife, they are not blessed, and therefore we have cause to mourn this day, for our often passions and fallings out, and learn to be meek and patient.

4. Again, They that hunger and thirst after righteousnesse are blessed: This is a day of hunger and thirst, and fasting for our bodyes, that we might mourn for our sins, but it is a day of feasting for our soules, and Christ doth here offer a great man blessings for our soules to feast withall, if therefore our souls be hungry after righteousnesse and godlinesse, then we are blessed.

5. Again, God is mercifull and commandeth us to be so too, and will therefore blesse those that are like unto himselfe.

6. They that are pure in heart are blessed, and this purity of heart the Spirit of God worketh in us, when he cometh and dwelleth in us (as we are taught in our Catechisme) and therefore Christ doth blesse them.

7. *Blessed are the peace-makers,* and who be peace-makers? I answer, that the Devil is the maker of strife, and he is alwayes so doing, sometimes in one place, sometimes in another, and so he is labouring to do in all the Towns of the praying *Indians*; but such as be wise and Godly will not suffer the strife to

continue, but will use such means as shall reconcile them, and make them friends againe, and this is a blessed worke so to doe.

The last that Exercised was *Wutasakompavin*, whom I formerly wrote of by the name *Poliquanum*.

The Text he spake of was,
Matth. 8.2,3.

2. *And loe there came a Leper and worshiped him, saying, Master, if thou wilt thou canst make me clean.*
3. *And Jesus putting forth his hand touched him saying, I will be thou clean, and immediately his leprosie was cleansed.*

A very little am I able to say, and besides it is late (for it was very neer night)

THis day is a day of fasting and prayer for many causes, and one is for the many sicknesses, and deaths among us, and this Text doth shew us the best Physitian in the world, and the best way of curing all diseases. Christ is the great Physitian, he healed many when he was on earth, and he healed this Leper. This sick man came to Christ and worshipped him and confessed his power to heal him if he would, which confession of his was so pleasing to Christ, as that he presently touched him and healed him. So let us this day cry to Christ, and worship him, and if we do it in faith then he will heal us.

Again, God doth chastise us with raine, and spoyleth our Corn, and Hay, but let us take heed that in our hearts we be not angry at God, for God is righteous, and we are sinners, let us be angry at our sins, and repent this day, and goe to Christ as this man did, and then he will blesse us.

Postscript.

UPon these exercises I will animadvert a little. These things argue a good savor of spirituall things in the speaker, and here is spirituall food for the hearer. I doe know assuredly that many Godly and savory matters and passages have slipped from me, and these expressions are but a little of a great deale. I know not that I have added any matter, which they spake not, but have let slip, much which they spake. I have cloathed it with our English Idiom which is the greatest difference which I have knowingly made, but their Idiom to them is, as ours is to us. They have none of the Scriptures printed in their own Language, save *Genesis*, and *Matthew*, and a few *Psalmes* in Meeter, and I blesse the Lord they have so much, and such as see these Notes may easily observe that they read them, and improve them, which putteth my soule into an earnest longing that they might have more zeal. I blesse the Lord, that the whole book of God is translated into their own language, it wanteth but revising, transcribing, and printing. Oh that the Lord would so move, that by some means or other it may be printed.

S O M E

H E L P S

F O R   T H E

I N D I A N S

S H E W I N G   T H E M

How to improve their natural *Reason*, To know
the *True* G O D, and the true *Christian Religion*.

1. By leading them to see the Divine Authority of the
Scriptures.

2. By the Scriptures the Divine Truths necessary to
Eternall Salvation.
Undertaken

At the Motion, and published by the Order *of the*
COMMISSIONERS of the United Colonies.

by A B R A H A M   P E I R S O N.

Examined and approved by *Thomas Stanton* Interpre-
ter-Generall to the United *Colonies* for the *Indian*
Language, and by some others of the most able
Interpreters amongst us.

L O N D O N,
Printed by *M. Simmons*, 1 6 5 9.

To the Reader.

WHO *have occasion to make use of this Book, may please to observe, that the accute or long accent thus noted (á) signifies that the syllable over which it is placed is to be pronounced* long, *the rest of the words be short, till the like, or a circumflex do regulate the sillables following. Words of two sillables most frequently be not accented at all, being commonly of equal measure, and hardly mispronounced. Also, sundry times the prepositions in, with, for from by, &c. be set after the Substantives in the* Indian *and before them in the* English, *that so no harshnesse (this caution remembred) may sound in either.*

Likewise sometime a phrase is used in the Indian, *which word for word can hardly be rendred in the* English; *but then, and ever, care is had that in every sentence, and with in the limits of every stop, the* Indian *doth truly answer the* English. *The Lord pardon, accept, and give successe, that this may be an help towards the spiritual good of* Indian-souls.

So prayes A. P.

Some   helps   for   the

P Oshshe Airenamàwetouwúngash wutche Eànske-

  Indians,   shewing them   how to improve

támbawg, Okkekôod múnganâuwaus ten auwórchan

their   natural   Reason   to know

nêjek arumbàuwe penauwuawunk wauhéan webe

the only   true   God,   and

waugh wauwérhummat Mando Jehovah, quah, wér-

the true   Christian   religion.   First   by

ramâuwe Christianâuwe routàsowank. Negónne spe

  leading   them   to see   the divine Autho-

pummóoawariánau nejekkenâwmen Màndowe tóuh-

    rity   of   the   Scriptures.

kretássowunk wutche God wuskwhégansh. Néesee-

Secondly by the   Scriptures   the divine

tetâuwe spe God wuskwhégansh màndowâious wér-

  Truths   necessary   to eternall

ramauwúngansh querûhikkamuks re michéme kejâ-

Salvation.

hiitawunk.

Question

Náttoohtemâuwetoowunk

How   prove you   that there is a God?

T *Oohgôkje korâmen neh átta Mandouh?*

Answer.

Anasquetâuweten.

From   the universal   and   constant agree-

Wutche wéwinnakommuk quah yeiache wérrawâ-

ment   of   all nations,   and   persons

wunk wutche wame arkèes, quah skeetambâwg mit-

in the   world, who are   not   void   of

tâuhkuk terre, owwànnak matta sâuwaiooguk wutche

right   reason   and humanity.

sompâio penauwáwuk quah renôowunk.

  For the things   which   are grounded

Wutche ai akquíiks chawgwunsh wekakontamoo-

upon   particular   mens   fancies
awk skeje nanseêawk rénwawk róytammoúngansh

and   opinions   are not   acknow-
quah wàtramawóytammoungansh matta wèrramattau-

ledged   of   all   men,   and   are
comunks wutche wame rènawawk, quah wegonje

often   changed   but   this notion   that
àssowunnamanôosh: webe (youhcôytámmoouk) neh

there is a God, is common   to all   men,   nor   is it chan-
Mandoo nànharwee re wâme rènawawk matta àssowú-

ged   by   the changes   of times;
numôoanas spe assowunnàmoûngansh quompaious;

therefore   it   must   arise   from
règouche youh paughke môuche songème wutche

some   light   which is common   to   all
chawgun nowèta wequá-ai, teou nannarwe re wame

men,   and   that   light   must   be   ei-
rènnawawk quah youh wequa-ai pahke mouche nuk-

ther   from   tradition   which   hath   flowed
qúddee wutche as-hittewunk wutche pommochawà-

                    from   the first   parents   of mankind to
shshâuwus wutche negonnii{?}ek oushwâwog rènawak re

all   their   posterity   from   age
wame nejik wúttansewú{?}gannôoawk wutche àntseun-

to   age   who   would   not lye
ganak, re àntsúnganak, ouwànnak matta pèpetruwâ-

to   their children   in   a matter
gup re núkkrassoowúnganòas rame ischâuwúnganak

of   so great   importance;   or from
terre wu chio rio shaiô shàramanwuganak; ux wutche

an inward light   implanted   in   the minds
ramiôak wequàai ramekèzekekózzo ramee útteoitúm-

                of   all   men   by   Jehovah
mooúnganoo wutche wame rènnawawk spe Jehovah

himself.   And   that   such   a light   is in
nagum. Quah neh nenar wequàii útteamopètàngua-

every   man   naturally   appeareth   by
nau wáme rènnawawk renámpaûwe; mouskème spe

the feares   that   are in   all
wèz-sassawungansh teous útteampèánguanau wame

men   when   they have done that which   they know
rénnawawk pókkatche rehit chawgun waughtassoo-

to   be evill, though   no man   knoweth
wawk matchreéwunk, mukko, renna matta waugh-

and   upon   extraordinary
tammóan, quah skeje chechége móncharawanúnguo-

accidents,   as   Thunder,   Earthquakes,
tush ahárrêmuks, arra Páddaquáhhum, Quequansh,

fights   in the   Aire,   blazing   Stars,
mázzenúnguottush késesusk terre, squárrug arráksak,

&c. which   shewes   that they   know
&c. youh kakkoodumchàmo neh nejek wautânnau

there is   a power   above   the creatures,   though
mouche milkissowunk ausin keizhittishànnuk, muk-

they see him not, who   will   punish   sin,
komatta naûwab, ouwun bitch arroutaûtak matcheré-

and can do it   when   he will. And
wunk, quah óm uttrên hanrúkkeque roytak. Quah

this   is   {God Jehovah.}
youh mutche God Jehovah.

Secondly,   from the beginning of all   things,
Nézetataûwe, waske noujàiitch wame aiakquiiks,

that   have   a dependant   being.   For
teous uttahhênau rambatsen pummaiawunk. Wutche

the things   which had a beginning   could not be cause
aiak quiiks teous noujaiiggishhansh, matta hom wâje

of their own being,   for   that which is not
pummaiawúnganoo, wutche ne matta pummaynook

cannot   act,   nor could any thing
matta hom rémanoo chaugun, matta hom chaugun

be   before   it   was   therefore it must
pummâio, askam pummây nóshan, newutche paughke

have   its beginning   from
[môuchh]outàhhèamo noujaiewunk wutche chaugun

some   other   cause   which is without beginning
nowêta perrewawhjaioohittit teou matta outchinoh,

and   therefore   the first
[mehchu noujaiewunk] quah nè-wutche negonne

being   and   efficient cause   of   all
pummayawunk quah kezkúwan waje wutche wame

other   being.
unkatagganakpum mayawúngansh.

There was a first man, and   a first   woman   and
Moh negônne ren, quah negônne kèrequabus, quah

a first   in   every   kind   of   liv-
negónn rame wame achabwehittawunk wutche púm-

ing   creatures,   but   that   first   man
pamantajek kezhittshaunak, webe youh negônne ren

and   woman   those   first   of
quah kerequãbus, quah yôujek negonnijek wutche

all   kinds   living
wame attchabrehittewúogansh púmpamántejek

creatures   could not   make   themselves
kezhittishanák matta hom kezhúwáwk hoggaûwâw-

therefore there was a first   being,   which
wo: negáuche moh negonne pummâyhuad, youh

absolute   and   independent
sunkaio [sambió] quah webe negamo tse wutchaiô

and   rests   upon nothing   that was
quah matta chetamssennómanah chaugun, nôh moh

before   them all,   and   made   them   all,
a kam wâme nejek, quah kezhûwushan wanne wame,

and   upon whom   all   other   beings
quah skeje youh wame kat{?}ággansh pummáyawú-

depend.   And   this   is   {God Jehovah}.
gansh korchetámsenak. Quah youh atta God Jehovah.

How can   you know   that there is a God, seeing
Ob: *Ten hôm kuttawáuhtaun ne atta Mando maetax*
you never saw him, nor   can   see him?
kekenâuwah, matta hôm nauwo?

I know   I   have   a reasonable
An. Nouwáuhtâun no wadjânaman penaunâuwe

soul,   though   I never saw it,   nor can
mittachonkq, mukko matta ne nauwah mátta hôm

see it.   The soul   were not   a spirituall
nauwo. Mittachonkq matta hom rasha wrándowe

substance   if it could be seen with bodily   eyes,
pummâyawunk hôm naûwit spe hoggâuwe skesuks,

and so no   soul. In like manner were not a Spirit
quáh riò matta oútachonq. Rio God matta rashau-

if he could be seen with bodily   eyes   and so
wandoo, om naûwit spe hoggâuwe skesuks; quah rio

no   God.
matta Mando.

But   no   man   can   fully   know
Ob: *Webe mata howan nowêta hom tabâre wauhtawn*

Gods   nature,   therefore   no   God?
Jehovah rièwunk [arándoit] nègouche matta Mando?

It   followeth not   for   an
An. Youh matta nôskommôenah, wutche wómar-

inferiour   nature   cannot fully   understand
remúggeree árrumâuit hommattátabaie wâuhtawn

the things   of   an higher   and more excellent
aiakquiiks wutche sháramúggesee quah arwenúngesee

nature,   then   itself.   Beasts
arrumbaúit, aúse nágamo hoggunk. Oppishshamok

cannot   understand   what   man is, much
hommatta wauhtàuóunau chawgun ren atta shareok-

lesse   how to plant   and   govern   Com-
kóssisse ten réokkechan, quah soudamotáuôan korta-

mon-weales   or to become learned
soôdomoúngansh; ux koodamanchan wnskwhagana-

or   sayl   over   the Seas, &c. For
kre, ux seboghómman akkómmuk kathans, &c. Wut-

these   things   exceed   their
che yous aiakquiiks [remuks] árrookawáuwáunk ne-

capacities   in like manner man seeing
jek waúhtammawúnganoo río ren nauwun ewo

himselfe to be made of   a more noble   nature
hogga kezhean wutche arwenúguot arrumbâuwunk

then   beasts,   and that not   of
aûsinre oppishimmok, quah youh matta wutche

him   selfe, must   needs   inferre   that he
nagum hogga, pauhke moushe pakadoowun ne hô-

who   made him   superior   to beasts, he
wan kezhuwusuwâio arrôokawah oppishim, ewo

no lesse above   man, then man   is above
ausinre arrôokawah renôok àrra ren arrôokawant

beasts;   and therefore that the full knowledge
oppishshim; quah nègouche ne tabâio wauhtawunk

of   his   nature
wutche uwio arrándoit [árrumàuwunk] âusin
exceeds mans   capacity.
errôokawah renna kitchshantàmmoowunk.

Are there many Gods? or is there but one
Q. *Sharaog Mandóak? ux webe àtta papâsaguun wah*
true   God?
wèrramat Jehovah?

There are not   many Gods, there is only one
An. Matta sharáou Mandoak, atta webe pâsuk wah
true   God.
wérremat Mando Jehovah.

How do you   prove that there is but one   true
Q. *To gonje korámen ne webe pâsuk wah werremat*
God?
Jehovah?

Because   the reason   why   singular
An. Wutche waiâiewunk tohódje nansâiewok
things   of   the same   kind   are multi-
aiakquíiks wútche anséjekmuche nenar kokkôodish-
plyed is not   to be found   in   the nature
ahéawk matta misskommauwaûoân râme àrumbâu-
             of {God} for   the reason
wunk [arándoit] wutche God; wuche wajâiewunk
why   such like things   are multiplyed   is
tohodje   arsôauk aiakquiiks kokkôodishhéauk atta
from   the fruitfulnesse of   their causes:
wutche hokkissègowunk wutche wajaiwunganooas:
but {God} hath   no   cause   of
webe God matta outáhe wajaiewunk wutche
his   being,   but   is of himself
uwâio   pummaîewunk, webe wutche nagum hogga
therefore   he is one.
negôuche papasaqun.

Because   singular   things   of
2. Newutche nansâioaks aiàkquiiks wutche

the   same   kind   when they are multiplyed,   are
nenar   ârak nantséjek kokkoodrishshahettit, chabis-

differenced   among   them   selves   by
sohèawawk   yarâuwe nàgamáuwo hoggâuwo weêche

their   singular   properties;   but   there
nejek nanseas artumbauhittaw úngansh webe muche

cannot   be   found   another   God   differenced
hom   matta skôwah   unkatak   Mando achabizhéan

from   this by   any   such like   propertyes.
wutche yôuh spe chawgunsh arrâious àchabissewún-
gansh [arrambâmuks{]}.

Because   its   proper   to   God
3. Nèwutche webe mohtantammim re   Jehovah

to do   whatsoever he willeth; if there were many Gods they
utèein   hanharroytaks, hom sharehit Mandoak hom

might will contrary things,   and   one might be hindred by
ópperrewórrantammock , quah   nejek hom wowotam-

another,   so that he could not do what he
hittawawk rêan chawgun rio matta hom re kaddau-

would, which can not   stand   with   the Omni-
werèatteou hom matta toukranah weeche wame keiz-

potency   and   nature of   God.
tauwunganuk quah arrandoit Jehovah.

But may there not   be many Gods: yet so that
Ob. *Webe hom matta sháraog Màndoak: narraio ne*

one   is the chiefest   and   greatest   of   all?
pasuk negónquassik quah oussewe kerik wutche wame?

No,   because the first   being   must
An.   Matta, wutshe negónne pummáyhuad pauke

be   absolutely   Supreame
mutche nàgamo utse oúsewe quonúnguoso [sqon-

because   he dependeth upon nothing,   he rests
guoso{]} wutche matta rambátsênno chawgun, muche

not   upon   any person   but   is alsufficient to
matta howáno káchetamsenno webe wame tabbaio re

him   selfe   and   to all   things;   and   all
nagamo hogga quah   wame re aiakquiiks; quah wame

things   depend upon him   that which   is not
aiakquiiks rambats'nnétankq' chawgun nowéta   matta

absolutely   chiefest   and   above   all
nagámo utse negónquasik quah árroukásso wame
cannot be   God.
matta hom Jehovah.

    Because   the Essentiall   pro-
2. Wutche Mándowâious pummáyaûwous árwe,
petties   of God   are such as cannot be
nunquesoûngansh Jehovah nearrious ar matta hom
given to any   more   then   one.
meríttonoush unkatágganak re ause pasuk.

    What are   those   Properties   which are
Qu. *Chaugunsh yous arwenunguesoungansh teous mou-*
peculiar   to God   alone?
tantamminoush Jehovah webe ise?

    There are many I   shall instance in three which include
An. Pharítchch' nen swanch mishom teous mínna-
        the rest.
mok únka{illeg.}ággansh.

    That   all   perfections   are
1. Neh wame arwénunquesoúngansh uttámous
in   him originally, and eminently   as   in
rame ewo negónne, quah wuna shí auwe a{r?}h' rame
the first   cause,   from which   heaven and earth
negónne wajáiewunk, ten wutche kesukq' quah ôhke
and all   things   in   them   receive
quah wáme ajakquiiks rame nejek uttúmmonúmmok
   what soever   good   they have that   all
nauweta châwgun warréguk uttáhéhit neh wame
    perfection   are   in [Jehovah]
àrwejanúnguesoúngansh uttámous rame Jehovah
      infinitely   the reason   why   the
wame árroukawáwe wajàiewunk to hodie pumma-
being and   goodnesse   of   all
yàwunk quah wurrégowunk wutche wame kei
   creatures   is limmited,   is because the
higwushánnak sachwhúngankâuwo, atta wutche wai-

cause   whereby   they exist   hath communicated
iewund spe teou poummàiomúauk maugamous

so much to them   and   no more, and
youche re neiek quah matta wunk, quah

hath made   them   capable   of so much
keí-heous neiek tabe àttumminúmmin youche

and   no   more, but [Jehovah] receiveth not
quah matta wunk, webe Jehovah matta attum-

any thing   from   another,   but is a Spirit
minsimmo chawgun wutche únkatak, webe Rash-

living   in   him selfe, or
shâuunk pómpemantammin nagamo ewo terre, ux

of himself   therefore God is   not lim-
nagamo utse negauche Jehovah matta sachwhún-

mitted   his   strength   is infinite
gankâuwo ewo milkissewunk wame arrôukassómo

whatsoever he willeth he doeth in heaven and   earth
hanharróytaks útteréen kesukuk quah okkêak-terre

his   knowledge   is   Infinite   he know-
ewo wéwaughtâuwunk wame arrôukassomo waugh-

eth   all   things; he heareth all   the words,
tâun wame aiakquiiks; padak wame ruwâuwun-

and he seeth   all   the works   of
gansh, quah wonaumen wame reúngansh wutche

all   men   in all   the world   his Goodnesse
wame renouh wame   mittâukuk terre, ouraiéwunk

is   Infinite   he is exceedingly good, he goes beyond all
wame arròkassòmo oussewewerrego, arrôukan wame

in   goodnesse   he doth good   towards
wahwórregewúnganak terre wauhwérrerêat rak'que

all   creatures,   the presence   of God   is
wame keisheaus-hannak taûterêit Jehovah wame

infinite,   he is every where in all the world   filling   all
arrôukâssómo wampsin wame mittauk remássen wame

places,   and goes not from place to place, as doth
ahapúmmuks, quah matta ahàntse aú,   arra rehit

the creatures   his   life   is
keizhíttishánnak uppomantammewunk wame arroù-

infinite,   he   is   Eternal,   without beginning,
kassòmo, ewo muche Micheme, matta nenóuj aíous,

and   without   end.

quah matta éakquíno.

That   the true   God   is   perfectly

3. Neh wauh wérramat Mandouh muche sonks

blessed   in himselfe,   Alsufficient   of himself,

waûwerrehea nâgamo utse, Wame tabaio nâgamo

he   needs not   supply   from an

utse, matta querâuhikquo áirananamàmauetounk paí-

other,   For,

uwutche, Wutche,

He knowes   all   things   at once

1. Waughtunk wame aiakquiiks, passukutte

and   together in all   the world,   without

quah nàppe wawa mittâukuk terre, matta keke-

discourse   by   the infinitenesse   of

tokaúanak terre spe wame arroukawaúwunk wutche

his   Essence.

ewo Pummayawuk.

He willeth   most   freely   whatsoever

2. Wórrantámmo oùssewe narraûwe chawgun

is good,   and so   perfectly   that whatsoever

nowêta warréguk, quah asonkkaioùwe neh chawgun

he willeth   is   good   so farre   as he

werrantámmo muche warreguk, rikqueque arróy-

willeth it, and because he willeth it,   For {Jeho-

tak,   quah wutche warrantámmen, Wutche Jeho-

vah} is simply and   Infinitely   good.

vah saíoo quah wame-arrôukowauwe werrego.

How do   you prove   that heaven and earth,   and

Q. Ten hom wutche korámen neh kesuk quàh ôhke, quah

all   things   in   them   have   the Originall

wame aiakquiiks rame nejek outâhhenau noujiewunk

of   their   being   from {Jehovah}?

wutche nejek pummayawungano wutche Jehovah?

This   followeth   from   what

An. Yowh nôskonsómo wutche chaw-

was   said   before,   for   we have proved

gun arwamacup negónne, wutche nôrramana-

that God   hath   his   being

nas neh Jehovah uttahe ewo pummâyawunk

of himselfe,   and is but one: therefore   all

nagamo utse, quah webe pasuk: negauche wame

Postcirpt. {sic}

T Here might have been much more printed concerning the progresse of this
work amongst the *Indians,* certified in other letters sent from *New-England,*
which would be too tedious to insert, only the Corporation established here think
fit, that the following Certificate lately received (which gives an account what
proficiency two of the *Indians* now at the University in *New-England* have made
in their learning) be printed, which is as followeth (*viz.)*

August 18. 1658.

T Hese are to testifie to all men to whom these presents may come, that two
of the *Indians* that are trained up at the Grammer-Schoole in *Cambridge* of
New-England, whose names were *Caleb* and *Joel,* were called forth upon tryall
at the publick Commencement before the Magistrates and Elders, and in the face
of the Country, and thereupon very little warning gave good contentment (for
their time) to them that were present, being examined by the Præsident of the
Colledge in turning a part of a Chapter in *Isaiah* into Latine, and shewing the
construction of it so that they gave great hope for the future of their perfecting.

Witnesse

Charles Chauncy,
Præsident of *Harvard Colledge,* in *Cambridge.*

A further Account of the progreſs

OF THE

GOSPEL

Amongſt the *Indians*

In New England :

BEING

A Relation of the Confeſsions made
by ſeveral *Indians* (in the pre-
ſence of the Elders and Members of ſeveral Churches) in order to their admiſſion into
Church-fellowſhip.

Sent over to the Corporation for Propagating the Goſpel of
Jeſus Chriſt amongſt the *Indians* in *New England* at *London*, by Mr *John Elliot* one of the Laborers in the Word
amongſt them.

LONDON,
Printed by *John Macock*. 1 6 6 0.

A further Account of the progress

OF THE

GOSPEL

Amongst the Indians

In New England :

BEING

A Relation of the Confessions made
by several *Indians* (in the presence of the Elders and Members of several Churches) in order of their admission into
Church-fellowship

Sent over to the Corporation for Propagating the Gospel of
Jesus Christ amongst the *Indians* of *New-England* at Lon-
don; by Mr. *John Eliot* one of the Laborers in the Word
amongst them.

LONDON,
Printed by *John Macock*. 1 6 6 0.

TO ALL

That love the Lord *Jesus Christ* in sincerity, and
have a zeal for the propagation of Gospel-light,
to those who sit in darkness, Grace and peace
be multiplyed.

Brethren,

I T *was the holy ambition and strife of the Apostle* Paul (*that chosen Vessel
to bear the Name of Christ before the Gentiles*) to preach the Gospel where
Christ was not named, lest hee should seem to build upon another mans
foundation, *Rom.* 15.20.

*To hand on a good work begun by another is very commendable, and shall
not loose its reward; but to break the ice and begin a good work is very
honourable, and shall surely have a great reward. I am much perswaded it hath
been the gracious strife, I am sure it hath been the lot of many of our faithful
Brethren, in* New England, *to preach the Gospel where Christ was not named
before; and the Lord hath given a signal Testimony, that they have not laboured
in vain. Wee reade of the* First-fruits *of Achaia unto* Christ (Rom. 16.5. *and
again, I Cor. 16.15.) Wee have also heard both of the* First-fruits *and* Second-
fruits *of India in* New England *unto* Christ; *and these are a fair assurance of a
plentifull harvest there in due time. A blessed Foundation is laid, yea, the
Building begins to appear above ground, in the visible profession or professed
subjection of many poor Souls unto the Gospel of Christ. May wee not therefore
hopefully expect, that the* Top-stone *shall be set up with a shout of* Grace, Grace
to it?

*Hee that attentively readeth the Report, which is made in the following
Collection of the Examinations and Confessions of several Native* Indians, *who
have been wrought upon by the preaching of the Word in the Wilderness, will
see much cause to admire the free grace and goodness of God to them, as also
his mighty power and the revealing of his arme in them. What strong and clear
convictions of sin, both of the sinfulness of their natures, and of the sins of their
lives have they been under; who lay (before) dead in trespasses and sins, wholly
alienated from the life of God through the ignorance that was in them? What
strugglings and strivings with corruption and temptation do they speak of,*

before they could come off from sin, and from that vain conversation received by tradition from their Fore-fathers? What wrestlings had they with unbelief, before they could close with Christ in the promise? What full resignations of themselves have they made to the commands of Christ after closing with him by faith in the promise? Yea, what hungrings and thirstings do some of them express for more intimate communion with Christ inattendance upon all his Ordinances in a Church-state or holy Fellowship with his People?

Surely, what these late Aliens from the Common-wealth of Israel *have found and declared (as their spiritual experiences) about the dealings of God with their hearts, in bringing them off from sin, and home to himself, may shame many among us, who have been born and bred up in the aire and sound of the Gospel all their dayes.*

I may, not unfitly, make use of those Prophesies of Moses *and* Esaias *concerning the Jewes and Gentiles (and so applyed by the Apostle* Paul, Rom. *10.19,20,21.) in this present case between us in* England *and the* Indians. *The Lord hath begun to* provoke us to Jealousie by them that were no people, and by a foolish Nation hee hath angred us, hee is found of them that sought him not, hee is made manifest to them that asked not after him, but all the day long hath hee stretched out his hands unto us a disobedient and gainsaying people. *Conversions are grown somewhat rare (that's sad) in* England; *and such accounts of Conversion much more rare. And as we finde but few able to give any passable account of their conversion to God, so wee finde not a few offended at the requiring and taking of it, before admission into compleat Church-communion. Wee have many who profess the Religion they were born in, but wee have (comparatively) only a few, who profess Religion upon the evidences of their New-Birth. And that's one great reason why the Church and the world, the pretious and the vile, are in so lamentable a mixture in most places at this day.*

It were a very desireable mercy, that the practise and example of our native Brethren, yea, of the native Indians *in* New England *might kindle in us the fire of a blessed emulation in this matter; and that the Ministers of the Gospel would every where expect and diligently enquire after some hopefull proofs of the work of Grace from all those, who, in their own right, partake of those higher Priviledges, the Seals of the Covenant of Grace. Doubtless, then, Churches would appear more like Churches in the beauties of Holiness, and the fruits of the presence of Christ would be more gloriously visible in them. The great thing which wee (upon whom the ends of the world are come) should earnestly pray, endeavour and wait for is, that the new* Jerusalem *may be seen coming down from heaven, like a Bride adorned for her Husband; and to be any way, rightly, instrumentall for the bringing in of this glory, is a piece of the best Glory which wee are capable of on this side our heavenly Glory.*

'Twas therefore a very gracious as well as a noble Design, to create and establish a Corporation in this our England, *to receive, improve, mannage, and issue a free contribution and the profits arising from it for the constant support, encouragement, and promotion of this work of Christ in That Other* England. *Nor can wee but with much thankfulness to God take notice of the liberal charity*

of many who have already contributed to it as also of the faithfulness, diligence, prudence, and Godly zeal of those worthy Persons who are entrusted with the disposal of those Contributions. And because, as the whole Work is great, so there are some great parts of it now in hand, as the Printing of Davids Psalms *and the* New Testament *(besides an intendment of printing the whole* Bible*) in the* Indian *Language, which must needs be a work of great charge as well as of excellent use, (for these reasons I say) it would be a most acceptable Charity, either to procure or advance additional Contributions. How can any honour the Lord better with their perishing substance, then by forwarding a Design which may be a means to keep thousands of Souls from perishing? Yea, what an honour will it be to this whole Nation, that the Holy Bible should be printed in our dayes and at our cost in a Language and for a Nation which never had it to this day? That this blessed and beautifull Undertaking for the gathering in of those poor Souls, who yet wander in that Howling wilderness, to the Flock and fold of Christ (the Great Shepherd of the Sheep) may not want their compassionate and chearfull assistance, who are already (through grace) gathered into his holy flocks and folds, is the hearty desire and prayer of*

The 6th of the first   *Sirs,*
   Moneth, 1659.

                          Your affectionate friend to serve you in the Lord,

JOSEPH CARYL.

A brief Relation received from Mr John Elliott *of the late Proceedings with the* Indians *in* New England, *in order to their admission into Church-fellowship. In the year of our Lord 1659. The fifth day of the fifth Moneth.*

His is the third time that the Praying *Indians* (some of them) have been called forth into publick, to make open confession of the Name of Christ, to come under the publick tryal of Gods people, whether they be indeed Christians, as fit matter for a Gospel Church. Truth loveth and seeketh the light.

I was stirred up hereunto and quickened by Letters from *England*. The Lord put it into the hearts of such as are honourable, reverend, and of eminent service to Christ in *England*, to move mee, before I moved. When I moved this last time, I perceived that it was the general inclination of the Spirit of the Saints, both Magistrates, Elders, and others, that (at lest some of the principal of them) should (for a season) be seasoned in Church-fellowship, in communion with our *English* Churches, before they should be Churches among them selves. And when it was *objected*, What should the rest of the people do, if the principal and most able should not keep their Sabbaths among them? It was *Answered*, That their usual Sabbath conversation should be at home among their own people, only sometime to be among the *English*; viz. for participation of the Seals, the Sacraments of Baptism and the Lords Supper, and for any special Exercise of Discipline. When it was Questioned what *English* Church they should joyn unto? All with one mouth said, that *Roxbury* Church was called of God to be first in that service of Christ to receive the praying *Indians.* In the accomplishment whereof, I yielded my self up to follow counsel in the Lord. The elders offered themselves, on some Lecture day, to meet (if need were) at *Roxbury* Lecture, then to speak with the Church, to perswade to an unanimous accord, in receiving the *Indians* for a season; which accordingly they did: and the Lord was so effectually present in that meeting, that all Objections, so far as I know, were silenced. Soon after, our Church passed a Vote for the receiving of the *Indians.* The Elders of *Roxbury* called eight of them to a private preparatory Confession, in order to our publick proceeding. Wee gave notice of the time and place of this meeting, and many were present to hear them, both men and women; which Confessions I shall here set down, for reasons which seem to mee to have much weight; and they are as followeth.

An Abbreviate of the Confessions of some of the Indians, *which they made before the Elders of* Roxbury, *(sundry Christian people being present, both men and women) the 15ᵗʰ day of the second Moneth,* 1659. *preparatory, in order to their admission into the Church.*

Nishohkou.

O H God of Grace and Salvation, help mee by thy spirit to confesse truth and grace, in the presence of God.

1. I confesse, that I have now learned out of *Gen.* 5.1. that God made man in the Image of God, and *Adam* lived 130 years, and begot a Son in his own Image, *ver*.3. which then was not the Image of God, but by reason of the fall, was the Image of *Satan;* and that Image of *Satan* hee did communicate to us, so that wee are all born in sin, and so I lived.

After wee pray'd to God about three years, my heart was not yet right, but I desired to run wilde, as also sundry others did. Then I understood, that the Lord did make heaven, earth, sea, and all creatures, and also man, and therefore I understood that God made mee. Yet I being young, I was still vain, and ran about; and I liked to do acts of youth and vanity, and lust, as others did. And I went to *Pawwauing* among others, and these things I loved throughly, and they grew in my heart, and had nourishment there, and especially lust; if I cut my hair, it was with respect to lust, to please women; if I had long hair, it was with respect to lust, and all I did was with respect to lust and women; when there was meetings, drinkings, sports, they respected lust, and these things I perfectly loved. When the Minister came to teach us, hee taught, and I came to meeting; but I came to look upon women, I understood not what hee taught; sometimes I came, and understood nothing at all, only I look't on women. About two years after, I began to understand what the Minister preached: I understood that Scripture *Jam.* 1. *Hee that doubteth is like a wave of the sea, driven of the windes and tossed; and if any man lack wisedom, let him ask it of God.* This I understood, yet I only understood it, but it was very hard to believe. Afterward, I heard out of *Gen.6.* that God spoke concerning man, *I will destroy man whom I have made, because God saw that the way of man was corrupt before him;* and this troubled mee. And again, in the same Chapter it is said, *That God saw that the iniquity of man was great upon the earth, and that every imagination of the thought of his heart is only evil continually;* this troubled mee, for I saw the roots of sin in my heart: yet it was hard to believe. Again, in that 6. of *Gen.* God rebuked that sin in man, which was my sin, and then my heart was troubled. Sometime my heart said, it is better to run wilde as I did before, then to pray to God; for if now I sin, or commit lust, I shall be punished, or put in prison; but if I run wilde, I have liberty to sin without danger: but I was ashamed of such thoughts, and repented; but yet I doubted.

After half a year I heard the Minister preach this; *That Christ his death is of infinite value, but our death is little worth; God is satisfied with the death of Christ, and promiseth to pardon our sins for Christ his sake, if wee believe in Christ: we deserve to die, but Christ standeth in our stead, and dyeth for us, and so saveth us from death.* Next time the Minister came, hee asked, what I remembred of this I now spoke of: and I did remember it, and do remember it to this day; and I desire to pray to God as long as I live. I believe Christ dyed for sinners, but I doubted concerning my self. Then I heard this promise; *If you repent and believe, you shall have pardon and be saved:* and therefore sometime I believe, and sometimes I doubt again. Afterward, I had temptation to drinking, and to vain courses, nigh half a year; yet when Sabbath came, my heart would turn to God; when the Soldiers came upon us on the Sabbath, while wee were at meeting, and made us bring our guns hither: then my heart said, Sure God hath not said, Keep the Sabbath day holy; and then my heart cast off God, yet it was only in my heart. When wee came to the Magistrates, and *Cutshamoquin* asked, Why they came on the Sabbath day? my heart was troubled, and I did believe, when wee went from the Magistrates. I was thirsty, and I drank a great deal; and I was drunk, and was carried before the Magistrates, and then I was ashamed. Then I came to the Ministers house, and I was greatly ashamed; and my heart said, Sure I have now cast off praying to God; but I repented and cryed to God, Oh God, pardon all my sins, and this my sin; for my sins are great. I had other temptations to drinking, and I found my heart weak, and doubting, but my heart was troubled, and I was ready to stumble like a little weake childe.

After this, I heard that word of God, Mat. 12. *Do yee not remember what David did on the Sabbath day, and was blamelesse?* Then I thought the

Souldiers did not sin; but then I saw that I was a great sinner, and that I had broken the Sabbath.

Again, I heard that word, Mat. 3. *Every tree that bringeth not forth good fruit is hewen down and cast into the fire:* and this troubled mee, because I had evil fruits.

Again, Mat. 6. Christ saith, *Be ye not like hypocrites, which seem to pray before men.* I thought this was my case, I did only pray before men, but I doubted of Christ and his Grace.

Again, Mat. 5. *Whoever breaks the least of Gods Commandements, and teach men so to do, shall be least in the Kingdom of heaven.* Then I was troubled, because I had been an active sinner, in lust, and other sins, and I was worse then a beast in my sins. Then I cryed to God, Oh Christ pardon all my great sins, Oh Christ have mercy on mee, Oh God remember mee, to pardon all my sins. Thus I cryed and desired pardon, but I was weak in believing. But then, about two years after, I was greatly troubled about my weakness: I desired to do well, but I was weak: Then I cryed to God, Oh God help mee by thy spirit in mee, and send thy spirit into my heart. Sometimes I read and taught on the Sabbath day, but weakly. Then I heard, *Mat. 23.* Christ bid the people *do what the Scribes and Pharisees said, but not do as they do.* I said (Lord) that is my case; I teach better then I do: and therefore I desired repentance for my sin, and to forsake my sin. Then *Mat. 7.* Christ saith, *Thou hypocrite, first cast the beam out of thy own eye, and then thou mayst see clearly to cast the mote out of thy brothers eye.* My heart said, Truly it is so; I teach others, but I do not well my self; I reprove sin, and yet I do it. Then was my heart weary, and I desired again to do well, and amend, but I found my self very weak. Sometime my heart hated praying to God, and meeting on the Sabbath dayes; and therefore I see I deserve hell torments: and then I cryed, Oh Christ pardon all these my sins. Then afterward my heart desired strongly to pray unto God, but I saw I deserved misery and punishment, and I was weak. Then I desired my heart might be made strong by Church-covenant, Baptism, and the Lords Supper, which might be as a Fort to keep me from enemies, as a Fort keepeth us from our outward enemies. Yet my heart was sometime backward, and said, No matter, do it not, but still do what thy heart would have thee. And I saw Satan did thus follow mee with these temptations to misbelief and doubting. But now I see Satan tempteth mee, because hee desireth I should be ever tormented with him. Then I learned that in *John 6. I am the true bread, and hee that eateth mee shall live for ever, and hee that drinketh my blood shall have life; but hee that doth not eat my flesh and drink my blood shall not have life.* Then my heart saith, Truth Lord, that is my case. Again I learnt, *John 3. Hee that believeth shall not perish, but have eternal life:* And my heart said, Yea Lord, let it be so.

Again, *Mat.* 16. Christ saith, *Thou art* Peter *a Rock, and on this Rock I will build my Church, and the gates of Hell shall not prevail against it:* Therefore my heart said, I desire this; because *Christ dwells in the Church, and in the midst of them where two or three are met together in my name.* Oh! I do therefore desire Church Ordinances, that I might be with Christ, and that I might have the Seals. *Mat.* 3. Christ sayes, *Let it be: for it is necessary that I should fulfill all righteousness:* My heart said, Oh that I might also so do O Lord, now my heart desireth and thirsteth; Oh God have mercy on mee and pity my weakness, that I may have pardon in Christ, and strength from Christ in all his Ordinances, and that I might leave all my sins; and Oh God pardon all my sins for thy mercies sake; I know not what to do I am so weak, Oh God help, and have mercy on mee. And the same I desire of you, before whom I am in this house, help mee; for *Mat.* 16. *whom yee binde on earth are bound in heaven, and whom yee loose on earth are loosed in heaven:* and my desire is, that Christ would pardon all my sins, and that I may be helped.

Elder Heath *propounded this Question, which hee answered in broken English.*

Question.   *Whether doth Satan still tempt you with former lusts and temptations? and what do you when you are tempted?*
Answer to the first part. Yes, alwaies to this day. *To the second part:* When Devil comes, I sometime too much believe him, but sometime I remember to do Gods Word, because Gods Word is all one a sword, and breaks the Devils temptations.
Deacon *Park* propounded this Question. *What is it in sin, why hee hateth it now more then before?*
Answ. his answer in broken English. I did love sin, but now not all one so, because I hear Gods Word, and that shewes mee, that which I loved is evil, and will bring mee to hell, therefore I love it not now.
Deacon *Park* urged, *Doth hee hate sin because it is against God?*
Answ. That chiefly.

Anthony.

F Irst, I make confession in the presence of God, and of all these Elders: and this I confesse, that I am not able to speak before the Lord, yet I do it according as God requireth I should. Assuredly I am a sinner, but now I hope Christ hath taught mee his Word; Oh let him (my Lord!) help mee to speak it.

I confesse, that in my mothers belly I was defiled in sin: my father and mother prayed to many gods, and I heard them when they did so; and I did so too, because my parents did so: and in my childhood, (afore I could act sin) I did delight in it, as dancing and Pawwaug: and when they did so, they prayed to many gods, as Beasts, Birds, Earth, Sea, Trees, &c. After I was born, I did all such things: I loved lust when I was a youth, though I did act these lusts but a little. But when I had a little begun, my heart did very much desire more to do such sins: I saw the *English* keep Sabbath; I cared not, but played, and catch't birds, or any thing: yet when I saw *Englishmen*, I ran away, on the Sabbath day, because they should not see mee. As yet I knew not of great sins, as Murder,

Adultery: then some *Indians* said we must pray to God. When I was in *English* houses, I saw them pray, and I thought it a vain work. They said there was but one God; I thought, nay, there be many Gods. When *Indians* said, Wee will pray, my heart said, No; I will not so long as I live. Yet I heard more and more of praying to God, and that my brothers prayed to God; but my heart said, Praying to God is vain. After I heard *Waban* did pray, and my brothers, *Wompooas,* and *Toteswoomp*; yet my heart said, No: I am well enough, I have not so sinned as other men, I am no Murderer, Adulterer, &c. Then I ran away; yet I was not much troubled, because my brothers prayed. A little after I came, and my brother said to mee; I pray you pray to God. I answered him not, but my heart said, No: yet I was troubled, because I heard my brothers. I thought, if any should kill my brothers, I would kill him: if any Warrs were, I would go with my brothers; only I thought of my love to my brothers: and then that, if my brother make Warr, I would go with him, to kill men. Now he prayes, shall not I go with my brother? And my brothers love me, and they both pray to God, why should not I? They prayed morning and evening; and when they eat, and on Sabbath dayes, then I thought I would do so: but it was not for love of God, or fear of God, but because I loved my brothers. Again, when I came to *Noonantam* I heard the Minister preach, and I desired to hear what he taught: and he taught, but I understood not, but thought they were vain words, because I understood not. Then after I coming to hear, I heard some youths must go dwell at *Roxbury.* My brother said to me, Go you; because you may learn *Smithery:* For that reason I did go, but desired not to learn to pray: all these things were vain. When we came to *Roxbury*, I said, I desired to learn *Smithery:* But my Master said, I may not teach him my Trade, lest *Indians* learn to make Locks and Guns. Then I would not dwell with him, and thought to cast off praying, and thought I would forsake my brothers. My brother perswaded mee to dwell one year there, but I would not: yet at last I did dwell there one year, and went to meeting, but in vain, for I understood not one word. After that year, I returned to *Noonantam,* and then I heard that God made all the world, but yet I did not pray to God one jot, but still I sinned, and especially the sin of Lust, & I made light of any sin. I heard, and understood the Commands of God, *Thou shalt not murder, commit adultery, steal, bear false witness, covet;* and that made me afraid to commit sin afore man, lest I should be punished or put to death, but I feared not God. After I heard the Minister ask, *Who made you?* A. *God:* and *Who redeemed you?* A. *Christ:* and *Who must sanctifie you? The holy Ghost,* and that God made Heaven, Earth, Sea, &c. then I a little considered of God, who made all this world, and then I was afraid. I saw that no man could make these things, and that therefore we must pray to God. Then my heart said, Assuredly it is so; God made all things, and made mee, and I must pray to him. After this, my brothers were sick, and I prayed God, Oh that they may live! and then I heard, that now God tryeth mee whether I will pray or no. I confesse I have done many sins, especially lust, though I had not been a Murderer, or the like. But then my brothers and kindred dyed: then my heart said, Sure it's a vain thing to pray to God; for I prayed, yet my friends dye: therefore I will run wilde, and did cast off praying, I did not pray morning and night, and at meat, only on the Sabbath day I came to meeting, but I cared not for hearing, nor did I believe anything I heard, but I still lived in sin, and my heart said, I will run away; for here we are hindred from sin, in other places I may freely sin. Then my brothers which lived were troubled for mee. Then I said I will abide with my brothers, because I love them, but not because I would pray.

Then that Winter God broke my head; I knew but little, I was almost dead: Then my heart said, Now I know God is angry with mee for my sins, and hath therefore smote mee; then I prayed hard, when I was almost dead. I remembred my sins much, and considered them much: I remembred that God made all the world, and therefore assuredly there is a God. I heard that God made *Adam*, and made him in his own image, *Gen.* 1. and assuredly none but God could make all the world, heaven, earth, sea, &c. then I did believe that God did make the world.

Again, I confesse, I saw that I had offended against God, and sinn'd against him, and that I had the root of sin in me, and that I had deserved all miseries, and death, and hell. I heard, that God made a Covenant with *Adam*, and forbad him to eat of the Tree in the midst of the Garden; and yet he did eat, and therefore God was angry with man: and I was born in sin, and therefore God was angry with me: and because I have sometime forsaken God, and run wilde, therefore I now know my sin and my offence against God. I desire no more to cast off God and prayer, for now I know my sins, and that I have deserved misery: therefore now I desired to pray to God, as long as I live. I desired pardon of my sins, and I thought it may be God will pardon mee: and my heart prayed to God, Oh God if thou give mee life again, I will assuredly believe and obey; and now I know my sins by the sin of *Adam*: but when I had thus done, quickly my heart would be vain again. After my wound, when I came to my self and awaked, I saw my sin, and promised God to pray unto him, when I saw the mercy of God was so great unto mee: I heard that word, Say not, I will pray hereafter, but now, *Today if yee will hear his voice, harden not your hearts,* but pray to God; and that made my heart to yield to do it. Then I understood, *Gen.*2. that *God formed man out of the dust of the earth, and breathed into him a living soul:* by this I did believe that God made me. And I heard that *God* caused Adam to sleep, and took out a rib, and made it a woman: and by this I believed, that surely this is the work of God. Again I heard, that *wee are born in sin, under the guilt of Adams sin:* and by that I believed that I was a sinner. Again I heard, *Gen.* 6. that *all the thoughts and imaginations of the heart of man, are only evil continually;* and that God did threaten *to destroy man whom hee had made, and all beasts and living creatures which hee had made:* and by this I saw, that surely sin is a very great evil.

Again I heard, that *Noah found grace, and hee onely was upright before God,* and that *God drowned all the world, except Noah, and his sons, and their wives, eight persons:* this did make mee remember my sinnes, and confesse them, and I saw that God is angry with sin. *It rained forty dayes, and so drowned all the world:* then I said, Surely this is Gods work, and hee doth as he threatned to do to sinners; and the same may God do to me, who am a sinner; and my heart is full of sin, and evil thoughts, &c. And then I prayed, Oh God be not angry with mee, but be mercifull to mee, and shew mee what I should do. Then I considered why did God bid *Noah* make an Ark, and saved *Noah* and his Sons, and their Wives: and by it my heart saw, that this is Gods work, who does what hee speaketh, and hath mercy on whom hee will. And my heart thought, does God pardon mee, and love mee? It may be God will have mercy on mee. I heard that promise, Mat. 3. *Repent and believe, for the Kingdom of heaven is at hand:* then my heart said, Oh that God would help mee, and pardon my sins. And God made mee wonder at Gods mercy to mee. I heard of *Sodom,* and their great sin, and destruction, and that did make me to remember my great sins, and the great work of God that hee had almost kill'd mee; Oh, I thought this is Gods work, to shew mee my sinnes: and as God saved *Lot* by the Angels, and sent him out of the place, but burnt *Sodom* and all the people, this I saw to be Gods work, & now I desired to fear God and pray unto him all the dayes of my life.

Again I heard, Mat. 3. *The axe is laid to the root of the tree, every tree that bringeth not forth good fruit is hewen down, and cast into the fire:* then I feared my own case, because my fruits were sin, and I deserved to be cut down; then I desired to believe in Christ. I did believe that Christ is the Son of God, by that word *Matth.* 4. Satan tempted Christ, *If thou be the Son of God, &c.* but Christ conquered Satan; and therefore assuredly hee is the Son of God. Then I considered that place, Mat. 11. Many came to Christ, the halt, and blinde, and lame, and deaf, and sick, and hee healed all, and if they did but touch Christ they were healed; and therefore my heart believed assuredly, hee is the Son of God: and therefore now I will pray, and Oh let Christ save mee. And Christ hath promised, *Whatever yee ask in my name, it shall be done:* therefore now I prayed, Oh Christ Jesus pardon mee; but my heart is weak and doubting, and I cannot believe. And I heard that word, that *every tree that bringeth not forth good fruit, is cut down and cast into the fire:* then I said, I deserve that. Again, that word, *Not every one that sayeth, Lord, Lord, but hee that heareth the Word, and doeth it.* Assuredly it is so; and I desire not only to hear the Word, but to do it: then my heart was ashamed of my sinnes, and grieved. I heard that word, Matth.6. *Blessed art thou Simon bar-Jonah, flesh and blood hath not revealed this unto thee, but my heavenly Father:* then my heart said, Yea Lord, no man has taught mee Christ, onely God hath taught my heart to know Christ.

Again, I heard that word, Mat. 1. *Hee will save his people from their sins:* then my heart said, Be it so to mee, Oh Lord. Again, I heard that Christ rose again the third day with an Earth-quake; and the Watchmen were afraid, and fled: then my heart said, Surely this is Christ the Son of God; and whosoever believeth in Christ, his soul shall go to heaven: For again, I heard of the Ascension of Christ, and more then five hundred saw him ascend; and therefore I believe this is Christ the Son of God. Again, I heard that in John 14. *No man cometh unto the Father, but by mee:* my heart answered, Yea assuredly, Oh Lord, Christ is the way, to believe in, and come to God.

Again, I heard that *Mat.* 25. Christ saith to the wicked, *Depart yee cursed:* I said, God might justly say so to mee, and send mee to eternal death. But I earnestly cryed to God, Oh God, set mee into the right way, and give mee Christ, that I may ever walk with Christ; for I am poor and weak: and Christ promiseth, that *what wee ask hee will grant;* and I say, Let God do with mee what hee will: but I beg mercy in Christ, onely I desire to pray to God as long as I live.

John Speen.

THis I confess, that I assuredly am a great sinner before the Lord: but now I beseech God to help mee; Oh Christ, lead mee in the right way, that I may speak that which is right.

This I confesse, that before wee prayed to God, I was wholly a sinner, and not only before, but since praying to God, I have been a great sinner: and now I desire to make a short confession [for we desired that they would be shorter, the time requiring so]. At first when I prayed, my prayer was vain, and only I prayed with my mouth; and on the Sabbath, only I came to the House of Prayer. I prayed morning and evening, and when I eat, but I considered not what I prayed for; I was sometime angry and passionate about wordly matters; and I was troubled when I saw my brother was chosen to be a Ruler, who was younger then I; because now I saw that I was a sinner; and though I repented, yet presently again I fell into sin: therefore I thought, surely God hath cast me off, because I thus sin; and still my heart was full of sin, all my thoughts were full of sin, all my talk and doings were sinfull.

But now of late, about 2 yeares ago, I heard this word, Mat. 12. *When the unclean spirit was cast out, hee went up and down unquiet; then hee returned and took 7 devils with him, worse then himself, and dwelt in that man, and the latter end of that man was worse then his beginning.* When I heard this I feared, my heart feared; I feared that my repentance and praying and all was nought, and that God hath almost quite cast me off. Then I considered how I fell into these sins: I remembred that the Serpent did deceive the woman, & she the man, and thereby brought sin; and thereupon God punished both the man and the woman. Hearing this, my heart thought, Surely I am a great sinner, and I was born in sin, because my parents were sinners, and so am I. I have sinned against God, and I was born in sin. My Parents broke that Command, *Thou shalt have no other gods but Mee;* but they served many gods, and so did I, and therefore the earth bringeth forth thorns and weeds unto man, when he laboreth: therefore by this I remembred my troublesom life, and all is because God is offended at me, because of my sins. And then I remembred that many of my children are dead; this is Gods punishment on me, because of my sins. Sometime men punished me, and were offended at me, but now I remembred my sins against God, and I saw that the punishments of God are a greater matter. Again, I heard that word, that *hee that keepeth his word shall finde mercy.* I thought so it is indeed; but I am a sinner. I considered what I should do, because I was a sinner, and born in sin, and have lived in sin. I considered assuredly there is a God, and God made heaven and earth, and all that is therein, and all destructions and deaths are the work of God. I remembred my vain praying to God, and considered what to do. I confessed my sins before God, and begged pardon for Christ his sake. I did finde I could not deliver my self, but Christ only is my deliverer; and my heart desired to believe, and pray to him, and yet knew not what to do, nor how to please God, and get pardon; only I prayed, Oh Christ deliver mee, because I am a sinner, and know not what to do.

Then I remembred that God layeth on us two deaths in this world: First, the soul is dead, and wee are made guilty of *Adams* sin, and have lost Gods Image, and hereby my soul is a fool, and hereby my soul is dead: and a man dead can do nothing, nor speak, nor go, nor stand, and verily so is my soul dead, and I shall fall to eternal damnation by sin. Therefore now I cry to God to help mee, for I am throughly a sinner. After I heard that God pardoneth penitent believers: and I remember the word of *Jonas*, when he was almost cast off, he repented, and God made a Whale to eat him up; and then he looked to God, and cryed for mercy; and then I saw that if I cry for mercy, and believe, I shall have pardon. I heard that Christ healed all manner of diseases; therefore I believed that Christ is the Son of God, able to heal and pardon all. Now I confess I know nothing, almost nothing at all. Again, Christ saith, *Hee that is not with mee is against mee;* my heart said, True it is so, so must I do, I must be with Christ: and, *Hee that gathereth not, scattereth;* I said, So it is with mee, I have so done; I scatter, and am a stranger to Christ. And I did not truly love them that prayed to God, but I was a stranger in heart unto them. But now I desire in my heart to do as they do; and our poor teaching, I desire to obey it, and do what God bids; and what he saith you shall not do, that I desire not to do: But yet again I do sin, and my sins troubled me by hearing the word of God, and yet I would do them. I heard that God will pardon all kinde of sins, that men sin, *but the sin against the Holy Ghost shall not be pardoned in this world, nor in that which is to come.* Then I fear'd that I was such an one, and that God would not pardon me. Then I earnestly entreated God to pardon and deliver me, because he was the true deliverer. Again, I heard that word, that *they that are well need not the Physitian, but the sick.* My heart said, True; I did even so, I sought not help when I was well, but now I remember my sins, and now my soul is dead, and now I desire that my soul may live, and I desire the Physitian of my soul to heal mee; and Christ will not in vain heal souls, but such as convert from sin, and believe in Christ, their sins Christ pardoneth: this my soul doth earnestly beseech of Christ, and else I know not what to do. Again, I heard that *Christ dyed for our sins,* when we are sinners. Again, *Mat.*26. *Christ saith, This is my blood of the New Testament, which is shed for many, for the remission of sins:* my heart said, Yea (Lord) let it be so for my soul, and let me not be a stranger any more before thee. I know now what to do, Lord help. I desire to be washed from all my filthy sins, and to be baptized, as a sign of it. I am as a dead man in my soul, and desire to live.

Ponampam.

A Little I shall speak. I was young, about 8 years old when my father lived. I did play as other children did, and my father did chide me for playing. I wondered at it, for he said we shall all die. I wondered and sat amazed about half an hour, but I soon forgot it. That Winter the Pox came, and almost all our kindred dyed. I and my mother came to the Bay, and there dwelt till we pray'd to God; but I did nothing but sin, as the rest of the world did. Then hearing the word of God, I heard that *from the rising of the sun to the setting thereof, my Name shall be known among the Gentiles:* therefore all must pray to God. But my heart did not desire that, but to go away to some other place. But remembring the word of God, that all shall pray to God. Then I did not desire to go away, but to pray to God. But if I pray afore the Sachems pray, I fear they will kill me, and therefore I will not pray. But yet when others prayed, I prayed with them; and I thought, if I run away to other places, they will pray too, therefore I will pray here. Then on a Sabbath, none taught, and some bid me teach, what the Minister had taught us; but I feared, and durst not for fear of the Sachems, yet they urged me, and I did. And I taught them what I remembred, and they were angry at me, and we fell out, and I went away. I thought that my praying would be in vain, and I laid by praying; and there was Pawwauing, but I doubted to do that, because I had prayed, and I did think they would laugh at me. After I returned again, and was among them which prayed, but my heart did not rightly pray, though I came on the Sabbath day. Then about the time that my Son (who was at School) was born, the Minister taught on I Chron. 28.9. *Thou Solomon my son, know the God of thy fathers, &c. if thou seek him, hee will be found of thee; if thou forsake him, hee will cast thee off for ever:* Then I feared, for I said, This already I have done, I have cast off God, and therefore he will cast off me; for every such one God will cast off, I know not what to do. It repented me for my sin, I feared Gods wrath and damnation. Then I prayed, and call'd upon God, yet only sometimes I repented, and after I found my heart full of sin again: But then I was angry at my self, and knew not what to do; alwayes I did fear, God hath cast me off, for all my many sins which I have done. Hereby I was troubled and angry at my self. Then I heard that word, *Who ever repent and believe shall be saved, Il'e pardon them:* Then my heart cryed, Oh Christ let it be so, that my sins may be pardoned, and that I may pray alwaies. Then I begged, Lord give me repentance and faith, and I did pray to God much. Then I did beg, that I might give up my self, wife, and children to God as long as we live; and then I prayed. Then I heard that word, *Mat.* 5. *Hee that looks on a woman to lust after her, hath committed adultery in his heart.* I then remembred my sins; that though I had promised to pray, yet I had thus sinned, and my heart was now troubled about this. My heart said, Cast off praying, because you are filthy in lust, your heart and eyes still commit adultery; therefore run away from these that pray to God, and go to *Qunniticot,* or some other place; and if you be in other places, you may do what you will, and my heart almost inclined to this sin: But after that, this merciful word of God I heard, That *Satan led Christ into the wilderness to tempt him,* and so I thought hee would do me. Then I desired God to be merciful to me; then I turned to God, and cryed, but knew not what to do, for I feared God had cast me off, and I shall perish for ever; God has cast me off, and I have deserved hell fire. Then I heard that word, Joh. 14.6. *None come to the Father but by me:* I did pray, Oh

Christ let it be so, that by thee I may come to God; and I pray Christ Jesus pardon all my sins, this mercy I beg. Then I repented my casting off praying to God; then I promised I would not return again to sin, and if Christ help me, I and children shall serve God. Then that Spring my mother and two children dyed, and I was troubled, and knew not what to do; my heart said, Lay by prayer, but that I did not: but I saw Christ came to give eternal life, and therefore what Christ will do for me, so let it be. Therefore I believe only in Christ for eternal life; and what Christ will do with my soul, so let it be; and my soul desireth that I may receive the Seals to make strong my heart.

Piumbuhhou.

A Ssuredly, I have nothing that I should confesse as I ought, for my heart is full of foolishness and darkness; stopt up is my heart, and deaf are my ears. I know not by what way I can get life. I was born in sin into this world, and therefore I am in folly, and I know my heart is full of foolishness and ignorance. I am a great sinner ever since I saw light in this world; my foolishness appeareth in every thing I do in this life. I know not what God hath given me, but now I hear of the mercy of God, who hath made the world, and all things in it; by this great work of his I know there is a God, and because my heart checketh mee for sin, and I fear the punishment of God: And the Word of God now sheweth me that there is a God; therefore my heart sayes, I desire to pray to God: and because God is angry with me for all my sins, I know nothing by my self but that which is evil. I heard that word Mat. 5. *Blessed are the poor in spirit, for theirs is the kingdom of heaven.* Then my heart said, So be it Oh Lord to me, and I love thee as long as I live. Then said my heart, I am a poor man, and desire to pray to God. Again, God said, *Blessed are they that hunger and thirst after righteousness, for they shall be filled.* Then when I heard that word, my heart rejoyced; and yet again I doubted, and my heart misbelieved and feared. Then that word came, that Christ saith, *Be ye mercifull as your heavenly father is merciful.* And again, *Hee maketh his sun to rise on the evil and on the good; and sendeth rain on the just and on the unjust.* When I heard it, my heart rejoyced to hear of the mercy of God; yet I doubted, and my heart was hard again. Now I confess before God, because God is a great God, and a mercifull God, and I pray to him. I heard of Gods great mercy, to give us his only Son to dye for us; therefore I loved God, and I begged, Oh God pardon all my sins, and I give up my self to Jesus Christ.

Monotunkquanit.

B Efore I prayed to God, I lived at *Nipmuk.* I did not know that there was a God, only I lived for nothing, for no end or purpose; but I alwaies did wilde actions. I kept no Sabbath, nor Lecture, nor any work of Prayer; nor did I remember my works. I now know that all my words and works are naught, my eyes and ears are stopped, and mad works I dayly did. After I went to *Dorchester* Indians, the praying Indians; and they that were my friends, did say it was good to pray to God; and said, To morrow is our Lecture, and the Minister cometh to teach us; then my heart desired to see the Minister, and hear what he said: next day he came, and taught the Indians; I went and desired to see: when I came, my son *Sam* came with mee; the Minister call'd my son, and set him afore, and asked him, *Who made him?* and he was taught to answer, *God.* Then he commended my son, and asked whose son he was; they said, *Mine.* The Minister gave him two apples: then the Minister said to me, Do you pray to God? you see your childe saith, God made him; and therefore it is your duty to pray to God: *[Note here that God hath so blessed this youth, that hee is one of our School-masters, and an hopefull young man.]*

Then I considered what he said, I could not sleep that night. I considered whether I should pray to God; my heart did much doubt that night. Shall I pray? my heart said, No; yet I doubted. Then *Waban* came to my house to *Nipmuk,* and perswaded me to pray to God; I said, I know not how to pray. Hee said, God will teach you; God is a great God, and made all the world. I answered, Who knoweth that? and who can witness that? He said, The Minister is sent of God, and sheweth us Gods Word, and hee by that teacheth us, Then I promised *Waban,* that when hee came again I would pray to God. Then *Toteswamp* came, and exhorted me to pray to God, and told me of Christ, and pardon of sin; and then almost my heart prayed to God. Then I said, *English* men understand not me, and does God understand me? They said, God made all, and understands all: then I said, I will pray to God. Then I heard first, that *God made heaven, and earth, and all things, and in six dayes finished them;* and also *made man in his own Image,* wise and holy like God. Then I heard that *Satan came and tempted Eve,* and cozened her, and she tempted the man. And God had said, *Eat not of the tree in the midst of the Garden, if yee eat thereof yee shall dye;* yet she did eat, and gave unto man, and he did eat: and thereby he sinned, and all his posterity became sinful, and deserved damnation. Then my heart said, What shall I do? and I prayed for my children, for now I hear of eternal damnation, and sure I am a great sinner. Again, I heard the Minister preach, That Christ was born like a man, and was both God and man, and dyed for us, and sheweth us the way of eternal life. Then I cryed, Oh Lord give me Christ, because Christ hath dyed for us, and hath made his righteousness ours, and our sins are Christs, as *Adam* made his sin ours. Now my heart was broken, and I saw that I was a great sinner. When I heard of the great works of Christ, I said, Oh what shall I do, that I may get Christ? & I said in my heart, Oh let the holy Spirit help me, for I am ashamed of my sins; melted is my heart, and I desire pardon of all my sins; now I desire to forsake all my sins, and now I desire dayly to quench lusts, and wash off filth, and cast out all my sins, by the blood of Jesus Christ, and this I do by believing in Jesus Christ. *Gen.* 6. there was only one *Noah* righteous, and God saved him: then my heart said, Oh mercifull God, who savest them that trust in thee, save mee. Again, *God made his Covenant with Abraham, and with all the seed of Abraham:* now I desire to have this Covenant, and to receive this Commandement of Christ. *Abraham* was strong in faith, and followed Christ; and my heart doth desire to follow Christ, because he hath dyed for us.

Wutásakómpauin.

OH Christ help mee! I confess my sins before God, and before men. We are all born in sin, because *Adam* sinned, and made his sin ours. Our Parents knew not God, nor the way of life; we Indians are all sinners, and did all sins, afore we heard of God; we did pray to every thing that is in the world, and knew not the way of life. When *English* men came first, we did pray to the Devil, and many were our sins; and God doth know all our sins, all which we have committed, before the *English* came. After the *English* came, I went to *Sudbury*, to Mr *Browns* house, and he said to me, Pray to God; but I did not like it, nor to hear of praying to God; but afterwards I heard *Waban* prayed to God, and I was not glad of it; yet after *Waban* prayed, he told us of it, and that the Minister came to *Noonantam.* I heard him, and he taught, that the souls of good men die and go to heaven, the souls of the wicked, when they die, they go to hell; but I only heard it. Then we resolved we would pray to God, and carry our children to *Roxbury,* that they might learn to pray, but we feared that we should not learn to pray. After the Minister taught that word, that every man himself must pray and believe to be saved; and though your sons be at *Roxbury*, and learn to pray, yet if you pray not, you must be damned.

Again, I heard many words of God; this was one, *Therefore watch, for ye know not the day, or hour, when the Lord will come:* When I heard that, I knew not what to do, nor do I know when is the day of death. But I am full of sin, and when I die Christ will not receive me, because I am so full of sin. After that my wife dyed, and then weak was my heart, almost I left praying to God, but yet I did not not so. But after, I heard that word of God, *Who ever heareth the word, and doeth it, is like a wise builder, who built on a rock; and when the storms and floods came and beat upon the house, it stood, because it was built upon a rock: But hee that heareth the word, and doth it not, is like a foolish builder, who built upon the sand, and the storms and floods came and beat upon that house, and it fell, because it was built on the sand.* By this I saw that I was a foolish builder, because the death of my wife did almost make me leave praying to God. After I had another wife, and shee dyed also: Then I heard that word, That it is Gods love, by afflictions, to call us to repentance; and therefore my heart said, Oh Lord I will pray, Oh Lord help me. Again, I heard another word, that *at the end of the world all must appear before the Judgment Seat of Christ:* and therefore now confess all your sins, and repent, because Christ hath writ down all your actions, both good and bad, and all shall be opened; and therefore repent of your sins, that they may be pardoned.

Then I said, I am a great sinner, and ever I commit sin; I confesse I have deserved hell, and I cannot deliver my self; but I beg of God, Oh Lord give me Christ; and I give my soul to Christ, that all my sins may be pardond, and I now confess my sins before man but at the end of the world I must be judged by Jesus Christ. Now I desire the spirit of God would help me to confess all my sins to God, that they may be pardoned in Jesus Christ.

T Hese Confessions I wrote in English *from their mouthes with the best of my endeavours, both for diligence and also faithfulness; and so soon as they had done, I read them unto the Elders and Brethren and Sisters there present, and that the substance hereof was delivered by them, and faithfully translated and delivered by me (to the best of my understanding) I do here before the Lord testifie.*

JOHN ELIOT.

I *Did understand most things that some of those* Indians *spake; and though others spake not so well to my understanding, yet many things I understood of what they all spake: and thus much I may testifie, that (according to what I understood) the substance of their Confessions is here truly set down.*

JOHN ELIOT, jun.

Waban being sick when the rest made their Confession, after the Lord had restored him, came to *Roxbury*, and before the Elders made his Confession as followeth.

U Nto this day I do understand but little of the *English* Language; the Word of God came not first unto my heart by the *English* Language. I did not know what state I was in at my first birth, and my sin by birth I knew not: When I was young I knew not what I was, as now I do know; for now I know that I am a sinful man. Since I prayed to God, I know more of my self; but afore, I cared not for such things, nor what they said. If I heard any thing, I took no heed to it; if any asked me whether I knew God, I did not regard it; yea, I hated the knowledg of God, nor did I regard any word of God: but other kinde of praying (which we used) I did love; to pray to the Devil, this I loved.

But afterward, I began to think; it may be they say true, that speak of God; it may be it is true, that God is in heaven; and should any teach me in my language, I might know God: but if I should pray, it may be it is in vain to pray in my language; could I speak *English,* I might learn to pray. And I see the *English* love us, and therefore it is like, that is true which they say of God, and I desire to live for ever where they do. When I first heard the Word, it said, God is good; a little I believed it, but I did more doubt.

Mr *Jackson* asked me if I did pray to God: I asked him whether God understood our language, if I prayed to him: Hee said, yea, all things God doth know, and all languages. Then my heart said, It may be I may attain to pray.

know, and all languages. Then my heart said, It may be I may attain to pray. But my heart was hard, and therefore I could not pray, afterwards it may be I may. Sometime I thought if we did not pray, the *English* might kill us; but if I prayed, I thought I did not pray right. When I saw, and considered, that all men in the world dyed, I knew not how I might come to live for ever, how my soul might live, and therefore I desired I might pray to God aright; because they that so pray, are all one as if they dyed not, but live for ever. I wish'd I could pray aright, but could not tell how to do it. I did in my heart love wandering about, and our wilde courses alwaies; and when I did pray, it was but out-side praying, for in my heart I understood not right praying to God; I understood not how to pray, and I regarded not my weariness of that which was good, many things hindred my heart; I was ashamed, because my heart was full of evil. Sometimes I thought of my sins, but it was but a little, and I was soon weary of any good. I did not think God was not mercifull, but I saw my heart was naught, and very little did I know the evils of my heart. No humility was in my heart, and to this day my heart is evil, and hard is my heart, When you taught us the Word of God, my heart did not believe, but went contrary to the Word of God. I saw my mourning for sin was not good: I do confess my heart did not submit to God, only I hoped I might might learn the Word of God, which you taught us. My heart did afore love praying to the Devil, but I do not finde that I so love praying to God: therefore I did pray, Lord break my heart, that I may pray to God aright. My heart was weary of praying quickly; and therefore my heart said, Surely my heart is nought, and I am like a dead man: and therefore I prayed, Lord help me now to pray aright to God. Now I knew that God knoweth all the thoughts of my heart, and my many sins, and contrary doings, and how little I know of God. Surely I am a great sinner, and this I do throughly know, that great are my sins, and that my heart is contrary to praying to God, and my heart desired wilde courses, and I see that my heart loveth not praying to God. Yet now my heart began to desire to pray, and to love those things which are according to right praying; but I knew not what to do. Then I asked what I should do; then I heard this answer, I should desire Christ to break my heart by his spirit, none else in the world could do it; no man could work faith in me, but the Word which I heard doth it. I could not my self repent of sin, or be ashamed; but this I know, that the Word of God saith, *Those that believe in Christ shall not perish, but have eternal life*: Then my heart said, Oh Lord, let it be so to me, and let not my heart say contrary. Again I heard, *If any be foolish, let him ask wisedom of God, who giveth freely:* Then my heart said, I am foolish, Oh Lord teach me. Then I feared that my heart in vain seeketh, and then I desired humility, and that I might not pray in vain, and that I might not pray only outwardly. But my heart had contrary and misbelieving thoughts dayly, and my heart did not dayly desire after God, and but a little could I remember of God. Sometime my heart desired not to be like to such as prayed aright unto God; therefore I desired the Image of God upon me, and that I might be like to them which prayed to God aright; alwaies I thought that what God said in his Word was right. I heard this word, *The Foxes have holes, and the Birds have nests, but the Son of man hath not where to lay his head:* Then my heart said, Truth (Lord) the riches of this world are of no value; and therefore I desire not this worlds goods, but only heavenly blessings and grace, & I desire the way to the Heavenly Kingdom. And always my heart saith, touching my poverty and misery, I give my self and my soul to God and to Christ, because that is right. Again, I learn in the Catechize, Q. *What hath Chrsit done for us?* A. *He dyed for us, hee was buried, he rose again for us, and by his resurrection hee raiseth our souls unto grace, and also at the last day:* And my heart said, Oh let it be so in me! Again it is said, *What else hath Christ done for us?* A. *He ascended to heaven, to raise our hearts first to heaven, and then to carry us to heaven also, to be with him for ever.* My heart saith, Oh God I am not able to save my self, I cannot save my own soul, this is only thy work Oh God, and my heart believeth it; and with God is mercy and goodness, but in this world is nothing but weariness, and I know my weakness; therefore I am ashamed, and Oh let God put grace into my heart; and my heart saith, Oh let me not say in vain that I believe, Oh Lord help that I may truly believe, not by my works, but by thy Word Oh God. Again it is said in Catechism, *Why is Christ a Prophet?* A. *To teach me the way to heaven:* therefore my heart desireth that Christ may ever lead me by his Word; and it is only the mercy of Christ that must do this for me, and he giveth me true comfort only by believing in him.

THe Lord was so graciously with them in these Confessions, that they had good acceptance. Wee advised with the Church touching our further progress; the conclusion whereof was, that we sent Letters to all the neighbor Churches, informing them of our progress in this matter, in order to our receiving them; desiring them, or any among them, that had any just offence against any of these eight Indians, whom we named, that they would orderly communicate the same unto us, and seasonably; or if they had such knowledg of any of them, as to give us encouragement, we should be thankfull; or their silence, we should take in good part also. We had both incouragement and testimony from some Churches, only the paucity of Interpreters to co-attest with my Interpretation, was a matter of much difficulty, and no small impediment; for which cause I sent to Mr *Peirson*, to old Mr *Mayhu*, to *Thomas Stanton,* to be present with us, losing no known opportunity to bring our waies into the light, and to make all things clear. We proposed it to our Church, to agree about the publick day of Confessions; the conclusion was, that a Council was called, we sent unto ten Churches about us, requesting them by their Messengers to be present on *Roxbury* Lecture day, being the 5th of the 5th Moneth, 1659. acquainting them that that day was set apart to hear the Indians Confessions, and we requested counsel and direction from them, and concurrence with us.

After Prayer, I first declared to the Congregation what supply of Interpreters we had for co-attestation with my Interpretation of the Indians Confessions.

First, here was Mr *Peirson*, and we had (for clearness of our way, because of his unacquaintance with our dialect) ordered the confessing Indians to keep Sabbath at *Roxbury*; we spent half the Sabbath among them, a good part whereof was spent in hearing some of their Confessions, and all the second day we so spent, so that Mr *Peirson* had taken in writing all their Confessions; so that, if the Assembly pleased, they might hear the Confessions which they made before the Elders of *Roxbury*, which I have here in writing, and had been already seen by sundry of the Elders; also they might hear the Confessions which Mr *Peirson* and I had taken yesterday; which (compared with what the Lord shall assist them to utter this day) may help to clear up the verity and reality of their hearts in these their Confessions.

Moreover I declared, that here was a godly brother of *Martyns* Vineyard, named *Peter Fouldger*, who had for many years taught the Indian School in Mr *Mayhu's* life time; & since, he hath been by the Comissioners imployed to teach the Indians each other Sabbath; who told me, when I spake unto him about this work, that by reason of the different dialect, he durst not alone undertake to give in a testimony; but if he brought one of his Indians with him, (as need might be to help him) then he durst undertake to give a testimony upon Oath, if need were. This man, and his Indian with him, are this morning come, and are present in the Assembly, and set in a convenient seat together. Again I declared, that my son was present, who doth in some measure understand the Language: Also here are present two sons of *Thomas Stanton,* one of which the Commissioners maintain at the Colledg. And lastly, here are the Indian Scholars present; so that if the Assembly think meet to make use of any of these youths in this grave business, they might so do.

Further I declared, that in all this matter we did submit our selves to the guidance of the Reverend Council here present, and desired them to direct us and order us, as they saw meet to do in the Lord.

Then we proceeded to hear the Indians Confessions, which are as followeth.

Nishóhkou.

I called him forth, and said, Stand up and make your Confession before the Lord and his people.

Hee said, I Desire to confess before God and all these wise men, and God helping by the mercifull help of his gracious spirit, that I may confess all my sins.

I heard that word, Gen. 5. that *God made Adam in his own Image, both male and female;* and after many years *Adam* begat a son in his own Image, having lost Gods Image. And God did form man in the womb of our mother, in *Adams* Image, and so I was formed in the Image of *Adam;* and when I was born I lived in the same way, in the Image of Satan, and original sin was rooted in my heart, and grew up there; also I confess, that when I was a Child, my Parents and I were all wilde, we prayed to many Gods, and many other sins we did, and all the people did the same, both men and women, they lived in all lusts, they prayed to every creature; the Sun, Moon, Stars, Sea, Earth, Fishes, Fowl, Beasts, Trees, &c. all these things I saw when I was a youth, and all these things I liked and loved to do, and was delighted with these things; in all these things I lived, and with these things my memory was exercised, and in my youth I did what I listed, as *pauwauing,* or what else I would; when I was grown up, I loved lust, and delighted in it, I knew it not to be a sin, but an excellent delight: I loved all sin, but especially lust, and all that I did, was for the sake of lust, such things as women might like of; if I cut my hair, it was to please women, if I cut my hair in another fashion, and left a Lock on one side, it was with respect to lust; if I got fine cloaths, stockins, shoes, all was for to serve lust; our meetings and drinkings were with respect to lust: so that this was the chief thing I did delight in; and these things were in my bones, and there grew; then the Minister came to *Channit* to teach us: I came to the Meeting, but in vain; I came for lust to look on women, always I did thus, and I thought teaching to be madness, and so I continued two years after we prayed to God; after two years I heard a little, my ears were a little opened; I first understood that word, *He that doubteth, is like a wave of the Sea, driven to and fro, and tossed;* and that word, *If any man lack wisdome, let him ask it of God, who giveth freely, and unbraideth no man.* Also the same Winter I heard that word, *Gen.* 6. *God said, I will destroy man whom I have created, and he repented that he had made him.* These things I understood and remembred, but I confess before God, that I did only hear and know these things, as I did sometimes speak of what I did remember, but I believed not, yea I laughed, as other youths did, at all these things, because thereby did original sin grow in me, and hard it was to root it out, and hard to believe. After this I heard still, and more I understood; I heard, *Gen.* 16. that the people were full of sin, lust, and all other sin, and therefore the Lord destroyed them; and I knew that I had the same sins, and therefore I was afraid; but I feared only this bodily life, and not for my Soul: After this, my heart did a little desire to pray to God, because God found *Noah* righteous, and did save him, therefore I desired to pray; but again I laid it by, and I said it is vain to pray, for if I pray, and should commit sin, I shall be punished, or imprisoned, but if I pray not, I may commit what sin I will, and have no punishment for it. About a year after, I heard the Minister teach another word, that the Death of Christ is precious, and our death is nothing worth, therefore God promiseth pardon of all sins for Christ his sake; he bid us remember this against next time: When he came again, he asked me, and I did remember it, and do to this day; but I confess I did not believe, only I did remember it, and answered when I was asked: And then again, I desired to pray to God, and would not go away, but it was because I loved our place and dwelling; I prayed, but I believed not, I considered not Eternal Life, but only this worldly life: And thus I went on, till they chose Rulers at *Natik,* they chose me, and I refused, because I believed not: After that, my Wife and Child died, and I was sick to death, but lived again, and being well, I thought I could not pray, I was a Child, and therefore could not, I put off praying to God, my Relations died, and why should I pray? but then I considered, why does God thus punish me; yea, the Minister spake to me about it, and said, it may be it was because I refused to do Gods work, as *Moses,* when he first refused, God was patient, but when he persisted in his refusal, God was angry; and then my heart saw my sin, and then my heart almost believed: I desired to do right, and to keep the Sabbath, for I further heard in the 4th Commandment, *Remember the Sabbath to keep it holy;* and *Psa.* 101. *I will walk wisely in a perfect way:* Also in *Isay* 58. *If thou turn away thy foot from the Sabbath, and do not thy own works, nor find thy own pleasure, nor speak thy own words;* therefore my Soul desired to keep the Sabbath, then the Souldiers came upon us on the Sabbath-day, while we were at meeting, and took away our Guns, and caused us to bring them as far as *Roxbury;* that night my heart was broken off, my heart said, God is not, the Sabbath is not, it is not the Lords Day, for were it so, the Souldiers would not have then come; then my heart cast off praying, then we came before the Magistrates, and *Cutshamoquin* asked, Why they came on the Sabbath day: It was answered, that it was lawful; but I did not understand it: That day I being very thirsty, did drink too much, and was brought before the Magistrates, and was ashamed: I came to *Roxbury* to the Minister, and there I was ashamed also, because I had greatly sinned; then I cried to God for Free-mercy, because precious is the Death of Christ, oh pardon this my sin: Yet again I had temptations to drinking, and then I considered what a great sinner I was, even like a beast before God: Then I heard that word, *Mat.* 5. *He that breaketh the least of Gods Commands, and teacheth others so to do, shall be the least in the Kingdome of Heaven*: My heart said, Lord, such an one have I been, for I have been an active sinner; yet I cried again for mercy, O Lord freely pardon my great sins. Again, I confess I am very weak, even like a very child, and I so walk, and know not what to do; if I die, I fear I shall die in my sin; yet I cried again, O God pardon me for Christ his sake. Again, further I confess, that when I was troubled about our wants, poverty, and nakedness, I considered that text, *Foxes have holes, and Birds have nests, but the Son of man hath not whereon to lay his head.* And again, *Mat.* 6. *The Birds plough not, and the flowers spin not, and yet God doth both feed and cloath them;* and therefore be not over-much troubled about these things, yet I desire to follow labour with my hands, because *Gen.* 1. God gave *Adam* dominion over the creatures, and commanded him to Till the ground: And *Gen.* 2. He set him in the Garden, and commanded him to dress it, and keep it: Also *Gen.* 3. he said, *Thou shalt eat thy bread in the sweat of thy face all thy dayes, till thou returnest to thy dust.* When I remember these things, my heart doth bow to labour: also I heard that riches were the root of all evil, and *Dives* with his fine apparel, and dainty fare, was in hell, and poor *Lazarus* was in heaven: When my heart is troubled about our Land and about riches, I quiet my heart with these meditations. Also I further heard, when my heart was troubled about Salvation, and doubted, I heard that there is no means of Salvation but Christ, not any thing in the world can carry us to heaven, only Christ, which I did believe, by *Gen.* 28. where *Jacob* dreamed a dream, and he saw a Ladder which stood on earth, and the top reached up to heaven, and that Ladder is Christ; who is Man, and so toucheth the earth; and God, and so is in heaven, and by believing in him, we ascend to heaven as by a ladder. This helped me almost to believe, and I cried, Oh Christ be thou my Ladder to heaven! Again, *Joh.* 14. Christ saith, *None cometh to the Father, but by me*; therefore I believe, nothing can carry me to God, but only Christ, if I penitently believe in him. Again, I confess I do still find my self very weak to resist sin, for if I read, and teach on the Sabbath, I teach indeed, but I do not as I ought; and therefore that Word of Christ doth rebuke me, *Mat.* 23. Hear, and do what they say, but do not as they do. When I do, among others, reprove sinners, that Word of Christ reproveth me: *Thou hypocrite, first cast the beam out of thine own eye, and then thou mayest see clearly to cast the moat out of thy brothers eye.* Again, when I pray, I find hypocrisie in my heart, to do it to be seen of men, and that Word of Christ reproveth me, *Mat.* 6. *They pray to be seen of men, verily they have their reward;* and then I cryed mightily to God, O Lord help me, pardon me, what shall I do. Again, I heard *Mat.* 9. The Son of Man hath power to pardon sin on earth, and therefore me O Lord; then my heart did desire Christ, and to pray as long as I live, and my heart was stirred up thereunto, by *Luke* 18. Christ spake a parable, that we should pray, and not be weary, because the Widdow tyred the unjust Judge, and made him help her; how much more shall God the righteous Judge, hear and help his children, that cry night and day, therefore I desired to pray unto God as long as I lived: Then my heart said, What shall I do, for I am weak, and I fear I shall perish; then I heard that word, *Joh.* 3. *God so loved the world, that he gave his only Son, that whosoever believeth in him should not perish, but have Eternal Life.* And again it is said, that God loved his Son, and gave all things into his hand: I am weak, and though I pray, yet I am weak, therefore I desired to be in Christs hand, as in a Fort; in a Fort we are safe from exercise, they cannot easily catch us; out of a Fort we are open to them: So I desire Church-Estate, the Seals of Baptisme, and the Lords Supper, and all Church-Ordinances, as a Fort unto my Soul: I heard that Word of Christ, *Mat.* 16. *Thou art* Peter, *and on this Rock I will build my Church, and the gates of hell shall not prevail against it:* Oh I desire to be there kept! Again, I heard *Mat.* 3. *God is able of these stones to raise up seed to* Abraham; therefore raise up me O Lord: And again, Christ came to *John* to be baptized, *John* refused, but Christ said, *Suffer it to be so:* It is necessary to fulfill all unrighteousness, therefore so I desire to do all that is right, and I desire to be baptized. Again I confess, I fear I shall sin again, and defile my self, after I washed and baptized, even as the dog returneth to his vomit; therefore I cry, O God help me for thy free mercies sake. Again, I heard that in *Mat.* 18. *where two or three are met together in my Name, Christ is in the midst of them:* Therefore I desire to have the Ordinances of Christ, to be with Christ; but my heart saith, if I be bound by Ordinances, then I shall be imprisoned, but yet I desire to be there in prison with Christ; if my heart say, I shall be as dead, but yet I desire to be so with Christ. Again, I heard in *John*, Christ saith, *Who ever cometh to me, I cast him not away, but he shall have life:* But *Joh.* 5. Christ doth say, *Ye will not come unto me, that you might have life:* Therefore my heart did greatly fear, and pray, Oh that I might come to Christ! and Christ is the everlasting Son of God; therefore my Soul desireth to be with him: And this I confess, that though I believe in Christ, yet I am still weak; and therefore I desire to be made strong by the Seals; but I fear I am unworthy, because of that word, *Mat.* 7. *Cast not Pearls before Swine, nor holy things to dogs;* yet my heart saith, O Lord remember me, and yet let me a dog come under thy Table to get a crum; and I cry to God because of all my weakness: I confess I cannot deliver, or help, or save my self, only Christ Jesus can do it, and let Free-grace pardon me, and save me, O God have mercy on me! Again, *Mat.* 18. *Whatever ye bind on earth, is bound in heaven; and whatever ye loose on earth, is loosed in heaven;* therefore I desire to be loosed both in earth, and in heaven, and to be sealed with Gods Seal.

When I had read this Confession of his, I said, because the Lord hath said, that in the mouth of two or three Witnesses, every Truth shall be established; *therefore I desired that the rest of the Interpreters might attest unto this which I had read.*

First, Mr. *Peirson* said, so far as I discern, I doubt not of the truth of what Mr. *Eliot* hath delivered, and for that which he hath now uttered, though some things the *Indian* hath added more then he spake in private, and somethings left out, and some things otherwise placed, yet for the substance of his present Confession, it is the same with that which he delivered in private, where we did carefully try all things, that we might be sure that we understood him right. Then Bro. *Fouldyer* was desired to speak; who saith, That he did not expect to have understood so much of his speech, and so plainly as he did, and his Interpreter did perfectly understand all; and to his best understanding, that which Mr. *Eliot* had delivered, was the very same which he spake.

I said unto the Assembly, In that he spake so plain to his understanding, it is because I had advised him, and so all the rest, to express themselves in the most plain and familiar words and expressions they could, for my more easie and perfect understanding. Again, for that my Bro. *Peirson* observed, that they left out something, and added other, and varied in sundry expressions: It is true, I observed the same, and it may well be so, for they have not any writing, or like helps, only their memory, and the help of Gods Spirit, to read in their own hearts, what they utter.

Then the two Sons of *Thom. Stanton* were called, to testifie the Schollar spoke first, and said, that he did understand perfectly all that the *Indian* said, and he did not observe any difference in what Mr. *Eliot* had delivered, but it was the same which the *Indian* spake.

The other spake, and said, he did not perfectly understand all that the *Indian* said, but so far as he did understand, Mr. *Eliot* had delivered the truth.

My Son was called to speak, who said, I did, for the most part, well understand the *Indian*, and to my best understanding, my Father hath given a true interpretation thereof.

Antony.

He was next called, who thus spake.

I Confess my sins before the Lord, and all these people and godly men, for ye throughly know that we are great sinners, not only before God, but before man also.

I confess that in my Mothers Womb I was conceived in sin, and that I was born in iniquity; my Father and Mother were sinners, and lived in sin, they prayed to many Gods, the Sun, Heavens, Beasts, Trees, and every thing in the world, they made them their Gods, and throughly we followed these sins: When I was born, I was in the Image of Satan, I knew not that God made all this world, I was only wise to sin, and I did all those things which I liked to do, even all lusts, from my youth up; and now I confess my sins before God, and all men, for God and men do know them: I did all my delights. When I was a youth the English came, but I regarded them not: Afterward I heard that the *Indians* prayed, but my heart said, I will not pray so long as I live, for they be vain words to pray unto God, my Parents taught me to pray unto many Gods: Sometime I came to English Towns on the Sabbath day, and I played, for I did not regard that sin; I thought it vain to keep one day, yet I feared that the English should see me play, least they should be angry, but not because I offended God. Afterwards I heard that my Brothers prayed, and therefore I disliked them, and I thought I will forsake my Brothers, because they do a vain work, and I did run away into the Country, but they soon found me, and asked me to pray, and they pitied me, and loved me, and therefore I returned, not because I loved God, but because I loved my brothers: My brother said, Go dwell with the English, and learn their manners; I yeilded, because I loved my brother: I dwelt here at *Roxbury,* and came to this meeting house, but in vain, I prayed not one word, and my heart did misbelieve; I heard the Minister preach that there is one God, and he made the World, and all things in it, but my heart thought it was a vain word; I thought my Father made me, and not God. Again, I returned from this Town, but yet I did not pray; I heard the Commandements, *Thou shalt not murder; Thou shalt not commit adultery; Thou shalt not steal; Thou shalt not bear false witness against thy neighbour; Thou shalt not covet,* &c. and other sins and punishments I heard of, and I feared to sin because of man, and because of punishment, but not for fear of God; therefore vain were all my wayes. When I came back to *Noonantam,* I did the same sins again, especially I loved lust; yea, after my praying and being among them, I loved it more then before: When the Minister came and taught, I went to the meeting, but in vain; I learned nothing, but I still loved all our sins and lusts: Afterward hearing the Catechism, *Who made you?* God. *Who redeemed you?* Jesus Christ, &c. my heart misbelieved, and said, I will not believe, I will go away into the Country. Again, I heard that God made all the world, and then a little I believed, and thought I will pray to God, but weak it was. Again, I heard *Mat. 7. Ask, and ye shall have, seek, and ye shall find, knock, and it shall be opened to you:* Then I prayed a little, and then I thought there was a God who made the whole world, I thought man could not make the world, but only God; and therefore I did pray unto him. Afterward my Brothers were sick, and others also, I remembered that word, *Ask, and ye shall have;* then I prayed, to try if that word was true, but they dyed; then I thought that was a vain word, and that God heareth not our prayers, and that God is not; therefore I thought I will cast off praying, and run away. I did not believe in God; my heart said, I shall die, whether I pray, or not pray, all is one: Then I heard that praying was the way to Everlasting Life, but yet I regarded not praying, I thought of running away, and yet I thought, whether I go or stay I shall die, and therefore I was troubled, but I did not pray: Afterward I was at work, and my head was broken in the Saw-pit, and then I knew God was angry with me, because I prayed not; and then I did much know my sins, I thought surely God is angry; I remembred that I had heard that Word preached, *Watch, for ye know not the hour that the Son of Man cometh;* this I remembred when my head was broken, I heard that God made all the world, and *Adam*, and set *Adam* in Paradise, and bid him eat of all the Trees, saving of the Tree in the midst of the Garden, if he eat thereof he should die; but *Adam* did eat thereof, and died; then my heart believed, surely God is, and he made the world, and man, and me. I heard *Gen.* 1. God said, *Let us make man in our own Image, and let him have dominion over all the creatures*: Then my heart believed, sure God is good to man, and man is a sinner against God; and therefore God is angry with me for my sins. I heard that God formed man of the dust of the earth, and breathed into him the breath of Life; and then my heart said, surely God made the world, and man, and me, and all things, and my heart believed: And now I know God is angry with me; now I will pray to God as long as I live, and no more return to sin, but I will do Gods Word all my daies. Again, I heard that God made *Adam* sleep, and took out of him a rib, made it a woman, and brought her to man; then I thought, sure God made us, and the world, and these great works shew, that there is a God. Again, I heard that God called her the Mother of all living, and by that means we have life, and then I believed that God made us; and therefore I will pray to God as long as I live, and no more cast it off. Again, I heard *Gen.* 6. that *God saw the sin of man, that it was great, and that all the thoughts and imaginations of his heart are only evil continually; and therefore God was angry, and repented that he had made man, and therefore drowned the world, and every living creature; he caused it to rain fourty dayes on the earth;* then my heart said, sure there is a God, and he will perform all his threatnings, he is God, and therefore he will do it. Again, I heard that God found *Noah* righteous, and he found favour in his sight; he believed in God, and did obey his Word, and God saved him: Then my heart desired to believe that God is, and to pray unto him. Again, I heard *Gen.* 19. that the Angels of God came to *Lot* in *Sodom,* and delivered just *Lot,* but did burn up with the wicked *Sodomites* with fire from heaven, who had cast off praying to God, and did commit great sins against God; therefore I saw that I had deserved to be burnt, because I had done their sins: And when God sent his Angels, and did deliver just *Lot,* and then the rest were burnt, then I saw in my heart, sure God is merciful to them that love him; and therefore my heart said, I will no more return to sin, but I will follow God; but yet sometimes I doubted, but I believed the mercy of God, according to that I heard, *Mat.* 1. *she called his Name* Jesus, *for he saveth his people from their sins:* Then my heart thought, surely it is true, that Christ is the Son of God, and was made man, and is merciful; but yet I still did doubt whether Christ was the Son of God. Again, I heard *Mat.* 3. *Repent, for the Kingdome of Heaven is at hand.* And again, *The voice of one crying in the Wilderness, prepare ye the way of the Lord, and make his paths straight:* My heart said, I desire to repent, and to make ready my heart for God, that I may have mercy and pardon in Christ Jesus. Again, the word saith, *The Tree that brings not forth good fruit, is cut down, and cast into the fire:* My heart said; sure so is my heart, and I have deserved to be cast into the fire; I have brought forth such fruits as may justly cut me down. Again, I heard the word of Christ, *He that heareth the Word, and doeth it, shall be blessed:* Then my heart said, I have deserved not to be pardoned, but I beg for mercy. Again, the word saith, *This is my beloved Son, in whom I am well pleased:* My heart said, sure God is merciful to send his own Son, and Christ is merciful that he came and died for us. Again, I heard that the Tempter came to Christ, and said, *If thou be the Son of God, make these stones bread:* But Christ said, *man liveth not by bread only, but by every word which cometh out of the mouth of God:* Then I believed that Christ was the Son of God, and that my Soul liveth not by bread, but by the Word of God. Again, *Mat.* 8. the Leper came to Christ, and said, *Lord if thou wilt, thou canst make me whole, and Jesus touched him, and he was healed:* Then my heart said, surely Christ is the Son of God, and he only can heal my sins. Again, I heard in *Mat.* 6. *If ye forgive one another, God forgiveth you:* Then my heart said, I desire to do this, else God will be angry with me. Again, I heard *Mat.* 9. all diseased came to Christ, the blind, halt, &c. and he healed them; therefore I believed that he was the Son of God, and I begged of Christ to pardon my sins, and save me, because sure he is Christ the Son of God. Again, the word saies, *Not every one that saith Lord, Lord, shall enter into the Kingdome, but he that doth the will of my Father:* Then my heart said, I do fear, because I do very weakly obey the Word of God; and therefore Christ saith, *Depart ye workers of iniquity:* My heart said, such an one am I but now I cry to, and trust to Christ, to pardon all my sins. Again, I heard *Mat.* 11. that Christ said *Capernaum* was lifted up to heaven by the Gospel, but should be cast down to hell, for refusing it: I thought I did now pray, if I now fall off I shall perish. And again, Christ saith, *It shall be easier for* Tyre *and* Sidon *in that day:* Then my heart said, I have deserved the worst of Gods wrath, so I believed not the great works of God; and therefore I desire pardon of all my sins, and to forsake all my sins, and to pray to Christ as long as I live. Again, I heard *Mat.* 5. *That Heaven and Earth shall pass away, but not one jot or tittle of the Word of God, but all shall be fulfilled:* Therefore my heart did desire, that I may both hear and do the Word of God, which will never perish. Again, I heard *Mat.* 16 Christ saith, *Who say ye that I am?* Peter said, *Thou art Christ, the Son of the living God;* Christ said, *Blessed art thou* Peter, *flesh and blood hath not revealed this to thee, but my Father, and on this Rock I will build my Church, and the gates of hell shall not prevail against it:* Therefore my heart believed that God helped me to receive Christ, and I desire to take that promise to *Peter,* and my heart joyed more and more in Christ, and in the Word of God. Again, I heard *Mat.* 26. *Jesus took bread, and blessed it, and brake it, and gave it, and said, Take eat, this is my body which is broken for you, and likewise the Cup, &c. saying, This is my blood in the New Testament, which was shed for remission of sins, &c.* My heart said, sure Christ is full of love, and hath given us great mercy, and I desire to partake of it. Again, the wicked did kill Christ, but he rose again, and ascended to heaven; then my heart believed Christ. Again, I heard *John* 14. *No man cometh to the Father, but by me:* My heart said, so be it Lord; I desire to come to God by Christ; and I said, Why did the wicked kill Christ? My heart said, I believe that Christ died for my sin; and therefore I desire to believe in Christ: Then my heart did joy in Christ, and to hear the Word of God; but yet to this day I have doubts in my heart, my heart is weak to this day: And now I know that in six daies God made the world, and before that God I desire to confess my sins, and forsake them, and no more to do them. Sometimes my heart is in an ill frame, and loveth sin, and my heart hateth good; therefore I desire the free Mercy of Christ to hold and keep my Soul.

When he had finished, and I had read before the assembly this confession of his, we called upon the witnesses to co-attest. Who did in the same order as before express themselves to the like purpose. Only when we called for Tho: Stanton *his* sonnes, *they were not present, nor did they any more appeare in the Congregation, to attest the* Indians *confessions all the day.*

Ponampiam

He was next called forth, and thus spake.

I Confess my sinnes before the Lord, and his people this day. While my Father lived, and I was young, I was at play, and my Father rebuked me, and said, we shall all die shortly. [In private we asked him what ground or reason moved his Father so to speak? he answered, it was when the English were new come over, and he thinketh that his Father had heard that Mr *Wilson* had spoken of the flood of *Noah,* how God drowned all the world for the sinnes of the people.] Then I was troubled, and thought sure what God saith, shall be, and not what man saith; but I quickly forgot this, and thought not of any good. That same Winter the pox came; all my kindred died, only my Mother and I lived, we came to *Cohannit,* by *Dorchester,* where I lived till I was a man, and married. All those daies I sinned, and prayed to all gods, and did as others did; there I lived till the Minister came to teach us. When I heard that they prayed, my heart desired it not. Sometime I prayed among them, and sometime I neglected it. I feared to pray because of the *Sachems,* therefore I put it off, for the fear of man. Afterward I considered in my heart, to pray to God, not because I loved the word, but for other reasons. I heard that Word, *Mal.* 1. *From the rising of the sun to the going down thereof, my name shall be great among the Gentiles, and in every place incense shall be offered unto my name, and a pure offering, for my name shall be great among the heathen, saith the Lord of hosts.* Then I was troubled in my thoughts about running away, yet then I thought if I should go to another place, they must pray also, and therefore I cannot flie from praying to God, therefore I tarried, and when others prayed, I prayed with them, only I still feared man; after I heard the same word again, to perswade us to pray to God; and I did so, but not for Gods sake, only it was before man. I remembred the Sabbath, and I heard Mr *Mathews* also preach of it, and therefore I thought I would keep the Sabbath, but still I feared man. Upon a Sabbath, they wished me to teach what I remembred, that the Minister had taught. I did so, and we had talk about what I said, and we fell out. Thereupon I went away, and left praying to God. I went into the Countrey, but I remembred my wife and children, and quickly returned, but not for Gods sake. Again the Minister preached on *I Chron.* 28.9. *And thou Solomon my son know the God of thy Fathers, and serve him with a perfect heart, and with a willing mind, for the Lord searcheth all hearts, and understandeth all the imagination of the thoughts; if thou seek him, he will be found of thee, but if thou forsake him, he will cast thee off for ever.* This greatly troubled me, because I had left praying to God, and I had deserved eternall wrath. Then I desired to pray, I begged mercy, but I knew not what to do, for my sins were many, my heart was full of originall sin, and my heart was often full of anger; but then I was angry at my self, for I found my heart quickly carried after sin. Afterward, through the free mercy of God, I heard that word, *He that penitently believeth in Christ shall be pardoned and saved;* then my heart did beg earnestly for pardon and mercy. I heard *Joh.* 15. *Whatever ye ask the Father in my name, he will give it you;* therefore my heart did now greatly beg for mercy in Christ and pardon. Afterward I heard *Mat.* 5.28. *Who ever looketh upon a woman to lust after her, hath committed adultery in his heart.* Then my heart was troubled, because many were my sins, in my eies, and heart, and actions too. My heart did love the having of two wives, and other lusts of that kind: Then Satan said to me, You are a great sinner, and God will not pardon you, therefore cast off praying, and run away, it is a vain thing for you to pray. Here you want land, but in the Countrey there is land enough, and riches abundance, therefore pray no more. My heart did almost like it, but I heard that word, *Mat.* 4. *Satan tempted Christ, and shewed him the Kingdoms of the world, and the glory thereof, and promised to give them to him, if he would worship him.* Then my heart said, that even thus Satan tempteth me to cast off praying to God; and therefore my heart desired to believe that word of Christ, *Thou shalt worship the Lord thy God, and him only shalt thou serve.* Then I prayed again, but still I was full of sin, and very weak I was, and I loved sin. Again I heard, *Joh.* 14. *I am the Way, the Truth, and the Life, no man cometh unto the Father but by me.* Then I fully saw that Christ only is our Redeemer, and Saviour, and I desire to believe in Christ; and my heart said, that nothing that I can do can save me, only Christ: therefore I beg for Christ, and a part in him. Then said my heart, I give my heart and my self to Christ, and my wife and children, let him do with us what he will. Then my mother and two children died, and my heart said, What Christ will do, so be it; I have given them to him, and I begged pardon and mercy, if God will please to pardon me a poor sinner, blessed be his name.

When I had read this Confession in the Assembly, we called upon the witnesses, as before we did, whose answer was like as before it was.

John Speen
Hee was next called forth, and thus spake.

I Confess my sins this day before the Lord, and not only before God, but before all these people. Before I prayed, verily I was a great sinner, yea, in my mothers womb I was a sinner: my sins are such as not only God knows, but people also know them. Before our praying, I did thorowly sin, and did commit all sins; and now I confess these my sins before God. After I prayed, I did also live in sin. At first when I prayed, I did not worship God, nor believe in Christ; but I did therefore pray, because my brothers, and friends, and *Waban*, and the rest did pray, for their sakes I prayed. And again I therefore prayed, because many *English* knew me, and that I might please them; and because I saw the *English* took much ground, and I thought if I prayed, the *English* would not take away my ground, for these causes I prayed. When I prayed, it was but with my mouth, yet I thought I do well enough in that I pray thus, and I thought, that for it God will pardon all my sins; and I thought that my praying was good enough. But yet again I sinned, and did the like sins as before, only I did outwardly pray, but I mourned not for my sins. I thought, if we pray and leave Pauwauing, who shall make us well when we are sick. But again, I thought man could not make us well, because he must die himself, and therefore Pauwauing is a vain thing, and they die though they Pauwau. But still my heart did not believe praying to God: then I heard that word, *Repent and believe; and if we repent and believe, God will pardon all our sins.* Then sometimes I repented, yet again quickly I committed sin; and sometimes I thought I am throughly a sinner. I heard that God made the world, and all things in it, and lastly man, and that God formed him of the dust of the earth, and breathed into him the breath of life, and he became a living soul, and that God made a Covenant with *Adam*, that he should eat of all the Trees of the Garden, save one in the midst of the Garden, and if he eat of that Tree, he should die. Then I understood that *Adam* sinned, & fell, and thereby I uneerstood that I became a sinner, born in sin, my heart full of sin, and God will not pardon sinners; and yet again I sinned, and therefore I feared that God will not pardon me, because more and more I sinned: and thus I sinned after praying, as well as before praying. When they chose Rulers, and chose my brother, and not me, my heart was in an evil frame, and then I thought sure I am a great sinner, and yet still I was more and more a sinner. After my brothers loved me still, and then I repented of my sins, but not for Gods sake, but for my brothers sake; then I desired to pray as long as I live. My brother died, which troubled me; the people said, Be you in your brothers place: then my heart thought, I will no more do as I had done, but sure I was weak, my praying was but words, I was a great sinner. After this, a while since I heard that word, Mat. 12. *The unclean spirit being cast out of a man, he walketh about seeking rest and findeth none; then hee returneth and bringeth 7 other spirits with him worse then himself, and the end of that man is worse then his beginning.* When I heard this, my heart feared. I thought now I repent of my many sins, for verily I am a great sinner, & I have offended, I am 7 times worse then before I prayed; then I repented.

Again I heard that Word, *He that penitently believeth shall be saved,* and then my heart did desire to repent and believe, then I thought that men will not forgive me, and therefore it is not good to abide in this place, but I remembred that I had learned to read the Word, and if I should forsake my friends, I should lose the Word of God. Then I heard that Word, *Repent, for the Kingdome of Heaven is at hand,* my heart said ô let it be so, and then my heart rested; but yet quickly it was unquiet again. Then I did strongly desire to repent my sinnes. I heard that Word, that *God sowed good seed, but evill seed was sowen by the Enemy*, and such were in my heart, as in my field there were many roots, and weeds which spoyled the corne, and I plucked them up, and cast them out; my heart said, verily just so is my heart, the Word is but a little in my heart, and there be many ill roots in me, and therefore God may justly cast me out from among his people, because of my many sinnes. Then my heart said, I desire to pray to God as long as I live, and now I forsake my sins, who have been a great sinner. Now I beg of Christ, O give me thy spirit, that I may confess my sins before God, and not only before men; again I remember that I cannot pardon or help my self, but only Christ must help me. Again I heard that Word, *All manner of sin shall be forgiven to a man, but the sin against the Holy Ghost, shall not be forgiven in this world, nor in the world to come.* Then my heart feared, because many and great were my sins since I prayed to God, and I cried to God for mercy and pardon: and then I thought I will pray to God as long as I live. But verily I am a sinner, for I am guilty not only of *Adams* sin, but of my own sins also, and they are many. I remember that in Catechisme I learn, that God made a Covenant of works with *Adam, Do the Commands, and thou shalt live, and thy seed also; but if thou sin, thou shalt die, and thy seed also;* therefore by that I know I am a sinner, and have deserved to die. Then I crie to God, O God have mercy upon me, and pardon me. Again, I heard of the mercy of God, but I am forgetfull, and cannot remember Gods mercies to me. God made a Covenant with *Abraham* and said, *I will be thy God, and the God of thy seed after thee,* then my heart said, O let it be so to me O Lord. And now *Abraham* is in heaven, who believed, and kept Gods Covenant; So I, if I believe and keep Gods Covenant, God will have mercy on me. I remembred the Covenant of Circumcision to him, and all his family; and such a Covenant I desire for me and mine. Again I heard, Mat. 3. In those daies *John* baptized in *Jordan:* saying, *Repent for the Kingdome of God is at hand.* When I heard this my heart said, the same is now with us, not *Abrahams* signe but baptisme, and therefore I desire to repent, and Confess before God, and before the Church:

and I desire not only to confess, but to have repentance, and faith, that I may have grace, mercy, and pardon: and such repentance as workes obedience. Again, the same Word saith, vers. 6. *They were baptized confessing their sins;* So I desire to do. I do confess before God, and desire to cast off, and forsake my sins, and to go to Christ. The promise of pardon is to them that penitently believe, and rest on Christ. In the same Baptism of *John*, he said, *I baptize you with water, but he that cometh after me, is mightier then I , he shall baptize you with the Holy Ghost and fire.* Now this Baptism I desire, and not to receive the signe in vain: I desire to purge out evill thoughts, and therefore I confess these sins before God, that they may be purged, and I desire the spirit of God may dwell in me for ever, to turn me to Christ. I cannot of my self do any of these things, but only Christ Jesus can by his spirit in me.

Again I heard another word, *As the Eagles are about a carkass, so believers come to Christ:* then my heart said, So be it Oh Lord; when I receive the Covenant of God, I am like the Eagles; when I come to Christ, I desire not to come in vain; but if I feed not, I shall die, my soul will die. Then I greatly begged that I might feed my soul on Christ; and Oh Christ send thy spirit into my heart, that I may not only know, but do the Word of God. Again, *Christ, near his death, took bread, and blest it, and broke it, and gave it to his disciples, and said, Take yee, eat yee, this is my Body which was broken for you:* And so also he did the Cup, *and said, Drink yee of it, this is the Cup of my blood in the New Testament which is shed for the remission of sins.* Now this believers in Christ must do, not only to eat Bread, and to take the Sign, but soul food: therefore Christ sending his spirit, and helping me, I desire to receive the Sign, not in vain, but to help my faith.

When I had read this Confession in the Assembly, we called upon the witnesses, (as before wee did) whose answer was to the like purpose as before.

Wutasakompauin

He was next called forth, who thus spake.

HElp me Oh Jesus Christ, to confess before the Lord; Oh I am full of sin, because *Adams* sin made mine, and so was a sinner in my mothers womb. When I was a youth I found many sins, and after I was grown up, I did the same alwaies, all the daies of my life I lived in sin. After the English came I went to their houses; they would teach me about God but I hated it and went out, I did not love such teaching. Afterward the Minister taught, and at first *Waban* perswaded me to pray, and taught us; I did not at first like it, yet afterward I did. Four years the Minister came to *Noonantam;* I came, but I only came, I lost all he taught. After I considered one word; the Minister said, That God sent him to teach us; then I thought surely there is a God, therefore I must believe and pray: a little I believed, but when I heard, I did only outwardly hear. After, my wife and children died, and then I almost cast off praying. I had another wife, and she died also; and then my heart said, Surely God is angry with me, who doth thus afflict me. Then I heard that word, *Mat.* 22. God made a Feast, and invited his Guests, and they would not come, and therefore God was angry with them: So did I; for I came not to the Word of God, when he called me, I cared not for the Feast of Christ. Again, after many of my friends were destroyed, I thought it was because they prayed not to God, therefore I feared that God is angry with me also, because of his punishments. I fear, I believe not Christ; and my heart feareth, because of my sins; daily I break Gods Commands. Another Word I heard, Mat. 5. *Blessed are they who hunger and thirst after righteousness, for they shall be satisfied;* this is the Word of Christ, and I desire to hunger for Christ, and begged O Christ help me. Again, I remembred that Word, *Blessed are the pure in heart, for they shall see God;* my heart saith, O Christ, help me to be so, that cleane may be my heart. Again, I heard that Word, *Blessed are the peace-makers, for they shall be called the Children of God;* then my heart thought, O that I had peace with God in Christ, that I might have that blessing; and therefore I now confess my sins before God, and I beg mercy from God in Jesus Christ. When I had read this short confession, (for the day spent, and brevity was called for) we called upon the witnesses who spake as formerly.

Monotunkquanit.

He was next called, who thus spake.

I Have heard the word, and prayed to God several yeares. And I confess that before I prayed, I was full of sin, and yet I do not know my sins. I thought they were all good waies, and therefore I did them. I knew not the Sabbath, nor Lecture daies, nor any good, only I knew wild Actions, daily I desired falshood, vile actions, singing *Indian* songs, these things I desired to do: but all good things I was ignorant of, and very much I sinned, daily. Then I heard of praying to God. I came to *Cohannit* at *Dorchester*, from *Nipmuk* where I lived, but my heart laughed at praying, and said its a vain action, only those actions that I was bred up in, I liked and esteemed, but these new things I derided. The *Sachims* disliked it, and therefore so did I. The rich men disliked it, and therefore so did I. I believed not, that God is; I went to *Cohannit,* not for praying, but to gather clams. When I came thither, they exhorted me to pray: and said, The Minister cometh to morrow to teach, it is lecture day. I desired to see him: he came, they met together. I went, and carried my son *Samuel:* I saw the Minister, he called my son; asked him, *Who made you;* they bid him say *God;* but I had not so taught him. He asked, whose son he was, they said mine: he said, *do you pray to God?* I said no, for I am a poore man, and naked: they that pray are cloathed.

Therefore I will not pray, can poore men pray? Therefore I would not pray: I went home. Then *Waban* and *Totherswamp* came to my house, and taught me to pray. They intreated me, now pray *to God*; My heart liked it not. They said, *God is a great God, and made all the World.* I said, who is witnesse of that? They said, the Minister will answer you. Again, *they taught me the Commandments of God*; but I did not believe. *Totherswamp* promised to come again, he did so; and said, *now pray to God*, because *God is good.* I thought it a teadious thing to pray to God. Then he strongly intreated me: I said I will try; but not for praying, but in vain. Then my kindred said, praying is a vain thing, why will you pray? therefore returne again: then I went, and prayed. When I first came, *Waban* taught that Word. *The night is farre spent, the day is at hand, therefore let us cast off the works of darkness, and let us put on the Armour of light.* My heart asked what are dark workes? They answered, *sinnes;* and what is day? they answered, *praying to God*, and the wisdome of the Word *is light*: And this is now almost come unto us. Then my heart smile, I will pray to God. Again, I heard the Minister who said, these words, *Thou shalt have no other Gods but me; thou shalt not make to thy selfe any graven Image, nor the likeness of any thing in Heaven above, in the earth below, in the waters under the earth: thou shalt not bow down to them, nor worship them;* Then my heart said, that I did worship many false gods, therefore if I pray, it may be God will kill me: but they said no, he is a good God; then I prayed, and then my kindred hindred me. Therefore my heart said, If my kindred pray, then I will pray. Then I was taught more, and I did heare the Word, that *God made Adam of the dust, and made him sleep, and took out a rib, and made a woman,* and thus God made man. My heart said, It may be God made English men, but not us poore naked men, as we are of a strange language; and therefore I doubted to pray. Then I heard of *Nimrod* his building of *Babel*, and that God was angry, made strange to each other their language, and brake their work: Then my heart said, Surely so it is, as I did believe. Againe I heard, that *God found one man just, Noah, and saved him in his Ark, and did drown the world:* then my heart said, I desire that God may find many just persons with us, therefore I pray to God: then I more prayed. Again I heard, *that God made a Covenant with Abraham and his seed, to be their God.* My heart said, so let it be: I desire to be in this Covenant of God, and to pray so long as I live. I thought, if I do well, God will pardon all my sinnes: the Minister said no; If you do all good, as perfectly, yet God will not pardon: God will pardon, only *for Jesus Christ his sake.* Then I believed *Jesus Christ was both God and man, and made peace betwixt God and man: Christ* did for us *all the Commandments of God, and died for us, he payed death for us;* and therefore for his sake God will pardon us, if we believe in Christ. I heard that which Mat. 7. *Ask and ye shall have, seek and ye shall find, knock, and it shall be opened, &c.* Then my heart said, I will pray as long as I live, and knock at heaven dore. Again I heard that word, *Enter in at the streight gate, &c.* My heart said, Sure it is so, *narrow and hard is the way to Heaven, broad and easy is the way to hell;* I desire to walk in the narrow way to heaven. Again, *Christ died for us,* and thereby saveth us; and saith, *Come to me all that are weary, and I will give you rest.* Then my heart said, Great is my weariness, for many are my sinnes, and I desire rest in Christ. I heard that Christ only is our redeemer and Saviour, my heart did much joy in it; and I desired to pray and heare the Word as long as I live. Another Word of Christ I heard, *Whoever forsaketh father or mother, or brother or lands for my sake, &c.* My heart said, ô Lord let it be so, I have for Christ his sake left all, and come to pray. And I desire now to confess before the Church of *Roxbury*, and do submit to your government, and Gods Ordinances among you. He was going on, but shortness of time made me take him off. When I had read this confession, and the witnesses had spoke as before, some of the Elders present, did move that seeing there be two more to speak, and the time streight; and seeing Mr *Peirson* had in private taken in writing their confessions, which they perceived by his testimony, to be for substance the same which they expressed in publick; What if the Assembly should heare Mr *Peirson* read those two remaining confessions, according as he had taken them? The motion was acceptable to the Assembly, and he did read them, which are as followeth.

Piumbuhhou.

First, THis I say in the presence of God, and in your presence, Verily I knew not how or what to confess of God, before I prayed. I knew not who gave me life and being, but I thought my life was of my self. I confess I was born in sin, my Parents were sinners, and I thought I had life from none but my Parents, therefore my sins were very great: from the first time that I saw light, untill this day, I do nothing else but sin; hard is my heart, proud is my heart, and hypocriticall: I do hypocriticall acts, to this day. I act foolishly, and deceitfully; therefore so many are my sinnes, that I am not able to express them; only this I say, that I am naught. Then I heard that *Waban* prayed, and they said to me, pray to God: but I hated it, for I had a wife, and many children, and therefore I cared not for praying. I thought if they were any of them sick, the *Pauwaus* could make them well, therefore I believed not *Waban*, when he exhorted me to pray to God. Then my wife and children died: then my afflicted poore heart came in, and the Minister came to me and said, pray to God, because *God afflicteth and tryeth you;* my heart said, when the Minister spake to me, let it be as you say, that God may shew me that mercy: then my heart said, I will pray to God, from henceforth, as long as I live. Then I heard the Minister Preach of the great works of God, *in making Heaven and Earth,* and therefore fear the great punishments of God; and because my heart so feared, and condemned me, therefore I did believe that God is, who had punished me, and took away my children. Again, I heard from Mat. 5. *Christ* saith, *Blessed are the poore in spirit, for theirs is the Kingdome of God: and blessed are the mercifull, for they shall find mercy;* my heart said, I am a poore man, and therefore I will pray to God so long as I live: and I desire to find mercy with God. Again, now my heart saith, I am weak and doubting, and full of misbelief. Again, I heard that Word of Christ, which saith, *Come unto me all yee that are weary and heavy laden, and yee shall find rest;* my heart said, be it so O Lord: and now I will pray to God, as long as I live; my heart said, surely I am greatly laden with many, and great sins: and therefore I will go to Christ, and pray unto him, as long as I live. Again, Christ saith, *Take up my burden, and learne of me, for I am humble and meeke;* then my heart said, surely I am a great sinner, and therefore I desire to learne of Christ, and to follow him. Again Christ saith, *Yee shall find rest to your soul;* and therefore my soul desired to pray as long as I live, that I may find rest to my soul in Christ. Again, my heart did gladly hear the Word of Christ, and the great redemption of Christ. Again, I learned in a Catechism, that Christ sendeth his Spirit into my heart, to break it, to make it repent, to convert me, to cause me to believe: my heart said, therefore I desire to pray to God, and to believe for pardon, and adoption, and peace with God. Then hearing of the mercy of Christ, my heart said, I am like a dead man, and therefore I desire to be with Christ as long as I live: my heart did not know how to Convert, and turn to God, therefore my heart did gladly pray to God for it; my heart did desire to pray, because I heard, Christ is our redeemer, and doth deliver our soules. I cannot deliver my selfe, therefore I desire that Christ may be my deliverer: therefore I betrust my soul with Christ as long as I live; and because Christ is my mercifull God, therefore let him do with my soul what he will.

When Mr Peirson *had read this Confession, he was desired to go on, and read the last which was* Wabans *Confession, and is as followeth.*

Waban.

First, I Confess, that before I prayed, it was hard to love another fashion then my old course: my Parents were sinners, and in my Mothers belly I was in sin: after I was born, the same way of sin I followed. When I was a child I grew up in sin, and I did not know that they were sins, but now of late I know them; in my youth also, in the same sins I lived, and did not know them to be so, but by the remembrance of my waies, I do remember my sins, and hereby I am made to understand, that my Parents taught me to love sin. And after they were dead, others taught me to sin: I liked to be taught to commit sin; those that taught me, said to me, Choose to be a Pauwau: they said, If you be a Pauwau, you may make others to live and if you be a Pauwau, God will blesse you, and make you rich, and a man like God. Then I desired so to do: also I alwaies desired other sins, for my heart did desire to grow up in those sins, alwaies lust I desired, alwaies my heart labored and desired to know how to adde to, and to multiply my sins. Thus it came to pass that I knew abundance of sins, before I knew my waies were sin. When the English came hither, they said, when I came to the English houses, that I loved the Devil: then I was very angry, and my words were, You know the Devil: I do not know the Devil, and presently I would go out of the house. Sometime they spake meekly to me, and would say, God is in heaven, and he is a good God: yet I regarded not these words, but strongly I loved my sins: it was hard for me to believe what the English said: after many yeares, I sometime believed a word, but I left not my sin. When I began to understand more, I began to doubt, but I desired not Conversion from sin. Afterward, when the English taught me, I would sit still, because they would give me good victuals; then I sometimes thought, certainly God is in heaven: then my thoughts said, It may be I have sinned.

Again I thought, if I prayed, God could not understand mee; then I found it hard to believe, and love God, because I was almost an old man, because I thought, if any could read the book, he would love God. I asked Mr *Jackson*, Whether God knew our language? Hee answered, Yea: God knoweth all languages in the world, and therefore now pray unto God; then I first thought, I will pray unto God; a little I thought of praying; sometimes I would a little pray when I eat; about that time you came to teach us; then I remembred the Word, *Glad tidings was sent us from Heaven*; then my heart said, Now I will pray, because the Minister is come to my house, now I heard the Word of God. Then you called the Children to Catechism: and one question is, *Who redeemed you?* then you taught that *Christ died for our sinnes.* Then my heart thought, that Christ is a very great life-giving God. Then I feared not Pauwaus, nor loved them; and the Minister taught, that we must take heed of all these sins. Then my heart said, I will leave off my sins; and again my heart said, I will pray to God as long as I live. Further you taught, that *Christ died for sin, was buryed, rose again, ascended:* then my heart hoped and desired, Oh that it might be so, that I might have eternall life by Christ, because Christ is a great life-giving God. But then I found that I did not understand right words, and therefore I walked not in the right way: when the Word of God said, *six daies shalt thou labour,* then I was strong, yet I did not labour; and I was soon weary of praying to God: and therefore I saw, I found not the right way unto righteousness; therefore now I verily see that I am a sinner, and did not believe: my heart feared because of my great sins, and my heart feareth that I do not yet much know the Word of God. Sometime my heart saith I believe, I am a believer: but my heart wandereth away, and the deceits of my heart I sometime know, and my poverty I know, but my heart careth not for that; I reject riches, but my heart saith strongly, I will pray to God so long as I live; I do not throughly know the vanity of my mind. I have heard the Word but believed it not. I remember that Word of Christ, the *Pharisees* said, *Why doth your Master eat with Publicans and sinners:* Christ said, *Those that are not sick need not the Physitian, but they that are sick.* My heart said, sure I do not need the Physitian: but my desire is now, that I may need him, and spirituall life by him. Again, I heard that Word of Christ, *A leper came to Christ, and worshiped him, saying, Lord if thou wilt, thou canst make me cleane: and Christ touched him, and he was perfectly healed.* Then my heart said, that outward healing which he had, my soul desireth, that I may have it in my soul: for Christ healeth the outward diseases of the body, but especially the inward filth of the soul; this I desire may be healed. Again I heard that Word, go learn what that meaneth, *I desire mercy and not sacrifice: I came not to call the righteous, but sinners to repentance.* Then my heart said, my own righteousness cannot obtain mercy for me; then my heart said, Oh I fear that Christ the truest righteousness is not in my heart: I am almost ready to die; and now I desire to know Christ.

W Hen Mr *Peirson* had done reading these two last Confessions. Mr *Wilson* spake to this purpose, though they have all spoken well of Jesus Christ, in their Confessions, and especially the last viz: *Monotunkanit,* yet he desired further to heare how they were instructed in the knowledge of Christ. This question touching Christ, I called *Piumbathou* to answer, and his answer was to satisfaction: and then many other Catecheticall questions were propounded, which would be too long to rehearse, as touching Grace, Ordinances, Sacraments, Baptisme and the Lords Supper: about Repentance and Faith, all which they readily answered, & so as that there was no reply. *Nishohkou,* answered the question what Faith is, Mr *Allin* asked him, whether he had that Faith in his heart, which he now spake off; to which after a pause, he answered to this purpose, that he feared himself about it, and if he spake, he must say no! but he hoped in the Lords mercy that he would work it in him, and help him to believe.

Then Mr *Danforth* said, I ask you *Nishohkou* this question, and answer me in English whether the same lusts which you have so much confessed, do not follow you still; and what you do to resist them? I said that a question to the like purpose was asked him, when he made Confession in private, to which he answered in broken English, if the Assembly pleased I would read that: but he was desired to answer now, and his answer was to this purpose; that the Word of God is all one like a sword: and he did with that, resist his temptations. He was asked further, if he did diligently watch against his sins: he answered, he did not well know what a diligent watch is, but he hoped that Jesus Christ would keep him.

Then Mr *Danforth* called *Anthony* and asked him, whether he believed that it was the duty of men to labour six daies in the week? After a pause, he answered, he believed it was Gods command, but he confessed he did not obey it so much as he ought to do; and saith Mr *Danforth*, that I would have asked you next, whether you obey it, for you ought to do so; and follow labour, and cloath your selfe and family better, and you ought to give towards the maintenance of Gods Ordinances. After this I remember no more questions.

Then I declared to the Congregation, that they having heard their Confessions; if they thought meet, they might hear what testimonies we have to produce touching their Conversation, but it went not forward, and so we ceased the work, and Reverend Mr *Wilson* concluded with prayer. After the publick meeting, the messengers of the Churches met together, and considered what answer to give to our Church: and the vote among them all was, that as touching their Confessions, which was the work of the day, they were satisfactory, and they appeared in that respect, to be fit matter for Church estate.

The End

Hese are to testify to all men whom it may concern, That two of five *Indian* youths, viz. *Cales* and *Joel*, that are instructed and educated in the Grammer School at *Cambridge,* were publiquely examined at the Commencement in *Cambridge* (mon. 6.9.59.) concerning their progress in the learning of the Latine Tongue, out of *Buchanans* Translation of *Davids* Psalmes, and they gave good satisfaction unto our selves, and also to the Honorable Magistrates, and Reverend Elders that were present, and others that were judicious, as we have had opportunity to inquire off: and we conceive, that the other three *Indian* Youths, that are trained up in the same School, have made some competent proficiency, for the short time that they have been with us: In witness whereof we have subscribed our hands.

Camb. *Sept.* 6. 1659.

> *Charles Chauncy*
> Præsident of *Ha-*
> *ward* Colledge in
> *Cambridge.*
>
> *Elijah Corlet* Lon-
> dinensis olim & jam
> Ludimagister Can-
> tabrigiensis.

A BRIEF
NARRATIVE

OF THE

Progreſs of the Goſpel amongſt
the *Indians* in *New-England*, in
the Year 1 6 7 0.

Given in

By the Reverend Mr. JOHN ELLIOT,
Miniſter of the Goſpel there,

In a LETTER by him directed to
the Right Worſhipfull the COM-
MISSIONERS under his Majeſties
Great-Seal for Propagation of the
Goſpel amongſt the poor blind Na-
tives in thoſe United Colonies.

LONDON,

Printed for *John Allen*, formerly living in *Little-Britain* at
the Riſing-Sun, and now in *Wentworth ſtreet* near *Bell-
Lane*, 1671.

A BRIEF

NARRATIVE

OF THE

Progress of the Gospel amongst

the *Indians* in *New-England*, in

the Year 1 6 7 0 .

Given in

By the Reverend Mr. J O H N E L L I O T,
Minister of the Gospel there,

In a L E T T E R by him directed to
the Right Worshipfull the C O M –
M I S S I O N E R S under his Majesties
Great-Seal for Propagation of the
Gospel amongst the poor blind Na-
tives in those United Colonies.

LONDON,

Printed for *John Allen*, formerly living in *Little-Britain*
at the Rising-Sun, and now in *Wentworth Street* near
Bell-Lane, 1671.

To the Right Worshipful the Commissioners under his Majesties Great-Seal, for the Propagation of the Gospel amongst the poor blind Indians in New-England.

Right Worshipful and Christian Gentlemen,

That brief Tract of the present state of the *Indian-Work* in my hand, which I did the last year on the sudden present you with when you call'd for such a thing; That falling short of its end, and you calling for a renewal thereof, with opportunity of more time, I shall begin with our last great motion in that Work done this Summer, because that will lead me to begin with the state of the *Indians* under the hands of my Brethren Mr. *Mahew* and Mr. *Bourn.*

Upon the 17th day of the 16th month 1670, there was a Meeting at *Mak{?}epog* {i.e., Mahshepog, or Mashpee} near *Sandwich* in *Plimouth-Pattent,* to gather a Church among the *Indians*: There wee present six of the Magistrates, and many Elders, (all of them Messengers of the Churches within that Jurisdiction) in whose presence, in a day of Fasting and Prayer, they making confession of the Truth and Grace of Jesus Christ, did in that solemn Assembly enter into Covenant, to walk together in the Faith and Order of the Gospel; and were accepted and declared to be a Church of Jesus Christ. These *Indians* being of kin to our *Massachuset-Indians* who first prayed unto God, conversed with them, and received amongst them the light and love of the Truth; they desired me to write to Mr. *Leveredge* to teach them: He accepted the Motion, and performed the Work with good success; but afterwards he left that place, and went to *Long-Island,* and there a godly Brother, named *Richard Bourne* (who purposed to remove with Mr. *Leveredge,* but hindred by Divine Providence) undertook the teaching of those *Indians,* and hath continued in the work with good success to this day; him we ordained Pastor; and one of the *Indians,* named *Jude,* should have been ordained Ruling-Elder, but being sick at that time, advice was given that he should be ordained with the first opportunity, as also a Deacon to manage the present Sabbath day Collections, and other parts of that

Office in their season. The same day also were they, and such of their Children as were present, baptized.

From them we passed over to the *Vinyard*, where many were added to the Church both men and women, and were baptized all of them, and their Children also with them; we had the Sacrament of the Lords Supper celebrated in the *Indian-Church*, and many of the *English-Church* gladly joyned with them; for which cause it was celebrated in both languages. On a day of Fasting and Prayer, Elders were ordained, two Teaching-Elders, the one to be a Preacher of the Gospel, to do the Office of a Pastor and Teacher; the other to be a Preacher of the Gospel, to do the Office of a Teacher and Pastor, as the Lord should give them ability and opportunity; Also two Ruling-Elders, with advice to ordain Deacons also, for the Service of Christ in the Church. Things were so ordered by the Lord's guidance, that a Foundation is laid for two Churches more; for first, these of the Vinyard dwelling at too great a distance to enjoy with comfort their Sabbath-communion in one place, Advice was given them, that after some experience of walking together in the Order and Ordinances of the Gospel, they should issue forth into another Church; and the Officers are so chosen, that when they shall so do, both Places are furnished with a Teaching and Ruling-Elder.

Also the Teacher of the *Praying Indians* of *Nantuket*, with a Brother of his were received here, who made good Confessions of Jesus Christ; and being asked, did make report unto us that there be about ninety Families who pray unto God in that Island, so effectual is the Light of the Gospel among them. Advice was given, that some of the chief Godly People should joyn to this Church, (for they frequently converse together, though the Islands be seven leagues asunder) and after some experience of walking in the Order of the Gospel, they should issue forth into Church-estate among themselves, and have Officers ordained amongst them.

The Church of the *Vinyard* were desirous to have chosen Mr. *Mahew* to be their Pastor: but he declined it, conceiving that in his present capacity he lieth under greater advantages to stand their Friend, and do them good, to save them from the hands of such as would bereave them of their Lands, &c. but they shall alwayes have his counsel, instruction and management in all their Church-affairs, as hitherto they have had; he will die in this service of Jesus Christ. The *Praying-Indians* of both these Islands depend on him, as God's Instrument for their good.

Advice also was given for the setling of Schools; every Child capable of learning, equally paying, whether he make use of it or no: Yet if any should sinfully neglect Schooling their Youth, it is a transgression liable to censure under both Orders, *Civil* and *Ecclesiastical*, the offence being against both. So we walk at *Natick.*

In as much as now we have ordained *Indian Officers* unto the Ministry of the Gospel, it is needful to add a word or two of Apology: I find it hopeless to expect *English* Officers in our *Indian* Churches; the work is full of hardship, hard labour, and chargeable also, and the *Indians* not yet capable to give considerable support and maintenance; and Men have bodies, and must live of the Gospel: And what comes from *England* is liable to hazard and uncertainties. On such grounds as these partly, but especially from the secret wise governance of Jesus Christ, the Lord of the Harvest, there is no appearance of hope for their souls feeding in that way: they must be trained up to be able to live of themselves in the ways of the Gospel of Christ; and through the riches of God's Grace and Love, sundry of themselves who are expert in the Scriptures, are able to teach each other: An *English* young man raw in that language, coming to teach among our Christian-*Indians*, would be much to their loss; there be of themselves such as be more able, especially being advantaged that he speaketh his own language, and knoweth their manners. Such *English* as shall hereafter teach them, must begin with a People that begin to pray unto God, (and such opportunities we have many) and then as they grow in knowledge, he will grow (if he be diligent) in ability of speech to communicate the knowledge of Christ unto them. And seeing they must have Teachers amongst themselves, they must also be taught to be Teachers: for which cause I have begun to teach them the Art of Teaching, and I find some of them very capable. And while I live, my purpose is (by the Grace of Christ assisting) to make it one of my chief cares and labours to teach them some of the Liberal Arts and Sciences, and the way how to analize, and lay out into particulars both the Works and Word of God; and how to communicate knowledge to others methodically and skilfully, and especially the method of Divinity. There be sundry Ministers who live in an opportunity of beginning with a People, and for time to come I shall cease my importuning of others, and onely fall to perswade such unto this service of Jesus Christ, it being one part of our Ministerial Charge to preach to the World in the Name of Jesus, and from amongst them to gather Subjects to his holy Kingdom. The Bible, and the Catechism drawn out of the Bible, are general helps to all parts and places about us, and are the ground-work of Community amongst all our *Indian*-Churches and Christians.

I find a Blessing, when our Church of *Natick* doth send forth fit Persons unto some remoter places, to teach them the fear of the Lord. But we want maintenance for that Service; it is a chargeable matter to send a Man from his Family: The Labourer is worthy of his Hire: And when they go only to the High-wayes and Hedges, it is not to be expected that they should reward them: If they believe and obey their Message, it is enough. We are determined to send forth some (if the Lord will, and that we live) this Autumn, sundry ways. I see the best way is, *up and be doing*: In all labour there is profit; *Seek and ye shall find*. We have Christ's Example, his Promise, his Presence, his Spirit to assist; and I trust that the Lord will find a way for your encouragement.

Natick is our chief Town, where most and chief of our Rulers, and most of the Church dwells; here most of our chief Courts are kept; and the Sacraments in the Church are for the most part here administred: It is (by Divine Providence) seated well near in the center of all our praying *Indians*, though Westward the Cords of Christ's Tents are more enlarged. Here we began Civil Government in the year 1650. And here usually are kept the General-Trainings, which seven years ago looked so big that we never had one since till this year, and it was at this time but a small appearance. Here we have two Teachers, *John Speen* and *Anthony*; we have betwixt forty and fifty Communicants at the Lord's Table, when they all appear, but now some are dead, and some decriped with age; and one under Censure, yet making towards a recovery; one died here the last Winter of the Stone, a temperate, sober, godly man, the first *Indian* that ever was known to have that disease; but now another hath the same disease: Sundry more are proposed, and in way of preparation to joyn unto the Church.

Ponkipog, or *Pakennit* is our second Town, where the *Sachems* of the Bloud (as they term their Chief Royal-Line) had their Residence and Rights, which are mostly Alienated to the English Towns: The last Chief Man, of that Line, was last year slain by the *Manquaogs*, against whow he rashly (without due Attendants and Assistance, and against Counsel) went; yet all, yea his Enemies say, He died valiantly; they were more afraid to kill him, than he was to die; yet being deserted by all (some knowingly say through Treason) he stood long, and at last fell alone: Had he had but 10 Men, yea 5 in good order with him, he would have driven all his Enemies before him. His Brother was resident with us in this Town, but he is fallen into sin, and from praying to God. Our Chief Ruler is *Ahauton*, an old stedfast and trusty Friend to the *English*, and loveth his Country. He is more loved than feared; the reins of his bridle are too long. *Wakan* is sometimes necessarily called to keep Courts here, to add life and zeal in the punishment of Sinners. Their late Teacher, *William*, is deceased; He was a man of eminent parts, all the *English* acknowledge him, and he was known to many: He was of a ready wit, sound judgment, and affable; he is gone unto the Lord; And *William*, the Son of *Ahauton*, is called to be Teacher in his stead. He is a promising young-man, of a single and upright heart, a good judgment, he Prayeth and Preacheth well, he is studious and industrious, and well accounted of among the *English*.

Hassunnimesut is the next Town in order, dignity, and antiquity; sundry of our chief Friends in the great work of Praying to God, came from them, and there lived their Progenitors, and there lieth their Inheritance, and that is the place of their desires. It lieth upon *Nichmuke* River; the people were well known to the *English* so long as *Connecticot* Road lay that way, and their Religion was judged to be real by all that travelled that journey, and had occasion to lodge, especially to keep a Sabbath among them. The Ruler of the Town is *Anuweekin*, and his Brother *Tuppukkoowillin* is Teacher, both sound and godly Men. This Ruler, last Winter, was overtaken with a Passion, which was so observable, that I had occasion to speak with him about it; he was very penitent; I told him, That as to man, I, and all men were ready to forgive him. *Ah!* said he, *I find it the greatest difficulty to forgive my self.* For the encouragement of this place, and for the cherishing of a new Plantation of Praying Indians beyond them, they called *Monatunkanet* to be a Teacher also in that Town, and both of them to take care of the new Praying-Town beyond them. And for the like encouragement, Captain *Gookins* joyned *Petahheg* with *Anuweekin*. The aged Father of this Ruler and Teacher, was last year Baptized, who hath many Children that fear God. In this place we meditate ere long (if the Lord will, and that we live) to gather a Church, that so the Sabbath-

Communion of our Christian *Indians* may be the more agreeable to the Divine Institution, which we make too bold with while we live at such distance.

Ogquonikongquamesut is the next Town; where, how we have been afflicted, I may not say. The *English* Town called *Marlborough* doth border upon them, as did the lines of the Tribes of *Judah* and *Benjamin*; the English Meeting-house standeth within the line of the *Indian* Town, although the contiguity and co-habitation is not barren in producing matters of interfering; yet our godly *Indians* do obtain a good report of the godly *English*, which is an argument that bringeth light and evidence to my heart, that our *Indians* are really godly. I was very lately among them; they desired me to settle a stated Lecture amongst them, as it is in sundry other Praying Towns, which I did with so much the more gladness and hope of blessing in it, because through Grace the Motion did first spring from themselves. *Solomon* is their Teacher, whom we judge to be a serious and sound Christian; their Ruler is *Owannamug*, whose grave, faithful, and discreet Conversation hath procured him real respect from the *English*. One that was a Teacher in this place, is the man that is now under Censure in the Church; his sin was that adventitious sin which we have brought unto them, Drunkenness, which was never known to them before they knew us *English*. But I account it our duty, and it is much in my desire, as well to teach them Wisdom to Rule such heady Creatures, as skill to get them, to be able to bridle their own appetites, when they have means and opportunity of high-spirited enticements. The Wisdom and Power of Grace is not so much seen in the beggarly want of these things, as in the bridling of our selves in the use of them. It is true Dominion, to be able to use them, and not to abuse our selves by them.

Nashope is our next Praying Town, a place of much affliction; it was the chief place of Residence, where *Tahattawans* lived, a Sacham of the Blood, a faithful and zealous Christian, a strict yet gentle Ruler; he was a Ruler of 50 in our Civil Order; and when God took him, a chief man in our *Israel* was taken away from us. His only Son was a while vain, but proved good, expert in the Scripture, was Elected to Rule in his Fathers place, but soon died, insomuch that this place is now destitute of a Ruler. The Teacher of the place is *John Thomm*, a godly understanding Christian, well esteemed of by the *English*: his father was killed by the *Mauquaogs,* shot to death as he was in the River doing his Eele-wyers. This place lying in the Road-way which the *Mauquaogs* haunted, was much molested by them, and was one year wholly deserted; but this year the People have taken courage and dwell upon it again.

In this place after the great Earthquake, there was some eruption out of the Earth, which left a great *Hiatus* or Cleft a great way together, and out of some Cavities under great Rocks, by a great Pond in that place, there was a great while after often heard an humming noise, as if there were frequent eruptions out of the Ground at that place: yet for Healthfulness the place is much as other places be. For Religion, there be amongst them some Godly Christians, who are received into the Church, and baptized, and others looking that way.

Wamesut is our next Praying-Town; it lyeth at the bottom of the great Falls, on the great River *Merymak,* and at the falling-in of *Concord* River; the Sachem of this Place is named *Nomphon*, said to be a Prince of the Bloud, a Man of a real Noble Spirit: A Brother of his was slain by the *Mauquaogs* as he was upon a Rock fishing in the great River.   In revenge whereof he went in the forementioned rash Expedition, but had such about him, and was so circumspect, that he came well off, though he lost one principal Man. This place is very much annoyed by the *Mauquaogs*, and have much ado to stand their ground.

In this Place Captain *Gookins* ordered a Garrison to be kept the last year, which Order while they attended they were safe; but when the Northern Sachems and Souldiers came, who stirred up ours to go with them on their unsuccessful Expedition, the Town was for the most part scatter'd, and their Corn spoyled.

The Teacher of this Place is named *George*: they have not much esteem for Religion, but I am hopefully perswaded of sundry of them; I can go unto them but once in a year.

Panatuket is the upper part of *Merimak*-Falls; so called, because of the noise which the Waters make. Thither the *Penagwog Indians* are come, and have built a great Fort: Their Sachems refused to pray to God, so signally and sinfully, that Captain *Gookins* and my self were very sensible of it, and were not without some expectation of some interposure of a Divine-Hand, which did eminently come to pass; for in the forenamed Expedition they joyned with the Northern Sachems, and were all of them cut off; even all that had so signally refused to pray unto God were now as signally rejected by God, and cut off. I hear not that it was ever known, that so many *Sachems* and Men of Note were killed in one imprudent Expedition, and that by a few scattered people; for the *Mauquaogs* were not imbodied to receive them, nor prepared, and few at home, which did much greaten the Overthrow of so many great Men, and shews a divine over-ruling hand of God.   But now, since the *Penaguog-Sachems* are cut off, the People (sundry of them) dwelling at *Panatuket*-Fort do bow the Ear to hear, and submit to pray unto God; to whom *Jethro*, after he had confest Christ and was baptized, was sent to preach Christ to them.

Magunkukquok is another of our Praying-Towns at the remotest Westerly borders of *Natick*; these are gathering together of some *Nipmuk Indians* who left their own places, and sit together in this place, and have given up themselves to pray unto God.   They have called *Pomham* to be their Ruler, and *Simon* to be their Teacher.   This latter is accounted a good and lively Christian; he is the second man among the *Indians* that doth experience that afflicting disease of the Stone.   The Ruler hath made his Preparatory Confession of Christ, and is approved of, and at the next opportunity is to be received and baptized.

I obtained of the General-Court a Grant of a Tract of Land, for the settlement and encouragement of this People; which though as yet it be by some obstructed, yet I hope we shall find some way to accomplish the same.

Quanatusset is the last of our Praying-Towns, whose beginnings have received too much discouragement; but yet the Seed is alive: they are frequently with me; the work is at the birth, there doth only want strength to bring forth. The care of this People is committed joyntly to *Monatunkanit*, and

Tuppunkkoowillin the Teachers of *Hassunemesut,* as is abovesaid; and I hope if the Lord continue my life, I shall have a good account to give of that People.

Thus I have briefly touched some of the chiefest of our present Affairs, and commit them to your Prudence, to do with them what you please; committing your Selves, and all your weighty Affairs unto the Guidance and Blessing of the Lord, I rest,

Your Worships to serve you in the
Service of our Lord *Jesus,*

Roxb. this 20th of
the 7th month,

1 6 7 0.   *John Elliot.*

Books sold by John Allen.

V I Z.

Cotton on the Covenant, new printed.

Confession of Faith of the Congregational Churches,

Mr. *Hook* and Mr. *Davenports* Catechism.

Astrologers Routed: shewing that divining by the Stars hath no solid foundation from Scripture, Reason, or Experience, &c.

Letters

J E W S

IN

A M E R I C A,

OR

Probabilities, that those Indians are

Judaical, made more probable by some Ad-

ditionals to the former Conjectures.

An Accurate D I S C O U R S E is premised of
Mr. *John Elliot,* (who first preached the Gospel
to the Natives in their own Language) touching
their Origination, and his Vindication of the
P L A N T E R S.

Psal. 59.11. *Slay them not, lest my people forget, scatter them*
    by thy power.
Ezek. 34.6. *My sheep wandred through all the mountains, my*
    flock was scattered upon all the face of the earth, and none
    did search or seek after them.
Greg. in Cant. 6. 13. *Bene quater reverti unamitisadmonetur,*
    quod in quatuor mundi partes Judæi dispersisunt, qui
    ubicunq; fuerint, in fine convertentu. —
Hæc scripsit, non ut Doctor perfectus, sed cum docendis
    perficiendus. Aug. Epist. 130.
    THO. THOROWGOOD *S.T.B Norfolciencis.*

LONDON,
Printed for *Henry Brome* at the Gun in Ivie-Lane. 1660.

The learned Conjectures of Reverend Mr. John Eliot *touching the* Americans, *of new and notable consideration, written to Mr.* Thorowgood.[*]

S I R.

BY reading your book, intituled, *Jews in America, or Probabilities that the Americans be of that Race,* the Lord did put it into my heart to search into some Scriptures about that subject, and by comparing one thing with another, I thought, I saw some ground to conceive, that some of the Ten Tribes might be scattered even thus far, into these parts of *America,* where we are according to the word of God, *Deut.* 28.64. I wrote unto you these few weak meditations about it, according as the streights of my time, and manifold imployments would give way, there is a great distance of place betwixt us, and I perceive it was a long time ere they came to your hands. Though the Lord hath scattered the Ten Tribes into corners, and made their remembrance to cease among men, as he threatned, *Deut.* 32.21. in so much as that they are lost, and no man knowes where to find them; yet the Lord hath promised to bind them up again, and to gather together those dry and scattered bones, and bring them to know the Lord, and to be known, and acknowledged among men again. He that can gather together the scattered dust of the dead bodies of men, and raise them up at the resurrection, he also can find the lost Israel: and now the time is even at hand, wherein the people of God do waite for the accomplishment of that great work, which appeares not only by the interpretation of the holy prophesies, but also by the spirit of prayer, which the Lord hath poured out upon his servents on that behalf, as also by the spirit of search, and inquiry after them, which is of late more stirring, then in former times. Among whom the Lord hath put it into your mind to take pains to inquire after them in *America.* In which search, you professing to shoot your arrowes only at rovers, presenting only probabilities to break the ice into this strange disquisition, have thereby provoked others to follow this chase; It's not to be thought, but that some others, who see no reason to search for them that way, especially such who may think, that God calleth not, to make any search at all after them, such may conceive all these arrowes to be wide off the mark. That if the Apostle, *Rom.* 11.25. *until the fulness of the Gentiles be come in,* is fit to be remembred, and so *all Israell shall be saved,* viz. Israel shall come in under the Gentiles skirt, being some of the croud, whereas others, and that general do

---

*In Thorowgood 1660, 1-28

apprehend that Israel shall be brought in by their own covenant, and that the Gentiles shall be blessed, quickned, and brought in by vertue of their coming in, and come in as under the skirt of their Covenant, *seven men shall take hold of the skirt of one Jew:* to which purpose many passages of the same, *Rom.* 11 are very considerable, as *ver.* 12,15,16,23,24,27. and glad shall he be, that can get hold on the skirt of a Jew, I have some cogitations, as well as others, of the first peopling of America by the posterity of *Sem;* though in sundry particulars, I have some different thoughts touching the story of those first times. I have not the help of variety of Authors, my only guide is the holy Scriptures, which is the best and surest record of all. And by the conduct of that sure guid, I conceive that the first planters of America, to be not only of *Sem,* but *Ebrew* as of *Eber,* even as *Abraham* and *Israel* were though not in the same line, of which if I misremember not, I did give a touch in my former letters to you, and now I shall write a little more.

The chief record of those times are left unto us in the names of the holy line of Christ, in whose families, chiefly the Church was preserved, and the holy worship of God upheld in the world. Out of these records we may read some of the most remarkable providences that befell the Church, both in the old world before the flood, and in the first times after it. The history of the first times after the flood, as touching our present purpose in hand, is as followeth.

The Ark landed Eastward first of the land of Eden, as the text prooves, and *Sir. Walter Raleigh* doth clear, whose judgment herein is considerable. *Noah* and his three sons did dwell there quietly, and prosperously, multiplying of posterity, rather then fixing his habitations and possessions for the space of above 30. years: for a few people in a wast country, have more desire to procure company to them, then possesse lands other then for their presant use: this their peaceable and succesful progresse in replenishing the world is recorded in the name of, the sone of hope in the holy line of the promised seed, whom they hoped for, and believed; *Arphaxad,* [*Arphaxad,* i.e. healer of ruines.] which signifieth a healer of ruines, shewing that the Church looked on the dispensations of providence in those times, the ruined World, and the ruined Church were in the healing, growing, and rising hand, and therefore they did record it to Gods praise, in the holy line of Christ, which record, though it was first wrote but two years after the flood, yet there is no reason but to think that they so continued, saving that there was one sad affliction fell out in those first times, namely, that *Noah* having planted a vineyard (finding the soil replenished with such plants and pregnant in such fruits, the flood not destroying vegetables) he was drunk with the wine thereof, not because he knew not the strength of the fruit of the vine, unless we should think the old world so foolish, as not to improve the fruit to an use so easily invented, when as they had inventions of far greater considerations, and difficulty, but out of an unwatchfulnesse over his own waies, for the humbling of his own heart, and trial of his Sons; though this may excuse him *a tanto,* because he now began to be an husbandman, as all men usually do in new plantations, what ever their occupations were formerly; for in the old world *Noah* was a *Father,* a *Judge,* a *Ruler,* and eminent in the Church, and if he attended to any occupation manual, it was Carpentry (of which calling our Lord Jesus was) especially he attended thereunto for a hundred years before the flood, and more. But his awakening and repentance was so deep and spiritual, as that the spirit of prophesie came upon him, to dispence and declare Gods blessings, and works among his children, and posterity. The time when this fell out, was before the great expedition, and sending forth of *Sem* and his Sons (of which anon) because all the Sons of *Noah* were yet at home together: and it was after *Canaan, Chams* youngest Son was borne, because *Cham* is cursed in him, and his posterity, shewing, that he was then, as it is probable, an ill qualified, unpromising, unhappy boy, and it might be, he that first told his father *Cham*, yea, and it may be uncovered his grandfather, lying in a posture capable of being uncovered, because in him falleth the curse.

After thirty yeares cohabitation, or there abouts, they beginning to grow numerous, found not only need to disperse and spread themselves further upon the face of the earth, but also a desire was in them, especially in *Sems* familie, where the Church most flourished, to visit, and inhabit the land of *Eden*, where the garden of *Eden* had been, and where abouts, it is most like *Adam,* with the other Patriarks, the chief Rulers of the old world had dwelt; all which saving the first three, *Noah* had known, and among whom, it is like, he, and his Sons had dwelt, which might well breed in them a desire to possesse, at least to send forth his Sons to possesse those desirable places of the earth, and to leave that Easterne world, the cursed habitation of *Cain* and his posterity, and where the floud-growing sins did first spring up, as appeareth in the history of the old world. So great a business of dispersing themselves, and removing unto so remote a place, no question, did cause them, with prayers, and sacrifices unto the Lord, to consult seriously upon it, the issue of which consultation was this, that *Sem,* in whose familie the holy line of the promised seed was, did first attempt this removall *Westward*, towards the land of *Eden*, and his Sons with him, unlesse they might go before to beat the way for them: So that there was an eminent sending forth of people into the new plantation of the old world; which did cause *Arphaxad*, in whom the line of the promised seed did run, to call his Son, in whom they hoped for the promise, *Shalack*, [*Shalack* sent.] which signifies sent, for their grandfather *Noah*, and their father *Sem* in a counsel of the Fathers, did send forth all the family of *Sem* westward, even all the five Sons of *Sem*, namely, *Elam, Ashur, Arphaxad, Lud*, and *Aram,* as after will appear in the possessions, and habitations they setled upon.

The time of this great removal, and sending forth was between thirty and forty years after the floud, for *Arphaxad* begat *Salah* at his fifteenth year, and that sons name bore the record of that great enterprise. The successe of this voyage appeareth in the Scriptures to be as followeth, *Elam*, the eldest Son finding a commodious situation about the East borders of the *Persian* gulph (now so called) there he settled himself, and his posterity, for it is most manifest that *Persia* is in Scripture called *Elam*, he proceeded no further in that Westerne expedition: The rest of his brethren abode in those parts above twenty years, but at the last finding cause to prosecute the enterprise and plantation of the world, which they had been so solemnly sent forth about: the great river *Havilah*, or

Tigris (which maketh the *Persian* gulph by empting it self into it) was a great impediment unto their progresse, they were a great while, in getting, and using means to passe over that river with their women, and little ones, with their flocks and heards: But at last by the great mercy of God they got well over, which was so remarkable a mercy of God, that the son of hope in the holy line, being about that time born unto *Salah*, in whom the promise was, he called his name in remembrance of this mercy *Eber*, [*Eber*, passing over.] which signifieth passing over. The time of this great, and observeable providence was about the thirtieth year of *Salah's* age, thirty years after they had been sent forth upon that expedition, and about the 67. year after the floud.

Their proceeding in plantation after they had gotten over those great waters, appeareth to be this, that *Ashur*, the second son of *Sem*, took possession of *Shinar*, that pleasant and fertil country in the land of *Eden*, where afterward *Nimrod*, the rebel, found him possessed, and out of which country he drove him, *Gen.* 10.11. *Arphaxad*, the third son of *Sem* (in whose family was the line of the promised seed) went lower upon that river, and possessed *Ur* of the *Chaldees* which appeareth by this, because there the Church of God in that line and family abode untill *Abraham*, and out of that country God called him. *Aram* the fifth son of *Sem* sate down in the land, afterward called *Mesapotamia*, I say afterwards so called, because that is a Greek name, and this possession was transacted before the confusion of languages, when all spake *Hebrew*: he taking up this possession before *Lud* who was his elder brother, did it no doubt, with his consent, who went further westward, and planted himself, and posterity in *Lydia*, the most westerly skirt of *Sems* posterity. And this is the issue of the great expedition, upon which all the sons of *Shem* was sent forth in the beginning of *Salah* his daies: All those plantations were setled soon after *Eber's* birth, about seventy years after the floud. In all this story it is observeable, that the Church, and its posterity, had a spirit in them to goe westward, and so had all the rest of the *sons of Noah* afterwards, as doth appear by the holy story, for they multiplyed in the place of the resting of the Arke, but did not fix themselves and posterity till the earth was divided, by a counsel held by the fathers, & given unto them for their own possession, only those forenamed sons of *Sem* did fix themselves in possessions, being sent forth for that purpose, as it is said before. About the time when *Eber* was born or soon after, *Nimrod the Rebel* was born, which appears, *Gen.* 10.6,7,8. his Father *Cush* was coetaneous with *Arphaxad, Cush* had five sons, the fourth of them had two sons, all borne before *Cush* had *Nimrod*; so that *Nimrod* was rather younger then the grandchildren of *Arphaxad* and *Cush:* now *Eber* was *Arphaxads* grandchilde, and therefore *Nimrod* was somewhat younger then *Eber*, and was born about, or soon after the time when *Ashur, Arphaxad, Lud, & Aram* made their new plantations above mentioned: and hence it must needs appear, that when afterwards *Nimrod* drove *Ashur* out of *Shinar*, he did very unjustly, and therefore was called a mighty hunter; *Ashur* was a good man, and of the Church, but *Nimrod* called a hunter before the Lord. *Gen.* 10.10,11. These new and fixed plantations of the world had quietness and prosperity, for the space of more then twenty years, until *Nimrod* made a disturbance among them.

The fame of the good successe of the westerne plantations, & contentment of the people in their pleasant places, going back unto the place of their first landing of the Arke (so they could not but hold intercourses) where *Noah, Ham, Japhet,* and all their Sons were yet abiding, not fixed, but waiting, which way they should be sent forth to people and possesse the world: it moved in them an earnest desire to go Westward also, which desire was so effectual, as that they did at last accomplish their desires, as we shall hereafter see.

The aged Fathers (who were Rulers in chief in that paternal government) being slow to send out the sons of *Japhet,* and *Ham,* as they had done the Sons of *Sem,* the young men grew impatient of such delays, and were madly desirous to run into the land of *Eden,* and being still curbed, and stayed by the paternal government of the Fathers, *Nimrod* a proud ambitious young man, between twenty, and thirty years old, entertained thoughts of casting off the yoke of the paternal government, and would no longer be curbed from his desires of going into the land of *Eden:* he soon found a crew of young fellowes like himself, that were as weary of government as he, and as desirous to goe Westward, to the land of *Eden,* as he, whereupon much company gathered to him, and he took upon him to be their Captain, leader and Monarch, changing that form of government which had been in force ever since the World began, and was still in force, namely paternal government: but he takes upon him Kingly government, gathering up a confused company out of many families, who rebelled against their aged parents, and followed this young upstart, among whom a great part of the sons of *Ham,* and *Japhet* were, a scattering they had out of most of the Easterne people, having this advantage, that they all spake one language, out of what coast so ever they came *Gen.* 11.1 that language was *Hebrew,* which the old world, before the floud did universally speak, being necessary in the paternal government thereof, and the new world also, until the confusion of *Babel.* The end, & scope of this enterprise was not to make war, the new world yet knew no war, but their ends were to break away from their Fathers to goe dwell in the land of *Eden,* and to change government, or rather to cast off the paternal government, without considering of the issue of such a change. The rebellious company of youth marched along from the *East, Nimrod* being their Captain, and arived at *Shinar,* a place where *Asher* and his posterity had been planted before *Nimrod* was born; they take likeing to that place, and there would dwell, *Ashur* refuseth, and pleadeth his true possession, & that by the authority of the Fathers, who had sent them forth to that purpose, and therefore they had no right to disposess them, especially not being sent forth by the counsel of the Fathers so to do: but the young proud men put little weight in *Ashers* being sent by the Fathers, from whose authority they had broken away, and having so much hight of mind, and wickedness, as to break the fift commandement, and was as little careful to be ruled by the justice of the eighth: no bonds of justice can bind them, whom the awe of authority cannot bind, and therefore there they would dwell. And not onely so, but that they would no longer be governed by the Fathers, but they would have a Prince to governe them, and *Nimrod* should be the man. *Ashur* seeing this division grow high, and great, and full of danger, and fearing it might come to some violence, and blood at last, like a wise and godly man he departed out of that land, he, and his, and went into another country, and that he named after his own name, *Assyria,* and there he built cities. And now *Nimrod* began to reigne as King, and the first act he did after he was thus made their King, was to build cities *Erac, Accad*, and *Calneh,* in the land of *Shinar,* Gen. 10.10. Though this great distemper was so far quieted by the wisdome, and self denial of *Ashur,* in giving place to this boistrous crew of rebellious youth, yet there were great divisions still, by reason that the two families of *Ham* and *Japhet,* had not their habitations and possessions assigned them by the Fathers, as the family of *Sem* had, which troubles were not appeased, until a great counsel of the Fathers sate upon this businesse, and agreed upon the division and distribution of the whole earth. Men of new plantations are subject to much disrest, and unquietnesse, until all common lands be divided, an humor which after nations have no occasion to see into. And though I have on the by touched this grave counsel of the Fathers, and the quieting conclusion they made, yet I have not brought down the story of these times so far: besides the unsettlement of those two families, for want of their portion in the division of the earth: *Nimrods* rebellion brought the world into a great disturbance and tended to whet up the family of *Ham* (of which he was) to be discontented for not having their portion of the world laid out unto them, the not doing whereof gave occasion to this rebellion: and *Japhets* family likewise, desiring to go Westward, would lay in for their parts too, so that the division grew great and full of trouble. Mean while *Nimrod* thought it his safest way to make sure unto himself his new upstart government, and perceiving that *Sem* was in great repute in the world for his Religion, and foreseeing that his neer neighbourhood in *Ur,* and the authority of his name might soon weken the affections of his people to him, seeing also the unreplenished earth gave occasion to his fickle minded young crew, to be roving and scattering to every new place they heard of to be fit for plantation, and so he might come to be diserted by them, and his kingdom ruined, therefore he (with the counsel of such as were chief about him, and firme to his designe) used the best humane policy they could to prevent these mischiefs, hereupon they concluded, that they would build a city, and a tower of a huge hight, and magnitude, whereby to attain these two ends, first to procure unto themselves a *Sem*, a great name to balance the potent name of *Sem*, and secondly to keep the people together from being scattered from him, having with him both greatnesse, strength and safty. But this is to be observed that the very plot and policy which he used to establish his kingdome, was the very way, and means to bring it to utter ruine, insomuch that his kingdome lasted but a very few years: when foundations are laid without God, the building is unstable, and not durable; for the Lord looking upon the great divisions and discontent afore named, as also upon this proud rebellion, he wrought that strange work of confounding their language, whereby they were not only hindred in their intended building, and setling together, but on the contrary were broken into so many several companies as they spake languages; and were thereby necessitated to be scattered abroad over the face of all the earth, to break their plots, and accomplish Gods end in replenishing the earth, thus *Nimrods* policy turned to his ruine, and his kingdome came to an utter end and confusion, God from heaven blasting that his rebellion against the ancient government of the Fathers. This confusion of languages fell not only upon *N{i}mrods* crew of builders but also upon all the discontented people above mentioned, yea and afterwards upon others according as they apostatized from the Church, and from paternal government. By this means now they were necessitated, not only to be quiet from the great division that were among them, because they could not understand each others language, but now they were by a divine hand prepared to be sent out with quietness into all parts of the earth, to possesse, and subdue the same. And now was the season of that fore-named counsel of the Fathers, for now the Fathers might with more freedome and quiet come together, and agree about the division of the whole earth, which agreement in brief was this. They understanding how the midland Sea did cut in two the whole Continent of the Western world, (the coasts which they all thirsted after) they appointed *Japhet* to possesse all the Isles of the Sea, and the Northside thereof, which (being elder brother) he first chose, as *Sems* sons above named chose by their seniority: the South side of the *Mediterranean* Sea was assigned to *Ham,* the places already possessed, as also the deserted Easterne part of the world was left unto *Sem:* I say, the deserted Eastern part of the world; for they being discontented with their place, and so vehemently desiring to go westward, they would not leave a child, nor house behind them; nor do we read of any cities they built, until they were fixed in their own deserted possessions: and furthermore, because afterwards in *Abrahams* time *Sem* is found at *Salem* in *Canaan*, under the title of *Melchisedeck*, as it is conceived among some of the sons of *Cham*, it may well be, that this great counsel of the Fathers, afore mentioned, who divided the earth, and appeased the divisions of men, seeing an unjust spirit in the familie of *Cham*, out of which *Nimrod* the rebel sprung, and fearing some after disturbance by them, they did request *Sem* to goe, and dwell in that place, there to be a King of righteousnesse and peace among them, and to keep quietness in their posterity; that place being much about the centre, where all the three families were bordering upon each other, though I refuse not also a prophetical foresight of the holy land, and holy City in that place, as some think, to be a motive for his residing there. The place where this council of the Fathers was held, was *Ur*, because there was the Church, Gods worship, and presence most eminently, and the confusion of languages fell not upon them, nor was the discontent, and division among them, nor any sparks of the rebellion, but quietness, and place therefore; that was the only place, where the great councel could be held, and it is most like that thither came *Noah, Sem,* and other of the godly Fathers to dwell, all giving occasion for the council to be held there. These manifold and memorable works of God, the Fathers saw good to record in the holy line of the promised seed, for *Eber* his son of hope, being about that time borne, he called his name *Peleg*, [*Peleg.* i.e. division.] which signifies division, recording the great division in those daies, both among the People, and especially of the division of the whole earth among them, for to make peace, and also the division of languages, *Gen.* 10.25. In his daies the earth was divided. Again, there being now many languages in the earth, the Fathers thought good to call the holy language, which still continued in the Church by the name of *Eber*, who was then in his flower, and stood against *Nimrod*, and kept the sparkes of his rebellion from poysoning the youth of the Church, whereby the Church was, by the favour of God, kept from the confusion both of rebellion and discontent, and also of language; that language therefore left in the Church, beareth his name *Ebrew, Japhets* family spake *Greek, Latine,* &c. *Chams* family *Syriack, Egyptian,* &c. The time when these great agitations were, is thus made manifest: It was before proved that *Nimrod* was about the age of *Eber*, who, in the thirty fourth year of his age, begat *Peleg*, who beareth the record of this confusion, and conclusion thereof: hence therefore *Nimrod* might be about twenty four years old, when he began his rebellion in the East, and by such time as he was thirty four year old all the storme was over, and his company scattered over all the earth, and his upstart kingdome quite ruin'd, about 101. years after the floud; so that there may be ten years more or lesse, allowed him for that action, the beginning of it being about ninty one years after the floud.

This is also considerable in the holy story, that by the same it doth appear, that none of *Sems* family were in this rebellion, because it rose in the *East*, and they were all removed westward about sixty years before, and were setled in their possessions, as is above said. Again it is not like, that any of the ancient Fathers of the familie of *Japhet*, no, nor of *Ham*, in whose familie the rebellion sprung, were consenting in it: for who can think that the wise Fathers would so betray their authority, as to subject themselves to a boy of twenty four yeares old, which was a small age in those long lived times. And thus it doth now appear that the same ground of faith, by which we believe *Europe* to be of *Japhet*, and *Africa* of *Ham*, we also believe all the *East* parts of the world to be peopled by the posterity of *Sem*, for though *Elam* or *Parsia*, be the furthest Easterne bounds that were so early planted, yet in as much as all the Eastern world was deserted totally by the other two families, and the Scripture guideth us to further notice of planting the Easterne world by the posterity of *Sem*. And seeing I have undertaken to shew that the first planters of *America* were *Ebrewes* of *Eber*, who was of the line of *Sem*, I must bring down this history of the first planting the world a little further.

When the Lord had thus from heaven blasted *Nimrods* rebellion against the government of the Fathers, by confounding their language, and thereby utterly disabled, and disappointed those that affected it from proceeding, terrified others from affecting it, and strengthened the Church in their opposing of it, then was that troublesome and terrifying mischief, for the presant, utterly suppressed, dissolved, and scattered away, like a black cloud from before the bright Son, and this did minister great tranquility of mind to the wise, and peaceable among the people: Moreover that bone of discontent, and division of heart about dividing the empty earth, and assigning to each family his desired possession, and hab itation being by the wisdome of the Fathers taken out of the way, and all the (erewhile unaccommodated) families, and companies scattered and disperced into their several appointed, and desired habitations, the earth grew calm and quiet like the smooth waters, by degrees asswaging their tumultuous minds, and composing themselves into good agreement and accord, their minds being now diverted, and taken up with the multifarious business of new plantations. So that the Fathers did now see another calm season in the daies of their government, their children and families making considerations for peace, and good agreement according as vicinity of place, or affinity by marriages, or consanguinity did minister occasion thereunto. And this peaceable state did (not only the more eminent Church in *Sems* familie but) all the world enjoy for more then thirty years together, which great mercy of God unto all, and comfort to the good old Fathers who sat at the helme, and ruled the World, they did think meet to leave upon record to all ages, in the name of the next son of hope, in the holy line of the promised seed: therefore at thirty years of age *Peleg* begat his son, whom upon the forenamed ground he called *Reu* or *Regnu* [*Reu* or *Regnu* i.e. consociation among the divided.] as some pronounce that ע, which signifies consociation, or confederation among the divided. Moreover this tranquility and rest, which both Church and world had so long enjoyed, was not yet of a good time longer expired; for partly the remembrance of the ten years trouble and strife, which rose by reason of the unsettlednesse and discontent of the two families of *Japhet*, and *Ham*, for want of their desired westerne habitation, which also gave advantage unto that daring tumult of *Nimrods* rebellion, was not easily, nor quickly forgotten, but the remembrance of it kept all wise mens minds in a continual fear of any occasion presented, that might move a like division, discontent, or rebellion, the burnt child dreads the fire: and now likewise all the people of the earth having their desired places of habitation, and vast bounds to spread themselves unto, according as the unity of language, or other relations might mould them into fit companies, & societies, the whole bent of mens mindes, in such exigents, are to build, plant, fixe, and settle themselves in the places of their desire. And no sooner could there be a company of young plants sprung up, fit for a new plantation, but the new divided world did afford them some desirable place or other, to draw them forth unto further and further spreadings, and dispersions, insomuch that mens minds being thus taken up, and their hands imployed, and now also living at great distances from each other, whereby all occasion of strife was taken away, hence the peace of all nations was not only continued, but grew stronger and stronger, and all remembrance of former strife, and anger, buried and forgotten: And thus the daies of peace and rest under the government of the Fathers were still further continued, for the space of more then thirty years longer, which long continued mercy the Fathers were so affected with, and took such eminent notice of, that they thought meet to leave a record of it to Gods praise, unto after ages, in the name of the next son of hope, in the holy line of the promised seed, whom therefore his father called *Serug*, [*Serug.* i.e. ful agreement.] which signifies full agreement, which was more then sixty years after *Nimrods* rebellion was scattered, and one hundred sixty three years after the floud.

And thus have we brought the story of the first times of the world after the floud, recorded truly in no book, saving in the holy book of God, thus far finding them still in peace and good agreement, I will so leave them, and not proceed to the after corruptions, and troubles that did arise, because my scope is, not to prosecute and set forth this story, but only shew how the world was first planted, and by whom the Easterne parts of the earth, and *America* were first peopled, and possessed.

Gen. 10.25,26,27,28,29,30. We read that *Eber* his second son was *Jocktan*, who had thirteen sons, now this is to be considered, that it appeareth by the issue, and effects; that the same spirit and desire was in all the Sons of *Noah*, namely to goe westward, from the place where the Ark did rest, and that they did quite desert the Easterne world, as not being affected there to fix themselves, which consideration doth afford several consequences of weight in this story. But for our present purpose consider this, *viz.* that seeing the family of *Sem* was first sent forth upon this westerne expedition to replenish the world, they did take the next and nearest parts for their possession, as appeareth before in the possessions of *Elam*, and *Ashur*, &c. Afterwards the rest of the westerne world being divided to *Japhet*, and *Ham*, and possessed by them, hence it doth follow, that the whole Easterne world is left to the familie of *Sem*. Now the most considerable places being taken up, and possessed by the elder Sons of the family, it remaineth that these younger Sons, namely the Sons of *Joktan* must be sent back into the Easterne parts of the world, which had before been deserted, and unto the possession of which, none of the familie of the Sons of *Noah* had any affection or desire. Hence therefore it may appear, that when this long tranquilitie of sixty years and upward (after *Nimrods* rebellion was brought to nothing) did give oportunity of promoting plantations in the world, and of quiet and peaceable transplanting themselves from place to place, for the injoyment of their inheritances assigned them by the Fathers; These Sons of *Jocktan*, about the time of *Serug*'s birth, might be up-grown, and present their desires to the Fathers, to assigne unto them a portion in the possession of the earth, which might well produce another great councel of the Fathers, to settle so great a family: the conclusion and product whereof was this, that in as much as all the westerne parts of the world were divided unto the two families of *Japhet* and *Ham*, and the *East* left unto *Sem*, therefore they could not expect any westerne possessions to be assigned unto them, there were no more westerne expeditions to be made: seeing also that all neer parts unto *Ur* (where the Church and Fathers of the holy line did live, and it is like, this and other councels were held) were already taken up and possessed, it remaines therefore, that now the Fathers must assigne them possessions in the East parts of the world, and whereas all former expeditions for plantations were westward, now they make an expedition Eastward, and send forth a great familie, the grandchildren of *Eber*, to possesse the Easterne world, which though it had been deserted in former times, out of a thirsty desire after the westerne parts of the earth, yet now all other parts being divided) here is a great family that like to travel Eastward for their inheritance: and as the Fathers of this familie were the first that had a spirit to go Eastward, to possesse the Easterne world, so they are the last that received their portions by the council of the Fathers, among these families unto whom the Lord saith, the whole earth was divided. *Gen.* 10.

This great Easterne expedition had this thing memorable in it, that they journeying from their grandfather *Eber*'s possessions, they must of necessity, at least sundry of them, passe through several possessed and planted countries, and especially through the vast countrey of *Elams* possession, which yet, through the wisdome, and the care of the Fathers, they did safely perform, which was especially furthered by the opportunity of the great peace and tranquility, that all the world did injoy in those daies, through the good blessing of the Lord, they did peaceably, and with good accord and agreement every family past into his own place to take up his assigned possession, which great favour of God, for furtherance of the plantation of the World, no doubt is comprehended in the signification of *Serug*'s name, because that was a great signe and fruit of full agreement, and peace, thus to further the passage of people through planted nations to take up their Easterne possessions. And thus it appeareth by the holy story, that as the whole Easterne world is the portion of *Sem*, so all the Easterne world eastward of *Elam* is the portion of *Eber*; and no other family could be sent beyond them, because soon after this expidition great corruptions, oppositions, and divisions did arise, as might be shewed, which would have shut the door against any more such undertakings; nor need we give reasons, that there were no more plantations and distributions made by the Fathers, because the word of God saith, that those were the last, and all: Hence therefore we may, not only with faith, but also with demonstration, say, that fruitful *India* are *Hebrewes*, that famous civil (though Idolatrous) nation of *China* are *Hebrewes,* so *Japonia*, and these naked *Americans* are *Hebrewes*, in respect of those that planted first these parts of the world: The family of *Sem* was the chiefest Church of the world since the flood, among the Sons of *Noah*, because the holy line of Christ did run in his family, yet the policy of the Church was, as was also the civil policy paternal, and that was the universal policy after the floud among all the Sons of *Noah,* as it had been through all the old world: and though the Church held, by Gods gracious, providence its greatest glory in the holy line of Christ, yet it is true that godliness, and Religion was in many other families, even in the posterity of *Canaan:* That policy therefore, Religion, and language did *Ebers* sons bring into the Easterne world, and planted the same from its first beginning of plantation; this policy was in force till God shooke it, and disalowed it, by the comming in of *Moses policy*, which he did appropriate to the familie of *Abraham*, which familie, and the Church in it, the Lord sent westward, and planted them in *a Skirt of Hams* inheritance: And although the Lord still followed the line of *Sem*, and *Eber,* until *Christ*, yet he shook off all *Sems* posterity, save that one line of *Abraham* in *Moses* daies: And when Christ came and changed the policy of *Moses*, which was national, into the Gospel-policy of congregational Churches, and spread it into the world, the Church still went westward into the families of *Japhet,* and *Ham,* and *Sems* familie was wholy deserted, saving that once mention *is made* of Saints at *Babylon*, and history telleth of *Thomas* the Apostle, in one part of *India,* but these are small matters in comparison of the vast Easterne world, the huge posterity of *Sem*, and oh the depth of Gods divine wisdom, and counsel! that his first-born Church should be so long neglected by him, and when will it be Gods time to open the door of grace to them? May it not be worthy of consideration, that when *Ezekiels* Gospel-temple (a misery yet unto us) shall be measured, the Easterne gate is first measured, *Ezek.* 40.6. again when the glory of the Lord cometh into that glorious Temple, he is upon his Westerne progresse, and first enters that Temple at the Easterne gate, *Ezek.* 43.1,2,3. &c. again the frontispeece of that Temple is *Eastward, Ezek.* 47. and those pretious waters of that Sanctuary, so wholsome, powerfull, and pretious, they run *Eastward* into the *East* land, and the further *Eastward* the more deep & wonderful they be: doth not all this shew, that there shall be a glorious Church in all the Easterne world? And God grant that the old bottles of the Westerne world be not so uncapable of the new wine of Christ his expected Kingdom, that the Easterne bottles be not the only entertainers thereof for a season.

Remember Lord the everlasting Covenant and Priesthood of *Melchisedeck,* to whom they paid Tithes in the lines of *Abraham,* and let all the earth again say, blessed be the Lord God of *Sem,* and when shall all ancient *Hebrewes* again speak the language of *Canaan.* It is worthy of consideration, that seeing the confusion of languages fell not upon *Ebers* family (a work of God so eminent that the Fathers have left it upon record, by calling the ancient holy language by *Eber's* name) how it should come to passe that his posterity have lost his language, and is fallen under the breach of that confusion. If the holy language was kept for the Churches use, as it seemeth to be, thence it might follow, that as they degenerated from the Church, and the ancient government and the holy waies of God, so they fell under the reach of that confusion: and may it not be worth the searching after, whether all the Easterne world, the posterity of *Eber,* have not more footsteps of the *Hebrew* language, at least in the gramatical frame of the language than the westerne world hath. It seemeth to me, by that little insight I have, that the gramatical frame of our *Indian* language cometh *neerer to the Hebrew,* than the *Latine,* or *Greek* do: and if so, then may it not be considerable, that the dispersion of the Ten Tribes to the utmost ends of the Earth eastward, into the Easterne world (which the Scripture threatneth first, *Deut.* 28.64. and after testifieth that way, 2 *Kin.* 17.6-23. hath lesse severity of punishment in it, being dispersed into the countries of *Sem,* and among the posterity of *Eber,* whose language and spirit was not wholey strange unto them: whereas *Judah,* when they were dispersed, it was westward, to the uttermost ends of the Westerne world, and among a people whose language was utterly strange unto them, being children of another stock and spirit, and among whom they found greater affliction, in as much as her sins were greater than the sins of her sister *Samaria. Ezek.* 1.46,47,51,52. Is not this also considerable, that as *Samaria* and the Ten Tribes were first in the captivity, and least in the offence, so may she not be first in the return? *Ezek.* 16.53,54,55. seemeth to speak that way: and doth not the Lord seem to say, *Ezek.* 37.19. that he will first lay hold on the stick of *Joseph* in the hands of *Ephraim,* who was the head of the Ten Tribes? and lastly, doth not the Lord seem to say, *Ezek.* 16.61. that after *Judah* is converted, how ever *Ephraim* may have priority of time, yet *Judah* shall have priority of eminency in all other respects; Touching the Ten Tribes, these considerations may seem not unworthy to be thought upon.

1. That the Ten Tribes are dispersed and scattered into other Nations.

2. That they were scattered Eastward.

3. That it was for their sins, for which God did threaten them to be scattered

to the utmost ends of the earth.

4. That they shall be found again, and called into Christ his kingdome.

5. *Judah* being scattered westward, and were scattered to the utmost ends of the Westerne world.

Hence why ought we not to believe, that the ten Tribes being scattered Eastward, are scattered to the utmost ends of the Easterne world? and if so, then assuredly into *America,* because that is part of the easterne World, and peopled by Easterne Inhabitants, as aforesaid.

It is one of the great works of Christ in the last daies to finde up lost Israel, and bring them into his kingdom? and this moveth the hearts of many of the good people of the Lord to search after them: and in this search I would propound this to consideration, that the surest thread to guid us in this darke inquiry is, to follow the line of the Scriptures, for Scripture notes and markes will be best evidences to move Gods people to believe, whether this, or that people be of the remnant of lost Israel, or no; Now the Scripture doth describe lost Israel in three estates, which descriptions, when they shall be all seen accomplished upon a people, it may seem to be a ground of faith to believe, that they indeed are of that people that have been so long lost, and through free grace found again. Those three estates are these first, the state of their misery, while they are lost, and scattered in the world, and that thread the Lord guided you, in your book, happily to lay hold upon, and how far that thread will guid in this scrutiny, I undertake not to say, aftertimes may say more.

2. The manner, meanes, and way of their returne and recovery.

3. Their deportment after conversion, in their correspondence with converted *Judah,* and subjection unto *David* their King, as the Scriptures do mysteriously speak of the Kingdome of Christ. But these things I leave, and yet being but in the twilight, if so neer approaching, and being a subject not yet capable of a judgement to be passed in the case. And this is all I shall at present say about this matter. But seeing there are some, that do not approve of the cause of our coming into *New-England,* no, though it were that we might be freed from the ceremonies, and have liberty to enjoy all the pure Ordinance of Christ; and that they doubt of our sincerity, and that under a needless pretence of conscience we came hither, indeed and in truth, for wealth, and matters of this world; and most especially the Ministers, who, had it not been to better their living, would not have come hither, and that they have spoken too unreverently of that holy man of God, Mr. *Cotton,* now at rest with the Lord, and lastly, they call into question, at least, seem to doubt of the equity of our titles unto the lands we possesse among the *Indians,* in these respects therefore I shall add a little more.

For the grounds and the reasons of our coming hither, no doubt but they were manifold, according to the manifold conditions, temptations, trials, hopes and expectations that were prevalent in in the mindes of them that came, yea, among the godly, there may well be conceived variety of grounds moving to this vast and difficult undertaking, and among the Christian and religious grounds and reasons, which swayed in the hearts of good men, they may not be thought to be unmixed with some thing of another nature, which the world, or flesh, or outward being in this life might present or suggest, our best actions are mixed with that mud which followeth from the unmortified principles of corrupt nature, therefore pleads for Christian grounds and ends of coming hither, must be understood with that caution. Nor would I take the imputation of carnal ends with the left hand, but rather as an intimation from God to try our ends and grounds, and cast out such things as do offend. Grounds and ends are secret things from the sight of other men, who will ever judge of them by their fruits, and therefore our best way to prove unto men that our grounds and ends are Religious, is, to let it appear to be so, by our religious waies and works, that here we do walke in. Assuredly, if any do come hither to greaten their wealth, and comforts in this world, who had any considerable being in *England,* I believe by such time as he had conflicted with our wildernesse wants, difficulties, uncertainties, temptations, & raw beginnings, he wanted not matter of abundant conviction of the great folly of coming out of an old setled and cultur'd land into a wildernesse to mend his means of living; that this is also true, that such as lived in *England* upon their handy labours, and had nothing to live on, have not a little mended their outward meanes of living: But that was not the condition of such upon whose shoulders the weight of this great work hath lyen, who have, by coming hither, changed a comfortable being for the outward man into a condition full of labour, toile, sorrow, wants, and temptations of a wildernesse, which dwellers in *England* cannot so well see, weigh, or pitty, but the Lord can. We were not ashamed in *England* (and we have lesse cause now) to owne our distastes of mens imposing their ceremonies in the holy worship of God, and the non-conformity both of our judgement, and practice unto such a way; nor did the terrors of a prison, or whatever else might follow, answer or conquer our consciences in that cause, for the cause was Gods: and yet when God opened a door of quiet departure, and liberty to enjoy the holy worship of God, not according to the fantasies of man, but according to the word of God, without such humane additions and novelties, we thought it better for us to give way by departing quietly and leaving the field to them that were masters of it, than to stand up longer in opposition; and I cannot see why any should cast upon this our quiet departure the imputation of rending: We have reason to think, that many who sate at that helm, did like well of that our departure, and said let them go in peace, expecting to have stood their ground the more firme by our removal. Some have blamed our departure upon another point, *viz.* a giving back in the cause, and deserting them in the conflict, but such should have done well to consider, that the cause was not the same, nor the state of times alike, when we departed, and they complained. Assuredly the better part of our plantations did undertake the enterprise with a suffering minde, and who ever shall do such a thing, must be so armed or else he will not be able to hold out in the work: to part with our native country, a setled habitation, dear friends, houses, lands and many worldy comforts, to go into a wilderness where nothing appeareth but hard labour, wants, and wildernesse-temptations (stumble not countrymen, at the repetition of that word, wildernesse-temptations) of which it is written, that they are trying times, and places, *Deut.* 8. there must be more then golden hopes to bear up the godly wise in such an undertaking, but when the injoyment of Christ in his pure Ordinances is better to the soul, than all wordly comforts, then these things are but light afflictions, come they never so big in the eye of reason: I remember, we were wont to use unto each other this proverb, before we came, that brown bread and the Gospel is good chear, and through grace we have learned that lesson a little further in this place, namely, that no bread and the Gospel is so good a choise, as that we have been (in our poor measure) thankful for the one when we have been crying for the other. Had our aime, and desire been gold or tobacco, wherewith many have inriched themselves in *America,* and more destroyed their souls, we should not have come into so Northernly a climet, where the eagernesse of the cold doth so vehemently resist the Sun in that royal generation of gold, or high concoction of the plants, or had our aime been to inrich our selves with rich Furs, we must not have come into so Southerly a climet, the heat whereof gives not so acceptable entertainment unto those richly clad creatures, as colder places do; But we chose a place where nothing in probability was to be expected, but Religion, poverty, and hard labour, a composition that God doth usually take most pleasure in, and therefore chosen by the undertakers of this plantation, and accordingly as the bounty of the Lord hath blessed our labours unto any degree of plenty and prosperity, it is too visible, and apparent, that we are ready to grow worse in point of Religion; and that convicteth us, that if Religious men make the world their aime, it will prove destructive to Religion, ye cannot serve God and Mammon. And hence charity may not think, that wise godly men should look so low in this great enterprise, and if any did make that their mark in coming to this place, let that suffice to convince their folly, in that so many have returned home from us, who might take up the saying of *Naomi,* I went forth full, and am returned empty. But above all other men, Ministers that came to *New-England* to get a benefice there, because they could get none in old *England,* or to get a better here than they had, they did quite misse the make, for if a man were so undesireable that he could not get imployment in *England,* his labours would be of lesse accompt here, among so many seeing eyes; and sure he had but a very mean benefice, that could not afford as comfortable a subsistance, as most places here. I thank the Lord, I am not in a temptation to complain, either of Gods bounty, or the peoples love, and yet I know Ministers that are necessitated to labour with their hands, and do many mean offices for meer necessity, both through want of servants, and some other comforts too, and yet I do think, that the brightness of the grace and power of Jesus Christ hath shined in their Ministry more than ever, and the more (I believe) for their tryals. And *New-England* can name many learned, holy, and peaceable, and self-denying Ministers, who wanted no means of plentiful livelyhood in *England,* and are contented with poor matters. It is true, we had that vented among us, their new-fangles, unto much grief, and offence of the godly, but they have felt the power of the discipline of Christ in the Church, and of civil government in the common wealth unto the reclaiming of some, and therefore God will not charge their sin upon *New-England,* what ever men may do, when sin shall receive its due censure, the land will be innocent; and because, in allusion to your old kingdome of *Eastangles,* you called us *Novangles,* the world of New-fangles is put upon us, but it is a more happy and true cadency of the word, *Novangles* into

No fangles, thus they torture the word to make it speak us so bad. There was indeed one, many years since, an uncomfortable paroxisme among us, though the erring party abused Mr. *Cottons* authority further then he approved of, and by this the Lord taught us, that we are all but men, and Mr. *Cotton* was but a man, though far from that corruption of judgement, or pertenacity of defence that is reported of him. But let all men take notice what end the Lord made of those troubles, and were that well observed, such as hope for pardon of their own swervings from the mercies of Jesus Christ, who useth to blot out our iniquities, and remember them no more, would not, yea could not so rake up those buryed bones, long since pardoned both by God and man, to cast an *odium* upon such a man, whose name will be a pretious oyntment poured forth, do what they can. Nay, it will unavoidably reflect upon themselves, and fall upon their own heads, who ever shall with such fingers touch such Prophets of God, as that good man was: he after bewailed those evils in publick, and especially on daies of humiliation, publick, or private, and when he lay upon his death-bed, many Elders of the Churches about, being at the lecture, went together to visit him, unto whom, among other gracious words, he did make an holy and humble remembrance of those daies, so as that caused much weeping among us. He is now at rest, and beyond the reach of such arrowes, which, being out shot will return, and pierce the hearts of such as shoot them, which wounds ending in true repentance, they will then forgive Mr. *Cotton*, and God for Christ his sake will forgive them.

As for that great question of our Title to the lands we here possesse, our general practice hath been to purchase of the natives what we enjoy; and not only so, but it is frequent also with them to invite the *English* unto fit places for Townes, because of the benefit they receive by our neighbourhood, and so long as we hold to these principles, and walk by them, no man can have any thing justly to impeach our Titles so far as I conceive; but if we should recede from those principles and practices, I know not what apologie may be made to such a case. Some expresse their fears of some corruption to be the latent springs, that move in the worke of preaching to the *Indians,* and this I take with my right hand, as an wholsome advertisement, and submonition, I beg of God to help me sincerely to say as *David, Psal.* 141.5. such smitings shall not break my head, but be as a pretious ointment. I am but a man, and am sensible, that I need such advertisements or any other that may help me in my dayly conflict with the body of sin, I do dayly fear such evils, and many more because of such feares, for it may be some quick-sighted men have seen some such hints unseen by me, in some of my letters which my friends have printed. One evil feared, is spiritual pride, a sin incident to mans nature, and to mine. I do perceive that the worke of preaching to the *Indians* is greatly accepted among the people of God, which is a temptation to me to lift up my heart with pride; But this I say I foreknew not, nor forethought any such thing, therefore it was no first mover, it is an intruder if it do prevail, and, I trust in the Lord, it shall not have dominion, and I beg prayers against it; and I can, through grace, say, that when here other magnifie their works, it doth abase me; and I wondred a thousand times, why the Lord should set such a poor wrech as I am on work in this matter, the most unfit of all my brethren, and so much unfitness and frailty I see in my self, and weakness in that little I do, as that I cannot but ascribe the whole glory of the work unto the Lord, who alone is the worker of what is done. Another evil feared, is the sacred thirst of Gold, of which I say as of the former, I neither did nor could expect reward from the *Indians,* but the contrary; nor did I foresee, or forethink, that there would have been such thoughts of incouragement to the work in our native country, it was a consequence of my preaching, and therefore was not the first mover, and indeed great things are done already from *England,* among us and the *Indians,* blessed be God; But this I can say, that the Lord God who, did at the first set me on work without worldly incouragements, or expectations, he hath never failed to supply and help me in such waies, and by such means, as I had no knowledge of: and blessed be his name that hath hitherto made every passage in this work, both towards them and me (as his manner is in these daies) beyond mine, and other mens expectations. The godly undertakers of this plantation had it so much in their hearts, to make the conversion of the *Indians* one end of their coming, as that they made it one clause in their patent, which did lay a publick ingagement upon us thereunto: and when God was pleased to put me upon that work of preaching to them, that publick ingagement, together with pitty to the poor *Indians,* and desire to make the name of Christ chief in these darke ends of the earth, and not the rewards of men, were the very first, and chief movers, if I know what did first, and chiefly move in my heart. As for the foundations that are laid among them, I shall say but little, because these foundations, of repentance from dead works, of faith in the Lord Jesus, and of holy working with God, may be best seen in the *Indians* own confessions of their faith, which they have made before the Lord, and I have, by advise, this year made publick, if the Lord please to send them safe to Mr. *Winslowes* hands. For the foundation of their government they have by covenant solemnly given up themselves unto the Lord, to be ruled in all things by the word of his mouth, a short touch of that Scripture-form of their civil government, upon which they have entred, is already published: and for the Church government it may be gathered, what that is like to be, by what is known to be our opinion, and practice in the *English* Churchs in *New-England:* briefly, my scope is, to write and imprint no nother but Scripture principles in the *abrasa tabula sraped board* of these naked people, that so they may be in all their principles a choice people unto the Lord, owning none other Lord or law-giver, but the Lord alone, who is the King of Saints. I cannot ere I have done but bewail also the vaine, & frothy fashions, follies wanton dresses, and madnesses of the times, which shews mens brains to be more exercised about their breeches, and heels, than about better matters, which might be either to the praise, of God, or for good service unto their generation [This passage was occasioned by a printed book that seemes to asperse the planters, &c.]: nay, it is spoken, as if some carried it, that their religion doth sublimate their spirits, as that they can suffer their flesh to be bedangled from head to foot with the fashions of the vainest men, and wel it is, if they have not, upon the same grounds, a commission to pollute themselves with the like lusts: this is an evil fitter to be ejected with loathing, and derision, than confuted with sober reason.

It seemeth men may be said in some respects to be even bewitched with fashions, when they wil disguise and dishonour their own bodies, rather than not to be fashioned like the world, they will cut off their own beards, and old men cut off all gravity, that nature & gray haires would honour them with all, and cover the honour of their gray heads with counterfeited and youth full periwigs, as if all the grave affaires of the land were managed by green-headed youth. [*De Cul. Fœm. p.* 183. *Hœc est eternitas nostra, de capitis veritate, &c.*] An evil it seems in *Tertullians* time, elegantly and earnestly scorned by him, to such he writes, We youthfullize our heads, as if that were our eternity: If you be not ashamed of the enormity, be ashamed of the pollution, vex not an holy and Christian head with the perriwig and refuse of another mans hairs it may be a filthy person, perhaps a wicked man, ordained to damnation, cast off from your free heads, this slavish excrement, and oh to be lamented! they say the pulpits are much of the same guise. Sundry come over hither from *England* in such dresses, that the sight of our eyes might move us to lay to heart the sins of *England*, and yet sundry of ours, yea, of the more ungirt sort of professors too, are more ready to imitate, then bewail them: and were not such sins cryed against by some, there be that would spare no cost, to shew their frothy minds, by such flags, when it were far better to be bestowed in paying their debts. But Christ hath his pretious ones among us, who do continually bewail, and resist these things. And thus, reverend and dear Sir, I have made bold to trouble you with a larger discourse than I intended when I set pen to paper, yet I was willing to intimate thus much unto your self, having sundry motives thereunto. The Lord reward your love, and blesse all your holy labours. Amen. So prayeth

> *Your unworthy brother*
> *and fellow-labouror in*
> *our Lords Vineyard.*

John Elliot.

F I N I S.

Reliquiæ Baxterianæ:

OR,

Mr. *RICHARD BAXTER's*

NARRATIVE

OF

The most Memorable Passages

OF HIS

LIFE

AND

TIMES.

Faithfully Publish'd from his own Original Manuscript,

By *MATTHEW SYLVESTER.*

Mihi quidem nulli satis Eruditi videntur quibus nostra ignota sunt.
Cic. de Finib. lib. I.

Quibus [ergò] recte dem, nou prætermittam —— Sic habete, me, cum ille re
sæpe communicata, de illiue ad te sententià atque authoritate Scribere ——
Cic. Epist. 7. ad Lentul. Lib I.

LONDON:

Printed for *T. Parkhurst, J. Robinson, J. Lawrence,*
and *J. Dunton.* **M DC XC VI.**

For the Reverend and his much honored Friend Mr. Baxter, Chaplain in Ordinary to his Majesty*

Reverend and much esteemed in the Lord!

HOwever black the Cloud is, and big the Storm, yet by all this the Work and Design of Jesus Christ goeth on, and prospereth, and in these Clouds Christ is coming to set up his Kingdom. Yea, is he not come, in Power and great Glory? When had the Truth a greater, or so great and glorious a Cloud of Witnesses? Is not this Christ, in Power and great Glory? and if Christ hath so much Glory in the slaughter of his Witnesses, what will his Glory be in their Resurrection! Your Constancy who are in the heat of the Storm, and Numbers, ministers matter of humbling and quickning to us, who are at a distance, and ready to totter and comply at the noise of a probable approach of our Temptation. We are not without our Snares, but hitherunto the Lords own Arm hath brought Salvation. Our Tents are at *Ebenezer*. However the trials and troubles be, we must take care of the present Work, and not cease and tarry for a calm time to work in. And this Principle doth give me occasion to take the boldness to trouble you with these Lines at present. My Work about the *Indian* Bible being (by the good hand of the Lord, though not without difficulties) finished, I am meditating what to do next for these Sons of this our Morning: they having no Books for their private use, of ministerial composing. For their help, though the Word of God be the best of Books, yet Humane Infirmity is, you know, not a little helped, by reading the holy Labours of the Ministers of Jesus Christ. I have therefore purposed in my heart (seeing the Lord is yet pleased to prolong my life) to translate for them a little Book of yours, intituled, [*A Call to the Unconverted*]: The keenness of the Edge, and liveliness of the Spirit of that Book, through the blessing of God, may be of great use unto them. But seeing you are yet in the Land of the Living, (and the good Lord prolong your days) I would not presume to do such a thing, without making mention thereof unto your self, that so I might have the help and blessing of your Counsel and Prayers. I believe it will not be unacceptable to you, that the Call of Christ by your holy Labours shall be made to speak in their Ears, in their own Language, that you may preach unto our poor *Indians*. I have begun the Work already, and find a great difference in the Work from my former Translations: I am forced sometime to alter the Phrase, for the facilitating and fitting it to our Language, in which I am not so strict as I was in the Scripture. Some things which are fitted for *English* People, are not fit for them, and in such cases, I make bold to fit it for them. But I do little that way, knowing how much beneath Wisdom it is, to shew a Man's self witty, in mending another Man's Work. When this Work is done, if the Lord shall please to prolong my Life, I am meditating of Translating some other Book, which may prescribe to them the way and manner of a Christian Life and Conversation, in their daily Course; and

---

*Letter from John Eliot to Richard Baxter, Baxter 1696, 293-295; Baxter's reply, 295-297.

how to worship God on the Sabbath, fasting, feasting Days, and in all Acts of Worship, publick, private, and secret; and for this purpose I have Thoughts of translating for them, the *Practice of Piety*; or some other such Book: In which Case I request your Advice to me; for if the Lord give opportunity, I may hear from you (if you see cause so far to take Notice hereof) before I shall be ready to begin a new work; especially because the Psalms of *David* in Metre in their Language, are going now to the Press, which will be some Diversion of me, from a present Attention upon these other proposed Works.

Sir, I am very well satisfied with your Explications of the Point of Free-will in fallen Man, which I have read in a small Treatise of yours, which I once had the happiness to see. I doubt not but you will give me leave to talk a little according to my weakness, *Gen.* 1.26. *God made Man after his own Image/ Likeness.*

I have oft perplexed my mind to see the difference of these two Divine Stamps upon Man. That God's Image consisteth in Knowledge, Holiness, and Righteousness, is clear and agreed, expressed in Scripture. But what our likeness to God is, is the Question: Why may it not admit this Explication? that one chief thing is, to act like God, according to our light freely; by choice without compulsion, to be Author of our own act to determine our own choice: this is spontaniety. The Nature of the Will lyeth in this.

Between God's Image in Man, and the Likeness of God, in Man, are these two Differences:

1. God's Image was lost and changed, and in the room of it, Original Sin was infused, inflicted upon the Soul; and in this Change the Will suffered.

But the Spontaniety was not lost; nor changed. But the Will doth freely act according to these new ill Qualities, and freely chooses to Sin, as afore this Change it freely acted according to the good Qualities which it was endewed withall.

So likewise at Conversion, and in Sanctification, the Will suffereth the Powerful Work of the Spirit to change these Qualities, to kill the old Habits of Sin, and to create the new Habits of Grace; that it may freely act according to Grace, as afore it freely acted in Sin.

2. Difference is, that God's Image are separable Qualities of the Will, and the moral Ground which maketh our Actions good, legal, regular, and virtuous: As original Sin is the ground that maketh our Actions illegal and sinful. But Spontaniety is the Form and Nature of the Will, which if it cease, we should cease to be Men, and to act by Choice; and so not capable to sin, or to act virtuously.

Sir, I pray pardon my Boldness and Weakness thus to talk; but it is for my Information in this Point. I observe also in yours, a thing which I have not so much observed in other Mens Writings; *viz.* That you often inveigh against the Sin of Gluttony, as well as Drunkenness. It appeareth to be a very great point of Christian Prudence, Temperance and Mortification, to rule the Appetite of eating as well as drinking, and were that Point more inculcated by Divines, it would much tend to the Sanctification of God's People, as well as to a better Preservation of Health, and lengthening of the Life of Man on Earth.

I lately met with an excellent Book of learned Dr. *Charleton*'s, about the Immortality of the human Soul, composed in a gallant Dialogue, where speaking of the admirable Advancement of Learning in these late Days, he, among other excellent matters, speaketh of that long talk'd of and desired Design of a universal Character and Language, and what Advance hath been made towards it, by some of the learned of these Times, and that by the way of Symbols. Of this he speaketh, *p.* 45, 46. I doubt not, but that it is a divine Work of God, to put it into the Heart of any of his Servants, to promote this Design, which so great and eminent a Tendency, to advance the Kingdom of Jesus Christ, which shall be extended over all the Kingdoms and Nations of the Earth, *Rev.* 11.15. Not by the personal Presence of Christ, but by putting Power and Rule into the Hands of the Godly, Learned in all Nations: Among whom, a universal Character and Language, will be both necessary, and a singular Promotion of that great Design of Christ: Now, whereas the Proposal of it is by way of Symbols, I would make bold to propose a way, which seemeth to be of more Hopes of Success, and that is by the *Hebrew* Language, which above all other Languages, is most capable to be the Instrument of so great a Design. If you please to look into a Book called *Jordini Hebreæ radices*, composed by *Decads* into Heroick Verses; the Hebrew *Radix*, with the Signification in Latin, helping to smooth it into a Verse; a worthy Work, wherein *bene meruit de Lingua Hebraica*. This Author in his Preface, speaketh most honourably of the Hebrew Tongue; and sheweth that by the trigramical Foundation, and divine Artifice of that Language, it is capable of a regular Expatiation into Millions of Words, no Language like it. And it had need be so, for being the Language which shall be spoken in Heaven, where knowledge will be so enlarged, there will need a spacious Language; and what Language fitter than this of God's own making and composure? And why may we not make ready for Heaven in this Point, by making and fitting that Language, according to the Rules of the divine Artifice of it, to express all imaginable Conceptions and Notions of the Mind of Man, in all Arts and Sciences? Were this done, (which is so capable of being done, and it seemeth God hath fitted Instruments to fall to the Work) all Arts and Sciences in the whole Encyclopædie would soon be translated into it; and all Paganish and prophane Trash would be left out: It would be (as now it is) the purest Language in the World: And it seemeth to me, that *Zeph.* 3.9. with other Texts, do prophesie of such a universal and pure Language. Were this done, all Schools would teach this Language, and all the World, especially the Commonwealth of Learning, would be of one, and that a divine and heavenly Lip.

Moreover, This learned Doctor speaketh very honourably of that renowned Society, the Colledge of Physicians in *London*, and no whit above their Deserts, as appeareth by the admirable Effects by the blessing of God, upon their Studies and Labours, which they have found out and produced for the Benefit of the Life of Man. In which Art, by the Blessing of God upon them, they seem to me to design such a Regiment of Health, and such an exact Inspection into all Diseases, and Knowledge of all Medicament, and Prudence of Application of the same, that the Book of divine Providence seemeth to provide for the lengthning of the Life of Man again, in this latter End of the World, which would be no small Advantage unto all kinds of good Learning and Government. And doth not such a thing seem to be Prophesied, *Esay.* {Isaiah} 65.20. *If the Child shall die one hundred Years old, of what Age shall the old Man be?* But I would not be too bold with the Holy Scriptures.

If unto all this, it may please the Lord to direct his People into a Divine Form of Civil Government, of such a Constitution, as that the Godly, Learned in all Places, may be in all Places of Power and Rule, this would so much the more advance all Learning, and Religion, and good Government; so that all the World would become a Divine Colledge. And *Lastly*, when Antichrist is overthrown, and a divine Form of Church-Government is put in practice in all Places; then all the World would become Divine: or at least, all the World would become very Divine or very Prophane, *Rev. 22.*11,15. And so the World should end as it began, *Gen.* 4.26. some calling on the Name of the Lord, and some prophaning it; eminently distinguish'd from each other. I rejoice to see and taste the wonderful gracious Savour of God's Spirit among his Saints, in their humble Retirements. Oh! how sweet is the trodden Cammomile! How precious and Powerful is the Ministry of the Cross! It is a dryer time with us, who are making after Compliances with the Stream. Sir, I beseech you, let us have a share in your holy Prayers, in your holy Retirements, in your blessed Chambers, when the Lord shuts the Door, and yet is among you himself, and maketh your Hearts to burn by the Power of his Presence. Thus commending you and all your holy Labours to the Lord, and to the Word of his Grace, I rest

Roxbury, this 6th of the 5th.   *Your unworthy Fellow-Labourer*
     1663.

In the Lord's Vineyard,

John Eliot.

To his Reverend Friend and Brother, Mr. *Baxter.*

The Answer.

Nov. 30. *from* Acton, *near* London.

Reverend and much honoured Brother,

T Hough our Sins have separated us from the People of our Love and Care, and deprived us of all publick Liberty of preaching the Gospel of our Lord, I greatly rejoice in the Liberty, Help and Success which Christ hath so long vouchsafed you in his Work. There is no Man on Earth, whose Work I think more Honourable and Comfortable than yours: To propagate the Gospel and Kingdom of Christ, unto those dark Parts of the World, is a better Work than our hating and devouring one another. There are many here that would be ambitious of being your Fellow-Labourers, but that they are informed, you have access to no greater a Number of the Indians, than you your self, and your present Assistants are able to instruct. An honourable Gentleman (Mr. *Rob. Boyle*, the Governor of the Corporation for your Work, a Man of great Learning and Worth, and of a very publick universal Mind) did Motion to me a publick Collection, in all our Churches, for the maintaining of such Ministers, as are willing to go hence to you, partly while they are learning the Indian Language, and partly while they after labour in the Work, as also to transport them: But I find those backward to it, that I have spoke to about it, partly suspecting it a Design of those that would be rid of them; (but if it would promote the Work of God, this Objection were too carnal to be regarded by good Men) partly fearing that when the Money is gathered, the Work may be frustrated by the alienation of it (but this I think they need not fear, so far as to hinder any); partly because they think there will be nothing considerable gathered; because the People that are unwillingly divorced from their Teachers, will give nothing to send them further from them, and those that are willingly separated from them, will give nothing to those that they no more respect: But specially because they think (on the aforesaid Grounds) that there is no work for them to do if they were with you. There are many here I conjecture, that would be glad to go any whither (to *Persians, Tartarians, Indians*, or any unbelieving Nation) to propagate the Gospel, if they thought they could be serviceable, but the Defect of their Languages is their great Discouragement: For the universal Character that you speak of, many have talked of it, and one hath printed his Essay, and his way is only by numeral Figures, making such and such Figures to stand for the Words of the same signification in all Tongues; but no body regards it. I shall communicate your Motion here about the Hebrew, but we are not of such large and publick Minds as you imagin; every one looks to his own Concernment, and some to the things of Christ that are near them, at their own Doors. But if there be one *Timothy* that naturally careth for the State of the Churches, we have no Man of a Multitude more likeminded, but all seek their own things; we had one *Dury* here, that hath above thirty Years laboured the reconciling of the Churches, but few regarded him, and now he is glad to escape from us into other Countries. Good Men that are wholly devoted to God, and by long Experience are acquainted with the Interest of Christ, are ready to think all others should be like them, but there is no hope of bringing any more, than here, and there an experienced, holy, self-denying Person, to get so far above their personal Concernments, and narrowness of Mind, and so wholly to devote themselve to God. The Industry of the Jesuits and Fryars, and their Successes in *Congo, Japan, China, &c.* shame us all, save you: But yet for their personal Labours in the Work of the Gospel, here are many that would be willing to lay out, where they have Liberty and a Call, though scarce any that will do more in furthering great and publick Works. I should be glad to learn from you, how far your Indian Tongue extendeth; how large or populous the Country is that useth it (if it be known); and whether it reach only to a few scattered Neighbours, who cannot themselves convey their Knowledge far, because of other Languages. We very much rejoice in your happy Work (the Translation of the Bible) and bless God that hath strengthened you to finish it. If any thing of mine may be honoured to contribute in the least measure to your blessed Work, I shall have great cause to be thankful to God, and wholly submit the Alteration and use of it to your Wisdom. Methinks the *Assemblies Catechism* should be next the holy Scriptures, most worthy of your Labours. The Lord prolong your Days, and prosper you.

As to your Case about God's Image and Likeness, 1. The Controversy *de Nomine* is of no great Moment: I know the Schoolmen make the two Words signifie two things: I think it's a groundless Conceit. But *de re* (call them what you will, Image or Likeness) it consisteth of three parts, or a Trinity in Unity. 1. The natural substantial Part. 2. the qualitative moral part. 3. The relative honorarary part. (I rather call them three Parts of God's Image, than three Images, though here also the Controversy *de Nomine* is small) 1. Man's high superanimal or rational Life in *Unity*, hath his Trinity of noble Faculties; an Intellect or Reason capable of knowing God, a free or self-determining Will, capable of adhearing to him, and an executive Power capable of serving him: That these Natural Essential Powers, are the Natural Part of God's Image, appears, *Gen.* 9.6. where Man, as Man is supposed to have it; else the Murder of none but Saints is there forbidden: This no Man loseth. 2. *Holiness*, or the *Spirit* in *Unity* containeth 1. The *Wisdom of the Mind*, which is the *Knowledge of God*. 2. The *Rectitude of the Will*, which is the *Love of God*. And 3. The *Promptitude, Obedience and Fortitude of the Executive Power, in and for the Service of God*; and this is the *moral Part of God's Image*. 3. *God,* having the *only Aptitude* by his three great Properties, Infinite POWER, WISDOM, and GOODNESS, and the *only Right Jure Creationis* [and since *Redemptionis & Regenerationis*] immediately stood related to Man, in the three great Relations contained expressively in the Name *God*; 1. Our *absolute proprietary Owner* or Lord. 2. Our *Supreme Rector*. 3. Our *bountiful Benefactor*, or *Father*, and *End*, all flowing from his Relation, of our most potent, wise, good CREATOR. Man is related to him, 1. As his *own*, to be wholly at his dispose. 2. As his *Subject*, to be wholly at his Government. 3. As his *Beneficiary*, or *Child* to love him with all the Heart. Now God hath given Man to bear his Image in these Relations, which is in Unity caled his *Dominion over the bruit Creatures*, And in Trinity containeth, 1. That we are their *Owners*, and they our *own*. 2. we are their *Governors* (according to their Capacities). 3. We are their *Benefactors*, and they have (and had more) dependance on us, and were made for us as their *End,* as we were *immediately* for God as our End. This part of God's Image is partly, not totally lost. The *moral* part is that which the Spirit restoreth: The Wisdom of the Mind, the Righteousness or Rectitude of the Will, and the Holiness and Obedience of the Life. If we had a right Scheme of Theology (which I never yet saw) Unity in Trinity would go through the whole Method: It's easy to follow it a little way, and to see how God's three grand Relations of Owner, Ruler, and Father or End and chief God, and the Correspondent Relations in Man, and the mutual Expressions go far in the great parts of Theology: but when we run it up to the Numerous and small Branches, our narrow Minds are lost in the search. But the Day is coming when all God's Works of Creation and Providence, and all his Truths shall be seen to us *uno intuitu*, as a most entire, perfect Frame. Pardon my too many words to you on this.

As for the divine Government by the Saints which you mention, I dare not expect such great Matters upon Earth, lest I encroach upon the Priviledge of Heaven, and tempt my own Affections downwards, and forget that our Kingdom is not of this World. Certainly if Christianity be the same thing now that it was at first, it is much unsuitable to a reigning State on Earth: Bearing the Cross, Persecution, Self-denial, &c. found something of another Nature. The Rich will rule in the World, and few rich Men will be Saints. He that surveyeth the present State of the Earth, and considereth that scarcely a sixth Part is Christian, and how small a Part of them are reformed, and how small a part of them have much of the Power of Godliness, will be ready to think that Christ hath called almost all his Chosen, and is ready to forsake the Earth, rather than that he intendeth us such blessed Days below as we desire. We shall have what we would, but not in this World. As hard as we think God dealeth with us, our King's Dominions are yet for the Power of Godliness, the Glory and Paradise of the Earth. Success tempted some here into reigning Expectations, and thence into sinful Actions and Attempts, and hardened them in all; but God hath done much already to confute them. Through Faith and Patience we must inherit the Promise. May I know Christ crucified on Earth, and Christ glorified in Heaven, I shall be happy. Dear Sir, the Lord be your Support and Strength: I rest

Your Weak Fellow-Servant,

Richard Baxter.

Index

ABOUT THE EDITOR

Michael P. Clark is Associate Executive Vice Chancellor for Academic Planning and Professor of English and Comparative Literature at the University of California, Irvine.

ABOUT THE EDITOR

Michael P. Clark is Associate Executive Vice Chancellor for Academic Planning and Professor of English and Comparative Literature at the University of California, Irvine.